# Offshore
# Island Politics

The Constitutional and Political
Development of the Isle of Man
in the Twentieth Century

CENTRE FOR MANX STUDIES MONOGRAPHS 3

# Offshore Island Politics

## The Constitutional and Political Development of the Isle of Man in the Twentieth Century

### David G. Kermode

LIVERPOOL UNIVERSITY PRESS

First published 2001 by
LIVERPOOL UNIVERSITY PRESS
4 Cambridge Street
Liverpool L69 7ZU

**British Library Cataloguing-in-Publication Data**
A British Library CIP Record is available

ISBN 0-85323-777-8 (hardback)
0-85323-787-5 (paperback)
Typeset in Galliard
by BBR Solutions Ltd, Chesterfield
Printed by Bookcraft, Midsomer Norton, Bath

*To the memory of Herbert and Elsie Kermode*
*(1903–87 and 1907–87)*

# Contents

# Acknowledgements

I would like to place on record my thanks to all those people who have helped me during the writing of this book. Particular thanks are due to Alistair Ramsay for the many helpful discussions of the project while exploring the Island's hills and hostelries; to Professor St John Bates, Clerk of Tynwald (1987–2001), and William Cain, First Deemster, who read and made constructive comments on an earlier draft of the book; to the staff of the Tynwald and Manx National Heritage Libraries, especially Geoffrey Haywood, without whose patient and informed responses to endless requests for information this book could not have been written; to Martin Caley for supplying the Price Index that forms Appendix 1 to this study; to the Centre for Manx Studies, Liverpool John Moores University, the Manx Heritage Foundation and the Manx National Heritage Library for material and financial support; to Isle of Man Newspapers Ltd for the complimentary subscription to the *Isle of Man Courier*, the *Isle of Man Examiner* and the *Manx Independent*; to Phil Cubbin at LJMU's Centre for Social Science for preparing the maps and to all those who helped me in finding and selecting photographs to illustrate the book.

Special thanks are due to Maureen for both encouragement with the book and distraction from it.

None of the individuals or organisations mentioned bear any responsibility for any residual errors of fact or judgement.

# Figures

# Tables

# Photographs

I would like to thank all the individuals and organisations listed below, especially Manx National Heritage (MNH) and Island Photographics (IP), for permission to publish selected photographs. Particular thanks are due to Aerofilms Ltd, Douglas Bolton, William Cain, Arthur Bawden and colleagues in the Clerk of Tynwald's Office, Dudley Peck of the Department of Agriculture, Fisheries and Forestry (DAFF), Derek Hudson and Maureen Harris of the Department of Health and Social Security (DHSS), Daphne Caine and Terry Toohey of the Department of Tourism and Leisure (DTL), Ken Bawden of the Department of Trade and Industry (DTI), David Cannan, Speaker of the House of Keys, Monica Clark and colleagues at Island Photographics (IP), Frank Johnson, Lionel Cowin of Isle of Man Newspapers, John Maddrell, Roger Sims and colleagues at the Manx National Heritage (MNH) Library, Christopher Norris, Rosemary Penn, Colin Bagshaw of the Ronaldsway Aircraft Company (RAC), Ian Qualtrough, Kathleen Smith and Fred Stephen.

## Chapter Four: 1919–39

## Chapter Five: 1939–58

## Chapters Six and Seven: 1958–81

# Chapters Eight and Nine: 1981–2000

# Note on Sources

There are very few good secondary sources on twentieth-century Manx history and politics and almost no detailed political memoirs, that of Samuel Norris being the notable exception. Accordingly, with the exception of the Home Office material deposited in the Public Record Office at Kew, the main items consulted for this study were published Manx sources, the Reports of the Debates in the Manx Legislature (the Manx Hansard), reports of legislative committees and boards of Tynwald, government reports, including the annual budget books and audited accounts, and the Manx press. The 118 volumes of the Manx Hansard were used extensively and constitute an extremely rich source of information about political history and the beliefs and commitments of Manx politicians. When the research was undertaken it was not possible to complement this with material from internal government records. With the passing of the Public Records Act 1999 and the formal opening of the Public Record Office at Spring Valley in April 2000, it should soon be possible to fill this gap. It is already possible to see a basic list of the files held (from circa 1914 to the 1950s) and obtain approval from the Chief Secretary to see specific files, but this facility was not available to the author when carrying out the main research for this book.

With three important exceptions, endnotes provide details of the sources consulted. The exceptions relate to biographical details of members of Tynwald, aspects of electoral history and financial data extracted from public accounts. Unless indicated to the contrary, biographical details were obtained from the various Isle of Man yearbooks, notably the *Examiner Annuals*, the *Norris Modern Press Yearbooks*, successive editions of *The Tynwald Companion* (1980, 1982, 1983, 1986, 1993, 1999 and 2000) newspapers, obituaries in the press and the Manx Hansard. Except where stated to the contrary, details of Manx electoral history are taken from the *Isle of Man Examiner* and her sister newspapers, the only newspaper providing coverage for the whole of the twentieth century, election manifestos available for consultation in the Manx National Heritage Library and Tom Sherratt (comp.), *Isle of Man Parliamentary Election Results 1919–1986* (unpublished, Warrington, 1986). The sources of raw expenditure data were the annual *Financial Statements* up to 1919/20, the *Accounts of the Government Treasurer* from 1920/21 to 1985/86, the *Isle of Man Government Accounts* 1986/87 to 1992/93 and the *Detailed Government Accounts* 1993/94 to 1999/2000; the level of spending at March 2000 prices was calculated with the help of the Price Index supplied by Martin Caley of the Economic Affairs Division of the Manx Treasury; it forms Appendix 1 to this study.

# Abbreviations

The Home Office correspondence files consulted in the Public Record Office at Kew are referred to by their PRO file reference number, commencing with the series number HO 45 or HO 284. Reports of the Debates in the Manx Legislature are referred to by the volume number, followed by *Manx Deb.*, the date and page number(s); after October 1970, the page number is preceded by C for Legislative Council, K for the House of Keys and T for Tynwald. Acts of Tynwald are printed in volumes of *Statutes of the Isle of Man* up to 1970 and in annual volumes of the *Acts of Tynwald* from 1971.

Most of the abbreviations used in the book are explained in the text. The following are some of those that appear a long way from the explanation:

| | |
|---|---|
| APG | Alternative Policy Group until 1999; Alliance for Progressive Government thereafter |
| CEA | Customs and Excise Agreement |
| CPA | Common Purse Arrangement or Agreement |
| DAFF | Department of Agriculture, Fisheries and Forestry |
| DHSS | Department of Health and Social Security |
| DLT | Department of Tourism and Leisure |
| DHPP | Department of Highways, Ports and Properties |
| DOLGE | Department of Local Government and the Environment |
| DTLT | Department of Tourism, Leisure and Transport |
| DTT | Department of Tourism and Transport |
| EC | European Community |
| EEC | European Economic Community |
| EPAC | Expenditure and Public Accounts Committee |
| EU | European Union |
| FSC | Financial Services Commission |
| IPA | Insurance and Pensions Authority |
| IRIS | The Integration and Recycling of the Island's Sewage |
| MCA | Manx Constitutional Association |
| MDP | Manx Democratic Party |
| MER | Manx Electric Railway |
| MHK | Member of the House of Keys |
| MLB | Manx Law Bulletin |
| MLC | Member of the Legislative Council |
| MLP | Manx Labour Party |
| MLR | Manx Law Reports |
| MNRL | Manx National Reform League |
| MPPA | Manx People's Political Association |
| NHI | National Health Insurance |
| NHS | National Health Service |
| LGB | Local Government Board |
| OAPNHIB | Old Age Pensions and National Health Insurance Board |
| PAC | Public Accounts Committee |
| SMS | School Medical Service |
| STV | Single Transferable Vote |
| TGWU | Transport and General Workers' Union |
| VAT | Value-Added Tax |

# CHAPTER ONE

# Introduction

## *Offshore Island Politics*

*Offshore Island Politics* is a study of the constitutional and political development of an island whose fortunes during the twentieth century were inextricably linked to those of its much larger neighbour, the United Kingdom. While that development might be portrayed as a struggle, albeit an erratic one, for greater autonomy from the UK, progress towards that goal in formal constitutional terms stopped short of full independence. Territorial proximity, political history, cultural affinity, social links and economic integration combined to persuade Manx decision-makers to choose a dependent political relationship with the UK.

Geographically the Isle of Man is part of the British Isles. While location in the middle of the Irish Sea clearly separates it physically from the main islands in the group, small size and population have made it vulnerable to the wishes of the dominant island in the group. The Isle of Man is 221 square miles or 572 square kilometres. Figures 1.1 and 1.2 show its location within the British Isles and Western Europe. The Island's population in 1901 was 54,752; it declined to 48,133 in 1961 before rising steadily to 74,900 by 2000.[1] Tables 1.1 and 1.2 detail the changes over the course of the century.

Notwithstanding that vulnerability, a remarkable feature of Manx political history over the course of the millennium was the retention of a separate political identity. At no stage was the Island fully assimilated into an external political system. On the contrary, during most of her history the Isle of Man enjoyed some measure of internal self-government. Whether the ultimate authority over the Island rested with Norway, Scotland, England or the UK, considerable power was devolved to insular institutions. Although the extent and pattern of that devolution varied over the centuries, the survival of Tynwald, the Manx Parliament, from its emergence during the tenth century to the present day at the centre of Manx affairs, was the hallmark of a special relationship with successive sovereign powers. During the period covered by this study that special relationship was with the UK. Although the Island was never formally described as a colony of the UK, for much of the period under discussion the Island's political relationship with the UK bore all the hallmarks of a colonial relationship, policy making by the UK institutions of government in which the Manx people were not represented, the dominant position of UK-appointed officials in Tynwald and local legislation and taxation subject to Home Office or Treasury approval.

In the course of the twentieth century the Isle of Man was a Crown dependency whose relationship with the UK during the century developed very gradually from one of strict UK control to one of almost complete autonomy insofar as purely domestic

Figure 1.1. Isle of Man in the British Isles

P.G.Cubbin, FBCart.S - 2001

Figure 1.2. Isle of Man and Europe

| | | |
|---|---|---|
| 1957 EEC 6 | 1981 EC 1 (10) | 1990 E. GERMANY (12) |
| 1973 EEC 3 (9) | 1986 EC 2 (12) | 1995 EU 3 (15) |

500km

P.G.Cubbin, FBCart.S - 2001

matters are concerned. The UK retained responsibility for the Island's international relations, external defence and certain other matters of a nonlocal character. Increased autonomy did not always result in separate development; in many major policy areas the Island chose to keep very closely in line with UK developments and in more recent years with European developments. Even in such areas as direct taxation and economic support for tourism and industry, where the Island pursued a distinctive path, policies were designed to exploit the Island's close relationship and attract new residents, investment and tourists from the UK.

The essence of the Isle of Man's separate political identity lay in Tynwald. The last hundred years saw major changes in the membership and powers of Tynwald and its constituent branches, the Legislative Council and the House of Keys. Domination by an externally appointed Lieutenant-Governor and Legislative Council gave way gradually to a more democratic system with power in the hands of the directly elected representatives of the Manx people sitting in the House of Keys. Throughout the century the Island also maintained a system of local government with between 24 and 26 local authorities; Figures 1.3 and 1.4 show the local authority boundaries and population at the beginning and end of the century.[2]

One effect of distinctive political institutions and the emulation of major UK policies was the perpetuation of attitudes and values supportive both of the Manx

**Table 1.1. Population change 1901–2000[1]**

| Census Year | Census Population | Resident Population[2] | Percentage of Population born[3] Isle of Man | UK |
|---|---|---|---|---|
| 1901 | 54,752 | n/a | 82.0 | 17.2 |
| 1911 | 52,016 | n/a | 80.4 | 17.7 |
| 1921[4] | 60,284 | n/a | 60.4 | 35.9 |
| 1931 | 49,308 | n/a | 74.1 | 23.4 |
| 1939 (estimate)[5] | 52,029 | n/a | n/a | n/a |
| 1951 | 55,253 | 54,024 | 64.3 | 30.6 |
| 1961 | 48,133 | 47,166 | 67.4 | 29.7 |
| 1966 | 50,423 | 49,312 | n/a | n/a |
| 1971 | 54,581 | 53,288 | 59.3 | 34.7 |
| 1976 | 61,723 | 60,496 | n/a | n/a |
| 1981 | 66,101 | 64,679 | 53.2 | 42.7 |
| 1986 | 66,060 | 64,282 | n/a | n/a |
| 1991 | 71,267 | 69,788 | 49.6 | 44.8 |
| 1996 | 74,680 | 71,714 | 49.9 | 44.1 |
| 2000 (estimate)[6] | | 74,900 | | |

1　Data derived from Isle of Man Census Reports 1901–96.

2　Figures not available for 1901–31

3　The figures in these two columns are percentages of the census population up to and including 1971 and of the resident population from 1981.

4　While all the other censuses were held in April, that of 1921 was conducted on 19/20 June and included an exceptional number of visitors (18 per cent compared with the more usual figure of 2 per cent).

5　No census was held in 1941 because of the war.

6　An April 2000 estimate, see Isle of Man Government, *Policy Review 2000*, vol. 1, p. iii.

political system and a close working relationship with the UK. Inhabitants of the Island and their representatives in Tynwald are very conscious of being both Manx and British. This dual culture was reinforced by the media, a vigorous local press and, after 1962, a local commercial radio station, Manx Radio, promoting Manx culture, and the daily press and main radio and television services, British culture. It was also reflected in the Island's extraparliamentary political institutions. Although the Island did not see the development of a party system, let alone one along UK lines, there were periodic attempts to organise parties with an ideological affinity to one of those in the UK, but with an independent Manx organisation as in the case of the Manx Labour Party. More important than parties were the host of interest groups that developed over the course of the century. Many of these were distinctively Manx, but others, in particular the labour unions, were affiliated to or part of larger British organisations.

The free movement of people between the Isle of Man and the UK provided the basis of strong social as well as cultural links with the population of the UK. It also proved one of the most powerful rationales for the Island's pursuit of UK policies in such areas as social security, health and education. Demands for reciprocal agreements and standards at least equivalent to those of the UK were to the forefront of the campaigns for social and educational reform in the Island. The outstanding changes in the population of the Isle of Man over the course of the century were the result of either

Table 1.2. Population change in the four towns 1901–2000[1]

| Census Year | Isle of Man Population | Castletown[2] | Douglas[3] | Peel[4] | Ramsey[5] |
|---|---|---|---|---|---|
| 1901 | 54,752 | 1,965 | 19,223 | 3,304 | 4,729 |
| 1911 | 52,016 | 1,817 | 21,192 | 2,605 | 4,247 |
| 1921[6] | 60,284 | 1,898 | 27,604 | 2,690 | 4,642 |
| 1931 | 49,308 | 1,713 | 19,328 | 2,477 | 4,198 |
| 1939 (estimate)[7] | 52,029 | n/a | n/a | n/a | n/a |
| 1951 | 55,253 | 1,755 | 20,361 | 2,612 | 4,621 |
| 1961 | 48,133 | 1,536 | 18,821 | 2,483 | 3,789 |
| 1966 | 50,423 | 2,378 | 19,517 | 2,739 | 3,880 |
| 1971 | 53,288 | 2,671 | 19,163 | 2,911 | 4,807 |
| 1976 | 60,496 | 2,788 | 19,897 | 3,295 | 5,372 |
| 1981 | 64,679 | 3,141 | 19,944 | 3,688 | 5,818 |
| 1986 | 64,282 | 3,019 | 20,368 | 3,660 | 5,778 |
| 1991 | 69,788 | 3,152 | 22,214 | 3,829 | 6,496 |
| 1996 | 71,714 | 2,958 | 23,487 | 3,819 | 6,874 |
| 2000 (estimate) | 74,900 | | | | |

1 Census population up to 1961; resident population from 1971.
2 The Castletown boundaries were extended in 1966; see Appendix 3, Figure A3.1.
3 The boundaries of Douglas were extended in 1904, 1937, 1952, 1969 and 1985; see Appendix 3, Figure A3.2.
4 Peel's boundaries were extended in 1956 and 1971; see Appendix 3, Figure A3.3.
5 Ramsey's boundaries were extended in 1970 and 1993; see Appendix 3, Figure A3.4.
6 While all the other censuses were held in April, that of 1921 was conducted on 19/20 June and included an exceptional number of visitors (18 per cent compared with the more usual figure of 2 per cent).
7 No census was held in 1941 because of the war.

## Figure 1.3. Local Authorities and Census Population, 1901

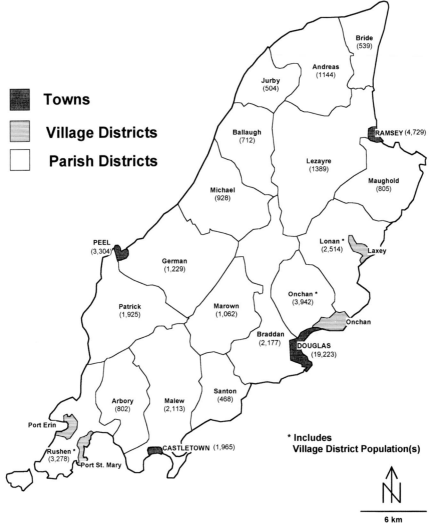

P.G.Cubbin, FBCart.S - 2001

Source of Census data: *Census 1901, Islands in the British Seas*, Cd. 1473 (London, 1903).

Manx residents moving to the UK for higher education, employment and onward migration or UK residents responding to the Island's attractions as a place for retirement, work and investment. In 1996, out of a total resident population of 71,714 people, 44 per cent were born in the UK (mainly England) compared with 49.9 per cent in the Isle of Man.

The attraction of new residents and investment from the UK was facilitated by the continuing strength of economic ties with the UK. Throughout the century there was free trade between the Isle of Man and the UK, monetary union, a largely common

Figure 1.4. Local Authorities and Residential Population, 1996

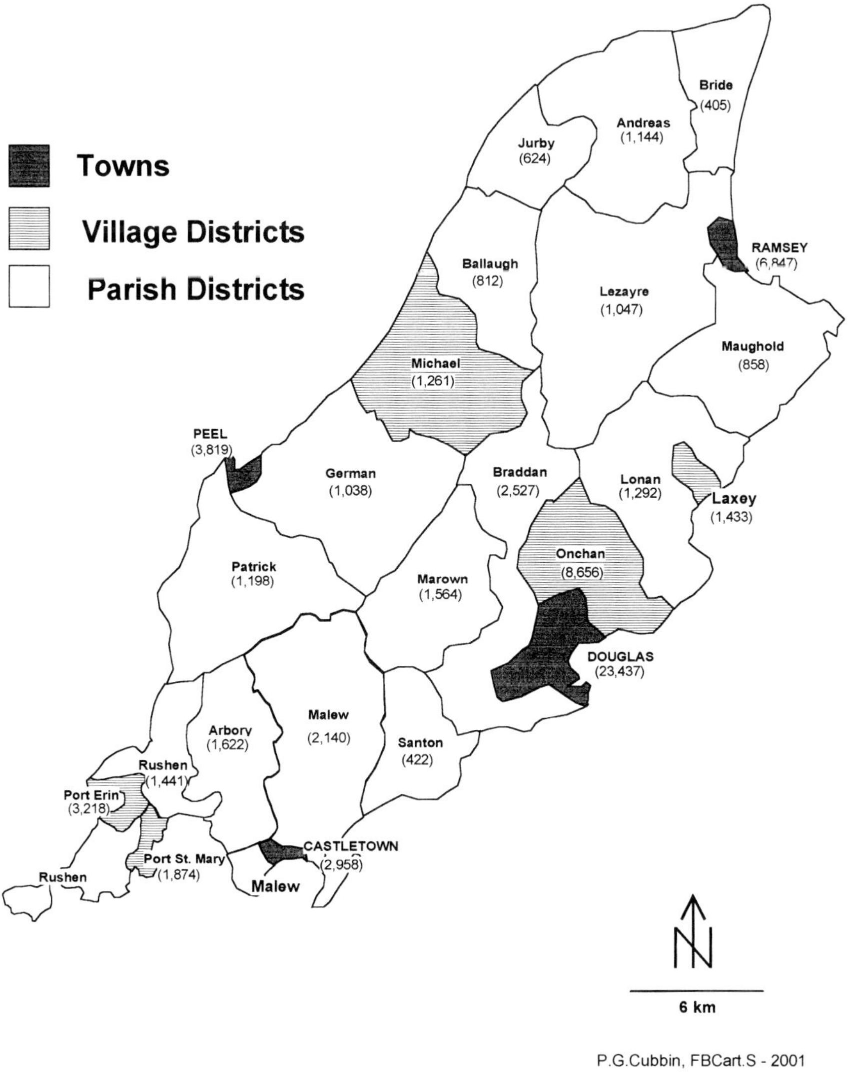

Source of Census data: *Isle of Man Census Report 1996* (Douglas, 1996).

policy in respect of indirect taxation and similar levels of subsidy and support for agriculture and fisheries. For much of the century there was free movement of labour between the UK and the Isle of Man; despite the Island's introduction of work permits in 1954 and Manx exclusion from the European Economic Community in 1973, there were no barriers in the way of people from the Isle of Man entering or returning to the UK labour market. Until 1958 Manx finances were formally subject to UK Treasury control; subsequently the UK was able to exercise control informally and indirectly as a result of intergovernmental agreements on indirect taxation and the Island's pursuit of

UK-based policies in expensive areas like social welfare, health and education. Social and economic ties with the UK were reinforced by the UK origin of most of the new residents to and investment in the Island since the 1960s.

Although there can be little doubt about the tremendous influence of the UK on offshore Isle of Man and the Island's vulnerability to policy change within the UK and Europe, it would be misleading to leave this preliminary discussion without reference to the benefits that have accrued from its special relationship with the UK, especially in the aftermath of the considerable devolution of power effected by the Isle of Man Act in 1958. The detail of that measure and subsequent reforms will be considered later; suffice it to say here that within an overall framework of policies influenced by the UK, the Island was able to protect and promote its interests and wellbeing in ways denied to the many offshore islands that form part of the UK. The Island was for the most part free to choose whether and when to follow UK initiatives, to tailor legislation derived from the UK to meet particular Manx needs, to introduce distinctive policies to assist the Manx economy and to promote Manx heritage and culture. At no time was such freedom more important than in 1973 when the UK joined the EEC; on that occasion the negotiation of a special relationship with the Community was in no small measure the result of the special status already enjoyed with the UK.

## *Major Themes and Periods*

This study analyses three broad aspects of twentieth-century political development: constitutional progress towards Island self-government, elections and public policy and the changing role of the state in Manx society. In doing so the focus is on the politicians of Tynwald rather than their official advisors or the many interest groups that seek to influence them. Although such advisors—notably the Government Secretary/Chief Secretary, the Attorney General and his staff, the Clerk of Tynwald, the Clerk to the Legislative Council and senior civil servants—have played an important role, it is beyond the scope of this study. While reference is made to some of the more influential interest groups, the complex interactions between such groups, civil servants and politicians could not have been analysed without extensive further research. Each of the themes is examined with reference to five periods.

The analysis of the Island's constitutional development has two main strands, the devolution of power from the UK to the Isle of Man and the transfer of power within the Island from the Lieutenant-Governor and Crown-appointed officials to directly elected members of the House of Keys. Consideration is also given to the growing tensions in the area of international relations, which remain a UK responsibility. Simultaneously with the Island's struggle to maximise its autonomy in domestic affairs, international agreements and interpretations of those agreements brought into question exactly what is and what is not domestic to the Isle of Man.

One of the most important political changes of the twentieth century was the gradual ascendancy of the directly elected House of Keys in Manx politics. The second major aim of this study is to examine the role of elections both in recruiting members of the House (MHKs) and setting the agenda for public policy. Changes in the franchise, the distribution of seats and the electoral system are studied as a necessary prerequisite to an analysis of the century's 18 general elections. The absence of a party system in the Island makes the relationship between elections and public policy much more tenuous

Lord Henniker (Lieutenant-Governor 1895–1902) with the Legislative Council in July 1900. At the time of the first Tynwald ceremony of the twentieth century the Lieutenant-Governor as chief executive and the Legislative Council were very much the senior partners in Tynwald. The three in the front of the picture are Bishop Straton, Lord Henniker and the Clerk of the Rolls, Sir James Gell; in the background are Deemster Thomas Kneen, the Vicar General, Samuel Harris, the Archdeacon, the Reverend Hugh Stowell Gill and the Attorney General, George Alfred Ring.

The Council of Ministers in June 1999. By the end of the twentieth century power had been transferred to the Chief Minister and the Council of Ministers with members drawn primarily from the House of Keys. From left to right those standing are Stephen Rodan (Education), Tony Brown (Transport), Richard Corkill (Treasury), Clare Christian (Health and Social Security) and David Cretney (Tourism and Leisure); those sitting are Alex Downie (Agriculture, Fisheries and Forestry), Walter Gilbey (Local Government and the Environment), Donald Gelling (Chief Minister), Allan Bell (Home Affairs) and David North (Trade and Industry).

than in the UK. Nevertheless, the study of successive elections does reveal their importance as a vehicle for placing issues on the public agenda, as a source of new public policies and both explicitly and implicitly as a mechanism for legitimising continuity of policy. Although no attempt will be made to analyse Manx voting behaviour, it is important to be aware that the policy commitments and manifestos of candidates cannot by themselves explain voting behaviour. For the electorate the attractiveness of a candidate's manifesto may be judged side by side with the candidate's personality and political record, campaign performance, standing in the community and social background; moreover for individual voters the relative weight of these factors may vary. Manx electoral history provides many examples where two or three candidates in a multimember constituency stand on a joint manifesto, but fare very differently on polling day, attracting more or less support for reasons unrelated to policy and sometimes succeeding or failing in spite of as well as because of policy commitments. There is no reason to suppose that the situation is any different in single member constituencies.

The third major aim is to describe and explain the changing role of the state in Manx society. Three broad aspects of public policy are considered, the development and persistence of the welfare state, the changing pattern of government support for the economy and the funding of public policy. The first is studied by reference to five main policy areas, social security, education, health, housing and employment, the second by

Government Office with the 1894 Legislative Buildings, Douglas circa 1900. In 1900 central government used Government Office and 23 other buildings, most of which were concerned with the law and order service—the prison, courthouses and police stations.

Hillary House with the old Government Office, the Legislative Buildings and the new Government Offices opened in 1975. By the turn of the century, central government administration and service delivery involved over 300 buildings or parts of buildings, most publicly owned like Illiam Dhone House, Homefield House, Markwell House, Murray House and the Sea Terminal Building, and some, like Hillary House, leased from the private sector.

focusing both on general economic policy and specific support for agriculture, tourism, light industry and the financial sector and the third by discussing the means adopted for the funding of the ever more expensive policies agreed by Tynwald.

The periodisation used in this study is broadly the same as that adopted by the author in *Devolution at Work* in 1979[3] and his contribution to John Belchem (ed.), *A New History of the Isle of Man: The Modern Period 1830–1999* in 2000.[4] The twentieth century is divided into five periods of roughly equivalent length. Chapter Two is a historical introduction, looking at the Island's position during the latter part of the nineteenth century. Chapter Three studies the Raglan era from 1902 to 1919. Lord Raglan's appointment as Lieutenant-Governor coincided with the commencement of the Keys' campaign for constitutional reform; his resignation in 1919 came immediately after the end of the First World War as the Island was about to embark on a major programme of constitutional, electoral and social reform. The interwar period, which is the subject of Chapter Four, is one that has been widely used by historians of other countries and regions and makes eminent sense in the case of the Isle of Man, given the landmark political developments of 1919 and war in 1939. The combination of the years of the Second World War with the postwar period up to 1958 in Chapter Five is perhaps more controversial. However, the war did see the resumption of the Keys' campaign for an executive council and for the removal of UK Treasury control and the promise by the UK of progress on both fronts. It also heralded a radical shift in the role of government and people's expectations of government as the Island followed the major social reforms of the Coalition and Labour Governments. Parliament's Isle of Man Act in 1958 marked the culmination of the negotiations to give effect to the UK's promise. Chapters Six and Seven cover the years of internal political reform between 1958 and 1981, the main feature of which was the gradual transfer of power from the Lieutenant-Governor to bodies that were responsible to Tynwald. Chapters Eight and Nine look at the final two decades of the century, a period of population growth and unprecedented prosperity for the small offshore island. Constitutionally and politically the main features were the emergence of a ministerial system and the retention of a strong public sector. Chapter Ten offers some concluding comments.

## Notes

1   An estimate of the residential population in April 2000; see Isle of Man Government, *Policy Review 2000*, vol. 1, p. iii.
2   There were 25 local authorities in 1900, the number rising to 26 with the creation of Michael Village District in 1905 and falling to 24 as the result of the amalgamations of Onchan Parish and Village District in 1986 and Michael Parish and Village District in 1989. Periodic approval was also given by Tynwald to requests from the urban authorities for boundary extensions; for further detail in the case of the four towns, see Appendix 3.
3   D. G. Kermode, *Devolution at Work: A Case Study of the Isle of Man* (Farnborough, Hampshire, 1979).
4   Volume 5, Liverpool, 2000.

# CHAPTER TWO

# Nineteenth-Century Background

The nineteenth-century background to this study is one of colonial rule by or on behalf of the United Kingdom. Lieutenant-Governors acted as sole executives subject to the often strict control of the UK authorities. The opportunities for Manx participation in government except in an advisory capacity were quite restricted and the role of Tynwald fell far short of what might have been expected in a 'Land of Home Rule'.[1] The period after 1866 did see an enhanced role for Tynwald and within Tynwald for the House of Keys now that it was directly elected, but only in the context of a political system dominated by a UK-appointed Lieutenant-Governor and 'his' Legislative Council. Part of that enhancement was the result of the changing role of the state in Manx society. As government became increasingly active in promoting the welfare of both the Manx people and the Manx economy, so the opportunities for members of the Keys to share in decision making increased, both as legislators and members of new boards of Tynwald.

## *The Myth of Home Rule 1866–1902*

The 1866 changes were mainly the result of efforts by the House of Keys and Sir Henry Loch who had been appointed Lieutenant-Governor in 1863.[2] Following the Isle of Man Purchase Act of 1765[3] the Isle of Man had been subjected to the general financial control of the British Government and, although Tynwald had continued to legislate for the Island on a limited range of domestic matters, the lack of control over customs and finance had limited its real room for manoeuvre. Sympathising with the Keys' desire for Tynwald to be able to control the expenditure of insular revenue and convinced of the need for this revenue to improve the Island's economy, Loch wrote to the Home Office on 21 March 1865 submitting proposals for an increase in insular customs duties on condition that the increased revenue be at the disposal of the Isle of Man Government. The Treasury agreed to introduce the necessary legislation at Westminster if the Keys consented to become an elective body and subject to the Island bearing any financial risk and paying to the UK a fixed annual contribution of £10,000 for defence and common services. Tynwald approved the proposals on 20 March 1866.[4]

The resultant Isle of Man Customs, Harbours and Public Purposes Act 1866 provided for the increase in the customs tariff originally proposed by Loch, separated Manx finances from those of the UK and gave to Tynwald a share in determining the expenditure of the surplus customs revenue left after meeting the essential costs of

Sir Henry Loch, Lieutenant-Governor
1863–82.

Spencer Walpole, Lieutenant-Governor
1882–93.

Sir West Ridgeway, Lieutenant-Governor
1893–95.

John S. Goldie-Taubman, Speaker of the
House of Keys 1867–98.

government and certain statutory expenses.[5] The latter included the sum of £2,300 per annum which had been set aside each year since 1844 for harbour maintenance and the ninth of the total gross revenue made available each year for harbours and other public works since 1853;[6] on security of a further two ninths the Harbour Commissioners were empowered to borrow money for harbour improvements with the approval of Tynwald and the UK Treasury; the Island was also to pay the fixed sum of £10,000 demanded by the Treasury as an annual contribution to the UK for common services. Section 8 of the Act made very clear the formal limits of Tynwald's new financial powers:

> The surplus, if any, of the duties of customs of the Isle of Man, after deducting the sums herein-before directed or authorised to be paid or set aside thereout or charged thereon, shall be applied for such public purposes of the Isle of Man to be approved of by the Commissioners of Her Majesty's Treasury, as the Court of Tynwald shall from time to time determine, the Lieutenant-Governor having a veto upon such decisions.[7]

What was the significance of the changes? First, the separation of Manx finances from those of the UK helped to ensure that Manx revenues were at least used for Manx purposes. Second, the increase in revenue enabled the Island to proceed with a series of breakwater projects that were to prove of immense value to the Manx economy and the tourist industry in particular. Third, Tynwald was given a share in the control of expenditure of the surplus revenue; however, because the expenditure of this surplus was subject to the approval both of the Lieutenant-Governor and the UK Treasury, the actual powers of Tynwald remained subject to the goodwill of the colonial authorities. In practice Tynwald's position after 1866 was better than it was in theory, due to the Island's largely good relations with the UK Treasury and the sympathetic attitudes of Lieutenant-Governors Loch and Walpole who between them held office for the 30 years from 1863 to 1893.[8] Indeed, Walpole, describing the effects of the 1866 Act, talked of a transformation from a position where the Isle of Man was 'little more than a department of the Home Office' to one where 'Tynwald was practically given a free hand and was allowed to manage its affairs in its own way'.[9] Such a description tends to neglect the important role of the externally appointed Lieutenant-Governor and the reality of UK Treasury control which was far from a formality, but it does give some idea, if an exaggerated one, of the significance of the changes. A. W. Moore wrote of the Act as having provided 'home rule during pleasure',[10] but even that gives a misleading impression of the extent of Tynwald's freedom. The UK remained responsible for the good government of the Island and continued to appoint and remunerate out of Manx revenue such officers as were deemed necessary for carrying on the insular government, including the judiciary, the law officers and the police. Parliament retained the power to legislate for the Island on any matter. Manx harbours were still under UK control. Crown lands in the Island were administered by the UK Department of Woods and Forests and the revenues received kept by the UK. Even the size and expenditure of the surplus revenue was largely determined by the Lieutenant-Governor in his capacity as the Island's Chancellor of the Exchequer. In conflict with a Lieutenant-Governor or the UK Treasury, Tynwald remained extremely weak.

Following the reforms of 1866 a series of developments, both formal and informal, resulted in further increases in the authority of Tynwald. In addition to the right to decide what harbour works should be undertaken, which had been gained in 1866, an Act of Parliament in 1872 gave to Tynwald control of the Island's harbours and the right to vote on the Lieutenant-Governor's nominations for membership of the

Harbour Commissioners.[11] In 1878 it was admitted by the Law Officers of the Crown that Tynwald was competent to pass measures relating to church temporalities.[12] The church had been one of the main spheres in which Parliament had legislated for the Isle of Man since the Revestment in 1765. As a result of the decision the insular Bishop Temporalities Act of 1878 was given the Royal Assent.[13] A major grievance under the 1866 Act was Tynwald's lack of control over what were deemed to be the essential costs of government. In 1886, when his attention was drawn to the fact that increases in the salaries of officials had been made without Tynwald being consulted, Walpole, while reserving the rights of the UK authorities and his successors, gave an undertaking not to increase the costs of government without first consulting Tynwald and to defer to any objection that was supported by a majority in Tynwald.[14] While the latter change was an informal one, only guaranteed as long as Walpole was Lieutenant-Governor, Parliament's Isle of Man (Customs) Act 1887 empowered Tynwald to impose, abolish and vary custom duties by means of resolutions.[15] In practice, Tynwald was still only able to propose changes indirectly through and with the support of the Lieutenant-Governor. Moreover, in most instances the Island followed the UK tariff very closely and there is good reason to believe that the Treasury would have disallowed major departures from the UK tariff for fear of a recurrence of illegal trading.[16]

The only question that seriously disturbed relations with the UK in the latter part of the nineteenth century was that of the Port Erin breakwater. The incident highlighted the considerable constraints on Tynwald's freedom to cater for the general welfare of the Island. A breakwater had been recommended in 1791, 1835 and 1859, but was only seriously considered following a petition from 700 fishermen to Tynwald in 1861. In return for its erection, they offered to pay annual dues of £2 on each fishing boat entering the harbour until the costs of the project were covered. Tynwald asked the UK authorities to introduce legislation authorising the toll. The resultant Isle of Man Harbours Act of 1863 authorised the collection of harbour dues at Port Erin and empowered the Harbour Commissioners, with the approval of the Board of Trade, to borrow on the security of the dues collected.[17] In 1864 the Isle of Man Harbours Amendment Act enabled the Commissioners to borrow too on a collateral security of £1,600 per annum from the Island's surplus customs revenue.[18] A loan of £58,200 was thus obtained and work commenced in 1864.[19]

It had been expected by both governments that, once the breakwater had been built, harbour dues would provide sufficient money for maintenance costs, interest charges and the repayment of the loan, but they were soon proved wrong. Damage to the breakwater by storms in 1868 and 1869 and the scanty receipts from harbour dues made both governments realise that dues alone would not be sufficient to fund the breakwater. Although Treasury approval was given to £13,000 voted by Tynwald for repairs and completion in 1870, on 30 November of that year the Treasury complained to the Home Office about the 'nominal' dues being collected and the fact that the entire cost of the interest and sinking fund on the £58,200 loan was being met 'out of Imperial revenue'.

A lengthy controversy ensued. The UK Government, on the plea that it had been misled about the harbour dues and that the Island was being subsidised out of taxes it did not pay, demanded that the interest and repayment of the loan be charged on the insular revenue. It admitted legal liability but claimed that the insular authorities were morally responsible. Tynwald's answer to this, in addition to the legal argument, was that the breakwater served Imperial as well as Manx shipping. In 1875 the Treasury offered to concede to the Island certain other financial claims that had been made by Tynwald, including the right to revenue from Crown lands in the Island, the refunding of duties paid in the UK on goods afterwards imported to the Island and an additional payment by the Post Office towards the cost of providing a daily mail service, on condition that the Island assumed full responsibility for the Port Erin loan. In December 1876 Tynwald rejected these proposals, with the result that the Treasury announced its refusal to sanction further expenditure and loans for public works in the Isle of Man. After much negotiation the dispute was finally settled in 1879. It was agreed that the £58,200 loan should be liquidated by a payment by the Island of £20,000. In return, the Island would be credited with £2,000 per annum in respect of the duty paid in the UK on goods subsequently imported into the Isle of Man, Crown property in the Island would be subject to local rates and the Island would have a daily mail service provided at the expense of the Post Office. The breakwater was destroyed in a storm in 1884 and was not rebuilt.

While the controversy was the exception to an otherwise harmonious relationship with the UK, it was far from being the only example of the tightness of UK financial control. Between 1866 and the turn of the century each of the four Lieutenant-Governors periodically found themselves fighting for the Island against the UK. For example, when in 1870 Tynwald voted £14,200 to buy a site and erect legislative buildings and law courts in Douglas, the Treasury expressed doubts as to whether the Island could afford them and undertook a review of the Island's finances. In a letter dated 30 November 1870, it concluded that it was 'evident that the large powers lately bestowed upon the Government have been freely used' and until it was 'clear beyond question' that the finances of the Island could bear the charge, it could not be sanctioned. In the same letter the Treasury also refused to sanction two loans that had been requested for harbour works at Ramsey and Castletown. Loch made repeated protests against the decisions and even asked the Home Office to support him against the Treasury, but to no avail.[20] During his administration Loch made several requests for increases in the salaries of government officials, but these were invariably turned down or substantially reduced on the grounds that unless there was an increase in their duties there was no justification for an increase in pay.[21]

In a strongly worded letter to the Home Office on 20 May 1885 Walpole objected most strongly to the interference of the Treasury 'with small additional expenses which I consider it necessary to incur for the efficiency of the administration'. He alluded to the fact that he had promised Tynwald that he would not increase salaries of officials without their approval, 'a much more effective restraint on my action than any mere approval or disapproval of the Treasury can be'. In a letter to the Home Office the Treasury privately conceded that there was no point in interfering 'beyond seeing that the £10,000 is properly received'.[22] For the rest of his administration Treasury control relaxed considerably and Walpole himself acknowledged that he encountered no more interference.[23]

During the last decade of the century the finances of the Island deteriorated. As a result, Sir West Ridgeway (1893–95) and Lord John Henniker (1895–1902) encountered a tightening of UK control.[24] When Ridgeway forwarded a resolution of Tynwald voting £2,000 for the purpose of advertising the Island as a holiday resort, the Treasury withheld its sanction on the grounds that such expenditure was 'not absolutely necessary for the wellbeing of the Island'. Although on receipt of the estimates for 1894/95 it amended its position, approval was only given on the understanding that after three years evidence must be produced to show the real value of the expenditure. The Treasury made very clear that it viewed advertising as something 'better left to private enterprise'.[25] Continuing concern about the state of the Island's finances during Henniker's term of office resulted in an additional constraint being imposed on the Island by the Treasury in 1899:

> The surplus of revenue over expenditure provided in the estimates of recent years is considerably smaller than is consistent with sound finance. Their Lordships are of the opinion that the surplus should not be less than £5,000 in addition to the receipts from interest on local loans and they will not be prepared to approve the estimates for the coming financial year unless they show a surplus of this amount, which should be secured either by increased taxation or preferably by a reduction in expenditure.[26]

Given this stricture, it is hardly surprising that the Treasury should reject a series of requests from Lord Henniker in 1899, 1900, 1901 and 1902 for an end to the £10,000 contribution.[27]

Thus when Lord Raglan became Lieutenant-Governor in 1902 the constitutional authority of Tynwald was severely constrained. The UK Parliament retained the right to legislate for the Island on any matter and all Manx legislation required the Royal Assent, which was by no means a formality. The Crown, through the Home Office and Lieutenant-Governor, remained responsible for the good government of the Island and continued to appoint and control such officers as were necessary for carrying on the insular government, including the judiciary, the law officers, the police and civil servants. The Lieutenant-Governor was the Island's sole executive and Chancellor of the Exchequer. He presided over Tynwald and dominated the Legislative Council, made up as it was almost exclusively of Crown-appointed officials. The Council enjoyed parity of powers with the House of Keys and provided an effective means for the colonial government to control the legislature without recourse to such extreme measures as denial of Treasury approval or the Royal Assent. While members of the House of Keys could reject legislation and refuse to sanction financial resolutions, positive initiatives depended for their success on a sympathetic Lieutenant-Governor and the backing of the UK authorities.

Notwithstanding these formal constraints, there were limited opportunities for members of the Keys to participate in the administration of the Isle of Man, outside of the House itself and the full assembly of Tynwald, in committees and boards of Tynwald. For example, in anticipation of reductions in the surplus revenue and following criticisms from MHKs about the lack of a clear financial policy, Lord Henniker proposed the establishment of an expenditure committee to advise Tynwald on expenditure and taxation. Accordingly, in 1901 and again in 1902 Tynwald appointed the Speaker of the House, Arthur W. Moore, and four other MHKs to serve with two MLCs on such a committee; even though the anticipated decline in revenue did not materialise, the committees' recommendations regarding priorities for capital spending were acted upon by Lord Henniker and without objection from the UK authorities.[28]

Prior to Tynwald's appointment of a Lunatic Asylum Committee in 1864, the only example of delegation of authority to an executive body appointed by Tynwald was that of the Highway Board. After 1864 there was a gradual increase in opportunities for MHKs to share in the administration of the Island through membership of bodies with an executive and advisory role. The reconstitution or establishment of eight such bodies between 1872 and 1894, each involving MHKs, marked the beginnings of the board

Arthur W. Moore, Speaker of the House of Keys 1898–1909, with other MHKs at St Johns on 5 July 1900. On his left is his eventual successor as Speaker, Dalrymple Maitland. Moore represented Middle from 1885, becoming Speaker on the death of Goldie-Taubman and a leading spokesman for the House in their negotiations with Lord Raglan and the Home Office. He is also remembered for a series of learned publications on Manx history and culture, including *A History of the Isle of Man* which was published in two volumes in 1900.

system that was to be a distinctive feature of Manx politics for most of the twentieth century. Although not formally a board of Tynwald until 1948, the Harbour Commissioners were reconstituted in 1872 as a result of the transfer of responsibility for Manx harbours to Tynwald under the UK Harbours Act of that year; Tynwald gained the power to approve the nominations by the Lieutenant-Governor for four of the five members; by statute the chair was the Receiver-General, an appointee of the Crown and an ex officio MLC.[29] In the same year the Board of Education was established under Tynwald's Elementary Education Act. It was renamed the Council of Education in 1893, but retained a composition of five members appointed by Tynwald, the appointees selecting their own chair.[30] Tynwald's Highways Act 1874 reconstituted the Highways Board, with six members appointed by Tynwald and the appointees selecting their own chair.[31] In 1882 the Salmon and Freshwater Fisheries Act provided for the Board of Fishery Conservators, made up of five members appointed by Tynwald, the appointees choosing their own chair.[32] With the introduction of poor relief and the completion of a poor asylum, the Lunatic Asylum Board became the Asylum Board. Under the Poor Relief Act 1893 the Board selected its own chair from among the five members appointed by Tynwald.[33] A Fisheries Committee with a similar composition was set up under the Sea Fisheries Act 1894.[34] In the same year two other bodies were established, one reflecting the considerable expansion of local government in the field of public health, the other the concern of the Island to promote itself as a holiday resort. The Local Government Board was set up under the Local Government Amendment Act 1894, with the Lieutenant-Governor as ex officio President, two members elected by the Legislative Council and two by the House of Keys.[35] The Advertising Committee, set up under the Advertising Rate Act 1894, comprised nine members, five appointed by Tynwald and four by local authorities, and the members selected their own chair.[36]

It is perhaps a reflection of the times that, on the eve of Raglan's appointment and the 1903 general election, all but one of these eight bodies were chaired by a member of the Legislative Council. In two cases this was a statutory requirement, the Receiver General, Colonel W. J. Anderson, chairing the Harbour Commissioners and Lord Henniker presiding over the Local Government Board. In each of the other cases it was the choice of the members selected, the Receiver General chairing the Highways Board and the Asylum Board and Bishop Straton the Education Council and the Fisheries Committee. Politically, as opposed to constitutionally, the Legislative Council was the superior chamber of Tynwald and members were salaried officials. By contrast MHKs were unpaid and most served in the legislature while continuing to work as farmers, lawyers and businessmen. While being a Ramsey merchant had not precluded John R. Cowell (Ramsey) serving as chair of the Advertising Committee from its inception in 1894, his successor in 1902, John T. Cowell (North Douglas) was one of several 'gentlemen' of the House. MHK membership of the eight bodies was between two (LGB) and five (Advertising Committee), giving the House a majority on all but the LGB. Not all MHKs served and several, notably Speaker Moore (Middle) and 'gentlemen' members like John T. Cowell, John C. Crellin (Michael), John R. Kerruish (Garff) and Dalrymple Maitland (Middle) served on more than one.

## *An Unrepresentative Tynwald*

The Tynwald of the nineteenth century was presided over by an externally appointed Lieutenant-Governor, who was also president of the Legislative Council. Lieutenant-Governors were appointed by the Crown on the advice of the Home Secretary, usually after consultation with other departments of the British Government that might have been able to help in finding a person for the job. The four holders of the office between 1863 and 1902 were colonial appointees and in no way representative of the Manx people. Loch, Walpole and Ridgeway were appointed on the advice of Liberal governments and Henniker on the advice of a Conservative government. None had any Manx connection, although both Loch and Walpole had served as private secretaries to a British Home Secretary. Immediately prior to appointment, Loch had been private secretary to Sir George Grey, the Liberal Home Secretary, Walpole an experienced civil servant and academic historian, Ridgeway a distinguished colonial servant and diplomat and Henniker a Conservative member of the House of Lords and Lord-in-Waiting to Queen Victoria.[37] On appointment each represented the interests of the Island in dealings with the British authorities, but that was not representation in any elective sense.

All the members of the Legislative Council held their positions ex officio. They were either Crown or Church appointees. Even though most were recruited locally on the advice of the Lieutenant-Governor, they were very much part of the colonial apparatus of government. Of the eight members four held high judicial or legal office, the Clerk of the Rolls, the First and Second Deemsters and the Attorney General; three were senior members of the established Anglican church in the Isle of Man, the Lord Bishop of Sodor and Man, the Archdeacon and the Vicar General; the remaining member was a Crown civil servant, the Receiver General. Like the House of Lords in the UK, albeit without the hereditary members, the Legislative Council had equal powers with the elected chamber and the ability to frustrate the wishes of the elected members. By the turn of the century both its membership and powers were being questioned by more radical elements both within the House of Keys and outside of Tynwald.

For much of the nineteenth century the members of the House of Keys were scarcely more representative of the Manx people than the official members of the Legislative Council. Prior to 1867 MHKs were selected by the Lieutenant-Governor from nominees chosen by existing members and held their seats until resignation or death. Tynwald's House of Keys Election Act 1866 provided for a more representative House of Keys, but fell considerably short of the hopes of liberal reformers.[38] The combination of a limited franchise, plural voting and a distribution of seats that favoured rural areas reflected the importance of property and rural interests at the time, but was to provide ammunition for reformers for the rest of the century and beyond.

The 1866 Act gave the vote to all males over 21 owning real estate of a net annual value of not less than £8 and to all male tenants over 21 liable to a net annual rent of not less than £12. In fact, 4,500 or just under 20 per cent of the adult population recorded in the 1871 census were eligible to vote under the Act.[39] Appropriately qualified persons were entitled to vote in more than one constituency and for as many candidates as there were seats in the constituency or constituencies. Figure 2.1 shows the constituencies established under the Act, the six sheadings and Douglas with three seats and the towns of Castletown, Peel and Ramsey one.[40] This built into the system the inherent inequality of allowing voters in seven constituencies three votes while restricting those in the smaller towns to a single vote. It also provided for the disproportionate representation of

**Figure 2.1. House of Keys Constituency Boundaries, 1866**

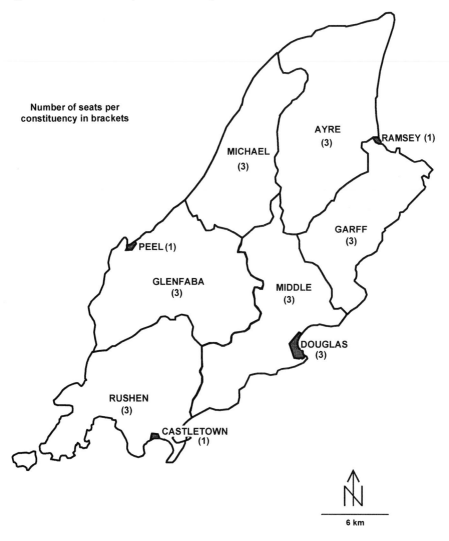

Number of seats per
constituency in brackets

AYRE
(3)
RAMSEY (1)

MICHAEL
(3)

GARFF
(3)

PEEL (1)

GLENFABA
(3)

MIDDLE
(3)

DOUGLAS
(3)

RUSHEN
(3)

CASTLETOWN
(1)

N

6 km

P.G.Cubbin, FBCart.S - 2001

rural areas. Again using the 1871 census, the six sheadings had 18 seats for 2,370 electors and the four towns six seats for 2,130 electors. In Douglas and Ramsey with 1,540 and 338 electors respectively, the number of electors per seat was 513 and 338 compared with figures for the six sheadings and the smaller towns of between 100 (Garff) and 150 (Rushen).

If the restrictions on the franchise were severe, those in relation to candidates for election were even more so. Candidates had to be owners of real estate of an annual value of £100 or £50 plus personal estate or effects delivering an annual income of £100, over 21, male and British subjects. Clergymen and holders of office of profit under the Isle of

**Figure 2.2. House of Keys Constituency Boundaries, 1891**

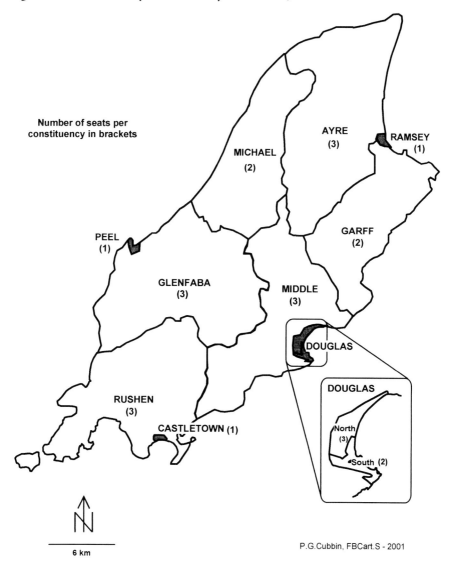

Number of seats per
constituency in brackets

AYRE
(3)

RAMSEY
(1)

MICHAEL
(2)

PEEL
(1)

GARFF
(2)

GLENFABA
(3)

MIDDLE
(3)

DOUGLAS

RUSHEN
(3)

CASTLETOWN (1)

DOUGLAS

North
(3)

South (2)

6 km

P.G.Cubbin, FBCart.S - 2001

Man or UK governments were not eligible to stand. As a result only a tiny proportion of the adult male population were qualified to contest elections.

Under the 1866 Act there was no secrecy of ballot. All votes had to be recorded in poll books incorporating the personal details and voting decisions of voters. The candidates with the most votes were declared elected on the first-past-the-post principle.

Between 1866 and 1902 electoral reform was an important election issue and a series of changes were introduced in respect of the franchise, the distribution of seats, the qualification for candidates and the method of voting. There were extensions of the franchise in 1881 and 1892. The House of Keys Election Act 1881 extended the franchise to males, spinsters and widows over 21 who owned or, in the case of the former, occupied real estate of a net annual value of not less than £4, some 37 years before any women were granted the vote in the UK.[41] Under the new Act, 6,788 persons or 29 per cent of the 1871 adult population became eligible to vote.[42] The House of Keys Election Act 1892 further extended the franchise to spinsters and widows occupying real estate of a net annual value of not less than £4 and male lodgers who were the sole tenants of lodgings with a yearly value unfurnished of £10 or more,[43] although the newly enfranchised had to wait until 1897 for a general election under the new law. In that year there were 10,498 eligible electors, just over 40 per cent of the 1891 adult population.[44]

Attempts were made to redress the imbalance of representation of seats in the House in favour of Douglas, Ramsey and Peel in 1884, 1886 and 1890. Most were unsuccessful. However, in 1887 the rejection by the Keys of an 1886 bill promoted by Walpole to increase the representation of Douglas to six and each of Ramsey and Peel to two at the expense of four of the sheading constituencies persuaded him to dissolve the House. In the ensuing election there were unopposed returns in every constituency except Ayre, leaving the rural majority free to defeat whatever proposal came forward. Eventually in 1891 the extent of the under-representation of the rapidly growing town of Douglas convinced a majority of the House to support a limited reform. In 1890 John R. Cowell, MHK for Ramsey, and Major Robert S. Stephen, MHK for Douglas, introduced a bill modelled on that of 1886; although unsuccessful, a compromise increasing the representation of Douglas was agreed by a substantial majority.[45] The House of Keys Election Act 1891 provided for one member to be transferred from each of Michael and Garff to Douglas, which was then divided into the separate constituencies of North Douglas with three members and South Douglas with two members.[46] Figure 2.2 shows the 1891 distribution of seats.[47] The change improved the representation of Douglas in the 1891 general election, but fell far short of what the two towns had demanded. By the time of the last general election of the century in 1897, the two towns accounted for 47.8 per cent of the electorate and 25 per cent of the seats. For the politicians of Douglas, and to a lesser extent Ramsey, redistribution was to be a central political issue for much of the twentieth century.

The liberal spirit that was abroad in the 1890s also saw the removal of the special property qualification for candidates. Between 1866 and 1881 candidates had to have real estate or a mixture of real and personal estate. In 1881 it was modified to allow the alternative of personal property alone yielding a yearly income of £150.[48] Notwithstanding the criticisms of the pre-1867 House as a self-perpetuating elite, the members elected after 1866 were drawn from the same social group of 'gentlemen', farmers, advocates and businessmen, the restrictions on standing and the lack of pay for members effectively precluding all but the wealthy from becoming members. In 1892 all enfranchised males, other than clergy or holders of offices of profit under the Isle of Man or UK Governments, became eligible to stand for election,[49] but they had to wait until 1897 for a general election to be held under the new law. Dissolving the House in January 1897, Henniker expressed astonishment at the failure of his two predecessors to call an election following the reforms of 1892 both in terms of fairness to the new electorate and the greatly enlarged field of potential candidates.[50]

The Island also had a long wait for the introduction of secrecy of ballot. Tynwald first legislated in 1883,[51] 11 years after the UK. However, the first general election under the new law was not until 1887, when, due to unopposed returns, it only proved necessary to hold a ballot in one constituency. It was not unusual during the latter part of the nineteenth century for candidates to be elected unopposed. The pool from which they were drawn was very narrow and it was common practice for public meetings in a constituency to approve a single candidate who was then declared elected by the returning officer. Although 1887 was exceptional, the figures for unopposed returns in the six elections after 1866 were nine in five constituencies in 1867, 12 in six in 1874, 11 in five in 1881, 21 in nine in 1887, seven in three in 1891 and five in three in 1897.

Despite the lack of competition in many of the constituencies, elections in this period did begin to inform policy making in a way that was not possible before 1867. Whether or not they faced opposition at the polls, candidates were expected to comment on the issues of the day at public meetings and the publicity engendered—they were reported in the local press in considerable detail—certainly influenced Lieutenant-Governors when introducing legislation and determining priorities for public expenditure. Detailed comment on the relationship between elections and public policy in this period would be out of place without further research. Nevertheless a number of general observations can be made. The outstanding feature of the relationship was uncertainty, the result of the lack of a disciplined party system. Candidates were for the most part Independents with their own policy priorities. None could be sure of being part of a majority on any of the issues of the day and even a majority in the Keys could not be sure of support either from the Legislative Council, the Lieutenant-Governor or the UK authorities. In areas of evident consensus the relationship could appear to be strong, but on controversial issues candidates could never be sure of achieving more than a hearing for a particular point of view. Policy statements of candidates were often vague, saying little more than that they promised to do what was good for the constituency, local industry or the Island, but without spelling out in detail what might be involved for fear of alienating a small minority of voters. It is also important to remember that people's expectations of government were considerably less than during the twentieth century and that for many, both politicians and electorate, the least government was the best government.

Before leaving this section on elections, it will be worth commenting further on the 1897 general election, the most competitive since 1866 and the one that recruited members to serve in the House into the new century. The central issue was that of licensing, an ongoing source of conflict between the rural areas and the tourist dependent towns, especially Douglas, and between Methodists advocating or inclining towards temperance and those adopting a more *laissez-faire* attitude on the subject of drink. Although it was not a single issue election, the decision of Lord Henniker on 14 January 1897 to dissolve the House of Keys before the end of its seven-year term followed the House's rejection, by 17 votes to seven, of a resolution to extend the operation of the Boarding House Act 1894. The question of whether or not to allow boarding houses permits to sell beer became the dominant election issue.[52] The election proved something of a stalemate in terms of the particular issue with the new House refusing to extend the legislation in March 1897.[53] It did, however, show that candidates and members had to tread very warily on this extremely sensitive subject, one that was to remain a major source of division in Manx society and elections for many years to come.

Other issues, for the most part already on the political agenda, included further electoral reform, government support for the Manx economy, the development of public works, new sources of taxation and social reform. Each appeared on the agenda of Tynwald between 1897 and 1903. The franchise was extended in 1903 in time for the next election, although further attempts to redistribute seats in favour of Douglas and Ramsey met with the hostility of the House's rural majority. Support for the economy was reflected in decisions to approve the funding of harbours, advertising the Island as a resort, investigating Manx industries and, albeit in a very small way, assisting agriculture and fishing. Initiatives in relation to security of tenure for tenant farmers, employers' liability for the health and safety of their workers and factory legislation were debated and rejected as too were demands for the introduction of some form of direct taxation.

Thirty-seven candidates contested the 1897 election, those in Castletown, Garff and Michael being returned unopposed. Seventeen members were re-elected, all but one having served at least since 1891. Among those elected were figures who were to assume a prominent role in early twentieth-century politics, including future Speakers of the House, Arthur Moore and Dalrymple Maitland and campaigners for constitutional and social reform such as Joseph Qualtrough, William Quine, John R. Kerruish and John T. Cowell. Between the general elections of 1897 and 1903 deaths, including that of Speaker Goldie-Taubman in 1898, retirements and resignations in the wake of the collapse of Dumbell's Bank in February 1900 necessitated 11 by-elections and these saw the election of three more of the leading reformers of the Raglan era, William Goldsmith (North Douglas, June 1900), William Crennell (Michael, October 1900) and Hall Caine (Ramsey, October 1901).[54]

## *The Foundations of a Welfare State*

The late nineteenth century saw a major extension in the role of the state as government began to respond more positively to the social needs of the Island. The response to social problems was by no means a comprehensive one, but it is possible to see in a series of nineteenth-century initiatives the foundations of a welfare state.

The Poor Relief Act of 1888 marked the first small step by government as opposed to charities to address the problem of poverty.[55] It provided for the establishment of a poor asylum and empowered local authorities to set up poor relief committees and levy a district poor rate to cover the costs of maintaining the poor from that area. The measure did not have an easy passage through Tynwald.[56] Most of the MLCs and a minority of MHKs would have preferred to retain a voluntary system. The majority of MHKs favoured a compulsory poor rate and a centrally funded poor asylum. The eventual compromise preserved as far as possible a voluntary system of poor relief, while establishing a means of addressing the problem of poverty where a voluntary arrangement was clearly not working. In contrast to the position in England since 1834, the legislation was permissive, with the Island's 21 local authorities free to decide whether to provide a rate-funded public service. Only Douglas and Ramsey chose to appoint poor relief committees immediately, Castletown and four parishes following suit between 1894 and the turn of the century, when the committees were renamed boards of guardians.[57] The Poor Asylum operated as 'the hospital and infirmary of the destitute',[58] accommodating on average around 80 residents during the 1890s. It was redesignated the Home for the Poor in 1900.[59] The total number of people on relief in the late 1890s was around 1,000, with two thirds of those based in Douglas.[60] Poor relief remained the Island's only form of social security until after the First World War.

The most extensive and expensive social intervention by the state in the latter part of the nineteenth century came in the field of education.[61] Heavily influenced by the

English Education Act of 1870, Tynwald's Elementary Education Act of 1872 provided for compulsory elementary education and that of 1892, free elementary education.[62] Under the 1872 Act local authority-based school committees were empowered to remedy deficiencies in the availability of elementary schools by public provision, waive school fees for the poor and enforce attendance of children aged 7–13 (5–13 after 1878). The revenue costs of such provision were to be borne partly by fees and voluntary subscriptions, partly by the product of a school rate and partly by insular government grants, the latter not to exceed other sources of revenue and conditional on adherence to Whitehall regulations. The capital costs were to be covered half by borrowing and half by similarly conditional government grants. Section 87 of the Act was remarkable from a constitutional point of view in that it formally tied the Island to the English educational system by making grant aid conditional on adherence to the English Educational Code. It was also significant for future educational progress that local responsibility was divided between a relatively weak board of Tynwald and 21 powerful school committees.

The legislation encouraged an expansion of the state sector at the expense of the voluntary sector. Between 1872 and 1887 the old parochial schools were transferred to school committee control and by the turn of the century 63 per cent of the 8,154 elementary school pupils were in state schools.[63] However, outside of Douglas progress in enforcing attendance and providing for the education of those who attended was extremely slow. A damning report prepared for Loch by the English Education

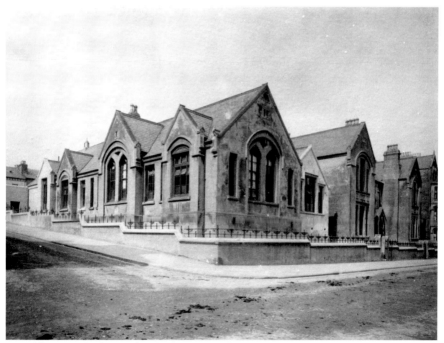

Tynwald Street School, Douglas, the first purpose-built board school, opened in 1882. Legislation was passed by Tynwald in 1872 making elementary education compulsory, and in 1892 making it free. Provision was placed in the hands of local school boards, but was partly funded nationally, making education the largest single call on the general revenue in the latter years of the nineteenth century.

Department in 1880 referred to average attendance of only two thirds, poor standards, inadequate premises and school committees outside of Douglas that were characterised by disinterest and parsimony.[64] Considerable progress was made after 1880, with Board of Education support for new purpose-built schools in Douglas, the appointment by the Board of attendance officers in 1884, the introduction of free elementary education in 1892 and the raising of the school leaving age to 14 in 1893.[65] By 1900 both levels of attendance and standards of achievement were comparable with those of England.[66] Government spending on public education more than trebled between 1878 and 1900 and in the year ended 31 March 1900 totalled £14,493 or 20 per cent of total revenue expenditure by Tynwald.[67]

The latter half of the nineteenth century saw a serious response by Tynwald to the squalor and disease prevalent in the Island's towns, involving legislation in three broad areas, water supply, the quality of food and drink and local government. Already, in direct response to an outbreak of cholera, the Douglas Waterworks Act 1834 had enabled the private Douglas Waterworks Company to provide Douglas with clean piped water.[68] In 1851 the Nuisance Removal and Diseases Prevention Act was the first of many with the aim of promoting environmental health.[69] The Act enabled persons to seek the removal of insanitary conditions through legal action against offenders and authorised the Lieutenant-Governor to issue directives and regulations for the prevention or mitigation of disease. A more positive role for government was envisaged by the Towns Act 1852.[70] This enabled inhabitants of the four towns to elect commissioners who would have rating powers and the responsibility to provide the town with paving, cleansing, lighting, sewerage and other environmental improvements.

Between 1857 and 1886 the Douglas Waterworks Act 1834 was followed by six similar measures regulating the activities of private water companies in Castletown, Ramsey, Peel, Port Erin and Rushen.[71] In each case subsequent legislation empowered the local authorities to purchase and operate the waterworks as public utilities.[72] By 1900 water supply in Douglas was in local authority hands, while in Port Erin and Rushen it was under the joint control of the Port Erin Commissioners and the Rushen Water Company.[73]

A second group of measures was designed to prevent the adulteration of food and drink and followed English legislation albeit with local variations and an elapse of time. From 1869 it became illegal to adulterate food and drink, complaints could be heard in the courts and products analysed, and the Lieutenant-Governor was empowered to appoint public analysts.[74] Subsequent legislation in 1874 and 1888 extended the scope of the original Act to include tobacco and increased the powers of the authorities in respect of food and drink.[75] The Bread, Flour and Corn Act 1880 regulated the composition and sale of bread.[76] This combination of regulation, analysis and the threat of prosecution proved a vital if relatively inexpensive contribution to public health.

The final group of legislation provided for the development of local authorities whose main responsiblities were in the area of public health. The Douglas Town Act 1860 and a series of amendment Acts empowered Commissioners to exercise a wide range of public health functions including the paving, cleansing and lighting of streets, making and keeping in good repair drains and sewers, ordering the cleansing of premises, removing refuse, the erection and maintenance of public urinals, the maintenance of a public fire service and the regulation of house-building.[77] The Ramsey Town Act 1865,[78] the Castletown Town Act 1883[79] and the Peel Town Act 1883[80] did likewise for the other three towns. Insofar as public health was concerned most of this early local government provision was repealed and extended by the Public Health Act 1884.[81] This in turn was repealed and modified by the Local Government Act 1886.[82] The legislation of 1884–86 formally recognised the commissioners of the four towns as sanitary authorities and enabled ratepayers in other areas to petition Tynwald for similar recognition, Port Erin gaining recognition in 1884, Port St Mary in 1890 and Laxey and Onchan in 1895.[83] Armed with extensive powers under these Acts, urban local authorities were able to transform sanitary conditions for much of the Island's population, building modern sewers and sewage works, enforcing the provision of privy accommodation for houses and factories and their proper drainage into sewers, cleansing streets, removing refuse, restricting the establishment of offensive trades and responding to complaints about 'nuisances' injurious to the public health. Local government, at least in the towns and larger villages, had begun to accept responsibility for environmental health and this was reflected in rapidly increasing levels of expenditure and debt.[84] Between 1880 and 1895 total expenditure by the four towns, Port Erin and Port St Mary increased more than five-fold from £13,634 to £72,591, while their debt escalated from £45,201 to £370,353.[85]

Progress was much slower in the rural areas. Although the 1886 Act empowered Tynwald to grant selected powers under the Local Government Acts to districts outside of the four towns, much of the Island remained without a local public health authority. The Local Government (Amendment) Act 1894 went some way towards remedying this.[86] First, it provided for the Local Government Board of Tynwald that was to become the key player in public health provision, especially through powers of inspection and reporting to Tynwald. Second, it introduced elective local government to the rural areas by creating parish commissioners, albeit with few responsibilities, a reluctance to spend and parish boundaries that were to prove inappropriate for major public health purposes.

While the state assumed responsibility for environmental health, the treatment of ill health was, with few exceptions, left to the voluntary sector. The exceptions were in the areas of mental health, infectious diseases and medical treatment for the poor. The Lunatic Asylum Act 1860 provided for the erection and maintenance of an asylum for criminal and pauper lunatics, funded partly out of the general revenue and partly by a lunatic asylum rate.[87] The asylum opened at Strang in the parish of Braddan in 1868. Major outbreaks of infectious diseases resulted in a series of public initiatives to prevent and contain such disease. The Vaccination Act 1876 empowered the Lieutenant-Governor to appoint general practitioners as public vaccinators with authority to vaccinate all persons resident in a district.[88] The Public Health Act 1884 authorized the Lieutenant-Governor to make, alter and revoke regulations for the prevention of disease, on such matters as the treatment of infected persons, the interment of the dead, provision of medical aid and accommodation and cleansing areas.[89] The Public Health (Amendment) Act 1885 gave to sanitary authorities the power to establish fever hospitals and provided for up to 50 per cent grants from the general revenue towards the costs of purchasing suitable premises.[90] This led to the establishment by the Douglas and Ramsey Commissioners of isolation hospitals at White Hoe in 1888 and Cronk Ruagh in 1896. In practice these hospitals served the whole Island, other authorities being charged for their use. The Local Government Act 1886 provided for the establishment of boards of health in the various districts operating under the Act, with the responsibility for ensuring the enforcement of government regulations for the prevention of diseases;[91] half of their operating costs were to be borne by the general revenue and half by local rates. Following its appointment in 1894 the Local

Government Board began to assume responsibility in this area and in 1897 formally replaced the Lieutenant-Governor as the regulatory authority under the Local Government (Amendment) Act 1897.[92]

Reference has already been made to the poor asylum becoming a hospital for the destitute and at its inception provision was made for the appointment of a medical superintendent. Section 46 of the Poor Relief Act 1893 placed on local authorities a duty to provide medicine and medical attendance for those on relief.[93] Apart from 'indoor' medical relief provided in the poor asylum, White Hoe and Cronk Ruagh, the level of spending on medical relief was very low,[94] a reflection perhaps of the extent to which the voluntary sector fulfilled this need. Medical practitioners and town nurses frequently provided the poor with treatment free of charge.[95]

The Island's first public sector housing was built in Douglas under the Douglas Town Improvement Act 1889.[96] Promoted in Tynwald by the Douglas Commissioners and modelled on English local authority schemes,[97] the Act gave the Commissioners powers, subject to schemes being approved by Tynwald, to improve 'unhealthy' districts and to provide for the accommodation of displaced working-class persons in suitable dwellings. In 1892 the Commissioners petitioned Tynwald for authority to clear and rebuild the James Street, King Street and Lord Street area and to erect artisans' dwellings for the 970 persons who would be displaced by the scheme. Initially the housing was to be undertaken by private enterprise, but a committee of Tynwald recommended public housing.[98] Tynwald approved the recommendation on 25 May 1892[99] and between 1895 and 1899 a total of 66 tenement flats were erected in four blocks on what became James Street and King Street.[100]

## Government Support for the Manx Economy

With increased economic powers after 1866, the Manx authorities were able to provide support for the economy in a variety of ways. There were three particular areas where intervention became increasingly important as the Island approached the twentieth century: paving the way for private enterprise by means of legislation and regulation, investing in infrastructure, social policy and public buildings and providing economic support for local industries.

Notable areas of enabling and regulatory activity were seen in relation to traditional local industries, urban development, transport and the private utilities and services. While agriculture remained in private hands, a series of legislative measures between 1851 and 1900 dealt with land drainage, land settlement, farm sales, leases and improvements, cattle diseases and the adulteration of agricultural products.[101] Sea fishing was also the subject of legislation and attempts at regulation, although because of the unwillingness of the UK Government to restrict fishing by non-Manx fishermen in Manx waters, these proved of little practical value in limiting the steady decline of the industry.[102] Between 1860 and 1897 Tynwald empowered new local authorities and, after 1894, the Local Government Board to regulate aspects of urban and rural development. The private development of a network of steam railways and electric tramways between 1870 and 1898 was facilitated by legislation, regulation and inspection.[103] In a similar vein, Tynwald authorised and regulated the private supply of water and gas, further legislation in the case of water providing for some public ownership and control.[104] The expansion of Manx trade also brought with it regulatory

Victoria Pier, Douglas, between 1890 and 1900. One of the most important contributions made by government to the Manx economy between 1866 and 1900 was investment in harbour improvements. The Victoria Pier was opened by Loch in 1872, but was extended and modified between 1886 and 1890.

The Port Erin Breakwater, between completion in 1876 and destruction in 1884. The building and financing of the breakwater was the subject of prolonged negotiations between the UK and Manx authorities between 1861 and 1879.

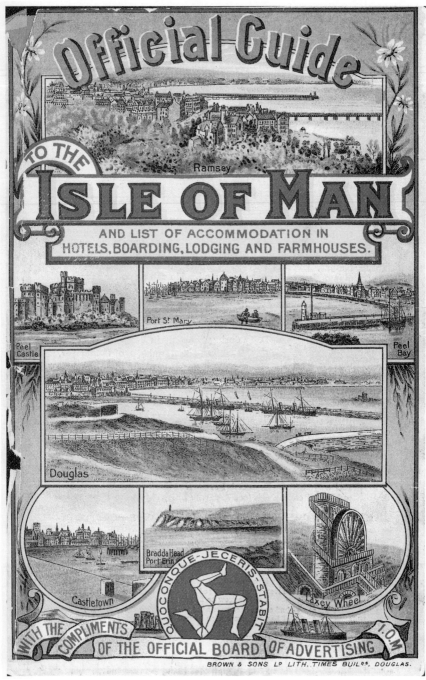

*The Official Guide to the Isle of Man*, 1898. The first Government support for advertising the Island was provided through Tynwald's Advertising Committee, which was set up under the Advertising Rates Act 1894. This picture shows the front page of the Committee's first official guide to the Island.

measures relating to the operation of companies, financial transactions, sale of goods and weights and measures.[105] Tourism, the Island's major growth industry in the latter years of the nineteenth century, benefitted directly or indirectly from most of this enabling and regulatory activity.

While regulatory endeavours made relatively few demands on the public purse, investment in infrastructure, public buildings and social policy was a different proposition. Public investment in infrastructure during this period was primarily on highways and harbours. In the case of highways quite modest levels of capital investment were funded partly by borrowing and partly by grants from the general revenue, the latter including £6,000 between 1893 and 1896 for the express purpose of opening up new roads for the benefit of tourists.[106] Harbour projects included the Victoria Pier, which provided Douglas with landing accommodation that could be used independently of the prevailing tide, the Battery Pier in Douglas, a new breakwater at Peel, the Alfred Pier at Port St Mary, the Queen's Pier at Ramsey and modifications to Castletown Harbour. Between 1866 and 1900 capital expenditure on harbours totalled 'more than £400,000', all but the £45,000 spent on the Port Erin Breakwater before it was finally destroyed in 1884 being productive investment of benefit to commerce, fishing and tourism. During the same period more than £146,000 was spent on public buildings.[107] Local authorities too invested in public buildings, Douglas building a town hall, a library and new market halls within a few years of achieving borough status in 1896.[108] Policy commitments in the fields of education, public health, water supply and, in the case of Douglas, housing also made heavy demands both on Tynwald and local government. Thus, while in 1880 local authority debt was a mere £50,402, by 1895 it had increased almost eight-fold to £396,304.[109]

Government spending in direct support of local industries was minimal before 1900. Apart from extremely small grants in aid of planting trees[110] and improving the breed of horses and cattle, only tourism benefitted directly from public subsidies. Following a petition to Tynwald in April 1893 from local authorities, public companies and inhabitants, the Advertising Rate Act 1894 enabled Tynwald to levy a rate for the express purpose of publicising the Island and to supplement the rate by a grant from the revenue of £750 per annum.[111] Although government funding in this area was initially turned down by the UK Treasury as something better left to private enterprise, conditional approval in 1894 marked the beginning of a role for government that was to increase dramatically in the next century.

## *Manx Finances at the Turn of the Century*

Although Manx finances were separated from those of the UK after 1866, there remained an extremely close financial relationship with the UK. While the Government derived revenue from a miscellany of sources (e.g. fees, fines, rents and interest on loans) and could borrow on the security of that revenue, the main sources of current revenue were customs and excise duties. After 1866 the revenue from these duties together with the miscellaneous receipts from other sources constituted the General Revenue of the Island. Any surplus over current requirements became part of the Isle of Man Accumulated Fund, the contents of which were available for expenditure in subsequent years. In the year ending 31 March 1900 current government revenue totalled £84,759, of which £78,230 or just over 92 per cent came from customs duties.[112]

Although free to establish and maintain duties at a different level from the UK, the Island tended to follow changes in the UK tariff fairly closely either because it needed the extra revenue or felt it had to allay UK fears of illicit trade. Indeed the origins of an almost complete customs union with the UK are to be found in the final decade of the nineteenth century. The practice of maintaining duties at UK levels, paying revenue into a 'common purse' and dividing it between the Island and the UK originated with tea in 1890 and was quickly extended to include tobacco, wines and a few less important items where duty was already at the UK level.[113] By 1900 some 41.6 per cent of total customs revenue was accounted for by the Common Purse Arrangement.[114] The Island's share was based on its resident population plus a fiscal equivalent for visitors. Increases in the volume of trade and keeping or coming into line with a rising UK tariff proved an indispensable source of funding for new or more expensive services. For example, bringing the tobacco duty up to the UK level in 1891 enabled Walpole to find an additional £3,000 per annum to meet the costs of free elementary education.[115]

A significant proportion of revenue spending was also accounted for by the practice of emulating UK policies. Again colonial control was a significant factor, legislative constraints and gubernatorial power combining to limit the scope for independent initiatives. The Isle of Man Customs, Harbours and Public Purposes Act made it clear that the first calls on customs revenue should be the cost of collection and other necessary expenses of government as determined by the Lieutenant-Governor, statutory payments for harbours and public buildings and an annual contribution of £10,000 to the UK for defence and other common purposes. In 1899/1900 these items accounted for 75 per cent of a total expenditure from the General Revenue of £72,635.[116] A further 20 per cent was spent on public education where levels of funding were largely determined by English policy. The Island authorities were, subject to UK Treasury approval, able to determine priorities within these areas of expenditure, including the commitment of funds from the Accumulated Fund or through borrowing for capital purposes,[117] but the scope for independent initiatives was very limited indeed.

As one important measure of change in the role of government is financial, it is proposed to draw this section to a close by providing a rough approximation of the levels of revenue and expenditure just discussed at March 2000 prices. Of course changes in the level of expenditure were not just the result of intervention by government into new arenas of activity; they were also the result of improvements in the quality and standard of services and real increases in the costs of labour and capital. Appendix 1 details a price index going back to 1899/1900. According to the index £1 in 1899/1900 would be worth £54.03 at March 2000 prices. Between 1899/1900 and 1999/2000 total revenue spending by Tynwald rose from £86,411 or £4,668,873 at March 2000 values to £291,804,905, a 62.5 fold increase in real terms.[118] One of the primary aims of this study is to describe and explain this massive increase in expenditure.

# *Notes*

1  The term used by Spencer Walpole, *The Land of Home Rule* (London, 1893).
2  For a discussion of Loch's contribution as Lieutenant-Governor, see Derek Winterbottom, *Governors of the Isle of Man since 1765* (Douglas, 1999), pp. 63–96 and John Belchem, 'The Onset of Modernity' in J. C. Belchem (ed.), *A New History of the Isle of Man: The Modern Period 1830–1999*, vol. 5 (Liverpool, 2000), pp. 72–93.
3  1765 (5 Geo. 3 c. 21).
4  For details of the lengthy correspondence leading to the agreement, see HO 45/OS 7686.
5  1866 (29 and 30 Vic. c. 23).
6  Under Acts of Parliament; 1844 (7 and 8 Vic. c. 43) and 1853 (16 and 17 Vic. c. 107) respectively.
7  For details of the legislative background to the 1866 Act, see D. G. Kermode, *Devolution at Work: A Case Study of the Isle of Man* (Farnborough, Hampshire, 1979), pp. 30–31.
8  For a discussion of Walpole's governorship, see Winterbottom, *Governors of the Isle of Man*, pp. 96–106.
9  Winterbottom, *Governors of the Isle of Man*, p. 256.
10  A. W. Moore, *A History of the Isle of Man* (London, 1900), p. 812.
11  1872 (35 and 36 Vic. c. 23).
12  See Sir James Gell, 'Memorandum on Ecclesiastical legislation', *Manx Society Publication*, vol. 31, pp. 21–32.
13  *Statutes*, iv, pp. 514–19; see also Gell, 'Memorandum on Ecclesiastical legislation'.
14  Moore, *History of the Isle of Man*, pp. 813–14.
15  1887 (50 and 51 Vic. c. 5).
16  Kermode, *Devolution at Work*, n. 36, p. 49.
17  1863 (26 and 27 Vic. c. 16). Although an Act of Parliament, the Bill was prepared by the insular authorities at the request of the Board of Trade, who felt that the Bill should be 'determined by those who have local knowledge'. For details of the negotiations, see HO 45/OS 6919.
18  1864 (27 and 28 c. 62).
19  Unless indicated to the contrary, what follows is taken from two reports that were presented by Loch to the Home Office on 17 November 1873 and 13 September 1879; *Periodical Reports on Progress and Condition of Island*, HO 45/9524/28724.
20  See HO 45/9282/1586 and 9286/3663.
21  See HO 45/OS 8192 and HO 45/9502/10135.
22  See HO 45/9654/A40068.
23  Walpole, *The Land of Home Rule*, p. 274.
24  For a discussion of their governorships, see Winterbottom, *Governors of the Isle of Man*, pp. 106–25.
25  See HO 45/10134/B16342 A/3.
26  See HO 45/10134/B16342 A/50.
27  William Cubbon in 'Another Home Rule Crisis', *Truth* (London), 26 December 1917, p. 905.
28  For details of the committees and reports, see 18 *Manx Deb.*, 21 May 1901, pp. 726–28 and 744–59; 19 *Manx Deb.*, 13 December 1901, pp. 60–62; 19 *Manx Deb.*, 2 May 1902, pp. 479–80 and 504–08; 27 May 1902, pp. 564–73 and 576–90.
29  See 1872 (35 and 36 Vic. c. 23).
30  *Statutes*, iv, pp. 57–94.
31  *Statutes*, iv, pp. 352–66; instead of five members as had been the case under the Act of 1776.
32  *Statutes*, v, pp. 157–73.
33  *Statutes*, vi, pp. 524–44.
34  *Statutes*, vi, pp. 613–18.
35  *Statutes*, vi, pp. 562–78.

36 *Statutes*, vi, pp. 611–12.

37 For further detail on their background, see Winterbottom, *Governors of the Isle of Man*, pp. 63–125.

38 *Statutes*, ii, pp. 372–421.

39 For a detailed breakdown of the figures used here and in the rest of this paragraph, see *Isle of Man Times*, 19 March 1881.

40 Although nominally this distribution survived until 1891, Tynwald's approval of local authority boundary extensions—for Castletown in 1883, for Douglas in 1868 and 1882, for Peel in 1883 and for Ramsey in 1881 and 1884—increased the size of the town constituencies at the expense of the adjacent sheading constituencies. For further detail, see Appendix 3.

41 *Statutes*, v, pp. 95–100.

42 See *Isle of Man Times*, 19 March 1881.

43 *Statutes*, vi, pp. 379–89.

44 See *Isle of Man Times*, 21 November 1903.

45 By 16 votes to six, the main opposition coming from the members of the two sheadings which stood to lose a member; see 8 *Manx Deb.*, 13 January 1891, pp. 7–33. The original proposal was to increase the membership of each town by one.

46 *Statutes*, vi, pp. 232–33.

47 Although nominally this distribution lasted until 1956, Tynwald's approval of local authority boundary extensions—for Douglas in 1904, 1937 and 1952 and for Peel in 1956—had the effect of increasing the size of three of the five town constituencies. For further detail, see Appendix 3. In 1929 Tynwald also agreed to modify the boundary between the constituencies of North Douglas and South Douglas; see 46 *Manx Deb.*, 9 April 1929, pp. 740–42.

48 By the House of Keys Election Act 1881, *Statutes*, v, pp. 95–100.

49 By the House of Keys Election Act 1892, *Statutes*, vi, pp. 379–89.

50 14 *Manx Deb.*, 14 January 1897, pp. 178–81.

51 By the House of Keys Election Act 1883, *Statutes*, v, pp. 244–62.

52 The Act had been passed amid considerable controversy in 1894, when it was agreed that it would only remain in force until 30 September 1895 unless extended by resolution of Tynwald. It was renewed on 8 November 1895 for the period up to 5 July 1897; see *Statutes*, vi, pp. 605–11.

53 In March 1897 the House of Keys refused a further extension—the voting was 12 to 12 and the Speaker did not exercise his casting vote; see 14 *Manx Deb.*, 16 and 23 March 1897, pp. 203–311.

54 The failure of Dumbell's Bank alone resulted in five resignations and by-elections.

55 *Statutes*, vi, pp. 55–62.

56 See 2 *Manx Deb.*, 17, 24 and 31 January 1888, pp. 1–39, 51–82 and 100–70; 8 February 1888, pp. 171–80.

57 *Report of the Poor Law Commission*, 27 March 1940 (Douglas, 1940), para. 39. The poor relief committees became board of guardians in 1900 under Section 12 of the Poor Relief Amendment Act of that year; see *Statutes*, vii, pp. 340–46.

58 *Isle of Man. Annual Report of the Asylum Board Year Ending 31 March 1896* (Douglas, 1896).

59 Under Section 12 of the Poor Relief Amendment Act 1900; *Statutes*, vii, pp. 340–46.

60 See Moore, *History of the Isle of Man*, p. 691. The total cost of state poor relief in the year ended 31 March 1900 was £5,537, of which two thirds was spent by the Douglas Board of Guardians; see *The Reports and Annual Statement of Accounts of the Isle of Man Asylums Board and Assessment Board for the Year ended 31 March 1900* (Douglas, 1900), pp. 74–86.

61 For a detailed discussion of the history of education in the Isle of Man from 1872, see Hinton Bird, *An Island that Led: The History of Manx Education*, vol. 2 (Port St Mary, 1995).

62 *Statutes*, iv, pp. 57–94 and vi, pp. 379–88. These measures were consolidated and amended to raise the school leaving age to 14 by the Education Act 1893; *Statutes*, vi, pp. 454–508.

63 Bird, *Island that Led*, pp. 61–65.

64 Bird, *Island that Led*, pp. 46–47.

65 Bird, *Island that Led*, pp. 48–55.

66 Bird, *Island that Led*.

67 See Moore, *History of the Isle of Man*, p. 696 and *Financial Statement for the Year ended 31 March 1900* (Douglas, 1900), p. 9.

68 *Statutes*, ii, pp. 47–58.

69 *Statutes*, ii, pp. 288–89.

70 *Statutes*, ii, pp. 297–303.

71 The Castletown Waterworks Act 1857, the Ramsey Waterworks Act 1859, the Peel Water Act 1862, the Port Erin Waterworks Act 1885 and the Rushen Waterworks Act 1886.

72 The Castletown Town Act 1883, the Ramsey Town Act 1865, the Peel Town Act 1883 and the Port Erin Waterworks Act 1900. The latter dealt with both Port Erin and Rushen.

73 In the case of Douglas the option of full public ownership was exercised in 1890 at a cost of £144,000; see 6 *Manx Deb.*, 11 May 1890, pp. 472–79.

74 *Statutes*, iii, pp. 497–500.

75 *Statutes*, iv, pp. 316–29 and vi, pp 75–84.

76 *Statutes*, v, pp. 77–82.

77 *Statutes*, iii, pp. 1–13. Amending legislation was passed in 1864, 1874, 1882, 1884, 1886, 1889, 1890, 1891 and 1892.

78 *Statutes*, iii, pp. 196–203. Amending legislation was passed in 1874, 1882, 1885, 1886, 1889, 1891 and 1892.

79 *Statutes*, v, pp. 267–84.

80 *Statutes*, v, pp. 286–303.

81 *Statutes*, v, pp. 374–400.

82 *Statutes*, v, pp. 512–630. Amending legislation was passed in 1889, 1890, 1894 and 1897.

83 Port Erin acquired this status in 1884 prior to the first published volume of the *Manx Debates*. For Port St Mary, see 6 *Manx Deb.*, 23 January 1890, pp. 35–36; for Laxey and Onchan, see 12 *Manx Deb.*, 5, 9 and 23 July 1895, pp. 539–40, 564–66 and 633–34.

84 For further detail, see Moore, *History of the Isle of Man*, pp. 705–06; G. N. Kniveton (ed.), *Centenary of the Borough of Douglas 1896–1996* (Douglas, 1996), pp. 8 and 28–30; Constance Radcliffe, *Shining by the Sea: A History of Ramsey 1800–1914* (Douglas, 1989), pp. 111–21.

85 Moore, *History of the Isle of Man*, p. 732.

86 *Statutes*, vi, pp. 562–79.

87 *Statutes*, iii, pp. 43–73.

88 *Statutes,* iv, pp. 468–77.

89 *Statutes*, v, pp. 374–400.

90 *Statutes*, v, pp. 431–32.

91 The Lieutenant-Governor's powers to issue such regulations under the Public Health Act 1884 were incorporated in the 1886 Act.

92 *Statutes*, vii, pp. 224–30.

93 *Statutes*, vi, pp. 524–44.

94 See *Annual Reports of the Asylum Board 1896–1900*. For example, in 1896 the Douglas Poor Relief Committee spent a total of £3,167 of which a mere £12 was on medical expenses.

95 C. G. Pantin, in an interview with the author, 11 November 1996.

96 *Statutes*, vi, pp. 118–30.

97 Developed under the Artisans and Labourers Dwellings Improvement Acts 1875 and 1879 (Acts of Parliament).

98 Chaired by Deemster Gill, 9 *Manx Deb.*, 25 May 1892, p. 813.

99 9 *Manx Deb.*, 25 May 1892, p. 813–14.

100 See *Report of the Local Government Board on the petition for leave to borrow a sum not exceeding £8,000 for the purpose of defraying the cost of providing a hot water supply, new sink and tiled fireplace in each of 66 single flats in King Street/James Street* (Douglas, 1949).

101  See Moore, *History of the Isle of Man*, pp. 939–34.

102  Moore, *History of the Isle of Man*, pp. 953–59.

103  See G. N. Kniveton, *The Isle of Man Steam Railway: Official Guide* (Douglas, rev. ed. 1993), pp. 1–11; G. N. Kniveton and A. A. Scarffe, *The Manx Electric Railway: Official Guide* (Douglas, rev. ed. 1994), pp. 1–16.

104  The activities of gas companies had been regulated since the passing by Tynwald of the Douglas Gas Act in 1835 and the Peel Gas Act, the Castletown Gas Act and the Ramsey Gas Light Act in 1857.

105  See Moore, *History of the Isle of Man*, pp. 710–11.

106  Moore, *History of the Isle of Man*, p. 722.

107  Moore, *History of the Isle of Man*, pp. 714–15.

108  See Kniveton, *Centenary of the Borough of Douglas*, pp. 15–17.

109  Moore, *History of the Isle of Man*, p. 732.

110  These grants were made to the Isle of Man Arboricultural Society, commencing in 1898. A Tree Planting Committee of Tynwald was established in response to the Society's invitation to nominate six members to work with the Society. De facto this Committee became an official board, but did not have the de jure status until 1931. The Commissioners of Woods and Forests were also responsible for the development of plantations on Crown lands during the 1880s—at Archallagan, Greeba and South Barrule; these plantations and the Crown lands were formally transferred to Tynwald in 1949.

111  *Statutes*, vi, p. 611–12. For further details, see J. G. Beckerson, *Advertising the Island: The Isle of Man Official Board of Advertising 1894–1914* (MA thesis, University of East Anglia, 1996); see also 10 *Manx Deb.*, 28 April 1893, pp. 748–49 and 14 July 1893, pp. 1015–28; and 11 *Manx Deb.*, 16 March 1894, pp. 228–34.

112  See *Financial Statement for the Year ended 31 March 1900*, p. 8.

113  See Kermode, *Devolution at Work*, pp. 117–18.

114  See *Financial Statement for the Year ended 31 March 1900*, p. 8.

115  Kermode, *Devolution at Work*, p. 117.

116  See *Financial Statement for the Year ended 31 March 1900*, p. 9.

117  In the Isle of Man during this period capital expenditure by the Isle of Man Government came partly from savings in the Accumulated Fund and partly through borrowing. While at the end of 1867/68 there was no Manx national debt, between then and 1893/94 the net debt rose steadily to a high of £219,531 before falling to £186,322 in 1899/1900; see Moore, *History of the Isle of Man*, p. 729.

118  The current expenditure figure for 1899/1900 was derived by adding the expenditure from the General Revenue Account and the Accumulated Fund; for 1999/2000 the figure used was the total expenditure from the General Revenue Account. See *Financial Statement for the Year ended 31 March 1900*, p. 11 and the Isle of Man Government, *Detailed Government Accounts for the year ended 31 March 2000* (Douglas, 2000). Grateful thanks are due Martin Caley of the Economic Affairs Division of the Manx Treasury for supplying the Price Index in Appendix 1 to this study; with a letter, dated 11 April 2000. This Index has been used to to calculate real changes in the levels of spending; the resultant figures should be treated cautiously as the index is a retail price index and not one that can accurately portray the changing value of items that loom large in government spending such as labour.

# CHAPTER THREE

# The Raglan Era 1902–19

The weakness of Tynwald when confronted with a hostile Lieutenant-Governor was revealed during the governorship of Lord Raglan between 1902 and 1919.[1] Immediately prior to appointment at the age of 45, Raglan served in Lord Salisbury's Government in the UK as Under Secretary of State for War. He was an hereditary peer and a staunch Conservative. Despite the supposed political neutrality of the post and a change of government in the UK in 1906, Raglan governed the Isle of Man as a Conservative politician. While the Liberal government in the UK was embarking on a major programme of social reform, MHKs became embroiled in a serious constitutional confrontation with Raglan over the powers of the Lieutenant-Governor and Legislative Council, financial control and social reform. Involving extraparliamentary groups such as the Manx National Reform League (MNRL) and trade unions as well as members of Tynwald, the conflict dominated Manx politics between 1903 and Raglan's resignation in 1919 and delayed the introduction of Liberal reforms in the Isle of Man, although the delay was in part due to the conservatism of members of Tynwald, for example in the field of education, and to the war after 1914.

## *Constitutional Conflict*

Raglan interpreted his role firmly in the colonial tradition. He was responsible for the good government of the Island and implacably opposed to the ideology that had given the Liberals an overwhelming victory in the British elections of 1906. He believed in the superiority of the colonial administration and had a jaundiced view of the ability of the elected members of Tynwald. His appointment at a time when members of the Keys were anxious to expand their role proved a recipe for constitutional conflict.

Following an extraparliamentary initiative by 28-year-old journalist and printer, Samuel Norris, the establishment of the Manx National Reform League made constitutional and social reform the central issues in the general election of 1903.[2] The MNRL programme was influenced by Liberal demands for political change in the UK and built on the spirit of reform among progressives already in the Keys. During a successful by-election campaign in Ramsey, Hall Caine had advocated dominion status for the Island with a Manxman as Lieutenant-Governor, a directly elected Legislative Council and departmental officials appointed by and responsible to Tynwald.[3] In 1903 the Keys had supported a proposal by J. D. Clucas for the removal of the Archdeacon and the Vicar-General from the Legislative Council and their replacement by nominees of the House of Keys, but the Home Office saw no reason for change.[4] Legislation extending the franchise to include nearly half of the Island's adult population (46 as

Lord Raglan, Lieutenant-Governor 1902–19.

opposed to 40 per cent in 1897) had been introduced by J. T. Cowell and approved without division before the 1903 general election.[5] Although initiatives by Lord Henniker in 1900/01 to introduce UK-based legislation on employers' liability and safety in factories and workshops were defeated in the Keys, there had been substantial minority support for both. Following a report from a divided committee of the House, supporters of reform were narrowly defeated on the Employers' Liability Bill by 11 votes to nine.[6] There was considerable sympathy in the House for the aims of the UK-based Factories and Workshops Bill, but not for the detail. J. T. Cowell, who proposed the motion not to proceed, claimed it was 'like taking an eighty ton gun to scare rooks', an allusion to the complete absence of large scale industry in the Isle of Man.[7] When the search for new sources of revenue in 1903 led to a proposal to impose a tax of four shillings and two pence per hundredweight on sugar, initially the voting in the House was 11 to eight in favour, two votes short of what was necessary for a financial resolution to be approved. Although the next day the requisite number of signatures was obtained, the removal of what the minority regarded as an inequitable tax on consumption became one of the central demands of the MNRL at the ensuing election.[8]

Norris was successful in welding these disparate strands into a programme that was adopted by the MNRL in October 1903. On the constitutional front, the League sought the preservation and extension of the right of the Island to regulate its internal affairs, the reform of the Legislative Council so that two thirds of the members were directly elected, the appointment of Lieutenant-Governors for a term not exceeding five years, the establishment of an executive of not more than seven members drawn from and responsible to Tynwald for particular departments (Commerce, which was to include agriculture, fisheries, mining and the visiting industry, Education, Finance, Harbours, Highways and Local Government) and the reform of the judiciary by relieving the Lieutenant-Governor of his judicial duties, reducing the number of High Court judges and appointing one stipendiary magistrate in place of the four High Bailiffs. On finance, it proposed that all taxes and expenditure be levied annually by Tynwald, that no more taxes on food be imposed pending the introduction of death duties and other forms of direct taxation and that expenditure on the civil list be reduced by the abolition of unnecessary and obsolete offices, including those of the Receiver General, the Vicar General and one of the three High Court judges. The League also demanded legislation, tailored to Manx needs, on employers' liablity and factories and workshops, permanent funding for technical education and advertising the Island and funds for improved postal and steamship services.[9] The MNRL's contribution was to attract support for the main ingredients of the reform programme from the overwhelming majority of successful candidates. Although Norris and the League campaigned in a similar fashion at elections in 1908 and 1913, after 1903 the impetus for reform shifted to the House of Keys.

On 1 March 1904 the new House established a seven-person committee on constitutional reform. Chaired by Hall Caine, the membership included five other supporters of reform, John T. Cowell, William T. Crennell, William Goldsmith and Joseph Qualtrough, who like Caine had been members of the old House, and one new member, Tom H. Cormode.[10] The Committee reported on 13 December 1904, and the following March the House began debating the proposals, starting with four relating to the civil list. They followed those of the MNRL very closely but did not include relieving the Lieutenant-Governor of his judicial duties. The House supported replacing the High Bailiffs by a single stipendiary magistrate, reducing the number of Deemsters from three to two, prohibiting the Attorney General from private practice and requiring him to be available to advise both branches of Tynwald and the boards of Tynwald and appointing an English barrister of standing to serve on the Court of Appeal in place of the judge whose decision was the subject of appeal.[11]

Perhaps unwisely, given the delays that followed and the eventual response from the Home Office, the House accepted Speaker Moore's advice to petition the Home Secretary on these proposals before proceeding with the rest of the Committee's Report. In a letter dated 12 September 1905 the Conservative Home Secretary, A. Ackers Douglas, refused to support the proposals, but agreed to review the Attorney General's role on the occasion of the next appointment to the office. Following the announcement of the decision to the House, a resolution in the names of Cowell and Goldsmith was carried, regretting the decision and, in view of the pending vacancy in the office, reiterating the demand for the removal of the Archdeacon from the Legislative Council. Responding to the demand in February 1906, the new Liberal Home Secretary, Herbert Gladstone, was unwilling to contemplate such a reform except 'as part of a scheme for the general revision of the constitution of the Isle of Man'.[12]

It was at this point, a full year after the House Committee had reported, that the House turned to the main proposals for reform. On 27 March 1906 the House carried a series of resolutions, moved on behalf of the Committee by Cowell and Goldsmith. Once these had been agreed, in most instances without either amendment or division, a committee led by Speaker Moore met with Lord Raglan to discuss the proposals.[13] When the Speaker reported back to the House on 11 May 1906 he expressed regret that, with the exception of the proposed change in the duties of the Attorney General which Raglan was prepared to consider, 'on all other points his views are not those of the majority of the House'.[14]

Following their failure to gain Raglan's approval, the House appointed a committee, whose members included Caine, Cormode, Cowell, Goldsmith and Qualtrough, to draft a petition to the Home Secretary. Based on the proposals already agreed, the petition was approved by the House on 19 February 1907 with the aim of obtaining for the Manx people 'fuller control of insular affairs than they have yet enjoyed'.[15] The petitioners sought to limit the power of the Lieutenant-Governor by means of a fixed term of office, the appointment of an executive council to assist in all questions of government and finance and the transfer of responsibility for the police to a board of Tynwald. They wanted a majority of MLCs to be elected and only a minority appointed by the Crown. They asked for economy and fairness in the administration of justice, notably the involvement of an English barrister in hearing appeals in place of the judge whose decision was being challenged, the replacement of the four High Bailiffs by a single stipendiary magistrate and prohibiting the Attorney General from engaging in private practice. On finance they demanded that the approval of Tynwald be required 'before any alteration is made in the salaries of insular officials and before the imposition of any new charges for the government of the Island and for the administration of justice'.

Forwarding the petition to the Home Office on 1 March 1907,[16] Raglan indicated his strong opposition to the proposals, saying that it would be quite inappropriate to grant financial control to a legislature 'which does not enjoy responsible government'. Opposing changes to the composition of the Legislative Council, he argued that 'there is not a man in the House of Keys and hardly one outside it in the Island, who would strengthen the Council if summoned to its deliberations'. Nearly a year later on 13 February 1908, Speaker Moore, Cowell and Goldsmith met the Home Secretary to

Hall Caine, MHK for Ramsey 1901–08. Caine was a Manx novelist who entered the Keys in 1901, became President of the Manx National Reform League in 1903 and chair of the Keys' Committee that prepared the 1907 petition for constitutional reform. He retired from active politics in 1908.

William T. Crennell, MHK for Michael 1900–05 and Ramsey 1908–18. A Ramsey grocer, Crennell was one of the most effective leaders of the Keys' campaign for constitutional, fiscal and social reform, especially between his re-election to the House in 1908 and his death in May 1918.

John T. Cowell, MHK for North Douglas 1891–1909 and MLC (Receiver General) 1909–19. A retired insurance agent, Cowell was a member of the Keys' Committee that prepared the 1907 petition for constitutional reform and, after becoming Receiver General in 1909, was the Legislative Council's lone voice in support the Keys' reform campaign.

William Goldsmith, MHK for Douglas 1900–13. Goldsmith, a Douglas jeweller, was also a prominent leader of the Keys' reform campaign until his defeat in the general election of 1913.

Arthur W. Moore (SHK 1898–1909) in the House of Keys. Moore, who became Speaker in 1898, was re-elected to the post after the general election in 1903 and again in 1908, but died in office in November 1909 at the age of 57.

Thomas Kneen (left), First Deemster 1900–05 and Clerk of the Rolls 1905–16, and George Alfred Ring (right), Attorney General 1898–1920, were Raglan's principal advisors, dominant in debate in the Legislative Council and the Council's chief spokesmen in Tynwald.

discuss the petition. According to Moore they received a sympathetic hearing,[17] but it was over a year before a formal response to the petition was received.

The delay was due to Raglan's continuing hostility towards reform.[18] After receiving the deputation, the Home Secretary instructed Raglan to submit for consideration a scheme of reform along the lines demanded by the Keys, subject to the Crown continuing to appoint a majority of MLCs and retaining control over the insular finances. In talks at the Home Office on 27 November 1908, Raglan persisted in his outright opposition to the Keys' proposals, even as qualified by the Home Office and despite support for reformist candidates in the general election that had been held earlier that month.

The 1908 general election was the second to be held with constitutional reform as a central issue. Once again the overwhelming majority of those elected were supporters of reform in general and the 1907 petition in particular. Thus, when on 12 January 1909 Goldsmith and Qualtrough asked the House to reaffirm its commitment to the petition, their resolution was welcomed by all but a small minority. A lengthy debate saw strong speeches in favour of reform by the chief drafters of the petition, Cormode, Cowell, Crennell, Goldsmith and Qualtrough and by two new members who were to play a major role in the House in the coming years, William M. Kerruish, who had been successful in a by-election in 1905, and G. Frederick Clucas, a new member and future Speaker of the House. The resolution was carried by 18 votes to 5 and transmitted to the Home Office.[19] In a letter to Raglan on 3 March 1909, the Home Office informed the Island of its decision on reform: it accepted a fixed term of office for Lieutenant-Governors and the introduction of a minority of indirectly elected MLCs, but was unwilling to see any dilution of colonial control over finance.[20] The letter was silent on much of the detail of the petition and did not go far enough for MHKs. Later in the year, the Keys welcomed a Home Office deputation to the Island to consider the matter further, but no agreement was reached.

Matters came to a head two years later over the question of financial control, as a result of a proposal in Tynwald by William Kerruish to increase a financial vote for advertising the Island from £750 to £1,750 without prior consultation with the Lieutenant-Governor. During a debate in Tynwald on 31 January 1911 it became apparent that, while the Advertising Board would as in previous years receive £1,750, £1,000 would not be available until the budget at the end of March, by which time it would be too late to make best use of the money. Kerruish's amendment was duly seconded, but ruled out of order by Raglan on the grounds that it was 'improper' to propose a financial vote without prior consultation with the Lieutenant-Governor. This led to a refusal on the part of the Keys to participate in any further business until the matter was settled.[21] On 2 February 1911, a resolution moved by Kerruish, supporting the amendment and reaffirming the decision not to proceed with any other business, was approved unanimously by the House. In a speech widely praised by other members, Kerruish objected strongly to the Lieutenant-Governor having a double veto, both before and after financial resolutions are considered.[22] On the same day the Legislative Council, following lengthy speeches by the Clerk of the Rolls, Thomas Kneen, and the Attorney General, George Alfred Ring, declared its unanimous support for the Lieutenant-Governor's ruling.[23] The following day, in a letter to the Home Secretary, Raglan explained what had happened and asked for guidance.[24] Initially the Home Office supported his ruling.[25] However, the reply did not satisfy the House of Keys and Raglan was obliged to adjourn Tynwald 'sine die' in view of their continuing refusal to transact business.[26]

The crisis continued through February and March, the Keys, with the support of the insular press, still refusing to do business. Faced with this impasse, on 12 April 1911 the Liberal Home Secretary, Winston Churchill, announced the appointment of a Home Office Departmental Committee under the chairmanship of retired civil servant, Lord MacDonnell, to enquire into the petition of the House of Keys and other representations made to the Home Office respecting constitutional reform and to report whether any alterations were desirable and practicable.[27] After taking evidence from interested parties in both the UK and the Isle of Man, the MacDonnell Committee reported to the Home Secretary on 31 August 1911.[28] It opposed any reduction in the powers of the Lieutenant-Governor or the Legislative Council, but recommended a fixed term of office for future Lieutenant-Governors and the introduction of indirectly elected MLCs. It supported a reduction in the number of Deemsters from three to two and the number of High Bailiffs from four to two, the removal of the Lieutenant-Governor from the judicial bench and measures to guarantee the independence of those hearing criminal and civil appeals. The Committee rejected the Keys' proposals for an executive council to advise the Lieutenant-Governor and a board of Tynwald to control the insular police, feeling that there should be no question as to the supreme controlling power of HM Government over the insular administration. On the composition of the Legislative Council its recommendation also fell short of what the Keys had sought. It proposed a

The Home Office Departmental Committee on the Constitution etc of the Isle of Man, 1911. The MacDonnell Committee was appointed in April 1911 by the Home Secretary, Winston Churchill, to report on the 1907 petition of the House of Keys and other constitutional representations. It reported in August 1911. From left to right those standing are Sir William Byrne, Assistant Under Secretary of State at the Home Office, Frank Elliot (Secretary) and Roland Wilkins of the Treasury, and those sitting, Neil Primrose MP, Lord MacDonnell (Chair) and Sir Ryland Atkins MP.

10-member Council presided over by the Lieutenant-Governor with two Deemsters, the Lord Bishop, the Attorney General, two nominees of the Lieutenant-Governor and four members elected by the House of Keys from among their own members or the body of the electorate. The Archdeacon, the Vicar General, one of the Deemsters and the Receiver General would lose their seats.

The Committee felt that 'in ordinary times' Tynwald should be allowed a greater measure of financial control. Because of the Common Purse Arrangement the Island had little real control over its revenue and, because the UK Treasury could charge any expenditure it deemed fit on the insular revenue, Tynwald's control over expenditure was also small. The Committee believed that in recent years expenditure not voted by Tynwald was unnecessarily large and included charges for the civil establishment which should be subjected to the scrutiny and vote of Tynwald. Accordingly it suggested an alteration in the form of the Manx budget, Part One of which—the necessary costs of government[29]—should not be discussed in Tynwald, while Part Two—all other items including increases in Part One—should be subject to the scrutiny and vote of Tynwald. To enable Tynwald to perform this new financial role, the Committee proposed the establishment of a finance and general purposes committee of Tynwald with freedom to initiate expenditure policy, subject to not raising estimated expenditure above estimated revenue 'by a larger sum than is available from the accumulation of realised surpluses'. The Committee argued that the statutory control exercised by the UK Treasury should continue, as too should the Treasury stipulation to budget annually for a surplus of at least £5,000 and a balance in the Accumulated Fund by the end of each financial year of at least £20,000. However, the Committee did believe that the balance of £78,439 in the Accumulated Fund on 31 March 1911 was unnecessarily high and that as long as a reserve of £20,000 was maintained, Tynwald should be free to frame its budget 'according to its income and available surplus'.

The decisions of the Home Office with regard to MacDonnell were taken after consultations with Raglan and the Treasury and announced in a minute of the Lieutenant-Governor on 17 July 1913, almost 10 years after the election that had set the reform ball rolling.[30] Raglan opposed the MacDonnell proposals en bloc, feeling strongly that they would be detrimental to the Island, but his reactionary views were ignored by the Home Office.[31] The Treasury on the other hand was 'in entire agreement with the general spirit of the Committee's Report', but strongly opposed to the suggestion that Tynwald should be able to initiate expenditure, believing it necessary to retain financial responsibility in the Lieutenant-Governor and arguing that informal consultations and procedural devices, such as the declaratory resolution or a proposed reduction in expenditure, could afford ample opportunity for Tynwald to make its feelings known to the Lieutenant-Governor. Furthermore, while approving of the proposals regarding the form of the budget, it opposed the suggestion that increases in expenditure under Part One should be laid before Tynwald for approval in Part Two on the grounds that it 'might be inconvenient from a practical point of view'.[32]

The Home Office announced four major outcomes and support for a number of controversial recommendations that had arisen from the Committee's investigations rather than the original demands of the House of Keys. First, future Lieutenant-Governors were to be appointed for a fixed term of seven years. Second, Tynwald was to reform the Legislative Council along the lines recommended, the result after a long delay being the Isle of Man Constitution Amendment Act of 1919.[33] Third, Tynwald was to reform the judiciary, the result, again after protracted delays, being the Isle of Man

Judicature (Amendment) Acts of 1918 and 1921.[34] Fourth, on the subject of finance the Home Office accepted the Treasury view that the initiation of expenditure should remain the prerogative of the responsible executive and rejected the idea of a finance and general purposes committee. It accepted the Committee's recommendation that, so long as there was £20,000 in the Accumulated Fund, there should be no restriction in framing the budget according to income and available surplus except that there should be no budgeting for a deficit. The Committee recommendation regarding the form of the budget was implemented by means of a further Government Minute on 11 December 1913.[35] This divided the estimates into two parts, the reserved services over which Tynwald had no control and the voted services, in respect of which a vote of Tynwald was necessary. On the insistence of the Treasury, the recommendation that increases in the reserved services should be the subject of a vote in Tynwald was not accepted. Finally, Tynwald was to introduce legislation to centralise the administration of the Island by replacing the local highway and poor relief rates by central rates levied by Tynwald, establishing a single education authority and transferring the powers of the boards of guardians to the Asylum Board.

Although the position of the House of Keys and Tynwald was improved by these changes, the main objects of the 1907 petition had been defeated. The Lieutenant-Governor remained a strong executive, invariably supported in Tynwald by the 'official' majority on the Council and thus able to defeat even a unanimous House of Keys. The demands for an executive council and a police board had been rejected. In the field of finance real power still resided with the Lieutenant-Governor and the UK Treasury. As the Keys pointed out in a letter to the Home Office on 17 August 1917, it remained theoretically possible for every penny of Manx revenue to be spent 'not only without the consent, but without any reference to the representatives of the Manx people'.[36]

In the general election of November 1913, many candidates accepted that the decision of the Home Office had effectively brought to an end the current campaign for constitutional reform and that the immediate priority was for Tynwald to carry out the reform of the Legislative Council. For a minority the case for more radical reform remained a strong one. After the election, which saw the defeat of two of the leading advocates of reform, Goldsmith and Kerruish, the branches of Tynwald turned their attention to the legislation necessary to implement the reform of the Legislative Council and the Manx judiciary and to centralise aspects of Island administration. Conflict between the branches resulted in delays, and the intervention of the war made those delays much longer than they might otherwise have been. The problem was that Raglan had prepared a single bill for the whole package of reforms, some of which had never been sought by the House, and, rather than consider such a diverse bill, the House of Keys divided it into seven separate bills.

The Isle of Man Constitution Amendment Bill provided for the reform of the Legislative Council along MacDonnell lines: five ex officio members, reducing to four as soon as one of the three judicial posts became vacant, two members appointed by the Lieutenant-Governor and four indirectly elected by the Keys. It was taken through the House by Crennell with support from Cormode and Qualtrough, the three members of the Committee that had initiated the demand for reform in 1904 who were still in the House. After extensive debate, the third reading was eventually carried by 18 votes to 6 on 3 March 1914.[37] However, before the Bill was considered by the Legislative Council, the House also considered the other six bills. Cormode, Crennell and Qualtrough were again jointly responsible for the measures. It was the fact that only two of these bills were approved and the manner in which the other four were rejected that ushered in the next round of conflict over constitutional reform. The Isle of Man Judicature and the Criminal Code Amendment Bills received a smooth passage through the House. The main purpose of the former was to relieve the Lieutenant-Governor of his role as a judge of the High Court, reduce the number of Deemsters and provide for the appointment of an English barrister to the Court of Appeal; that of the latter was to simplify procedures in respect of criminal cases coming before the courts. On 10 March 1914 each of the other bills was rejected at second reading. Three of the bills, the Poor Relief Amendment Bill, the Finance Bill and the Education Bill, were part of the centralisation package that had been recommended by the MacDonnell Committee and the fourth, the Highways Act Amendment Bill, was designed to abolish the system of commuted labour, whereby labour could be furnished for road repairs in lieu of paying the highway rate. These reforms had not been sought by the House and, whatever their merits, the House made it clear that it was not willing to discuss them at this juncture. Thus, when the motions for the second readings were moved, the proposers made it clear that they were doing so formally out of courtesy to the Lieutenant-Governor and that they hoped the House would join with them in rejecting the legislation. There was almost no debate and the rejections were either without division, in the case of the Finance Bill, or by an overwhelming majority.[38]

Much to the chagrin of the House, the Legislative Council rejected each of the three bills that had been passed. The reasons were made clear during the second reading debate on the Isle of Man Constitution Amendment Bill on 17 April 1914. The debate was dominated by Attorney General Ring, who condemned the Keys for their initial refusal to bring proposals for reform before Tynwald, their decision to invite the UK authorities to intervene in matters domestic to the Island and their treatment of the reform legislation, in particular their decision to split the original bill into seven and reject four without debate, thereby denying to the Legislative Council the opportunity to consider the Home Office proposals as a whole. He saw the refusal to debate much needed reforms to centralise the administration of the Island as illustrative of an unhealthy parochialism that pervaded the deliberations of the House. Ring's amendment to reject the Bill was carried without division; only the Receiver General, J. T. Cowell, a former leader of the reform movement, spoke in support of the Keys.[39]

Raglan sought advice from the Home Office and was instructed to introduce the seven bills into the Legislative Council so that each could be considered on its merits.[40] Although they received a formal first reading on 12 June 1914, further discussion was postponed until the end of the war.[41] In the event the Island had to await Raglan's resignation in 1919 before most of these issues were addressed and implemented. The Highways Amendment Act 1916 did provide for the abolition of commuted labour for the duration of the war, a response to the scarcity of labour resulting from the war, rather than a response to MacDonnell.[42] A much truncated Judicature Act was passed in 1918, reducing the number of Deemsters and providing for an English barrister to serve on the Court of Appeal, but not relieving the Lieutenant-Governor of membership of the High Court as recommended by MacDonnell. William Crennell did move an amendment to remove the Lieutenant-Governor from the list of High Court judges, but it was unsuccessful.[43] The Isle of Man Constitution Amendment Act 1919, which provided for the reform of the Legislative Council, was passed immediately following Raglan's departure with the full backing of the new Lieutenant-Governor, Sir William Fry, but did not come into operation until after the postwar election of November 1919. It fell to the new House to consider the other reforms requiring legislation in Tynwald.

Simultaneously with the struggle for constitutional reform and financial control, MHKs campaigned for the removal of taxes on food and the selective adoption of the social reforms that had been introduced in the UK from 1906 onwards.[44] Here too the House found itself powerless in the face of a Lieutenant-Governor, who not only controlled the Island's purse strings but made no secret of the fact that he was ideologically opposed to social reform. Finding new sources of taxation to fund such economic and social reforms was the subject of discussions in Tynwald throughout the Raglan years, but without success until 1918 when the intervention of the labour movement and the UK authorities eventually persuaded a majority of members to support reform.

Following an initiative by Speaker Moore in July 1904, Tynwald set up a committee to consider whether there should be any changes in the system of taxation. It brought together Attorney General Ring with six supporters of the MNRL who had advocated tax reform during the 1903 election, Moore himself, Cowell, Cormode, Goldsmith, Qualtrough and Dalrymple Maitland. The Committee recommended the replacement of taxes on food by estate duties along the lines introduced in the UK in

Dalrymple Maitland, SHK 1909–19, from a painting by R. E. Morrison in House of Keys. Maitland, a successful businessman who represented Middle between 1890 and his death in March 1919, has the distinction of being the only 'come over' to gain election as Speaker since the House of Keys became an elected chamber in 1867.

1894.[45] However, in spite of the acceptance of the recommendation by the House of Keys, Raglan refused to introduce legislation. 'Sufficient unto the day is the evil thereof' was his response to questioning in Tynwald in May 1907.[46] Two years later a deputation from the House persuaded the Lieutenant-Governor to prepare an estate duties bill as a means of funding old age pensions, although Raglan personally remained opposed to both estate duties and old age pensions.[47] Such legislation was introduced in 1910 and passed by both branches, but foundered because of the Keys' refusal in May and June 1912 to give their final approval to the Bill as amended in Council, because of the lack of progress with legislation to provide for old age pensions.[48] Despite efforts to pass the legislation before the election of November 1913, no further progress was made until 1915, when Raglan had to inform Tynwald that, even without the additional cost of emulating the social policies of the UK, the Island had nearly run out of money and needed to find new sources of revenue. He had been obliged to budget for a deficit in 1915/16 and this had resulted in the Treasury refusing to approve the estimates. Accordingly, on 31 August 1915, Raglan asked Tynwald to appoint a committee to consult with him on ways of raising new revenue.[49] Having explored the alternatives with the Committee of Tynwald, on 5 October 1915 he successfully urged members of Tynwald to accept the principle of direct taxation and an increase in indirect taxation.[50] However, the legislation to provide for particular forms of direct taxation ran into difficulties, either because of opposition in the Keys or because of Keys' amendments stipulating that the expenditure of the proceeds of the new taxation be determined by Tynwald without reference to the UK Treasury. Thus began another stage in the Keys' long struggle for financial control.

The first move was to consider the Revenue Rates Bill, a measure designed to tax the considerable profits being made by farmers because of the war by levying a rate on real estate. It was taken through all its stages in the Legislative Council without dissent in March 1916, only to meet with fierce opposition and defeat by 12 votes to 10 at the third reading in the Keys on 20 June 1916, the rural members seeing the proposed rate as an unjust tax on agriculture.[51] The second was to approve the Estate Duty Bill incorporating an amendment moved by William Crennell and strongly supported by the House, reserving to Tynwald the right to spend the proceeds without reference to the UK Treasury.[52] The Keys' views were presented in a letter to Raglan which was forwarded to the Home Office on 17 August 1917.[53] They claimed that the Treasury had no statutory authority for the control of Manx finances other than customs duties, that general supervision of insular finances was claimed because of practice, that Tynwald had raised and spent money without reference to the UK in the past, exemplified by the Lunatic Asylum rate, and that there should be no limitation on the right of Tynwald to control the raising and expenditure of revenue from direct taxation other than Lieutenant-Governor's veto. On 12 November 1917 the UK Government objected to the legislation, insisting that Manx finances remain subject to Treasury control, asserting that the Lieutenant-Governor's veto was to be seen as an emergency power and that Tynwald's power to raise and expend rates could not be regarded as a precedent or justification for sole control of direct taxation.[54] As neither party was willing to modify its stand, the Bill was lost.[55]

The same constitutional principle lay at the heart of the conflict over the Income Tax Bill that was introduced in 1917. When in 1917 the war led the British Government to subsidize flour to reduce the price of a loaf from one shilling to ninepence, pressure from the newly formed Workers Union and a series of protest meetings across the Island demanding a similar subsidy in the Isle of Man persuaded Tynwald to vote £20,000 from the Accumulated Fund to fund a similar subsidy.[56] To continue the subsidy after the initial six months, the Government introduced its Income Tax Bill. As with the Estate Duty Bill, the Keys decided to insert a clause providing that the expenditure of all income tax revenue should be determined by Tynwald.[57] Once again the Treasury objected and financial deadlock ensued. In his budget speech on 28 June 1918, Raglan announced that, given the deadlock and the refusal of the Treasury to sanction further expenditure from the Accumulated Fund, the subsidy was to be stopped immediately. At a private sitting later that day the Keys demanded that the subsidy continue to be funded out of the Accumulated Fund and determined not to approve taxation of any sort until the matter had been resolved. A deputation met with Raglan, who advised that the Keys' demands would not meet with Treasury approval. Both Tynwald and the House of Keys then adjourned until 2 July 1918. Before either could meet the Island's bakers announced their decision to increase the price of bread to one shilling; the Lieutenant-Governor responded by issuing a proclamation fixing the maximum price of bread at ten pence halfpenny; the bakers immediately refused to bake any more bread until the subsidy had been restored. On 2 July 1918 the Keys unanimously reaffirmed their decision not to support any taxation measures until the subsidy issue had been settled. Two days later the Island was facing a general strike, with trade union leaders campaigning for the restoration of the subsidy.[58] On 5 July 1918 Raglan, on his own initiative, capitulated and made immediate arrangements for the restoration of the subsidy.[59]

Following meetings with Raglan at the Home Office on 8 and 10 July, the UK response was to blackmail the House of Keys into submission, by threatening to impose UK rates of income tax.[60] By the end of July the Income Tax Act 1918 had been passed and given the Royal Assent. The Keys did emerge from the dispute with some success. While the entire Manx budget was to remain subject to Treasury control, the revenue from income tax was at least reserved for use 'for such purposes as may be determined by Act of Tynwald'.[61] A mechanism was now in place for Tynwald to identify policy priorities and, subject always to the approval of the Lieutenant-Governor, to earmark funds for such purposes. The way was open for Tynwald to overcome some of its long-standing frustrations in the arena of social policy.

While the Keys were struggling for constitutional and fiscal reform, the distress caused by the wartime collapse of the visiting industry gave rise to a very different challenge to established authority, including the Keys, from outside of Tynwald. Once again Samuel Norris was involved in establishing and organising an extraparliamentary protest movement.[62] It began life in December 1915 as the War Rights Union (WRU) with the limited goal of obtaining relief from the distress being experienced by boarding house keepers and others dependent on tourism and by local authorities suffering a serious loss of rate income; but, in conflict with Raglan and Tynwald, it became the Redress, Retrenchment and Reform Campaign with much broader constitutional and political goals. The political tactics employed and the constitutional solutions offered did not endear the movement to most members of Tynwald, but they did attract mass support, highlight the undemocratic nature of the Manx political system and provide an impetus to the cause of constitutional change.

Tynwald's initial response to the distress in June 1915 had been to reduce rents and rates for boarding house keepers by two thirds and offer them the option of a loan against the security of furniture and other assets. It was the lack of help for traders,

Top left: Samuel Norris with his wife, Margaret, circa 1914; top right: Norris Modern Press, 6 Victoria Street, Douglas; above: Demonstration at Tynwald Hill, 5 July 1916 (from Samuel Norris, *Manx Memories and Movements*, 3rd ed. 1941, p. 376).

Samuel Norris, who had moved to the Island as a teenager in 1894, was a successful printer and journalist, an active agitator for constitutional and social reform during the Raglan years and the driving force behind the establishment of the Manx National Reform League in 1903, the War Rights Union in 1915 and the Redress, Retrenchment and Reform Campaign of 1916. After a period of extraparliamentary agitation, Norris became an MHK for North Douglas in 1919.

shopkeepers and local authorities and the harsh terms of the loans that provided the impetus for the WRU, with its demands for fair rents and rates and help for local authorities, the encouragement of local authorities and ratepayers to refuse to collect or pay more than a fair rate (one third of the full amount) and requests for the intervention of the Home Office. Tynwald did eventually respond by passing the War Emergency (Relief of Rates) Act 1916,[63] but this was seen as too little and too late. It provided for rates to be reduced to one third, for loans to ratepayers against the security of furniture and other assets and for grants to local authorities in respect of one third of their rate income. The relief would only be available from 1916/17 and, to add insult to injury, it would be funded by increasing the duty on tea. Public meetings followed, culminating in a mass demonstration on Tynwald Hill on 5 July 1916 and a memorial to Tynwald seeking the redress of grievances relating to war distress and taxes on food, retrenchment in government and reform of the Manx political system including the replacement of Raglan by a financially able and sympathetic Lieutenant-Governor. Immediately after the Tynwald ceremony, demonstrators approved the appointment of a Redress, Retrenchment and Reform Committee. The strength of feelings expressed at the demonstration, the refusal of Tynwald to discuss the memorial which was ruled out of order on a technicality and the prosecution of the Douglas members of the Reform Committee, including Norris, for refusing to pay the balance of their rate demand for 1915/16 opened up a more militant phase of the struggle.

In July 1916 petitions were sent to the Home Secretary and the House of Commons demanding the replacement of the Lieutenant-Governor, drawing attention to the unfairness of taxation, the inadequacy of war relief, the urgent need for social reform and the use of the Manx courts to crush the reform movement. More controversially the petitioners sought, in the absence of local action, the suspension of the Manx constitution and a period of direct rule. The campaign was widely publicised in both the Manx and the UK press. When members of the Reform Committee had goods seized by the coroner for failing to pay outstanding rate demands, they attempted to persuade people attending the auction on 6 October 1916 not to buy the seized goods. On 21 October 1916 they were found guilty of contempt by a court presided over by the Lieutenant-Governor, the very man they were campaigning to replace. While other members were simply fined and threatened with prison if they did not pay, Norris received an open-ended prison sentence, to be served until such time as he had purged his contempt. A further petition to the Home Secretary reiterated earlier demands, drew attention to the parody of justice that had led to Norris's imprisonment and demanded his immediate release. Ironically the Home Secretary referred the petition to Raglan, the Lieutenant-Governor being responsible for the exercise of the prerogative of pardon in such cases, provoking the following observation by Norris:

> Lord Raglan had prosecuted me; Lord Raglan had presided over the Court which sentenced me to prison; Lord Raglan alone was now capable, according to the Home Secretary, of giving me my release ... He was Caesar in the Isle of Man.[64]

Raglan refused to pardon Norris, but did agree to convene a court to hear a petition for release and on 17 November 1916, after four weeks in prison and an apology for contempt, Norris was released.

The various petitions for reform and UK intervention were unsuccessful, the Home Secretary honouring the constitutional status of the Island and accepting that the lack of progress with reform was the result of the war. Nevertheless, the Reform

Committee's campaign and the publicity generated, especially by Norris's imprisonment, did much to highlight the case for constitutional and social reform. Taken with the Keys' own campaign, it made the Home Office more sympathetic to Manx demands for reform and a sympathetic Lieutenant-Governor, and almost certainly influenced Raglan's decision to resign once the war was over.

Before that, however, the death in November 1916 of the Clerk of the Rolls, Thomas Kneen, provided the Reform Committee with an opportunity to press the Home Secretary for the abolition of this office and the implementation of the MacDonnell recommendation for the appointment of an English barrister to the Court of Appeal. On 27 February 1917, shortly after the promise of action by the Home Secretary, Sir George Cave, the Isle of Man Judicature Bill was introduced into the Legislative Council. Raglan, who had wanted temporary arrangements to cover the vacancy until the end of the war, informed the Council that he was bringing in the Bill on the instruction of the Home Office and that 'in obedience to their command … I could do no less'.[65] The Bill provided for the reduction in the number of Manx judges and the appointment of an English barrister as a judge of the High Court and the Court of Appeal; but, despite the adverse publicity surrounding the Norris case, it did not provide for the removal of the Lieutenant-Governor from the judicial bench. The Council was clearly determined not to be railroaded into reform by the Home Office and referred the Bill to a committee. Nine months later, and only then after complaints to the Home Office by the Reform Committee about the lack of progress with the Bill and telegraphed instructions from the Home Office to Raglan, the Bill completed its passage through the Legislative Council. Attempts were made by William Crennell during the second reading in the Keys to amend the Bill to provide for the removal of the Lieutenant-Governor from the High Court and the Court of Appeal, but the amendment was lost. Despite further objections during the third reading, the Bill was approved by 15 votes to six as a step in the right direction.[66]

The responses of the Home Office to the 1907 petition, to the MacDonnell recommendations, to the Keys' stance on direct taxation and to Norris's wartime campaign were illustrative of their stand on more routine matters. The turn of the century seems to have coincided with a change of attitude on the part of the Home Office towards the Isle of Man, the official correspondence files for the period showing it adopting a much more interventionist role. It began scrutinising the Isle of Man estimates and financial resolutions very closely and only then forwarding them to the Treasury with firm recommendations, which were invariably accepted. Thus it was the Home Office which, in 1904, recommended the postponement of a £1,500 vote for improvements to Laxey harbour on the grounds that the Island was drawing too heavily on the Accumulated Fund; the Treasury agreed, feeling that it would be unwise to allow the Fund to drop below £20,000 in any year. Raglan opposed the decision, but even a visit to the Home Office on 22 November 1904 did nothing to change their mind.[67] While Raglan was displeased at being overruled, in the Isle of Man discontent was being expressed at the excessive powers of the Lieutenant-Governor. To the reformist MHKs it was of little consequence whether financial control was being exercised by the UK Government or by its representative in the Island, for what they wanted, and what they were sure Raglan did not, was for Tynwald to be in control of insular finances.

Although Tynwald was able to influence financial policy through legislation, debates on financial resolutions and the Lieutenant-Governor's annual budget statements, the opportunities for democratic control were limited. Raglan repeatedly refused to introduce or support legislation if he thought the Island could not afford the expense and a study of the debates on the annual financial statements show very clearly the weakness of his critics. One part of the problem was Raglan's oft stated belief that he was the responsible executive, able to reject or ignore requests from MHKs with impunity. Another was the Island's dependence on customs and excise revenue and the attraction of gaining additional revenue through the Common Purse by following slavishly the changes initiated by the UK. Thus attempts by MHKs after 1903 to persuade Raglan to abolish duties on food, especially sugar, met with a resounding failure and the Island kept in line with UK sugar duties until their abolition after the First World War. A few reformist MHKs were critical of aspects of Raglan's budgets, none more so than William Kerruish, who protested about the cost of government, the lack of detail in budget statements, proposals to increase taxation without reference to purpose, unnecessarily large surpluses while refusing to introduce social reforms and Raglan's lack of support for the financial ambitions of the House of Keys, but to little real avail.[68] During the war there were fewer critics inside Tynwald; a number of Raglan's critics had been defeated in the 1913 election, including William Kerruish, and MHKs had to acknowledge that without new sources of revenue, they had little choice but to go along with Raglan's determination not to countenance major new expenditure and to raise duties in line with the UK.[69]

Outside of the full assembly of Tynwald, the Island's board system continued to provide members with limited opportunities to share in the administration of the Island. There was little change in the system during Raglan's governorship. The two boards concerned with fisheries were amalgamated to form the Fisheries Board in 1904, with seven members elected by Tynwald and selecting their own chair.[70] Of considerably more importance in the longer term was the decision in 1914 to set up a board of agriculture. The Agricultural and Rural Industries Act 1914 provided for a nine-member board, five elected by Tynwald and four representing agricultural interests; as with most of the existing boards the members appointed their own chair.[71] While providing for a measure of power sharing in the Manx political system, by modern standards the jurisdiction of the boards was limited and their budgets small. The Advertising Committee, which was renamed the Board of Advertising in 1904, was narrowly concerned with publicising the Island. The Board of Agriculture, although set up during the war, did not really get under way until the war was over. The role of the Asylum Board was also narrow and, as has been seen, the Keys rejected out of hand the MacDonnell recommendation to transfer to it responsibility for the administration of poor relief from the boards of guardians. Even in the relatively expensive field of education, the Council of Education shared power with the many local education authorities and the prospects of a centralised administration had been dashed by the House of Keys both in 1905 and again in response to the MacDonnell Committee.

During the Raglan administration the pattern of power sharing remained one in which the chairs of the boards were recruited primarily from the Legislative Council, the result of choice by members save in the case of the Harbour Commissioners, where the Receiver General continued as ex officio chair and the LGB, where the Lieutenant-Governor continued to preside, although in practice its meetings were chaired by one of the Deemsters. MLCs also provided the chairs of the other boards for much of the period. Only six MHKs chaired one of the boards between 1902 and 1919. J. T. Cowell chaired the Advertising Committee from 1902 until his death in 1917, although as an MLC from 1909 when he became Receiver General. William A. Hutchinson chaired the

Fisheries Board between 1904 and the election of 1908. Speaker Maitland was chair of the Asylum Board from 1909 until his death in 1919. Finally, MHKs occupied the chair of the Council of Education from 1912 to 1918, William Kerruish for one year prior to his defeat in the 1913 election, John R. Kerruish the following year and Crennell from 1914 until his death in 1918. By the time of Raglan's resignation in 1919 all but the Asylum Board were being chaired by MLCs, although most MHKs served on at least one of the boards and several on more than one.

## The Elections of 1903, 1908 and 1913

The recruitment of members of Tynwald during this period was partly in the gift of the Crown and partly by election under the House of Keys Election Acts. The appointments of the Lieutenant-Governor and the various officials in the Legislative Council did not commit the individual appointees to particular policies. Raglan and officials such as Attorney General Ring—who held the post from 1897 to 1920, was an ardent supporter of the Lieutenant-Governor and the leading spokesman for the Government in the Legislative Council and Tynwald—held their positions in Tynwald and the Legislative Council ex officio. They enjoyed considerable power, able to initiate policy on the basis of what they thought was best for the Island. Although influences behind their policy initiatives and their reactions to those of the Keys may have included public and electoral opinion, unlike MHKs they did not owe their position to the electorate. The primary focus of this section is on the recruitment of members of the House of Keys and the impact of their relationship with the electorate on public policy.

Between Raglan's appointment in 1902 and his resignation in 1919 there were three general elections, each held under the extended franchise introduced in 1903 and in the constituencies established in 1891.[72] The House of Keys Election Act 1903 became law on the eve of the first of these elections, a useful reminder of the liberal credentials of a majority of MHKs well before the intervention of Norris and the MNRL. The Act reduced the normal interval between elections from seven to five years and extended the franchise by adding a residential qualification. As well as adults who qualified as owners or occupiers of real estate or as male lodgers in unfurnished lodgings under the 1892 Act, the vote was given to adult males, widows and spinsters who were resident, as owner or tenant ratepayers, in a dwelling house or part of a house in the Isle of Man for at least 12 months prior to the May preceding a particular election. Further, the clause relating to the eligiblity of lodgers was modified to apply to all males, spinsters and widows who were the sole tenants of unfurnished lodgings with a yearly value of at least £10. As a result of the modified franchise 14,373 persons or 46 per cent of the adult population of 1901 were eligible to vote in the 1903 election.

The 1903 Act provided the basis of the franchise until 1919, when the Island introduced universal adult suffrage, immediately following the UK insofar as men were concerned, but nine years earlier in the case of women. The House of Keys had approved a motion by William Crennell in favour of the principle of universal adult suffrage as early as November 1912, but the following February less than a majority were prepared to support the necessary legislation.[73] With the war reopening the question of suffrage in the UK, Crennell tried again. On 20 November 1917 a resolution in favour was approved by the Keys by 19 votes to two and led to the House of Keys Election (Amendment) Act 1919.[74] Unfortunately Crennell did not live to see the fruits of his labours, having died in 1918 after successfully seeing the Bill through the Keys. Universal adult suffrage on the basis of a residence qualification came into force in time for the 1919 general election. The Act also gave the vote to resident males aged 18 or over who had served in HM forces during the war. The property qualification was unaffected by these changes and continued to provide for extensive plural voting until its abolition in 1969. With the introduction of universal adult suffrage in 1919, the entire adult electorate, except for clergymen and holders of offices of profit under the UK and Manx Governments, became eligible to stand for election to the House of Keys.

The distribution of seats in the House of Keys was not changed in this period. Attempts were made by town members in 1908 and again in 1918 and 1919 to achieve a fairer distribution, but on each occasion a defensive rural vote was easily large enough to defeat the proposals. In 1908 a divided committee of the House reported in favour of giving Douglas two additional members and Ramsey one, but the recommendation was defeated by 14 votes to six. Ten years later an attempt by Douglas MHK, Mark Carine, to have a House committee appointed to investigate redistribution was narrowly defeated by 10 votes to nine. On 15 April 1919 a proposal by Ramsey member, Hugo Teare, for an extra seat for North Douglas, South Douglas and Ramsey at the expense of Ayre, Glenfaba and Michael, was defeated by 14 votes to seven. In 1919 the number of electors per seat in North Douglas, South Douglas and Ramsey was 3,482, 1,997 and 2,961 respectively, compared with figures for the sheadings of Ayre, Glenfaba and Michael of 743, 872 and 682. Despite the blatant unfairness of the 1919 distribution, only one member from outside the two towns was prepared to support the Teare proposal.[75]

The dominant issues before the electorate in 1903 were those highlighted by the MNRL policy programme and campaign, constitutional and fiscal reform, economy in government, social reform and support for local industries. Individual candidates felt obliged to talk about these issues even if they did not reflect their own priorities. Outside of the MNRL programme, the advocacy of redistribution by candidates in Ramsey and Douglas and the demands for stricter controls over licensing by Methodist and temperance candidates ensured that these became all-Island issues. On constitutional reform the MNRL initiative was the real talking point, with many candidates indicating their support even though they did not go along with every detail of the programme. On redistribution the battle was essentially between the towns and the rural areas rather than within individual constituencies, although there were occasional claims for separate representation for particular village districts. The debate on tax reform centred on the relative merits of indirect and direct taxation, existing members in particular having to defend their support or opposition to the tax on sugar levied earlier in the year. In the social field the MNRL demands for legislation to protect working men were widely debated, the defeat by the outgoing House of the Employers' Liability and Factory and Workshop Bills being particularly controversial. Although support for technical education figured in the MNRL list of demands, a minority of candidates had much more to say on the subject of education, seeking improvements to elementary schools, the introduction of 'higher' or secondary education and the centralisation of the education service as a prerequisite to educational advance in the Island. There was similar minority advocacy of a national poor relief system. Support for local industries was expressed either in very general terms or with specific reference to such areas as advertising the Island, developing infrastructural services and improving postal and steamship communications with the UK. In the area of licensing the central issues were the licensing of boarding houses, Sunday opening and the local option, whereby individual local authorities could decide on licensing hours.

Thirty-one candidates contested the election, 13 in the constituencies of Garff, Glenfaba, Michael, Middle and North Douglas being returned unopposed. Nearly all stood as Independents, although they were variously labelled in the press as progressives, moderates and constitutionalists, the latter being supporters of the existing constitution. Some had their candidature endorsed by associations such as the Political Progressive Association in Rushen, the Douglas Trades and Labour Council and the Peel Temperance Society. Leaders of the reform movement also appeared on each other's election platforms. Of the 21 members who sought re-election, 18 were successful, providing a high level of continuity in the House. These included Moore, a 51-year-old manufacturer, and Maitland, a 55-year-old retired businessman, both representing Middle and returned unopposed. Also included were five of the six postelection leaders of the reform movement: Caine, 50 years old, a distinguished author and President of the MNRL, representing Ramsey, Cowell, a 54-year-old retired insurance agent, JP and by far the most experienced, having served in the House since 1891, returned unopposed in North Douglas, Crennell, a 36-year-old Ramsey grocer returned unopposed in Michael, Goldsmith, a 52-year-old jeweller and Methodist lay preacher who was returned unopposed in North Douglas and Qualtrough, a 44-year-old timber merchant, Methodist lay preacher and one of the two successful candidates sponsored by the Rushen Political Progressive Association. The sixth member who came to prominence within the leading group of reformers was one of the six new members, Tom Cormode, a 41-year-old blacksmith and Methodist lay preacher who was the first member of the working class to sit in the House. His candidature was endorsed by both the Douglas Trades and Labour Council and the Peel Temperance Society.[76] Not all the supporters of reform were successful and notable among these was the 37-year-old William Kerruish, a surveyor who was dubbed the 'oratorical hero' of the campaign by the *Isle of Man Examiner*, but who came bottom of the poll in South Douglas. He entered the House following a successful by-election campaign in 1905. With the exception of Caine who was an Anglican, the leaders of the reform group were Methodists.

Immediately following the election the House re-elected Moore as Speaker. During the election, Moore had remained noncommittal on the subject of reform, but in his capacity as Speaker became one of the chief spokesmen for the reform platform adopted by the House. Born in 1853, he had been an MHK since 1881, becoming Speaker on the death of Sir George Goldie-Taubman in 1898. He was also the author of several prestigious academic publications, including the two-volume *A History of the Isle of Man* (1900).[77]

The success in the election of a clear majority of candidates more or less committed to MNRL policies—Hall Caine claimed that 19 of the successful candidates had indicated their support for the the main aims of the MNRL[78]—ensured that reform issues dominated the political agenda over the next five years although, in a range of areas such as local government, public health and the regulation of commerce, the main initiatives were governmental and unrelated to the election. Although there were several by-elections during this period, the balance of opinion in favour of reform was not disturbed. In spite of the many hours devoted to constitutional reform, an investigation into redistribution on the eve of the 1908 election and periodic debates on taxation, the reformists were unable to deliver change in these areas. The supporters of workmen's protection were successful in passing the Employers' Liability Act 1904 and the Factories and Workshops Act 1909. In the field of education the proponents of a national education service were defeated in the Keys in 1905, while limited provision for 'higher' education was made in 1907. Towards the end of the quinquennium Tynwald approved an amendment to the Poor Relief Acts, but that did not provide for a national service. The advocates of greater restrictions on licensing were successful in passing the Licensing Act 1907, which provided for an end to Sunday opening and a reduction in weekday opening hours outside of the tourist season.[79] Overall these were years of frustration for the supporters of reform and this guaranteed reform a central place in the election of 1908.

Constitutional reform dominated the 1908 election. While candidates were still being asked by Norris to support the MNRL programme, it was the Keys' petition of 1907 that assumed centre stage. All but the handful of constitutionalists indicated their support for the stand taken by the Keys and for the policies advocated in the petition to the Home Office. The failure of the 1908 committee on redistribution made this an important issue for candidates in Douglas and Ramsey. Tax reform remained on the political agenda, in the absence of progress in introducing direct taxation and removing taxes on food. With the Liberal government in the UK committed to radical social reform, Manx reformers widened their own programme of social reform to include the introduction of old age pensions. The conflict between supporters of a local education service and those seeking a national service continued, as did the debates about further legislative protection for Manx workers. Public health was an issue for a minority of candidates, with demands for the appointment of an all-Island medical officer of health and the inspection of dairies meeting with opposition in the rural communities. Support for local industry, a perennial issue in twentieth-century elections, included demands for improvements in the conditions of tenant farmers, the appointment of a board of agriculture and greater financial support for advertising the Island.

There were 35 candidates in the 1908 election, of whom nine were returned unopposed in Ayre, Castletown, Middle and Peel. Although most were Independents, the mainstream conflict was one between progressive and moderate supporters of reform and the Manx Constitutional Association (MCA), formed by R. D. Farrant, a wealthy advocate and landowner, to fight for the status quo.[80] In Douglas and Rushen candidates were, with one exception, labelled either progressives or constitutionalist, but these labels did not denote membership of a political party in the modern sense of that term. The exception was Walter C. Craine, an Independent Labour Party candidate, who would eventually enter the House as one of the first representatives of the MLP in 1919. All but three of the retiring members contested the election and 15 were successful. In addition, William Crennell and Joseph Qualtrough, who had resigned their seats in-between the two elections, were re-elected.[81] Overall it was a mixed set of results for the reform movement. It retained a clear majority in the House and managed to secure the re-election of its leading figures. The new House had 13 progressive members, five moderates and six conservatives, the latter figure including the three MCA-sponsored members and the conservative representatives from the sheading of Ayre. Both Moore and Maitland had come out in favour of moderate reform and were returned unopposed. Cormode in Peel and Crennell in Ramsey—Hall Caine did not seek re-election—were also returned unopposed. In the strongly contested constituencies of North and South Douglas and Rushen, MCA candidates, Armitage Rigby, Robert Moughtin and J. D. Clucas, topped the polls, but in these two- and three-member constituencies the progressives Cowell, Goldsmith, Kerruish and Qualtrough were also re-elected.

Among the new members supporting reform, 38-year-old advocate Frederick Clucas stands out. A progressive, he was returned unopposed in Middle, but prior to election had conducted an impressive campaign, delivering some of the best informed speeches of the whole campaign. He had been involved with the reform movement since its inception in 1903 and now joined his MHK colleagues as a leading influence in the House. Unfortunately for the reform movement, he resigned his membership in 1910 for family reasons and, although he kept in close touch with Manx affairs from his home in Bristol, presiding over meetings and speaking during the 1913 election campaign, he did not return to the House until 1919. The MCA was able to build on its 1908 successes through a series of three by-election victories, in November 1909 in Middle following the Moore's death, May 1910 in Glenfaba and November 1910 following Clucas's resignation. However, following the death of Rigby the MCA lost a seat in North Douglas to the reformist William J. Corlett in a by-election in 1909.

Moore was re-elected Speaker, but died on 12 November 1909 at the age of 57. He was replaced by Dalrymple Maitland. Although not a Manxman by birth—he was born in Liverpool in 1848—his success as a businessman in Union Mills placed him well to serve as one of the three members for Middle. He became a member of the House in 1890 and combined that role with a distinguished business career which took him to the chairmanship of each of the Isle of Man Steam Packet Company, the Isle of Man Bank and the Isle of Man Railway. He served as Speaker until his death on 25 March 1919.[82]

Initially well placed to dominate the proceedings of the House, the reformers faced an uphill struggle on the road to reform, facing opposition from within the House, the Legislative Council, the Lieutenant-Governor and the UK authorities. Constitutionally, limited success followed the MacDonnell Report, although the decision on the form of the Manx budget came just after the 1913 election. The House was similarly frustrated over tax reform, passing an Estate Duties Bill only for it to be shelved in the Legislative Council, and, in the absence of new sources of revenue, there was little prospect of members persuading Raglan to end the taxation of food. Redistribution, a live issue during the election, was not even placed on the agenda of the House in this period, possibly because of the known opposition of the House's rural majority.

In the economic and social sphere the story was mixed. The long-awaited Factories and Workshops Act, which had been passed before the election, became law in 1909, but an initiative by the reformers in 1911 to bring the Island into line with the UK with regard to workmen's compensation narrowly failed to get a third reading in the House. In 1910 the Keys passed its Old Age Pensions Bill, only to see it denied even the usual formality of a first reading in the Legislative Council. An eve-of-election attempt to have a committee investigate sources of funding for old age pensions was defeated in Tynwald in May 1913. The reorganisation of Manx education as a national service was not the subject of serious debate until after the 1913 election. A government measure to provide for an all-Island medical officer of health and the inspection of dairies was passed by the Legislative Council, but defeated in the Keys in April 1913. Members' promises of support for agriculture was reflected in the their approval of the Agricultural Holdings Bill in 1909 and their initiative in the establishment of a committee of Tynwald in July 1911 to confer with Raglan about setting up a board of agriculture, but the Bill was defeated following a tied vote in the Legislative Council and action to set up a board of agriculture was not taken until after the 1913 election. The campaign for additional funds for advertising the Island was moved forward when, in May 1912, Tynwald approved in principle the levying of a penny rate to provide extra funds. However, the legislation needed for this purpose was not forthcoming until after the 1913 election.

Thus by the autumn of 1913 there was every expectation of progress on a number of the issues that had been raised five years earlier, in some cases 10 years earlier, and this was reflected in the 1913 campaign. Constitutional reform assumed centre place in the campaign, progressives supporting action to implement the MNRL programme, moderates favouring the limited reforms approved by the Home Office in response to the MacDonnell Report and constitutionalists generally opposed to all constitutional reform. Redistribution continued to arouse support in the towns and defensive posturing in the sheadings. More equitable taxation remained an important aim of the reformists, but they encountered growing opposition from the MCA and other conservative candidates anxious to resist the imposition of estate duties or income tax.

In the social arena the progressives campaigned for old age pensions and national insurance along UK lines and justice for workers, including the establishment of a labour exchange, other measures to relieve unemployment and improvements in hours and pay. They also sought action on measures that had been defeated by the outgoing House on public health, tenants' rights and workmen's compensation. The Douglas Trades and Labour Council was particularly active in seeking support for social reform. MCA candidates opposed such reform as unnecessary and expensive. There was some support and considerable local opposition to the MacDonnell proposals for the centralisation of the Island's education and poor relief services.

Economically, there were demands for increased support and public funding for local industries, in particular agriculture, fishing, the visiting industry and mining, and the Island's highways and harbours. In the case of agriculture the pre-election support for a board of Tynwald to promote the industry gathered momentum in the course of the campaign with the Farmers' Club anxious to discover where candidates stood on this and other agricultural issues. One industry aroused very strong feelings both for and against, namely the liquor trade. The Temperance Legislation League attempted to persuade candidates to support the local option in respect of licensing, leaving local communities to decide whether to go for more or less liberal licensing regimes or even total prohibition.

There were 40 candidates in the 1913 election and contests in every constituency except Castletown. Most were Independents, standing as progressives, moderates or constitutionalists. Exceptions among the progressives included the three candidates selected by the Rushen Constitutional Reform Association and William P. Clucas who contested the election in Glenfaba and narrowly failed to gain election as an Independent Labour Party candidate. Like Craine in 1908, he too would eventually enter the House as a member of the MLP. Exceptions among the conservative candidates were those standing under the banner of Farrant's MCA. All of the retiring MHKs contested the election and 18 were successful, leaving the political balance in the House after the election pretty much as it had been before with 12 progressives, six moderates and six constitutionalists. Maitland topped the poll in Middle and was chosen as Speaker for a second term. Although generally the progressives fared well, in Douglas the reverse was true. There the success of MCA candidates, Mark Carine and Joseph Garside in North Douglas and Robert Moughtin and Robert Clucas in South Douglas, left the progressives with a solitary representative, William Corlett. Three others lost their seats, including William Goldsmith and William Kerruish. Their defeat was a major loss to the reform movement and the House and neither stood for election again. After the election the *Isle of Man Examiner* on 22 November 1913 referred to Kerruish as 'the most brilliant debater and the most constructive legislator that the House has known in modern days', explaining his defeat as the result of alienating several groups of voters through his opposition to live music in public bars and professional betting on Manx racecourses—unpopular decisions taken as a nonconformist member of the Licensing Bench—and his fervent advocacy of estate duties.

By-elections during and immediately after the war did not significantly affect the political balance of the House, but those following the deaths of Crennell in May 1918, Maitland in March 1919 and Lieutenant-Colonel Moore and Robert Moughtin in August 1919 brought into the House three leading politicians of the interwar period and saw the first attempts by Manx Labour Party members to gain election. In the Ramsey by-election in June 1918, Crennell was succeeded by 41-year-old businessman and journalist, A. Hugo Teare, a key figure in the House between 1918 and 1929. The Middle by-election in April 1919 saw the return to the House of Frederick Clucas; he became Speaker after the 1919 election and served in that capacity until his death in 1937; in the meantime the House had chosen John R. Kerruish, a progressive member for Garff since 1897, to succeed Maitland as Speaker until the dissolution. In the Castletown by-election in August 1919, Moore was succeeded by the 34-year-old Joseph Davidson Qualtrough, son of the member for Rushen, Joseph Qualtrough, and employed in the family timber business. Qualtrough's record over the next 18 years made him the obvious successor to Clucas as Speaker in 1937, a post he filled with distinction until his death in 1960.

The Castletown and South Douglas by-elections in August 1919 were significant, not only for the election of J. D. Qualtrough and Leigh Goldie-Taubman, but also for the entry of the MLP into Manx electoral politics.[83] The first serious attempts to establish island-wide organisations to represent Manx labour had resulted in the formation of a branch of the Workers' Union in March 1917 and the Manx Labour Party in September 1918. The following August two of the founding members of the MLP were nominated by the Party to contest the by-elections, James R. Corrin in Castletown and Alfred J. Teare in South Douglas; although neither was successful, three months later at the general election they were and went on to serve the Party and the Island over long and distinguished political careers.

The opportunities for action on electoral commitments made in 1913 were severely limited by the war and Raglan's refusal to contemplate major new expenditure until after the war, as well as by the lack of a disciplined majority in the House and conflict between the branches. Even so, some progress was made. Constitutional reform was further delayed by the Legislative Council's decision not to proceed with the reform bills until after the war. The Isle of Man Judicature Act 1918 and the Isle of Man Constitution Amendment Act 1919 were eventually passed before the 1919 election, but both fell short of what the Keys had originally demanded. Moreover, the former only went through the Legislative Council under duress and the latter after Raglan's resignation in March 1919. There were eve-of-election attempts to redistribute the seats in the House, but these met with resounding defeats. After a lengthy conflict with the Lieutenant-Governor and the UK authorities, which saw the refusal of the Royal Assent to the Estate Duties Bill in 1917, legislation to provide for income tax was passed in time for the tax to be levied in 1918/19.

There was a similar story of frustration in respect of social policy, for reasons related to the war and the failure to agree who should control the proceeds of direct taxation. While successes included the Education (Provision of Meals) Act 1915, the

Education (Aid Grant) Act 1918 and the Workmen's Compensation Act 1919, progress on the main issues of old age pensions, national health insurance and public sector housing had to wait until after the next election. On the economic front Tynwald passed the Agricultural and Rural Industries Act 1914, which paved the way for a much more interventionist role by government in agriculture through a new board of Tynwald and higher spending on advertising the Island. Unfortunately the war delayed the operation of the Board of Agriculture and brought to a temporary halt all expenditure on advertising the Island.

An attempt in 1918 by two of Rushen's Methodist members, Joseph Qualtrough and Thomas Quine, to honour their promise of legislation to provide for the local option with regard to the sale of alcohol was almost successful, at least in the Keys. The Liquor Traffic (Local Control) Bill was given a second reading by 14 votes to seven, but an amended version failed to obtain the 13 votes necessary to carry a bill at third reading.[84] Much to the relief of the liquor trade, the prospect of parts of the Island following the prohibition pathway was avoided.

## The Absence of Social Reform

In marked contrast to the UK where radical reform came in the wake of the 1906 parliamentary elections, the Manx story was one of continuity rather than change. Circumstances combined to frustrate demands for social reform and the Island emerged from the First World War with the role of the state little changed.

When Parliament passed the Old Age Pensions Act in 1908, Tynwald was very quick to respond. On 27 July 1908 William Kerruish moved a resolution urging the Court to provide pensions for the over-70s. He argued that it was the duty of the Government to see that the old were not impoverished and provided figures which suggested that a third of the Manx people who were over 70 depended on charity, relations or poor relief. He stressed the importance of keeping in line with the UK given the close links and movement of people between the islands. Despite general support for the resolution, Raglan was not prepared to bring forward a scheme when he had no inkling of the likely cost or where the money for it would come from. He advised Tynwald to wait and see how the UK scheme was going to be financed and warned that it was going to be 'exceedingly expensive'.[85] At the end of a subsequent debate on 26 January 1909, Raglan again warned of the dangers of embarking on legislation without any idea of either cost or source of funding. On that occasion a motion requesting legislation was defeated as the result of a unanimous decision by the Legislative Council to support Raglan's stance.[86] During the year alternative sources of funding pensions were explored, but Raglan concluded that 'he did not see his way to obtaining the money; consequently he was not prepared to introduce legislation'.[87]

Frustrated at waiting for the Government to act, the House of Keys introduced and passed two bills, one to provide for pensions on English lines, the other to levy estate duty to pay for them.[88] However, the Legislative Council gave their backing to Raglan and effectively quashed the bills by agreeing on 5 April 1910 to adjourn consideration 'sine die'.[89] Raglan had expressed serious doubts about the capacity of the Island to fund a pensions scheme similar to that of its wealthy industrial neighbour and suggested that death duties were unlikely to raise enough revenue to cover the costs of collection, let alone pensions. Two years elapsed before the matter was raised again.

By this time Parliament had passed the National Insurance Act 1911, a landmark reform providing for unemployment and health insurance and reflecting the determination of the Liberal Government to find a nonsocialist answer to the problem of poverty.[90] Within weeks members of Tynwald were asking Raglan not only about his plans to introduce old age pensions but also about national insurance. On 15 May 1912, nearly four years after Tynwald had urged him to introduce old age pensions, Raglan announced the appointment of a commission to investigate the likely costs of a pensions scheme.[91] Chaired by Deemster Callow, the Commission reported that it would cost approximately £20,085 per annum to provide pensions for the 2,262 people aged 70 or over.[92] However, in his budget speech on 4 March 1913 Raglan identified the costs of a range of social reforms—old age pensions, health insurance, medical inspection in schools and the appointment of a medical officer of health—that had been requested by Tynwald and the 'crushing taxation' that would be necessary to meet them.[93] To cover additional annual expenditure in excess of £31,000 on these items, it would be necessary to bring certain customs duties into the Common Purse and to legislate for new forms of taxation. Following two inconclusive debates in Tynwald during 1913,[94] which revealed a broad consensus in favour of social reform but a need for further research into sources of revenue, in June 1914 Raglan appointed a commission to investigate the matter.[95] At this point war intervened. Although attempts were made to keep the Commission alive 'until happier times',[96] it effectively ceased operations for the duration of the war. Protests in Tynwald fell on stony ground, Raglan refusing to contemplate major additions to the Island's financial burden for the duration of the war.[97]

In the meantime the Island's poor, a significant proportion of whom were the elderly, were obliged to rely on charity and poor relief. The period saw two major changes in the operation of the poor law. The Poor Relief Amendment Act 1908 extended the responsibility of the family for the maintenance of the poor.[98] Fathers, mothers or children with appropriate means who failed to maintain poor relations were made liable to imprisonment with hard labour for up to three months. Secondly, the number of local authorities choosing to appoint boards of guardians increased from seven in 1900 to 16 by 1918.[99] As a result of these changes and the social instability immediately after the war, total expenditure on poor relief rose from £5,537 in 1899/1900 to £10,288 in 1918/19.[100]

If, by contrast, public education remained a relatively expensive service, for most of the period the Island visibly failed to keep pace with developments in England. Hinton Bird refers to 'the wasted years', progress being frustrated by the division of responsibility for education and the hostility of many of those in power to any expansion of provision.[101] While Parliament's Education Act 1902 transferred responsibility for education to the county borough and county councils and required them to provide and coordinate all forms of education including secondary, the House of Keys rejected a bill based on the UK Act and paid the price of uneven and limited development, especially at the secondary level. In England the Education Act 1918 made it the duty of every education authority to provide for the progressive development and organisation of all public education in their area, for populations that were generally much higher than that of the Island as a whole. Manx provision remained in the hands of 'twenty five boards of very mixed diligence supervising the education of not many more than six thousand pupils',[102] a contrast that can be explained by the defeat in the House of Keys of Education Bills in 1905 and 1914, the uneven response of the four higher education boards to the opportunities provided by the Higher Education Act 1907, the lack of funds for expansion during the war and, above all, the conservatism or lack of interest of many of those responsible for education.

The Education Bill passed by the Legislative Council in 1905 was designed to improve elementary education, extend public provision into the secondary or 'higher' sector along the lines of the English Act of 1902 and end the fragmentation of responsibility for public education by establishing an all-Island authority. Attorney General Ring, a former chair of the Douglas School Board, saw such an authority as a 'fundamental' component of the educational reform package.[103] Debate in the Keys focused exclusively on the replacement of the 21 school boards by a single authority or five district authorities. Both proposals were defeated, on the casting vote of the Speaker in favour of the status quo, as a result of which the whole Bill was lost.[104] Opponents were suspicious that a single authority would favour the interests of Douglas at the expense of the rest of the Island; they were also opposed to public funding of secondary education, being more interested in economy and the availability of children for work.[105]

Two years later, following the publication of the Jackson Report on Secondary and Higher Education, the Island attempted to make good the loss of the 1905 Bill with regard to secondary education. The Higher Education Act 1907 provided for four higher education boards with powers to provide secondary education, raising to 25 the number of local education authorities.[106] The new boards were empowered to levy a rate of up to two pence in the pound and to borrow against the security of that rate. Secondary schools operating under English Board of Education regulations would qualify for grant aid from Tynwald, in addition to which the Council of Education would receive a special grant to enable it to support 'higher' education initiatives. The Higher Education (Amendment) Act 1909 enabled elementary schools to obtain rate and grant support for providing 'higher' education for older pupils in areas where there was no secondary provision.[107] When in 1913, following the recommendation of the MacDonnell Committee, a second attempt was made to centralise educational administration, it was rejected by the House of Keys without debate and subsequently deferred by the Legislative Council until after the war. The impact of the legislation that did reach the statute book was very limited outside of the Douglas dominated Eastern District.[108] Some 'higher' provision was introduced in schools throughout the Island, but only the Eastern District Board, with responsibility for the Island's sole state secondary school, chose to levy a two pence rate and make a real commitment to secondary education. The secondary school in Douglas was in fact attracting pupils from all parts of the Island and having difficulty in meeting growing demand. Following English Board of Education concern over the size of classes, recommendations from the MacDonnell Committee for greater investment in secondary education and pressure from the Eastern District Board, in 1914 the Council of Education obtained the approval of Tynwald for expenditure of £21,000 on a new secondary school for Douglas. Fifty per cent of this sum was to be paid by Tynwald. Unfortunately for Douglas and the Island as a whole, the hopes of the educational reformers were dashed by the war, leaving Douglas struggling to manage with temporary additional accommodation and the Island as a whole with 'very inadequate' provision.[109]

While many in the Island were only too well aware of the urgent need for educational reform, it was perhaps the mainland Education Act of 1918 that proved a catalyst for action.[110] The Fisher Act was seen as a means of establishing a national system of education available for all persons by imposing on the education authorities the duty to provide for 'the progressive development and comprehensive organization of education in their areas'.[111] Moreover, the prospect under the Act of compulsory education for the 14–18 age group 'more or less compelled the Isle of Man to review its system of education'.[112] That review was under way before the end of the war and although real progress had to wait until the 1920s, the 1914–18 period did see action on a number of long-standing issues. The Education (Provision of Meals) Act 1915, based on Parliament's Education (Provision of Meals) Act 1906, empowered school boards to provide meals for children at school and to levy a halfpenny rate to provide free meals for children in need.[113] More significant was the Education (Aid Grant) Act 1918,[114] which empowered the Council of Education to award grants for elementary and secondary education at the rates laid down in Parliament's Education Act 1902, overcoming a serious hindrance to the progress of education on the Island. It also enabled teachers to benefit from the level of grant aid in support of salaries that had been available in England and Wales since 1902. One result of the Act was to increase national spending on public education from £14,764 in 1917/18 to £22,538 in 1918/19. Finally, in February 1918, a conference of the school and higher education boards carried a resolution in favour of their replacement by a single central authority, paving the way for the postwar Tynwald to remove what had been seen as the major structural obstacle to educational progress since 1872.[115]

Fragmentation of responsibility also hindered progress in the field of public health, especially in rural areas. Small local authorities often lacked the powers and resources to tackle problems such as water supply and sanitation. Local authority boundaries meant that solutions to such problems required cooperation between authorities, the creation of ad hoc authorities or even the modification of boundaries, none of which were easily achieved. Local authority commissioners frequently prided themselves on keeping budgets low and encouraging self-reliance and voluntary endeavour. Reporting in 1918 on the need for local government commissioners to be more active in the public health arena, the LGB Inspector, Herbert Faragher, regretted to observe 'that the majority of the Boards of Parish Commissioners are inert and are, in some cases, dead.'[116] Even so, the Island generally was able to build on the achievements of the late nineteenth century and to advance the cause of public health in a variety of ways. These advances, especially outside of the towns, were often the result of long campaigns by the LGB and its inspectors, anxious to see the Island emulate the best of mainland practices.

Legislation, regulation and inspection were the main vehicles for action centrally, albeit often with the cooperation of local authorities. The Local Government Acts of the late nineteenth century continued to provide the main legislative framework for action, with few amendments between 1900 and 1919. The Local Government (Amendment) Act 1904 empowered the LGB to create special districts for the purpose of water supply and drainage where existing local authority boundaries were inappropriate for the purpose.[117] The Local Government (Highways and Streets) Act 1908 gave to local authorities enhanced powers to regulate and inspect public highways and streets in their area.[118] The Local Government Act 1916 was a massive consolidation measure, much of which was to remain in force until the 1990s.[119]

There were two substantial legislative measures in this period concerned with safeguarding the public health. The Factories and Workshops Act 1909 made registration of factories and workshops compulsory and provided the LGB with powers of inspection in respect of sanitation, safety and working hours.[120] By the end of the war 172 factories and 750 workshops had been registered and inspected. A large number of improvement orders had been issued and acted upon to the satisfaction of the inspectors.

Relatively few cases necessitated prosecution, the threat of such action usually proving an adequate incentive to remedial action. The Children Act 1910 consolidated existing legislation concerned with the protection and welfare of children and brought the Island into line with recent UK legislation, the Children's Act 1908 and the Probation of Offenders Act 1908.[121] It recognised that children had individual rights and were not simply the property of their parents. It provided for the distinctive treatment of juvenile offenders and introduced the option of placing offenders on probation. The LGB was given powers of inspection in respect of children placed in care. This measure was introduced in the House of Keys and passed despite Raglan's doubts about the value of such 'grandmotherly legislation' for the working classes.[122]

One attempt to legislate in the field of public health was unsuccessful. The Local Government (Medical Officer of Health and Inspection of Dairies) Bill was defeated in the Keys on 1 April 1913.[123] The Bill was a hybrid, seeking to respond both to the recommendations of the LGB for the appointment of a full-time medical officer of health with powers of inspection anywhere on the Island and independent of the local authorities, and to a long campaign by LGB inspectors for the regulation and licensing of dairies. After a successful second reading of the Bill, a committee of the House recommended acceptance of an all-Island MOH whose powers would include dairies, but rejection of the licensing of dairies as unnecessary. Following a protracted debate, spread across four sittings of the House and revealing strong opposition from the rural constituencies, it proved impossible to obtain agreement and the Bill fell. The Island had to wait until 1934 for the licensing of dairies and 1949 for the appointment of an all-Island MOH.

The annual reports of the LGB 'on matters relating to public health' provide a useful summary of progress in relation to the prevention of disease and the related issues of water supply and sanitation.[124] Although the incidence of acute infectious disease varied over the period, the Board was able to report the success of preventative action—through improvements to water supply and sanitation in the urban areas, vaccination programmes, enhanced awareness of public health in local government through the appointment of MOHs and sanitary officers in every local authority and campaigns by the LGB and improved ventilation in schools—and the promptness of action in response to reports of disease—through notification, inspection, isolation of patients, disinfection of premises and, where appropriate, vaccination. These successes were offset by the lack of progress in reducing the incidence of tuberculosis, a major cause of death and illness on the Island with between 120 and 160 deaths a year between 1900 and 1918.

In 1901 the LGB Inspector reported that 60 per cent of the Island's population were served by 'a proper system' of water supply and drainage and that there was a pressing need to make similar provision for the rest of the Island. In spite of repeated pressure for action, very little progress was reported. Apart from comments on improvements to existing provision as the urban authorities agreed to serve new areas, the main thrust of the reports was about the lack of progress with both water supply and sewerage in what the LGB regarded as priority areas, Ballasalla and Derbyhaven, Crosby, Michael and Laxey. Eventually, in the case of Laxey, the Board was able to report progress, a public water supply in place by 1911, some 15 years after the LGB had first pressed the Commissioners for action, and a modern sewage system working effectively by 1914. Further progress was not reported until after the war.

The Board also reported with satisfaction the considerable improvements in the sanitary conditions of private housing, state schools, factories and workshops, slaughterhouses, dairies and cowhouses. The Board acknowledged that a lot more needed to be done to make some of the Island's older housing fit for human habitation, both in rural and urban areas, and lamented the lack of by-laws regulating building in rural areas.

Public policies regarding the treatment of ill health did not change markedly. One of the few advances came with legislation promoted by the Ramsey Commissioners, the Local Government (Isolation Hospitals) Act 1911, which empowered local authorities to provide a free service in the isolation hospitals for all their residents and not just those on poor relief.[125] Whereas on the mainland the Education (Administrative Provisions) Act 1907 provided for the medical inspection of children in state schools and a system of school clinics, marking 'the beginning of a national health service',[126] and the National Insurance Act 1911 included provision for a scheme of national health insurance partly funded by the state, in the Isle of Man equivalent legislation was not passed until 1920. Although Tynwald expressed a desire to adapt both of these provisions for the Isle of Man, the necessary legislation was not forthcoming because of the refusal of the Lieutenant-Governor to give such measures priority in a period of financial hardship and war. Tynwald did approve funding for a pilot medical inspection of schoolchildren in 1913 and a report on the results was presented to the Lieutenant-Governor in November 1913,[127] but no action was taken until after the war.

Housing was an area of great social need, especially in Douglas where the older parts of the town 'abounded' with housing that was unfit for human habitation.[128] For the most part housing was seen as a matter for the private sector. Government's only routine involvement was that of regulation, inspection and associated action. Douglas was the exception, having pioneered the development of public housing in the 1890s with remarkably little opposition. In contrast, the Lord Street phase of the same development provoked considerable hostility. Because of the value of the land and the strength of commercial interests on the Borough Council, petitions were presented to Tynwald, initially for permission to build shops on the ground floors of the tenement blocks and subsequently for permission to sell the land for private development and build in another part of town.[129] The result was a prolonged argument between those who believed the Corporation had a duty to provide accommodation for the displaced working-class families in accordance with the 1892 plan and those who questioned the wisdom of increasing an already excessive rate burden to provide modern accommodation for the undeserving poor.[130] The Lord Street tenements were eventually completed in 1911.[131] Even with this development, insanitary conditions and overcrowding remained a problem for the Island in both urban and rural areas.[132] The complete absence of building work during and immediately after the war made matters much worse, so bad in fact that the arguments in favour of public investment in housing were to become irresistible.

Although there was no public investment in new housing until after the war, 1918 did see the introduction of rent control in respect of working-class housing. Initially UK legislation restricting rent increases on houses with an annual rental below £26 was applied to the Island, before becoming the subject of Manx legislation in 1921.[133] While this helped to prevent profiteering at a time of housing shortage, it in no way removed the need for additional housing.

There was little in this period that could be described as an employment policy. Although the Government influenced employment practices by the terms offered to public sector workers and those employed on public contracts and by the range of public health and safety measures already discussed, little progress was made in addressing the issues of unemployment or the pay and conditions of workers. The concerns expressed over unemployment in 1913 were largely overtaken by the war and the shortages of labour it produced. A Labour Exchange was established in 1916, but demands by the labour movement for a minimum wage and better pay and conditions fell on deaf ears. The one area where progress was made was in relation to the liability of employers for their workforce, but even here progress was slow. Attempts were made by Henniker in 1900 and 1901 to bring Manx law into line with that of the UK by making employers liable for employment related deaths and injuries to workmen, and for compensation to workers regardless of who had caused the death or injury. The Employers' Liability Bill had a smooth passage in the Legislative Council and was strongly supported in the Keys by Cowell and other members for Douglas. However, most of the House's rural majority was opposed and the preamble to the Bill was defeated by 11 votes to nine.[134] The Keys' rejection of the Bill led to the abandonment of its 'twin', the Workmen's Compensation Bill. Immediately following the 1903 election, Cowell asked for leave to reintroduce the Bill on behalf of the five Douglas members. With more progressives in the House, the Bill had a relatively smooth passage in the Keys, was welcomed by the Legislative Council and became law as the Employers' Liability Act 1904.[135] No attempt was made to resuscitate the 'twin' measure until 1911 when the Keys approved a resolution moved by William Goldsmith asking the Lieutenant-Governor to introduce legislation. The Workmen's Compensation Bill was duly passed by the Legislative Council, only to meet with defeat at the third reading in the Keys by 12 votes to 10.[136] Opponents of the legislation saw it as prejudicial to the interests of employers, although some like Crennell believed that national health insurance would be a more effective way of addressing the problem. Eventually, with the change of climate generated by the war, the Government succeeded in getting the measure accepted. The Bill had a relatively smooth passage and became law as the Workmen's Compensation Act 1919.[137]

## The Protection and Promotion of Manx Economic Interests

The early years of the twentieth century did not see any major changes in the role of government in the economy, although the war and the rising prices and distress that came with it did lead to a reduction in spending on infrastructure and advertising and new spending on the relief of distress.

Perhaps the most important area of difference between the late nineteenth and early twentieth centuries was the sheer volume of enabling and regulatory legislation, especially that providing for the public regulation of private enterprise. Between 1900 and 1919 the scope of such legislation included agricultural and rural industries, the ownership and operation of the Island's railways and tramways, local government and a public water supply for Laxey; legislation also regulated the operation of companies and financial institutions, conditions in factories and workshops, landlord-tenant relationships, gaming and betting, licensing and a range of individual traders, notably brewers, pharmacists, pedlars and street traders, dental practitioners, money-lenders, conveyancers and boarding house keepers.[138]

The promotion of agriculture was the subject of two major legislative initiatives, one narrowly defeated, the other successful but only really so after the war. In 1909 the Keys passed the Agricultural Holdings Bill, the first of many attempts to improve the quality of Manx agriculture by providing tenant farmers with the right to compensation for 'unexhausted improvements' in the event of having to leave the farm. According to William J. Radcliffe, the member for Ayre who had introduced the Bill on behalf of a group of northern farmers, the Island had 1,398 tenant farmers on approximately 75 per cent of the Island's farmland and such legislation would be a major incentive to more efficient farming.[139] Another group of owners and tenants from the northern sheadings begged to differ and petitioned the Legislative Council to defeat the Bill, for which they claimed there was no general demand and which they believed would be harmful to Manx agriculture. Voting on the second reading in the Council was tied, three votes to three, and the Bill fell. Raglan could have used his casting vote to support the wishes of the Keys, but chose not to do so.[140]

The second initiative was successful, in large part because it was a hybrid bill designed to help both agriculture and the visiting industry, thereby attracting the support of both rural and town members. In July 1911 Lieutenant Colonel George Moore, MHK for Castletown, proposed the establishment of a board of agriculture with funding to promote improvements in the industry and Tynwald agreed to appoint a committee to confer with the Lieutenant-Governor on the matter.[141] In May 1912 Tynwald was asked to approve an all-Island penny rate to provide an additional £1,600—the current level of funding was £1,750 per annum—for the purpose of advertising the Island. Moving the proposal, the chair of the Board of Advertising, J. T. Cowell, argued that the whole Island stood to benefit from a healthy visiting industry. Although the proposal was carried in the Legislative Council, the majority of the House were not convinced, seeing such a rate as an unfair burden on the rural areas, and defeated the proposal by 13 votes to 11.[142] The Committee set up in 1911 reported in June 1912, recommending legislation in support of the agricultural industry. Both the Committee's recommendation and the proposed increase in funding for the visiting industry were widely supported in the ensuing general election. Immediately following the election, on 3 February 1914, Tynwald supported the levying of a halfpenny rate to provide an extra £800 for advertising the Island.[143] When the Agricultural and Rural Industries Bill was published in 1914, it was designed to implement both the recommendations of the agricultural committee and the improved funding for advertising the Island. It had an easy passage through the Legislative Council and attracted the support of a clear majority of the House of Keys where the voting was 16 to five at the second reading and 15 to eight at the third.[144] The Agricultural and Rural Industries Act 1914 provided for the establishment of the Island's first Board of Agriculture, with the responsibility for collecting statistics, maintaining an experimental farm and promoting agricultural improvement.[145] It was to receive £1,600 funding per annum, half out of the general revenue and half from the product of a halfpenny rate on property outside of the towns and the village districts. An equivalent rate in the towns and village districts was to provide £800 of additional funding for the Advertising Board. Although the benefits of the legislation were not felt immediately because of the war, this was a significant commitment by Tynwald to increased government support for the Island's two main industries.

Tourism, which benefitted from much of the general enabling and regulatory activity, was also the focus of specific legislation. The Highways (Light Locomotives) Act 1904 provided for the Island's first motor racing on public roads.[146] The Villa Marina Act 1910 enabled Douglas Corporation to purchase the Villa Marina estate, open the Villa Marina Park and, with funding from the Noble Trustees, build the Villa

Lord Raglan inspecting the roads before the Island's first motor races in 1904. In 1904 Tynwald passed the Highways (Light Locomotives) Act empowering the Highway Board to close public roads for racing purposes, paving the way for these races and the first TT motorcycle races in 1907. From left to right are George Drinkwater (standing), Sir Julian Orde (owner and driver of the car), Lord Raglan (Lieutenant-Governor 1902–19), Deemster Thomas Kneen and Chief Constable Frith.

Marina Royal Hall.[147] The Ramsey Mooragh Improvement Acts of 1912 and 1915 were the latest in a series of measures enabling the Ramsey Commissioners to 'improve' the Mooragh for the benefit of the town and its visitors.[148]

Public investment by the Island's authorities was on a smaller scale than in the later years of the nineteenth century and the war brought to an end public works that might otherwise have provided both employment and other benefits. Capital spending by Tynwald was almost exclusively on harbours and public buildings. Between the turn of the century and March 1919 over £171,000 was spent on improvements and repairs to harbours and almost £43,000 on public buildings. Investment by the local authorities during the same period declined in the urban areas as major water and sewerage projects were completed and as local debt imposed a growing burden on ratepayers. Capital spending in the rural areas remained extremely small.

Government expenditure in direct support of local industries was negligible. Apart from minor spending on improving the breed of horses and cattle, planting trees,[149] the Port Erin Fish Hatchery and, after 1916, the Labour Exchange, Tynwald's only increased commitment came with the Agricultural and Rural Industries Act 1914. Grant aid towards the cost of advertising the Island rose from £750 per annum in 1899/1900 to £2,550 in 1914/15, when the grant was stopped for the duration of the war. Local authorities too were concerned to make their areas more attractive to visitors. Although a wide range of local authority activity was of direct benefit to the tourist industry, for example, clean water, better sanitation and the promotion of public health generally, authorities also invested explicitly in tourist projects. Douglas was prominent in this respect.[150] For example, in 1902 the Corporation became a transport authority, when, following the collapse of the Isle of Man Tramways and Electric Power Company, it purchased the local tramways for £50,000. The following year, with financial assistance from the Noble Trustees, the Corporation acquired and redeveloped the privately owned swimming pools in Victoria Street at a cost of £17,000. The property left by Henry Bloom Noble on his death in 1903 included the Villa Marina estate and, after protracted negotiations and special legislation, the Corporation agreed in 1910 to purchase the site for £60,000 and develop it with the help of grants totalling £45,000 from the Noble Trustees.

The pattern of public spending between 1914 and 1919 was radically altered as a result of the war.[151] Capital investment declined rapidly as scarce resources were directed towards the relief of distress caused by the collapse of the tourist industry and rampant inflation. On 22 June 1915 Tynwald adopted a report of a committee set up to investigate the impact of the war on local industries.[152] The Committee was chaired by the Clerk of the Rolls, Thomas Kneen, and included Speaker Maitland, Cowell, Crennell, Qualtrough and Cormode. Although the committee acknowledged that, with the possible exception of agriculture, the entire Manx economy was adversely affected, it targeted its recommendation at boarding-house keepers. In December that year Tynwald voted £25,000 for loans to enable boarding-house keepers to retain their tenancy and render the sale of furniture unnecessary.[153] Between December 1915 and March 1919

Knockaloe Camp for civilian internees. During the First World War, the UK authorities required the use of the Island for the detention of enemy aliens. Over 30,000 civilians were imprisoned in two internment camps, the vast majority at the specially constructed Knockaloe Camp near Peel.

the War Distress (Loans) Committee authorized £12,500 worth of such loans. After a long campaign by the War Rights Union and the Island's rating authorities, Tynwald passed its War Emergency (Relief of Rates) Act 1916.[154] Between the granting of the Royal Assent in May 1916 and March 1919 Tynwald provided needy authorities with £57,072 in grants and £25,029 in loans. Reference has already been made to the controversy surrounding the Island's subsidisation of flour, but it is worth noting here that in the final 18 months of the Raglan Administration this cost the Island £46,511. At the end of the war the Island followed the UK in voting moneys for demobilised servicemen who were without employment. In 1918/19 the 'out of work donation' scheme cost the Island £4,500. In the same year the total committed to these war-related schemes was £67,781, a massive 42 per cent of total expenditure.

Table 3.1. Central Government Spending 1899/1900 to 1918/19

| Financial Year up to 31 March | Total Expenditure £ | Expenditure at 2000 Prices £ |
| --- | --- | --- |
| 1900 | 86,411 | 4,668,873 |
| 1901 | 82,602 | 4,499,331 |
| 1902 | 88,047 | 4,910,469 |
| 1903 | 81,517 | 4,360,589 |
| 1904 | 92,779 | 5,058,775 |
| 1905 | 89,519 | 4,861,240 |
| 1906 | 84,311 | 4,456,764 |
| 1907 | 91,716 | 4,777,670 |
| 1908 | 82,277 | 4,236,690 |
| 1909 | 79,897 | 4,055,811 |
| 1910 | 81,793 | 4,419,358 |
| 1911 | 78,959 | 4,309,582 |
| 1912 | 85,647 | 4,604,468 |
| 1913 | 96,094 | 5,054,737 |
| 1914 | 88,002 | 4,120,606 |
| 1915 | 98,461 | 4,015,240 |
| 1916 | 105,718 | 3,672,432 |
| 1917 | 162,863 | 4,492,739 |
| 1918 | 134,415 | 3,317,765 |
| 1919 | 191,819 | 4,183,956 |

The sources of the raw expenditure data were the annual *Financial Statements* up to 1918/19. The level of spending at 2000 prices was calculated with the help of the Price Index supplied by Martin Caley of the Economic Affairs Division of the Manx Treasury. The real expenditure figures should be treated with caution as they are derived with the help of an index designed for a different purpose.

To avoid double counting, expenditure facilitated by borrowing is not included in the totals

i)  1899/1900–1917/18 The sum of expenditure from the General Revenue Account and the Accumulated Fund.

ii) 1918/19 The sum of expenditure from the General Revenue Account, the Income Tax Fund and the Accumulated Fund.

## Manx Finances 1900–19

A close financial relationship with the UK remained the dominant feature, characterised by tight colonial control and Tynwald's lack of real success in enhancing its financial role. The one major change was the introduction of income tax in 1918. For most of the period the lion's share of the insular revenue came from customs and excise duties; even with the introduction of income tax, they accounted for 71 per cent of total revenue in 1918/19. Moreover, the proportion of customs revenue derived from the practice of keeping in line with the UK tariff rose from 41.6 per cent in 1899/1900 to 47.8 per cent in 1918/19.

Notwithstanding changes in the form of the Manx budget in 1913 and the introduction of income tax in 1918, Manx Government spending continued to be heavily influenced by colonial controls and UK policies. Although the 'reserved services', over which Tynwald had no control, only accounted for 23 per cent of total spending in 1918/19, the major items of 'voted' expenditure—education (from the General Revenue), the relief of distress (from the Accumulated Fund) and the subsidisation of flour (initially from the Accumulated Fund and subsequently from the Income Tax Fund) and several lesser items were the result of pursuing UK policies, albeit with the blessing of Tynwald. If the Keys had had their way over social policy the extent of UK influence would have been even greater. The scope for genuinely independent initiatives remained extremely small.

Changes in the level of spending in this period are summarised in Table 3.1. A modest increase in spending prior to the war, from £86,411 in 1899/1900 to £88,002 in 1913/14, represented an 11.7 per cent reduction in real terms. By 1918/19, following a period of rapid war-induced inflation, the level of spending had risen to £191,819, but was still over 10 per cent below the 1899/1900 level in real terms.

## Notes

1   For a discussion of Raglan's governorship, see Derek Winterbottom, *Governors of the Isle of Man since 1765* (Douglas, 1999), pp. 125–54.
2   For details, see S. Norris, *Manx Memories and Movements* (Douglas, 3rd ed. 1941), Chapter 12; see also G. N. Kniveton (ed.), *A Chronicle of the Twentieth Century: The Manx Experience*, vol. 1: 1901–50 (Douglas, 1999), p. 14.
3   See Norris, *Manx Memories and Movements*, pp. 133–34.
4   The motion was approved by 12 votes to five; see 20 *Manx Deb.*, 30 May 1903, p. 998 and 21 July 1903, pp. 1176–77.
5   The House of Keys Election Act 1903; *Statutes*, vii, pp. 445–51.
6   See 18 *Manx Deb.*, 19 March, 2 and 30 April 1901, pp. 547–57, 573–98 and 657–96.
7   The Factories and Workshops Bill had been passed by the Legislative Council in January 1901, but fell at second reading in the Keys; 18 *Manx Deb.*, 5, 6 and 12 February 1901, pp. 336–59, 361–81 and 383–95.
8   The Financial Statement delivered in Tynwald on 29 May 1903 by Deputy Governor, Sir James Gell, was followed by this controversial resolution to impose a tax on sugar; see 20 *Manx Deb.*, 29 and 30 May 1903, pp. 898–99 and 949.
9   The full programme is included as Appendix A to Norris, *Manx Memories and Movements*.
10   See 21 *Manx Deb.*, 1 March 1901, p. 260.

11  See 22 *Manx Deb.*, 13 December 1904, pp. 106–08; 22 *Manx Deb.*, 21 March 1905, pp. 524–34 and 534–39 and 18 April 1905, pp. 787–89.

12  In a letter dated 26 February 1906; see 22 *Manx Deb.*, 24 October 1905, pp. 29–39 and 23 *Manx Deb.*, 27 February 1906, pp. 273–75.

13  See 23 *Manx Deb.*, 23 March 1906, pp. 437–79. The members of the committee were Speaker Moore plus T. H. Cormode, J. T. Cowell, R. Cowley and Joseph Qualtrough.

14  See 23 *Manx Deb.*, 11 May 1906, p. 692.

15  See 25 *Manx Deb.*, 18 February 1908, pp. 550–61 where the petition is reprinted in full.

16  The details in the rest of this paragraph are taken from HO 45/10492/113941.

17  See 25 *Manx Deb.*, 18 February, 1908, pp. 546–61.

18  See HO 45/10492/113941.

19  See 26 *Manx Deb.*, 12 January 1909, pp. 76–145. Hall Caine did not seek re-election to the Keys in 1908.

20  See HO 45/10492/113941.

21  See 28 *Manx Deb.*, 31 January 1911, pp. 129–45.

22  See 28 *Manx Deb.*, 2 February 1911, pp. 148–77.

23  28 *Manx Deb.*, 2 February 1911, pp. 190–209

24  See *Correspondence relative to the originating of Financial Proposals in the Tynwald Court* (London, 1911), Cd. 5663, No. 1.

25  Cd. 5663, No. 2.

26  See 28 *Manx Deb.*, 21 February 1911, p. 258; also Cd. 5663, No. 3.

27  Born in Ireland in 1844, Lord MacDonnell served in the Indian Civil Service before becoming Permanent Under Secretary of State for Ireland from 1902 until retirement in 1908; see *Report of the Departmental Committee on the Constitution, etc. of the Isle of Man, 31 August 1911*, Cd. 5950 (1911). Evidence to the Committee was published in a separate volume, Cd. 6026 (1912).

28  The details in the rest of this paragraph are taken from the Report.

29  The cost of collecting revenue, the servicing of public debt, the grant of £2,300 for harbours and £10,000 for the Imperial Exchequer, pensions, the cost of audit and the decennial census, the salaries of the Lieutenant-Governor, the Secretary to the Government, judges and their office expenses.

30  *Government Office Minute No. 2. Cor. No. 2847*, 17 July 1913 (Douglas, 1913).

31  See correspondence in HO 45/10492/113941/129–32.

32  In a letter to the Home Office dated 22 February 1911; HO 45/10492/113941/129–32.

33  *Statutes*, x, pp. 390–98.

34  *Statutes*, x, pp. 261–63 and xi, pp. 95–103.

35  *Government Office Minute No. 3 GO 2847*, 11 December 1913 (Douglas, 1913).

36  *Government Office Minute No. 6 GO 9220/14*, 14 November 1917 (Douglas, 1917).

37  See *Manx Deb.*, 6 January 1914, pp. 8–10; 20 January 1914, pp. 20–29; 17 February 1914, pp. 125–61; 25 February 1914, pp. 163–86 and 3 March 1914, pp. 191–204.

38  See 31 *Manx Deb.*, 10 March 1914, pp. 232–34. In the case of the Poor Relief Bill the defeat of the second reading was by 17 votes to four; in that of the Education Bill, by 18 votes to five and the Highways Act Amendment Bill, by 16 votes to four.

39  For details of the debate, see 31 *Manx Deb.*, 17 April 1914, pp. 272–92.

40  See 31 *Manx Deb.*, 26 May 1914, pp. 389–91.

41  Although it was over two years into the war before the de facto decision was formally agreed; see 34 *Manx Deb.*, 14 November 1916, pp. 15–16.

42  *Statutes*, x, pp. 50–52. The sections of the 1889 Highways Act providing for commuted labour were finally repealed in 1924; *Statutes*, xi, pp. 587–90.

43  See 35 *Manx Deb.*, 18 December 1917, pp. 161–62; *Statutes*, x, pp. 261–64.

44  For a useful summary of these reforms, see Kathleen Jones, *The Making of Social Policy in Britain 1830–1990* (London, 2nd ed. 1994).

45 See 21 *Manx Deb.*, 6 July 1904, pp. 937–64 and 22 *Manx Deb.*, 24 October 1905, pp. 22–28.

46 See 24 *Manx Deb.*, 29 May 1907, p. 1100.

47 The deputation comprised G. F. Clucas, J. D. Clucas, Cormode, Crennell, Goldsmith, W. M. Kerruish and Maitland; see 26 *Manx Deb.*, 20 April 1909, pp. 673–84 and 1 May 1909, pp. 809–16.

48 See 29 *Manx Deb.*, 15 May 1912, p. 492 and 16 June 1912, p. 123.

49 See 33 *Manx Deb.*, 31 August 1915, pp. 24–28. The Committee comprised two MLCs (the Clerk of the Rolls Kneen and Attorney General Ring) and five MHKs (Speaker Maitland, Crennell, M. Carine, R. S. Corlett and W. F. Cowell).

50 33 *Manx Deb.*, 5 October 1915, p. 38.

51 See 33 *Manx Deb.*, 20 June 1916, pp. 454–59.

52 See 33 *Manx Deb.*, 11 April 1916, pp. 372–73.

53 The details of this letter and the response of the UK Government are taken from *Government Office Minute No. 6 GO 92240/14* (Douglas, 1919), pp. 1–4

54 See also 35 *Manx Deb.*, 20 November 1917, pp. 113–14.

55 35 *Manx Deb.*, 20 November 1917, pp. 113–14.

56 For a discussion of the role of the labour movement in persuading Tynwald to fund the subsidy, see A. J. Teare, *Reminiscences of the Manx Labour Party* (Douglas, 1962), pp. 16–20.

57 35 *Manx Deb.*, 20 November 1917, pp. 100–13. The ensuing details are taken from D. G. Kermode, *Devolution at Work: A Case Study of the Isle of Man* (Farnborough, Hampshire, 1979), p. 43.

58 For a discussion from the perspective of the labour movement, see Teare, *Reminiscences of the Manx Labour Party*, pp. 20–25 and Robert Fyson, 'Labour History', in J. C. Belchem (ed.), *A New History of the Isle of Man: The Modern Period 1830–1999*, vol. 5 (Liverpool, 2000), pp. 289–96.

59 See Kermode, *Devolution at Work*, pp. 43–44; 35 *Manx Deb.*, 2 July 1918, pp. 444–52.

60 See Norris, *Manx Memories and Movements*, p. 444. The Home Office files for this period contain only newspaper reports of the discussions; see HO 45/11015/348878.

61 *Statutes*, x, pp. 292–321.

62 Much of the detail that follows is taken from Norris's own detailed account of the campaign in *Manx Memories and Movements*, Chapters 18–39.

63 *Statutes*, x, pp. 43–46.

64 Norris, *Manx Memories and Movements*, p. 385.

65 See 34 *Manx Deb.*, 27 February 1917, pp. 73–75; see also Norris, *Manx Memories and Movements*, pp. 414–18.

66 See 35 *Manx Deb.*, 18 December 1917 and 15 January 1918, pp. 161–62 and 170. All but one of the opponents at the third reading were constitutionalists opposed to the whole Bill. The only progressive to oppose the Bill, on the grounds that it left the Lieutenant-Governor as a judge, was Ambrose Qualtrough, one of the members for Rushen. He was the only member to be closely associated with Norris during his trial and imprisonment.

67 See HO 45/12279/446999/10–15.

68 See for example, 24 *Manx Deb.*, 29 May 1907, pp. 1092–101; 27 *Manx Deb.*, 7 June and 12 July 1910, pp. 1063–67 and 1166–272.

69 Early in the war Raglan did keep duties on tea well below UK levels, but by 1916 felt obliged to raise the duty to within a penny of the UK rate. This decision provoked one of the few attempts in the Raglan era to amend a financial resolution. The amendment in the name of W. T. Crennell was defeated by 13 votes to seven in the Keys and unanimously in the Council; see 33 *Manx Deb.*, 17 and 21 March, 1916, pp. 292–319.

70 Under the Fisheries Authorities Amalgamation Act 1904, *Statutes*, vii, p. 476.

71 *Statutes*, ix, pp. 390–96. Two of the non-Tynwald members were to be appointed by Nobles Trustees and one each by the Northern and Southern Agricultural Societies.

72  For a discussion of these three elections, see Jeffrey Vaukins, 'The Manx Struggle for Reform' (M.Phil., University of Lancaster, 1984).

73  The resolution in favour of the principle was carried by 16 votes to eight; 30 *Manx Deb.*, 19 November 1912, pp. 11–23. The second reading of the House of Keys (Adult Suffrage) Bill in February 1913 went to a vote without any debate and was defeated by 13 votes to 10; 30 *Manx Deb.*, 18 February 1913, p. 203. The main reason for the defeat of Crennell's Bill was that it also provided for the abolition of plural voting.

74  See 35 *Manx Deb.*, 20 November 1917, pp. 120–27; *Statutes*, x, pp. 342–46.

75  For a summary of attempts at reform between 1884 and 1919 see 36 *Manx Deb.*, 15 April 1919, pp. 345–47. The Teare proposal also offered the options of redistribution within three of the sheadings so that their urban areas might have their own seat, Laxey in Garff, Onchan in Middle and Port Erin and Port St Mary together in Rushen.

76  For an interesting working-class perspective on the Peel election, see Teare, *Reminiscences of the Manx Labour Party*, pp. 5–6.

77  For an assessment of Moore's contribution to Manx politics, see *The Manx Quarterly* (Douglas), No. 7, November 1909 and Kniveton, *Chronicle of the Twentieth Century*, vol. 1, p. 33.

78  See *Isle of Man Examiner*, 28 November 1903.

79  *Statutes*, viii, pp. 83–84.

80  The language in use at the time denoted progressives as those who fully supported the reforms being advocated in the Keys' petition and moderates as those who supported some of the reforms.

81  Crennell resigned because his views on the 1905 Education Bill (in favour of a single authority and a uniform education rate) were 'hopelessly at variance with those of a huge majority of my constituents'; 23 *Manx Deb.*, 12 December 1905, pp. 103–04. Joseph Qualtrough resigned in June 1907 for very different reasons. During a by-election in Rushen in 1907, he was accused by one of the candidates, Ambrose Qualtrough, of being a liar when he denied having interests in Castletown Brewery. Joseph Qualtrough said he would resign from the Keys rather than sit with a colleague who had called him a liar. His letter of resignation was read out to the Keys the day Ambrose was sworn in as the new member for Rushen; see *Isle of Man Examiner*, 1 June 1907 and 24 *Manx Deb.*, 4 June 1907, p. 1139.

82  For an assessment of Maitland, see *The Manx Quarterly* (Douglas), No. 21, April 1920.

83  See Teare, *Reminiscences of the Manx Labour Party*, pp. 9–12 and 26–32.

84  See 35 *Manx Deb.*, 12 February, 5 March, 30 April and 2 July 1918, pp. 214–15, 266–68, 400–03 and 453; 36 *Manx Deb.*, 27 May 1919, pp. 454–77.

85  Kerruish's resolution was supported by all but three MHKs and unanimously in the Legislative Council. For details of the full debate, including Raglan's reactions, see 25 *Manx Deb.*, 27 July 1908, pp. 1282–302.

86  See 26 *Manx Deb.*, 26 January 1909, pp. 220–52.

87  27 *Manx Deb.*, 2 November 1909, p. 5.

88  For details of the debate on the Old Age Pensions Bill, see 27 *Manx Deb.*, 15 and 22 March 1910, pp. 682–94 and 807–35; for the Estate Duties Bill, see 27 *Manx Deb.*, 1 and 15 February and 8, 15 and 22 March 1910, pp. 353–409, 621–44, 656–82, 774–803 and 809.

89  27 *Manx Deb.*, 5 April 1910, pp. 837–50.

90  See Jones, *Making of Social Policy in Britain*, Chapter 8.

91  29 *Manx Deb.*, 15 May 1912, pp. 485–86.

92  *Isle of Man. Report of the Commission on Old Age Pensions* (Douglas, 1913).

93  30 *Manx Deb.*, 4 March 1913, p. 233.

94  See 30 *Manx Deb.*, 8 April 1913 and 20 May 1913, pp. 323–37, 340–48 and 443–58.

95  See 31 *Manx Deb.*, 12 June 1914, pp. 516–17.

96  32 *Manx Deb.*, 6 July 1915, p. 404.

97  See 33 *Manx Deb.*, 11 August 1916, p. 585.

98   *Statutes*, viii, pp. 272–91.

99   See *Report of the Poor Law Commission, 17 March 1940*, para. 39.

100  See *The Reports and Annual Statement of Accounts of the Isle of Man Asylums Board and Assessment Board for the Year ended 31 March 1919* (Douglas, 1919), p. 61. Douglas accounted for 51 per cent of total expenditure.

101  Hinton Bird, *An Island that Led: The History of Manx Education*, vol. 2 (Port St Mary, 1995), p. 176.

102  Bird, *Island that Led*, p. 177.

103  See 22 *Manx Deb.*, 21 March and 18 April 1905, pp. 458–98 and 733–59.

104  23 *Manx Deb.*, 28 November, pp. 58–102.

105  See Bird, *Island that Led*, pp. 148–51.

106  *Statutes*, viii, pp. 97–117.

107  *Statutes*, viii, pp. 296–97.

108  See Bird, *Island that Led*, pp. 159–61.

109  Bird, *Island that Led*, p. 184.

110  Bird, *Island that Led*, p. 177.

111  Education Act 1918, s. 1.

112  Bird, *Island that Led*, p. 181.

113  *Statutes*, ix, pp. 425–28.

114  *Statutes*, x, pp. 264–66.

115  Bird, *Island that Led*, p. 181.

116  *Summary by the Local Government Board of the Annual Report of their Inspector as to the Public Health in the Isle of Man for the Year ended 30 September 1907*, 26 November 1907 (Douglas, 1907), p. 8.

117  *Statutes*, vii, p. 491.

118  *Statutes*, viii, pp. 263–65.

119  *Statutes*, x, pp. 57–233.

120  *Statutes*, viii, pp. 297–311.

121  *Statutes*, ix, pp. 15–81.

122  See 27 *Manx Deb.*, 26 November 1909, p. 107.

123  See 30 *Manx Deb.*, 1 April 1913; pp. 307–08.

124  Annual reports were published up to 1906 and LGB summaries of their Inspector's reports in subsequent years. The material in the next three paragraphs is taken from these reports.

125  *Statutes*, vii, pp. 581–92.

126  Jones, *Making of Social Policy in Britain*, p. 96.

127  See 30 *Manx Deb.*, 28 January 1913, p. 147; *Report of the Test Medical Inspection of Scholars*, 9 November 1913 (Douglas, 1913).

128  G. N. Kniveton (ed.), *Centenary of the Borough of Douglas 1896–1996* (Douglas, 1996), p. 15.

129  See 15 *Manx Deb.*, 15 July 1898, pp. 499–504 and 17 *Manx Deb.*, 7 November 1899, pp. 9–10.

130  See n. 129 and Kniveton, *Centenary of the Borough of Douglas*, p. 15.

131  Kniveton, *Centenary of the Borough of Douglas*.

132  See Local Government Board summaries of their Inspector's reports for the period.

133  The Increase of Rent and Mortgage Interest (War Restrictions) Act 1915 was extended to the Isle of Man by SRO 1918/469 and remained in force until its repeal by SRO 1921/1287 and replacement by Manx legislation; *Statutes*, xi, pp. 79–90.

134  See 18 *Manx Deb.*, 30 April 1901, pp. 657–96.

135  *Statutes*, vii, pp. 537–41; see also 21 *Manx Deb.*, 2 December 1903, p. 6; 4 February and 8 March 1904, pp. 72–127; and 15 March 1904, p. 389.

136  See 30 *Manx Deb.*, 14 and 21 January 1913, pp. 85–99 and 111–28.

137  *Statutes*, x, pp. 346–72.

138  *Statutes*, vii-x.

139 See 27 *Manx Deb.*, 2 November 1909, pp. 6–50 and 1 February 1909, p. 344. The second reading was approved without division and the third by 15 votes to eight.

140 See 27 *Manx Deb.*, 22 February 1909, pp. 486–509.

141 See 28 *Manx Deb.*, 11 July 1911, pp. 677–88.

142 See 29 *Manx Deb.*, 15 May 1912, pp. 486–90.

143 See 31 *Manx Deb.*, 3 February 1914, pp. 70–84.

144 See 31 *Manx Deb.*, 26 May 1914, pp. 376–98 and 2 June 1914, pp. 407–31.

145 *Statutes*, ix, pp. 390–96.

146 By empowering the Highway Board to close public roads; *Statutes*, vii, pp. 468–70.

147 *Statutes*, ix, pp. 97–107.

148 During the 1880s the Commissioners had purchased the Mooragh and adjacent lands for the purpose of housing and tourist developments; see Constance Radcliffe, *Shining by the Sea: A History of Ramsey 1800–1914* (Douglas, 1989), pp. 111–15.

149 This period saw the development of forestry plantations by the newly formed Arboricultural Society. Under the auspices of Tynwald's Tree Planting Committee and with grant aid from Tynwald, this Society embarked on a programme of planting. The two main plantations were at Slieu Whallian in 1906 and Sulby in 1907; they were formally transferred to Tynwald with the establishment of the Forestry Board in 1931.

150 For further detail, see Kniveton, *Centenary of the Borough of Douglas*, pp. 25–27 and 54.

151 For further information on the Manx experience of war, see Kniveton, *Chronicle of the Twentieth Century*, vol. 1, pp. 53–66.

152 32 *Manx Deb.*, 22 June 1915, pp. 324–36.

153 33 *Manx Deb.*, 14 December 1915, pp. 114–25.

154 *Statutes*, x, pp. 43–46.

# CHAPTER FOUR

# The Interwar Years 1919–39

The immediate postwar years were a turning point in Manx history every bit as important as the prewar period had been for the UK. A new Lieutenant-Governor, a reform-minded House of Keys and a reconstituted Legislative Council cooperated to deliver a package of social and economic reforms that were to transform the role of the state in Manx society. While the recession of the 1920s and 1930s limited the extent and impact of the reforms, a successful tourist industry, buoyant customs revenues and a flexible income tax base gave the Manx Government the capacity to consolidate its welfare role and tackle economic problems. The enhanced role of government was not matched by any formal diminution of the powers of the Lieutenant-Governor or UK control.

Four Lieutenant-Governors were responsible for the good government of the Isle of Man over this period.[1] They were appointed for fixed terms of seven years, although one resigned before his term was up and another had his term extended because of the Second World War. They were aged between 50 and 60 on appointment, after distinguished careers either in the armed forces or the colonial service. By comparison with Raglan they were liberal in outlook, sympathetic to the interests of the Island and more willing to be advised by the elected representatives of the Manx people.

Major General Sir William Fry (1919–26) was born in 1858 and had served in the army from the age of 20; immediately prior to appointment, he had been military administrator of Ireland. His wife, Ellen, was the daughter of a former Speaker of the House of Keys, Sir John Goldie-Taubman. He came to the Island with instructions from the Home Office to take early steps to bring about a greater measure of contentment to the Island and immediately promised Tynwald that he would do his utmost to advance the welfare and wellbeing of the Island.[2] He was succeeded by Sir Claude Hill (1926–33). Born in 1866, he enjoyed an outstanding career in the Indian civil service from 1885 to 1920, when he became Director-General of the League of Red Cross Societies, a nongovernmental post. Hill was replaced by Sir Montagu Butler (1933–37). Born in 1873, he too came to the Island after a successful career in the Indian civil service from 1896 until his retirement in 1933. He resigned his position as Lieutenant-Governor in 1937 to become Master of Pembroke College, Cambridge. Butler was followed by former naval officer, William Leveson-Gower (1937–45), who became the fourth Earl Granville on the death of his brother in July 1939. Born in 1880, he joined the navy as a young man and by the time of his retirement in 1935 had reached the rank of Vice Admiral. He came to the Island with a background that was to serve the Island well during the Second World War.

Sir William Fry, Lieutenant-Governor
1919–26.

Sir Claude Hill, Lieutenant-Governor
1926–33.

William Leveson-Gower (Earl Granville), Lieutenant-Governor 1937–45, welcoming the
Norwegian Ambassador to London, Erik Colban, to the Island in July 1939. From left to right,
William Cubbon, head of the Manx Museum, Professor Mahr, Director of the Irish National
Museum in Dublin, Lieutenant-Governor Leveson-Gower, Erik Colban, Speaker Qualtrough and
High Bailiff Ramsey Johnson, a former MHK (1924–29) and Clerk of Tynwald (1929–38).

Throughout the interwar period the Lieutenant-Governor remained the sole executive, presiding over government without the help of the executive council that had been sought by the MNRL in 1903 or the much weaker advisory body, for which the Keys had petitioned in 1907. Attempts to reform the executive during this period were also unsuccessful, but the establishment of advisory committees and new boards of Tynwald led to a new level of partnership in government between the externally appointed official at the helm and members of Tynwald.

The period opened with the much delayed legislation to reform the Legislative Council and this was followed by the first general election to be held under universal adult suffrage. With the installation of a new Lieutenant-Governor in April 1919, these developments brought about a remarkable change in the personnel of Manx politics. Most of those who had led the struggle for reform over the previous two decades had either retired from politics or died—of the original leaders of the reform movement, Caine had retired from politics in 1908; Kerruish and Goldsmith had suffered electoral defeat in 1913; Cowell had died in 1917 and Crennell in 1918; Cormode was too ill to continue in politics and died in 1920; only Joseph Qualtrough successfully contested the 1919 election, but even he left the House of Keys on becoming one of the first four MHKs to be elected to the Legislative Council. Sir William Fry, who thought of himself as a progressive, now occupied the post of Lieutenant-Governor. Although the powers of the Legislative Council were unaltered, the membership was transformed. By December 1919 the only members who had served in the unreformed Council were Bishop Thompson, the two Deemsters and the Attorney General, George Ring. They remained ex officio members. The Clerk of the Rolls, Thomas Kneen, had died in 1916

Sir Montagu Butler, Lieutenant-Governor 1933–37, at the Tynwald Ceremony, July 1934.

Joseph D. Qualtrough (SHK 1937–60) with his family at the time of his election as Speaker in December 1937. Qualtrough was elected MHK for Castletown in a by-election in 1919 and served the constituency with distinction until his death in 1960. His performance in the Keys and Tynwald made him the obvious choice to succeed Clucas in 1937. From left to right are his son, Ian, wife Ethel, daughter Cicely, Speaker Qualtrough and daughter Eileen.

and the post absorbed with that of First Deemster; Ring would retire in 1920 and be replaced in 1921 by Ramsey B. Moore; three officials, the Receiver General, the Archdeacon and the Vicar General, ceased to be ex officio members in 1919. Six new members were appointed in December 1919, two by the Lieutenant-Governor, Richard B. Quirk and George Drinkwater, and four by the House of Keys, Joseph Qualtrough, Joseph Cunningham, John R. Kerruish and William C. Southward. Only time would tell whether the new membership would be more amenable to the reform initiatives of the elected chamber. The membership of the House of Keys was also radically changed; following the 1919 election and the four by-elections necessary as a result of the elevation of four members to the Legislative Council, there was a new Speaker, 15 new members and six others who had been in the House for less than a full term. It was from this group of 21 that a new generation of reformist leaders emerged, the Speaker, Frederick Clucas, who had been associated with the reform movement since its inception in 1903, Samuel Norris, the extraparliamentary agitator for reform who now continued the struggle from within the House of Keys, Richard Cain, who had also been active in the MNRL, Joseph Davidson Qualtrough, one of the most effective MHKs of the interwar period, eventually succeeding Clucas as Speaker in 1937, and the four members of the MLP, Gerald Bridson, James R. Corrin, Christopher R. Shimmin and Alfred J. Teare.

Left: Ramsey B. Moore, Attorney General 1921–45. A liberal committed to social reform, Moore was elected to the Keys in 1919 and appointed Attorney General in 1921, an office he held until retirement in 1945.

Right: G. Frederick Clucas, Speaker 1919–37. Clucas was MHK for Middle from 1908 to 1910 and from 1919 until his death shortly after being knighted in 1937. He was one of the outstanding political leaders of the interwar period, successfully combining the roles of leadership in the House and on boards of Tynwald.

## *Limited Constitutional Progress*

Constitutionally the period was dominated by a renewed campaign for an executive council and the question of financial control. Even following the MacDonnell reforms and the introduction of income tax in 1918, the role of Tynwald in general and the elected members in particular remained dependent on the goodwill of the Lieutenant-Governor on the Island and the Home Office and Treasury in London. The first that a major programme of expensive social legislation was passed and implemented was the result of a consensus between the elected and official members of Tynwald and the UK authorities in favour of UK-based reforms. However, faced with conflict, the MHKs were very conscious of their and Tynwald's weakness both in matters of legislation and finance.

Constitutional reform was not the major issue in the interwar elections that it had been before the war, but a minority did press for further action on the MacDonnell recommendations, for the establishment of an executive that was responsible to Tynwald and for Tynwald's control of the Island's finances to be enhanced. At the first sitting of the Legislative Council after the election, Fry raised the question of the legislation that was still hung over from before the war. Much of this, although arising out of the MacDonnell Committee's recommendations, was not strictly constitutional and it was agreed not to proceed further with it, except that the proposal to centralise educational administration would be tackled in a new Education Bill.[3] The one outstanding constitutional matter concerned the Manx judiciary and a new bill was introduced to remove the Lieutenant-Governor from the High Court of Justice. With Fry's full backing, the Bill had a smooth passage through the Legislative Council on 17 February 1920. The main provision of the Bill was welcomed in the House of Keys, but conflict over provisions relating to the office of Vicar General culminated in the Bill's defeat at third reading. It was reintroduced by Norris, modified to provide for the abolition of the office of Vicar General and approved by the House. The Legislative Council agreed to go along with the amended version, subject to the public salary of the Vicar General continuing for a period of three years. The Isle of Man Judicature (Amendment) Act became law in 1921.[4]

An opportunity to press the case for a responsible executive came in 1921, when Fry introduced legislation to formally recognise the reformed Legislative Council as the Executive Council. Fry's purpose was not to meet the demands of reformers, but to legalise the long-standing practice of regarding the Legislative Council as the Executive Council that Lieutenant-Governors were obliged by statute to involve in decisions on a very narrow range of matters, such as the granting of bankers' licences, the approval of

Left: Samuel Norris, MHK, 1934. A determined and persistent campaigner for constitutional and social reform between 1903 and his death in December 1948 at the age of 73, Norris served in the Keys (1919–29 and 1934–43) and the Legislative Council (1943–46). He was the author of one of the few detailed accounts of Manx politics, *Manx Memories and Movements* (Douglas, 1938).

Right: John Donald Clucas, first Chair of the Keys Finance Committee 1920–24. Clucas was MHK for Rushen (1897–1903 and 1908–13) and Ayre (1906–08 and 1919–24). The first Committee also included four figures who were pre-eminent in Manx politics during the interwar period: Speaker Clucas, his eventual successor J. D. Qualtrough, Samuel Norris and Ramsey Moore, at that time an MHK but moving to the Legislative Council on becoming Attorney General in 1921.

burial ground closures and the issuing of orders under the Cattle Diseases Acts. For these purposes the Executive Council was any two MLCs acting with the Lieutenant-Governor. The aim of the Isle of Man Constitution (Amendment) Bill 1921 was to enable the Lieutenant-Governor to summon any two members of the reformed Legislative Council to assist him and not just the ex officio members.[5]

When the Bill came before the Keys, successful amendments moved by Norris provided for an executive council with three members from the Legislative Council, other than the Deemsters, and three members from the Keys, and with the responsibility to advise the Lieutenant-Governor on the whole range of government matters.[6] In the Legislative Council, Fry made it clear that the Norris amendments were unacceptable and the Bill fell. Further attempts by Norris to achieve the same reform in 1922 and 1927 had the overwhelming backing of the House of Keys, but were unacceptable to Fry and a majority of the Legislative Council.[7] The following year, and partly in response to the Keys' wishes to be more involved in government, Hill offered to consult regularly with a committee of the House on matters relating to the government of the Island and this stemmed the demands, temporarily at least, for an executive council.

Following the news of Butler's pending resignation, the question was reopened. On 13 April 1937 Norris and J. D. Qualtrough obtained the support of the House for a resolution asking the Home Office to require future Lieutenant-Governors to consult and be advised by an executive committee that was responsible to Tynwald. Norris had been in the vanguard of those pressing for a system of responsible government in the Island for over 30 years. Qualtrough, by this time one of the leading spokesmen on constitutional matters, felt the time was ripe for such a development and that there were sufficient capable men in the Island to warrant a greater measure of self-government. The resolution was carried by 15 votes to seven.[8] The response of the Home Secretary, Sir Samuel Hoare, in a letter dated 21 August 1937, was an emphatic 'no'. He did give assurances that the consultative mechanisms introduced by Fry and developed by Hill and Butler would be maintained by future Lieutenant-Governors, but did not think any useful purpose could be served by receiving a deputation on the subject.[9]

The policy on consultation initiated during Fry's administration was a response to the Keys' campaign for greater financial control to be placed in the hands of the elected representatives. When Norris discovered by questioning in Tynwald that there had been an increase in the number and salaries of government officials on the eve of Raglan's resignation without the knowledge of the House of Keys, in January 1920 he moved a resolution of protest on the subject in Tynwald. Following the defeat of his motion of protest by a unanimous vote in the Legislative Council, Norris moved successfully that the Keys retire to their own chamber.[10] He then moved, again successfully, that the House refrain from meeting in Tynwald until their rights both to consider and approve increases in salaries were recognised and their demands for increased financial control met.[11] This 'strike' action, reminiscent of that initiated by William Kerruish in 1911, was approved without division. On receipt of the Keys' complaint the Home Office commented privately that it was 'unfortunate that Lord Raglan did not exercise a little statesmanship and avoid trouble by taking Tynwald into his confidence over these matters'.[12] Following a meeting with a five-man deputation from the House of Keys— led by Speaker Clucas and with J. D. Clucas, Moore, Norris and J. D. Qualtrough in support—and consultations with the Lieutenant-Governor and the Treasury, a way forward was suggested by the Home Office and accepted by the Keys on 1 June 1920. It was agreed that in future the Lieutenant-Governor put all financial proposals to both

*Offshore Island Politics*

Houses for private discussion and response, consider the responses and if necessary discuss them with a deputation to reach agreement and that, in the event of disagreement, the matter be referred to the Home Office. It was also accepted that proposals from the Keys for expenditure from the surplus revenue be made in the form of a declaratory resolution, submitted to the Lieutenant-Governor and dealt with in a similar manner.[13] As a result of the agreement the House of Keys set up a standing finance committee to undertake this new role. The full Legislative Council took on a similar role.[14]

The initial Finance Committee comprised the members of the deputation to the Home Office. Both Fry and members of the Committee spoke in Tynwald of the immense value of the new machinery of consultation. Presenting the first budget in Tynwald after the establishment of the Committee, Fry spoke of 'their very valuable advice' and stated that he had been able to accept most of their suggestions.[15] Reporting to the House on their meeting with Fry, Committee members explained that they had protested against the large increases in the expenditure on the reserved services in 1919/20 without a vote in Tynwald and asked the House to endorse their action.[16] Fry agreed to allow votes on such increases in 1921/22, a decision that was warmly welcomed in Tynwald. However, when presenting his budget for 1922/23, he had to inform Tynwald that the Home Secretary had decided that in future the views of the two branches on proposed increases in expenditure on the reserved services should be obtained through private sittings, but that there should be no vote on the increases in Tynwald.[17] While this was clearly a setback for the reformists, the establishment of the Finance Committee and private consultations over the reserved services were major steps forward on the position that had obtained since 1913.

In October 1927 Hill invited the Keys to appoint a consultative committee, a small 'unofficial' committee of five members with whom he could consult on matters relating to the government of the Island. Hill was anxious to develop closer cooperation with the Keys, saying that current reliance on 'irregular and informal consultations leaves a good deal to be desired'. He needed to benefit from their experience and knowledge of the questions of the day and wanted MHKs to be aware of the facts and reasoning behind policy initiatives or the lack of such initiatives.[18] Hill made it clear that such a committee would in no way prejudice the rights of MHKs. They would still be free to ask questions in Tynwald, appoint deputations to meet with him on any issue and accept, amend or reject policy resolutions and legislation. The committee would be advisory and, except when requested to treat matters confidentially, would be free to report to the House. It was to be seen as an experiment and without prejudice to any other development of the constitution. After a lengthy debate on 17 January 1928 the House agreed by 11 votes to seven to accept the offer.[19] The initial membership was quite different from that of the Finance Committee, only one member, J. D. Qualtrough, serving on both. After the 1929 general election, Qualtrough moved that the two committees be amalgamated to become the Consultative and Finance Committee.[20] After a debate, in which there were complaints about unnecessary secrecy on the part of the Consultative Committee since its establishment in 1928, the House agreed to the amalgamation proposal and proceeded to appoint the existing members of the Finance Committee plus the two members of the Consultative Committee who had survived the election. The seven-member Consultative and Finance Committee, chaired initially by Speaker Clucas and from 1935 by J. D. Qualtrough, became the main vehicle of consultation between Lieutenant-Governors and the House until the creation of the War Consultative Committee in 1939.

Leading MHKs were happy to place on record their appreciation of the new consultative mechanisms. Speaking in Tynwald on 31 May 1921, Norris thanked Fry for working so closely with the Finance Committee: 'You are the first to recognise the value of that cooperation, the value of that conference.'[21] J. D. Qualtrough, after eight years of experience on the Finance Committee, claimed that the mere existence of the Committee and its standing under the Home Office letter of June 1920 was 'sufficient protection' against the dangers of any abuse of power.[22] On the occasion of Butler's final budget in 1937, Speaker Clucas commented on his 'genius' at leadership and said how much the Keys appreciated the way he had developed the practice of consultation:

> There is really no step which has been taken upon which you have not consulted us, and in the many conferences we have had with you, you have always put the matter clearly before us, and asked our individual opinions, and, we believe, largely governed yourself accordingly.

Norris followed this by congratulating Butler on the great strides made under his leadership in enabling Tynwald to exercise financial control through the work of the Consultative and Finance Committee, and Qualtrough, the current chair of the Committee, thanked him for consistently trying to find out 'what Tynwald desires' and acting accordingly.[23] On the occasion of Leveson-Gower's first budget in 1938 Speaker Qualtrough thanked the Lieutenant-Governor for 'so very fully' consulting with the House and 'almost completely' meeting their wishes.[24] A year later Norris, a member of the Committee, welcomed the opportunity availed to members of the Committee to learn about and comment on the Island's financial situation:

> Members have had the opportunity of learning and examining what is in the coming budget, and we have had something more important still, consultation in the very earliest stages ..., consultation as to how the finances are turning out, and to some extent what proposals are being made ... There is greater consultation than ever.[25]

Membership of these committees between 1920 and 1939 came from a broad political spectrum. The first Finance Committee included veteran constitutionalist, J. D. Clucas, as chair and progressive reformers like the Speaker, Moore, Norris and J. D. Qualtrough. After the appointment of Moore as Attorney General in 1921, the trio of progressives was joined by Richard Cain, a progressive representing Ayre, who had entered the House following a by-election in December 1919. After the 1924 general election, Clucas was replaced by wealthy businessman, Arthur B. Crookhall, one of two new conservative members representing North Douglas. In January 1928 the Consultative Committee elected a conservative, the advocate Ramsey Johnson, as chair and the members included another conservative, Daniel J. Teare, J. D. Qualtrough and MLP member William P. Clucas. In 1929 the first membership of the Consultative and Finance Committee included the Speaker as chair, J. D. Qualtrough, Cain, William Clucas and three conservatives, Crookhall, W. F. Cowell and Daniel Teare. In 1935, with Qualtrough in the chair and the Speaker still a member, Norris rejoined the Committee and served with MLP member, Alfred Teare, on the left and Daniel Teare on the right. This 'coalition' dimension to the membership of these early advisory bodies is best explained by the lack of a party system, the concern to provide representation for different parts of the Island and the search for the best qualified people for the job. It remained a feature of Manx politics right through to the contemporary Council of Ministers.

Although the informal developments of 1920 and 1928 were welcomed by the Keys, they fell short of their aspirations for a more democratic system of financial control. Manx hopes had been raised by Hill in 1926 during discussions in Tynwald about a UK request for a substantial contribution towards the cost of the war. Between 1866 and 1914 the Island's contribution to defence and common services had been a statutory sum of £10,000 per annum, but with the onset of war this was considered by the UK to be inadequate.[26] In September 1914 Tynwald voted an extra £10,000 towards the cost of the war.[27] In April 1921, Tynwald undertook liability for the payment of interest and sinking fund on £250,000 of the UK Government's 1929–47 War Loan. This was effected by the War Contribution and Income Tax (Appropriation) Act 1922 and involved the Island paying £20,000 per annum to the UK over and above the £10,000 payable under UK statute. This contribution was made under pressure from the Home Office, which regarded it as 'belated and not too liberal'.[28] Because of Tynwald's failure to meet requests for a further contribution, in 1923 a committee of the Privy Council was appointed to enquire into the matter and recommended an increase in the fixed contribution to £50,000 per annum plus a further £50,000 for a period of 50 years.[29] This was quite unacceptable to the Island, where following consultations with the Committee of Tynwald appointed to advise on the matter, Hill proposed a compromise to Tynwald. On 22 October 1926 he urged Tynwald to assume responsibility for the payment of interest and sinking fund on a further £500,000 of UK war stock, £100,000 of which could be paid out of surplus revenue and the remainder by annual payments of £30,000 over a period of 25 years. Making it clear that he was not acting on instructions from the UK Government, Hill commented:

> I feel able to assure you of my personal conviction that all matters outstanding, including the application of financial control, will be most favourably and sympathetically considered by the Home Office and the Treasury. My personal view is that the submission of this offer will result in the creation of an atmosphere of mutual trust between ourselves and the British Government, which cannot fail to facilitate the solution of all problems.[30]

In November 1926 Hill's proposal was the subject of a protracted debate spread over four days. The motion to approve was moved with a powerful speech by J. D. Qualtrough, which was applauded by other members. He felt that it was a realistic proposition, could be afforded and would sweeten relationships with the UK. All but four members of Tynwald joined in the debate, several questioning the Island's capacity to pay and dubious about the prospects of progress on financial control. In the end the resolution was carried by 15 votes to nine in the Keys and unanimously in the Legislative Council.[31] The War Contribution and Income Tax (Appropriation) Act 1927 provided the statutory basis for the new contribution.[32]

The doubts expressed about the prospects of progress on financial control proved to be well founded. At informal discussions with the Home Office in 1928 a committee of the Tynwald, comprising Attorney General Moore and J. D. Clucas from the Legislative Council and Speaker Clucas, Corrin, Norris, J. D. Qualtrough and Hugo Teare from the Keys, proposed the removal of Treasury control and the transfer of financial power to an executive council or committee that was responsible to Tynwald. However, the Home Office was unwilling to discuss such a radical proposal and, despite the resignations of Norris and Qualtrough from the Committee in protest, no further progress was made until the Second World War.[33] Almost as if to compensate for the rejection of Tynwald's proposal, the following year three properties that had come under English control in 1765 were returned to the Island as a gift from King George V; however, while the symbolic value of insular ownership and control of the Tynwald Fairground, Castle Rushen and Peel Castle was considerable, the transfer did little to advance the Keys struggle for financial control.[34]

The financial weakness of Tynwald was further highlighted in the early 1930s as the Island sought to modify its laws on taxation. In 1930 the House of Keys passed an Income Tax Amendment Bill with the aim of securing the payment of Manx income tax on the profits earned in the Isle of Man by non-Manx companies, on dividends paid by Manx residents to persons outside the Isle of Man and on dividends received by Manx residents from investments outside the Island. The UK authorities objected strongly to the Bill on the grounds that it would deprive the UK Treasury of income and insisted on the removal from the Bill of the provisions relating to the two categories of dividends and the payment of the revenue from the taxation of the Manx profits of non-Manx companies into the General Revenue rather than the Income Tax Fund.[35] In 1931 the Isle of Man Government drafted estate duty and surtax bills only to be told by the Home Office 'to drop any idea of resorting to super-tax or estate duty' and to 'refrain from suggesting them in any way' to the Legislative Council or the Consultative and Finance Committee of the House of Keys. The reason given was that such measures would result in a significant loss of revenue for the UK. Even though this reasoning was challenged, the Island was obliged to abandon both bills.[36] In rather different circumstances and with the aim of financing contributions towards the cost of UK rearmament, surtax was eventually introduced in 1939.[37]

The Island's experience of Treasury control was in part a reflection of the unfavourable economic circumstances of the interwar years. The tightness of control was a regular source of controversy, sometimes involving relatively minor sums, and was one of the factors leading to wartime demands for radical constitutional reform, in particular an end to Treasury control.[38] Most of the decisions regarding UK control were in practice taken by the Treasury on the advice of the Home Office. For example, on 8 November 1923, three declaratory resolutions of Tynwald were forwarded to the Home Office, proposing expenditure of £7,000 towards the cost of renewing water mains in Douglas, £5,000 for the construction of a new reservoir in Rushen and £2,000 for the resurfacing of two roads in Ramsey not classed as main roads. The Home Office response on 16 November 1923 was that the items should be charged against the local rates. As a result of a meeting on 4 December 1923 between a deputation from Tynwald and seven UK officials (four from the Home Office, two from the Treasury and one from the Ministry of Health) approval was subsequently given to two of the proposals, but the Home Office insisted that no case had been made for the full grant in respect of the Douglas water mains and that half of the cost should be borne by the rates. Tynwald agreed 'under protest'.[39]

In 1925, on receipt of a draft declaratory resolution expressing the desirability of spending £17,500 on a new school in Laxey, the Home Office argued that the Laxey and district ratepayers should assume responsibility for half of the cost as was the usual practice under the Island's Education Acts since 1920. Despite explanation that schools in Douglas and Rushen had been wholly financed out of the General Revenue, the Home Office refused to modify its views. The Government Secretary then argued that if the 'normal procedure' was adopted, there would be no new school in Laxey because of the poverty of the area. The Home Office stood its ground. On 15 August 1925 the declaratory resolution was forwarded to the Home Office with a promise that after Laxey future schemes would conform with the 1923 Education Act. The Home Office was still unhappy about the entire cost falling on the General Revenue, ordered an inquiry into the state of the Laxey lead mines and asked Fry for details of the economy of Laxey and district. On learning that the lead mines were likely to be exhausted within six years and of the poverty of the area generally, the Home Office finally relented and recommended to the Treasury that approval be given, on condition that the proceeds of the sale of the existing schools be paid into the General Revenue and that no further schemes of the kind be introduced. On the advice of the Home Office, Treasury approval was duly given on 4 December 1925.[40]

Proposed expenditure on advertising the Island, which had been the subject of conflict with the UK authorities in 1894 and 1911, met with further opposition during the interwar period. Early in 1924 a vote of £2,000 for the purpose of publicising the Island at the British Empire Exhibition was only approved on condition that the regular vote for publicity in 1924/25 be reduced by £500. Instead of lowering the vote, Tynwald, with Fry's approval, voted £8,357 for the purpose, an increase over 1923/24 of nearly £1,500. The Treasury, on the insistence of the Home Office, approved only £7,000. The Home Office reminded Tynwald that advertising by English local authorities was restricted to the revenue from a penny rate, which in the Island's case would be approximately £1,900 per annum. The Island's Board of Advertising protested that it was already committed to expenditure on the scale approved by Tynwald and in these circumstances the full vote was allowed, subject to expenditure in future years being resticted to £7,000. This incident caused considerable resentment on the Island and was one of several in which the UK authorities insisted on reductions in proposed expenditure as a condition of approval. Requests to the UK authorities in 1927, 1931 and 1938 for the issue of special postage stamps to advertise the Island were turned down by the Home Office on the recommendation of the General Post Office.[41]

In 1938 a relatively minor issue illustrated just how restrictive financial control could be. A request had been received from the National Trust for a government grant of £150 towards the cost of maintenance and repairs of its buildings on the Calf of Man, attempts to raise money by public subscription having failed. On 23 April 1938 the Government Secretary asked the Home Office to sound out the Treasury semiofficially on the subject and received this reply:

> No grant from public revenues should be made. The Isle of Man taxpayer was presumably not consulted when the property was presented to the National Trust and it scarcely seems right that in such circumstances any expenditure should be imposed upon him. Moreover, I doubt whether the Isle of Man taxpayer has any substantial interest in the use to which the Calf of Man is put. No grants have been made from the UK Exchequer to the National Trust … and I think we might be embarrassed if any grant were made [in the Isle of Man].[42]

On 8 May 1938 the Government Secretary wrote to the Home Office, seeking the Treasury's reactions to the proposal if the control and management of the Calf as a bird sanctuary were handed over to the Trustees of the Manx Museum, who were responsible to Tynwald. The Treasury remained unwilling to authorise the grant. On 5 September 1938 a third letter was sent to enquire if approval would be given if the Manx Government obtained a 99-year lease on the Calf, but once again the response was a very firm 'no'.[43]

It would be misleading to leave this discussion without reference to the fact that the UK authorities did approve legislation and expenditure that contributed to a major expansion in the role of government. Moreover, the changes provided members of Tynwald with increased opportunity to participate in the administration of the Island through the developing board system, the various commissions appointed by Lieutenant-Governors and committees appointed by Tynwald. The major developments came in the social arena. The Old Age Pensions and National Health Insurance Act 1920 provided for the creation of the Old Age Pensions and National Health Insurance Board (OAPNHIB) with 14 members, of whom eight were from Tynwald including the chair.[44] In the same year the Education Act created a new role for the Council of Education in relation to the directly elected Education Authority, although its statutory composition was unchanged.[45] The Local Government Act 1922 removed the Lieutenant-Governor from the Local Government Board, over which he had presided since 1894, and allowed the seven members appointed by Tynwald to elect their own chair.[46] Finally, following the increased role of the state under the Mental Diseases Acts of 1924 and 1932, the Asylum Board was renamed the Mental Hospital Board.[47]

A second series of developments resulted from Tynwald providing greater economic support for the economy. The Board of Agriculture became fully operative after the end of the war and in 1923 its membership was reduced to seven, all appointed by Tynwald.[48] 1919 saw the creation of a Tree Planting Board, initially a semiofficial voluntary society, but formally established as the Forestry Board in 1931 with seven members and responsible for electing its own chair.[49] Also in 1931 the Advertising Board was renamed the Publicity Board and reconstituted with 14 members, of which seven were from Tynwald including the chair.[50] A third set of changes involved the establishment of commercial boards with responsibility for managing publicly owned utilities. The Electricity Board was set up under the Isle of Man Electric Light and Power Act 1932 with a chair appointed by the Lieutenant-Governor and four members appointed by him with the approval of Tynwald.[51] In practice the chair and one other member were recruited from Tynwald. A similar pattern was adopted for membership of the Northern and Southern Water Boards when they were established in 1936 and 1939 respectively under the Water Supply Act 1936.[52] Thus, during the interwar period the number of boards increased from eight, including the Board of Agriculture, to 13, including the three commercial boards.[53]

The respective roles of the two chambers in providing chairs of the boards changed markedly after 1919, the Keys taking on much greater responsibility. The increased number of boards, the practice of no longer involving the Deemsters in the work of the boards, the introduction of members' pay in 1922 and choosing the best man for the job, all contributed to the change. The Receiver General continued as statutory chair of the Harbour Commissioners, although after 1919 he did so as an unpaid official recruited from among the indirectly elected MLCs, Joseph Qualtrough until his death in 1933 and Robert C. Cain for the rest of the interwar period. Qualtrough also chaired the Fisheries Board until his death, but was succeeded by John F. Crellin, an MHK. In fact most of the Boards experienced periods of leadership from both branches as the following examples show. The Board of Agriculture had 10 chairs in 20 years, including three MLCs. The Council of Education was chaired by Speaker Clucas from 1920 until his death in 1937, when the leadership passed to Attorney General Moore until the end of the war. After 1922 the leadership of the LGB was assumed by J. D. Clucas, initially as an MHK and after 1924 as an MLC; it passed briefly to Robert Cain, MLC, until after the 1929 election, when Crellin was chosen; he held the post as an MHK until appointed by

Granville to the Legislative Council in 1943 and as an MLC until 1960. The OAPNHIB was led briefly by Speaker Clucas with Ramsey Moore as one of the members, but, shortly after becoming Attorney General in 1921, Moore was asked to take over and remained chair until his retirement in 1945. The Advertising/Publicity Board was chaired by J. R. Kerruish, MLC, from 1920 to 1924 and Samuel Norris, MHK, from 1924 to 1929; then, after a year under Edward Callister, MLC, the leadership passed to J. D. Qualtrough, MHK/SHK, who served as chair from 1930 until 1957. The only exceptions were the Asylum/Mental Health Board, which was chaired by Speaker Clucas until 1937 and Walter Craine, MHK, until 1946, and the Highways Board, which chose one of the indirectly elected MLCs, William Southward, as chair for the whole of the interwar period.

Given the size and number of boards, the positions available ensured that each member of Tynwald other than the Deemsters served on at least two and sometimes as many as four boards. While few members of Tynwald achieved the distinction of Speaker Clucas, in terms of the number of boards of which he was a member his position was by no means exceptional. For most of the period he was a member of four Boards and chair of two of them, the Council of Education and the Asylum/Mental Hospital Board. As with the advisory committees of the House, the political make-up of the boards was as wide as that of Tynwald itself. MLP members sat side by side with other progressives and conservatives and, although for most of this period they were not selected for leadership positions, Corrin was appointed by Butler to chair the Electricity Board in 1935 and in 1937 Craine was selected by fellow board members to succeed Speaker Clucas as chair of the Mental Health Board.

Without considerably more research, it would be difficult to generalise about the contribution of board members to public policy. The boards were just one of several sources of public policy and on occasions the real drive for policy development came from specially appointed commissions and committees. However, within the framework of existing policy, the boards enjoyed considerable freedom to get on with the job. Expressing his admiration for the board system in Tynwald in May 1937, Butler explained that almost half of total annual expenditure was to pay for established policies being implemented by the various boards:

> I hope the system will never be sacrificed without the most careful scrutiny of the benefits likely to accrue from any change ... Under the system now in force, these boards and not the Government administer the various departments in their charge. For example, normally the Highway Board does not consult the Government about the roads it wishes to repair or improve, the staff it wants to employ or the quarries it intends to work. It makes up its mind, frames its estimates and sends them into the Government Treasurer ... Insofar as the estimates submitted have [been] similar to the amounts voted by Tynwald in previous years and have been on account of activities approved generally by Tynwald, it has been my practice to accept them.[54]

The role of policy commissions and committees in advising Tynwald assumed greater importance as government activity increased. Chairs and members of commissions were appointed by Lieutenant-Governors and usually included MHK members. This period saw commissions reporting on social security, education, public health, housing, unemployment, agriculture and fishing; most were chaired by one of the Deemsters. Committees of Tynwald usually selected their own chair and had a majority of MHK members. The role of such bodies is well illustrated in the case of agriculture, where three major investigations during the interwar period helped shape policy, the Agricultural Committee of Tynwald reporting in 1926, the Industrial Commission on Agriculture in 1930 and the Agricultural Commission in 1939.

## The Four Interwar Elections

Even though the recruitment of the Legislative Council changed in 1919, none of the ex officio, appointed or indirectly elected members owed their positions directly to the electorate. While in this section the focus is on the House of Keys, it should be remembered that most policy was initiated by the Government in the Legislative Council, which continued to enjoy equal powers with the Keys and some of whose members enjoyed a leading role in Manx government.

Between 1919 and 1939 there were four general elections, held under universal adult suffrage and in the 11 constituencies established in 1891.[55] There were no changes in the franchise, except that with the passage of time there were no 18–20 year olds qualified to vote by virtue of having fought in the war. The qualifications for standing as a candidate were also unchanged, but the introduction of members' pay in 1922 did make it easier for the less well off to contemplate membership of the House. There were attempts at redistribution, but these were unsuccessful.

The payment of members had been raised as an issue in the 1919 election by MLP and other progressive members. Ramsey Moore took the matter up in the House on 2 November 1920, when he moved a resolution requesting the Lieutenant-Governor to introduce legislation to provide for the payment of MHKs and the nonofficial MLCs. It was carried by 13 votes to nine.[56] Legislation was duly introduced and passed by the House. This was one of the few occasions when the prime mover of a proposal in the Keys was also the chief supporter of it, as Attorney General, in the Legislative Council, where it was approved by six votes to four, the opposition coming from the indirectly elected members.[57] Prior to 1922, Tynwald had provided for the payment of limited expenses to chairs and members of certain boards, but no pay that was independent of board service. The Payment of Members Expenses Act 1922 provided £50 per annum for MHKs and indirectly elected MLCs, plus £10 travelling expenses for members living outside of Douglas or Middle. In addition chairs of boards were to get between £20 and £40, subject to no one receiving more than £100 in total.[58]

Redistribution was an issue at each of the four elections, with the Douglas members at the forefront of the campaign for reform. An attempt by Norris in 1922 to obtain support for the principle of reform was defeated by 12 votes to 10.[59] Bills introduced by Norris in 1923 to provide two extra seats for Douglas and one extra for Ramsey were both defeated at second reading by 12 votes to 10.[60] A bill, similar to those of Norris except that it provided three extra seats for Douglas, was introduced by Ramsey Johnson in 1928, but met a similar fate, being defeated by 16 votes to 6.[61] In 1938 the House did at least agree to ask a committee to report on the matter, but the Committee concluded that no case had been made. The Douglas members disagreed, but an amendment by Norris in favour of redistribution along the lines of the 1928 Bill was defeated by 13 votes to 7.[62] By the time of the 1934 election, there were 39,090 voters, of whom 38.5 per cent were in the two Douglas constituencies and 8 per cent in Ramsey. The numbers of electors per seat in the constituencies of North Douglas, South Douglas and Ramsey were 2,827, 3,286 and 3,119 respectively compared with 834 in

Glenfaba, 754 in Ayre and 655 in Michael. The proposals for reform were quite moderate and were not seeking to equalise the ratio of seats to electors, but they met with the opposition of the House's rural majority, especially from those sheadings which stood to lose a seat at the expense of either Douglas or Ramsey. Even the representatives for Ramsey, Hugo Teare in the 1920s and William Alcock in 1938, opposed reform, seeing Ramsey and its agricultural hinterland in Ayre, Garff and Michael as well represented in the House.[63]

Before looking at the four elections in detail, it is worth noting the pressures favouring consensus in a number of important policy areas. After 1919 few politicians were prepared to argue with those campaigning actively for more self-government. The political agenda at election time was heavily influenced by debate and policy in the UK and, even though policies may have been the subject of bitter conflict inside the UK, in the Isle of Man consensus often replaced conflict. The development of the welfare state after 1919 was a case in point. Candidates and MHKs were so anxious to keep in line with the latest UK developments, that they were prepared to forget their ideological differences. In other areas the fact that the UK had pioneered reform was insufficient to persuade Islanders to abandon their differences, differences between socialists, progressives and conservatives, between business and labour, between town and country and over particular issues such as licensing. Again, while there were major differences between candidates and members over the role of the state in the economy, there was an acceptance that public funds should be used to develop the Island's infrastructure, advertise the Island, provide services in areas such as water supply where the private sector had failed and help industries such as agriculture remain competitive in the face of public support and protection in the UK and elsewhere.

The 1919 election was a landmark election, heavily influenced by the frustrations of the Raglan era, the First World War and the progress made with social reform in the UK. By November 1919 there was a new Lieutenant-Governor, who had already demonstrated his support for reform, the prospect of a reconstituted Legislative Council and a general determination that the Island should not deny its people the welfare services available in the UK. Indeed for a time it looked as if Manx politics might begin to look more like those of the UK, with Norris variously proclaiming himself to be a Liberal or a Progressive Independent and seeking support for an Island-wide programme of constitutional, fiscal and social reform, the Manx Labour Party fielding candidates for the first time and various conservatives, including five former constitutionalists in Douglas, campaigning as members of the National Party, implicitly identifying with UK Conservatives. However, while the attempts by Norris and the MLP to create a national election agenda were successful, Independents held their own both in the campaign and the election. What made Norris and the MLP so distinctive was the comprehensiveness of their manifestos and their approach to the election. Norris not only published a detailed manifesto, but also a national programme and policy for all progressives, identifying for electors across the Island the issues to raise and the questions to ask candidates. As in 1903 this tactic helped to nationalise the campaign. There was a significant overlap between this call to progressives and the programme and tactics of the MLP. On policy the MLP went much further in demanding state intervention to address social problems. The fact that the Party fielded candidates in every constituency except Ayre ensured that their radical manifesto became part of a national debate.

What were the issues? There was little controversy over demands for further constitutional reform, although for some the establishment of an executive council and democratic financial control was not high in their order of priorities. Closely related to the debate about financial control were widespread demands for fiscal reform, in particular an end to the taxation of food and a more equitable income tax structure. The MLP also wanted to see the taxation of land values. Redistribution was a priority in Douglas and Ramsey, but elsewhere most candidates simply promised to oppose changes that might adversely affect their area.

With very few exceptions, there was a consensus in favour of UK-style social reform. An Education Bill had already been published before the election and most candidates were supportive of the twin aims of the Bill, the centralisation of educational administration and the expansion of educational provision. While conservatives wondered whether the Island could afford old age pensions and national insurance, for the overwhelming majority of candidates the Island could not afford not to follow the UK. In the field of public health there was widespread support for national health insurance, a school medical service and measures to tackle insanitary conditions and tuberculosis. MLP candidates went further and argued in favour of the nationalisation of the Island's hospitals and the establishment of a national TB sanatorium. Support for public housing was especially strong in the towns, where candidates found the idea of 'homes for heroes' returning from the war hard to resist. On the employment front it was the MLP that led the way and offered the most radical combination of proposals, a minimum wage, a 48-hour week, the arbitration of workplace disputes, the regulation of shop hours and policies to tackle unemployment.

Although deep differences of opinion were expressed over the role of the state in relation to the economy, there was a general recognition of the need to support the visiting industry, with increased spending on advertising and improvements to the Island's harbours and highways, and agriculture by funding the sort of improvements already envisaged before the war. The MLP and some other progressive candidates campaigned for security of tenure for tenant farmers, compensation for unexhausted improvements and land rent courts. MLP candidates, strongly influenced by the British Labour Party, also pressed for public ownership of land, steamship and railway services and the liquor industry. As in the earlier elections of the twentieth century, licensing remained a divisive issue with opponents of drink pressing for the local option and others favouring more or less liberal Island-wide regulation.

There were 47 candidates in the 1919 election and contests in every constituency except Castletown, where the recent by-election victor, J. D. Qualtrough, was returned unopposed. Of these, 31 stood as Independents, 11 as members of the MLP and five as members of the Douglas-based National Party. Among the Independents, three were endorsed by the Progressive Party of Douglas and five were associated with the Rushen Political Progressive Association. Success was achieved by 19 Independents, including two of both the Douglas and Rushen Progressives, four MLP candidates and one of the five National Party candidates. Of the 19 members of the old House who sought re-election only 13 were successful, including six who had entered the House since the 1913 election. This represented the biggest change in membership since 1867 and more was to come; the election of four re-elected members to the Legislative Council paved the way for by-elections in December 1919 and the election of another four new members, including a third member of both the Douglas and Rushen Progressives. This brought the new membership of the House to 15 or 62.5 per cent of the total. In 1921 by-elections brought in three more new members.

Among those re-elected and who stayed in the House were 49-year-old advocate,

Frederick Clucas, who topped the poll in Middle, 34-year-old timber merchant and methodist lay preacher, J. D. Qualtrough, who was returned unopposed in Castletown and 42-year-old journalist, Hugo Teare, who comfortably defeated the MLP candidate in Ramsey. Among the 15 new members, four individuals and one party group deserve particular mention. After many years of political campaigning from outside Tynwald, 40-year-old printer, Samuel Norris, topped the poll in North Douglas. In North Douglas, 39-year-old advocate, Ramsey Moore, was successful in the December by-election and was already making his mark in the House when in 1921 he succeeded Ring as Attorney General. Moore was one of the most influential and respected figures in Manx politics for over a quarter of a century. His successor in North Douglas was 51-year-old businessman and Douglas town councillor, Arthur Crookall. Richard Cain was also successful in one of the December 1919 by-elections, this time in Ayre. Born in 1864 and like Norris a founder member of the MNRL, he was a progressive with business and farming interests. In addition to these individuals, four members of the House's first true political party, the MLP, were elected in November 1919.[64] Although as individuals they did not immediately assume leadership positions, as a group they were an important force for change, albeit only effective when they could persuade or join with others to achieve their goals. T. Gerald Bridson, a 26-year-old farm bailiff, narrowly won the third seat in Middle; James R. Corrin, a 41-year-old joiner and methodist lay preacher, topped the poll in Rushen; Christopher S. Shimmin, a 49-year-old monumental mason and playwright, succeeded Tom Cormode in Peel; and Alfred J. Teare, a 40-year-old printer and trade union organiser, topped the poll in South Douglas. Corrin was President of the MLP at the time and Teare its chief link with the union movement.

A clear majority of the new House were progressives favouring political and social reform. According to Norris, there were four Labour, two liberal, including Norris himself, eight progressives, including Clucas, Moore and J. D. Qualtrough, six moderates and four conservatives, although only the MLP group were members of an Island-wide political party.[65] Reference has already been made to the limited progress with constitutional reform in 1920 and the lack of success on the part of the Douglas members in their campaign for a redistribution of seats. Some of the fiscal objectives were met when taxation on food was brought to an end in 1920 and from 1921 income tax allowances were increased in line with UK legislation. The real breakthrough came in the social arena with the Education and Old Age Pensions and National Health Insurance Acts of 1920. As well as providing for educational reform and social security, these two measures brought about a major advance in health provision with the introduction of a partly state funded national health insurance scheme and a school medical service. On housing there was legislation for Douglas in 1922 and the Island as a whole in 1924. The two important advances with respect to employment came with the Shop Hours Act 1921 and the development after 1921 of winter work schemes. Government support for the economy was increased, with extra spending on advertising the Island, infrastructure and agriculture; in 1924 legislation was passed to provide agricultural land with further relief from local rates. Licensing was the subject of regulatory legislation in 1921 and 1922 and unsuccessful attempts to introduce the local option and state liquor control boards in 1923.

The 1924 election was characterised by demands for consolidation and improvement, rather than radical reform. The major exceptions were the 11 MLP candidates, who campaigned in nine constituencies on a radical manifesto. Most of the retiring members made it clear to the electorate that a tremendous amount had been achieved since 1919 and, that, if re-elected, they would be well placed to build on that progress. A minority of candidates reiterated their desire for further constitutional reform, individuals pressing for the establishment of an executive council and an end to UK Treasury control. UK requests for a substantial annual contribution towards the cost of the war were widely regarded as unreasonable and a few began to see such a contribution as something to offer in exchange for financial control. Norris also sought the removal of the Deemsters from the legislature. Redistribution remained a paramount issue for Douglas candidates and one of a long list for the MLP. Several candidates, including the MLP, advocated a more progressive income tax structure and the MLP repeated their commitment to the taxation of land values. The MLP were also to the fore in demanding improvements to the welfare state, an end to means testing for old age pensions, pensions at 65 instead of 70, pensions for widows and orphans and an increase in the pension from 10 shillings to one pound; they wanted a nationally funded education service, improvements in the quality of public education, health and housing and the restoration of rent controls which had been allowed to lapse in May 1924; in the employment field, they retained their commitment to a minimum wage, a 48-hour week and policies to tackle unemployment, and presented the case for an employment board of Tynwald. While other progressives and some conservatives went along with particular parts of the MLP's social policy, the differences in economic policy were as marked as in 1919. Most agreed that some extra economic support was required for the visiting industry and agriculture, but more controversial were MLP demands for a fair deal for tenant farmers by providing security of tenure, compensation for unexhausted improvements and rent courts and advocacy of public ownership. Licensing and the related question of Sunday trading were especially hot issues and for some candidates the issues of the election.

There were 43 candidates in the 1924 election and contests in all constituencies but Castletown, where J. D. Qualtrough was returned unopposed for a second time. All but the 11 MLP candidates were Independents, although two were adopted by the Rushen Progressive Association and others shared platforms and manifestos with colleagues in the same constituency. Twenty members of the old House sought re-election and 16 were successful, including Richard Cain, Frederick Clucas, Norris and J. D. Qualtrough. Three of the four MLP members were re-elected, only Bridson losing out in Middle. Corrin, Shimmin and Teare were joined in the House by three new MLP members; William P. Clucas, a 65-year-old retired Liverpool police officer, won a seat in Glenfaba; Walter K. Cowin, a 53-year-old village shoemaker, topped the poll in Garff; and Walter C. Craine, a 47-year-old commercial traveller and insurance agent was elected as the second member for South Douglas. The MLP now had a quarter of the members of the House, placing them in a strong position to influence policy in an often divided House.[66] Among the other new members was a 34-year-old advocate who only entered the election in North Douglas when it seemed likely that an MLP candidate might be elected unopposed; Ramsey G. Johnson very quickly joined his conservative campaign partner, Crookall, by this time also Mayor of Douglas, as a leading figure in the House until 1929, when he became Secretary of the House of Keys and Clerk to Tynwald. Following the election Frederick Clucas was re-elected Speaker of the House.

As in 1919, a clear majority of the new House were progressives. Norris described the membership as six Labour, nine liberals, including the Speaker, Richard Cain, Norris and J. D. Qualtrough and nine conservatives, including Crookall, Johnson, Crellin and Hugo Teare, although it should be stressed again that the liberals and conservatives were

Manx Labour Party members elected to the House of Keys in 1924. From left to right they are Walter K. Cowin (Garff), Walter C. Craine (South Douglas), Alfred J. Teare (South Douglas), William P. Clucas (Glenfaba), James R. Corrin (Rushen) and Christopher R. Shimmin (Peel). Corrin, Shimmin and Teare were first elected to the Keys in 1919 and the others in 1924.

not members of disciplined political parties but independent members of a liberal or conservative persuasion. There was a slight change in the political balance of the House in 1928 following Corrin's appointment to the Legislative Council and the narrow defeat of Richard Kneen of the MLP by a progressive in the ensuing by-election, one of only two held between the elections of 1924 and 1929. Notwithstanding the progressive majority in the House, the reforms delivered were modest by comparison with the previous House. The Consultative and Finance Committee was the only important constitutional development and no progress was made over redistribution. The Widows, Orphans and Old Age Pensions Act 1929 introduced a contributory pensions scheme, old age pensions at 65, pensions for widows and orphans and the removal of the means test for noncontributory pensions at 70. There was a major schools building and modernisation programme and improvements in the provisions of the national health insurance scheme and the school medical service. The Housing Act 1924 was extended to 1929 and the Housing (Rural Workers) Act 1929 designed to assist with the housing of agricultural workers. The temporary lapse in rent controls was remedied by the Increase of Rent (Restrictions) Act 1925 and the Act extended in 1927 and 1929. The Report of the Unemployment Commission in 1928 led to the establishment of a new Unemployment Committee and a new approach to the funding of unemployment relief and winter work.

Insofar as other aspects of the economy were concerned, Tynwald approved increases in funding for advertising the Island, harbours and highways and devoted considerable time to investigating and debating the future of Manx agriculture. Following the report of a committee of Tynwald, eight agricultural bills were debated and four of these had become law by 1929. There was no action on MLP demands for more public ownership, although the Water (Supply) Act 1929 did pave the way for an increase in public water supply. In the sensitive areas of licensing and Sunday opening, a committee of Tynwald set up to review the operation of the 1921 Shop Hours Act came up with a split verdict, which became a major issue in the 1929 general election.

The 1929 election took place against the backcloth of a world economic recession. In the Island, however, relatively well insulated from the rapidly rising unemployment being experienced in the UK, local issues predominated. The Home Office's refusal to agree to the removal of Treasury control and conflict between some MHKs and the Lieutenant-Governor and the Legislative Council provided ammunition for those, like Norris, who wished to make constitutional reform one of the central issues. MLP candidates supported democratic financial control as a necessary means to achieving a redistribution of wealth in Manx society. The campaign by Douglas candidates for a redistribution of House seats continued.

There was a general desire for improvements to the developing welfare state, even conservatives welcoming the progress made since 1919 and seeing the value of keeping in line with the UK. It was the MLP candidates who placed greatest emphasis on providing a fairer system, seeking increases in pensions, a more egalitarian education system with free and compulsory education to the age of 16, better care for the sick, a national housing scheme and the retention of private sector rent controls. They also reiterated their demands for a statutory board to tackle unemployment, a minimum wage and a shorter working week.

The role of the state in the economy continued to give rise to conflict, especially between the MLP candidates and a variety of antisocialist candidates, representing both business and farming interests. Most accepted that the state should support industries in need; the real controversy was over the nature and extent of that support. With an extra £5,000 spent on supporting the TT races in 1929, the level of funding in support of tourism aroused little controversy. The poor state of Manx agriculture and the recent defeat in Tynwald of legislation designed to help tenant farmers and agricultural workers led to renewed demands for and opposition to legislation to improve the lot of these two key groups. All but a few conservatives supported the public provision of Island-wide electricity and clean water. By contrast, few agreed with the MLP policy of taking other industries, including the liquor trade, into public ownership. Candidates also disagreed strongly over the way in which the liquor trade and the retail trade generally should be regulated, the focus of conflict being on the Sunday opening of public houses and the extent to which there should be restrictions on Sunday trading generally.

There were 40 candidates in the 1929 election and contests in nine of the 11 constituencies. J. D. Qualtrough was returned unopposed for the third time in Castletown and, more surprising given the usual intensity of competition in Douglas, the sitting MLP members for South Douglas, Teare and Craine, were also returned unopposed. Eight MLP candidates contested seats in seven constituencies. All the other candidates were Independents, including three in Rushen endorsed by the Rushen Progressive Association. Twenty-one members of the old House sought re-election and 17 of these were successful, including progressives, Richard Cain, Frederick Clucas and J. D. Qualtrough, and conservatives, Crookall and Crellin. Norris was not only ousted from his previous position at the top of the poll by Crookall, but came fourth and lost his seat by just four votes to the MLP member, John Kelly. Equally unexpected was the defeat in Ramsey of leading conservative, Hugo Teare. There victory was gained by a retired civil engineer of Irish descent, William H. Alcock, 66 years of age and standing as an Independent but with the endorsement of the Ramsey branch of the MLP. He quickly became an effective campaigner for reform. Each of the five MLP members were re-elected and were joined by two new members, Kelly, a 48-year-old general worker and member of the Transport and General Workers' Union, and Richard Kneen, a 49-year-old fisherman from Port St Mary who topped the poll in Rushen. The Party now had a record seven members in the House and Corrin in the Legislative Council. Following the election Frederick Clucas was elected for a third term as Speaker of the House.

As in 1919 and 1924, the majority of the new House were progressives, seven Labour, nine liberals and eight conservatives. The five by-elections between 1929 and 1934 only marginally affected this political balance. On the death of Christopher Shimmin in 1933, his 55-year-old wife Marion Shimmin was returned unopposed as the MLP member for Peel and the first woman MHK. Following the death of William Clucas in 1933, the MLP did not even contest the Glenfaba by-election and corn and seed merchant, James Clinton, was elected unopposed. On the death of William F. Cowell in 1933, 34-year-old advocate John H. L. Cowin defeated the MLP opposition in Middle. Following the elevation of Crookall to the Legislative Council in 1934, Norris returned to the House, a comfortable winner in the ensuing North Douglas by-election.

The period between 1929 and 1934 was not especially productive. No progress

Members of the House of Keys outside the Speaker's house at Cronkbourne, 1929. From left to right, standing: the Reverend C. A. Cannan (chaplain), John F. Crellin and Daniel J. Teare (Ayre), Alfred J. Teare (South Douglas), Robert Kneen (Glenfaba), Joseph D. Qualtrough (Castletown), Arthur B. Crookall and Samuel Norris (North Douglas), Thomas Callow (Garff), Richard Cain (Ayre), Walter K. Cowin (Garff) and F. Samuel Dalgleish (Glenfaba); sitting: A. Hugo Teare (Ramsey), Ramsey G. Johnson (North Douglas), John W. Cannan (Michael), G. Frederick Clucas, SHK, Charles Gill (Middle) and Christopher Shimmin (Peel).

was made with constitutional reform or redistribution. Moves in 1931 towards a more progressive system of taxation were thwarted, when the Home Office instructed Hill not to proceed with plans for estate duties or surtax. This was a quiet period in respect of welfare reforms. Social security legislation was kept in line with the UK by the Widows, Orphans and Old Age Contributory Pensions Act 1930. An attempt to set up a new board of education in place of the Council of Education and the Education Authority was defeated in the Keys in 1934. The Education (Extension of Medical Treatment) Act 1932 provided for improvements to the School Medical Service. Despite a continuing housing problem, little progress was made with building or renewal during the 1930s. Attempts to make Tynwald fully responsible for the cost of unemployment and remove the financial burden from the boards of guardians were unsuccessful.

Economic support for Manx industries was increased in a variety of ways. Funding for publicising the Island rose from £7,000 to £10,000 per annum and in addition an annual grant of £5,000 was paid to support the TT races. Expenditure on infrastructure, especially highways, was also increased. Manx agriculture was investigated by an Industrial Commission in 1930 and various recommendations made. The Legislative Council defeated two attempts to provide a better deal for tenant farmers and after protracted debates on other recommended measures, three eventually became law on the eve of the next election, the Agricultural Marketing Act 1934, the Agricultural Rates and Improvement Act 1934 and the Local Government (Milk and Dairies) Act 1934. Also

Marion Shimmin being sworn in as a member of the Keys by Deemster Frederick Lamothe, 19 February 1933. She was the first lady member of the House of Keys, having been elected unopposed as the MLP member for Peel following the death of her husband, Christopher Shimmin. She served until her death in 1942.

on the eve of the election, Tynwald approved a declaratory resolution moved by Marion Shimmin seeking the payment of grants to assist Manx fishermen. Public ownership was extended in the Island with the completion of public water supply schemes in Ballasalla/Derbyhaven, Crosby and Michael and the decision in 1932 to opt for a public rather than a private electricity supply for the Island. Five attempts to modify the licensing laws and two attempts to amend the Shop Hours Act 1921 foundered because of opposition within the House to increases in opening hours and Sunday trading.

The 1934 election was the last until after the Second World War. The focus of this chapter will be on the election itself and policy up to the outbreak of war in 1939. The distinguishing feature of the election was Norris's attempt to influence voters across the Island. Two weeks after the *Isle of Man Examiner* had referred to the lack of burning issues, Norris published his *Manx National Programme and a Policy for the People* (Douglas, 1934), a 14-point manifesto that was issued as a free supplement to the *Isle of Man Weekly Times* on 27 October 1934. This programme and Norris's campaigning style attracted both support and opposition; they certainly generated debate on the issues highlighted. On many of the issues raised there was a wide measure of agreement across the Island, but the emphasis he gave to Douglas, the visiting industry and redistribution, and the hostility he showed towards agriculture aroused criticism not only from rural conservatives, but also MLP candidates and other progressives. The only other attempt at Island-wide campaigning was the MLP with a manifesto little changed from that of 1929.

Constitutional reform was a high priority for Norris, seeking increased financial control through the more effective use of the Consultative and Finance Committee and the replacement of the Deemsters and the indirectly elected MLCs by six directly elected members. While few disputed the need for more effective financial control, there was little support from other candidates for this particular reform of the Legislative Council. Redistribution once again divided the Island and Norris's threat to lead Douglas MHKs out of Tynwald and refuse to do business until Douglas was given its just deserts merely deepened the division.

On welfare reform there was a large measure of agreement. There was widespread support for an eve-of-election report by a committee of Tynwald in favour of extending the Island's social security scheme to include voluntary contributors (one of Norris's 14 points), providing pensions for all at the age of 65 and increasing pensions from 10 shillings to one pound. Norris's advocacy of a single Island-wide rate for poor relief aroused considerable hostility in the rural areas where current rates were much lower than in Douglas. Education and public health did not figure in Norris's list, but there was considerable support for increased investment in education and the raising of the school leaving age to 16, the nationalisation of White Hoe Hospital and improvements to water supply, drainage and sanitation in the rural areas. Although Norris supported 100 per cent funding of public housing by Tynwald, it was left to MLP candidates, other progressives and some conservatives to prioritise additional investment in public housing. Unemployment was a major concern for most candidates, but a priority for the MLP and a handful of other progressives. Their demands included a board of Tynwald with responsibility for employment and development, 100 per cent funding of unemployment relief by Tynwald (one of Norris's points), increased investment in public works and government support for the diversification of the Manx economy.

For many candidates the state of the Manx economy was the main election issue. Norris's prioritisation of the visiting industry's needs over those of agriculture was not well received, most candidates seeing both industries as deserving of support. For Norris and the MLP, the outstanding need for Manx agriculture was legislation to protect the tenant farmer. Candidates were broadly in agreement about the need for more public investment in water supply and electricity. It was almost taken for granted that, like the Island's highways and harbours, the much talked about national aerodrome would be publicly owned; the major point of disagreement was over the best site. The regulation of the liquor trade and retail trades generally remained a live issue because of continuing conflict over Sunday trading.

There were 40 candidates in the 1934 election and contests in nine constituencies; in Castletown and Peel candidates were returned unopposed, J. D. Qualtrough for a fourth time and Marion Shimmin for a second time. There were seven MLP candidates in just six of the 11 constituencies and 33 Independents.[67] There was an extremely high level of continuity from the old House; 22 members sought re-election and 20 were successful. In addition the election saw the return to the House of former member, Ambrose Qualtrough. There were no surprise results. Despite the controversy surrounding Norris's campaign, the voters of North Douglas placed him at the top of the poll. Five of the seven MLP candidates were successful, Kelly losing his seat in North Douglas and Bridson unsuccessful in Middle.[68]

Although the progressives retained a majority in the new House, Labour's reduced representation left the rest of the House evenly divided between liberals and conservatives. This political balance was not disturbed by the three by-elections held between 1934 and the outbreak of war. One of these was caused by the death of the House's most distinguished member, Sir Frederick Clucas. Knighted shortly before his death in 1937, he had been a member of the House from 1908 to 1910, its Speaker from 1919 to 1937 and a major contributor to the work of the House and Tynwald. He was replaced as Speaker by J. D. Qualtrough and as MHK for Middle by another advocate, Eric W. Fargher.

No progress was made with constitutional reform or redistribution before the war. While attempts by Teare and the MLP to increase old age pensions were defeated in 1934, legislation in 1938 extended the scope of the old age pensions and national health insurance scheme in line with the UK to include voluntary contributors, juveniles and young persons. In 1939 a resolution in Tynwald led to the appointment of a commission to investigate poor relief, but its work was interrupted by the war. A major reorganisation of the Island's schools into primary and secondary and the implementation of legislation to raise the the school leaving age to 15 were also disrupted by the war. Public health was given a high priority by Tynwald, with increased expenditure on water supply, drainage and sanitation. The nationalisation of White Hoe Hospital was considered but deferred on grounds of cost in 1935. Although there were no other election related successes in the field of employment, a strike by the Transport and General Workers' Union in 1935 did lead to a substantial increase in the pay of public sector workers and a shorter working week.

Economic support for Manx industries increased in response to members' demands. Funding for the Publicity Board was retained at pre-election levels. The depressed state of Manx agriculture led to the adoption of far-reaching reforms, with an Agricultural Holdings Act in 1936 and a programme of subsidies along UK lines in 1937 and 1939. On a much more modest scale, Tynwald also began to subsidise the Manx fishing industry. Demands for improved water supply led to more public investment through the Northern and Southern Water Boards, set up in 1936 and 1939 respectively. A proposal for a publicly owned aerodrome was defeated in Tynwald in March 1935. Finally, after all the heat devoted to debating Sunday trading, in 1939 legislation was approved providing for a significant relaxation of the restrictions that had been in force since 1921.

## Social Policy: Reform and Consolidation

The political circumstances of 1919 were generally favourable to reform. The UK had already introduced reforms and was unlikely to object to the Island following suit. Fry was sympathetic to the aspirations of Tynwald and wasted no time in responding to the demands for social action. Reform-minded candidates in the election of November 1919 emerged with a majority in the Keys; the Legislative Council now included four members chosen by and sympathetic to the House of Keys and Crown-appointed officials who, although loyal to Lord Raglan, were known to favour reform. War proved a major stimulus to reform, highlighting the poverty and poor health of many volunteers and conscripts and their families and leading to a determination by the Island's politicians to respond to these social needs. The healthy state of the Island's finances immediately after the war, with buoyant customs revenue and the availability of income tax revenue for selected purposes, meant that the Island could afford the high cost of reform.

The initial priorities for action were old age pensions and national insurance. One of Fry's first acts was to appoint a 24-member commission to report on the best means of making such provision. Chaired by Deemster Callow, the Commission reported in favour of old age pensions at 70 and national health insurance for all employed persons over 16, including the self-employed who were not covered by the UK scheme and with a scale of contributions and benefits identical to the UK.[69] The Commission also recommended a scheme of unemployment insurance embracing all trades and persons, but not until such comprehensive provision was in place in the UK. The scheme introduced in the UK in 1912, limited as it was to a few high risk industries, was felt to be inappropriate for the Isle of Man.

The reaction of Tynwald was twofold. In December 1919 Tynwald accepted a resolution moved by Norris for a temporary pensions scheme on UK lines pending the introduction of legislation for the longer term.[70] The first old age pensions (10 shillings per week or less depending on means) were paid out of the General Revenue with effect from January 1920. When legislation was introduced, Fry asked for it to be passed as a matter of urgency and the Bill had a smooth passage through both branches. The responsibility for steering the Bill through the House fell to Ramsey Moore, who was subsequently chosen to chair the OAPNHIB from 1921 to 1945. The Old Age Pensions and National Insurance Act 1920 received the Royal Assent on 28 June 1920, less than three months after its first reading in the Legislative Council.[71] The Act provided for old age pensions to be paid to persons aged 70 or over at the prevailing UK rate and subject to a similar means test. Tynwald agreed subsequently that two thirds of the cost should come from the Income Tax Fund and one third from the General Revenue. The Act also provided for national health insurance, with contributions and benefits at UK rates and covering all employed persons aged 16–70 with earnings up to £200 and all manual workers. Contributions from employees and employers were to be the main source of funding for the scheme, with two ninths of the cost of benefits and administration being

The first old age pensions being paid by postal order in 1920 (from Samuel Norris, *Manx Memories and Movements*, 3rd ed. 1941, p. 481). The picture shows Samuel Norris shaking the hands of some new pensioners outside the Widows House, Cambrian Place, Douglas.

borne by Tynwald out of the General Revenue. Benefits were to include financial payments in respect of sickness (initially 15 shillings per week for men and 12 shillings for women) and disability (initially seven shillings and sixpence) and medical attendance and treatment. While the Act did not include provision for unemployment insurance, in other respects it marked the beginning of a long period of harmony and reciprocity with the UK.[72]

Subsequent changes followed those introduced in the UK. The Widows, Orphans and Old Age Contributory Pensions Act 1929 extended the insurance principle to the provision of pensions.[73] A new contributory scheme provided for old age pensions to be paid at the age of 65, still at the rate of ten shillings a week, to insured persons and the wives of insured men; at the age of 70 and above the original noncontributory scheme would apply but without the restriction of means testing. The Act also provided for pensions for widows and dependent children. The delay in following the UK legislation of 1925 was partly the result of the unexpected defeat of the initial Bill in the Legislative Council and partly the amendment of the Bill to include voluntary contributors. On 19 January 1926 the second reading in the Legislative Council had been moved by Attorney General Moore and seconded by Deemster Farrant, when to their surprise and Fry's amazement no one else spoke and the Bill was rejected by five votes to two.[74] The same bill was then introduced into the House, with Hugo Teare in charge and a committee chaired by J. D. Qualtrough playing a decisive role. During debates spread over seven sittings of the House between February 1927 and February 1928, there were three main concerns over the Bill, the cost to the Island, the fact that it was a contributory scheme and the lack of provision for voluntary contributors. Following a report by the Committee, most members were satisfied that the Island could afford the new scheme, that if the Island was to maintain reciprocity with the UK the scheme would have to be a contributory one and that a new clause be added to the Bill to include voluntary contributors. The third reading was carried by 16 votes to six, two members opposing the scheme on grounds of cost and four of the six MLP members objecting to the contributory principle at the heart of the legislation.[75] The amended Bill had a smooth passage through the Legislative Council following a strong speech in support by Hill,[76] only to run into difficulties at the Home Office. This Act was refused the Royal Assent in 1928 because of the embellishment of the UK scheme to include voluntary self-employed subscribers without a previous period of employment insurance; the voluntary provision of the UK scheme related only to those who had fulfilled a specified period of insurance while in employment and the Home Office did not see how the Isle of Man could afford to do what was considered 'economically impossible' in the UK.[77] The Island had little choice but to pass the measure without the offending clause. Ten years later, after equivalent legislation at Westminster, the Widows, Orphans and Old Age Pensions (Voluntary Contributors) Act 1938 did offer the self-employed the option of joining both the contributory pensions scheme and the national health insurance scheme.[78] In the same year the National Health Insurance (Juvenile Contributors and Young Persons) Act provided for the admission to the national health insurance scheme of young employees between the ages of 14 and 16.[79]

The outstanding difference between the UK and the Isle of Man related to unemployment insurance. Despite the recommendations of the 1919 Commission and a widening of the UK scheme in 1920 to cover around 12 million workers, roughly three quarters of the UK workforce,[80] the Island did not follow the UK example. In 1928 the Commission on Unemployment, chaired by the High Bailiff for Ramsey and Peel, W. Percy Cowley, concluded that the mainland scheme was unsuited to a small island

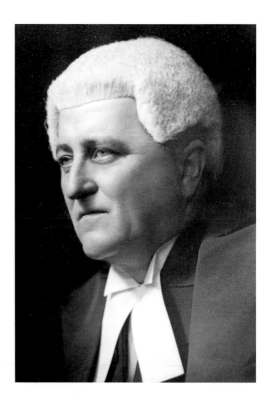

W. Percy Cowley, Deemster and MLC 1934–58. A key figure during the interwar period, who went on to chair the War Consultative Committee and play a major role in the constitutional negotiations with the UK prior to his death in 1958.

with a very different occupational structure and a distinctively seasonal unemployment problem.[81] Even though the 1931 Commission on Unemployment Insurance, chaired by Deemster Farrant, disagreed, arguing that a sound insurance system was 'a necessary and desirable part of any good scheme for abating the hardships of unemployment',[82] the Island continued to rely on noncontributory methods, in particular public works investment and poor relief.

There were three main developments in respect of the system of poor relief during the interwar period. First, four more parishes appointed boards of guardians, leaving only Maughold maintaining its poor by voluntary endeavour by 1939. Second, the Poor Relief Amendment Act 1923 gave to the OAPNHIB responsibility for ensuring an effective poor relief service across the Island.[83] It was authorized to carry out inspections, investigate complaints, conduct inquiries and require remedial action of the boards of guardians.[84] Third, rising unemployment caused a steady increase in the financial burden of relief. Prior to 1928 this was borne entirely by the boards of guardians. After the Report of the Cowley Commission in 1928, the burden was shared, with Tynwald bearing 50 per cent of the costs incurred in the relief of unemployment.[85] Attempts by MLP and Douglas members to increase Tynwald's share to 75 or 100 per cent had mixed results. In 1933 a proposal by MLP members to increase Tynwald's share to 75 per cent in the particular cases of Peel and Lonan was defeated in Tynwald by an adverse vote in the Legislative Council.[86] In 1934 an attempt by Norris to persuade the Keys to push for 100 per cent funding by Tynwald led to acceptance of an amended resolution in favour of Tynwald bearing 'a considerably larger share of the burden of unemployment' and a subsequent increase in Tynwald's share to 75 per cent.[87] In 1935 separate attempts were made by MLP members and Norris to increase Tynwald's share to 100 per cent, but both were defeated by the Legislative Council.[88] Even with the support from Tynwald, net expenditure by the boards of guardians continued to rise, from £12,650 in the year ending March 1920, to £20,841 by 1930 and £29,148 by 1940, a real increase over 1919/20 of 196 per cent. The figures for Douglas alone were £6,359, £9,592 and £13,642 respectively, with a growing proportion accounted for by unemployment.[89]

These changes to the Island's social security provision involved a significant proportion of the Island's population. From a situation in 1919 where the only public provision was that provided by the boards of guardians, by 1939 over eight per cent of the Manx population (4,287 persons) were in receipt of pensions and a further 35 per cent (18,390) were paying contributions for pensions and health insurance.[90] During the same period expenditure by Tynwald on social security rose from nothing in the year ended 31 March 1919 to £45,109 in 1921, the first full year of provision, and £87,905 in 1939, a real increase over 1920/21 of 207 per cent and making social security Tynwald's most expensive service.

For the Island's public education service this period was one of 'remarkable progress'.[91] The Island's education laws were brought into line with those of the UK, political responsibility for education centralised, the quality of provision greatly improved and a school medical service developed. Behind this progress was a surprising generosity of funding given the worldwide recession. The Education Act 1920 assimilated Manx law to that of England by applying, with necessary modifications, the provisions of Parliament's Education Acts of 1902 and 1918 to the Island.[92] A government measure, it had a smooth passage in both branches with Moore steering it successfully through a very supportive House. The Act required the education authorities to provide for 'the progressive and comprehensive organisation of education

Northwest front of the Douglas High School for Boys, St Ninians, 1927. This photograph of the Island's long-awaited new secondary school was presented to the School with the compliments of the architect, J. Mitchell Bottomley.

in the Island', including secondary education which had hitherto been so neglected. Responsibility was to be shared between a new directly elected education authority and the Council of Education. The Education Authority was made responsible for policy, subject to the consent and control of the Council of Education. Although conflict between the two interfered with progress on occasions and led to proposals for further reform,[93] the outstanding achievement of the 1920 Act was the creation of an all-Island authority that was able to transcend 'the pettiness of local politics and parsimony' associated with the the 25 local education boards it replaced.[94]

The Island's achievements under these new arrangements were as impressive as the relative lack of progress in the Raglan years.[95] The Island invested heavily in both elementary and secondary education. A programme of rationalisation of elementary provision saw the amalgamation of schools, the closure of uneconomic schools and the building of new schools serving more than one local authority area. There were new secondary schools in Douglas in 1927 and Ramsey in 1933, and opportunities for secondary study across the Island by the late 1930s. The pay and conditions of teaching staff were improved, with all teachers being placed on the Burnham scale following a mass resignation of teachers in 1920[96] and with the Island subsequently resisting reductions in pay imposed in the UK at the height of the recession.[97] The proportion of free places at secondary schools increased from the 25 per cent figure laid down in 1907 to well over 50 per cent by the mid-1930s.[98] Private education suffered as public provision improved, the private grammar schools in Douglas, Ramsey and Castletown closed by 1931 and the Peel Clothworkers Schools transferred to the public sector in 1936.[99] The result was the emergence of a unitary secondary school system that was to provide the basis for the postwar adoption of comprehensive education.

In March 1937 Tynwald approved the principle of reorganising Manx schools, at a total cost of £80,000, into primary schools for children up to the age of 11 and secondary schools, serving much larger areas, for children up to the age of 15. Moved by Speaker Clucas in his capacity as chair of the Council of Education, the resolution was carried without division.[100] By May 1937 Tynwald had voted the first tranche of £20,000 towards new secondary schools in Douglas and Ramsey and by 1938 had passed the necessary legislation to raise the school leaving age to 15.[101] The Education Act 1938, based on UK legislation and approved without a division in either branch, was to come into effect in September 1939,[102] but both the reorganisation and the raising of the school leaving age were delayed by the war.

There was ample testimony to the effectiveness of the interwar changes. By 1927 the Council of Education was able to report that English Board of Education standards were being met in the Island's secondary schools.[103] In 1933 the Commission on Manx Education, chaired by Sir Edmund Phipps, a former Assistant Secretary to the English Board of Education, reported that the Manx education system was 'well-conceived' and commended the Island on the 'remarkable progress' made since 1920.[104] Hinton Bird echoed these conclusions by saying that 'there would be no injustice in updating to 1940 the praise of the Phipps Commission for "the remarkable progress made"'.[105] The progress was all the more remarkable for having been achieved during a major recession and in a period of tight UK control.

The funding for Manx education increased dramatically during this period. Tynwald's 50 per cent share of revenue spending rose from £22,538 in 1918/19 to £63,688 in 1938/39, a threefold increase in real terms despite reservations by the UK authorities over levels of spending that would not have been tolerated at home. Fortunately for Manx education the Island's wishes were generally if somewhat reluctantly respected. 'Unlike us they have the money to spend' was the private response of the Home Office to Treasury criticisms of the 'lavish' expenditure estimates for 1923/24.[106] These and other controversially high (by English standards) estimates were eventually approved, but only after a lengthy exchange of correspondence and a spirited defence by the Island of its rights and needs.[107] The proportion of capital spending to be borne by rates and associated borrowing also caused friction between the Island and the UK. Section 58 (1) of the Education Act 1920 provided that half of all capital expenditure should be borne by the education district concerned and the UK objected to a series of capital projects where the full costs were to be borne by Tynwald. After much hard argument, approval was given during the 1920s for 100 per cent central funding of new secondary schools in Douglas (because they served the whole Island) and elementary schools in Laxey and Rushen (because they served rural areas unable to bear the cost) and in 1939 for 75 per cent of the capital costs of new elementary schools in Douglas, Ramsey and Peel.[108]

Progress in the field of public health was partly under legislation passed before 1919 and partly the result of new legislation concerning both the protection and promotion of public health and its treatment. Pressures from the LGB and its Inspectors, from the larger local authorities and from public health interest groups provided the impetus for action and legislation. Progressive opinion in Tynwald was in favour of building on earlier successes, benefitting from relevant UK experience and enhancing the powers of the LGB and local government to tackle public health problems. However there were obstacles to overcome. There was strong local opposition to the growth of central government in the Isle of Man, especially from the rural local authorities and constituencies. In the rural areas many local commissioners still believed in the maxim that the least government was the best government and were reluctant to incur unnecessary expenditure. Many of the powers of the parish commissioners were permissive, so it was open to the authorities to adopt a *laissez-faire* approach. The fragmentation of responsibility between small parish authorities continued to create difficulties in areas like water supply and drainage where problem-solving required a broader territorial framework.

Notwithstanding the obstacles, the interwar period did see important changes. Between 1919 and 1939 legislation provided for increases in the LGB's powers of regulation and inspection, with respect to drainage (1922),[109] the quality and standards of food and drink (1922 and 1925),[110] the notification, treatment and prevention of tuberculosis (1922 and 1929),[111] town improvement (1922 and 1936),[112] the safety of mechanical contrivances (1923),[113] urban housing (1924–28 and 1936),[114] rural housing (1929 and 1934),[115] the registration of dairies and the sale of milk (1934)[116] and the extermination of rats (1938).[117] The Local Government (No. 4) Act 1938 empowered the LGB, subject to the approval of Tynwald, to issue orders enabling or requiring joint action by authorities in carrying out any of the provisions of the Local Government Acts.[118] During the same period, powers given to the four town authorities by the Local Government Act 1916 were gradually extended to the rest of the Island (1922, 1931 and 1938).[119] In addition local authorities were given enhanced powers of regulation and inspection over private housing and common lodging houses (1922)[120] and the opportunity to become housing authorities (1922, 1924–28 and 1936).

Not all legislative initiatives were successful, the Keys resisting a series of attempts to increase the powers of central government at the expense of local authorities. In 1927 the Water Undertakings Bill, which sought to increase the powers of the LGB in respect of water supply, was rejected in the House of Keys by 16 votes to three, following representations on behalf of the local water authorities, who saw the Bill as 'unwarranted interference' in an essentially local matter.[121] In 1930 the Public Health Bill, the main purpose of which was to provide for an all-Island Medical Officer of Health, met a similar fate and for similar reasons.[122] In 1934 a proposal, to enhance the effectiveness of public health provision by replacing the parish authorities with five sheading authorities, was rejected in Tynwald on the advice of a select committee. In the Committee's view the parish commissioners were performing well except in relation to water supply and drainage, where it was felt that there should be a transfer of responsibilities to larger specialist authorities as subsequently provided for by the Water Supply (Amendment) Act 1936.[123]

The Annual Reports of the LGB on public health provide a useful summary of progress in relation to the prevention of disease and the related issues of water supply and sanitation. The Board reported further success in preventing disease and promoting health as a result of continuing improvements to water supply, sanitation and the quality of food and drink, especially milk, improved access to medical advice and treatment with the introduction of National Health Insurance, the School Medical Service and a free vaccination service and prompt action in response to reports of disease. The major advance reported related to the prevention and treatment of tuberculosis, the annual death toll falling steadily from 140 in 1918 to 28 in 1939. On water supply and drainage the Reports refer to successful renovation work on the part of the urban authorities and extremely slow progress in extending provision to the villages and the rural areas. Although the LGB made such provision its priority after the war, the responsibility for progress remained in the hands of local authorities who were either reluctant to commit funds for such expensive purposes or unable to act without the cooperation of adjacent authorities. Very little progress was made until the 1930s, when, with encouragement from the LGB and specialist advisors, financial help from Tynwald and the creation of the Northern and Southern Water Boards in 1936 and 1939 respectively, real progress was achieved. By 1939 the main gaps in public provision had either been filled or, in the case of certain southern parishes, would shortly be so as a result of the wartime endeavours of the new Southern Water Board. The Annual Reports also record improvements in sanitary provision and standards in cowsheds and dairies, factories and workshops, housing, schools, methods of refuse disposal and rodent control, and the availability of public conveniences.

Despite these improvements public health remained a cause of serious concern in the late 1930s. The LGB was pressing for further centralisation with a view to achieving a more effective service. Parliament's Local Government Act 1933 and Public Health Act 1936 raised the possibility of a new set of responsibilities for local government in the field of welfare. Both members of Tynwald and the LGB were anxious to see greater investment in public housing and regretted the complete lack of response by local authorities to the slum clearance provisions of the Housing Act 1936. In 1938 Leveson-Gower responded to these concerns by appointing the Public Health Commission, chaired by Deemster Cowley. Unfortunately, war intervened, the work of the Commission was suspended and the much needed policy developments had to wait until the end of the war.

In relation to health treatment the interwar years saw the evolution of a limited but fragmented public service. While general hospitals and medical practice remained in private hands, public access to treatment was greatly enhanced by the introduction of National Health Insurance (NHI), the School Medical Service (SMS) and increased state funding of specialist medical services. Provision for NHI was made in 1920 and people began to receive medical benefits in January 1921.[124] Initially these were restricted to attendance and treatment by the Island's 21 GPs but, following negotiations with GPs in 1921, Tynwald agreed to fund additional benefits that were not available in the UK, including access to special surgical and x-ray treatment at local hospitals and part-time medical and surgical consultants.[125] Between 1921 and 1939 the range and quality of benefits was increased, dental treatment being included from 1927 and pathological and electro-cardiographic examinations from 1938. As in the UK benefits did not include hospital or maternity treatment and were open only to insured persons, some 20 per cent of the population in 1921 (12,101) rising to 35 per cent by 1939 (18,390).[126] Dependent relatives were not included in the scheme.

From 1923 some of those dependents gained access to medical and dental treatment through the SMS, provision for which had been made, with the unanimous support of both branches of Tynwald, in the Education Act 1920.[127] Fifty per cent of the costs were to be paid by Tynwald out of the General Revenue and the balance by the Education Authority. Initially it was solely for schoolchildren. It provided free medical and dental inspections, free treatment of minor ailments and means tested treatment for other ailments (free for children of parents with a weekly income of less than £2, suitable adjustments being made for families with more than three children, and modest charges for others). In 1932, following a conference of members of Tynwald and health specialists,[128] the scope of the service was extended to include preschool children and young persons up to the age of 21. As with the NHI the nature of the treatment available improved with time, a major advance occurring in 1932 when Tynwald agreed to fund the full costs of a comprehensive orthopaedic service for children and young persons up to the age of 21.[129] The proportion of the population gaining access to a medical service through the SMS rose from 13.5 per cent in 1924 to 32 per cent in 1939.[130]

The third strand of state provision involved a miscellany of ad hoc services, some like the mental hospital, the isolation hospitals and poor relief dating from the late nineteenth century and others resulting from initiatives by Tynwald in the interwar years, of which the most important related to the treatment of tuberculosis. The Local Government Amendment Act 1922 empowered the LGB to make regulations and orders concerning the notification, treatment, general supervision and prevention of the disease.[131] In addition to the general public health measures already discussed, Tynwald agreed to fund a special TB consultancy service, a state sanatorium at Cronk Ruagh and a TB dispensary at Murray House in Douglas.[132]

One of the major impediments to public health during this period was the poor quality of working-class housing, both in urban and rural areas. Overcrowding, poor sanitation and inadequate water supplies were endangering not only the health and welfare of working-class people but also the image of the Island as a resort. Whereas before the war only Douglas had initiated a public housing programme, the seriousness of postwar conditions, described as 'appalling' by LGB Inspectors in the early 1920s and by a special committee of Tynwald in 1922,[133] persuaded Tynwald of the need for a series of housing initiatives throughout the Island.

The first was to replace wartime controls on rents for private accommodation with peacetime controls. The Increase of Rent and Mortgage Interest (Restrictions) Act 1921,[134] based on similar UK legislation, regulated rents on both unfurnished and furnished accommodation and the circumstances under which tenants could be evicted. It applied to two thirds of the Island's dwellings. With the exception of an extremely controversial period between May 1924 when the Act expired and June 1925 when a replacement measure came into force, rent control remained a feature of the Manx housing scene throughout this period. The temporary lapse became a major issue in the 1924 general election with both MLP candidates and individual conservatives pledging to restore the legislation. Immediately following the election, a new bill was introduced and steered through the Keys by Ramsey Johnson without a division; however, it was lost in the Legislative Council on Fry's casting vote. Fry saw such legislation as an unwarranted interference with individual property rights.[135] The Bill was immediately reintroduced in the Keys by Alfred Teare, who saw the Council's rejection of the Bill as 'an insult to the people of this Island'. Following a debate with strong speeches by J. D. Qualtrough, Norris and MLP members, the Bill was passed without division.[136] A deputation led by Qualtrough met with Fry, who later responded by saying that the Legislative Council still opposed the Bill, but that he would dissolve the House to test public opinion if that were the wish of a substantial majority of the House.[137] Qualtrough urged the House to reiterate its commitment to the Bill and to be prepared to reintroduce the measure in the event of a dissolution; a resolution to that effect, in the names of Qualtrough and Johnson, was carried by 20 votes to two. Faced with such resolve on the part of the House, the Legislative Council reluctantly agreed to pass the Bill and, after a conference with the Keys to resolve differences of detail, it became law in June 1925.[138]

By contrast legislation paving the way for public sector housing had a relatively smooth passage through both branches of Tynwald. Following a debate on the housing crisis in February 1921, a majority of both chambers approved Qualtrough's proposal for a committee to devise a national housing scheme.[139] Chaired by Joseph Cunningham, the Committee issued three reports that were widely welcomed, one on 12 July 1921 resulting in the Douglas Town Improvement and Artisan Dwellings Act 1922,[140] the second on 8 March 1922 leading to the more broadly based Housing Act 1924[141] and the third on 30 January 1923 resulting in a scheme to provide government aid to private builders.[142] Initially Douglas was the only authority prepared to undertake a building programme, as a result of which Tynwald agreed to authorise a Douglas scheme. The 1922 Act enabled the Corporation to carry out a street improvement scheme between the pier and the railway station and to provide housing for displaced artisans. The Act was the first to provide for the payment of government grants in support of housing, in this case to cover one third of the cost of the street scheme and half the net costs of the housing. The Housing Act 1924, modelled on UK legislation of 1890 and 1923 and passed without a dissenting vote, placed a duty on local authorities to prepare housing schemes to meet local needs and provided the LGB with default powers in the event of their not doing so. Under the scheme the Government was to meet 50 per cent of the net costs, up to a maximum of £250 per house, although under pressure from the UK Treasury this maximum figure was progressively reduced to £200, £140 and eventually £125.[143] Between 1922 and 1939 a total of 904 public sector houses were built by eight local authorities; 82 per cent were completed by 1930; Douglas accounted for 609 dwellings, 76 per cent of the total.[144] Under the private enterprise scheme, finalised in 1923, Tynwald provided low interest loans to Manx residents wishing to build their own house (repayable over 20 years) and to builders building private houses for sale to Manx residents (repayable on the sale of the house). Further encouragement to home ownership was provided by the Income Tax Act 1927, Section 6 of which introduced full mortgage interest tax relief.[145]

The next initiative, recommended by Tynwald's Committee on Agriculture in December 1926, was the Housing (Rural Workers) Act 1929,[146] the aim of which was to provide financial assistance towards the improvement of housing accommodation for agricultural workers. Local authorities were to submit improvement schemes to the LGB for approval and the authorisation of financial assistance, up to two thirds of the cost up to a maximum of £100 per dwelling. Between 1929 and 1938 56 agricultural cottages were improved under this scheme.[147]

Although the building work undertaken under the Acts of 1922, 1924 and 1929 resulted in the provision of satisfactory housing for around a thousand families, the Annual Reports of the LGB for the 1930s continued to refer to 'acute shortages'.[148] Such shortages were also the subject of debates in Tynwald,[149] investigation by a succession of special commissions[150] and further legislation in 1936. Based on UK legislation of 1930 and taken through the House by Alfred Teare, the Housing Act 1936 empowered local authorities to clear or improve 'unhealthy' areas or houses, the precise amount of financial subsidy from Tynwald being a matter for negotiation with the Lieutenant-Governor.[151] Despite the continuing social need, however, not a single authority came forward with a clearance scheme prior to the outbreak of war in 1939. There is no simple explanation for the lack of progress. MLP members initiated debate after debate on housing but, faced with Treasury insistance on lower levels of subsidy and the reluctance of local authorities to commit funds, their efforts were largely unsuccessful. Housing was still seen by many as a matter for private rather than public enterprise. While the Isle of Man Government was willing to subsidise local authority schemes up to the level approved by the UK Treasury, local authorities were either unwilling to see housing as a priority or too poor to raise their share of the net costs. Real progress in tackling the outstanding problem of houses unfit for habitation had to await the much higher levels of national funding that were made available after the war.

The Island's interwar employment problem was seen by authorities both on the Island and in London as essentially a seasonal one, resulting from dependence on tourism. While some MHKs did press for investment in diversification, no progress was made on that front until after the war and the main thrust of the Island's employment policies was directed towards the relief of seasonal unemployment. At the end of the First World War the Island did follow the UK in providing 'out of work' donations for demobilised soldiers, but such unemployment relief was temporary and members of Tynwald made it clear that they would prefer work-based relief.[152]

Between 1921 and the outbreak of war the provision of work for the unemployed became one of Tynwald's highest priorities. Pressures from the trade union movement and MLP and other radical MHKs led to the the adoption each year of 'winter work' schemes to absorb surplus labour. In October 1921 the House of Keys appointed a deputation to ask Fry to timetable public works to relieve winter unemployment. Norris, as leader of the deputation, reported back to the House the following month that Fry had agreed to do so and thus began the 'winter works' schemes that were at the heart of the Government's response to unemployment through the rest of the interwar period. An attempt to pay winter workers at a rate 10 per cent below the going rate was defeated in Tynwald by 13 votes to seven in the House of Keys.[153] In April 1922 Tynwald agreed to appoint a five-member committee to advise the Lieutenant-Governor on 'winter works.' Chaired by the Receiver General, Joseph Qualtrough, the Committee on Unemployment consulted with Fry and the various employing authorities and reported to Tynwald with a series of recommendations, all but one of which were accepted. A proposal to pay those employed on winter work five per cent below the standard wage was rejected by a 12 to eight majority in the House and a split vote in the Legislative Council. Alfred Teare, the author of a minority report opposing the differentiation of pay, came into Tynwald from his sickbed to argue against the proposal. He explained that he was so 'disgusted' with the injustice of the proposal that it gave him the strength to fight it.[154] In February 1924 Tynwald agreed to transfer the responsibility for advising the Lieutenant-Governor and Tynwald on 'winter works' to the OAPNHIB. The Public Works (Advisory) Committee, a subcommittee of the Board, chaired by Richard Cain and for a short period by John T. Quilliam, carried out this role until 1928. Initially the 'winter work' schemes provided work for most of the unemployed, but rising costs, from £54,675 in 1921/22 to £124,000 in 1926/27[155] prompted Hill to appoint a special commission on unemployment, chaired by High Bailiff Cowley.

The result of the Commission's Report in 1928, Hill's response and debates in Tynwald was twofold, a more broadly based unemployment strategy and a new unemployment advisory committee.[156] There were five main parts to the new strategy. First, it was agreed to maintain a register of the unemployed. Second and more controversially, it was agreed by 11 votes to seven in the Keys and unanimously in the Council to retain the 'winter works' approach, with Tynwald providing 75 per cent of the wages bill for approved development schemes. Critics of this approach included both radicals like Teare and Norris who were advocating investment to diversify the economy, and some representatives of rural areas who saw such schemes as a public subsidy for Douglas. Third, it was agreed by 13 votes to seven and unanimously in the Council to provide unemployment relief for the minority not obtaining work. Relief was to be administered through the poor relief system, with Tynwald footing 50 per cent of the bill (75 per cent from 1934/35). Norris was the leading critic, objecting both to half the burden of a national problem falling on the boards of guardians and to the high proportion of that half falling on the towns. Although the Government promised to investigate alternative ways of dispensing relief, no change occurred until after the war. The maximum numbers on the new unemployment register for the winter months rose from 1,282 in 1928/29 to 1,878 in 1931/32 and remained at that level or slightly above for the rest of the decade. The 'winter works' schemes provided employment for between 50 and 60 per cent of those on the register, the rest being obliged to claim poor relief.[157] Tynwald's share of expenditure on the relief of unemployment through refunds to the boards of guardians rose steadily from £1,594 in 1928/29 to £10,700 in 1938/39. A fourth outcome was the establishment of a juvenile employment committee and the development of policies to help school-leavers to find work. A radical proposal to reduce juvenile unemployment at a stroke by raising the school leaving age from 14 to 15 was supported in Tynwald and referred to the Council of Education, where it was also approved, subject to a satisfactory scheme for the reorganisation of schools into primary and secondary schools. However, it was not proceeded with because of the shelving of the same idea in the UK at the height of the economic recession.[158] Fifth, and costing much less than the main proposals, was the provision of grants in support of emigration. Already in place when the Commission reported, Hill had no hesitation in continuing the scheme first introduced in 1923/24. After 1928 the Government employed both the stick and the carrot to encourage emigration. When the regulations governing the registration of unemployed men were laid before Tynwald on 6 July 1928, single men over 22 had to be able to demonstrate that they were fit, had no dependents, had made every endeavour to find work and were unable to emigrate.[159] Alfred Teare referred to these regulations as the 'most objectionable and obnoxious regulations ever placed before this Court'. While the regulations, including what amounted to the stick of compulsory emigration for single males over 22, were still approved, by 11 votes to eight in the Keys and with one vote against in the Council, within a very short time the compulsory provision had to be relaxed because of the lack of opportunities for emigration.[160]

The transfer of responsibility for advising on unemployment came about because of the Commission's view that the body entrusted with this politically sensitive role should be independent, with two members appointed by each of Tynwald, the Employers' Federation and the Workers' Union. In June 1928 Tynwald agreed, objections by Norris, Richard Cain and J. D. Qualtrough being dropped when assurances were given by Hill that the names of the members of the new advisory body would be submitted for the approval of Tynwald.[161] The Unemployment Advisory Committee, albeit without representation from Tynwald, was duly appointed and remained responsible for advising the Lieutenant-Governor until replaced by a committee of Tynwald in 1946.

During most of the interwar period employment policy was about responding to unemployment rather than regulating the conditions of those who were in employment. Certainly workers benefitted from the protective statutory controls introduced before the war and periodic amendments to the Factories and Workshops Acts and the Workmen's Compensation Acts did result in improvements in these areas. The Shop Hours Act 1921 extended statutory regulation into the major area that had been excluded from the Factories and Workshops Act 1909.[162] However, the majority of Tynwald remained hostile to MLP demands for legislation to provide for a minimum wage, a shorter working week and arbitration courts for resolving employment disputes. The closest Tynwald came to accepting the statutory regulation of wages and hours of work was in 1926, when the Committee on Agriculture recommended it for agricultural workers. In January 1929 the Agricultural Wages (Regulation) Bill narrowly failed to get a third reading, a number of liberals like Norris joining with conservatives to defeat the Bill by 12 votes to 11.[163] In the absence of statutory regulation it was left to employers and workers, either individually or through employers' organisations and trade unions, to negotiate terms of employment.

For the most part such negotiations were concluded without industrial action and without the need for modern regulatory legislation.[164] However, in 1935 the breakdown of negotiations between the Employers' Federation and the Transport and General Workers' Union over rates of pay and hours of work and the successful strike by the TGWU on 3 and 4 June 1935 obliged Tynwald to review its position on the regulation of trade disputes. The details of the strike need not concern us here; suffice it to say that prior to the strike workers in Douglas were being paid 40 shillings for a 49.5-hour week, that the TGWU claim was for 48 shillings for a 48-hour week and that the eventual settlement was for 46 shillings for a 48-hour week from March to October and 44 shillings for a 46-hour week from November to February; for workers outside of Douglas the figures were two shillings less both before and after the strike. For the Lieutenant-Governor and Tynwald the strike, associated disturbances and disruption to essential services highlighted the lack of emergency powers legislation and statutory provision for the arbitration of such disputes. Three Acts of Tynwald followed.

The Emergency Powers Act 1936 empowered the Lieutenant-Governor to take the steps to maintain essential services in the event of an emergency. Proclamations of emergency had to be laid before Tynwald within five days and emergency regulations approved by Tynwald within seven days.[165] It was opposed in the Keys by the five MLP members and Ambrose Qualtrough, following the defeat of an amendment requiring consultation with a committee of Tynwald before declaring a state of emergency.[166] The same six members also opposed the other two measures, which were designed to facilitate the peaceful settlement of trade disputes. The Trade Disputes Act 1936 empowered the Lieutenant-Governor, with the consent of the parties in conflict, to refer disputes for conciliation, arbitration or investigation by a court of inquiry.[167] Much to the dismay of MLP members, it did not provide for the permanent arbitration machinery, like the Whitley Councils in the UK, for which they had been campaigning since 1919.[168] The Trade Disputes (Regulation) Act 1936 sought to ensure that trade disputes were conducted with due regard to the rights and liberties of other people by means of penalties for intimidation or violence.[169] The MLP feared that interpretation by the police and courts of what constituted intimidation would prejudice the worker rather than the employer and opposed what they saw as 'class' legislation.[170]

## *The Changing Role of the State in the Manx Economy*

During the interwar years the role of government, both directly and indirectly through the multiplier effect, became absolutely pivotal to the health of the Manx economy, as regulator, provider of welfare, investor in infrastructure, owner of public utilities and supporter of local industries. Legislation enabling and regulating private and public enterprise remained an important feature, well over a hundred such Acts of Tynwald being passed between 1919 and 1939. It is not possible to comment on the detail, but notable among these were the Town Planning Act 1928 and the Town and Country Planning Acts 1934 and 1936,[171] the Island's first real attempts to try and ensure that developments were compatible with broader environmental and social considerations, the Shop Hours Acts of 1921 and 1939, controversial because of their provisions relating to Sunday trading,[172] and the Licensing Act 1923, which fixed the opening hours of public houses, including a total ban on Sunday opening, for the rest of the interwar period.[173]

New social policies brought with them a large increase in public spending, most notably on education, pensions and national health insurance. In addition, Tynwald committed unprecedented levels of capital expenditure on housing, schools and public health, providing both sought-after facilities and much needed employment. Between 1922/23 and 1938/39 Tynwald's share of expenditure on public housing totalled £258,370, over three quarters of this being committed between 1924 and 1930. In the same 17-year period Tynwald's share of spending on schools totalled £161,147, the heaviest outlays occurring between 1925/26 and 1933/34 and in 1938/39. Between 1930/31 and 1938/39 Tynwald also agreed to assist with a range of water supply and drainage projects for the villages and rural districts at a cost of £176,925.

Infrastructure accounted for even higher levels of spending. Harbours continued to be a major call on public funds, a total of £430,415 over the 20-year period. However, the biggest single call on central funds was highways. From 1920/21 Tynwald agreed to fund 50 per cent of the cost of the upkeep of public roads and from 1933/34 75 per cent, through grants to local authorities and the Highways Board. The total grant aid for the period was £1,539,904.

Public ownership was hardly to the forefront of Manx politics between the wars. However, Tynwald did agree to extend public ownership in order to progress the development of much needed utilities. In the case of electricity the choice facing Tynwald immediately after the war was to allow demand for electricity in the Douglas area to be met by a subsidiary of the Douglas Gas Company or by Douglas Corporation. In the event the Douglas Corporation Electric Light and Power Act 1921 granted monopoly power to the Corporation to supply the Douglas area, paving the way for subsequent developments to be within the public sector.[174] Although the Electricity Commission of 1929 reported in favour of a private company distributing power purchased from Douglas Corporation to the rest of the Island, the Isle of Man Electric Light and Power Act 1932 gave that power to the Isle of Man Electricity Board.[175] With the exception of small areas served by the Manx Electric Railway Company, Douglas Corporation and the new Board became sole suppliers, the two undertakings eventually amalgamating in 1984.

In the case of water, public supply had historically been provided by both private enterprise and local authorities. While this remained true of the whole interwar period, new initiatives were public rather than private and national rather than local, private companies and local authorities proving either unable or unwilling to fund the investment required to provide a modern water service. The way forward was for Tynwald to establish and fund special boards under the Water (Supply) Acts 1929, 1934 and 1936.[176] The Northern Water Board was set up in 1936 to serve the five northern parishes of Andreas, Ballaugh, Bride, Jurby and Lezayre which were still without a public water supply.[177] The establishment of the Southern Water Board in 1939 was a public acknowledgement both of the financial difficulties facing existing suppliers and the obstacles faced by small local authorities in supplying hitherto neglected areas. Thus the Board became responsible for supplying Castletown, Port Erin, Port St Mary and the parishes of Arbory, Malew, Rushen and Santon, a total of £74,384 being paid in compensation to the Castletown Water Company (£14,798), the Rushen Water Board (£50,266) and the Malew Commissioners (£9,320).[178] On the outbreak of war in 1939 responsibility for public water supply was still fragmented and shared between the private and public sectors, but the economics of the industry was pointing clearly in the same direction as electricity, namely of supply outside of Douglas by a single public board.

Whereas before the war the Government provided very little support for local industries, the economic circumstances of the war and recession resulted in increased levels of support, especially for agriculture. Boards of Tynwald had special responsibility for promoting agriculture, fishing, forestry and the visiting industry. Support for fishing, forestry and the visiting industry support was agreed without major controversy. In a state of almost terminal decline, the Manx fishing industry received very little support until 1934 when, on the eve of the general election, Tynwald gave unanimous approval to a declaratory resolution moved by Marion Shimmin, the member for Peel, in support of subsidies to Manx fishermen similar to those already available in the UK.[179] A commission chaired by Deemster Cowley reported in 1935, as a result of which Tynwald agreed to subsidise Manx fishermen and increase the powers of the Fisheries Board. From 1935/36 onwards small grants towards running expenses were made available to the remaining eight herring boats, at a cost of between £200 and £1,000 per year. The Fishing (Herring Industry) Act 1939, based on UK legislation and approved without dissent, empowered the Fisheries Board to regulate the marketing of fish, limit the number of boats fishing in Manx waters, provide loans for the construction, repair and equipping of boats and carry out research.

Support for forestry rose steadily during the interwar period, especially after the establishment in 1931 of the Forestry Board, total expenditure rising from just under £1,000 in 1920/21 to £4,976 in 1938/39. The development of a publicly owned forestry industry had its origins partly in the work of the Arboricultural Society, a voluntary organisation set up in 1897 which attracted small government grants for the purpose of planting trees, and partly in the afforestation policies of the Commissioners of Woods and Forests, who were responsible for the maintenance and development of Crown lands in the Island. While the Crown lands were not transferred to the Island until 1949, the plantations developed by the Arboricultural Society in conjunction with the Tree Planting Committee of Tynwald—Gob-y-Volley and Slieu Whallian—became the responsibility of the Forestry Board in 1931. With the additional funding after 1931, the Forestry Board was able to extend the established plantations and commence planting at Tholt-y-Will, Vaishmoar, Beary, Knockaloe and Axnfel.

The tourist industry benefitted both directly and indirectly from increased public spending, especially that on public health, water supply, harbours and highways. Support for Manx agriculture was given partly in recognition of its vital contribution to the success of the visiting industry. The Board of Advertising/Publicity Board continued to promote the Island as a resort, the grant for advertising the Island increasing from £2,550 in 1919/20 to £11,300 in 1938/39. In addition, starting in 1929/30, Tynwald agreed unanimously to provide up to £5,000 per annum in support of the TT and other races.[180]

The really important change in the role of the government in relation to private enterprise was in the agricultural sector. Alongside the visiting industry, agriculture was seen as one of the twin pillars of the Manx economy but, after a profitable interlude during the war, it was in danger of collapse, suffering from cheaper foreign competition, undercapitalisation, ineffective marketing, poor conditions for tenant farmers and agricultural workers and a steadily increasing rate burden. There were widespread calls from both inside Tynwald and the farming community for the government to intervene. The Board of Agriculture had powers and the product of a halfpenny rate in the rural areas to promote improvements in the industry, but these were totally inadequate. The result was that agriculture was rarely off the agenda of Tynwald, with new legislation in 1924 and three major investigations leading to recommendations for unprecedented levels of government intervention in the industry, deep divisions over what should be done and, eventually, radical legislation and increased expenditure.

Following similar UK legislation in 1923, the Agricultural Rates Act 1924 reduced the agricultural rates payable in respect of education and asylums to one quarter and required Tynwald to make good the revenue lost by the rating authorities, while the Agricultural Credits Act 1924 enabled the government to advance credit for the purpose of agricultural improvements. Both were approved without dissent.[181] In 1925 Tynwald appointed a committee, chaired by Ramsey Johnson, to inquire into the distressed state of Manx agriculture.[182] The Committee's report of December 1926 was received in Tynwald on 28 June 1927, when it was agreed nem. con. to ask the Lieutenant-Governor to introduce legislation to implement the Committee's recommendations.[183] Eight bills were prepared and introduced in the Keys by Johnson, a Douglas member but committed to the regeneration of the industry; only four became law, two being defeated in the Keys and two in the Council. The successful ones were accepted without controversy. The Agricultural Returns Act 1929 was a simple measure empowering the Board of Agriculture to collect agricultural statistics.[184] The Merchandise Marks Act 1929 made it necessary for imported goods to be marked with their country of origin.[185] The Agricultural Rates Act 1929 followed the UK in reducing all rates on agricultural land and buildings to one quarter, with Tynwald making good the deficiency in revenue to the rating authorities.[186] An attempt later that year to follow the UK with the complete derating of agricultural land proved altogether more controversial. Critics opposed relieving landlords of their share of taxation and favoured assistance to those who worked the land rather than those who owned it. The Rating Relief and Valuation Bill was defeated in the Keys by 13 votes to nine.[187] The fourth measure to be agreed was the Housing (Rural Workers) Act 1929.

Although the other four bills were rejected, the fact that they were being recommended by a committee of Tynwald was a mark of the growing support for radical measures to address the decline of Manx agriculture. The Agricultural Holdings Bill, which aimed to provide tenant farmers with the rights already enjoyed by their counterparts in the UK, failed by one vote to secure the absolute majority support required at the third reading of bills in the House and met the fate of earlier attempts to legislate in 1909 and 1922.[188] The Agricultural Wages (Regulation) Bill aimed to establish a representative committee with powers to fix minimum wages and hours of work, but for the majority of the House this was carrying regulation too far and the Bill was narrowly defeated on the third reading by 12 votes to 11.[189] The Agricultural and Rural Industries Amendment Bill was an attempt to lay down that no more than four of Tynwald's seven appointments to the Board of Agriculture should be engaged in agriculture, but was defeated in the Legislative Council, where Hill argued that Tynwald should retain an unfettered choice of members.[190] The Agriculture (Import of Stock)

Bill was designed to prohibit the import of stock into the Island, except by license from the Lieutenant-Governor. It had been approved by the Keys as a means of dealing with the dumping of livestock from Ireland to the detriment of local producers, but was rejected by the Legislative Council as a protectionist measure that would invite retaliation. Further attempts at legislation in 1930 were abandoned following an agreement by the Island's butchers to refrain from importing livestock except when there was insufficient local produce. The measure did eventually reach the statute book in 1934 with an amendment limiting its operation to two years.[191]

Following the 1929 election and in the light of continuing concern about the state of Manx agriculture, Hill appointed the Industrial Commission on Agriculture under the chair of James Corrin to investigate and report. In April 1930 it issued a short interim report devoted entirely to the rights of tenant farmers and recommending the establishment of rent courts and compensation for unexhausted improvements.[192] A new Agricultural Holdings Bill was introduced into the Keys by William Moore, himself a tenant farmer, for many years a campaigner for this reform and a member of the Commission. He saw it as a prerequisite to a flourishing agriculture. Unfortunately he had died by the time the House gave the Bill a third reading in January 1931.[193] This time the Bill's defeat was at the hands of the Legislative Council, where, despite the presence of the Commission chairman and the vocal support of the Lieutenant-Governor, a majority of five to three opposed the Bill.[194] A further attempt by the Keys in 1933 was also unsuccessful, except that this time the Legislative Council agreed that a decision on the Bill should be deferred until after the general election.[195]

However, three important measures were approved following a further report from the Commission in December 1930.[196] The Agricultural Marketing Act 1934, an enabling measure based on UK legislation of 1931, paved the way for the development of schemes for the more efficient production and marketing of produce. It created the Isle of Man Marketing Society, a body comprising members of the Board of Agriculture and representatives of the industry and consumers, with the responsibility for framing schemes for the approval of the Board and Tynwald. These were to be administered by associations with specified powers and duties. Within a year, three such schemes had been approved by Tynwald, the Milk Marketing Scheme, the Potato Marketing Scheme and the Fatstock Marketing Scheme.[197] The Local Government (Milk and Dairies) Act 1934 sought to eliminate TB in cattle and milk by providing for the registration and inspection of dairies and cowhouses and was approved only after considerable debate between the branches over the funding of improvements necessary as a result of inspection.[198] The Agricultural Rates and Improvement Fund Act 1934 became the vehicle for that funding. It provided for the complete derating of agricultural land and buildings and the payment by Tynwald of a sum equivalent to the lost revenue into an Agricultural Improvement Fund.[199]

Following the general election in November 1934, the pace of reform continued unabated. Security of tenure, fair rents and the right to compensation for unexhausted improvements were finally delivered by the Agricultural Holdings Act 1936, some 30 years after England.[200] Faced with overwhelming support for the measure in the new House, the Legislative Council abandoned its opposition and passed the Bill through all its stages without division.[201] In 1937 threats to Manx agriculture from foreign competition and the introduction of subsidies by the UK persuaded Tynwald to approve two landmark resolutions, without division and almost without debate, introducing subsidies for particular agricultural products. A fatstock subsidy of five shillings per live hundredweight and a fertiliser subsidy were the first in a series of protectionist measures and the first agricultural subsidies to be approved in peacetime. The following year saw the appointment by Leveson-Gower of a further commission to investigate both the general condition of the agricultural industry and the particular conditions of agricultural workers. It was chaired by Deemster Cowley. Its main recommendations were to extend the policy of subsidisation.[202] In April 1939 Tynwald approved without division the seven-point package of assistance to agriculture recommended by the Commission, a modified subsidy for cattle and fertilisers, a five-year scheme of bounties payable on the export of cattle, lambs and pigs, increased grants for the improvement of livestock, a subsidy of £1 per acre of land brought out of lea for cereal and vegetable production, up to £500 towards the cost of milk marketing and an assisted farm labour scheme with Tynwald paying 75 per cent of the cost of labour employed during the winter on farm improvement projects. The new subsidies were to be conditional on farmers paying farmworkers' wages commensurate with standard rates, not exactly the statutory regulation of wages sought but a powerful incentive to farmers.[203]

Thus by 1939 Tynwald had moved from a position of almost no intervention in the industry to one of actively promoting the industry through a board of agriculture and the agricultural research farm at Knockaloe, providing grants and loans for farm improvement, funding the derating of agricultural land, giving financial assistance towards the building and upgrading of agricultural workers' housing, facilitating the

Board of Agriculture visit to Knockaloe, 1936. Before the First World War the role of government in relation to agriculture was confined to occasional regulatory legislation; after the war there was a whole series of interventions. Although legislation providing for the establishment of a board of agriculture was passed in 1914, the new Board did not get under way until after the war, when it quickly became one of the most important boards as Tynwald sought to restore the health of an industry struggling in an increasingly competitive world. From left to right are W. A. Kelly, MHK (Chair), G. W. Howie (Agricultural Organiser), E. Corlett, A. H. Tyson (Secretary), W. C. Craine, MHK, E. B. C. Farrant, MHK, A. J. Cottier, MHK, J. H. L. Cowin, MHK, and R. Kneen, MHK.

marketing of Manx produce, registering and inspecting dairies and cowhouses, guaranteeing the rights of tenant farmers, operating an assisted farm labour scheme, protecting Manx agriculture through subsidies and at the same time influencing the wages paid to farmworkers. As a result of this change financial support for agriculture increased steadily from just under £2,000 in 1920/1 to £14,761 in 1938/9. In addition, the approximate cost to Tynwald of relieving the industry of the burden of rates was £5,000 per annum under the 1924 Act, rising to £15,000 per annum under the 1929 Act and £20,000 under the 1934 Act.[204]

## Manx Finances 1919–39

The financial relationship between the Isle of Man and the UK became even closer in the interwar period, partly as a result of Tynwald's social legislation and partly because of the further development of the Common Purse Arrangement. Spending was heavily influenced by colonial controls and UK-based policies. Although the 'reserved services' accounted for a diminishing proportion of the total budget, most major items of 'voted' expenditure were the result of emulating the UK. Education, pensions, national health insurance and law and order each fell into this category and, although policy on housing, roads and agriculture were distinctively Manx, in each case the Island had adapted UK legislation.

Insofar as sources of revenue are concerned, Lieutenant-Governors were also constrained by UK policy. Of the two main sources of revenue, customs was by far and away the most important, the average ratio of customs to income tax revenue being four to one; in 1938/39 their respective shares of total revenue were 73 and 19 per cent. By 1938/39 the proportion of customs revenue attributable to the Common Purse Arrangement had risen to over 90 per cent. The buoyancy of customs revenues for most of the period enabled the Island to manage with much lower rates of income tax than the UK. On introduction the rates ranged from 1s 6d to 2s 7.5d (7.5 to 13.125 per cent). However, for most of the period they were lower than this and, when in 1938/39 surtax was introduced on incomes over £2,000, the range was from 9d to 2s 7.5d (3.75 to 13.125 per cent).[205] Ironically, given the Keys' struggle for financial control, the policies for which the Income Tax Fund was used were heavily influenced by the UK, the flour subsidy until 1921/22, two thirds of the cost of old age pensions and national health insurance from 1921/22, contributions towards the cost of the First World War from 1922/23 to 1933/34 and towards rearmament in 1938/39 and part of the costs of servicing Isle of Man debt from 1933/34.

Again the level of spending—the sum of expenditure from the General Revenue, the Accumulated Fund and the Income Tax Fund—can be taken as a crude index of the changing role of the Manx Government. Table 4.1 shows the changes in spending over the 20-year period. There was a dramatic increase in spending during the 1920s from £191,819 in 1918/19 to £524,597 in 1926/27, representing a real increase over the eight-year period of 244 per cent. Between 1926/27 and 1937/38 spending fell slightly below the 1926/27 figure, before rising to the new height of £591,623 in 1938/39, a real increase over 1918/19 of 333 per cent.

**Table 4.1. Central Government Spending 1919/20 to 1938/39**

| Financial Year up to 31 March | Total Expenditure £ | Expenditure at 2000 Prices £ |
|---|---|---|
| 1920 | 273,454 | 5,575,727 |
| 1921 | 489,898 | 9,532,925 |
| 1922 | 304,377 | 7,674,257 |
| 1923 | 318,354 | 8,482,861 |
| 1924 | 398,304 | 10,494,115 |
| 1925 | 416,562 | 10,913,507 |
| 1926 | 442,326 | 12,060,460 |
| 1927 | 524,597 | 14,387,072 |
| 1928 | 486,542 | 13,913,155 |
| 1929 | 431,862 | 12,200,533 |
| 1930 | 430,451 | 12,538,176 |
| 1931 | 463,082 | 14,478,258 |
| 1932 | 417,889 | 13,423,012 |
| 1933 | 435,007 | 14,676,701 |
| 1934 | 495,902 | 16,611,725 |
| 1935 | 471,483 | 15,681,524 |
| 1936 | 509,456 | 16,364,236 |
| 1937 | 499,285 | 15,506,294 |
| 1938 | 522,548 | 15,708,837 |
| 1939 | 591,623 | 18,134,428 |

The sources of the raw expenditure data were the annual *Financial Statement* for 1919/20 and the *Accounts of the Government Treasurer* from 1920/21 to 1938/39. The level of spending at 2000 prices was calculated with the help of the Price Index supplied by Martin Caley of the Economic Affairs Division of the Manx Treasury. The real expenditure figures should be treated with caution as they are derived with the help of an index designed for a different purpose.

To avoid double counting, expenditure facilitated by borrowing is not included in the raw totals, which are the sum of expenditure from the General Revenue Account, the Income Tax Fund and the Accumulated Fund.

## *Notes*

1   For a recent account of their family background and careers both before, during and after service in the Isle of Man, see Derek Winterbottom, *Governors of the Isle of Man since 1765* (Douglas, 1999), pp. 157–97.
2   See 36 *Manx Deb.*, 15 April 1919, p. 322.
3   See 37 *Manx Deb.*, 9 December 1919, pp. 45–50.
4   *Statutes*, xi, pp. 95–103. For details of the main debate, see 37 *Manx Deb.*, 17 February 1920, pp. 311–12; 22 and 29 June 1920, pp. 836–44 and 853–54; and 38 *Manx Deb.*, 17 December 1920, pp. 229–34.
5   See 38 *Manx Deb.*, 8 February 1921, pp. 354–55.
6   See 38 *Manx Deb.*, 10 May 1921, pp. 754–61
7   For the 1922 attempt at reform, see 39 *Manx Deb.*, 25 April 1922, pp. 760–63, 2 May 1922, pp. 770–71 and 20 June 1922, p. 1002; for the 1927 attempt, see 44 *Manx Deb.*, 1 March 1927, pp. 475–87 and 15 March 1927, pp. 530–33.
8   See 54 *Manx Deb.*, 13 April 1937, pp. 254–70.
9   See 55 *Manx Deb.*, 12 October 1937, p. 7.

10  See 37 *Manx Deb.*, 13, 20 and 21 January 1920, pp. 159–63, 164–92, 195–221 and 222–26.

11  37 *Manx Deb.*, 13, 20 and 21 January 1920; see also HO 45/11568/406863.

12  HO 45/11568/406863.

13  See *Report of the Deputation from the House of Keys to the Home Secretary on Financial Control* (Douglas, 1920), pp. 50–52 where the Home Office proposals are recorded in full. For the reactions of the Keys to the proposals, see 37 *Manx Deb.*, 1 June 1920, pp. 777–88.

14  The minutes of the Executive Council meetings reveal that, in this capacity, the Legislative Council were consulted by Fry not only about financial resolutions but also from time to time on policy and legislation. After 1927 it was consulted more widely following Hill's invitation to the Keys to set up a Consultative Committee; see *The Executive Council Minute Book 1920–46*, which is lodged in the Manx National Heritage Library, MD 15045.

15  See 37 *Manx Deb.*, 29 June 1920, pp. 847–48.

16  37 *Manx Deb.*, 29 June 1920, pp. 849–60.

17  See 39 *Manx Deb.*, 6 June 1922, p. 884.

18  See 45 *Manx Deb.*, 21 October 1927, p. 57.

19  45 *Manx Deb.*, 10 and 17 January 1928, pp. 291–306 and 360–63.

20  See 47 *Manx Deb.*, 6 and 17 December 1929, pp. 7 and 86–97; see also HO 45/11568/406863.

21  38 *Manx Deb.*, 31 May 1921, p. 795.

22  47 *Manx Deb.*, 17 December 1929, pp. 95–96.

23  54 *Manx Deb.*, 25 May 1937, pp. 334–35.

24  55 *Manx Deb.*, 31 May 1938, p. 556.

25  56 *Manx Deb.*, 6 June 1939, p. 557.

26  For further detail relating to the communications between the Island and the Home Office between 1914 and 1926, see HO 45/11060/266137 and 12313/476642.

27  See 32 *Manx Deb.*, 18 September 1914, pp. 1–4.

28  See 38 *Manx Deb.*, 12 April 1921, pp. 636–53; *Statutes*, xi, pp. 260–61. In a draft of the minute expressing thanks to the Isle of Man, the Treasury used the words 'grateful' and 'patriotic', but both were removed on the advice of the Home Office which regarded the contribution to be too late and too small to warrant such 'effusion'.

29  See *Report of Committee of the Privy Council* (London, 1926), Cd. 2586, p. 30. The latter was to include the £20,000 paid under the 1922 Act.

30  See 44 *Manx Deb.*, 22 October 1926, pp. 28–33.

31  For the full debate, see 44 *Manx Deb.*, 5, 6, 9 and 10 November 1926, pp. 91–181; see also G. N. Kniveton (ed.), *A Chronicle of the Twentieth Century: The Manx Experience*, vol. 1: 1901–50 (Douglas, 1999), p. 97

32  *Statutes*, xii, pp. 162–64. In 1933 the balance of the loan was liquidated by means of a local loan raised under the War Contribution and Income Tax (Appropriation) Act 1933; *Statutes*, xiv, pp. 136–37.

33  See *Report of the Committee of Tynwald appointed to discuss informally with a Representative of the Secretary of State for Home Affairs the various Problems in Connection with Financial Control, 11 June 1928* (Douglas, 1928); see also 47 *Manx Deb.*, 10 December 1929, pp. 20–22.

34  Although the announcement of the gift was communicated to Tynwald by the Lieutenant-Governor on 16 October 1928, the property was officially transferred to the Island on 8 July 1929; see 46 *Manx Deb.*, 16 October 1928 and the *Annual Report of the Government Property Trustees*, April 1930.

35  The details of this controversy are taken from HO 45/15121-2/490074

36  The details are taken from HO 45/17484-5/588338.

37  See D. G. Kermode, *Devolution at Work: A Case Study of the Isle of Man* (Farnborough, Hampshire, 1979), p. 45 and n. 80 on p. 51.

38  Kermode, *Devolution at Work*, pp. 115–16.

39  See HO 45/12279/446999/10-15.

40  See correspondence in HO 45/12567/211309/78-84.

41  For the cases discussed in this paragraph, see HO 45/17885/253057.

42  Part of a letter from the Treasury to the Home Office, dated 6 May 1938; see HO 45/18015/563268.

43  HO 45/18015/563268.

44  *Statutes*, x, pp. 455–532.

45  *Statutes*, xi, pp. 4–34.

46  *Statutes*, xi, pp. 339–63.

47  Under the 1932 Act; *Statutes*, xiii, pp. 518–32.

48  Under the Agricultural and Rural Industries Act 1923, *Statutes*, xi, pp. 402–04.

49  Under the Forestry Act 1931; *Statutes*, xiii, pp. 193–201

50  By the Advertising Rate Act 1931; *Statutes*, xiii, pp. 202–04.

51  *Statutes*, xiii, pp. 541–65.

52  *Statutes*, xiv, pp. 470–71. Resolutions under the Act were approved by Tynwald; see 53 *Manx Deb.*, 10 July 1936, pp. 638–40 and 56 *Manx Deb.*, 22 March 1939, pp. 388–91.

53  There were, in addition, a number of other bodies on which members of Tynwald served but these, like the Food Council set up in 1931 and the Trustees of the Manx Museum reconstituted in 1922, did not have board status.

54  See 54 *Manx Deb.*, 25 May 1937, p. 331.

55  As can be seen from Appendix 3 the boundaries of some of the constituencies were modified as a result of local authority boundary changes. For the results of these elections, see Tom Sherratt (comp.), *Isle of Man Parliamentary Election Results 1919–1986* (unpublished, Warrington, 1986). An annotated version, which includes the elections between 1986 and 1996 is available in the Tynwald Reference Library.

56  See 38 *Manx Deb.*, 2 November 1920, pp. 56–69.

57  At second reading; see 39 *Manx Deb.*, 13 January 1922, pp. 335–44.

58  *Statutes*, xi, pp. 290–92. Prior to 1922 provision for the payment of board expenses had been made under the Highways Acts of 1874 and 1889, the Education Act 1893, the Local Government (Amendment) Act 1894 and the Old Age Pensions and National Health Insurance Act 1920.

59  See 39 *Manx Deb.*, 4 and 14 April 1922, pp. 648–77 and 714–22.

60  See 40 *Manx Deb.*, 8 May 1923, pp. 753–75 and 41 *Manx Deb.*, 18 December 1923, pp. 299–311.

61  See 46 *Manx Deb.*, 30 October 1928, pp. 75–99. Johnson was, however, successful the following year in obtaining the approval of Tynwald for a resolution modifying the boundary between North and South Douglas; 46 *Manx Deb.*, 9 April 1929, pp. 740–42.

62  See 56 *Manx Deb.*, 18 October 1938, pp. 11–38.

63  56 *Manx Deb.*, 18 October 1938, pp. 11–38.

64  For the recollections of one of those who were elected in 1919, see A. J. Teare, *Reminiscences of the Manx Labour Party* (Douglas, 1962), pp. 28–32

65  See *Manx Year Book, 1920* (Douglas, 1920), pp. 33–35.

66  See Teare, *Reminiscences of the Manx Labour Party*, pp. 37–40.

67  None of the candidates in Rushen had the endorsement of the Rushen Progressive Association, which had ceased to exist after the 1929 election.

68  The MLP did not contest the election in Glenfaba, where W. P. Clucas had held a seat for Labour from 1924 until his death in 1933. It is interesting too, that for the second general election in succession, the Party did not contest the election in Ramsey.

69  *Isle of Man. Report of the Commission on Old Age Pensions, National Health Insurance and Unemployment Insurance* (Douglas, 1919).

70  See 37 *Manx Deb.*, 16 December 1919, p. 81 and 30 December 1919, p. 117.

71  *Statutes*, x, pp. 455–532; see also 37 *Manx Deb.*, 6 April, 1 May and 18 May 1920, pp. 432–53, 587–612 and 691–711.

72  While it proved impossible to negotiate reciprocity in respect of the noncontributory pensions introduced in 1920 because of minor differences between the UK and Manx schemes, reciprocal arrangements were agreed in respect of national health insurance and the contributory pensions introduced in 1929; for details, see the *Annual Reports of the Old Age Pensions and National Health Insurance Board* for the interwar period.

73  *Statutes*, xii, pp. 495–540.

74  See 43 *Manx Deb.*, 19 January 1926, pp. 296–98. The three who voted in favour were ex officio members; those against were the indirectly elected members and one appointed member.

75  See 44 *Manx Deb.*, 1, 8 and 15 February 1927, pp. 375–423 and 433–47; 45 *Manx Deb.*, 6 December 1927, pp. 229–38, 17 January 1928, pp. 363–73, 7 and 14 February 1928, pp. 445–49 and 465–78.

76  See 45 *Manx Deb.*, 24 April 1928, pp. 719–32.

77  For details of the controversy surrounding the 1928 refusal of Royal Assent, see Kermode, *Devolution at Work*, pp. 144–45.

78  *Statutes*, xv, pp. 56–73.

79  *Statutes*, xv, pp. 31–34.

80  See Nicholas Timmins, *The Five Giants: A Biography of the Welfare State* (London, 1996), p. 27.

81  See *Isle of Man. Report of the Commission on Unemployment* (Douglas, 1927).

82  *Report of the Commission on Unemployment Insurance*, 12 November 1931 (Douglas, 1931). Legislation to implement the Commission's recommendations for a scheme targeted at seasonal unemployment was rejected by the House of Keys in 1933; see also HO 4515178/557114.

83  *Statutes*, xi, pp. 421–24.

84  Further legislation in 1939 introduced minor changes to the system of poor relief following recommendations from the Old Age Pensions and National Health Insurance Board; *Statutes*, xv, pp. 167–74.

85  See *Isle of Man. Statement by His Excellency the Lieutenant-Governor on the Report of the Commission on Unemployment*, 13 January 1928 (Douglas, 1928), p. 4 and 45 *Manx Deb.*, 17 and 24 February and 2 March 1928, pp. 502–14, 553–81 and 588–600.

86  See 51 *Manx Deb.*, 15 December 1933, pp. 139–45. The 1933 motion was moved by C. S. Shimmin and seconded by A. J. Teare, both of the MLP; it was carried by 19 votes to three in the Keys and defeated by four votes to three in the Council

87  See 51 *Manx Deb.*, 6 and 13 March 1934, pp. 327–39 and 425–28.

88  The first motion was moved by W. K. Cowin and seconded by J. R. Corrin; it was carried in the Keys by 14 votes to eight, but lost in the Council where only Corrin voted in support; 51 *Manx Deb.*, 20 April 1934, pp. 532–33. The second was moved by S. Norris and A. Qualtrough, carried in the Keys by 12 votes to six, but lost by a unanimous vote in a barely quorate Council; 52 *Manx Deb.*, 9 and 10 July 1935, pp. 566–79.

89  See *Annual Reports of the Asylum Board* up to 1923 and the *Annual Reports of the Mental Hospital Board* after 1923.

90  *Nineteenth Report of the Health Insurance and Pensions Board, Year ended 31 December 1939* (Douglas, 1940). The pensions data are in the main body of the report and those relating to contributors in Appendix G.

91  According to Hinton Bird in *An Island that Led: The History of Manx Education*, vol. 2 (Port St Mary, 1995), p. 233.

92  *Statutes*, xi, pp. 4–33.

93  On the recommendation of the Phipps Commission in 1933 legislation was introduced with the aim of replacing the two authorities with a single committee of Tynwald called the Education Council. However, the measure was rejected unanimously in the Keys as a retrograde and undemocratic step. For details, see 51 *Manx Deb.*, 8 May 1934, pp. 619–29; see also HO 45/17508/652103/10-23.

94 Bird, *Island that Led*, p. 209.
95 For a full discussion of these achievements, see Bird, *Island that Led*, pp. 181–233.
96 The mass resignation involved all teachers except those in Douglas and Onchan where the School Boards had agreed to increase pay in line with the Burnham scales. Faced with this threat and the inability of the remaining School Boards to fund the increase, Tynwald agreed to a request from Fry to vote the necessary funds. See HO 45/12567/211309/17.
97 See HO 45/12567/211309/39-40, 50 and 61 for details relating to 1923/24; and HO 45/17508/652103/2 for details relating to the early 1930s.
98 See Bird, *Island that Led*, pp. 227–30.
99 By the Education (Peel Clothworkers' Schools) Act 1936, *Statutes*, xiv, pp. 412–16.
100 See 54 *Manx Deb.*, 2 March 1937, pp. 210–24.
101 See 54 *Manx Deb.*, 26 May 1937, p. 379.
102 *Statutes*, xv, p. 21.
103 Bird, *Island that Led*, p. 190.
104 *Isle of Man Education Commission Report*, May 1933 (Douglas, 1933), para. 5.
105 Bird, *Island that Led*, p. 233.
106 In a letter to the Treasury dated 20 July 1923; HO 45/12567/211309/39.
107 See HO 45/12567/211309 for the period from 1919–25 and HO 45/17508/652103 for the 1930s.
108 See HO 45/12567/211309. Items 30–31 cover the Douglas case (1922); items 43, 52 and 73 the Rushen case (1923–24) and items 78 and 82 the Laxey case (1925).
109 The Local Government Amendment Act 1922, *Statutes*, xi, pp. 339–63.
110 The Local Government Amendment Act 1922, *Statutes*, xi, pp. 339–63, and the Adulteration Act 1925, *Statutes*, xii, pp. 83–108.
111 The Local Government Amendment Acts 1922 and 1929, *Statutes*, xi, pp. 339–63 and xiii, pp. 35–42.
112 Douglas Town Improvement and Artisan Dwelling Act 1922, *Statutes*, xi, pp. 283–89 and the Housing Act 1936, *Statutes*, xiv, pp. 434–60.
113 The Mechanical Contrivances Act 1923, *Statutes*, xi, pp. 404–06.
114 The Housing Acts 1924 and 1936, *Statutes*, xii, pp. 7–13 and xiv, pp. 434–60. The Acts of 1927 and 1928 merely extended the provisions of the 1924 Act for a further period.
115 The Housing (Rural Workers) Acts 1929 and 1934, *Statutes*, xiii, pp. 11–20 and xv, p. 158
116 The Local Government (Milk and Dairies) Act 1934, *Statutes*, xiv, pp. 279–82
117 The Local Government (Extermination of Rats) Act 1938, *Statutes*, xv, pp. 110–12.
118 *Statutes*, xv, pp. 116–20.
119 Under the Local Government Amendment Acts 1922 and 1931, *Statutes*, xi, pp. 339–63 and xiii, pp. 224–25; and the Local Government (No. 3) Act 1938, *Statutes*, xv, pp. 113–16.
120 The Local Government Amendment Act 1922.
121 40 *Manx Deb.*, 12 April 1927, pp. 653–68.
122 48 *Manx Deb.*, 4 November 1930, pp. 54–55 and 51 *Manx Deb.*, 5 January 1934, p. 182.
123 See *Report of the Committee of Tynwald appointed to consider the desirability of reducing the number of Local Authorities in the Island by establishing a Board of Commissioners for each Sheading or larger area to take over the functions of the Parish Commissioners*, 16 March 1934 (Douglas, 1934); see also *Statutes*, xiv, pp. 470–71.
124 Details of the medical benefits referred to below are taken from the *Annual Reports of the Old Age Pensions and National Health Insurance Board*.
125 30 *Manx Deb.*, 8 February 1921, pp. 369–72.
126 These percentages should be treated with some caution; that for 1921 was calculated using the census population which included an unusually high proportion of visitors, while that for 1939 used the government estimate of the population.
127 *Statutes*, xi, pp. 4–33.

128 *Report of the Conference of Representatives of Bodies interested in the Public Health service on Public Health ...*, 5 November 1930 (Douglas, 1930).

129 See the Education (Extension of Medical Treatment) Acts 1932 and 1933; *Statutes*, xiii, pp. 509–11 and xiv, pp. 8–10.

130 These figures must be regarded as approximations as they are derived from census data for 1921 (5–14 age group) and 1931 (0–21 age group) rather than actual SMS figures for the years in question; *Isle of Man. Census 1921* (London, 1924) and *Isle of Man. Census 1931* (1933).

131 *Statutes*, xi, pp. 339–63.

132 See *Summaries by the Local Government Board of the Annual Reports of their Inspector as to the Public Health in the Isle of Man.*

133 See *Summaries by the Local Government Board of the Annual Reports of their Inspector as to the Public Health in the Isle of Man* for the period between the end of the war and 1924; and 39 *Manx Deb.*, 8 March 1922, p. 546.

134 *Statutes*, xi, pp. 79–90; see also 30 *Manx Deb.*, 23 November and 7 December 1920, pp. 178–82 and 203.

135 See 42 *Manx Deb.*, 3 February 1925, pp. 152–67.

136 See 42 *Manx Deb.*, 10 February 1925, pp. 189–206.

137 In a letter dated 27 February 1925; for reference to the letter and the debate that followed, see 42 *Manx Deb.*, 3 March 1924, pp. 253–65.

138 See 42 *Manx Deb.*, 10 March 1925, pp. 280–86 and 17 and 24 March, pp. 290–318. The provisions of the 1925 Act (*Statutes*, xii, pp. 76–81) were kept in force, with some updating, by similarly titled Acts in 1927, 1929, 1930 and every two years until replaced in 1948.

139 38 *Manx Deb.*, 1 February 1921, pp. 331–35. The Committee comprised J. Cunningham, MLC, and four MHKs, R. Cain, C. Gill, J. D. Qualtrough and A. J. Teare.

140 38 *Manx Deb.*, 12 July 1921, pp. 949–57 and *Statutes*, xi, pp. 283–89.

141 39 *Manx Deb.*, 8 March 1922, pp. 546–50 and *Statutes*, xii, pp. 7–13.

142 40 *Manx Deb.*, 12 and 30 January and 15 May 1923, pp. 320–25, 420–29 and 781.

143 62 *Manx Deb.*, 6 February 1945, p. 295.

144 62 *Manx Deb.*, 6 February 1945, p. 295.

145 *Statutes*, xii, pp. 191–207. Between 1927 and 1966 tax relief on mortgage interest payments was deductible from income payable in respect of the gross value of residential property.

146 *Statutes*, xiii, pp. 11–23.

147 See *Summary by the Local Government Board of the Annual Report of their Inspector as to the Public Health in the Isle of Man for the Year ended 31 December 1938* (Douglas, 1939).

148 See for example, the Reports for the years ending 31 December 1932, 1934, 1938 and 1939.

149 See for example, 50 *Manx Deb.*, 11 July 1933, pp. 833–34; 52 *Manx Deb.*, 26 March 1935, pp. 291–92; 53 *Manx Deb.*, 1 November 1935, pp. 57–59; 53 *Manx Deb.*, 17 March 1936, pp. 321–24 and 55 *Manx Deb.*, 15 February 1938, pp. 295–99.

150 *Isle of Man. Report of the Housing Commission*, 24 February 1931 (Douglas, 1931). Butler appointed a further commission in 1935 which paved the way for new legislation in 1936, but no report appears to have been published; see 52 *Manx Deb.*, 25 January 1935. In 1938 his successor, Leveson-Gower, asked the Public Works Commission to report on the housing situation, but this Commission had not reported by the outbreak of war; see 55 *Manx Deb.*, 15 February 1938, p. 299.

151 *Statutes*, xiv, pp. 434–60.

152 38 *Manx Deb.*, 1 February 1921, p. 339. The scheme cost Tynwald £56,007 between 1919/20 and 1926/27, although nearly 90 per cent of payments were made during the first two years.

153 See 39 *Manx Deb.*, 18 October 1921, pp. 5–8 and 1 and 2 November 1921, pp. 25–26 and 50–103.

154 See 39 *Manx Deb.*, 7 April 1922, pp. 700–04; 40 *Manx Deb.*, 24 and 31 October 1922, pp. 37–60, 61–70 and 86–109.

155 See *Isle of Man. Statement by His Excellency the Lieutenant-Governor on the Report of the Commission on Unemployment*, 13 January 1928 (Douglas, 1928).

156 *Ibid.* and 45 *Manx Deb.*, 17 February, 24 February and 2 March 1928, pp. 502–14, 553–81 and 588–600.

157 See 'Comparative Figures re Unemployment. Winters 1928/9 to 1939/40' in *Isle of Man. Unemployment. Interim Report of the Commission appointed to consider and report upon the whole question of dealing with unemployment* (Douglas, 1944).

158 For a full explanation, see the speech of Speaker Clucas when moving the acceptance 10 years later; 54 *Manx Deb.*, 2 March 1937, pp. 210–14.

159 45 *Manx Deb.*, 6 July 1928, pp. 985–1000.

160 45 *Manx Deb.*, 6 July 1928, pp. 986 and 1000.

161 See 45 *Manx Deb.*, 13 June 1928, pp. 958–64.

162 *Statutes*, xi, pp. 106–14.

163 See 46 *Manx Deb.*, 15 January 1929, pp. 324–29.

164 See A. J. Teare, 'The Island's Immunity from Strikes' in *Reminiscences of the Manx Labour Party*, pp. 48–50. For a review of the 1935 strike, see Robert Fyson, 'Labour History', in J. C. Belchem (ed.), *A New History of the Isle of Man: The Modern Period 1830–1999*, vol. 5 (Liverpool, 2000), pp. 301–04, and Kniveton, *Chronicle of the Twentieth Century*, vol. 1, pp. 136 and 138.

165 *Statutes*, xiv, pp. 404–07.

166 See 53 *Manx Deb.*, 3 December 1935 and 4 February 1936, pp. 139–48 and 261.

167 *Statutes*, xiv, pp. 396–401.

168 See 53 *Manx Deb.*, 14 January and 4 February 1936, pp. 225–27 and 267.

169 *Statutes*, xiv, pp. 402–04.

170 See 53 *Manx Deb.*, 14 January and 4 February 1936, pp. 228–37 and 267–68.

171 *Statutes*, xii, pp. 435–47; xiv, pp. 163–75 and 329–31.

172 *Statutes*, xi, pp. 106–14 and xv, p. 144.

173 *Statutes*, xi, pp. 416–20. The most controversial provision of the Act was the Sunday closing of all premises in which alcohol was sold or consumed. During the summer—from Easter Sunday to the end of September—the opening hours for public houses on weekdays were 10am to 10pm except in the towns and certain village districts where the hours were 10am to 11pm. For the rest of the year public houses were allowed to open for 8–10 hours between 10am and 10pm, as determined by the District Licensing Courts.

174 *Statutes*, xi, pp. 201–49.

175 *Statutes*, xiii, pp. 541–65.

176 *Statutes*, xiii, pp. 46–56 and xiv, pp. 214–18 and 470.

177 53 *Manx Deb.*, 10 July and 15 September, 1936, pp. 638–40 and 662–69.

178 56 *Manx Deb.*, 22 March 1939, pp. 388–91 and 57 *Manx Deb.*, 31 October 1939, pp. 115 26; see also *Second Report of the Southern Water Board for the Year ended 31 March 1942* (Douglas, 1942).

179 See 51 *Manx Deb.*, 14 September 1934, pp. 955–58.

180 The reasons given were international goodwill and peace as well as economic self-interest; 46 *Manx Deb.*, 4 October 1929, pp. 1202–03.

181 *Statutes*, xi, pp. 646–50 and xii, pp. 1–6.

182 See 43 *Manx Deb.*, 22 December 1925, pp. 273–82.

183 See 43 *Manx Deb.*, 28 June 1927, pp. 851–62.

184 *Statutes*, xiii, pp. 8–10.

185 *Statutes*, xiii, pp. 24–34.

186 *Statutes*, xiii, pp. 43–6.

187 See 46 *Manx Deb.*, 7 and 14 May 1929, pp. 845–82 and 4 and 18 June 1929, pp. 896–916 and 1004–08.

188 See 46 *Manx Deb.*, 22 and 29 January 1929, pp. 368–76 and 409–27 and 5 and 19 February

1929, pp. 488–93, 495–500 and 503–10. The attempt in 1909 is discussed in Chapter Three. For details of the MLP attempt in 1922, see 39 *Manx Deb.*, 11 April 1922, pp. 722–34 and 737–57.

189  See 46 *Manx Deb.*, 13 and 27 November 1928, pp. 166–69 and 196–203, 11 December 1928, pp. 271–93 and 15 January 1929, pp. 324–29.

190  See 46 *Manx Deb.*, 23 April 1929, pp. 786–90.

191  *Statutes*, xiv, pp. 138–42; see also 46 *Manx Deb.*, 5 April 1929, pp. 712–20; 47 *Manx Deb.*, 25 April 1930, pp. 530–33 and 27 May 1930, pp. 689–91.

192  *First Interim Report of the Industrial Commission on Agriculture*, 26 April 1930 (Douglas, 1930).

193  See 48 *Manx Deb.*, 13 January 1931, pp. 177–81.

194  See 48 *Manx Deb.*, 10 March 1931, pp. 360–61.

195  See 51 *Manx Deb.*, 28 November 1933, pp. 84–90 and 8 May 1934, p. 604.

196  *Second Interim Report of the Industrial Commission*, December 1930 (Douglas, 1931)

197  See 52 *Manx Deb.*, 26 March 1935, pp. 278–85 and 14 June 1935, pp. 529–30; 53 *Manx Deb.*, 25 October 1935, pp. 31–44.

198  *Statutes*, xiv, pp. 279–82

199  *Statutes*, xiv, pp. 276–78.

200  *Statutes*, xiv, pp. 335–52.

201  The House approved the Bill without further debate, by 18 votes to three at the second reading and without division at the third; see 52 *Manx Deb.*, 26 March 1935, pp. 314–15. For the response of the Legislative Council, see 52 *Manx Deb.*, 28 May 1935, pp. 379–89.

202  *Report of the Commission on Agriculture*, 28 February 1939 (Douglas, 1939).

203  See 56 *Manx Deb.*, 18 and 19 April 1939, pp. 427–69.

204  *Statutes*, xi, pp. 581–83; xiii, pp. 43–46; xiv, pp. 276–83.

205  The data on levels of income tax were obtained from the *Accounts of the Government Treasurer*.

# CHAPTER FIVE

# War, Socialism and Devolution 1939–58

The period from the outbreak of war in 1939 to Parliament's Isle of Man Act in 1958 saw a major devolution of power to the Island and a great expansion in the role of the state. The Island's destiny both during and after the war was massively influenced by what was happening in the UK. The policies of the Coalition (1940–45), Labour (1945–51) and Conservative (1951–58) Governments not only determined the rate of constitutional progress, but also provided much of the agenda for social and economic reform. A war about self-determination and a postwar UK Government committed to decolonisation helped pave the way for the removal of important colonial controls. The circumstances of war, the socialist ideology of the Labour Government and Tynwald's belief that it could not afford not to keep in line with major UK policies led to a transformation of the role of the state every bit as significant as that which occurred in the 1920s. There was no postwar socialist victory in the Isle of Man; on the contrary, the MLP won only two seats in the 1946 general election. It was a liberal/conservative Tynwald that felt obliged to emulate UK policies. The irony is that as steps were being taken towards Island self-government in 1958, the real freedom of Tynwald was being progressively constrained by what it saw as a necessary harmonisation of major social and economic policy.

Within the Island three Lieutenant-Governors were responsible for good government during this period.[1] The UK practice of appointing individuals in their 50s with a distinguished career in the armed forces or the colonial service continued. Leveson-Gower, who had become Earl Granville in July 1939, remained in charge for the duration of the war. He was succeeded in October 1945 by Sir Geoffrey Bromet. Born in 1891, his career was initially with the Royal Navy and, after the First World War, the Royal Air Force, where he achieved the rank of Air Vice Marshall. Prior to taking up appointment he had been the senior British officer in the Azores Force. In September 1952 Bromet was followed by Sir Ambrose Dundas. Born in 1899 he joined the Indian civil service at the age of 23 and served there until 1949. Like Hill and Butler, he came to the Island with a wealth of administrative experience, both in India and, immediately prior to appointment, in the UK where for two years he was general manager of Bracknell New Town Development Corporation.

Inside Tynwald there were also changes in personnel, with the interwar generation of Manx politicians ascendant during the 1940s, but giving way during the 1950s to MHKs first elected just after the war. In the Legislative Council, which still enjoyed equal powers with the House of Keys, the leading officials were the Attorney General—

Sir Geoffrey Bromet,
Lieutenant-Governor
1945–52.

Sir Ambrose Dundas, Lieutenant-Governor 1952–59. The photograph shows Dundas at the Tynwald Ceremony in July 1959.

Deemster Percy Cowley chairing the War Consultative Committee, circa 1940. Cowley remained a key figure in Manx politics until his death in 1958; he was knighted in 1952. From left to right are James Corrin (MLC), Arthur Kitto (MHK), Daniel Teare (MHK), Deemster Percy Cowley (MLC), Ramsey Johnson (Secretary), Alfred Teare (MHK), Walter Craine (MHK) and Samuel Norris (MHK).

Ramsey B. Moore until 1945, Sidney J. Kneale from 1945 to 1957 and George E. Moore from February 1957—and the Deemsters—here the outstanding individual was Deemster W. Percy Cowley, who not only served in the Legislative Council throughout this period, but also as chair of the Public Works Commission, the War Consultative Committee and as a member of the first Executive Council.[2] The appointed and indirectly elected members were for the most part experienced politicians of the interwar period, including Norris (1943–46), MLP members Corrin (1928–55), Teare (1951–62) and Kneen (1950–54), Southward (1919–43) and Crellin (1944–61) Although there was no general election for the House of Keys in 1939 because of the war, by-elections during the war and the 1946 general election saw the election of 20 new members. Immediately after the war, the few remaining members elected during the interwar period continued to provide the leadership, none more so than J. D. Qualtrough, the Speaker of the House throughout this period. After the 1951 election, however, with Speaker Qualtrough still an active chair, the leadership of the House passed to the generation of MHKs first elected in 1946 or 1948. While only three of these—Thomas C. Cowin from 1949, Richard C. Cannell from 1950 and John B. Bolton from June 1951—served on the Executive Council before the 1951 general election, each of the six MHK members who served between the election and the selection or reselection of members in May 1958—Bolton, Cannell, Cowin, Henry K. Corlett, H. Charles Kerruish and Jack Nivison—were from this group.

## *The Devolution of Power*

As in 1927 when Hill took the initiative in proposing the establishment of the Keys' Consultative Committee, in November 1939 Granville initiated the establishment of the War Consultative Committee to advise him on 'the problems of the day'.[3] Although the membership was proposed by Granville, Tynwald approved his seven nominations in preference to four alternative names proposed. The Committee brought together senior politicians from all sides of the political spectrum, two from the Legislative Council— Deemster Cowley and James Corrin—and five from the Keys—Craine, Arthur E. Kitto, Norris, Alfred Teare and Daniel J. Teare. The Island's 'war cabinet' was, like its UK counterpart, a coalition cabinet, including three MLP members. It was chaired by Deemster Cowley and attended by the Government Secretary and the Attorney General in an advisory capacity.[4] The only changes in membership between 1939 and its replacement in 1946 followed the resignation of Norris in 1942 because of pressure of work and the death of Daniel Teare in 1943. They were replaced by MHKs, Arthur J. Cottier and George H. Moore.

The War Consultative Committee, although without formal constitutional status, played a central role in decision-making during the war. Welcoming Granville's initiative, Speaker Qualtrough expressed the hope that it would be 'so productive' that the Island would have 'an unanswerable case' for 'a permanent Cabinet'.[5] The Committee met regularly and reported periodically to Tynwald. It became the driving force behind public policy, liaising with the UK authorities and boards of Tynwald, advising the Lieutenant-Governor on policy and legislation, responding to specific war problems and undertaking an immense amount of preparatory work for postwar reconstruction. The war precluded its development as a responsible executive, all proceedings being strictly confidential. It came under criticism for unnecessary secrecy, insufficient reporting to Tynwald and the bypassing of the consultative mechanisms already in operation before the war.

The most serious criticism followed Granville's failure to consult the Consultative and Finance Committee over proposals to follow UK increases in taxation in 1943.[6] At an extraordinary meeting of Tynwald on 16 April 1943, Speaker Qualtrough explained that the House had agreed unanimously not to approve any taxation unless it received an assurance of consultation 'on all matters of taxation and expenditure'. Granville insisted that his instructions were to consult the House on expenditure only. During an adjournment the Keys despatched a memorandum to the Lieutenant-Governor seeking assurances of consultation on taxation as well as expenditure. Later that day, Granville indicated his readiness, if requested, to meet the Consultative and Finance Committee on any matter of public interest and that he 'would gladly meet them if requested on proposals for taxation, reserving always the same right as the Chancellor of the Exchequer has of maintaining secrecy on any proposal when the necessities of revenue so require until the morning of Tynwald.' Back in Tynwald the Speaker welcomed Granville's response and stated that the House was 'very satisfied'. As in 1911 and 1920 the threat of 'strike' action produced results.

For the most part, however, reactions to the War Consultative Committee were favourable. Both Granville and individual members welcomed the opportunities provided by the weekly meetings and the experience of the Committee was cited by MHKs in support of renewed claims for a responsible executive council. Following an initiative by Norris, the Keys agreed on 1 December 1942 to appoint a committee to consider the issue of reform. Norris's resolution included both a statement of principle and specific proposals for reform, fairer representation in the Keys before the next election, the direct election of two thirds of the Legislative Council, the removal of the Deemsters from the legislature, the establishment of an executive that was representative of and responsible to Tynwald and a Lieutenant-Governor shorn of political power. As agreed, the resolution was confined to the following statement of principle, members accepting that the detail should be a matter for the committee:

> This House believes that freedom of thought, freedom of speech, freedom from fear and freedom from want, and that government of the people by the people and for the people are as essential and as much the right of small peoples as for the biggest nations with whom we are now fighting as allies, and that for the democratic form of government the Manx people have fought in two great wars on equal terms with England, and are entitled to equal opportunities of life …
>
> This House is determined to secure these liberties under Manx Home Rule, and to bring about as great a measure of social service and housing and economic and industrial conditions as is provided for the people of Britain through Parliament, but asserts that it is necessary to bring into operation the same principles of democratic government as are enjoyed in England.[7]

This declaration of principle revealed an interesting combination of belief in the Island enjoying not only the same democratic rights as the people of the UK, but also equivalent social and economic benefits. While the Committee of the House of Keys concentrated on the former, the decisions of Tynwald during and immediately following the war revealed a determination to provide for the Island a similar programme of social and economic reform to that introduced by the Coalition and Labour Governments.

Norris refused to serve on the Committee, partly because of pressure of work and partly because he felt that his views were well known. The seven-member Committee was chaired by Speaker Qualtrough, who presented a unanimous report to the House in October 1943.[8] In an impressive speech, in which he confessed to being 'something of a Manx nationalist', the Speaker explained that the overriding goal was to enhance democracy in the Island. The central demand was an executive committee elected by and responsible to Tynwald and presided over by the Lieutenant-Governor. It would have seven members, five from the House, retain the advantages of an experienced administrator, combine in one body the responsibility for good order and government, including finance and the law and order services, and bring to an end the humiliation of being deemed incapable of self-government. The Committee did not support Norris's proposals for the reform of the Legislative Council.[9] After a debate spread over two meetings, the House approved the report in principle and appointed a nine-member committee, chaired by the Speaker, to prepare a petition to the Home Secretary.

Before the Committee was able to report, the appointment of a new Government Secretary and an Assistant Government Secretary, without any reference to members of the House, made the House even more determined to seek reform. In December 1943, the House gave its unanimous approval to three resolutions moved by Eric Fargher, the first objecting to the appointment of the Government Secretary without consultation and the failure to offer the post to a member of the Manx civil service, the second arguing that the temporary wartime post of Assistant Government Secretary be discontinued and the third protesting about the appointment of the Assistant Government Secretary in the face of the unanimous opposition of the House and without following the procedures of consultation laid down for increases in the reserved services by the Home Secretary in 1920.[10] The Home Secretary, Herbert Morrison, dismissed the Keys' complaints, pointing out that the House had been consulted about the decision to replace the Government Secretary and had expressed the view that the incumbent, Bertram Sargeant, be asked to serve until the end of the war, and that both appointments had been made with the approval of the Home Secretary and the Treasury.[11]

On 4 January 1944, acting on its Committee's recommendations and before receiving the reply of the Home Secretary to the complaints about these key government appointments, the House agreed unanimously to petition the Home Secretary to receive a deputation to discuss the broader issue of constitutional reform.[12] The debate was dominated by Speaker Qualtrough's impassioned plea for responsible government in the Isle of Man. He saw the Island as 'a conquered country' that could not be trusted to manage its own affairs, whose people were not deemed worthy of holding the post of Government Secretary and whose political destiny was in the hands of an externally appointed Lieutenant-Governor.

> The Lieutenant-Governor is sent here, he is not responsible to us. He is the head of the executive, he is the head of the police, he is Chancellor of the Exchequer, with control over finance and a complete veto over any proposals that may come before us; he is the head of the civil service; he may take our advice or he may not. He may ask for it, and after he has had it, he may not be guided by it.[13]

The petition was forwarded to the Home Secretary by the Lieutenant-Governor, who argued privately that such radical reforms did not have the support of the Manx people.[14] The Home Secretary suggested that it might be more appropriate to meet a deputation from Tynwald.[15] Accordingly Tynwald appointed a joint committee to prepare a common platform for the negotiations.

In order to present a united front at the talks, the Keys agreed to moderate their proposals in favour of those put forward by the Joint Committee of Tynwald.[16] In a report, accepted unanimously by Tynwald on 6 June 1944,[17] the Joint Committee maintained that the Keys' proposals were too radical, as the UK would never agree to finance being taken out of the hands of the Lieutenant-Governor. It did, however, believe that an executive council, made up of five board chairs and two members elected by Tynwald, one of whom would have responsibility for finance, was necessary to advise the Lieutenant-Governor and that it should have the right to be consulted on financial matters. It was also agreed to seek the devolution of the UK Treasury's powers in respect of the voted services to the Lieutenant-Governor. Only three members of Tynwald spoke in the debate, Speaker Qualtrough, Attorney General Moore and Norris; each gave their wholehearted support for the proposals. Given the Keys' initial demand for a system of responsible government, it is perhaps surprising that they accepted an advisory executive council. That acceptance did, however, mean that when a deputation was eventually received, it was representative of Tynwald and not just the House of Keys. It was agreed that the deputation should be the members of the Joint Committee, Deemster Cowley, Attorney General Moore and Corrin from the Legislative Council and Speaker Qualtrough, Fargher, Kitto and Alfred Teare from the Keys.[18]

The deputation was received at the Home Office by Herbert Morrison on 17 October 1944. After the Speaker had expressed the desire of Tynwald for a greater degree of responsibility, Tynwald's case was presented by the Attorney General:

> In form the Governor alone is responsible for policy and for government, for the initiation of legislation, the introduction of all financial proposals, both for the

imposition of taxation and for the expenditure of revenue. Now that form of government has one great drawback. It means that the representatives of the people in the House of Keys become a permanent opposition.[19]

Moore said that, while Tynwald accepted that ultimate responsibility for finance and government should remain with the Lieutenant-Governor, he should be fortified by the advice and experience of an executive council, disagreements being resolved by reference to the UK Government. Judging by the experience of the War Consultative Committee, such disagreements were unlikely, a consequence in part perhaps of the tendency for most Lieutenant-Governors to become staunch advocates of Manx interests. It was felt that in such circumstances Treasury control could cease.

The outcome of the talks was a letter from the new Labour Home Secretary, Chuter Ede, to the Lieutenant-Governor, dated 20 February 1946,[20] providing for the establishment of a seven-member executive council, drawn primarily from among the chairmen of the major spending boards and appointed by the Lieutenant-Governor on the recommendation of Tynwald. The letter itself was to provide the necessary authority for the appointment of the Council. The idea that one member might be made responsible for finance was rejected, but the letter promised that the whole issue of financial control would be dealt with later by the Treasury.

On 9 April 1946 Tynwald accepted this statement unanimously and, because chairs of the major spending boards were to become members of the Executive Council, asked the Lieutenant-Governor to prepare legislation for a rationalisation of the board system.[21] On 16 October 1946, following consultations between Bromet and representatives of the two branches of Tynwald, the first Executive Council was appointed.[22] Four individuals were proposed as chairs of the major spending boards on the understanding that they would also become members of the Executive Council, John Cowin (Agriculture and Fisheries), John Crellin (Local Government Board) and Charles Gill (Highways and Transport) from the Legislative Council and Richard Kneen (Social Services) from the House of Keys. Two other MHKs, Alfred Teare and George Higgins, were appointed who were not chairs of major boards. To provide continuity from the War Consultative Committee, maintained by Bromet under the name of Advisory Committee, Deemster Cowley became the seventh member. It was felt inappropriate for the Speaker, who had been selected as chair of the Board of Education, to serve on such a body, although Qualtrough did become a member following the resignation of Deemster Cowley in 1947. The Island's first Executive Council was very much a coalition of political interests and included the two MLP members of the House.

While the Executive Council represented an important constitutional advance, the relationship between the Lieutenant-Governor, the Council and the rest of Tynwald soon came in for criticism. For many of the new MHKs, elected in May 1946 but only commencing their five-year term in October 1946, the compromise agreed by the outgoing House in favour of an advisory body was quickly revealed to have been a mistake. The lack of representative and responsible government lay at the heart of their criticisms. In terms of representativeness, the first Executive Council did not have the five-to-two ratio of members originally sought by the Keys. The lack of experience of the new members in October 1946 had resulted in a majority of the Executive Council coming from the Legislative Council, an imbalance soon redressed with the replacement of Deemster Cowley by the Speaker in July 1947, John Cowin by Richard Cannell in 1950 and Gill by John Bolton in 1951; the ratio of five to two was honoured for the rest of this period.

In parallel with the redress of this imbalance came the recruitment of new members. In 1949 Bromet asked Higgins to withdraw to make way for the chair of the new Health Services Board, Thomas Cowin; with the resignation of John Cowin from the Legislative Council in April 1950, Cannell was chosen to succeed him both as chair of the Board of Agriculture and Fisheries and member of Executive Council; Bolton was appointed following the death of Gill in June 1951. Following the 1951 general election, the Speaker asked to be relieved of membership and, although Teare retained his seat, he did so as an MLC, Crellin keeping his seat as chair of the LGB. Each of the five MHKs appointed were new to the House in 1946 or 1948: Cannell (Agriculture and Fisheries), Henry K. Corlett (Education), Thomas Cowin (Health Services), Nivison (Social Services) and Bolton, who was not a board chair. These seven members were reappointed in December 1954. Following the death of Cowin in 1955, Charles Kerruish joined the Executive Council as chair of the Health Services Board. There were no further changes in membership until 1958, these seven being reappointed after the 1956 general election. While their reappointment in December 1954 and November 1956 suggested a measure of confidence in the members of the Council, there were criticisms of its operation.

There were improvements in response to criticism, but the basic demand for a system of responsible government was not met. In June 1951 the Consultative and Finance Committee complained that the Council was rarely consulted on the initiation of fresh legislation, police matters, official salaries and establishments and fiscal policy and that the Government was invariably fully committed to schemes long before proposals came before it. The Committee also asked for one of its members who was not the chair of a board to serve on Executive Council.[23] Although no progress was made with representation on the Executive Council, when Bromet presented his budget to Tynwald in June 1952, he explained that for the first time he had consulted the Executive Council about the budget and saw that as a great constitutional advance.[24] Concerned at the secrecy surrounding the activities of Executive Council, in May 1953 Kerruish asked Dundas if he would circulate the minutes of the Council to all members of Tynwald. The Lieutenant-Governor's answer was a categorical 'no'. However, when Kerruish returned to the issue six months later complaining of an 'iron curtain' between Council members and the rest of Tynwald, Tynwald formally requested the circulation of such information as the Lieutenant-Governor 'may consider expedient' and Dundas responded by arranging for monthly notes on the activities of Executive Council to be circulated to members of Tynwald.[25] In November 1956, newly elected MHK, Robert C. Stephen, attempted to have appointments to Executive Council deferred until the question of the Council's responsibility to Tynwald had been resolved.[26] While there was considerable sympathy for this position, it was agreed that such internal reform should await the imminent devolution of power from the UK.

The promised devolution of power, including the removal of Treasury control, had been delayed by the need for legislation at Westminster and a series of events both in Isle of Man and the UK. On 13 April 1949, the Home Office had made clear that the UK was prepared to sanction a major transfer of power to the Manx authorities, including the long sought removal of Treasury control,[27] but eight years elapsed before negotiations culminated in two agreements dated 30 October 1957 and the passage at Westminster of the Isle of Man Act 1958 and in Tynwald of the Isle of Man Contribution Act 1956, the Finance Act 1958, the Customs (Isle of Man) Act 1958, the Import Duties Act 1958 and the Loans Act 1958. The details of these negotiations are well documented in a series of reports to Tynwald between May 1949 and September 1956.[28]

In the Isle of Man the detail of the proposed devolution of power was not at issue, but the internal relationship between the Lieutenant-Governor, the Executive Council and Tynwald was. In 1951 the disagreement between Bromet and the House of Keys over the internal distribution of power, in particular the financial role of the Keys and the ineffectiveness of the Executive Council, delayed progress for almost three years. A report by the Consultative and Finance Committee in June 1951 led to the House adopting a series of resolutions critical of the excessive powers of the Lieutenant-Governor. The House condemned Bromet's decision to overrule the wishes of the House by applying UK scales (the Oaksey scale) to the salaries of the Island's Chief Constable and Superintendent of Police—the previous December when consulted by Bromet, the House had resolved by unanimous vote that the proposed increases in pay were excessive. The House demanded that in future the Executive Council should be more fully involved in government, with the whole range of policy matters being brought before it, including finance. It reiterated wartime demands for all financial matters to be discussed with the Consultative and Finance Committee and asked that a member of the Committee serve on the Executive Council. The Home Office response was to invite a delegation from Tynwald to discuss these and other constitutional questions, but that such a meeting be deferred until after the forthcoming general elections, in October 1951 in the UK and November 1951 in the Isle of Man. The elections brought about a change of government in the UK and ushered in a period of conflict between the branches of Tynwald over whether the deputation should discuss both progress towards the devolution of power to Tynwald and the specific Keys' complaints or just the latter. This conflict delayed the appointment of the delegation for two and a half years. In May 1954 the branches eventually agreed to concentrate on the transfer of powers from the UK on the understanding that internal constitutional reforms would be tackled following the removal of Treasury control.[29] Led by Speaker Qualtrough, the delegation reported to Tynwald in November 1954 that considerable progress had been made on the major issues, the removal of Treasury control, a revised contribution by the Isle of Man for defence and common purposes, policy on indirect taxation and insular legislation to be progressed once the 1866 Act and other UK legislation had been repealed.[30] Thereafter, progress was very much dependent on the UK, where a further general election and a busy UK Government meant that it was October 1956 before Tynwald's negotiating committee was able to report a final agreement.[31] Even after Tynwald had given its unanimous support to the report incorporating drafts of the two intergovernmental agreements, progress was further delayed by a congested parliamentary timetable and a lengthy process of interdepartmental and intergovernmental consultation on the complex detail of the proposed constitutional change.[32] The chief architects of these agreements—the first to be signed and agreed with another government—were Speaker Qualtrough and Deemster Cowley, albeit with the advice and assistance of other members of Tynwald's Constitutional Development Committee and the Committee's legal advisors, Attorney General Kneale and the Clerk of Tynwald, Frank B. Johnson.[33]

The first agreement concerned the annual contribution to the UK.[34] The amount was to be determined from time to time by Tynwald in accordance with the provisions of the Isle of Man Contribution Act 1956[35] and after consultation between representatives of the two governments. In the first instance it would be five per cent of net Common

Purse receipts and this remained the level of contribution until the Agreement was replaced by the Customs and Excise Agreement in 1979.

The effect of the second agreement was to pave the way for a major increase in the Island's control over its own affairs.[36] The UK Government agreed to repeal the 1866 Act and certain obsolete legislation and to empower Tynwald to impose its own customs duties and legislate on a range of matters that had hitherto been the preserve of the UK Parliament. Bills dealing with finance, the police, loans, the civil service and harbours had been in draft form for a number of years and Tynwald was to proceed with them as soon as the UK measures became law. Further the Isle of Man agreed to follow UK tariff changes in protective duties, Imperial preference duties and in pursuance of commercial treaties or international agreements, and not to introduce any fresh differences in other duties without first consulting the UK Government. The Island would keep its laws on customs administration in line with those in the UK, and the Commissioners of Customs and Excise would continue to collect all duties as before. The proceeds of 'unequal' duties would be paid straight to the Island, while those of 'equal' duties less the costs of collection and audit would be shared under the terms of the Common Purse Arrangement. There was provision for the review of the Agreement at the instance of either Government.

Of the legislation which followed this Agreement the most important was Parliament's Isle of Man Act 1958, which repealed the Isle of Man Customs, Harbours and Public Purposes Act 1866 and enabled Tynwald to legislate on such matters as customs, harbours, loans, mines and government officers.[37] One of the most significant changes effected by this Act was the removal of formal Treasury control over Manx finance and with it a situation where a large portion of Manx revenue was legally expended without reference to Tynwald. Between the end of the war, when the UK first agreed to its removal, and 1958, when it was actually removed, Treasury control had been more formal than real. Commitment to the principle of removal and the fact that immediately after the war the Island was doing well economically persuaded the UK authorities to respect the wishes of Tynwald. However, the fact that control had been more relaxed in no way diminished the significance for the Island of the formal removal of what had been a major constraint on Island self-government.

While the Isle of Man Act was an important milestone in the Island's campaign for self-government, it was by no means the end of colonial rule, as can be seen from the Manx legislation that followed. The Finance Act 1958 replaced the 1866 Act in providing the basis of the Island's financial system. The key provision was to place financial power in the hands of the Lieutenant-Governor.[38] Although, with the exception of Crown salaries and pensions and the interest and sinking fund payments in respect of Government borrowing, all expenditure had to be approved by Tynwald, the Lieutenant-Governor was still responsible for the Island's budget. He remained Chancellor of the Exchequer and there was no statutory provision for him to be advised by Tynwald in the execution of his financial duties; such provision as there was in the form of the Executive Council was very much reliant on the goodwill of the incumbent Lieutenant-Governor. The Act also provided for revenues from income tax and surtax to form part of the General Revenue and for surpluses to be transferred to the Isle of Man Accumulated Fund, £500,000 of which would be set aside as a strategic reserve, the Isle of Man Reserve Fund.

Based largely on Parliament's Isle of Man (Customs) Act 1955, which provided for the confirmation of Tynwald's customs resolutions by Order in Council instead of by Act of Parliament, the Customs (Isle of Man) Act 1958 made provision for Tynwald to impose, abolish and vary customs duties. It empowered the Lieutenant-Governor by Order approved by Tynwald to bring Manx duties into line with those of the UK. On paper, the Act clearly represented an increase in Tynwald's powers. In practice the change was of little immediate significance as Tynwald had agreed not to use this power without first consulting the UK Government and continued to impose, vary and abolish duties in complete accordance with the UK tariff, only beer remaining outside the Common Purse Arrangement. A further piece of customs legislation, the Import Duties (Isle of Man) Act 1958, gave legal effect to the Island's pledge to follow the UK in respect of all protective duties, Imperial preference duties and other duties imposed in accordance with international agreements.[39]

The third Manx Act resulting from the 1957 Agreement was the Loans Act 1958, making it possible for loans to be raised with the approval of Tynwald instead of Tynwald and the UK Treasury and to be charged against all or any part of government revenues instead of just customs revenue.[40] Extensive use would be made of these powers once outstanding domestic constitutional issues had been resolved.

Although the Keys were very dissatisfied with important aspects of the relationship between the executive and the legislature, the War Consultative Committee, the Executive Council and the developing board system provided for a greater measure of participation in government by MHKs than at any time in Manx history. This period saw some rationalisation of existing boards, the establishment of new boards as government assumed new responsiblities, a new role for the chairs of the major spending boards as members of the Executive Council and, after 1951, a shift in the leadership of the boards in favour of the House of Keys.

In 1946 steps were taken to rationalise the board system in anticipation of the recruitment of chairs to the Executive Council. The Board of Agriculture and Fisheries replaced the Board of Agriculture, the Fisheries Board and the Forestry Board; the Council of Education was renamed the Board of Education; the Highway Board became the Highway and Transport Board; the role of the LGB was extended to include development projects; and the OAPNHIB, which had become the Health Insurance and Pensions Board in 1939, was renamed the Board of Social Services.[41] These were the five main spending boards whose chairs became members of the Executive Council in 1946 or 1947. Among the other established boards, the Harbour Commissioners became a board under Manx rather than UK legislation in 1948 and the Publicity Board was renamed the Tourist Board in 1952.[42] Welfare reforms greatly added to the role and expenditure of the Boards of Education and Social Services and led to the creation in 1948 of another high spending board, the Health Services Board, which replaced the Mental Hospital Board and assumed responsibility for the whole of the national health service.[43] With the transfer of Crown lands to the Island, in 1950 the Forestry Mines and Lands Board was created to manage these lands and take over the responsibility for forestry from the Board of Agriculture and Fisheries.[44] There were also three new commercial boards, the Isle of Man Water Board replacing the various public and private water authorities outside of Douglas in 1946, the Airports Board being established in 1948 and the Manx Electric Railway Board in 1957.

The decision of the Home Office in 1946 that most members of the Executive Council should be chairs of the principal spending boards led directly to changes in the process of their selection. In 1946 Tynwald agreed to replace selection by board members with election in Tynwald and appointed a small selection committee to consult with the

Lieutenant-Governor prior to election and approval of the Lieutenant-Governor's nominations for the Executive Council.[45] Dissatisfaction with this ad hoc arrangement led to the Boards of Tynwald Act 1951, providing for the establishment of a selection committee of six MHKs and three MLCs, with the responsibility to consult with the Lieutenant-Governor and make recommendations to Tynwald for the chairs and members of boards. Tynwald was thus able to select chairs before members, knowing that the individuals proposed by the selection committee for the major spending boards, and accepted by Tynwald, would be nominated by the Lieutenant-Governor for membership of the Executive Council.

The respective roles of MLCs and MHKs in providing the chairs of the boards of Tynwald changed markedly as the postwar generation of MHKs asserted themselves. During the war the balance favoured the Legislative Council, the Keys providing the chairs of only one major spending board (Agriculture) and five others (the Fisheries, Mental Hospital, Publicity, Southern Water and, from 1943, Northern Water Boards). With the retirement of Attorney General Moore in 1945, the leadership of the Council of Education passed to Speaker Qualtrough and the Health Insurance and Pensions/Social Services Board to Richard Kneen, MHK. After the general election of November 1946, the inexperience of most MHKs left MLCs in many key positions, including the new Board of Agriculture and Fisheries, where the former chair of the Board of Agriculture, John Cowin, was chosen to lead, immediately following elevation to the Legislative Council. Indeed, the only MHKs to chair boards after the election were Cottier (Mental Hospital Board), Kneen (Social Services Board), the Speaker (Board of Education and Publicity Board) and Teare (Water Board). By 1951 the position had been transformed, with the Keys providing the chairs of all but the LGB and the Electricity and Water Boards. With the exception of the Speaker, who was first elected in 1919 (Publicity/Tourist Board up to 1957 and Electricity Board from 1956), they were first elected to the Keys during the war as in the cases of John W. Brew (Forestry, Mines and Lands Board 1950–53) and Frank H. Crowe (Highway and Transport Board 1951–56) or immediately after the war as with Bolton (Highway and Transport Board 1956–60), Cannell (Agriculture and Fisheries Board 1950–58), T. Ffinlo Corkhill (Forestry, Mines and Lands Board 1953–70), Corlett (Board of Education 1951–61), Thomas Cowin (Health Services Board 1948–55 and Airports Board 1949–55), A. Spencer Kelly (Harbours Board 1951–68), Kerruish (Health Services 1955–66), J. Harold Nicholls (Airports Board 1955–68) and Nivison (Social Services 1951–76).

While the constitutional changes between 1939 and 1958 fell short of the Keys' aspirations for a system of responsible government, the combination of the long-established rights to participate in the work of Tynwald and the House of Keys, the new opportunities provided by the War Consultative Committee, the Executive Council and an expanded board system, and participation in a series of policy commissions—on electoral reform, poor relief, public health, the health service, agriculture, fisheries, the visiting industry and the development of light industry—produced a partnership in government between the externally appointed Lieutenant-Governor and Tynwald. Set against the democratic ambitions of the wartime House of Keys, the immediate impact of the financial reforms of 1957–58 was limited given the powers of the Lieutenant-Governor. Progress in transferring powers, both general and financial, from the Lieutenant-Governor to bodies that were responsible to Tynwald had to await the outcome of the internal constitutional review that was set in motion in March 1958 under the chairmanship of Lord MacDermott.

# *The Elections of 1946, 1951 and 1956*

Between 1939 and 1958 there were three general elections held under universal adult suffrage, two with the distribution of seats laid down in 1891 and one following the redistribution effected by the Representation of the People Act 1956. There should have been an election in 1939, but the war led to an extension of the term of the 1934 House until October 1946.[46] There were no changes in the franchise or the qualifications for standing as candidates, MLP attempts to abolish the property vote in 1951 and 1956 and John Bolton's attempt to require candidates to pay forfeitable election deposits in 1951 proving unsuccessful.[47]

Bolton's other attempt at electoral reform, the redistribution of seats in favour of Douglas, was successful. Redistribution was a controversial issue for most of this period. A commission appointed by Granville in 1939 and chaired by the Clerk of Tynwald, Frank Johnson, had reported in favour of redistribution in 1944, but no progress was made with either of the schemes proposed.[48] In January 1946 legislation to implement one of the alternatives was introduced by Douglas MLP members, Teare and Craine, to provide two extra seats for Douglas and one extra for Ramsey by increasing the membership of the House to 27, but was defeated at the second reading by 10 votes to eight. Later in the same year Norris, a former Douglas MHK but now an MLC, introduced a bill based on the other alternative to provide a similar increase in the representation for Douglas and Ramsey, but at the expense of Ayre, Glenfaba and Michael; the Council agreed to adjourn consideration until after the general election, believing that initiatives for reform in this area should come from the House. No attempt was made by the House until the eve of the 1951 election, when a further attempt by MLP members to resolve the problem by increasing the membership of the House was defeated by 15 votes to four.[49] In December 1954 a resolution in the names of two Douglas members, Bolton and Teare, asking the Lieutenant-Governor to appoint a commission to investigate the fairness of representation, was carried unanimously in the Legislative Council and by 12 votes to 10 in the Keys.[50] Chaired by Charles Russell, QC, and with Ramsey Moore and Sir Sydney Wadsworth as members, the Commission reported in November 1955, recommending two extra seats for Douglas and the division of Douglas into four constituencies, one extra for Ramsey and the division of the town into two constituencies and one less for each of Ayre, Glenfaba and Michael.[51] Bolton introduced a bill to implement the recommendation, albeit with Ramsey as a two-member constituency. The second and third readings in the House were approved by 15 votes to eight, the only opponents being the members representing the three sheadings losing seats. After a smooth passage in the Legislative Council, the Representation of the People Act 1956 became law in time for the 1956 general election.[52] Figure 5.1 shows the results of the redistribution.[53] In 1956 the Island had 41,390 registered voters, of whom 40 per cent were in Douglas and 7.5 per cent in Ramsey. With the passing of the 1956 Act, their share of seats in the House rose from 20.8 and 4.2 per cent to 29.2 and 8.3 per cent respectively. The number of voters per seat in Douglas fell from 3,311 to 2,365 and in Ramsey from 3,070 to 1,537; the equivalent figures after redistribution for the three sheadings which lost a seat were 1,107 in Ayre, 1,088 in Glenfaba and 1,320 in Michael.

There is a temptation in analysing these postwar elections to focus on conflict, but underlying the conflict there was a high measure of agreement on major policy. There were differences of opinion over the timing and detail of internal constitutional reform,

Figure 5.1. House of Keys Constituency Boundaries, 1956

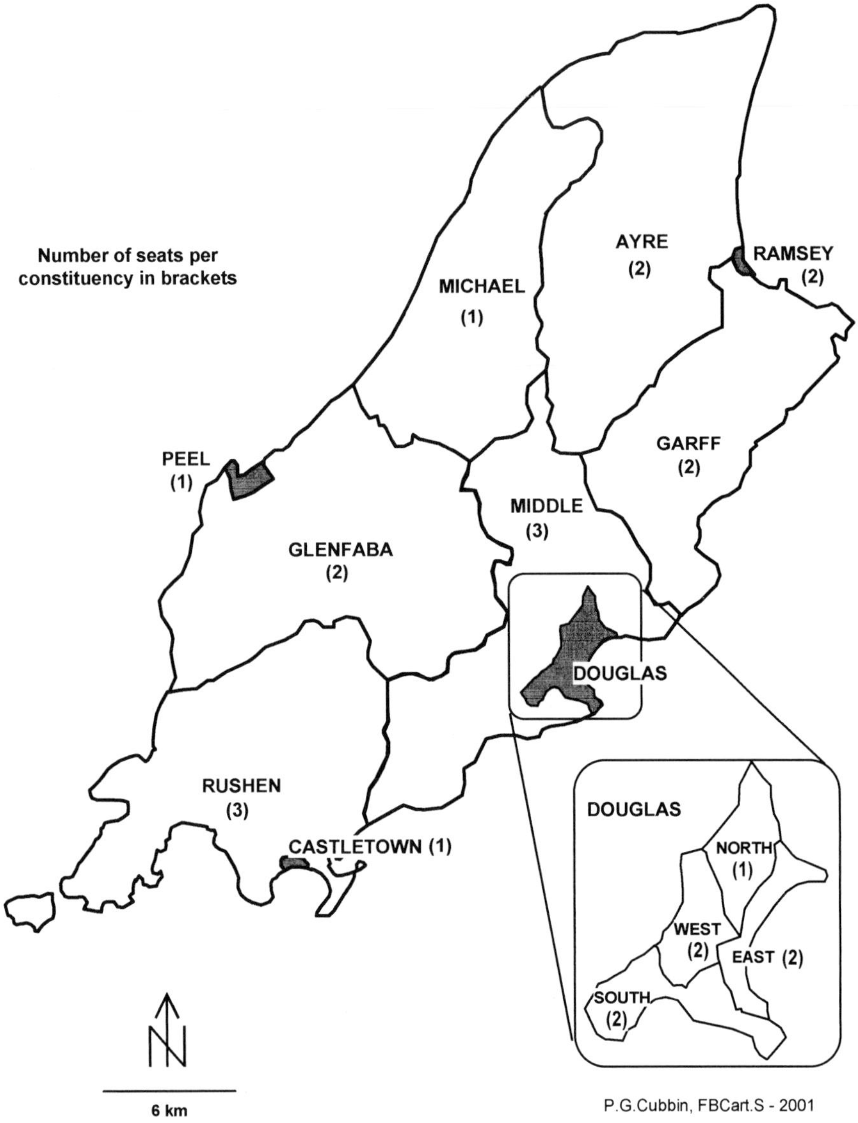

Number of seats per
constituency in brackets

AYRE
(2)

RAMSEY
(2)

MICHAEL
(1)

GARFF
(2)

PEEL
(1)

MIDDLE
(3)

GLENFABA
(2)

DOUGLAS

RUSHEN
(3)

CASTLETOWN (1)

DOUGLAS

NORTH
(1)

WEST
(2)

EAST (2)

SOUTH
(2)

6 km

P.G.Cubbin, FBCart.S - 2001

but broad support for constitutional devolution. While the UK parties were deeply divided over the role of the state, in the Isle of Man there was a consensus in favour of the development of the welfare state in line with the UK and increased economic support for Manx industries, in the case of agriculture, fisheries and light industry very much in response to developments in the UK.

Uniquely because of steps taken in 1945 to provide extra voting time for those serving in the armed forces and the merchant navy, the first postwar election commenced with voting in the constituencies in May 1946 and concluded with the announcement of results in September 1946.[54] It was a landmark election. The first for 12 years, it took place against the backcloth of increased government intervention in society during the war, the UK Labour Party's landslide victory in 1945 and the new Labour Government's commitments to a radical shift in the role of the state. In the Isle of Man MLP or Independent Labour candidates had contested all but one of the eight wartime by-elections, revealing a much higher level of MLP activity than in 1934, but with very mixed results. There was certainly no groundswell of opinion in support of the Party; even where Independent Labour or MLP candidates were successful, electoral turnout was low, 51 per cent in Garff in July 1942 and only 39.9 per cent in North Douglas in October 1943. While the resignation of Thomas Callow in 1942 paved the way for the return to the Keys of Gerald Bridson as Independent Labour member for Garff, in the by-election the following year caused by the death of sitting MLP member, Walter Cowin, the MLP candidate came a poor third to John L. Quine and runner-up, Charles Kerruish. The Party also lost its seat in Peel to an Independent, George H. Moore, following the death of Marion Shimmin in 1942. In October 1943, following Norris's elevation to the Legislative Council, former MHK, John Kelly, was elected for a second time as a member for North Douglas. Inspired by the success of Labour in the UK in July 1945, the MLP was determined to emulate that victory and fielded a record 18 candidates in nine of the 11 constituencies. In both towns and sheadings the opposition to the MLP was even more determined, pointing to the dangers of party government and to the excesses of the Labour Government in the UK. Although from constituency to constituency the detail of the conflict varied, everywhere the big issue was socialism and whether it was likely to help or injure the Island.

The only other political party to field candidates, the Douglas-based Manx People's Political Association (MPPA) was established in March 1946 with the aim of obtaining representation in the Keys for small businessmen on a private enterprise platform. Chaired by Thomas Cowin, it fielded four candidates, Bolton, Cowin and George Quine in North Douglas and George Higgins in South Douglas, each implacably opposed to the MLP and the Labour Government's emphasis on public ownership and control. Although the MPPA only contested the Douglas constituencies, its private enterprise and antisocialist stance was also adopted by most of the Independents fighting the election, whether in the towns or the sheadings.

Like most candidates, the MLP was silent on the constitutional question, the Home Secretary's promise of an executive council and further consideration of demands for the removal of Treasury control effectively removing the issue from the election. The MLP's commitments to redistribution and the abolition of plural voting were more controversial, the former attracting little support outside of Douglas and the latter little support outside of the MLP. A major part of the MLP manifesto was devoted to social reform along UK lines and few of their opponents were willing to be seen denying the Island a comprehensive social security scheme, educational reform based on the Butler Act of 1944, a national health service, a public housing programme and a commitment to full employment. The MLP's advocacy of government support for and regulation of the economy lay at the heart of the electoral conflict in 1946. While most candidates accepted the need for government help with revitalising traditional industries and promoting new industries, the MLP's proposals for greater regulation of the labour market to ensure better pay and conditions and for the public ownership of land, a national bank, transport and the public utilities were quite unacceptable to them and made the issue extremely heated. By contrast, licensing, which had been a central issue in almost every election since 1867, was scarcely mentioned, although a few candidates did stress the importance of continuing to oppose Sunday opening.

There was a record 54 candidates and contests in every constituency for the first time since the introduction of direct elections in 1866. There were 18 MLP candidates in nine constituencies, four MPPA candidates in the two Douglas constituencies, three candidates sponsored by the Ex-Servicemen's Association and 29 Independents. As in 1919 there was a low level of continuity from the old House; 16 members sought re-election and 11 were successful; two of these were immediately elevated to the Legislative Council and replaced by new members in by-elections in October 1946, making a total of 15 new members. Only two MLP members were successful, Teare in South Douglas and Kneen in Rushen. Each of the MPPA candidates and 18 Independents was also successful. After the election J. D. Qualtrough was re-elected Speaker for a second term. Three aspects of the results deserve particular comment, the poor showing of the MLP, the failure of Norris to be re-elected to the Legislative Council and the turnover of membership.

MLP performance was a function of the Party's programme and campaign, the personalities of its candidates, the social make-up of Manx society and the programmes, campaigns and personalities of opposing candidates. The misfortunes of the MLP in 1946 cannot be attributed solely to its political programme, as the controversial elements regarding public ownership had been present since 1919. What was new was the scale of the MLP campaign, creating fears of an MLP majority in the House, and the experience of the UK since Labour's victory in July 1945, causing concern lest a similar programme of state regulation and public ownership be introduced in the Isle of Man. It was these two fears, in particular, that motivated the campaigns of the MLP's opponents, especially

Awaiting election results in Athol Street, Douglas, September 1946.

the MPPA in Douglas. Historically, MLP successes have been heavily influenced by the personalities of rival candidates. This was demonstrated in 1946 by the very different results obtained by MLP candidates in the same multimember constituency, Teare topping the poll in South Douglas with 2,087 votes and Craine coming fourth with 1,603 votes, and Kneen's 1,779 votes being more than double the 836 votes gained by Mrs N. C. Shimmin in Rushen. The failure of the MLP to win a second seat in South Douglas was almost certainly the result of divisions within the Party, which resulted in the intervention of former and future MLP activist, Annie Bridson, as an Ex-Servicemen's Association candididate; it was almost certainly the three-way split of the Labour vote that accounted for the success of MPPA candidate, George Higgins. The importance of personality is also shown by the fact that there are no safe MLP seats; the Party has lost seats in every constituency where it has ever been successful, no matter how long and successful the service by the previous MLP members—in Middle in 1924 where sitting member Bridson was defeated, Rushen in 1928 after Corrin's appointment to the Legislative Council, Glenfaba in 1933 following the death of Walter Clucas, Peel in 1942 following the death of Marion Shimmin, Garff in 1942 after the death of Walter Cowin and North and South Douglas in 1946, where sitting members Kelly and Craine were defeated by MPPA candidates. The programmes, campaigns and personalities of the MLP's opponents were clearly more convincing in the eyes of the electorate. The example of Douglas is illuminating here, the MPPA candidates having already proved themselves in business and local government and going on to be four of the most effective members of the House. Finally, the Isle of Man had few areas where the social composition of the electorate alone was likely to generate majority support for a party associated so closely with the working class. As in the UK, small town, suburban and rural constituencies were much more likely to generate conservative or liberal members.

When the House decided in October 1946 to elect John Cowin and Joseph Callister and re-elect Charles Gill and Robert Cain to the Legislative Council in preference to Norris,[55] they effectively brought to an end a long and distinguished, if sometimes extremely controversial, political career. Between 1903 and 1946 Norris had campaigned consistently for constitutional, electoral and social change and had been a prime mover or supporter of many of the reforms that were implemented in the quarter of a century following his election to the House of Keys in 1919. He was the first to concede, however, in a treatise on Manx democracy published in 1945, that the Keys still had a long way to go to achieve their long-standing goal of representative and responsible government. In *This Manx Democracy* he looked forward to a new Manx National Reform League extending Manx home rule by making the branches of Tynwald more representative of the people, through the redistribution of seats for the House of Keys and the direct election of two thirds of the members of the Legislative Council, creating a responsible parliamentary executive and reducing the Lieutenant-Governor to a strictly ceremonial role.[56] Norris retired from public life in 1946 and died on 4 December 1948 at the age of 73.

The turnover of membership of the House between September 1939 and October 1946 was such that only four of the interwar generation survived, Cottier, Kneen, Qualtrough and Teare. While they continued to provide leadership in the House and Tynwald immediately after the 1946 elections, it was to the new generation of MHKs that the House would turn as it sought to achieve its goal of becoming the dominant branch of Tynwald. Six of the new intake and one unsuccessful MLP candidate were destined for leadership roles on the Executive Council during the late 1940s and the 1950s. George Higgins, a 64-year-old retired fishmonger, company director and former chair of the Education Authority, was the successful MPPA candidate in South Douglas and became one of the first members of the Executive Council in 1946. Thomas Cowin, a 47-year-old baker and confectioner, Mayor of Douglas and chair of the MPPA, was one of the three successful MPPA candidates in North Douglas; he became the first chair of the Health Services Board and in that capacity joined the Executive Council in 1949. Richard Cannell, a 45-year-old Lezayre farmer who topped the poll in Ayre, joined the Executive Council as chair of the Board of Agriculture and Fisheries in April 1950. Another of the successful MPPA candidates in North Douglas was John Bolton, a 44-year-old accountant, secretary of the Employers' Federation and a Douglas councillor since 1940; he became a member of the Executive Council in June 1951. Henry Corlett, a 50-year-old knitware manufacturer and company director who topped the poll in Glenfaba, joined the Executive Council in December 1951 as chair of the Board of Education. Jack Nivison, a 36-year-old Onchan insurance agent, also joined the Executive Council in December 1951 on succeeding Richard Kneen as chair of the Board of Social Services; one of the 16 unsuccessful MLP candidates in 1946, he became the third MLP member of the House on winning the Middle by-election in May 1948. Charles Kerruish, a 29-year-old Maughold farmer, was elected as a member for Garff and succeeded Cowin in 1955 both as chair of the Health Services Board and member of the Executive Council. Bolton, Kerruish and Nivison would be leading contributors to Manx political development over a much longer period.

In contrast to the UK Parliament at the time, the success of the conservative MPPA in Douglas and the election of conservatives in other constituencies gave the House a clear conservative majority. The MLP position in Tynwald did improve slightly with Kneen and Teare joining Corrin in the Legislative Council in 1950 and 1951 respectively, Nivison winning the Middle by-election in May 1948 following the resignation of Clifford Kniveton, Craine being re-elected in South Douglas in November 1950 following the elevation of Higgins to the Legislative Council and Thomas Moughtin winning the South Douglas by-election in April 1951 after the elevation of Teare. While the failure of the Party to contest the 1950 Ayre by-election following Cottier's elevation was understandable, the lack of a candidate in the Rushen by-election later the same year was quite remarkable given the Party's history of success in the sheading. Even with a conservative majority in the House, the five years from 1946 to 1951 saw a major transformation of the role of the state in Manx society.

There was little progress with constitutional reform and even less with electoral reform, but a plethora of legislation and action in the field of social policy. Building on developments under way during the war and following very closely the welfare reforms of the Coalition and Labour Governments, Tynwald passed legislation for the introduction of a comprehensive system of social security, free compulsory education from the age of five to 15 and the creation of the Manx NHS. The five-year period also saw massive investment in public housing, the formation of an Employment Advisory Committee of Tynwald and a commitment to full employment. Economically, Tynwald supported the visiting industry with increased funds for advertising the Island. It continued to subsidise the agricultural and fishing industries at similar levels to the UK and passed the Development of Industry Act 1949 to enable the Island to compete with the UK as it tried to diversify the economy. Finally, it is worth noting that, despite the strength of the opposition to nationalisation during the

Members of the House of Keys declared elected in September 1946, outside the Legislative Buildings. From left to right the front row (all those except the seven at the back and the Secretary to the House) comprises: T. Q. Cannell (Michael), C. Kniveton (Middle), A. S. Kelly (Ramsey), G. P. Quine and T. C. Cowin (North Douglas), A. J. Cottier (Ayre), J. D. Qualtrough (Speaker and member for Castletown), A. Moore (Rushen), A. J. Teare (South Douglas), G. H. Drummond (standing between Teare and the Secretary) (Middle), R. Kneen (Rushen), J. L. Quine (Garff), G. Higgins (South Douglas), R. C. Cannell (Ayre), J. B. Bolton (North Douglas) and H. K. Corlett (Glenfaba). From left to right the back row comprises T. G. Moore (Rushen), H. C. Kerruish (Garff), J. H. L. Cowin (Middle), T. F. Corkill (almost hidden behind the Speaker), J. Callister (Glenfaba), F. H. Crowe (Michael), J. W. Brew (Ayre) and F. B. Johnson (Secretary). G. H. Moore, the member for Peel, was absent when the photograph was taken.

election, Tynwald extended public ownership by taking over the remaining private water companies in 1946, the Crown's property interests in the Island in 1947 and Ronaldsway Airport in 1948.

The general election of 1951 came close on the heels of a change of government in the UK. As in 1946 the ideological and party conflict in the UK affected the election, the polarisation between right and left being very evident in the language of the campaign. The degree of conflict over what was best for the Island was much less than the language suggested. The MLP campaign differed from that of 1946 in two important respects; public ownership was removed from its programme and it fielded fewer candidates thereby removing possible fears of an MLP majority. Their leading opponents had been responsible for delivering a programme of reform that was broadly welcomed by the Party. Given the consensus about emulating so many UK policies, the scope for conflict was much less than in the UK and the Manx voter was often left with a choice between personalities and points of emphasis rather than fundamentally different policies. Having studied the programmes of all the candidates in the 1951 campaign, J. D. Qualtrough commented that he had 'never known such unanimity as there is in politics in the Isle of Man today … It almost boils down to a personal issue of who the electors think would make the best representative'.[57] The MLP was the only political group with a national campaign, fielding candidates in eight of the 11 constituencies. The MPPA limited its campaign to North Douglas and the fledgling Manx Conservative Association, which aspired to become a national party, ended up fielding candidates in only four constituencies. The overwhelming majority of candidates were Independents.

Reports by the Consultative and Finance Committee of the Keys and the Constitutional Development Committee of Tynwald in the months prior to the election guaranteed an airing for constitutional issues. The promise of a major devolution of power was welcomed, but only a few candidates prioritised internal reform. One who did was Charles Kerruish, who campaigned for the Lieutenant-Governor to be shorn of his political powers, a system of responsible government with the Keys in the dominant role and the reform of the Legislative Council so that two thirds of its members were indirectly elected by the Keys. Electoral reform remained a priority for the MLP and, insofar as redistribution was concerned, for most of the Douglas candidates. There was widespread satisfaction with the social reforms of the postwar period and agreement on the need to improve services and provide value for money; there were some differences of opinion over detail as evidenced for example by MLP opposition to NHS charges and the public funding of private schools. In the economic field too there was a remarkable consensus, support for subsidies to agriculture and fishing, more spending on tourism, moves to diversify the economy and improvements in the quality of transport to and within the Island.

There were 38 candidates in the 1951 election and contests in nine constituencies, J. D. Qualtrough being returned unopposed in Castletown and Cannell, J. W. Brew and E. B. C. Farrant in Ayre. There were 10 MLP candidates in eight of these nine constituencies (Michael being the exception), three MPPA candidates in North Douglas, four Conservative candidates, in Michael, Rushen and South Douglas, and 21 Independents. Continuity from the old House was high; 22 members sought re-election and 19 were successful, although Moughtin who topped the poll in South Douglas resigned almost immediately when it was disclosed that he was an undischarged bankrupt and ineligible for election; the ensuing by-election later in November 1951 brought in a sixth new member. The MLP won six seats, the MPPA three and Independents the remaining 15. By the time the MLP had won the South Douglas by-election, it had four new members in the House, George Taggart in South Douglas, a 59-year-old retired postal official, Annie D. Bridson in Garff, a 58-year-old housewife, Robert E. Cottier in Peel, a 66-year-old retired trade union official and Cecil C. Mcfee in Rushen, a 46-year-old master plumber. They joined Craine and Nivison in the Keys and Corrin, Kneen and Teare in the Legislative Council to make the largest MLP presence in Tynwald since the creation of the Party in 1919. Despite the MLP gains, the House retained its conservative majority and this changed little as a result of by-elections. However, by-elections did bring into the House three individuals who would assume leadership roles in Manx politics in the 1960s and beyond. A by-election in Ayre in November 1954 saw the return unopposed of Hubert H. Radcliffe, a 48-year-old retired member of the Royal Canadian Mounted Police; one in North Douglas in April 1955 resulted in the election of E. Clifford Irving, a 40-year-old Douglas merchant; and a third in Middle in April 1956, led to the election of William E. Quayle, a 37-year-old company manager.

During the five years from 1951 to 1956 real progress was made with both constitutional and electoral reform. At the last meeting before the dissolution of the House of Keys in 1956, Tynwald adopted the final report of its Constitutional Development Committee incorporating draft agreements that were to pave the way for a major devolution of power to the Isle of Man. Legislation in 1956 provided the first redistribution of seats in the House of Keys since 1891, although attempts to abolish the property vote were unsuccessful. The Manx welfare state was kept broadly in line with the UK, although rising unemployment did lead to the distinctively Manx Employment Act 1954. Economic support for the Manx economy was increased, agriculture benefitting from higher subsidies, investment in the electrification of farms and improved marketing, fishing from grants and loans to Manx fishermen and a fish meal factory in Peel, and light industry from funds available for diversification under the Development of Industry Act 1949. Faced with the steady decline of the tourist industry, members of the House honoured their election promises by providing government assistance for the improvement of hotels and boarding houses, supporting the establishment of a commission to investigate the industry and accepting the Commission's recommendations for a much higher level of government intervention in support of the industry. The state of the tourist industry and the Commission's far-reaching recommendations dominated the 1956 general election. Although Tynwald had accepted all but one of the Commission's 14 recommendations, they included highly controversial measures, such as increasing the powers of the Tourist Board, restoring and preserving amenities, the registration and grading of hotels and boarding houses and—the one recommendation to be rejected—the relaxation of the Island's licensing laws.

The 1956 election took place as the Island looked forward to signing two major constitutional agreements with the UK, but against a background of population decline and imbalance, a tourist industry that was struggling to hold its own and rising unemployment. Given the sure prospect of a major devolution of power, the attention of candidates turned to internal constitutional reform and the issues that had been deferred pending that devolution of power. The demand for responsible government, a reduction in the powers of the Lieutenant-Governor and the reform of the Legislative Council brought together the MLP and progressively minded Independents like Speaker Qualtrough and Charles Kerruish. There were also some demands for fewer members on boards of Tynwald. Devolution and internal reform were also seen as the means of dealing effectively with the Island's economic problems. While candidates continued to seek improvements in the welfare services, manifestos were dominated by demands and proposals for a healthier economy, a long-term programme of support for Manx agriculture, measures to revive the fishing industry, the implementation of most of the recommendations of the Visiting Industry Commission—there was some opposition to the grading of tourist accommodation and the relaxation of licensing hours—and increased incentives for light industry and economic diversification. More controversial was MLP advocacy of a publicly owned and integrated national transport system and an employment board to overhaul employment policy, although most candidates recognised the need for some intervention in these fields. The campaign also saw the first serious talk of encouraging new residents and investment by lower taxation. The conflict between left and right, while still evident in some constituencies, gave way to a much less ideological debate about how best to tackle serious economic problems.

Sir Joseph and Lady Qualtrough with their two daughters at Buckingham Palace, London, 1954. The Speaker was in London to receive a knighthood in recognition of his public service to the Isle of Man. He and Deemster Cowley were the two figures most deeply involved with the negotiations leading to the intergovernmental agreements of October 1957 and the ensuing devolution legislation. Qualtrough continued to serve as Speaker until his death in 1960.

There were 40 candidates in the 1956 election and contests in all but three of the 13 constituencies, Cannell and Radcliffe being returned unopposed in Ayre, Sir Joseph Qualtrough in Castletown—he had been knighted in 1954—and George Taggart and Robert C. Stephen representing the MLP in South Douglas. There were five other MLP candidates, in the new single seat constituency of North Douglas and the four constituencies outside of Douglas where the Party had been represented in the old House, two MPPA candidates in the new seat of West Douglas, one Conservative in Michael and 30 Independents, of whom five were Independent Progressives and one Independent Labour. The degree of continuity from the old House was slightly less than in 1951, but still quite high. Twenty-one members sought re-election and 16 were successful, including each of the five MHK members of the Executive Council and the MHK chairs of boards not represented on the Executive Council; in addition two former members were returned to the House. Five of the seven MLP candidates were successful, including sitting members, McFee, Nivison and Taggart, but the Party lost seats in Peel and Garff. The MPPA was reduced to a single member, Quine losing out to Irving and Bolton in a three way contest between sitting members in West Douglas. Eighteen Independents were elected, including three Independent Progressives, Irving in West Douglas, William B. Kaneen, a 55-year-old boarding house proprietor and local councillor, in East Douglas and Quayle in Middle. The new members included four

Sir Ambrose Dundas and members of Tynwald, July 1959. Those seated at the back are members of the Legislative Council, while those standing or seated at the front are members of the Keys. Legislative Council, from left to right: Alfred Teare, John Crellin, Deemster Bruce MacPherson, Bishop Benjamin Pollard, Sir Ambrose Dundas, Eric Davies (Government Secretary and Clerk to the Legislative Council), Deemster Sidney Kneale, Attorney General George E. Moore, Sir Ralph Stevenson, E. B. C. Farrant and George H. Moore. Keys standing, from left to right: messenger, J. L. Callister, A. H. Simcocks, J. C. Nivison, A. S. Kelly, E. N. Crowe, H. H. Radcliffe, T. F. Corkill, Cecil Teare, H. K. Corlett, Rev. H. Maddrell (chaplain), W. E. Quayle, H. C. Kerruish, G. C. Gale, W. B. Kaneen, T. A. Corkish, T. A. Coole, C. C. Mcfee, E. C. Irving, J. B. Bolton and messenger. Keys sitting, from left to right: Frank Johnson (Secretary), J. D. Qualtrough (SHK), J. L. Quine, J. E. Callister and J. M. Cain.

future members of the Executive Council. James M. Cain, a 58-year-old company director and aide de camp to the Lieutenant-Governor from 1945 to 1956, topped the poll in East Douglas. E. Norman Crowe, a 51-year-old sheep farmer, won the single seat in Michael. A. Howard Simcocks, a 40-year-old blind advocate, topped the poll in Rushen and Robert C. Stephen, a 54-year-old journalist and Douglas councillor, was returned unopposed in South Douglas. There was one other new MLP member, J. Edward Callister, a 64-year-old retired bank manager, who was successful in North Douglas and a persistent critic of government during his 15 years as an MHK. The new House retained its conservative majority, but with politicians of all political persuasions achieving high political office.

The period from 1956 to 1962 saw a reduction in the size of boards of Tynwald in 1957, a major devolution of power to the Island in 1958, the report of the MacDermott Commission on the Constitution in 1959 and major internal constitutional reforms in 1961 and 1962. While developments in social security, education, health and housing were kept broadly and for the most part uncontroversially in line with the UK, considerable attention was given to the relief of unemployment by investment in distinctively Manx development schemes. Increases in economic support for Manx industries were also delivered, agriculture and fishing benefitting from increased subsidies, grants and loans and investment in farm electrification and the kipper curing industry, and new industry being attracted under the Development of Industry Act 1949. The industry to receive most attention and support was the visiting industry, the recommendations of the Visiting Industry Commission leading directly or indirectly to a more powerful Tourist Board, increased regulation of the industry, a big increase in public investment in tourism and the nationalisation of the Manx Electric Railway (MER). Following recommendations by the Income Tax Commission, the Island embarked on a policy of lower direct taxation with the abolition of surtax in 1960.

## *The Welfare Revolution*

This period saw a remarkable degree of consensus in the area of social policy. Although local politicians had been struggling to improve social conditions for the Manx people both before and during the war, the radical shifts in policy that came after the war owed more to UK policies than to distinctly local initiatives. The Island's developing welfare state owed much of its postwar shape to the politicians and policies of the Coalition Government between 1940 and 1945, to Sir William Beveridge's 1942 report on social insurance and related services, with its emphasis on the need for a concerted attack by government on five giant social evils, physical want, disease, ignorance, squalor and idleness, and, above all, to the socialist ideology and policies of a Labour Government from 1945 to 1951 determined to eradicate those evils. The Island adapted UK policy to meet its own particular needs, but without challenging the fundamental principles underpinning the welfare revolution: social insurance backed by the state, free education up to the age of 15 and improved access to higher education, renewed emphasis on the public health role of local government, a comprehensive national health service free at the point of delivery, public sector housing for those in need and a commitment to government action to ensure full employment.

Social security policy between 1939 and 1958 followed closely that of the Coalition, Labour and Conservative Governments. The Island's politicians favoured keeping in line with the UK and the debates on legislation were marked by an almost complete absence of dissent. During the war the Island followed a series of improvements in provision initiated by the Coalition Government under Winston Churchill. Each measure was accepted without division. The Old Age and Widows Pensions Act 1940 lowered from 65 to 60 the age at which women could receive pensions and provided for the payment of supplementary pensions on proof of need, a measure which considerably reduced the number of elderly people on poor relief.[58] The Supplementary Pensions (Determination of Needs) Act 1941 meant that it would no longer be necessary to take account of the resources of the whole household in assessing individual needs.[59] The Old Age and Widows Pensions (Blind Persons) Act 1941 made blind persons eligible for supplementary pensions.[60] The National Health Insurance, Contributory Pensions and Workmen's Compensation Act 1942, as well as increasing benefits and contributions, extended the scope of the NHI scheme to include nonmanual workers earning between £250, the previous limit, and £420 a year.[61] The Blind Persons Act 1942 placed on the Health Insurance and Pensions Board the responsibility for preparing schemes for the general welfare of the blind[62] and a scheme was duly introduced during 1942, providing for the registration of the blind, financial and medical assistance and training.[63] The National Health Insurance (Disabled Persons) Supplementary Benefit Act 1945 made provision for supplementary disablement benefit and was unique among the legislation listed here in not being based on a UK measure.[64] The Family Allowances (Isle of Man) Act 1946 provided for the payment of family allowances with effect from 6 August 1946,[65] the same day as payments began in the UK under the Coalition Government's Family Allowances Act 1945. In addition to this legislation, Tynwald spent just over £35,000 on a War Distress Scheme between 1939 and 1947 by means of subsistence payments, lump sum grants and loans.[66]

Far-reaching though these wartime changes were, keeping in line with the Labour Government after 1945 ushered in a radical transformation of the Island's social security system. There were four main items of legislation, each taken through the Keys by MLP member, Richard Kneen. The Old Age, Widows and Orphans Pensions Act 1946 empowered Tynwald to increase pensions by resolution to accelerate the process of conforming with UK rates and enable changes to take effect at the same time as in the UK.[67] The first use of this power on 25 September 1946 enabled the Island's pensioners to benefit from the substantial increases in pensions introduced by the Labour Government with effect from 30 September 1946. The legislation was approved without division in either chamber and almost without debate and the basic pension rose from ten to 26 shillings.[68]

Based on the UK Act of 1946, the centrepiece of the reforms was the National Insurance (Isle of Man) Act 1948.[69] It provided for the compulsory insurance of everyone over school-leaving age and under pensionable age except for unemployed married women who were to be covered under their husband's insurance. In return for contributions, the insured would be eligible for unemployment benefit, sickness benefit, maternity benefit, widow's benefits, guardians' allowances, retirement pensions and a death grant. Notwithstanding the importance of the legislation it provoked very little debate in Tynwald. One MLC and a minority of the Keys objected to the introduction of unemployment insurance, preferring the existing Manx system,[70] but otherwise the provisions were accepted without division. Members of both chambers believed it was essential for the Island to follow the UK and maintain reciprocity. The agreed scheme was radical both in respect of the numbers compulsorily insured—23,147 in 1951, almost 42 per cent of the total population[71]—and in the scope and level of benefits, the most notable additions being benefit for uninsured married women and unemployment benefit.

The National Insurance (Industrial Injuries) Act 1948, based on a similar UK Act of 1946, replaced the Workmens' Compensation Acts of 1919 and 1946 and made industrial injury insurance compulsory for all employed persons, in return for which the insured would be eligible for greatly enhanced benefits where injury, disablement or death arose out of or in the course of employment.[72] Again, the emulation of UK policy met with the wholehearted support of Tynwald.

The fourth measure, the National Assistance Act 1951, replaced local poor relief and a range of supplementary national schemes with a single national assistance scheme and was based on the UK Act of 1948.[73] Assistance was to be primarily by way of financial aid to those in need, replacing poor relief, unemployment assistance to the uninsured, supplementary pensions and disablement benefits and allowances for the blind and those suffering from TB. Assistance in the form of residential accommodation and welfare service was to be available for the elderly and infirm. While this measure engendered considerable debate, this was due mainly to the distinctively Manx system being replaced and the extent of adaptations deemed necessary for a scheme, devised to be administered by local authorities in the UK, to operate in the Isle of Man. A handful of MHKs did speak against it on the grounds of expense and the adequacy of existing provision, but the second and third readings were approved without division.[74]

The result of the legislation passed between 1946 and 1951 was a comprehensive system of social security, providing for people in need 'from the cradle to the grave'.[75] Legislation in the 1950s provided for further increases in national insurance benefits and contributions and in family allowances in line with the UK, a process facilitated by the Old Age Pensions, Family Allowances and National Insurance (Isle of Man) Act 1956.[76] This empowered the Lieutenant-Governor, subject to the approval of Tynwald, to amend, vary or repeal enactments by order for the purpose of keeping in line with the UK. In 1954, following an initiative by MLP member, Cecil McFee, Tynwald agreed to fund a cost-of-living supplement for those in receipt of national assistance, in recognition of the higher cost of living in the Isle of Man.[77] National assistance rates remained higher than in the UK until April 1961 when the Island moved back into line with UK scales.[78] The radicalism of the changes over the period as a whole is evident in the changes in spending on the service, from £87,905 in 1938/39 to £486,824 in 1957/58, a real increase of 151 per cent.

The close links between English and Manx educational development continued both during and after the war. Wartime improvements in the funding of education, including substantial increases in teachers' salaries, were automatically followed in the Isle of Man.[79] Parliament's landmark Education Act 1944, as amended by the Education Act 1946, provided the impetus for the major educational reform of the postwar period. Tynwald's Education Act 1949 provided for free compulsory education from the age of five to 15, in primary schools up to the age of 11 and secondary schools up to the age of 15, subsidised milk and school meals and free medical inspection and treatment.[80] It required the Education Authority to provide further education opportunities for persons over compulsory school age. Manx educational institutions were to remain subject to Ministry of Education regulations and inspection by HMIs. Although there was extensive debate in Tynwald over the distinctively Manx provisions relating to educational administration, it was almost taken as read that the Island had to keep its education system 'very much in line with that on the mainland'.[81]

Aerial view of Ballakermeen Schools, Douglas, 1946. These two single-sex junior high schools were completed in 1939, requisitioned for use by the Admiralty for the duration of the war and only officially opened by the Labour Home Secretary, Chuter Ede, in October 1946. They combined with the Douglas High School for Boys at St Ninians and the Douglas High School for Girls at Park Road to form two comprehensive schools, each with its own headteacher.

In one important area the Island chose a distinctive path. Whereas nearly all UK local authorities devised educational development plans with a two tier system of secondary grammar and modern schools, the Island opted for a comprehensive system of secondary education,[82] a logical extension of the prewar practice of catering for all ability levels in the same secondary schools. In Douglas this involved new single sex junior high schools at Ballakermeen, completed in 1939 but only opened in 1946 having been requisitioned by the Admiralty for the duration of the war, and the established secondary schools at Park Road and St Ninians. Ramsey Grammar School became a comprehensive school, using its 1933 building and the new West Building, which was completed in 1940 but used by the RAF during the war and only officially opened as a school in 1947. In Castletown, Castle Rushen High School began life as a comprehensive in 1949, in converted huts that were built by the Admiralty during the war, before eventually obtaining purpose-built accommodation in 1962. In the longer term, acceptance of a comprehensive system was to insulate the Island from a major source of division in UK politics.

The cost of a greatly improved educational service was high. Tynwald's share of revenue spending on education—between two thirds and three quarters of the total[83]— increased from £63,688 in 1938/39 to £338,203 in 1957/58, a real increase of 141 per cent. During the same period Tynwald's share of capital spending, mainly in the 10 years from the end of the war, totalled £250,943.

The outstanding postwar change in the role of the state involved the creation of the Manx National Health Service in 1948. However, as this was just part of a series of changes during and immediately after the war, the reform should be placed in the broader context of public health developments. The war years saw a steady increase in the exercise of powers by the LGB and a concomitant increase in spending, usually following similar commitments by the UK authorities. From 1941 Tynwald agreed to provide a 50 per cent grant towards the cost of bringing nurses' pay into line with UK scales.[84] The Cancer Act 1942 empowered the LGB to make arrangements to fund the diagnosis and treatment of cancer.[85] In 1945 Tynwald agreed to fund a pathological service for the Island. Immediately after the war the Local Government Act 1946 empowered the LGB to provide the poor with milk, cod-liver oil, malt, medicine and medical assistance, the sick with hospital accommodation, the elderly and infirm with residential accommodation and mothers and young children with maternity care.[86] It also enabled the Board to maintain laboratories for the diagnosis and treatment of disease and a public ambulance service. As a direct result of the Act spending by the Board, which had more than doubled during the war, rose rapidly from £23,315 in 1945/46 to £50,888 in 1948/49.

The public health role of government was further extended following the recommendations of the Public Health Commission, set up before the war but not reporting under a new chair, Ramsey Johnson, until 1946.[87] The LGB assumed responsibility for the White Hoe Isolation Hospital in 1947, although it was October 1949 before Tynwald finally agreed to the payment of £10,573 to Douglas Corporation for the hospital.[88] The Local Government Act 1949 provided for the long sought appointment of an all-Island medical officer of health and increased the regulatory powers of the Board in respect of nursing homes and the appointment of local authority public health officers.[89]

The Annual Reports of the LGB are instructive as to the main achievements and outstanding problems of the period.[90] Report-worthy developments during the war included the funding by Tynwald of cheap or free milk, fruit juices and cod-liver oil for children, a successful immunisation programme against diphtheria, the introduction of free treatment for sufferers from cancer and the establishment of a pathological service under Dr C. S. Pantin. Further improvements in the public water supply were reported with the completion of the Block Eary Dam by the Northern Water Board and the Cringle Reservoir by the Southern Board. However, in 1946 the Board reported that, while the state of the Island's health was 'very satisfactory', there was a pressing need for improvements in the quality of housing, water supply, sanitation in rural areas, milk and the health of young children. Subsequent reports provide detail of progress in each of these areas. Demands for new housing had been substantially met by the late 1950s. The creation of the Isle of Man Water Board in 1946, with responsibility for the whole of the Island except Douglas, and a major programme of investment by Tynwald—£911,077 between 1946/47 and 1957/58—led to considerable improvements in water supply and sanitation. Better quality milk resulted from more rigorous inspections of farms and dairies, the regular testing of milk, the accreditation of supplies and the introduction of a scheme to eradicate TB from cattle. The health of children benefitted from all of these measures as well as from the introduction of a comprehensive health service.

The creation of the Manx National Health Service was perhaps the most radical of the postwar reforms and certainly the most expensive. The impetus was provided by the UK's National Health Service Act 1946 and a determination on the part of a majority in

Tynwald that the Island should follow the UK lead. A minority of MHKs opposed the second reading of the Manx Bill, because of the expense involved or because they believed that a better way forward would be to reform the NHI scheme to include wives and children, although they did not carry their opposition to the third reading which was approved without division.[91] Under the National Health Service (Isle of Man) Act 1948 the Health Services Board was given the responsibility for providing 'a comprehensive health service', free at the point of delivery.[92] While the existing public hospitals became the responsibility of the Board, the voluntary hospitals, unlike their counterparts in the UK, were allowed to continue as long as they cooperated 'fully' with the Board.[93] Specialist committees, with medical interest group representation, were given responsibility for making arrangements for the general medical, dental, pharmaceutical and opthalmic services. Specialist services were to be purchased from the UK. The entire service was to be funded by Tynwald. The special arrangements for the voluntary hospitals and the involvement of medical interest groups in planning the detail of implementation went a long way to avoiding the bitter conflict that had accompanied reform in the UK. There were short-term difficulties with these groups as a result of Tynwald's decision to bring the service into effect on 5 July 1948, simultaneously with the UK but before it had voted funds for the new service and before the Health Services Board had clarified with the voluntary hospitals and the medical practitioners an interim modus operandi. It was only the goodwill of the medical profession in deciding to stop charging patients on 5 July 1948 that enabled the Manx NHS to start on time.[94]

Between inauguration day and 1958 the Manx NHS developed along UK lines, providing or paying for a similar range of services, paying staff at the same rates as their UK colleagues and, after 1951,[95] imposing similar charges for dental treatment, spectacles and prescriptions. The main service remained free at the point of delivery, becoming the most expensive of all public services. In 1948/49 estimated expenditure in areas that were to become part of the comprehensive service—Tynwald's share of the cost

Thomas C. Cowin, first Chair of the Health Services Board 1949–55. Cowin was MHK for North Douglas (1946–55) and joined the Executive Council in 1949, in recognition of the importance of the new health service role.

Postwar council housing in Onchan, 1947. John Crellin, chair of the LGB, handing over the key to a tenant in Nursery Avenue, Onchan, the first council housing to be completed after the war, in the presence of Frank Johnson, chair of the Onchan Commissioners. Deemster Cowley, who as chair of the War Consultative Committee brought before Tynwald proposals for central government to assume a much more interventionist role in this area, is standing on the left.

of medical benefits under the NHI scheme, the miscellaneous health and welfare services managed by the LGB and the state hospitals at Ballamona, White Hoe and Cronk Ruagh—was approximately £80,000.[96] In 1949/50, the first full year of the NHS, revenue spending totalled £454,890, resulting partly from extra spending on established public services, but primarily from the funding of the general medical service and the three voluntary hospitals.[97] Although spending rose steadily to £606,869 by 1957/58, in real terms this constituted a nine per cent reduction on 1949/50. If critics like John Bolton had had their way, the real level of spending would have been reduced further. In response to initiatives by Bolton in 1953 and 1954, Tynwald agreed that the annual cost of the NHS was excessive given the parlous state of the Manx economy and asked the Health Services Board to investigate possible economies.[98] The Health Services Board reported that major savings were not possible without policy changes, as a result of which Tynwald agreed to ask Dundas to appoint a commission to investigate. Chaired by Deemster J. A. Cain, the Commission endorsed the plea for economies and, although Tynwald went along with this recommendation, in the final analysis it was unwilling to risk any major deviation from UK policy.[99] In contrast, the first 10 years saw very little capital spending on the service; although Tynwald did agree in principle to a £395,000 hospital modernisation programme in 1956,[100] it was two years before work got under way.

Health was in part dependent on living conditions. The war had delayed any response by government to the appalling housing conditions in the Island at the end of the interwar period. Although the Island's housing stock did not suffer the war damage experienced on the mainland, a six-year period of enforced neglect certainly exacerbated the problem. It was accepted by all concerned that the housing crisis could not be resolved without massive public investment. Before the end of the war the Government had embarked on discussions with local authorities and the UK Ministry of Health with a view to presenting proposals to Tynwald.[101] In the light of recommendations by the Commission on Agriculture in 1939,[102] consideration was also being given to the renewal of the rural housing scheme that had operated in the interwar period. The outcome was a five-pronged attack on the problem, a public authorities housing scheme, a temporary housing programme, investment in rural housing, assistance to private enterprise and a modified rent restriction scheme.

The public authorities scheme was presented to Tynwald on 6 February 1945 by the chair of the War Consultative Committee, Deemster Cowley, and amended on 17 April 1946 following advice from the Home Office that the new Labour Government was prepared to sanction higher levels of funding by Tynwald, thus making the rate burden on local authorities less of an obstacle to the development of public sector housing. Both resolutions were welcomed in Tynwald and approved unanimously.[103] There was to be no new legislation and the housing was to be solely for the working classes, a restriction which was removed in the UK in 1948 but which survived in the Isle of Man until 1955.[104] The LGB was to assume overall responsibility for housing development. Local authorities were to be invited to submit schemes for consideration by the Board and, where authorities did not submit schemes, the Board would become the functioning authority. Functioning local authorities were to receive 75 per cent of the net costs from Tynwald, the balance to be rate funded. Tynwald's share was to be five sixths for nonfunctioning town and village district authorities and 100 per cent for nonfunctioning parish authorities. The four towns, the village districts of Onchan, Port Erin and Port St Mary and the parishes of Braddan and Malew became functioning housing authorities, leaving the LGB to serve Michael and the remaining 16 parishes.[105] In 1947, following the report of a commission chaired by Ramsey Moore, Tynwald agreed that all public housing schemes should include houses or flats for the elderly.[106] Between 1945 and 31 March 1959 a total of 2,117 new houses were built, 1,221 by the local authorities and 896 by the LGB or other boards.[107] In addition, existing housing stock was maintained and upgraded as in the case of the 66 tenements built by Douglas Corporation before the First World War.[108]

Given the impossibility of meeting demand for houses overnight, the Government proposed to purchase and convert into temporary housing huts built for the armed services during the war. On 13 August 1946 Tynwald approved the development of the Royal Navy camps at Castletown and Ballasalla for this purpose[109] and on 8 July 1947 the Air Force camps at Andreas and Glen Maye.[110] The four sites provided temporary housing for 329 families, most of whom had been rehoused by 1958.[111]

Under the Rural Housing Act 1947, the LGB was required to inspect agricultural workers' dwellings, prepare improvement schemes for approval by Tynwald and authorise financial assistance in the form of grants and loans. The Board was also given the power to require owners to repair or demolish unfit dwellings.[112] The Rural Housing Act 1949 extended the Board's powers so that it could authorize and assist the construction of new dwellings.[113] Both measures were approved without division.

Between 1947 and 31 March 1959 assistance was provided in respect of 219 farmhouses and 132 agricultural workers' cottages.[114]

The assisted private enterprise scheme was approved by Tynwald on 16 October 1945.[115] It was designed to encourage individuals to build their own house with the help of grants covering 10 per cent of costs and interest-free loans covering a further 20 per cent of costs, subject to a maximum grant and loan of £250 and £500 respectively. The scheme ran for nine years, enabling the completion of 532 houses, just over one third of the 1,484 private houses built between 1945 and 31 March 1959.[116] Mortgage interest tax relief provided an additional incentive for home ownership.

The renting of private accommodation remained subject to statutory control, the major innovation being the Rent Restriction Act 1948.[117] This provided tenants with security of tenure, including the right to continue in possession of a property when a contractual agreement came to an end, and security from eviction except by court order, as well as the security against excessive rents that had been provided since 1918.

As a result of these schemes, net expenditure by Tynwald on housing, which had been virtually nil during and immediately after the war, rocketed from £197 in 1946/47 to £380,556 in 1950/51 before declining gradually as demand for housing was met. Net expenditure between 1946/47 and 1957/58 by Tynwald totalled £1,563,920, of which three quarters were in the five years from April 1947.[118] By the time Tynwald passed its Housing Act 1955, essentially a consolidation measure but also giving the LGB and local authorities the power to sell their houses, the worst of the housing crisis was over. Shortly afterwards the LGB was able to report that the demand for housing had been 'substantially met', the outstanding need being more bungalows for the elderly; a total of 3,601 houses had been built since 1945, of which 53 per cent were in the public sector and a further 17 per cent built with the help of public funds.[119]

The Isle of Man emerged from the war with a commitment to full employment. Ex-servicemen were helped to resettle, obtain training and resume apprenticeships. The raising of the school-leaving age increased opportunities for education and training after 15, and national service at the age of 18 helped alleviate the problem of youth unemployment. Social and economic reforms brought with them increased revenue and capital spending, generating employment both directly and through the multiplier effect. In spite of the best endeavours of government, however, continuing dependence on the tourist industry left the Island with persistent seasonal unemployment. The decline of tourism and the building industry in the 1950s gave rise to year-round unemployment. The recruitment of recent immigrants or personnel from outside the Island to fill job vacancies gave rise to demands for preference to be given to Manx workers. Towards the end of the 1950s increases in the number of school leavers, the result of higher birth rates during and immediately after the war, and the prospect of the end of national service in 1960 gave rise to serious concern about youth employment.

During the war Tynwald operated a scheme for the relief of unemployment based on that of the interwar period, except that relief was available throughout the year and at rates commensurate with the UK. These arrangements continued until the introduction of unemployment insurance in 1948 and, for the uninsured, until the replacement of poor relief by national assistance in 1951. The other major change after the war concerned the political management of unemployment. Following a resolution of Tynwald on 26 June 1946, the Lieutenant-Governor's Unemployment Advisory Committee was replaced by Tynwald's Employment Advisory Committee, whose role was to advise on employment policy and supervise the work of the Employment

Exchange which had been established at the onset of war.[120] Under the chair of MLP member, Alfred Teare, the Committee was instrumental in keeping unemployment high on the political agenda. Initially the chief concern was to provide for the large number of men registering unemployed during the winter season, a number which rose from 481 in 1946/47 to 2,347 in 1953/54 before settling around 2,000 for the rest of the decade. The short-term response was to maximise the public work that could be timetabled in the winter and to fund special 'development' schemes, although help was also given by the Employment Exchange to find other work both on the Island and the mainland. Between 1946 and 1958 roughly a third of the men registered were found work on the special 'development' schemes, another third found other employment, often in the UK, leaving a further third to claim unemployment benefit. The maximum numbers in receipt of benefit at any one time rose from 166 in 1946/47 to 860 (5.8 per cent of those insured) in 1953/54, falling thereafter to 667 (5.6 per cent) in 1957/58.

After 1952 male unemployment during the summer added to the problem. In 1953/54, the worst year of the decade, around 700 men were still registered unemployed in April and May, the number falling steadily during June to about 350 in July, before rising again to 500 by the end of August and the postseason peak of just over 1,200 by the end of September. As a result attention turned to the longer term strategies of diversifying the economy and regulating employment. The renewal of efforts to attract new industry are discussed below. Although by comparison the regulation of employment was an inexpensive option, over the longer term it proved an important protective measure for the Island. The Employment Act 1954 enabled the Lieutenant-Governor to regulate the engagement of workmen by employers.[121] Under the Regulation of Employment Order 1954 all male workers, except those exempted under the terms of the Order and Isle of Man workers resident in the Island for at least five years, had to obtain a work permit. Exemptions covered the police, civil servants, clergy, doctors and dentists and all employment of a temporary nature not exceeding two weeks. The Island was thus able to ensure that Manx men were given priority for employment over and above new residents and nonresidents.

Female unemployment received considerably less attention. Fewer registered unemployed during the winter—between 500 and 600 throughout the 1950s with about third of those receiving benefit—and almost none remained unemployed during the holiday season. Those who registered were helped to obtain work by the Employment Exchange and some obtained employment in the new industries, but there was no special winter work and no protection under the Employment Act 1954.

On 9 July 1957 Tynwald modified its approach to unemployment.[122] Responsibility for coordinating winter work schemes was transferred to the Board of Social Services, leaving the Employment Advisory Committee to organise training, place people in private employment, explore the possibilities of UK employment and devise means of creating new employment. In its Annual Report for 1957/58 the Committee reported that, while limited progress was being made in tackling unemployment, both seasonal and year-round unemployment were proving persistent. Moreover, it warned that matters were likely to get worse, as the numbers of children leaving school increased and national service ended, unless radical steps were taken. It fell to a Government and Tynwald with their authority greatly enhanced by the Isle of Man Act 1958 to come up with the answers.

## *Radical Change in the Economic Role of the State*

This period saw a radical transformation of the economic role of the state. War and the postwar 'emergency',[123] the influence of Keynesian thought and socialism on postwar UK policies and the conviction of Manx politicians that the Island should pursue mainstream policies very similar to those of the UK each contributed towards the transformation. Threats to the health of the Island's economy brought distinctively Manx responses, but most of these too were influenced by mainland developments. While the traditional role of government as regulator and developer of infrastructure remained important, what was really novel were the special measures taken in response to the war, the extent of intervention resulting from radical social policies and the dramatic increase in support for the local economy in response to war, UK policies and fear of the consequences of *laissez-faire*.

The circumstances of war necessitated an exceptional degree of intervention and regulation as the economy of the Island was switched to the war effort.[124] With the approval of Tynwald the UK Emergency Powers (Defence) Act 1940 was applied to the Isle of Man.[125] The requisitioning by the UK authorities of personnel, land and holiday accommodation for the armed forces, ships for the supply of goods and hotels and boarding houses for the accommodation of internees, prisoners of war and refugees was accompanied by a flood of regulations, emergency action and special legislation. While the end of the war brought a gradual relaxation of war-induced intervention, 'emergency' economic services were still being provided, albeit on a smaller scale, throughout the 1950s and other rationales for intervention quickly replaced that of war.

The welfare revolution brought with it huge increases in both revenue and capital spending as well as providing much needed employment and an increase in people's spending power. By 1958 revenue spending on the three main social services, education, health and social security had risen to over £1.4 million. Capital investment in education, housing and public health was crucial in terms of employment, as became evident in the 1950s when it proved impossible to sustain high levels of spending. Infrastructural investment on harbours, highways and local authority roads was also important in employment terms, highway and road projects in particular featuring in the Island's employment strategy. During the war spending on harbours was low compared with prewar levels, the £94,871 in the six years up to 1944/45 being largely attributable to maintenance. In the postwar years expenditure increased as a result of inflation and a series of harbour improvement projects, almost £1 million being spent in the 13 years to 1958. A similar pattern was seen with respect to highways and roads; after expenditure by Tynwald during the six war years totalling £227,831, the figure for the 13 years up to 1958 was £1,775,114.

The increase in economic support for local industries that came during and after the war was on a scale undreamt of before the war, the economic policy equivalent of the welfare revolution. Certain economic support operations were the direct result of the war and were phased out after the war; others reflected the Island's longer term concern to protect its vital industries and diversify a vulnerable economy.

During the war the Government developed an expensive programme of 'emergency services'. Their funding, which rose from £5,946 in 1939/40 to £251,995 in 1945/46, was approved wholeheartedly by a Tynwald anxious to support the war effort. The scale of spending was largely the result of following the UK in subsidising staple foods: cereals, meat, potatoes and milk products. The Island continued to follow UK policy on food subsidies after the war, as a result of which 'emergency services' expenditure remained one of the largest budget items for the rest of this period. In 1947/48 expenditure rose to £359,165 and continued to rise to £474,088 in 1951/52 before falling in the late 1950s; the figure for 1957/58 was £251,802.

Tynwald also approved less expensive schemes for the relief of economic difficulties caused by the war. The War Emergency (Relief of Rates) Act 1940 enabled local authorities to apply for grants and loans to cover the loss of rate revenue caused by the war, the grants totalling £63,983 over the seven years in which the scheme operated.[126] The War (Local Conditions) Act 1940 aimed to safeguard the assets of the tourist industry by providing loans and grants to those in financial need, the grants amounting to £69,233 over 10 years.[127] The Government also spent £35,035 on the relief of individual distress caused by the war emergency.

Prior to the war Manx agriculture had become uncompetitive. Influenced by the parlous state of much of the industry, the much higher levels of assistance to agriculture in the UK and recommendations by the Island's Commission on Agriculture in 1939, Tynwald agreed with relatively little dissent to an increase in agricultural subsidies.[128] When the UK increased the level of subsidies during the war as part of the push for food, the Island readily agreed to follow suit.[129] Similarly, when the Labour Government's Agriculture Act 1947 provided for the extension of subsidies into peacetime, the Island agreed to keep in line.[130] The developing policy of subsidisation provided the main reason for the steady rise in spending on the industry from £14,765 in 1938/39 to £80,539 in 1947/48 and the sharp rise thereafter to £209,524 in 1957/58, a real increase over the 20-year period of 543 per cent.

Having taken steps to keep agricultural prices low through a policy of subsidisation, Tynwald was urged by MLP members, Corrin and Teare, to introduce legislation to fix the price of labour. On 28 January 1941 Tynwald agreed without division to follow the UK in regulating agricultural wages.[131] The Agricultural Wages (Regulation) Act 1942 provided for a Wages Board with the task of fixing minimum wages both in agriculture generally or in any particular sector, so that farmworkers and their families could enjoy a reasonable standard of living.[132] Although passed during the war, this was not seen as a wartime measure, but a long overdue intervention by government in the interests of both a vital economic group and Manx society in general.

During this period the shape of Manx agriculture was significantly influenced by the recommendations of two commissions, the 1946 Commission on Agriculture and the 1950 Agricultural Marketing Commission.[133] Chaired by John Crellin, the former endorsed Tynwald's policy of subsidisation and recommended the derating of agricultural property and investment in the electrification of farms. The Rating and Valuation Act 1948 provided for the complete derating of agricultural land and buildings.[134] It brought the Island into line with the mainland, where derating had been introduced in 1929, and was broadly welcomed in Tynwald as 'long overdue'.[135] In 1948 Tynwald asked the Electricity Board to prepare a scheme to bring electricity to the vicinity of all Manx farms and agreed in principle to fund the extension of supplies.[136] It was left to individual farmers and landlords to pay for connection to the mains supply, but not all farmers and landlords were willing to invest. Tynwald responded with a mixture of the stick and carrot. The Agricultural Holdings and Dwellings Act 1951 empowered the Board of Agriculture and Fisheries to compel landlords to supply water and electricity to holdings where supplies were available[137] and from 1953/54 Tynwald agreed to subsidise the programme in the interests of agricultural efficiency.[138] The 1950

Marketing Commission, chaired by Henry K. Corlett, was concerned primarily with meat marketing and led directly to the abolition of private slaughterhouses and the establishment or modernisation of public abattoirs.[139]

By comparison, fishing received little support. The policy initiated in 1935 of providing interest-free loans and small grants for the purchase and equipment of boats continued. In addition, Tynwald's concern to protect what was left of a once flourishing industry led to £60,600 funding for the kipper industry between 1944 and 1958 and in 1957, following the lead of the UK, to the introduction of subsidies on fish landed and voyages undertaken.[140]

In peacetime, tourism reverted to being the Island's main source of income and employment. It provided an important part of the rationale for the increased public spending already discussed; issues of access, mobility, health and the cost of living were clearly important for the visitors. In addition, however, Tynwald felt obliged to take explicit steps to promote the industry in a rapidly changing world. After a six-year gap in funding except for the grants and loans provided under the War (Local Conditions) Act 1940, Tynwald restored funding for the industry at slightly above prewar levels. From 1946/47 to 1957/58 there was a steady increase in the funding of the Publicity Board/Tourist Board and the TT and other races from £18,885 to £84,000, a real increase over 1938/39 of 134 per cent. Much of the increase was in response to falling numbers of visitors during the 1950s. This was also the motive for other steps taken in the mid-1950s.

Low interest loans for the modernisation of tourist premises were discussed during the war by the War Consultative Committee but, with immediate postwar demand for accommodation high, 10 years were to elapse before legislation in 1954 and 1957 made such loans available.[141] Over the first four years of the scheme a total of £37,431 worth of loans were approved. Of much greater significance in the longer term was Tynwald's approval in February 1955 of a resolution by Jack Nivison proposing a commission to enquire into the state of the visiting industry.[142] The background to this initiative was mounting pressure, in particular from a tourism 'Action Group' led by Clifford Irving, for the revitalisation of the industry.[143] The Visiting Industry Commission was duly appointed by the Lieutenant-Governor in April 1955. It was chaired by an outsider, Gordon Davies, but included among its members three MHKs, Lawrence Gerrard, Charles Kerruish and Nivison. Evidence was submitted by local authorities, boards of Tynwald, interest groups (including five branches of the 'Action Group') and several individuals including Irving, who had been elected to the Keys—at the height of his tourism campaign—in the North Douglas by-election in April 1955. The Commission's report of 6 December 1955 made a series of general and detailed recommendations that proved a catalyst for a much higher level of state involvement in the industry.[144] After a lengthy debate on 17 and 18 April 1956, Tynwald accepted without dissent that steps should be taken to extend the length of the season, improve the state of the Island's natural amenities, provide support for the development of sport, register and grade hotels and boarding houses, help to improve the facilities of tourist accommodation, extend shopping hours, preserve the Manx Electric Railway (MER) and increase the powers of the Tourist Board. The Commission's proposal to liberalise the licensing laws to provide for limited Sunday opening was rejected as a result of opposition in the House of Keys.[145]

Although action was taken over the next few years in respect of each of these items, for the longer term the critical measure was the Tourist (Isle of Man) Act 1958.[146] Prior to this legislation the role of the Tourist Board, like the Publicity Board which it replaced in 1952, was restricted to publicising the Island. The 1958 Act required the Board to encourage, develop, protect, promote and facilitate tourism in the Isle of Man and to do so by means of publicity, advice, financial support, regulation and inspection, the latter in cooperation with the LGB. This was very much an enabling Act, paving the way for the development of the Tourist Board as the vehicle for a huge expansion of state involvement in the industry.

Public ownership did not assume the significance in this period that it had in the UK under the Labour Government. The Island had already shown, in the case of water supply, that it was not averse to public ownership or nationalisation where the private sector or local authorities were unable or unwilling to provide the quality of service or level of investment required. It was not surprising, therefore, given the scale of investment needed after the war, to see Tynwald assuming greater control of water

Ronaldsway Airport, 1949. Following the purchase of the airport for £200,000 in 1948, responsibility for its operation was vested in the Airports Board. Thomas C. Cowin became the first chair of the Board, combining this role with that of chair of the Health Services Board until his death in 1955.

supply. On 16 October 1946, on the initiative of the LGB and without division, Tynwald agreed to the establishment of an Isle of Man Water Board with full responsibility for public water supply outside of the Douglas area. It took over the public water undertakings of the Northern and Southern Water Boards and local authorities other than Douglas and the private undertakings of the Ramsey and Peel Water Works Companies for a total of £416,300.[147] As with the electricity industry, responsibility for the service was now shared by Douglas Corporation and a board of Tynwald. Both received subsidies from Tynwald for much needed development work after the war, a total over the 13-year period of £911,077 for improvements to water supply and drainage. In the same period the two electricity authorities received £312,078 for the supply of electricity to villages and farms. The extension of public ownership after the war to include Ronaldsway Airport, Crown lands and the Manx Electric Railway was in response to three quite different sets of circumstances. Insofar as there was an ideological motive it was again that each purchase was deemed to be in the national interest.

During the war the private airfield at Ronaldsway was taken over and developed by the Admiralty for military purposes. In 1945 it was offered to the Island for the sum of £1 million, considerably less than had been spent on it but more than the Island was prepared to pay. In March 1947 the Labour Government informed the Island that it was no longer willing to subsidise the airport and that it should be purchased and run by the Manx Government. On 8 July 1947, with scarcely a word of debate, Tynwald agreed to acquire the airport for the negotiated price of £200,000, knowing full well that it would be necessary to subsidise its operation.[148] The Isle of Man Airports Act 1948 provided for the establishment of an Airports Board to take on the responsibility for operating the airport.[149] After initial purchase and development costs, including investment in a new airport terminal which was opened in 1953,[150] every attempt was made to operate Ronaldsway as a commercial service. In the event Tynwald found itself having to approve an annual subsidy, which rose from £21,437 in 1950/51 to £97,128 in 1957/58, a real increase of 225 per cent.

In a similar vein Tynwald agreed on 21 October 1947 to purchase all the Crown's property interests in the Island for £75,000, resulting in the transfer of common lands, forest, minerals, quarries, foreshore and territorial sea.[151] The Forestry, Mines and Lands Act 1950 placed responsibility for these in the hands of a new board of Tynwald.[152] The Forestry, Mines and Lands Board was also given responsibility for forestry, under a separate Forestry Board until 1946 and the Board of Agriculture and Fisheries until 1950. Although the new Board, like its predecessors, engaged in commercial activity, gaining receipts for example from rents and the sale of trees, the nature of its work meant that some measure of public funding was taken for granted. By 1957/58 net spending by the Board had risen to £47,500, compared with £4,883 on forestry alone in 1939/40 and £15,000 on the extended service in 1951/52. Between 1952 and 1958 the Board also received £13,420 to purchase seven national glens. In supporting the purchase of Ballaglass and Tholt-y-Will Glens in 1952, Cecil McFee expressed the hope that 'this is the beginning of the day when all the glens in the Island will be publicly owned',[153] a view supported by the Visiting Commission in 1955 and reflected in the purchase of Colby and Molly Quirk's Glens in 1955, Dhoon and Laxey Glens in 1956 and Glen Helen in 1958.[154]

The needs of the tourist industry were also paramount in Tynwald's decision to purchase the MER in 1957. Faced with mounting losses and deteriorating track and rolling stock, on 14 December 1955 the MER Company notified the Government that it

Sir Ambrose Dundas at the wheel of a newly nationalised Manx Electric Tram, July 1957. With the Lieutenant-Governor is Sir Ralph Stephenson, MHK for Ramsey, who became the first chair of the Manx Electric Railways Board. The MER was purchased for £50,000.

would have to cease operations after September 1956 and that they were willing to sell the MER for £70,000.[155] After lengthy investigation, negotiation and debate and in spite of warnings by specialist advisors of the extremely high level of investment and subsidy required to restore and operate the railway, on 12 December 1956 Tynwald agreed by a substantial majority to purchase the MER for £50,000 and in doing so committed the Island to an estimated subsidy for capital renewal and maintenance of £25,000 for the next 20 years.[156] A national amenity had been preserved. It fell to the new MER Board, set up under the Manx Electric Railway Act 1957, to deliver Tynwald's ambitious plan in the face of a declining tourist industry and rapidly changing transport needs.[157]

In addition to supporting tourism, Tynwald was anxious to become less dependent on it. For many years politicians had spoken about the need to diversify the economy, but no concrete action had been taken. After the war firms interested in coming to the

The shop floor of the Ronaldsway Aircraft Company Factory, circa 1958. Opened in 1955 on a site adjacent to Ronaldsway Airport, the factory was the first to be established on the Island with help under the Development of Industry Act 1949.

Island were surprised to find that development incentives introduced by the UK in 1945 were not available in the Isle of Man. Bromet, with the full backing of Tynwald, sought to remedy this by means of the Development of Industry Act 1949.[158] The Lieutenant-Governor was given powers to provide financial assistance for the development of light industry, subject to funding not exceeding £100,000 in any one year without the approval of Tynwald. The immediate results were not very promising there being only one successful development in the first three years. Accordingly Tynwald agreed, on 21 January 1953, to offer a more attractive package of financial inducements; in addition to the loans and grants available under the 1949 Act, appropriate new industries would be offered relief from taxation and rates (other than water rates), subsidised freight and electricity, key worker housing, help in obtaining raw materials and access to sites purchased and developed by the Government.[159] By 1958 the growth of the Island's manufacturing sector was well under way, new industries accounting for the employment of 380 men and 218 women. There was, moreover, every prospect of further development and higher levels of employment in manufacturing.[160]

## *Manx Finances 1939–58*

The outstanding feature of Manx budgetary policy in the immediate postwar period was the continuing influence of UK policies both on spending and indirect taxation. Patterns of expenditure were influenced by both UK controls and the practice of emulating UK policies. The Lieutenant-Governor retained control of the Manx budget and Manx spending remained subject to UK Treasury control. Of much greater significance was Tynwald's acceptance of policies where both the focus and level of spending were determined by the UK. The most expensive services, education, health and social security, each fell into this category, as too did the policies of subsidising agriculture and food. Much other expenditure was committed under legislation modelled on that of the UK.

On the revenue side UK influence became even stronger than before the war. Indirect taxation remained the most important source of revenue, although less dominantly so. Whereas in 1938/39 it accounted for 73 per cent of total revenue and income tax only 19 per cent, by 1957/58 the figures were 60 and 30 per cent respectively. In absolute terms, of course, the revenue from indirect taxation increased dramatically as too did the UK Chancellor's influence. When purchase tax was introduced in 1941 to raise extra revenue during the war, the Island promised to keep rates in line with the UK in return for its inclusion in the Common Purse Arrangement.[161] As a result of negotiations in the 1950s and in the absence of evidence of benefit from lower duties on items other than beer, Tynwald agreed, on 9 October 1956, that all duties save those on beer should be kept in line with the UK.[162] Accordingly from 1 January 1957 only beer remained outside the Common Purse. Under the Customs Agreement of October 1957 the Island agreed not to deviate further from UK levels of taxation without prior consultation, in return for which the Common Purse Arrangement would continue. In 1957/58 the CPA accounted for 92 per cent of total customs and purchase tax revenue.

The revenue from direct taxation continued to be earmarked for purposes approved by Tynwald. In practice, however, the level of taxation remained at the level necessary to fund the shortfall in revenue from indirect taxation. Having agreed to keep in line with the UK in respect of indirect taxation, there was no scope for independence of action except in the field of direct taxation, but even here the Keys' wartime rejection of estate duties[163] and the desire to keep both income tax and surtax well below UK levels left little room for manoeuvre. Increases in direct taxation during the war were followed by temporary reductions in the late 1940s and further increases during the 1950s when the standard rate of tax was between 4s 6d and 5s (22.5 and 25 per cent). As in the interwar period expenditure from the Income Tax Fund was almost exclusively on items where the Island was determined to follow the UK, two thirds of the cost of health and social security, grants towards the cost of public housing, war-related contributions, loans and investments and part of the costs of servicing the national debt.

Taking the level of government spending over the period as a measure of the changing role of the state, Table 5.1 makes clear the magnitude of the change that occurred. There was a major increase in spending during the 1940s, especially during the middle war years, and immediately following the social and economic reforms towards the end of the decade, rising from £591,623 in 1938/39 to £2,740,004 in 1949/50, a real increase of 208 per cent. Over the next five years spending levelled out and fell well below the 1949/50 figure in real terms as spending failed to keep pace with inflation, before rising to the new height of £4,137,228 in 1957/58, a real increase over 1938/39 of 217 per cent.

## Table 5.1. Central Government Spending 1939/40 to 1957/58

| Financial Year up to 31 March | Total Expenditure £ | Expenditure at 2000 Prices £ |
| --- | --- | --- |
| 1940 | 571,204 | 14,964,973 |
| 1941 | 600,777 | 14,301,496 |
| 1942 | 898,443 | 21,066,691 |
| 1943 | 963,998 | 22,717,576 |
| 1944 | 1,739,848 | 40,795,955 |
| 1945 | 1,718,892 | 39,905,796 |
| 1946 | 1,394,891 | 32,224,771 |
| 1947 | 1,716,419 | 39,458,756 |
| 1948 | 2,044,179 | 44,383,214 |
| 1949 | 2,735,524 | 58,031,406 |
| 1950 | 2,740,004 | 55,770,041 |
| 1951 | 2,526,251 | 48,961,270 |
| 1952 | 2,895,661 | 50,184,700 |
| 1953 | 2,798,944 | 46,300,131 |
| 1954 | 2,678,250 | 43,805,457 |
| 1955 | 2,877,232 | 45,523,564 |
| 1956 | 3,277,080 | 48,707,240 |
| 1957 | 3,915,289 | 56,626,824 |
| 1958 | 4,137,228 | 57,466,096 |

The sources of the raw expenditure data were the *Accounts of the Government Treasurer* from 1939/40 to 1957/58. The level of spending at 2000 prices was calculated with the help of the Price Index supplied by Martin Caley of the Economic Affairs Division of the Manx Treasury. The real expenditure figures should be treated with caution as they are derived with the help of an index designed for a different purpose.

To avoid double counting, expenditure facilitated by borrowing is not included in the raw totals, which are the sum of expenditure from the General Revenue Account, the Income Tax Fund and the Accumulated Fund.

## *Notes*

1   For a recent account of their family background and careers before, during and after service in the Isle of Man, see Derek Winterbottom, *Governors of the Isle of Man since 1765* (Douglas, 1999), Parts 6 and 7; see also G. N. Kniveton (ed.), *A Chronicle of the Twentieth Century: The Manx Experience*, vol. 2: 1951–2000 (Douglas, 2000), pp. 14–15 and 49.

2   For an assessment of his contribution to the Island, see Kniveton, *Chronicle of the Twentieth Century*, p. 45.

3   57 *Manx Deb.*, 28 November 1939, pp. 167–68.

4   57 *Manx Deb.*, 28 November 1939, pp. 168–69. All seven members were approved by Tynwald with the chambers voting separately and agreeing six names and together to arrive at a seventh.

5   See 57 *Manx Deb.*, 28 November 1939, p. 190.

6   The details which follow are taken from 60 *Manx Deb.*, 16 April 1943, pp. 294–306.

7   60 *Manx Deb.*, 1 December 1942, p. 111.

8   For details of the two-day debate, see 61 *Manx Deb.*, 26 October 1943, pp. 32–42 and 2 November 1943, pp. 65–73.

9    *Report of the Committee of the House of Keys on the Constitution of the Isle of Man, 16 September 1943* (Douglas, 1943).

10   See 61 *Manx Deb.*, 7 December 1943, pp. 95–110 and 21 December 1943, pp. 118–29.

11   See 61 *Manx Deb.*, 18 and 25 January 1944, pp. 182–83 and 205–06; 15 and 22 February 1944, pp. 255–56 and 277.

12   61 *Manx Deb.*, 4 January 1944, pp. 141–56. See also *Petition of the House of Keys to the Home Secretary for Reforms in the Constitution of the Isle of Man*, 18 January 1944 (Douglas, 1944).

13   For the full debate, see 61 *Manx Deb.*, 4 January 1944, pp. 141–58

14   In a letter dated 28 January 1944; see HO 45/24990/689462/17.

15   In a letter dated 3 March 1944; see 61 *Manx Deb.*, 7 March 1944, p. 290.

16   *Report of the Committee of Tynwald on Manx Constitutional Development*, 23 May 1944 (Douglas, 1944).

17   61 *Manx Deb.*, 6 June 1944, pp. 462–66.

18   An attempt by MLP members to include Norris in the deputation was defeated by 14 votes to eight in the Keys and unanimously in the Council; see 62 *Manx Deb.*, 3 October 1944, pp. 16–20.

19   See *Notes of a Deputation to the Home Secretary on Proposed Reforms of the Constitution of the Isle of Man*, 17 October 1944 (Douglas, 1944).

20   *Letter … communicating the observations of the Secretary of State on the Report of the Committee of Tynwald on Manx Constitutional Development*, 20 February 1946 (Douglas, 1946); see also HO 45/24990/689462/30.

21   63 *Manx Deb.*, 9 April 1946, pp. 462–73.

22   64 *Manx Deb.*, 16 October 1946, pp. 20–21.

23   See *Report and Recommendations of the Consultative and Finance Committee …*, 26 June 1951 (Douglas, 1951) and HO 45/24990/689462/43; see also 68 *Manx Deb.*, 22 June 1951, pp. 899–902.

24   See 69 *Manx Deb.*, 17 June 1952, pp. 612–13.

25   See 70 *Manx Deb.*, 19 May 1953, pp. 674–75 and 71 *Manx Deb.*, 19 January 1954, pp. 296–306.

26   See 74 *Manx Deb.*, 27 November 1956, pp. 61–67.

27   See Appendix 7 of *Report of the Committee Appointed by Tynwald on 3 May 1949 with reference to Financial Relations between the Isle of Man and the Imperial Government*, 29 May 1949 (Douglas, 1949).

28   See *Report of the Committee appointed by Tynwald on 3 May 1949 with reference to Financial Relations between the Isle of Man and the Imperial Government*, 29 May 1949 (Douglas, 1949); *Report and Recommendations of the Consultative and Finance Committee of the House of Keys re the Constitutional Position*, 26 June 1951 (Douglas, 1951); *Further Report of the Committee Appointed By Tynwald on 3 May 1949 …*, 15 September 1951 (Douglas, 1951); *Report of the Deputation Appointed by Tynwald on 18 May 1954 to interview the Home Secretary on Matters Relative to the Constitution of Man*, 30 October 1954 (Douglas, 1954) and *Final Report of the Committee of Tynwald with Reference to the Constitutional Development of the Isle of Man*, 26 September 1956 (Douglas, 1956).

29   See Appendix B of the 1954 Report, pp. 4–6 and HO 45/24990/689462/43.

30   See 72 *Manx Deb.*, 23 November 1954, pp. 170–84.

31   See 73 *Manx Deb.*, 9 October 1956, pp. 997–1011.

32   See HO 284/17.

33   While Deemster Cowley and J. F. Crellin from the Legislative Council and Speaker Qualtrough and J. B. Bolton from the Keys served on the Committee from 1949 to 1958, the other three MHKs changed after 1951. G. H. Moore, J. L. Quine and G. P. Quine served until 1951 when they ceased to be members of the House; H. K. Corlett, H. C. Kerruish and G. Taggart replaced them when negotiations resumed in 1954.

34   *Agreement between the Governments of the United Kingdom and the Isle of Man regarding Payment*

*of an Annual Contribution to the United Kingdom Exchequer*, 30 October 1957, Cmnd. 317 (London, 1957).

35   *Statutes*, xviii, pp. 278–79.

36   *Agreement between the Governments of the United Kingdom and the Isle of Man regarding Customs and Other Matters*, 30 October 1957, Cmnd. 317 (London, 1957).

37   1958 (6 and 7 Eliz. 2), c. 1

38   *Statutes*, xviii, pp. 974–81.

39   *Statutes*, xviii, pp. 984 86.

40   *Statutes*, xviii, pp. 987–88.

41   Under the following Acts of Tynwald passed in 1946: the Isle of Man Board of Agriculture and Fisheries Act, the Isle of Man Board of Education Act, the Isle of Man Highway and Transport Board Act, the Isle of Man Local Government Board Act and the Isle of Man Board of Social Services Act; see *Statutes*, xiv, pp. 318–36.

42   Under the Isle of Man Harbours Act 1948, *Statutes*, xvii, pp. 34–39 and the Isle of Man Publicity Act 1951, *Statutes*, xviii, p. 95.

43   Under the Isle of Man Health Services Board 1948, *Statutes*, xvii, pp. 183–85.

44   Under the Forestry, Mines and Lands Act 1950, *Statutes*, xvii, pp. 923–37.

45   See 64 *Manx Deb.*, 15 October 1946, pp. 6–12 and 16 October 1946, pp. 20–21.

46   Under the House of Keys and Public Authorities Election Act 1939, *Statutes*, xv, pp. 248–49; a series of extensions of this measure were agreed by Tynwald in October 1942, October 1943 and October 1944; the Act was repealed in 1945.

47   For details of MLP attempts to abolish the property vote, see 68 *Manx Deb.*, 3 April 1951, p. 599 and 73 *Manx Deb.*, 28 February 1956, pp. 413–17. For John Bolton's attempt to require candidates to pay a deposit of £50, forfeitable unless they obtained one eighth of the votes cast divided by the number of seats in the constituency, see 68 *Manx Deb.*, 6 February 1951, pp. 331–38.

48   See *Report of the Electoral Reform Commission* (Douglas, 1944); 63 *Manx Deb.*, 15 January 1946, pp. 204–20 and 30 April 1946, p. 620.

49   By MLP members, J. C. Nivison and W. C. Craine; see 68 *Manx Deb.*, 3 April 1951, p. 597.

50   See 72 *Manx Deb.*, 14 and 15 December 1955, pp. 257–61 and 261–74.

51   See *Report of the Commission on Representation* (Douglas, 1955). The Commission also recommended the abolition of the property vote.

52   *Statutes*, xviii, pp. 712–19; for details of the debates in the Keys, see 73 *Manx Deb.*, 24 January 1956 and 28 February 1956, pp. 252–74 and 413.

53   Although nominally this distribution of seats survived until 1985, Tynwald's approval of local authority boundary extensions, for Castletown in 1966, Douglas in 1969 and 1985, Peel in 1971 and Ramsey in 1970, had the effect of increasing the size of the town constituencies at the expense of the adjacent sheading constituencies.

54   Although the House of Keys was dissolved on 1 May and the elections held between 17 and 23 May, the results were not announced until 26–28 September. The House of Keys (Votes of Members of HM Forces and the Merchant Navy) Act 1945 provided for the existing House to continue for a period of 130 days following the issue of writs for the election of new members and provided time for the overseas service vote to be cast. The Act was terminated on 4 October 1946 and the new MHKs were sworn in on 8 October 1946.

55   See 64 *Manx Deb.*, 8 October 1946, pp. 4–6.

56   *This Manx Democracy* (Douglas, 1945).

57   As quoted in the *Isle of Man Examiner*, 26 October 1951, p. 7.

58   *Statutes*, xv, pp. 462–72.

59   *Statutes*, xv, pp. 548–52.

60   *Statutes*, xv, pp. 566–67.

61   *Statutes*, xvi, pp. 34–41.

62   *Statutes*, xvi, pp. 124–25.

63 See *Twenty Second Report of the Health Insurance and Pensions Board*, 31 December 1943 (Douglas, 1944).

64 *Statutes*, xvi, pp. 281–83.

65 *Statutes*, xvi, pp. 496–516.

66 For details, see the *Annual Reports* of the National Health Insurance and Pensions Board up to 1945 and the Board of Social Services for 1946 and 1947; see also the *Accounts of the Government Treasurer* for the period.

67 *Statutes*, xvi, pp. 306–17.

68 See 63 *Manx Deb.*, 24 May 1946, p. 651 for all three readings in the Legislative Council and 11 June 1946, pp. 698–99 for the second and third readings in the Keys.

69 *Statutes*, xvii, pp. 197–286.

70 65 *Manx Deb.*, 9 December 1947, p. 187 and 2 March 1948, pp. 481–86.

71 See *Twenty Eighth Report of the Isle of Man Board of Social Services ... 1 January 1948 to 31 March 1954 ...* (Douglas, 1953), Appendix B, Table 1a.

72 *Statutes*, xvii, pp. 97–182.

73 *Statutes*, xvii, pp. 1008–60.

74 67 *Manx Deb.*, 27 June 1950, pp. 895–991 and 68 *Manx Deb.*, 28 November 1950, pp. 187–215 and 5 December 1950, pp. 218–35.

75 A phrase coined by Winston Churchill in responding to the Beveridge Report and quoted by Deemster Cowley during the second reading of the National Insurance Bill; see Nicholas Timmins, *The Five Giants: A Biography of the Welfare State* (London, 1996), p. 48 and 65 *Manx Deb.*, 9 December 1947, p. 186.

76 *Statutes*, xvii, pp. 735–37.

77 It was estimated that just under a thousand recipients of national assistance would benefit from the extra four shillings per week for married couples and two shillings for single persons; see 72 *Manx Deb.*, 18 May 1954, pp. 823–27 and 20 October 1954, pp. 68–73.

78 See 78 *Manx Deb.*, 21 February 1961, pp. 948–50.

79 See for example 62 *Manx Deb.*, 20 March 1945, pp. 387–93, when Tynwald voted an extra £15,000 to bring pay into line with the UK.

80 *Statutes*, xvii, pp. 516–645.

81 H. K. Corlett, moving the second reading of the Bill in the Keys, 65 *Manx Deb.*, 4 May 1948, p. 709.

82 See Hinton Bird, *An Island that Led: The History of Manx Education*, vol. 2 (Port St Mary, 1995), pp. 235–44 and G. N. Kniveton (ed.), *A Chronicle of the Twentieth Century: The Manx Experience*, vol. 1: 1901–50 (Douglas, 1999), pp. 219 and 227

83 See 62 *Manx Deb.*, 20 March 1945, p. 389.

84 See 59 *Manx Deb.*, 14 October 1941, pp. 43–44.

85 *Statutes*, xvi, pp. 66–69.

86 *Statutes*, xvi, pp. 344–55.

87 *Report of the Public Health Commission* (Douglas, 1946).

88 See 67 *Manx Deb.*, 26 October 1949, p. 90.

89 *Statutes*, xvii, pp. 444–70.

90 See *Summaries by the Local Government Board of its Inspector's Report as to the Public Health* for 1939 and 1940; *Annual Reports of the Local Government Board on Public Health in the Isle of Man* for 1941 to 1946 and *Report of the Isle of Man Local Government Board for the Period 1 January 1947 to 31 March 1958* (Douglas, 1960).

91 65 *Manx Deb.*, 29 June and 13 July, 1948, pp. 951–78 and 1028–54. The second reading was approved by 15 votes to eight.

92 *Statutes*, xvii, pp. 417–55.

93 The existing public hospitals were the Ballamona Mental Hospital, the White Hoe Isolation Hospital and the Cronk Ruagh Sanatorium; the voluntary hospitals were Noble's Isle of Man Hospital, the Ramsey Cottage Hospital and the Jane Crookhall Maternity Home.

94  See C. G. Pantin, *An Account of the Introduction of the Health Service on the Isle of Man in 1948* (unpublished).

95  Under the National Health Service (Isle of Man) Act 1950, *Statutes*, xvii, p. 962. This amending legislation was based on the Health Services Amendment (Northern Ireland) Act 1950.

96  A figure calculated with the help of the detailed estimates for the Social Services, Local Government and Mental Hospital Boards presented to Tynwald in March 1948; see 65 *Manx Deb.*, 16 and 17 March 1948, pp. 526–27 and 566–73.

97  The general medical service accounted for 39 per cent of the estimate and the voluntary hospitals 23 per cent; see 66 *Manx Deb.*, 26 April 1949, pp. 607–21

98  See 71 *Manx Deb.*, 17 November 1953, pp. 176–88 and 16 March 1954, pp. 509–40.

99  See 71 *Manx Deb.*, 18 May 1954, pp. 803–17 and 72 *Manx Deb.*, 17 May 1955, pp. 794–827.

100  See 73 *Manx Deb.*, 15 May 1956, pp. 740–45.

101  See 62 *Manx Deb.*, 6 February 1945, pp. 294–316 and HO 45/2298/588582/16 and 19.

102  See *Report of the Commission on Agriculture*, 28 February 1939 (Douglas, 1939)

103  62 *Manx Deb.*, 6 February 1945, pp. 294–316 and 63 *Manx Deb.*, 17 April 1946, pp. 459–61.

104  See Timmins, *The Five Giants*, p. 144. The Manx change came with the Housing Act 1955, *Statutes*, xviii, pp. 544–614.

105  See 64 *Manx Deb.*, 17 June 1947, p. 678.

106  See *Report of the Commission on the Housing and Care of Old People*, 29 January 1946 (Douglas, 1946) and 64 *Manx Deb.*, 21 January 1947, pp. 223–34.

107  *Annual Report of the Isle of Man Local Government Board for the Year ended 31 March 1959* (Douglas, 1960), p. 3.

108  On 25 October 1949 Tynwald granted a petition from the Corporation for permission to borrow £8,000 in order to supply each of these flats with a hot water supply, bath, new sink and tiled fireplace; 67 *Manx Deb.*, 26 October 1949, pp. 93–94.

109  63 *Manx Deb.*, 13 August 1946, p. 612.

110  64 *Manx Deb.*, 8 July 1947, pp. 719–20.

111  *Annual Report of the Isle of Man Local Government Board for the Year ended 31 March 1959* (Douglas, 1960), p. 3. All but 22 families had been rehoused by 1958.

112  *Statutes*, xvi, pp. 636–51.

113  *Statutes*, xvii, pp. 810–12.

114  *Report of the Isle of Man Local Government Board for the Year ended 31 March 1959* (Douglas, 1960).

115  63 *Manx Deb.*, 16 October 1945, pp. 60–62.

116  *Report of the Isle of Man Local Government Board for the Period 1 January 1947 to 31 March 1958* (Douglas, 1960), Appendix J.

117  *Statutes*, xvii, pp. 51–76. This Act was a consolidation of the English Rent Acts, undertaken by Deemster Johnson because of delays with a similar exercise in the UK.

118  These figures were derived from the *Accounts of the Government Treasurer* for the period, by adding the net expenditure incurred by the LGB on public housing to Tynwald's share of the deficiency payments on local authority housing.

119  *Report of the Isle of Man Local Government Board for the Year ended 31 March 1959* (Douglas, 1960), pp. 2–3.

120  63 *Manx Deb.*, 26 June 1946, pp. 768–69. The details which follow are taken from the Committee's Annual Reports for the period.

121  *Statutes*, xviii, pp. 418–23.

122  74 *Manx Deb.*, 9 July 1957, pp. 1041–54.

123  Emergency Services remained a major budgetary item until 1960.

124  For a journalistic review, see Kniveton, *Chronicle of the Twentieth Century*, vol. 1, pp. 156–217.

125  57 *Manx Deb.*, 12 June 1940, pp. 532–33 and 26 July 1940, p. 581.

126  *Statutes*, xv, pp. 473–75.

127 *Statutes*, xv, pp. 476–84.

128 See 56 *Manx Deb.*, 18 and 19 April 1939, pp. 427–69.

129 See comments by the Government Treasurer in *Isle of Man Estimates of Receipts and Expenditure for the Year ending 31 March 1942* (Douglas, 1941).

130 After 1947 most of the subsidy schemes operating in the Isle of Man were based on similar UK schemes; see for example, 65 *Manx Deb.*, 16 March 1948, pp. 531–45.

131 See 58 *Manx Deb.*, 28 January 1941, pp. 148–50, 17 June 1941, pp. 291–97 and 22 July 1941, pp. 351–70.

132 *Statutes*, xvi, pp. 43–50.

133 Postwar concerns over the state of Manx agriculture led to the appointment of the Commission on Agriculture; see *Report of the Commission on Agriculture 1946* (Douglas, 1946). The Agricultural Marketing Commission was set up on the initiative of the Lieutenant-Governor following a similar review in the UK; see *Second Interim Report of the Agricultural Marketing Acts Commission*, 17 July 1950 (Douglas, 1950).

134 *Statutes*, xvii, pp. 43–51.

135 65 *Manx Deb.*, 2 December 1947, pp. 169–75.

136 See 65 *Manx Deb.*, 18 February 1948, pp. 439–45.

137 *Statutes*, xvii, pp. 1063–67.

138 See 70 *Manx Deb.*, 21 April 1953, pp. 562–66 and 71 *Manx Deb.*, 15 June 1954, pp. 903–06.

139 See 68 *Manx Deb.*, 24 November 1950, pp. 165–70.

140 The support for the kipper industry was introduced on the recommendation of the 1944 Fisheries Commission, set up by Earl Granville following Tynwald's support for a resolution by the member for Peel, G. H. Moore; see 62 *Manx Deb.*, 31 October 1944, pp. 113–21, 63 *Manx Deb.*, 19 February 1946, pp. 289–90, 64 *Manx Deb.*, 18 March 1947, pp. 397–99, 66 *Manx Deb.*, 15 March 1949, pp. 451–56 and 71 *Manx Deb.*, 19 January 1954, pp. 317–18. The herring subsidy scheme was approved by Tynwald in May 1957; 74 *Manx Deb.*, 22 May 1957, pp. 783–86.

141 The Hotel and Boarding House Improvement Act 1954 and the Tourist Accommodation Improvement Act 1957; *Statutes*, xviii, pp. 351–53 and 904–08.

142 72 *Manx Deb.*, 15 February 1955, pp. 438–55.

143 See *Isle of Man Examiner*, 14 January 1955 for a report on a well-attended Action Group meeting, at which Irving presented 'The People's Plan for Progress', a programme for the development of the industry.

144 *Report of the Isle of Man Visiting Commission* (Douglas, 1955). The appendices to the Report incorporate the detailed recommendations.

145 73 *Manx Deb.*, 17 and 18 April 1956, pp. 601–47.

146 *Statutes*, xviii, pp. 957–65.

147 See 64 *Manx Deb.*, 16 October 1946, pp. 22–29. The breakdown of purchase costs was as follows: a) local authority undertakings in Laxey Village (£10,288), Michael Village (£4,593) and Marown (£3,668) and the St Johns, German and Patrick Water Board (£2,719); b) the Northern and Southern Water Boards for £117,025 and £199,607 respectively; c) the Ramsey and Peel Water Works Companies for £54,832 and £23,567 respectively. *Report of the Isle of Man Water Board for the Year ending 31 March 1948* (Douglas, 1949).

148 64 *Manx Deb.*, 8 July 1947, pp. 731–35. Prior to the vote Tynwald was informed of the full details of the negotiations leading up to the proposed purchase. For further detail, see Kniveton, *Chronicle of the Twentieth Century*, vol. 1, pp. 145, 189, 202, 209, 220–21 and 230.

149 *Statutes*, xvii, pp. 297–311.

150 See Kniveton, *Chronicle of the Twentieth Century*, vol. 2, p. 20.

151 65 *Manx Deb.*, 21 October 1947, pp. 14–17.

152 *Statutes*, xvii, pp. 923–37.

153 70 *Manx Deb.*, 21 October 1952, p. 13. The cost of the two glens was £2,250.

154 For details see the *Annual Reports of the Forestry, Mines and Lands Board* for the period. Colby

Glen was acquired by the Forestry Board in 1955 from Edward and Ethel Gawne for the sum of £20 (my thanks for the Colby Glen details are due to Robin Pollard, the Island's Chief Forestry Officer, in a letter dated 12 April 2000). Molly Quirk's Glen was transferred to the Board by the Trustees of S. A. Quirk in return for a payment of £100. The adjacent Bibaloe Walk was a present to the nation by ex-Deemster Ramsey Johnson in 1956. Dhoon Glen was purchased for £2,000 in 1955; see 73 *Manx Deb.*, 6 December 1955, pp. 163–64. Laxey Glen was bought for £4,750 in 1956; see 73 *Manx Deb.*, 9 October 1956, pp. 979–83. Glen Helen was transferred to the Board at a cost of £4,300; see 75 *Manx Deb.*, 20 May 1958, pp. 880–82.

155  See 73 *Manx Deb.*, 20 June 1956, pp. 882–912.
156  74 *Manx Deb.*, 12 December 1956, pp. 153–89; see also Kniveton, *Chronicle of the Twentieth Century*, vol. 2, p. 35.
157  *Statutes*, xviii, pp. 823–43.
158  *Statutes*, xvii, pp. 423–24.
159  70 *Manx Deb.*, 21 January 1953, pp. 321–30.
160  See *Report of the Employment Advisory Committee for the Year ended 31 March 1958* (Douglas, 1958).
161  Under the terms of the Purchase Tax Act 1940, *Statutes*, xv, pp. 488–97.
162  73 *Manx Deb.*, 9 October 1956, pp. 997–1101
163  See 59 *Manx Deb.*, 7 July 1942, pp. 382–90.

# CHAPTER SIX

# Towards Island
# Self-Government 1958–81

The Isle of Man Act 1958 provided for a major devolution of legislative power to Tynwald. However it did not meet the aspirations of the House of Keys for more democratic and responsible government. The period between 1958 and 1981 was marked by a lengthy but ultimately successful constitutional campaign by MHKs for a transfer of power within the Island, from the Lieutenant-Governor to Tynwald and within Tynwald to the elected chamber. Simultaneously, the Island was able to safeguard its newly won constitutional status in the face of threats posed by UK policies on devolution and Europe.

Political leadership was provided by Lieutenant-Governors and the most influential figures in the Legislative Council and the House of Keys, major changes in the balance of power between the Lieutenant-Governor and the branches of Tynwald helping to shape their respective roles. Four Lieutenant-Governors presided over Manx politics during this period,[1] coming to the Island following a successful career in the colonial or armed services. Sir Ronald Garvey (1959–66) was born in 1903. Immediately prior to retirement from the colonial service, between 1952 and 1958, he was Governor of Fiji. His successor, Sir Peter Stallard (1966–73), was born in 1915. His appointment followed a five-year stint as Governor of British Honduras. The third appointee was Sir John Paul (1974–80). Born in 1916, he arrived in the Island in 1974 after presiding over the independence of the Bahamas. Sir Nigel Cecil (1980–85), who was born in 1925, succeeded Paul in 1980 after a distinguished career in the Royal Navy. In 1975 he was promoted to the rank of Rear Admiral and served as the last Commander of the British Forces in Malta from 1975 until his retirement in 1979. This quartet did not preside over the independence of the Isle of Man, but it was during their administrations that the office of Lieutenant-Governor was shorn of most of its political power and executive authority placed firmly in the hands of politicians responsible to Tynwald.

Those politicians were recruited from both the Legislative Council and the House of Keys. While this period saw the end of equal bicameralism in the Manx legislature, there was no immediate or willing acceptance by MLCs of political inferiority and members continued to play an important role in the legislative process, the Executive Council and boards of Tynwald. The Attorney General—George E. Moore (1957–62), David Lay (1963–72), Arthur C. Luft (1972–74), John W. Corrin (1974–80) and T. William Cain (1980–93)—remained a key figure throughout the period, as too did the two Deemsters until their removal from the legislature in 1965 and 1975 respectively—

Sydney J. Kneale (1958–69), Bruce W. MacPherson (1958–63) and George E. Moore (1963–65 as Second Deemster and 1969–75).

Increasingly, however, the politically influential MLCs were the appointed (until their removal in 1969) and indirectly elected members. It was from this group, usually the Island's elder statesmen, that members were recruited to the Executive Council (the bracketed dates refer to membership of the Executive Council)—Sir Ralph Stevenson (1955–69), George Moore (1958–62), Harold Nicholls (1962–66), Cecil McFee (1962–66), John Bolton, who received a knighthood in 1977 (1966–79), Jack Nivison (1969–72), Hubert Radcliffe (1963–66), Norman Crowe (1970–78), R. Edward S. Kerruish (1978–85) and Percy Radcliffe (1980–85).

In the House of Keys the long-serving Speaker, Sir Joseph Qualtrough, died in 1960 and was replaced by Henry K. Corlett. However, Corlett's defeat in the 1962 general election paved the way for the election of Charles Kerruish, like Qualtrough an

Sir Ronald Garvey, Lieutenant-Governor 1959–66, welcoming the Home Secretary, Henry Brooke, at Ronaldsway, October 1963. The Home Secretary was on the Island to familiarise himself with the Island's problems, the background to the visit being the closure of Fleetwood in 1961, the UK veto of Manx plans for a powerful commercial radio station in 1962 and the pending closure of Jurby RAF station.

extremely influential figure as Speaker, if altogether more controversial. He was a member of Executive Council from 1955 to 1968, the leading chair of select committees of Tynwald and the recipient of a knighthood in 1979. Two other members of the 1946/48 intake, Bolton and Nivison, were also leading MHKs before being elevated to the Legislative Council; both served on the Executive Council as MHKs, Bolton from 1951 to 1962 and Nivison from 1951 to 1960.

Almost all the other leading MHKs of this period, defined as those elected at some stage to the Executive Council, were members first elected in the mid-1950s—J. Robert Creer (1975–76 and 1978–81), Norman Crowe (1964–70), Clifford Irving (1968–81), Howard Simcocks (1958–62 and 1970–74) and Robert Stephen (1962–64)—or the early to mid-1960s—R. G. J. Ian Anderson (1970–82), Edward Kerruish (1967–70), G. Victor H. Kneale (1970–74), Roy MacDonald (1975–78) and Percy Radcliffe (1967–80). The two exceptions were Noel Cringle, first elected to the Keys in 1974, the

Sir Peter Stallard, Lieutenant-Governor 1966–73, at the Tynwald Ceremony, July 1967. The Lieutenant-Governor is seen handing the staffs of office to the Island's six coroners.

Sir John Paul, Lieutenant-Governor 1974–80, at his desk for a meeting with the press shortly after appointment in January 1974.

chair of the Board of Social Security in 1976 and the Executive Council in 1978 (1978–81), and Edgar R. Mann, elected to the House in 1976 and to the chair of the Board of Agriculture and membership of the Executive Council in 1980 (1980–85).

## The Confirmation of Special Status

With the passing of the Isle of Man Act 1958, the Island's freedom to legislate included virtually all domestic matters. The next two decades were marked by campaigns to safeguard that position. Given the consensus between the UK and the Isle of Man over the extent of devolution delivered by 1958, one might have expected the issue to lose some of its prominence. Far from it, controversies surrounding the issue continued to dominate the relationship between the two territories. The period saw three further transfers of authority and concerted attempts by Tynwald to safeguard its autonomy in the face of the threats posed by UK foreign policy and a major review of the Island's relationship with the UK.

In 1966 the UK used the occasion of converting the Post Office into a public corporation to offer the Island the opportunity to assume responsibilty for its own postal and telecommunications services. Although Tynwald turned down the offer on 18 October 1967, the UK Post Office Act 1969 provided the Island with the option of a transfer of control.[2] By that time Tynwald had had second thoughts and, on 16 October 1968, accepted a resolution by Speaker Kerruish for the appointment of a select committee to investigate the desirability of the Isle of Man assuming responsibility for a) postal services and b) telecommunication services. The Committee was chaired by the Speaker and, after four years of negotiations and a series of reports from the Committee, Tynwald agreed to assume responsibility for its own postal services.[3] Initially the UK authorities had insisted on both postal and telecommunications services being transferred or no transfer at all, but in the course of protracted negotiations agreed to deal with the two separately. From Tynwald's point of view this was a major concession. While the transfer of postal services was seen as having tremendous potential in financial and publicity terms, the telecommunications sector, which was undergoing a major programme of capital intensive modernisation, held out the prospect of a serious financial and technical burden. The Isle of Man Postal Authority commenced operations on 5 July 1973.[4] The cost of transferring the buildings, equipment and materials from the UK to the Authority was £148,624 and this was paid out of the Authority's surplus income in the first year of operations.[5]

On 18 January 1977 Tynwald supported a futher resolution moved by Speaker Kerruish. Anxious to see the Island making greater use of the financial powers gained nearly 20 years earlier, he proposed a select committee evaluation of the Common Purse Agreement. The Committee was chaired by Percy Radcliffe. Its main recommendations, the outcome of extensive discussions between the two governments and accepted in full by Tynwald, were that a new Customs and Excise Agreement replace the CPA with effect from 1 April 1980 and that an Isle of Man Customs and Excise Service be established with responsibility in the Isle of Man for functions hitherto carried out by the UK. Interestingly Tynwald's acceptance of the recommendations on 10 July 1979, by 18 votes to three in the Keys and seven votes to two in the Council, came after a decision earlier during the same sitting to follow the Conservative Government's dramatic increase in VAT from eight to 15 per cent.[6] While the earlier decision was a necessary formality under the Common Purse Agreement, it did highlight the Island's lack of freedom in respect of indirect taxation. The CEA was duly signed by the Home Secretary for the UK and the Chairman of the Finance Board for the Island.[7] This was followed by enabling legislation at Westminster, the Isle of Man Act 1979, and in Tynwald by the Customs and Excise (Transfer of Functions) Act 1979.[8] The immediate effect of the changes was to symbolise the Island's fiscal freedom, as under the Agreement the Island agreed to keep in line with UK rates of duty and indirect taxation, save in respect of beer, and to ensure that the Manx Customs and Excise Service corresponded to that of the UK with regard to management, collection and enforcement. New differences between the UK and the Isle of Man were to be subject to a period of three months notice and the agreement of both governments. The Agreement was subject to review or termination at the behest of either party. Many in the tourist industry and a minority in Tynwald were disappointed with it, having seen differences in VAT rates or complete abrogation as a means of revitalising tourism and the economy generally. The issue continued to exercise the minds of the Island's politicians throughout the 1980s and 1990s.

The third extension of Manx legislative responsibility was in the field of merchant shipping, where the need for comprehensive legislation covering the management and control of merchant shipping in Manx waters led to an intergovernmental agreement that Tynwald should meet this need and bring the Island into line with the International Convention on Safety of Shipping at Sea. The result was a package of measures, replacing and updating a mixture of UK and Manx legislation and transferring to the Manx Harbour Board powers previously exercised by UK authorities. Relevant UK legislation was to be repealed by Order in Council. According to Harbour Board member, Edmund Lowey, the purpose of the package was to empower the Board to control the operation and standards of shipping using Manx ports and Manx territorial waters and to establish a Manx register of shipping with standards at least as high as those required by the UK.[9] The measures were noncontroversial, but provided a regulatory framework both for safety in Manx waters and in the longer term the development of the Island as a centre of excellence for shipping. The Merchant Shipping (Passenger Ships Survey) Act 1979 provided for an annual survey of all ships plying Manx waters with a view to ensuring minimum safety standards. The Merchant Shipping (Detention of Ships) Act 1979 transferred to the Island the powers to detain ships if found unsafe and to require appropriate action to render them safe; these powers were previously exercised by UK authorities under Parliament's Merchant Shipping Act 1947. The Merchant Shipping (Masters and Seamen) Act 1979 transferred to the Harbour Board the powers to control employment conditions on ships using Manx waters. The Shipping Casualties (Inquiries, Investigations and Reports) Act 1979 empowered the Board, with Tynwald's approval, to regulate arrangements for investigation of shipping casualties, in line with UK and international standards. The Anchors and Chain Cables Act 1979 empowered the Harbour Board to regulate the standards applying to anchors and chains. The Wreck and Salvage (Ships and Aircraft) Act 1979 was a consolidation measure and the Merchant Shipping (Load Lines) Act 1981, which brought the Island into line with UK legislation on the subject, completed the package.[10]

After 1978, Tynwald's Constitutional Issues Committee, established to consider ways of maximising self-government, undertook a review of the functions still administered for the Island wholly or partly by the UK under Acts of Parliament. Reporting a few months before the 1981 general election, the Committee noted with approval that a committee of Executive Council was currently exploring the possible transfer of responsibility for telecommunications and that further merchant shipping functions were in the process of being transferred. In addition it recommended the devolution of licensing powers in the controversial area of wireless telegraphy, further exploration of the potential for devolution of responsibility for civil aviation and the extension of Manx territorial waters to 12 miles. Tynwald accepted the Committee's recommendations in July 1981, but no further progress was made before the election.[11]

The controversies over commercial broadcasting, the European Economic Community and judicial corporal punishment illustrated well the vulnerability of the Island in areas transcending the boundaries of the Isle of Man either physically or as a result of international agreements entered into by the UK on the Island's behalf. The Island's struggle in the 1960s for permission to establish a powerful commercial radio station resulted in one of the few cases this century of the Royal Assent being refused to an Act of Tynwald, the single instance since the war of UK legislation being extended

Percy Radcliffe, Chair of the Finance Board 1976–81 (centre), with members of the Finance Board and customs officials on the occasion of the opening of the new Manx Customs House in December 1981. The opening was seen as the final stage in the transfer of responsibility for the customs service from the UK, initiated under the 1979 Customs and Excise Agreement and some 21 months after the formal transfer in April 1980.

to the Isle of Man without the concurrence of Tynwald, the establishment of constitutional machinery for the resolution of intergovernmental disputes and demands by Tynwald for a formal division of legislative competence between Westminster and Tynwald.[12] The Wireless Telegraphy (Isle of Man) Act 1962 was refused the Royal Assent on the grounds that broadcasting could not be considered 'solely domestic to the Isle of Man' and that Tynwald's plans were incompatible both with UK policy and international obligations accepted with membership of the International Telecommunications Union. The Island had to be satisfied with a strictly local commercial station. But Manx Radio had hardly commenced operations, in June 1964, when on Tynwald Day in 1964 the high-powered Radio Caroline began transmitting off the Manx coast in defiance of the regulations of the ITU. Early in 1965 the Island was asked by the Home Office to cooperate with the European members of the ITU in combatting pirate radio stations. However, by the time the necessary legislation reached the House of Keys in March 1967, Radio Caroline was proving an extremely valuable medium of publicity for the Island and there was a growing body of Manx opinion in favour of supporting Caroline. On 7 March 1967 the Keys discharged the Marine etc. Broadcasting (Offences) Bill at second reading by an overwhelming majority of 19 votes to three. The opposition to the Bill was led by Clifford Irving who argued forcefully that he was only prepared to torpedo Radio Caroline in return for support from the UK authorities for a powerful commercial radio station.[13] Despite warnings that UK legislation would be extended to the Island if it did not pass its own, members were unwilling to pass the Bill without first being granted greater transmitting power for Manx Radio.

On 19 April 1967 Tynwald, voting as a single body, agreed to petition the Queen not to apply the measure to the Island against the expressed wishes of Tynwald. The resolution, in the names of Howard Simcocks and Clifford Irving, had previously been defeated in Tynwald by an adverse vote in the Legislative Council, but voting as a single body the resolution was carried by 22 votes to eight.[14] On 5 June 1967, a delegation of five members of Tynwald, led by Simcocks, met a committee of the Privy Council, comprising the Lord President of the Council and three other UK Ministers. Not surprisingly given the political composition of the Committee, the petition was rejected and on 1 September 1967 the UK Marine etc. Broadcasting (Offences) Act 1967 was duly applied to the Island without the approval of Tynwald.[15] The Home Office reiterated that this was not a domestic matter for the Isle of Man and that the UK was internationally obligated to outlaw pirate radio stations. The response of the House of Keys, acting alone because of opposition in the Legislative Council, was to reject as 'incompatible with the freedom of a self-governing democracy the enforcement by Orders in Council of the domestic policies of Her Majesty's Government in the United Kingdom on the people of the Isle of Man against their wishes, as expressed by their elected representatives in Tynwald' and to seek the intervention on their behalf by the Commonwealth Prime Ministers.[16] While there was no way the UK authorities were going to countenance such intervention, the Keys' resolve did elicit a positive response from the Home Office. On 3 September 1967 the newly appointed Minister of State at the Home Office, Lord Stonham, arrived in the Isle of Man with instructions from the Home Secretary to establish a joint working party to examine the constitutional relationship between the UK and the Isle of Man, with a view to resolving differences of opinion over what was and what was not domestic to the Isle of Man. The following week Tynwald agreed to cooperate and appointed John Bolton from the Legislative

Arriving at Tynwald on 8 August 1967 for the so-called UDI debate, occasioned by the UK decision to impose Parliament's Marine etc. Broadcasting (Offences) Act on the Isle of Man against the wishes of Tynwald.

Top: Edward Callister, Labour MHK for North Douglas. At the front of the queue for the public gallery is a young Miles Walker attending his first ever Tynwald debate.

Bottom: Howard Simcocks, a blind advocate and MHK for Rushen, escorted by Mrs Julia Clague.

Top: The outlawed Radio Caroline, September 1967. Radio Caroline was outlawed for broadcasting in defiance of the International Telecommunications Union. The constitutional conflict between the Isle of Man and the UK over Radio Caroline was in large part the result of the UK's refusal to allow Manx Radio an equivalent transmitting power.

Bottom: Lord Stonham, Minister of State at the Home Office, with demonstrators, September 1967. Following the constitutional crisis over commercial broadcasting, Lord Stonham was despatched to the Island to seek the its participation in an intergovernmental review of the constitutional relationship between the Isle of Man and the UK.

Council and the Speaker, Norman Crowe, Edward Kerruish and William Quayle from the Keys to serve on the Joint Working Party.[17]

The Joint Working Party met on seven occasions between 6 November 1967 and 18 April 1969. The main result of its one report in 1969[18] was the establishment of the Standing Committee on the Common Interests of the Isle of Man and the United Kingdom, comprising three members elected by Tynwald and three members of the UK Government with a joint secretariat. It was to meet in London and Douglas alternately at six-monthly intervals or at the request of either side. Its terms of reference were to discuss matters of mutual concern and keep under review the practical working relationship between the two governments and those areas where the UK and the Island should pursue similar policies. The first members to serve on the Standing Committee, from its inception in July 1969 to the general election in 1971, were Bolton, Crowe and Edward Kerruish. After the election Bolton was joined by Speaker Kerruish and Percy Radcliffe and they represented the Island until 1977, when Bolton was replaced by the new chair of Executive Council, Clifford Irving. While the outcome of meetings over the first 12 years was mixed, favourable in connection with the EEC, completely unproductive in respect of Manx Radio, the new machinery helped create a better working relationship between the UK Government and Tynwald.

The Stonham Working Party did not resolve the problem of defining what was domestic to the Island. When the Isle of Man was included in the terms of reference of the Labour Government's Commission on the Constitution in 1969, Tynwald sought a formal agreement reserving to Tynwald the right to legislate on all domestic matters, including the purely local aspects of matters transcending the frontiers of the Island.[19] The Kilbrandon Commission saw this as a 'wholly impracticable' means of reconciling the Island's acknowledged autonomy in internal affairs with the UK's responsibility for international relations.[20] The problem of defining what was domestic to the Island was again evident in the negotiations with the UK on Tynwald's demands for the delegation to the Lieutenant-Governor of responsibility for granting the Royal Assent to Manx legislation. The demands were first made during the Stonham Working Party discussions and were identified in the Working Party Report in 1969 as worthy of further consideration. Although the UK saw no objection in principle, delegation could not be the vehicle for the Island to circumvent the UK's responsibility for matters that transcended the frontiers of the Island and would be inappropriate as long as the Lieutenant-Governor was closely involved in earlier stages of the legislative process. It was 12 years after Stonham before the principle was converted into reality. The transfer of gubernatorial power between 1976 and 1981 and further pressure from Tynwald during this period culminated in successful negotiations between Tynwald's Constitutional Issues Committee and the UK authorities. The Royal Assent to Legislation (Isle of Man) Order was made on 23 September 1981. It gave the Lieutenant-Governor powers to assent to Manx legislation, but subject to three qualifications, which taken together made it clear that Home Office approval would still be required for all Manx legislation. Under the Order the Lieutenant-Governor may be required by the Home Secretary to reserve particular bills for the traditional Royal Assent procedure; he is obliged to consult the Secretary of State about the possible reservation of bills dealing wholly or partly with international relations, defence, nationality, citizenship, the powers and remuneration of the Lieutenant-Governor and the Island's constitutional relationship with the UK; in addition he may reserve for the Crown's pleasure any bill he feels should be reserved.[21] The delegation of the Royal

Assent went a long way towards removing the often irritating delays in the grant of the Royal Assent before 1981, but it did little to meet Tynwald's aspirations for greater autonomy in those areas that in the view of the UK transcended the frontiers of the Island.

Without doubt the most serious threat to the Island's special relationship with the UK arose following the UK's application to join the European Economic Community.[22] During the negotiations from 1961–63 and 1966–67 Tynwald was consulted by the Home Office, who made it clear that while arrangements might be made to exclude the Isle of Man from the EEC, there was very little prospect of negotiating special terms. In the 1960s the choice facing the Island seemed to be one between evils. Entry with the UK would jeopardise rights of self-government, the source of the Island's developing prosperity, while exclusion appeared to threaten serious uncertainty for an economy and society so closely integrated with the UK. Thanks to France's vetoes of UK membership in January 1963 and November 1967, the Island did not have to face up to the dilemma. When the way to reopening negotiations was clear following De Gaulle's resignation as French President in 1969, the political climate proved much more favourable to the special problems facing dependent territories. In April 1970 Tynwald approved a resolution in the names of Speaker Kerruish and Clifford Irving affirming Tynwald's right to self-determination and appointing a five-member committee to undertake negotiations on Tynwald's behalf.[23] Chaired by Deemster Moore and with Bolton, Crowe, Irving and the Speaker as members, the Committee was assured by the new Conservative Government that Tynwald would indeed be free to determine its own future.[24] In the event, the UK was successful in negotiating special terms for both the Channel Islands and the Isle of Man. At a meeting on 28 July 1971 the EEC negotiators indicated that they were willing to adapt Article 227 of the Treaty of Rome to accommodate the islands' concerns. On 9 November 1971 they proposed special terms under which the islands would be included in the EEC solely for the purpose of free movement of industrial and agricultural products. To that end they would be required to apply the common external tariff and the agricultural levies on imports from third countries. Other parts of the Treaty of Rome would not apply. Tynwald approved these terms on 14 December 1971, well satisfied that a major threat to its special relationship with the UK had been avoided.[25]

Even though the Island had every reason to be pleased with these terms, the impact of the EEC during the 1970s was much greater than might have been expected from a simple reading of Protocol 3 to the Treaty of Accession, which provided the constitutional framework regulating the Island's relationship with the European Communities. Article 1 (1) of the Protocol provided for EEC rules on customs and quantitative restrictions to apply to the Island, making it part of a European customs union. Although this Article did not include excise duties and value-added tax, the Island became subject to EEC directives on VAT by virtue of its agreements with the UK on indirect taxation, the Common Purse Agreement up to 1979 and the Customs and Excise Agreement thereafter. Protectionist measures designed to shield local industries from competition elsewhere in the EEC were not permitted unless special sanction was given under Article 5 of the Protocol. Agriculture was the industry most directly affected, being subject to a special regime under Article 1(2) of the Protocol. This required free trade in agricultural products, including fish, and associated regulations laid down that government support for the industry must not exceed UK levels and that EEC rules relating to veterinary practice, animal health, plant health, seeds, food, feeding stuffs and marketing standards must be applied in respect of agricultural products imported into or exported from the Island. The Island was not subject to the financial provisions of the Common Agricultural Policy and was under no treaty obligation to provide support for the industry at particular levels; in practice, however, the Island continued its postwar policy of agricultural support broadly equivalent to that available in the UK. The EEC rules regarding the free movement of persons did not apply to the Isle of Man with the result that the Island was able to retain and extend its work permit system. The only proviso was that the Island treat all European persons equally. Although other aspects of EEC policy did not apply to the Island, the Island's tradition of emulating UK policies meant that gradually EEC policies and practices began to emerge as one of the major sources of Manx policy. In October 1981, with nearly nine years of experience under Protocol 3, Tynwald's Select Committee on the Common Market reported to Tynwald on the options of sticking with Protocol 3 or seeking one of the alternatives of full membership, renegotiation or withdrawal. The Report, which came down unequivocally in support of the status quo, was accepted by Tynwald on 14 October 1981 without debate or division.[26]

Tynwald was far less happy with the decision of the European Court of Human Rights in the case of *Anthony M. Tyrer v. the United Kingdom* on 25 April 1978.[27] When the European Convention on Human Rights was extended to the Isle of Man in 1951, few could have anticipated that it would be used in the 1970s to challenge the validity of Manx law concerning judicial corporal punishment and question once again the boundaries of domestic law. Even as late as 1969 when Tynwald was asked to approve an

Pro-birch protest march on Prospect Hill, 17 January 1978. The protestors, who were welcomed by Ian Anderson and other politicians outside the Government Offices and Legislative Buildings, were campaigning to preserve judicial corporal punishment in the Isle of Man at a time when Manx laws were seen to be under threat from the European Court of Human Rights.

extension of the individual's rights of petition under the Convention, members had no inkling of the controversy that was about to unfold and approved the resolution unanimously and without debate.[28] When in October 1976 members were asked to approve a further extension, the reaction was very different; with the Tyrer case under consideration by the European Commission on Human Rights, Tynwald approved the extension, but with an amendment moved by the Speaker seeking to exclude the right of petition against the imposition by a Manx court of a sentence of corporal punishment.[29] This highly sensitive case involved an appeal to the Court at Strasbourg against the UK for allowing judicial corporal punishment in the Isle of Man. The Court confirmed the preliminary opinion of the European Commission of Human Rights that such punishment was 'degrading' within the meaning of Article 3 of the Convention. By implication the Acts of Tynwald providing for corporal punishment were declared incompatible with the Convention. Tynwald saw the decision as a gross infringement of the Island's freedom to manage its own affairs and intensified its search for a formula that might facilitate the retention of judicial corporal punishment. Consideration was given to withdrawal from the European Convention and formulating a Manx Bill of Rights, but, with the UK making it clear that withdrawal was not an option, the Keys felt obliged to drop the idea.[30] Demands for a referendum on the issue did lead to the passing of the Referendum Act 1979, but no referendum was held because of the overriding effect of international law as it affected both the UK and the Isle of Man.[31] In July 1981 Tynwald accepted the recommendation of its Constitutional Issues Committee to press for a new constitutional status, as a fully self-governing territory save in respect of external affairs, defence and the royal succession which would remain the responsibility of the UK.[32] No progress was made with this request, but even if it had been, with the UK retaining responsibility for the Island's external affairs, it is difficult to see how it would have helped the Island retain corporal punishment.

The Tyrer case was a healthy reminder of the problems associated with defining what is domestic to the Isle of Man. International agreements invariably involve some erosion of domestic autonomy on the part of signatories as the price to be paid for the benefits of international cooperation. It is worth noting, however, that at no stage during the this period was there a serious questioning by the UK of the Island's right to self-government. Both the evidence from the Home Office to the Kilbrandon Commission and the general conclusions drawn by the Commission in 1973 were supportive of the Island's special status. Although Tynwald was disappointed not to receive backing for a formal definition of its legislative authority, the disappointment was tempered by the realisation that the Commission had in fact provided an authoritative seal of approval for Manx devolution.[33]

## *Towards Representative and Responsible Government*

In parallel with Tynwald's struggle to safeguard and enhance its authority, the House of Keys conducted a long but successful campaign to transfer power from Crown-appointed officials to the elected representatives of the people. The 'official' majority in the Legislative Council was still able to thwart the wishes of the elected chamber and the Lieutenant-Governor remained chief executive and Chancellor of the Exchequer. The impetus for reform came from a House of Keys determined to see the worldwide moves towards decolonisation and democratisation apply in the Isle of Man. Having shelved

Members of the MacDermott Commission, September 1958. The Commission was appointed by Sir Ambrose Dundas in March 1958 to report on the constitution of the Isle of Man; it reported in March 1959. The members are seated and from left to right are Sir Francis Mudie, a retired colonial official, Chuter Ede, Labour MP and former Home Secretary, Lord MacDermott, Chief Justice of Northern Ireland, Sir Lionel Heald, Conservative MP and former Attorney General and Sir Frederick Armer, a retired civil servant; the joint secretaries to the Commission are standing, Frank B. Johnson, Clerk of Tynwald, on the left and William B. Kennaugh, Assistant Government Secretary, on the right.

demands for internal constitutional reform so that Tynwald could present a united front during the devolution negotiations, members were quick to return to the subject once the Agreements of October 1957 had been signed. On 26 November 1957 Tynwald approved a resolution by Clifford Irving asking the Lieutenant-Governor to set up a constitutional commission.[34] On 18 March 1958, following consultations with the Home Office, Dundas announced the appointment of a five-man commission under the chairmanship of the Chief Justice of Northern Ireland, Lord MacDermott.

In January 1958 the House of Keys appointed a five-member committee to prepare evidence for submission to the Commission. The Committee was chaired by Speaker Qualtrough and included four MHKs known to favour constitutional reform, Irving, Charles Kerruish, Simcocks and MLP member George Taggart.[35] The Committee's recommendations were accepted by the House on 30 July 1958 by the slenderest majority of 11 votes to 10, although two absent members subsequently signified their support for the agreed recommendations.[36] The three main demands were for a Legislative Council with an indirectly elected majority, a reduction in the powers of the Legislative Council both in regard to legislation and resolutions in Tynwald and the establishment of an executive council that was representative of and responsible to the elected representatives. The Keys' demands for a reconstitution of the Legislative Council were motivated by a desire to bring to an end the official and appointed majority that had provided the basis of allegations about 'internal control' of Manx politics by the UK authorities. This term implied that the UK had been able, through the Lieutenant-Governor and other appointed members, to control Manx affairs without resort to the more overt means available to it such as refusing the Royal Assent to legislation. The Keys also wanted to see the removal of the Deemsters from the legislature as a means of guaranteeing the independence of the judiciary. In their evidence to the Commission, the Keys advocated an 11-member Legislative Council, the Lieutenant-Governor as chair with a casting vote, four members appointed by the Lieutenant-Governor, with the Bishop and the Attorney General eligible and the Deemsters ineligible for appointment, and six members elected by the House of Keys. The House was also concerned to end equal bicameralism and make it impossible for the Legislative Council to permanently defeat the wishes of the elected representatives. On legislation the demand was for the Legislative Council to have the power to delay the passage of a bill for a maximum of one year. Where the wishes of the majority of the House were defeated in Tynwald, the Keys proposed introducing a mechanism whereby a defeated resolution could be reintroduced at a later date when the wishes of the House would prevail. The final set of demands related to the Executive Council and the long-standing goal of representative and responsible government. They proposed a five-member Council with the chair elected by the House of Keys and the other members chosen by him in consultation with the Lieutenant-Governor. Executive Council members would not be eligible to serve on any board. The chair would then submit his policy and the individual members of his team to the House for approval. The Executive Council would then proceed to select chairs and members of boards for approval by Tynwald. The precise relationship between the reformed Executive Council and the Lieutenant-Governor was not spelled out in the memorandum, but Speaker Qualtrough made clear in oral evidence to the Commission that the House wanted to see the development of a cabinet system with the members accepting collective responsiblity for government and the Lieutenant-Governor acting on their advice.

The Legislative Council argued against changes to its own composition and powers, but agreed with the Keys that it was necessary to reform the Executive Council and place it on a statutory footing as a cabinet with collective responsibility to Tynwald for the government of the Island.[37] They also accepted that members should be free of board membership and duties, but that was the extent of their common ground with the Keys. While the Keys wanted the Council to be chaired by one of their own members, the Legislative Council argued in favour of it being chaired by the Lieutenant-Governor and envisaged eight members, five from the Keys, including the Speaker in an ex officio capacity, and three from the Council, the Attorney General ex officio and two nonofficial members.

On 14 March 1959, almost exactly a year after its appointment, the Commission reported.[38] It supported an evolutionary process and warned against 'too great haste' in moving towards a more representative form of government.[39] Its recommendations, while broadly sympathetic with the Keys' aspirations for greater democratic control, fell short of what the Keys had demanded. However, some of the recommendations, for example on finance, were to be seen as a staging post en route to greater self-government. The recommendation of the Commission on the composition of the Legislative Council was particularly disappointing for the reformists.[40] It was argued that the Bishop retain his seat for reasons of tradition, the ecclesiastical interests entrusted to him and 'his respected and authoritative personality'. The Commission saw no virtue in 'an absolute adherence to the theory of separation of powers', but proposed the removal of the Second Deemster to ensure that there was one judge 'who had not been involved in any legislative or executive action that might come into question'. As the legal advisor to the Government and the law officer responsible for the enforcement of the criminal law, the Attorney General should remain a member. Referring to the Lieutenant-Governor they felt that the advantages of contact and advice gained through his chairmanship were outweighed by the disadvantages of burden of work and being associated with one particular chamber of Tynwald; accordingly they recommended that, under normal circumstances, the First Deemster should preside and have a casting vote, but no other vote. In their conclusions about appointed members, the Commission commented thus on the Keys' allegations about 'internal control':

> While we think this fear is exaggerated and ought not to obscure the value of the accretion of strength which the Governor's power of appointment can bring about, we believe the time is opportune for an increase in the elected membership. We accordingly recommend that there should be five elected places and three appointed places.

Taken together, the recommendations were for a Legislative Council with the First Deemster and 10 other members, two ex officio, three appointed and five indirectly elected. If the Keys' fears about 'internal control' were well founded—and the Keys clearly believed they were—the proposals did not go far enough.

On the subject of the Legislative Council's veto over legislation and resolutions in Tynwald, the Commission was again wary of moving too fast, lest the benefits of a bicameral system be jeopardised. It did, however, agree that the capacity of the Legislative Council to defeat the wishes of the elected chamber should be limited in two ways. On legislation they recommended that 'a bill which has been passed by the Keys and rejected by the Council in two successive sessions, and which, in the next ensuing session, has been passed by the Keys but has not been agreed to by the Council within two months thereafter should for the purposes of enactment, be deemed to have been passed by the Council and to have been assented to by it in Tynwald.' This recommendation would have brought the Island into line with the UK position under the Parliament Act 1911 and allowed the Council to delay legislation for up to two years. In the case of conflict between the branches over resolutions in Tynwald, the Commission recommended that the MHK who had moved the proposal in question 'should be at liberty to move it again after giving due notice and within a time to be limited, and if, on his so doing, the proposal obtains the support of 18 members of Tynwald voting as a single body, it should be declared carried.' This was a slightly different formula to that requested by the Keys, designed to enable conflict between the branches to be resolved by an absolute majority vote in Tynwald.

The most far-reaching recommendations were for a reconstituted Executive Council and three new boards to share with the Lieutenant-Governor the responsibility for finance, police and the civil service. The Lieutenant-Governor would continue to preside over a Council with seven members of Tynwald, but with the chair of the Finance Board serving ex officio, four elected by Tynwald from among the chairs of other boards and two appointed by the Lieutenant-Governor. The Commission expressed the hope that, if the Council developed as an entity with a sense of collective responsibility, the Governor might at an appropriate stage designate 'one or more of the members to speak for the Government in Tynwald and the Branches'.[41] The Commission was unwilling to

198 *Offshore Island Politics*

recommend an immediate transfer of power from the Lieutenant-Governor, but talked of 'a period of transition during which conditions will be such as to provide for and encourage a gradual shifting of executive power from the Governor to a small body drawn from and answerable to Tynwald.'[42] The detailed recommendations reflected this cautionary position and provided for an extension of the partnership between Lieutenant-Governor and Tynwald, which had been facilitated by the board system and the formation of the Executive Council in 1946, into major new areas. The Commission's view was that the reconstituted Executive Council and the three new boards should be advisory to the Lieutenant-Governor and share power with him, thus precluding the Keys' demands for fully responsible government. There was no recommendation for an extension of the powers of the Executive Council, merely a reconstitution and a new method of appointment. The major innovations recommended were the establishment of a finance board 'to share, and eventually bear, the Governor's financial responsibilities', a police board to share responsibility for the administration of the police service, excluding appointments, promotions, discipline or the disposition of the force, and a permanent civil service commission, a positive if limited response to the Keys' lengthy campaign for control of these areas.[43]

The first phase of reforms came into effect immediately following the 1962 general election. Those dealing with the composition and powers of the Legislative Council were watered down and delayed by opposition from MLCs, whereas those providing for a sharing of executive power met with broad support in both chambers. This was to be the pattern for the next phase of reforms. Although the driving force for reforms in both areas came from the Keys, the initiative for further reform of the Legislative Council came from the House's own Constitutional Development Committee, set up in 1966, whereas that for the further transfer of power from the Lieutenant-Governor came from Tynwald's Select Committee on the Duties and Powers of the Lieutenant-Governor established in 1970. With the controversial legislation concerning the Legislative Council on the statute book by 1978, the stimulus for further internal reform came from Tynwald's Select Committee on Constitutional Issues. Set up in February 1978, it replaced the Keys' Constitutional Development Committee and the Constitutional Issues Committee that had been set up by Tynwald in 1973 in response to the Kilbrandon Report, and was responsible for the recommendations that led to the establishment of a ministerial system, which will be considered in Chapter Eight. There was considerable overlap of membership and within the committees leadership was provided by a small number of committed reformers from the House, notably Spencer Kelly who chaired the Keys Constitutional Development Committee from 1966 until his death in 1970, Victor Kneale, who was a member of each of the Tynwald committees throughout the period and chair of the Keys Committee until his elevation to the Legislative Council in 1974, and Speaker Kerruish, who chaired the Select Committee on the Powers and Duties from 1970 to 1981, the Keys Constitutional Development Committee from 1974 to 1978 and the Constitutional Issues Committee from 1978 to 1981. Change in the two decades after 1961 was gradual, but taken together the constitutional legislation passed effected a major transformation of the Manx system of government.

The Isle of Man Constitution Acts 1961–80 effected changes both to the membership and powers of the Legislative Council.[44] They provided for the gradual reduction in the official and nominated majority from seven, including the Lieutenant-Governor, to two, the Lord Bishop and the Attorney-General as a nonvoting member.

The Isle of Man Constitution Act 1961 provided for a fifth elected member, the measure being a compromise between what the Keys originally proposed and what the Legislative Council was willing to accept. When the Bill was introduced in the Keys by Clifford Irving, it provided for a sixth elected member in place of the Second Deemster and the replacement of the Lieutenant-Governor as nonvoting President of the Council by the First Deemster, a voting membership of nine and the removal of the possibility of 'internal control'. The Bill had a troubled but very speedy passage in the Legislative Council, emerging after third reading looking very different and not solely because of the opposition of the official and appointed members; even the indirectly elected members refused to support the Keys.[45] A conference of the Branches on 29 August 1961 produced a substantial measure of agreement, but the end product was for the Keys 'half a loaf' that was 'better than none'. The Keys' priority at the time was to replace the Council's legislative veto with the lesser power of delay. A second attempt to replace the Second Deemster was approved by the House without division in 1963, but the Bill did not become law until 1965 because of continuing opposition from the official and appointed members of the Legislative Council. Having twice rejected the Bill, the Council reluctantly approved it on 29 March 1965, knowing that after a third rejection the Bill would become law under Section 10(1) of the Isle of Man Constitution Act 1961.[46] Only the two Deemsters and appointed member, John Bolton, opposed the measure to the bitter end. Once the Isle of Man Constitution Act 1965 had received the Royal Assent—and there was no opposition from the UK authorities—it was no longer possible for the Legislative Council to defeat the Keys simply as a result of the official and appointed members acting in concert.

Following the success of 1965, the Keys' Constitutional Development Committee under the chair of Spencer Kelly set about extending the principle of indirect election to the whole Legislative Council. In a memorandum published on the eve of the 1966 general election, the Committee proposed that the indirectly elected membership be increased from five to 10 and that there be no official or appointed members.[47] After the election, while the memorandum remained the ultimate goal of the House, it was agreed to try and move forward in cooperation with the Legislative Council. Accordingly Tynwald established a Constitutional Development Committee, also chaired by Kelly and which came forward with a further compromise. The result was that on 28 January 1969 Tynwald agreed that the two appointed members be replaced by indirectly elected members and that the Attorney General become a nonvoting member of both the Legislative Council and Tynwald.[48] The Isle of Man Constitution Act 1969 provided for the replacement of the two appointed members and the Isle of Man Constitution Act 1971 for the nonvoting status of the Attorney General. During the debates on these two measures, notice was given by the Keys that moves would be made shortly to remove the remaining officials from the Council, including its President, the Lieutenant-Governor.

In fact the next initiative, to remove the First Deemster from the Legislative Council, came in 1974. On the recommendation of its Constitutional Development Committee, now chaired by Victor Kneale, the House approved an amendment bill providing for the replacement of the judge by an eighth indirectly elected member. Although rejected by the Legislative Council the first time round, the Bill subsequently passed through all its stages to become the Isle of Man Constitution Amendment Act 1975.[49] An interesting aspect of this change is that it was preceded by a critical change in the personnel of the Council. Kneale, who had piloted the Bill through the Keys, was elected to the Legislative Council in time to take charge of the Bill there too. The Keys' choice of Kneale and Simcocks for elevation to the Council in place of two opponents of reform was almost certainly responsible for the favourable outcome in the Council on 4 February 1975.

The final development relating to membership of the Legislative Council concerned the Lieutenant-Governor and resulted from the recommendations of Tynwald's Select Committee on the Duties and Powers of the Lieutenant-Governor, chaired by Speaker Kerruish. In its third report, the Committee recommended that the Council be requested to consider favourably the appointment of one of their members as presiding officer, a recommendation that was duly embodied in a resolution of Tynwald in February 1976.[50] The request was considered but turned down by a majority of the Legislative Council, whereupon the Select Committee agreed to reconsider the question prior to the appointment of the next Lieutenant-Governor.[51] Three years later the matter was reopened by Tynwald's Select Committee on Constitutional Issues, also chaired by the Speaker. Anxious to gain approval for their proposal for the Royal Assent to domestic legislation to be delegated to the Lieutenant-Governor, the Committee recommended that he should cease to preside over both the Legislative and Executive Councils. Tynwald approved the recommendation in June 1979 and the change became effective under the Constitution (Legislative Council) Act 1980.[52] Jack Nivison became the first Manx President of the Legislative Council in 1980.

The debate about the veto powers of the Legislative Council proved almost as controversial as that about membership. The 1961 Constitution Bill as passed by the Keys followed the recommendations of the MacDermott Commission with one important amendment, the requirement of a two thirds majority vote in support of the final third reading of any constitutional measure. The amendment was moved by James Cain and accepted by 16 votes to seven, with those in charge of the Bill prepared to support the change in order to maximise support for the Bill and make it more difficult politically for the Legislative Council to object.[53] The Legislative Council wanted to replace the provision enabling the Keys to override the Council by a requirement for a disputed bill to gain the support of an absolute majority of the full membership of Tynwald; as part of a compromise package, members eventually agreed to support the Keys' position, with the result that the Isle of Man Constitution Act 1961 brought to an end the formal parity of legislative power between the two chambers, broadly along the lines of the UK Parliament Act of 1911.[54] Under the 1961 Act the House of Keys was empowered to override the Legislative Council after it had rejected a bill in three successive sessions, a two thirds majority being required in respect of constitutional legislation. This left the Legislative Council with the power to delay legislation for two years. The requirement of a two thirds majority at the final third reading of constitutional bills proved instrumental in preventing a reduction in delaying powers in 1965. The House of Keys passed the Isle of Man Constitution Amendment (No. 2) Bill on 29 October 1965 with the express intention of reducing the delaying power from two years to one; it was rejected by the Council at second reading on 11 February 1964 and for a second time on 29 March 1965. On 7 December 1965, the voting in the House on the final third reading was 15 to seven, one vote short of the two thirds majority, and the Bill fell.[55] No further attempt was made to reduce the delaying power until the former Clerk of Tynwald, Edward Kermeen gave notice of intention to introduce a private member's bill on 8 March 1977. After a unanimous third reading in the Keys and a relatively smooth passage through a Council, that included among its members several former MHKs who had been at the forefront of the campaign for reform, the Isle of Man

Constitution Act 1978 provided for the reduction in delaying powers that had been denied to the Keys 12 years earlier; the power to override became available after rejection in two successive sessions, reducing the Council's power of delay to one year and bringing the Island broadly into line with the provisions of the UK Parliament Act 1949.[56] In marked contrast with the position when MacDermott reported in 1959, most members of the two branches of Tynwald were now in broad agreement about their respective legislative roles.

Side by side with legislation establishing the supremacy of the elected chamber in the legislative process were moves to transfer executive power to bodies with a majority from the House of Keys and responsible to Tynwald. The first phase of legislation in the 1960s followed the MacDermott Report and moderated the executive authority of the Lieutenant-Governor by establishing a much more formal advisory structure. The second phase between 1970 and 1981 followed recommendations of Tynwald's Select Committee on the Duties and Powers of the Lieutenant-Governor and provided for the formal transfer of power to these advisory bodies.[57] The associated legislation was broadly welcomed by members of both branches of Tynwald.

The Isle of Man Constitution Act 1961 placed the Executive Council on a statutory basis with the duty of advising the Lieutenant-Governor on all matters of principle and policy.[58] Under the Act membership comprised the chair of the Finance Board, the chairs of four other boards elected by Tynwald and two members of Tynwald, not being official members, appointed by the Lieutenant-Governor. Members were elected or appointed immediately after general elections for a period of five years and held office irrespective of the branch of the legislature in which they served. The Lieutenant-Governor, although not formally a member of the Executive Council, was to preside over meetings of the Council. In addition, the Executive Council was to appoint a chair from among its members to preside in the Lieutenant-Governor's absence.

The other part of the MacDermott package was legislation providing for an extension of Tynwald's system of boards into three areas previously reserved to the Lieutenant-Governor. The Finance Board Act 1961 provided for a finance board comprising a chair and two members to advise the Lieutenant-Governor on all financial matters.[59] The Police (Isle of Man) Act 1962 set up a police board with a chair and two members appointed by Tynwald and two further members appointed by the Lieutenant-Governor, its duties being to provide and maintain a constabulary in the manner required by the Lieutenant-Governor.[60] The Isle of Man Civil Service Act 1962 resulted in the establishment of a Manx Civil Service and transferred to a Civil Service Commission most of the powers of appointment previously reserved to the Lieutenant-Governor.[61]

During the 1960s there were two changes in the composition of the Executive Council, reflecting the concern on the part of the Keys to safeguard the House's representation and the political neutrality of the office of Speaker. The elevation of members to the Legislative Council without loss of their Executive Council seat had reduced the Keys' representation from five in 1962 to three by 1966, while the Speaker's activities as chair of the Executive Council convinced a growing number of MHKs that the Island should follow Commonwealth practice and make the office of Speaker and membership of the executive incompatible. The first attempt at reform came in 1966 when Victor Kneale introduced a private member's bill for both purposes, but it was referred to the Keys' Constitutional Development Committee and failed to reach the statute book before the 1966 general election.[62] After the election, the Isle of Man

The Executive Council with Sir Ronald Garvey presiding and Home Secretary Sir Frank Soskice in attendance, September 1965. Although set up in 1946, the Executive Council first became a statutory body in 1962. From left to right are a member of the Home Office visiting group, Norman Crowe, Hubert Radcliffe, Harry Nicholls, Sir Ralph Stevenson, Sir Ronald Garvey, Sir Frank Soskice, another member of the Home Office group, Attorney General David Lay, William Quayle, Charles Kerruish and the Assistant Government Secretary, W. B. Kennaugh.

Constitution Act 1968 provided for five members to be recruited from the Keys and two from the Legislative Council.[63] The chair of the Finance Board remained an ex officio member and counted as one of the representatives of the branch of which he was a member. Nominations for the other positions became the responsibility of the respective branches but required the approval of a majority of the members of Tynwald voting as one body. It was no longer a requirement for nominees to be chairs of boards. It also became mandatory for membership to be vacated on a person ceasing to be a member of the branch on which he was serving when elected. The Act became effective in January 1970. Part of the rationale for the concomitant removal of the Lieutenant-Governor's powers of appointment was Stallard's controversial appointment of Speaker Kerruish to the Executive Council against the wishes of Tynwald in January 1967.

That appointment also led to further amending legislation, making the Speaker ineligible for membership of the Executive Council. The active political role played by Speakers of the House was the subject of controversy long before 1967. The

MacDermott Commission received requests for the Speaker's political role to be diminished and his impartiality safeguarded, but recommended only that the Speaker be relieved of the obligation under standing orders, hitherto imposed on all members of both the House and Tynwald, to record his vote. That recommendation was duly implemented, but was to have little effect on the political role of the Speaker.[64] Following his election as Speaker of the House on 13 February 1962, Charles Kerruish was re-elected both as chair of the Health Services Board and as a member of the Executive Council, positions he had held since 1955. He also became chair of the Executive Council and, during Garvey's governorship, on occasions acted as spokesman for the Government in Tynwald. In July 1966 an attempt by Kneale, as chair of the Board of Education, to have the standing orders of Tynwald suspended to allow the Education Authority to purchase a site for a new College of Further Education brought the political role of the Speaker into the limelight on the eve of the general election. In his capacity as chair of the Executive Council, the Speaker opposed the suspension on the grounds that such a purchase was not part of the planned programme of development and expenditure for 1966/67 and found himself in direct confrontation with a majority of the House. The procedural resolution required a two thirds majority in both branches and this was clearly prevented by the disciplined vote of Executive Council members against the motion.[65] This vote made MHKs all the more determined to press ahead with legislation. During the 1966 election the Speaker campaigned not only in his constituency of Garff but across the Island defending and promoting the policies of the Government. For many candidates, such a role was incompatible with the traditional role of Speaker as defender of the interests of the House. Following the election, Tynwald decided that the Speaker should not be a chair or member of any board, thus depriving him of the necessary qualification for election by Tynwald to the Executive Council. When in January 1967 the new Lieutenant-Governor proceeded to appoint the Speaker to the Executive Council, MHKs asked the Speaker to resign and the Lieutenant-Governor to cancel the appointment; both refused. On 14 February 1967 the House was asked by Clifford Irving to approve a motion of no confidence in the Speaker and, although this was carried by 14 votes to nine,[66] the Speaker still refused to resign. Tynwald reacted by removing the Lieutenant-Governor's powers of appointment to the Executive Council and by passing the Isle of Man Constitution (No. 2) Act 1968 making the Speaker ineligible for membership both of the Executive Council and boards of Tynwald. The Speaker ceased to be a member of Executive Council on 9 April 1968, when he was replaced by his leading critic, Clifford Irving.[67]

During the 1960s Lieutenant-Governors acted increasingly on the advice of the Executive Council and the new boards, paving the way for a formal transfer of power during the 1970s. Tynwald's Select Committee on the Duties and Powers of the Lieutenant-Governor was established in 1970 and chaired by the Speaker Kerruish. With the controversy over Executive Council membership behind him, he devoted much of his energy to promoting the cause of constitutional development. The Committee's terms of reference were to come forward with recommendations for the further transfer of power to Tynwald, fulfilling the broad constitutional objective of promoting Manx self-government. The recommendations of the Committee, on finance, general functions, the police and membership of the Executive Council, met with overwhelming support in Tynwald and no objections from the UK authorities.

On 17 February 1976 Tynwald resolved that legislation be introduced to transfer the financial powers of the Lieutenant-Governor to the Finance Board. All bills and motions in Tynwald involving public expenditure required the concurrence of both the Lieutenant-Governor and the Finance Board, but formal responsibility for presenting the Island's budgets rested with the Lieutenant-Governor. The main purpose of the Governor's Financial and Judicial Functions (Transfer) Act 1976 was to make the Finance Board solely responsible for those financial functions that in the UK are the responsibility of the Treasury.[68] The Act marked the end of a long struggle by the Island for full control of its own finances.

Tynwald also committed itself in February 1976 to legislation transferring general executive functions, but action was delayed until after the general election in November of that year. The Governor's General Functions (Transfer) Act 1980 transferred a wide range of functions, under more than 200 Acts of Tynwald between 1691 and 1976, to boards of Tynwald or other appropriate authorities.[69] Where there was no appropriate body the functions were transferred to the 'Governor in Council', defined in the Act as 'the Governor acting on the advice and with the concurrence of the Executive Council'.

Charles Kerruish, Chair of the Executive Council 1962–67, welcoming Sir Peter and Lady Stallard and family to the Island at the beginning of his governorship, 7 September 1966. At the time Kerruish, a farmer and MHK for Garff, combined the roles of Speaker and chair of Executive Council. From left to right are Charles Kerruish, SHK, Stallard's son, Peter, Sir Peter and Lady Stallard, their daughter, Sarah, and the Acting Governor, Deemster Sidney Kneale.

The Act excluded the Lieutenant-Governor's responsibilities in respect of certain constitutional and ecclesiastical matters, the civil service and the police.

On 13 December 1977 Tynwald approved the transfer of police powers. As far back as 1907 the House of Keys had petitioned the Home Secretary for a police board responsible to Tynwald. However, when the Police Board was established in 1962 its powers fell far short of what the Keys had sought over 50 years earlier. The Lieutenant-Governor retained responsibility for appointments, promotions, discipline and disposition. The Police Board's role was restricted to that of a 'quarter-master's department', looking after 'pay, clothing, housing, equipment and so on'.[70] On 21 June 1978, in the wake of several officers of the Manx force being found guilty of criminal and disciplinary offences, Tynwald asked the Police Board to carry out a full review of the Police (Isle of Man) Act. A divided Board reported to Tynwald in July 1979, the majority favouring the transfer of powers to the Governor in Council rather than the Police Board, a minority of one preferring to see the Police Board assume full responsibility.[71]

Norman Crowe, Chair of the Executive Council 1967–71, with Lord Stonham, May 1968. Crowe, a farmer, was MHK for Michael; he had been chair of the Finance Board from 1964 to 1967. Lord Stonham, Minister of State at the Home Office, was on the Island to chair a meeting of the Joint Working Party. From left to right are Sir Peter Stallard, Lord Stonham, Norman Crowe and Percy Radcliffe, a member of Executive Council and chair of the LGB.

The Police (Amendment) Act 1980 implemented the majority recommendation, but only after the narrow defeat of amendments in favour of 'democratic devolution' to the Police Board.[72]

In the case of the police and a number of other areas where the transfer of powers was to the Governor in Council, it was not long before legislation was introduced to transfer responsibility for these services to new boards of Tynwald. In doing so the opportunity was taken to bring related services under one umbrella. The legislation had a smooth passage through both branches of Tynwald. The Home Affairs Board Act 1981 was promoted by the Executive Council and established a single board with responsibility for the full range of emergency and security services, including the police, fire and prison services, civil defence and civil aid, the probation and aftercare service and broadcasting.[73] It replaced the Police Board, the Civil Defence Commission, the Broadcasting Commission and a range of advisory committees as well as transferring a variety of functions still vested in the Governor or the Governor in Council. The importance of the new Board was reflected in the provision making the chair an ex officio member of Executive Council. The Industry Board Act 1981, also initiated by the Executive Council, provided for a board to replace the Industrial Advisory Council.[74] The Council was advisory to the Lieutenant-Governor until 1980, when it became advisory to the Finance Board. However, the inappropriateness of this interim arrangement and the increasing importance of government in supporting industrial development convinced the Executive Council of the case for the change in status and direct responsibility to Tynwald. The Board of Consumer Affairs Act 1981 resulted from a recommendation of the Select Committee on the Powers and Duties of the Lieutenant-Governor. It provided for the replacement of the Consumer Council, which had been set up in 1972 with a strictly advisory role, by a board with executive powers in relation to consumer protection, including responsibility for such powers and duties as were previously exercised by the Lieutenant-Governor in relation to consumer affairs.[75]

On 19 June 1979 Tynwald accepted the recommendation of its Select Committee on Constitutional Issues that the Lieutenant-Governor should no longer preside over the Executive Council. The rationale for this move was to gain approval for the delegation of the Royal Assent to domestic legislation to the Lieutenant-Governor. The change was given effect by the Constitution (Executive Council) (Amendment) Act 1980.[76] While the Lieutenant-Governor was still able to attend and participate in meetings, the Act ushered in a new era in Manx politics in which real executive leadership was firmly in Manx hands. The election of the chair of Executive Council remained the responsibility of its members, but was made subject to the approval of a majority of members of Tynwald voting as one body; the chair of the Finance Board was not eligible for election. Clifford Irving, who had been chair since January 1977, became the first chair under the 1980 Act when his election was approved by Tynwald on 18 November 1980.[77] In its final report to Tynwald the Select Committee recommended that legislation be introduced to transfer the power of electing the chair of Executive Council to Tynwald. The recommendation, designed to make the selection process more democratic and to enhance the authority of the chair, was accepted by Tynwald, but was only translated into law after a division between the branches over an amendment requiring the chair to be an MHK. The amendment moved by Clifford Irving was carried by 16 votes to four in the House, but reversed in the Legislative Council on the initiative of Eddie Kerruish. The House agreed to accept this reversal with the result that the Isle of Man Constitution (Amendment) Act 1981 provided for the chair to be a member of Tynwald elected by

Tynwald at the first sitting following a general election; the chair was a replacement for the Lieutenant-Governor and additional to the seven members nominated by the branches for approval by Tynwald; the office remained incompatible with that of chair of the Finance Board.[78] The authority of the chair was further enhanced by the provision making him ex officio chair of Tynwald's influential Selection Committee. Interestingly, bearing in mind the Keys' stand, the first chair to be elected under the 1981 Act was a member of the Legislative Council, Percy Radcliffe.[79]

The changing role of the Executive Council over this period was only partly the result of constitutional legislation. Lieutenant-Governors also followed the spirit of MacDermott by acting increasingly in partnership or on the advice of Executive Council and Finance Board. The interactions between individual Lieutenant Governors and the members of Tynwald with whom they had to work were for the most part cordial and reflected the personalities of those involved. While Garvey had been obliged to accept the reforms of 1961/62 and work increasingly with advisors appointed by Tynwald, a forceful personality and a well of ideas for the regeneration of the Manx economy combined to guarantee a continuing leadership role. He was nevertheless willing to allow his Manx partners an enhanced role, the chair of Executive Council increasingly taking on the role of Government spokesman in Tynwald. Stallard went out of his way to promote progress towards internal self-government, happy to see the transfer of financial power to the Finance Board in the late 1960s, well in advance of the legislation formalising the transfer, and openly supportive of Speaker Kerruish's 1970 initiative in proposing a select committee to report on the further transfer of gubernatorial powers.[80] Paul arrived in the Island in 1974 and immediately made known his support for the aspirations of Tynwald in reducing the role of governor to a largely ceremonial one;[81] by the time he left the Island in 1980, real executive power had indeed been transferred.

The MacDermott Commission's hopes for the reconstituted Executive Council were that it would develop a collective spirit and concentrate on 'the weightier questions of the day'.[82] Between the reforms of 1961 and the removal of the Lieutenant-Governor in 1980, the Executive Council met weekly and on other occasions when necessary, the Government Secretary, the Government Treasurer and the Attorney General attending in a consultative capacity. The confidentiality of proceedings and the lack of public access to records of meetings makes it difficult to be sure about the internal dynamics of the meetings. What does seem clear, however, is that the most influential figures were the chairs of the Executive Council and the Finance Board. Four individuals combined the former post with being the chair of a major board, Charles Kerruish (1962–67, Health Services Board), Norman Crowe (1967–72, Board of Agriculture and Fisheries), Percy Radcliffe (1972–76, Local Government Board) and Clifford Irving (1977–81, Tourist Board). There were also four chairs of the Finance Board over this period, former MLP member Bert Stephen (1962–64), Norman Crowe (1964–67), John Bolton (1967–76) and Percy Radcliffe (1976–81). With the exception of Stephen, who died while chair of the Finance Board, each of these five were long-serving members of Executive Council: Bolton (1951–62 and 1967–79), Kerruish (1955–68), Crowe (1964–78), Radcliffe (1967–85) and Irving (1968–81).

Although decisions were arrived at by agreement and usually without voting, the Executive Council was widely regarded as having failed for most of this period to provide the collective leadership associated with cabinet government in the UK. The absence of a disciplined majority party, the independence of members of Tynwald and the presence of certain board chairs and the absence of others, especially after 1968, made

Percy Radcliffe at Kella Farm, Sulby, March 1971. This photograph was taken shortly before Radcliffe (left), MHK for Ayre, became the third consecutive farmer to chair the Executive Council. He held the post 1972–76 and 1981–85, and in the intervening period chaired the Finance Board 1976–81. He is pictured with his son, Arthur Radcliffe.

consistent presentation of a united front a virtual impossibility. Members frequently reserved their right to oppose measures in Tynwald and there were many instances of split voting both in the branches and on the floor of Tynwald. Where measures were controversial, the agreed decision of Executive Council was often to let them go forward for Tynwald to decide.

   In many ways 1966–68 marked a turning point in the Council's development. For five years under Garvey and Speaker Kerruish, it had become an increasingly positive if controversial force in Manx politics. Important policy decisions still emanated from Tynwald, its boards and private members, but increasingly the Executive Council came to be seen as 'the Government'. Following the 1966 general election and, in the wake of growing public opposition to Executive Council policies and MHK dissatisfaction with the multiple roles of the Speaker, steps were taken to remove Speaker Kerruish from the Executive Council. With both Garvey and Speaker Kerruish replaced, the role of the Executive Council seemed to diminish. Neither Stallard nor the new chair of the Council, Crowe, were as forceful as the men they replaced and much of the real power seemed to

Clifford Irving, Chair of the Executive Council 1977–81, at the Tourist Board in May 1978. Irving, MHK for East Douglas, joined the Executive Council in 1968 and served as chair from 1977 until his defeat in the election of 1981. When the Lieutenant-Governor ceased to preside over the Executive Council in 1980, Irving became the first Manxman to chair the reconstituted Executive Council, a major landmark on the road to Island self-government.

pass to the Finance Board or back to Tynwald and its boards. With the Speaker's removal, the Finance Board, under John Bolton from 1967 to 1976 and Percy Radcliffe from 1976 to 1981, was allowed to assume the dominant role. Speaker Kerruish, meanwhile, made every effort to constrain the role of Executive Council by advocating, with considerable success, the more extensive use of alternative policy-making procedures, in particular that involving select committees of Tynwald. Between 1966 and 1981 important policy initiatives emanated from select committees established under resolutions moved by the Speaker and more often than not subsequently chaired by the Speaker. The latter alone covered such diverse issues as constitutional relations with the UK (set up in 1967), postal services and telecommunications (1968), the Common Market (1970), the Lieutenant-Governor's powers and duties (1970), constitutional issues (1973), indigenous power sources/energy (1977) and unemployment (1980). Shortly after becoming chair of the Executive Council in November 1981, Percy Radcliffe lamented the fact that 'in the last Tynwald we had the authority of Executive Council and Boards whittled away by select committees'.[83]

That is not to say that the Executive Council became unimportant, simply that it was more of a coordinator than a major initiator of policy. It considered and amended legislative and policy proposals from the boards and the Attorney General's department and established the order of priority for debate in Tynwald. It responded to requests for action by Tynwald. Support for proposals in Executive Council was a major step on the path to implementation, but no guarantee of it. When interviewed in June 1978, incumbent members were in broad agreement that the Executive Council should be, but was not in practice, the chief initiator of policies. According to the chair of the Finance Board, Percy Radcliffe, 'much greater power is enjoyed by the Finance Board. The Executive Council lacks punch.'[84] This view was also reflected in the interviews conducted with members of Tynwald not on the Executive Council. For example, Roger Watterson commented on the sheer length of Executive Council agendas and the fact that most of its work 'seemed to consist of noting the initiatives of others and the subsequent progress of such initiatives.'[85] Following the election of November 1981 and with Radcliffe as chair of both the Executive Council and six of Tynwald's most important committees there was a definite shift in power to the Executive Council.

The combined effect of the constitutional reforms and political developments between 1958 and 1981 was a remarkable transformation of the pattern of Manx

Left: Robert C. Stephen, Chair of the Finance Board, 1963. Stephen was an MLP member for South Douglas 1956–62 and Independent Socialist MHK 1962–64. He narrowly defeated John Bolton to become the first chair of the Island's Finance Board from 1962 until his death in January 1964.

Right: John B. Bolton, Chair of the Finance Board, January 1975. A conservative MHK 1946–62 and an MLC 1962–79, Bolton served on the Executive Council 1951–62 and again from 1967 until his retirement from politics in 1979. He was chair of the Finance Board 1967–76 and shortly after this exceptional term of office in 1977 received a knighthood in recognition of public service to the Island.

devolution. Whereas in 1958 the Lieutenant-Governor was the Island's chief executive and a dominant force in the legislative process, by the end of this period the Island's leading campaigner for reform, Charles Kerruish, was prepared to describe him as a 'rubber stamp'.[86] The chief beneficiaries of the reforms were the elected members of the House of Keys and the people they represented. The Manx political system underwent a process of democratisation, the reforms finally delivering the representative and responsible government that had been at the heart of the Keys' petition to the Home Secretary in 1907.

For members of Tynwald who were not chosen to serve on the Executive Council, the Island's board system continued to be an important vehicle for power sharing. In 1959 when the MacDermott Commission reported there were 17 boards and statutory bodies, of which four, the Airports Board, the Electricity Board, the MER Board and the Water Board were commercial bodies responsible for publicly owned utilities. The other 13 were the Board of Agriculture and Fisheries, the Assessment Board, the Board of Education, the Forestry, Mines and Lands Board, the Harbour Board, the Health Services Board, the Highway and Transport Board, the Local Government Board, the Board of Social Services (Social Security from 1970), the Tourist Board and, while not strictly boards of Tynwald, the Civil Defence Commission, the Government Property Trustees and the Manx Museum and National Trust. The MacDermott Commission recommended a reduction in the number of boards wherever feasible through amalgamation, but between 1959 and 1981 the number of boards and statutory bodies increased from 17 to 22. The MacDermott Commission itself led to the formation of three additional bodies in 1962, the Finance Board, the Police Board and the Civil Service Commission. A Broadcasting Commission was formed in 1965 and a Consumer Council in 1972, the latter giving way to the more powerful Board of Consumer Affairs, one of three new boards created in the aftermath of the Governor's General Functions (Transfer) Act 1980. The other two were the Home Affairs Board and the Industry Board. Extensions of public ownership led to the formation of the Isle of Man Postal Authority in 1972, the replacement of the Isle of Man Water Board by the Isle of Man Water Authority in 1972, the formation of the Isle of Man Gas Authority in 1972, the amalgamation of the Water and Gas Authorities to form the Isle of Man Water and Gas Authority in 1974 and the de facto establishment of an Isle of Man Railways Board in 1977 (although de jure the responsibility remained with the MER Board). While the principle of amalgamation was accepted in the field of education in 1968, in relation to water and gas in 1974 and home affairs in 1981, for most of the period the story was one of resistance to change and a continuing predilection for ad hoc development.[87]

Given the Keys' struggle for superiority in this period, one might have expected MHKs to be selected as the chairs of the principal boards, and generally speaking this was the case. The notable exceptions were John Bolton, who chaired the Finance Board for 10 years from 1967 to 1976, and Cecil McFee, the MLP member who chaired the Health Services Board from 1967 to 1971. Tynwald was also willing to see established chairs, such as Norman Crowe (Agriculture and Fisheries), Jack Nivison (Social Services/Social Security) and Percy Radcliffe (Finance Board) continue after election to the Legislative Council. These exceptions suggest that most members of Tynwald were happy to see the best person selected for particular posts rather than insist on an MHK. Even within the House, less than a majority were willing to support private members' bills introduced by Speaker Kerruish in 1972 and MLP member, Ted Ranson, in 1974 with the aim of reserving the position of chair of the major boards to MHKs; despite

MLCs chairing the Boards of Agriculture and Fisheries, Finance, Highways and Transport and Social Security at the time, these bills were defeated at second reading by 13 votes to nine in May 1972 and 15 votes to seven in January 1974.[88]

Even though the board system survived MacDermott and emerged from 20 years of constitutional reform largely unscathed, by the end of the 1970s it was sorely in need of the rationalisation that had been recommended 20 years earlier. The main criticisms of the boards were that they were too numerous, too large and too independent. The number of boards was widely believed to be too high for a small island. The scope for further amalgamations was considerable, as became evident in the 1980s when Tynwald began investigating replacing the boards by a system of ministerial departments. While the Boards Act 1971 had reduced the number serving on certain boards, the system still imposed a very heavy burden on members of Tynwald. In 1979 there were 74 positions on 22 statutory bodies to be filled by the members of Tynwald eligible for appointment; two members, the Speaker of the House and the Attorney General, were not eligible and, of the remaining 32, the three members of the Finance Board and the chair of the LGB were limited to serving on one board. In addition members were engaged extensively in the work of Tynwald, its branches and committees.

More serious than the number of boards or the burden of work they imposed was the fragmentation of government encouraged by the high degree of autonomy enjoyed by the separate boards. Each board possessed considerable freedom to make policy and carry out detailed administration within a framework laid down by Tynwald. Although in the final analysis Tynwald could change the membership or powers of boards and refuse them funding, in practice there was a reluctance to interfere. And yet there was a crying need for less fragmentation and more coordination in government. Nowhere was this better illustrated than in the field of public transport, where piecemeal development had resulted in the creation of separate boards for airports, harbours, highways and transport and railways and, after 1977, a publicly owned bus company, Isle of Man National Transport Limited. In 1966 the Commission on Transport, chaired by MLC member Hubert Radcliffe, had pointed to the advantages to be gained by having a single authority with general supervisory responsibility for transport but, while Tynwald accepted this as a long-term goal, in the short and medium term the task of supervision and coordination fell to Tynwald's Steering Committee on Transport, an additional body and an additional burden on members of Tynwald.

The Executive Council and the Finance Board went some way towards providing a central steer to the diverse activities of the boards, but for reasons already explained they were far less successful than had been hoped. The need to review or replace the board system was raised as an issue by a few candidates during the general elections of the period but, with the exception of the reductions in the membership of certain boards in 1971 and the amalgamations referred to above, little was achieved beyond the airing of ideas until Tynwald's decision in November 1980 to establish a select committee to investigate the entire board system. The initial proposal before Tynwald, in the names of Elspeth Quayle and Eddie Lowey, was for a committee to investigate the LGB with a view to rationalising its workload and responsibilities in relation to other boards, but an amendment moved by Speaker Kerruish and seconded by Dominic Delaney was carried extending the terms of reference to include all boards. Seconding the amendment, Delaney speculated 'that at some time we are going to have a system like a ministerial system … It would work more clearly and someone would have the responsibility.'[89] Although Tynwald already had a Constitutional Issues Committee, which could have conceivably taken on this investigation, at the time it was preoccupied with the general constitutional objective of maximising Island self-government and Tynwald proceeded to appoint a new committee, chaired by the President of the Legislative Council, Jack Nivison. In January 1981, at the request of the Committee, the terms of the investigation were further extended to include the Finance Board and other executive bodies. However, because of the radical and complex nature of the proposals being considered for streamlining the board system, no report was available for Tynwald before the November election. After the election, the initiative for reform passed to the Constitutional Issues Committee. That Committee's proposals for a ministerial system will be considered in Chapter Eight.

# *Notes*

1   For a discussion of their careers, see Derek Winterbottom, *Governors of the Isle of Man since 1765* (Douglas, 1999), Parts 7 and 8.
2   Section 87 of the Post Office Act 1969 empowered Her Majesty in Council to make the necessary provision if the Post Office were to surrender its privileges in respect of the Isle of Man or the Channel Islands. The surrender was effected by SI 1973/959 and SI 1973/960.
3   For details of the negotiations and final decision, see D. G. Kermode, *Devolution at Work: A Case Study of the Isle of Man* (Farnborough, Hampshire, 1979), pp. 57–58.
4   For a discussion of the transfer of power to the Isle of Man Postal Authority, see G. N. Kniveton (ed.), *A Chronicle of the Twentieth Century: The Manx Experience*, vol. 2: 1951–2000 (Douglas, 2000), p. 120.
5   See 91 *Manx Deb.*, 9 July 1974, pp. T971–72.
6   See 96 *Manx Deb.*, 10 July 1979, pp. T939–44 and 960–77.
7   William Whitelaw and Percy Radcliffe respectively. *Agreement between the Governments of the United Kingdom and the Isle of Man on Customs and Excise and Associated Matters*, Cmnd. 7747, November 1979.
8   *Acts of Tynwald, 1979*, pp. 259–61.
9   See 96 *Manx Deb.*, 28 November 1978, pp. K153–54; at the time the chair of the Harbour Board, Roy MacDonald, was an MLC.
10  See *Acts of Tynwald 1979*, pp. 71–84, 93–101, 105–41, 161–66, 181–84 and 209–31 and *Acts of Tynwald 1981*, pp. 319–35.
11  See *Second Interim Report of the Select Committee on Constitutional Issues*, 30 June 1981 (Douglas, 1981) and 98 *Manx Deb.*, 14 July 1981, pp. T1499–517 and 1531–42.
12  For details, see Kermode, *Devolution at Work*, pp. 59–63; see also Kniveton, *Chronicle of the Twentieth Century*, vol. 2, pp. 72, 89 and 93.
13  See 84 *Manx Deb.*, 7 March 1967, pp. 754–70.
14  See 84 *Manx Deb.*, 23 March 1967, pp. 955–76 and 19 April 1967, pp. 1207–18.
15  The Act was applied to the Isle of Man by Order in Council; SI 1967/1276.
16  See 84 *Manx Deb.*, 8 August 1967, pp. 1825–96
17  Interestingly the leading participants in the Keys' campaign of protest, Irving, MacDonald and Simcocks, were nominated for membership, but were unsuccessful; see 84 *Manx Deb.*, 12 September 1967, pp. 1908–11.
18  *Report of the Joint Working Party on the Constitutional Relationship between the Isle of Man and the United Kingdom* (Douglas, 1969).
19  For details, see Kermode, *Devolution at Work*, pp. 63–66.
20  *Royal Commission on the Constitution 1969–1973*, vol. 1, Cmnd. 5460 (HMSO, 1973), para. 1513.
21  For a discussion of the Royal Assent process before 1981, see the author's *Devolution at Work*,

pp. 142–46 and 'The Process of Royal Assent to Manx Legislation: A Study of Refusals since 1900', *Proceedings of the Isle of Man Natural History and Antiquarian Society*, VIII, 2, pp. 130–38.

22  For details, see Kermode, *Devolution at Work*, pp. 9–10 and Mark Solly, *Government and Law in the Isle of Man* (Castletown, 1994), pp. 147–77.

23  See 87 *Manx Deb.*, 21 April 1970, pp. 1366–402.

24  This was clearly stated to a special meeting of the House of Keys in August 1971 by Deemster Moore; 88 *Manx Deb.*, 23 August 1971, pp. 692–723.

25  89 *Manx Deb.*, 14 December 1971, pp. 179–234. See also *Treaty of Accession 1972*, Cmnd. 4862(1), Protocol 3, pp. 82–84. For a more detailed explanation of the Island's position under Protocol 3, see T. W. Cain, 'The Isle of Man and the European Union', 27 *MLB* (1 July 1996–31 December 1996), pp. 65–76.

26  See *Final Report of the Tynwald Select Committee on the Common Market*, October 1981 and 99 *Manx Deb.*, 14 October 1981, p. T139.

27  Council of Europe, European Court of Human Rights, *Tyrer Case: Judgement 25 April 1978* (Strasbourg, 1978), p. 16; see also Kermode, *Devolution at Work*, pp. 165 and 168–69; *The Manx Law Reports 1978–80* (Oxford, 1986), pp. 13–44 and Kniveton, *Chronicle of the Twentieth Century*, vol. 2, pp. 130, 136 and 150.

28  See 86 *Manx Deb.*, 21 January 1969, pp. 759–60.

29  See 94 *Manx Deb.*, 19 October 1976, pp. T114–28. The amendment was carried by 23 votes to nil in the Keys and by six to two in the Legislative Council, after which the amended resolution was approved without division.

30  See 99 *Manx Deb.*, 6 October 1981, pp. K1–41.

31  See the comments of the Attorney General, T. W. Cain, in reply to a question in Tynwald in May 1981, 98 *Manx Deb.*, 19 May 1981, p. T1242.

32  See *Second Interim Report of the Select Committee of Tynwald on Constitutional Issues*, 30 June 1981 (Douglas, 1981) and 98 *Manx Deb.*, 14 July 1981, pp. 1499–517 and 1531–42.

33  See comments by R. E. S. Kerruish, MLC: 'No one has queried the measure of independence which the Island possesses at this particular point in time'; 91 *Manx Deb.*, 20 November 1973, pp. T171–72.

34  75 *Manx Deb.*, 27 November 1957, pp. 279–89.

35  75 *Manx Deb.*, 28 January 1958, pp. 389–91.

36  Opponents included constitutional conservatives like Bolton, those for whom the changes proposed were too radical and others who wanted to leave the matter to the expert members of the Commission; 75 *Manx Deb.*, 29 and 30 July 1958, pp. 1160–208. The Keys' memorandum to the Commission is to be found in *Report of the Commission on the Isle of Man Constitution 14 March 1959* (Douglas, 1959), vol. II, p. 141. Speaker Qualtrough's comments while giving oral evidence are on pp. 142–52.

37  *Report of the Commission on the Isle of Man Constitution 14 March 1959*, vol. II, pp. 85–90.

38  *Report of the Commission on the Isle of Man Constitution 14 March 1959*.

39  *Report of the Commission on the Isle of Man Constitution 14 March 1959*, para. 19

40  *Report of the Commission on the Isle of Man Constitution 14 March 1959*, paras. 21–43.

41  *Report of the Commission on the Isle of Man Constitution 14 March 1959*, para. 88.

42  *Report of the Commission on the Isle of Man Constitution 14 March 1959*, para. 58.

43  *Report of the Commission on the Isle of Man Constitution 14 March 1959*, paras. 60–86 and 94–98.

44  The Isle of Man Constitution Acts 1961, 1965, 1968, 1969, 1971, 1975, 1978 and 1980; see relevant volumes of *Statutes of the Isle of Man* and the more recent annual volumes of *Acts of Tynwald*. For detail on the progress of the legislation in the face of opposition from the Legislative Council, see Kermode, *Devolution at Work*, pp. 72–79 and *The Changing Pattern of Manx Devolution*, Studies in Public Policy No. 52, Centre for the Study of Public Policy (Strathclyde, 1980) pp. 24–25; see also Solly, *Government and Law*, pp. 251–61.

45 See 78 *Manx Deb.*, 4 July 1961, pp. 1823–24.

46 See 82 *Manx Deb.*, 29 March 1965, pp. 954–55. The Bill had been rejected by seven votes to four at second reading the first time round; 80 *Manx Deb.*, 19 June 1963, pp. 1382–93. On 28 January 1964 the Bill was approved but with important amendments that were rejected by the House; see 81 *Manx Deb.*, pp. 622–23.

47 *Memorandum of the House of Keys appointed to examine Questions relating to Constitutional Development*, 1 November 1966 (an internal memorandum circulated to members of Tynwald).

48 See 86 *Manx Deb.*, 28 January 1969, pp. 766–77.

49 See 92 *Manx Deb.*, 4 February 1975, pp. C158–62. On the occasion of the second reading defeat, the voting was four in favour and four against. Of the seven indirectly elected members, four supported the change and three joined Deemster Eason in opposition. Sir John Paul did not use his casting vote and the Bill fell; see 92 *Manx Deb.*, 11 June 1974, pp. C379–94.

50 See 93 *Manx Deb.*, 17 February 1976, pp. T450–73.

51 See *Fourth Interim Report of the Select Committee on the Duties and Powers of the Lieutenant-Governor*, 29 November 1977, p. 5.

52 See *First Interim Report of the Select Committee of Tynwald on Constitutional Issues*, 6 June 1979 and 96 *Manx Deb.*, 19 June 1979, pp. T830–48 and 853–59.

53 See 78 *Manx Deb.*, 30 May 1961, pp. 1699–736.

54 *Statutes*, xix, pp. 586–97; see also 78 *Manx Deb.*, 4 July 1961, p. 2079 and 31 October 1961, pp. 99–105.

55 See 83 *Manx Deb.*, 7 December 1965, pp. 352–56.

56 *Acts of Tynwald 1978*, pp. 1–5.

57 Both phases are discussed in Kermode, *Devolution at Work*, pp. 57–59 and 96–97 and *Changing Pattern of Manx Devolution*, p. 25; see also Solly, *Government and Law*, pp. 251–61 and 309–12.

58 *Statutes*, xix, pp. 586–97.

59 *Statutes*, xix, pp. 597–605.

60 *Statutes*, xix, pp. 647–66.

61 *Statutes*, xix, pp. 666–74.

62 See 83 *Manx Deb.*, 5 April 1966, pp. 1269–72, 24 May 1966, pp. 1657–70 and 14 June 1966, pp. 1685–97. An eve-of-election report by the Constitutional Development Committee came down firmly in support of Kneale; see 84 *Manx Deb.*, 25 October 1966, pp. 191–210.

63 *Statutes*, xx, pp. 378–82. For background to this change, see 81 *Manx Deb.*, 11 February 1964, pp. 525–28 and 84 *Manx Deb.*, 25 April 1967, pp. 1256–58.

64 See *MacDermott Report*, vol. 1, paras. 47–49. The Standing Orders of the House of Keys and Tynwald were amended to allow the Speaker the right to vote or abstain.

65 See 83 *Manx Deb.*, 12 July 1966, pp. 1930–45; the voting in the House was 15 to five in favour, one short of the required two thirds majority, with the Speaker and the two other Executive Council MHKs opposed; the voting in the Legislative Council was four to five, with four of the five opponents being Executive Council members.

66 See 84 *Manx Deb.*, 14 February 1967, pp. 511–49.

67 See *Statutes*, xx, pp. 447–48 and 84 *Manx Deb.*, 9 April 1968, p. 1406; see also Kniveton, *Chronicle of the Twentieth Century*, vol. 2, p. 95.

68 *Acts of Tynwald 1976*, pp. 623–29.

69 *Acts of Tynwald 1980*, pp. 1–39.

70 Clifford Irving; see 95 *Manx Deb.*, 21 June 1978, p. T945.

71 *Report of the Isle of Man Police Board on the Transfer of the Governor's Functions relating to the Police and a Review of the Police (Isle of Man) Act 1962* (Douglas, 1979); 96 *Manx Deb.*, 10 July 1979, pp. T990–1000.

72 *Acts of Tynwald 1980*, pp. 183–92.

73 *Acts of Tynwald 1981*, pp. 181–99.

74 *Acts of Tynwald 1981*, pp. 65–69.

75 *Acts of Tynwald 1981*, pp. 107–16.

76 See 96 *Manx Deb.*, 19 June 1979, pp. T830–48 and 853–59; *Acts of Tynwald 1980*, pp. 151–55.

77 See 97 *Manx Deb.*, 18 November 1980, p. T236; Irving's nomination was approved by 23 votes to three.

78 See *Acts of Tynwald 1981*, pp. 163–67; for details of the conflict between the branches, see 98 *Manx Deb.*, 23 June 1981, pp. K987–1010 and C467–85 and 99 *Manx Deb.*, 6 October 1981, p. K55.

79 See 99 *Manx Deb.*, 24 November 1981, pp. T235–37.

80 See 85 *Manx Deb.*, 21 May 1968, pp. 1553–56 and 86 *Manx Deb.*, 20 May 1969, pp. 1735–40.

81 See 91 *Manx Deb.*, 15 January 1974, pp. C135–36.

82 *MacDermott Report*, vol. 1, para. 87.

83 See 99 *Manx Deb.*, 15 December 1981, p. T271.

84 In an interview with the author, on 21 June 1978.

85 In an interview with the author, on 26 May 1978

86 In an interview with the author, 15 September 1978.

87 See Kermode, *Devolution at Work*, pp. 126–28.

88 See 89 *Manx Deb.*, 2 May 1972, pp. K255–74 and 91 *Manx Deb.*, 22 January 1974, pp. K223–40.

89 See 98 *Manx Deb.*, 18 and 19 November 1980, pp. T247–78.

# CHAPTER SEVEN

# Devolution and Public Policy 1958–81

The constitutional reforms of 1958 did not lead to any weakening of the Island's strong ties to the UK. On the contrary, the UK's influence remained powerful, especially on welfare policies, spending and indirect taxation. The real value of the Island's special status was that it could choose when to follow the UK, when not to and when to develop distinctive Manx policies. Given the bitterly fought conflicts between the major UK parties, the Island was not affected by changes of government there as much as might have been expected, for there was a much higher level of consensus between the parties in the areas where UK influence was greatest than in either the immediate postwar period or following the election of a Conservative Government in 1979. By contrast, the conflicts between successive governments that dominated UK politics, over public ownership, comprehensive education, prices and incomes, industrial relations and the organisation of central, local and health service government, were seen to be of limited or no relevance to the Island. The Island chose not to follow UK social legislation in such areas as race, sex and abortion. Perhaps the most significant use of the Island's right to be different was in the way it sought to diversify the economy and assist tourism.

## *The Elections of 1962, 1966, 1971 and 1976*

While there were no changes in the distribution of seats in this period, there were important modifications to the franchise and the qualifications for being a candidate. There were two franchise reforms, the abolition of the property vote in 1969 and a lowering of the voting age from 21 to 18 in 1971, one the culmination of a lengthy struggle and 21 years after the UK, the other following the example set by the UK in 1969. There were also three reforms relating to candidates' qualifications; in 1971 membership of local councils was made incompatible with membership of the Keys, while 1976 saw the introduction of a three-year residency qualification and £100 election deposits. With the exception of the lowering of the voting age, each of these reforms had been considered and rejected on previous occasions. Surprisingly, given the number of unsuccessful attempts at reform, the Representation of the People (Registration of Electors) Act 1969,[1] which provided for the abolition of the property vote in national elections, became law after a relatively smooth passage. When abolition was recommended by a committee of Tynwald in 1963, the voting was nine to 13

House of Keys with Speaker Corlett, June 1961. First elected to the House in 1946, Corlett served as Speaker from 1960 until his defeat in the general election of 1962. The MHKs shown here were responsible for the raft of constitutional legislation that was passed between 1959 and 1962. Left back (front of photograph to rear): E. N. Crowe (Michael), J. L. Callister and H. H. Radcliffe (Ayre), messenger, A. C. Teare and A. S. Kelly (Ramsey); left front (front to rear): H. S. Cain, W. E. Quayle and J. C. Nivison (Middle), T. H. Colebourn (Castletown), G. C. Gale (Peel), T. F. Corkill (Glenfaba) and Frank Johnson (Secretary to Keys); speaker's chair: H. K. Corlett (Glenfaba); right front (front to rear): J. L. Quine and H. C. Kerruish (Garff), E. Callister (North Douglas), T. A. Corkish and R. C. Stephen (South Douglas) and W. B. Kaneen (East Douglas); right back (front to rear): T. A. Coole, C. C. McFee and A. H. Simcocks (Rushen), J. M. Cain (East Douglas), J. B. Bolton and E. C. Irving (West Douglas).

against in the Keys and two to nine in the Legislative Council.[2] The private member's bill introduced by Clifford Irving in 1967 received an easy passage in the Keys—where the voting on the third reading was 17 to three in favour—and acceptance without division in the Legislative Council.[3] The Representation of the People (Franchise) Act 1971 was one of the least controversial reforms, becoming law following a report by a committee of the House in favour of reducing the voting age to 18 in line with the UK.[4] The parallel legislation passed in 1971, precluding simultaneous membership of Tynwald and local authorities, marked the end of a long campaign by those who believed that the postwar growth in the responsibilities of Tynwald had made it impossible for individuals to do justice to both jobs and that members of Tynwald ought to be able to deal impartially with local authorities. Conflict between the branches had prevented legislation in 1964 and the Representation of the People (Members of Tynwald and Local Authorities) Act 1971 only became law after initially being rejected by the Legislative Council, the branch that had supported change in 1964. Victor Kneale's private member's bill had received the overwhelming backing of the House in 1970, but was defeated at second reading in the Legislative Council, where a split vote was followed by Stallard's refusal to exercise his casting vote. When the Bill was reintroduced, it was approved by the Council without division. On the subject of election deposits, the branches were divided over the proposal in 1964, very close to agreement with an Executive Council initiative on the eve of the general election in 1971 and united in support of a second Executive Council initiative in 1976.[5] Less controversially, the Representation of the People (Amendment) Act 1976 also introduced a residential qualification for aspiring candidates, the initial five-year proposal being moderated to three during passage in the Legislative Council.[6]

On four separate occasions during the 1970s members of Tynwald sought the establishment of a commission to enquire into aspects of electoral representation. On three occasions Tynwald opposed the resolutions in question before finally agreeing to a commission in 1979. The debates on these resolutions, moved by Clifford Irving in November 1970 and October 1971, Edward Kermeen in March 1977 and Roy

Members of the Commission on the Representation of the People Acts, February 1980. The Butler Commission was appointed by Sir John Paul in November 1979 and reported in March 1980. From left to right the members are Henry Kelly, David Butler and H. D. Teare. Michael Kinley (standing) was secretary to the Commission.

MacDonald in June 1979, revealed three main concerns, the unfair distribution of seats, the inegalitarian mix of single and multimember constituencies and the increasingly common election of members on a minority vote.[7] Chaired by the UK psephologist David Butler, the Commission reported on 26 March 1980 with three main recommendations. First, to guarantee fair representation there should be reviews of constituency boundaries at least every 15 years and more frequently in the event of major changes to local authority boundaries. The Commission suggested that deviations from the average number of voters per member should not exceed 15 per cent. In an Island the size of the Isle of Man there was no case for over-representation of rural areas. Second, while there were advantages for electors in having more than one representative, fairness demanded that the whole Island be divided into multimember constituencies. The Commission offered Tynwald a series of detailed options, including all two-, all three- or all four-member constituencies or a mixture of two- and three-member constituencies. Third, the Island should replace the first-past-the-post method of election by the single transferable vote (STV), thus honouring the principle of one person one vote and removing the possibility of electing members on a minority vote.[8] Tynwald was divided over each of these proposals, but agreed by the slenderest of majorities to support periodic review as recommended, the mixture of two- and three-member constituencies detailed in Appendix J to the Commission's Report and the adoption of STV.[9] However, bills introduced to provide for the agreed distribution of seats and the new method of voting were both defeated at second reading in the Keys, the Representation of the People (Redistribution of Seats) Bill by 12 votes to 10 in December 1980 and the Representation of the People (STV) Bill by 13 votes to nine in February 1981.[10] Accordingly, for the 1981 general election, the unfair representation identified in evidence to the Commission and in the Commission's Report continued. The number of electors per member varied widely, only Castletown, East and South Douglas and Ramsey falling within 15 per cent of the average of 1,977 per member. At one extreme the figures for Ayre, Glenfaba and Gafff were 1,113, 1,284 and 1,318 respectively; at the other the figures for Middle, Peel and North Douglas were 2,564, 2,672 and 3,127 respectively. The mixture of one-, two- and three-member seats continued to provide for unequal voting opportunities, just over 20 per cent having a single vote, 48 per cent two votes and nearly 32 per cent three votes. The retention of the first-past-the-post method of election made the election of candidates on a minority vote a continuing probability.

Between March 1958 and the general election in 1962 the deaths of George Taggart in 1958, Richard Cannell in 1959 and Speaker Qualtrough in 1960, and the elevation of Harold Nicholls and George Moore to the Legislative Council in 1958, led to a series of by-elections and the election of five new MHKs. Two were from the MLP, T. Albert Corkish replacing Taggart in South Douglas and George C. Gale recapturing Peel, thereby increasing MLP representation in the House to six; the other three were Independents. The death of Sir Joseph Qualtrough in January 1960, at the age of 74 and after 40 years as MHK for Castletown and 22 as SHK, brought to an end a long and distinguished political career. He was the outstanding politician of his generation, at the forefront of the Island's campaigns for constitutional and social reform, a highly respected Speaker of the House and a much admired chair of boards and committees of Tynwald. On his death members of Tynwald were united in their praise for Sir Joseph and, having studied the many reports, debates and decisions with which he was associated, one is left in no doubt that this praise was eminently deserved.[11]

The immediate background to the 1962 general election was the raft of constitutional legislation resulting from the MacDermott Commission. Indeed the life of the House had been extended by three months under the Representation of the People Act 1961 to enable the constitutional legislation to be completed prior to the election.[12] The reforms were due to be implemented after the election and there was little appetite for further reform shown during the campaign. A handful of influential figures in the reform movement did seek further change, but they were the exceptions—Bert Stephen and Charles Kerruish advocated the removal of the Deemsters from the Legislative Council and the further transfer of gubernatorial power; Stephen and Howard Simcocks campaigned for the replacement of the board system by a cabinet/ministerial system. MLP members continued their struggle for the abolition of the property vote. There was general support for the welfare state with candidates favouring particular improvements: a cost-of-living supplement for pensioners, more investment in technical training, the merger of the Board of Education and the Education Authority, a national housing policy, more housing for the elderly and a concerted effort to make full employment a reality. The central issue was how to promote the health of the ailing Manx economy. Most welcomed the abolition of surtax and the policy of attracting new residents and investment, wanted to see more new industries, including a commercial radio station, and saw no real alternative for agriculture and fisheries to the policy of subsidisation broadly in line with the UK. The area that aroused most controversy was tourism, proposals for a casino, the registration and grading of tourist accommodation and the removal of constraints on licensing proving especially divisive. Almost as controversial were demands for increased state intervention in the field of transport, ranging from public ownership of all local passenger transport to ownership or control of the Isle of Man Steam Packet Company.

Exceptionally the election was held in January/February, three months later than usual. There were 54 candidates and contests in each of the 13 constituencies. There were 10 MLP candidates, a solitary MPPA candidate and 43 Independents, of whom three were Independent Labour. All but two of the retiring members (Cecil Teare and Clifford Irving, the latter temporarily retiring from politics to devote more time to his business) sought re-election and 16 were successful, including three out of the five MHK members of Executive Council, Bolton, Charles Kerruish and Simcocks. The defeat of Cain in East Douglas, the first chair of the Tourist Board to serve on the Executive Council, came as no surprise, being the result of strong opposition, in particular to the Board's proposed registration of tourist premises. The narrow defeat of Speaker Corlett in Glenfaba was a complete surprise. Two of those who were successful, MPPA member Bolton and MLP member Nivison, were immediately elevated to the Legislative Council and replaced by Independents, Bolton's replacement being Cain, the previously defeated chair of the Tourist Board. The MLP won six seats and former MLP member, Stephen, one of the most active and effective MHKs prior to the dissolution, retained his seat as Independent Labour, although Labour's numbers were reduced following the Party's failure to retain the seat vacated by Nivison. The respect earned by Stephen on all sides of the House was rewarded when he was elected the first chair of the Finance Board. Eric R. Moore, a 30-year-old farmer representing Garff, was the Party's only new member. Among the other new MHKs were three future members of Executive Council, Edward S. Kerruish, a 54-year-old agricultural merchant who defeated one of the sitting members in Ayre, Victor Kneale, a 44-year-old insurance agent who topped the poll in West Douglas and Robert Creer, a 53-year-old master builder who was successful in Middle. On

13 February 1962 the 44-year-old member for Garff, Charles Kerruish, was elected as Speaker of the House. He was one of only four surviving members of the 1946 House and his nomination gained the unanimous support of the House. Following election he promised that, with the support of the House, he would endeavour 'to develop the power and authority of this House in keeping with modern democratic thought'.[13]

The political complexion of the new House was not markedly different from that of the old, a conservative majority, but with a significant minority of Labour and Independents with a progressive pedigree. In the course of the parliament, by-elections tended to favour the conservative wing of the House. The elevation of Hubert Radcliffe in 1963 paved the way for the election of a 47-year-old farmer, Percy Radcliffe, a future chair of Executive Council. When two more MLP members were elected to the Legislative Council, McFee in December 1962 and Gale in October 1964, both were replaced by Independents; surprisingly the MLP did not even contest the Rushen seat, a reflection of the Party's organisational weakness outside of Douglas. The Party's only by-election success in this period followed the death of Stephen in 1964, when master decorator, John J. Bell, recaptured the South Douglas seat for the Party. A second by-election in Peel in January 1966 saw the election of another Independent in the one-time Labour stronghold, Roy MacDonald, a 45-year-old retired RAF officer and also a future member of Executive Council. Again too much emphasis should not be placed on political labels, different issues before the House giving rise to different coalitions in support or opposition and individuals like Bolton and Stephen attracting support on the basis of their performance as much as their political leanings.

The preoccupation of the new House with constitutional reform stands in marked contrast to the low priority given to it by most candidates. The only positive outcome was the replacement of the Second Deemster on the Legislative Council by an indirectly elected member, attempts to reduce the Council's delaying power, slim down the membership of boards, fix the Keys' representation on the Executive Council and make the holding of executive office incompatible with the office of Speaker each proving unsuccessful prior to the 1966 election. While the advocates of electoral reform were successful in setting up a select committee to investigate the subject, only one of its recommendations for change, the provision for absent voters, became law in time for the 1966 election.[14] The impact of the election on welfare policy was varied. The Island kept in line with the UK in respect of social security, but did not introduce universal cost-of-living supplements for pensioners. Tynwald agreed in principle to support the establishment of a College of Further Education and the merger of the Board of Education and the Education Authority, but little progress was made on either front until after the election of 1966. The transfer of the voluntary hospitals to the Health Services Board in 1963 had not been an election issue. A national housing policy was agreed in 1963 with the needs of the elderly accorded the highest priority. Record levels of expenditure were voted for winter work schemes. The major economic initiative came with Tynwald's approval of a 14-point Development Plan with the aim of expanding light industry, attracting new residents and promoting tourism. Finally, in 1964 Tynwald asked the Lieutenant-Governor to appoint a Transport Commission, which in June 1966 duly recommended a major increase in the role of the state, a Transport Board with responsibility for the oversight and control of transport, government participation and a controlling interest in the operation of the Steam Packet and an extension of public ownership to include all the Island's railways and buses. No action was taken on these recommendations before the election in November 1966.

Events immediately prior to the 1966 election guaranteed a high profile for constitutional issues. Internally, the eve-of-election report by the Keys' Constitutional Development Committee, which had been approved by 18 members of the outgoing House, recommended changes to the role of the Speaker of the House and the composition of the Executive and Legislative Councils. Externally, the possibility of UK membership of the EEC, the determination of the UK authorities to outlaw Radio Caroline, a seven-week strike called by the UK-based National Union of Seamen and an eve-of-election report by the Finance Board opposing abrogation of the Common Purse Agreement, had each highlighted the vulnerability of the Island to UK decisions and contributed to demands for greater constitutional autonomy. Electoral reform attracted scant attention, although the abolition of the property vote remained MLP policy and some Douglas candidates pressed for a further redistribution of seats. There was a broad consensus over welfare policy, albeit with differences of emphasis and detail; while demands for improvements to the education and health services were widespread, the proposed abolition of the education rate and MLP demands for employment legislation covering health and safety at work and redundancy payments were more controversial. Interestingly there were no demands to follow the UK's decisions in 1965 to abolish the death penalty and outlaw racial discrimination.

The deepest conflict was over the role of government in support of the Manx economy. Speaker Kerruish's Island-wide campaign in defence of government policies attracted both support and opposition. However, even though opponents were critical of the waste and extravagance of particular elements of the Island's Development Plan, few were willing to challenge the principle of government support for the economy and most welcomed the twin goals of support for traditional industries and diversification. Low direct taxation was criticised by the MLP, but broadly welcomed as a means of attracting new residents, investment and industry. Candidates were divided over indirect taxation and whether to retain, amend or abrogate the Common Purse Agreement. MLP candidates sought the implementation of the recommendations of the Transport Commission, some of which took on new meaning after the the NUS strike at the beginning of the 1966 season. Many candidates expressed their support for government to take a controlling interest in the Steam Packet. Finally, there was controversy over the role of the state in permitting, regulating or prohibiting such activities as gambling and drinking; there were arguments for and against the more liberal policies of the 1960s, which had seen the development of the casino, public lotteries and Sunday opening, and demands for further liberalisation in the interests of the tourist industry.

There were 54 candidates in the 1966 election and contests in each constituency. There were nine MLP candidates, one Mec Vannin (nationalist) and 44 Independents. Nineteen members of the old House sought re-election and 15 were successful, including the MHKs on the Executive Council, Norman Crowe, Charles Kerruish and William Quayle. The election also saw the re-election of Clifford Irving, an influential member between 1955 and 1962 and a future chair of Executive Council. For the MLP the election was a disaster, the decline experienced after the previous general election continuing. It lost two of its four seats. Only Edward Callister in North Douglas and Albert Corkish in South Douglas were successful, leaving the Party unrepresented outside of Douglas for the first time since 1919. In contrast to the immediate postwar collapse, however, the Party was unable to recoup its losses in by-elections. Each of the five by-elections between 1966 and 1971 were won by Independents, including that in South Douglas in October 1968, where John Bell was returned to the Keys as an

Independent. Among the eight new MHKs were two future members of Executive Council, 50-year-old company director, Colin L. P. Vereker in Castletown and 45-year-old farmer, Ian Anderson, who topped the poll in Glenfaba; in Garff Jean Thornton-Duesbery became the third woman to sit in the House. Following the election, the other member for Garff, Charles Kerruish was elected Speaker for a second term.

The domestic constitutional concerns expressed during and immediately after the election led to changes in the role of the Speaker and the membership of the Executive and Legislative Councils, a reduction in the size of certain boards and the appointment of a select committee on the powers and duties of the Lieutenant-Governor. The external concerns led to a review of the Island's constitutional relationship with the UK, successful negotiations by a select committee on the EEC, the unanimous approval of the Finance Board's recommendation to stay with the Common Purse Agreement and an exploration of the costs of government acquiring a controlling interest in the Steam Packet Company. Electoral reforms were approved in 1969 and 1971. With respect to the welfare state, Tynwald agreed to increased investment in education, including the funding of a new college of further education, the raising of the school leaving age to 16 and the merger of the Board of Education and the Education Authority; it approved funding for a major upgrading and expansion of Noble's Hospital; it passed the Urban Housing Improvement Act 1969; however, it rejected MLP-inspired employment legislation. Economic policy reflected both the consensus in favour of support for the economy and the conflict over particular ways of providing that support. The continued subsidisation of agriculture and fishing aroused little conflict. Tourism, although generating much more debate, benefited from the appointment in 1968 of the Tourist Industry Development Commission and an increasingly interventionist regime, with investment in transport, accommodation and entertainment on an unprecedented scale. Electoral demands for a further liberalisation of the laws regulating gambling and drinking resulted in a series of measures, the Betting Act 1970 legalising cash betting, the Licensing Act 1969 allowing the issue of special amenity licenses to hotels and boarding houses and the Licensing Act 1970 providing for an extra hour of opening on Fridays and Saturdays out of season. However, attempts by a reasonably united House to liberalise shop hours were defeated in the Legislative Council in 1970 because of opposition to the proposed extension of shop opening hours and the further commercialisation of Sundays.

Despite the considerable economic progress made by the Island during the 1960s, economic issues dominated the 1971 general election. Even though the negotiation of a special relationship with the EEC removed one economic uncertainty, an eve-of-election report by PA Management Consultants was a useful reminder of the continuing fragility of the Island's economic base and the importance of the state in promoting the economic health of the Island. The successful outcome of the EEC negotiations also removed the one big constitutional issue. Beyond that constitutional reform was a priority for only a handful of candidates, most notably the three Mec Vannin candidates standing on a nationalist platform and Charles Kerruish, who campaigned for further reductions in the powers of the Legislative Council and the Lieutenant-Governor and for MHKs to chair all the major boards. Electoral reform was a priority for a few candidates, who demanded the redistribution of seats, single member constituencies and the introduction of a residential qualification for candidates. Much was said during the campaign about ways in which the welfare state might be improved both generally and in particular constituencies, but for the most part the proposals were uncontroversial. The MLP and several others sought a cost-of-living supplement for pensioners; there were demands for the full costs of education to be borne by Tynwald, for improvements to the service at all levels and for the establishment of a university on the Island; with health and housing too the plea was for better services, the MLP also seeking the restoration of private sector rent control; with unemployment virtually disappeared, there was almost no reference to employment issues, except for the MLP's reiteration of the need for legislation covering health and safety at work, redundancy payments and employment protection. At this juncture candidates were silent on two of the UK's most controversial social measures of this period, the legalisation of homosexual acts between consenting adults in 1966 and of abortion in 1967. On economic policy there was conflict over both taxation and spending. While most supported low direct taxation, the MLP argued for a more redistributive policy with higher overall levels and the introduction of estate duties. With the introduction of value-added tax about to accompany UK entry into the EEC, there were fresh demands for a review of the Common Purse and particular pleas for the tourist industry to be zero rated. There was widespread recognition of the importance of the state as regulator and investor in the economy, but differences of opinion over the nature, extent and detail of state intervention. Opinion was divided over population policy, with a small minority pressing for restrictions on the influx of new residents, over the extent to which economic development should be planned, with a few candidates advocating strict development planning, over the level of government support for tourist accommodation and facilities, over the degree of state involvement in transport, the MLP supporting the most radical options of subsidisation and public ownership of internal passenger transport and subsidisation and public control of sea and air transport, and over the regulation of gambling and drinking, a minority seeking a further liberalisation. The 1971 election campaign was also distinctive in being the first of the century in which law and order issues were prioritised by a significant minority of candidates. This was the result of publicity surrounding a petition to Tynwald on 5 July 1971 for the appointment of an independent commission to review the law providing for judicial corporal punishment in the Isle of Man.[15] The petition was the latest in a series of moves by Millicent Faragher, Angela Kneale and Valerie Roach aimed at the abolition of corporal punishment and provoked several candidates into defending such punishment for crimes of violence.

There were 52 candidates in the 1971 election and contests in 12 of the 13 constituencies, Roy MacDonald being returned unopposed in Peel. There were five MLP candidates, the lowest number since the Party first contested a general election in 1919, three Mec Vannin candidates and 44 Independents. Twenty-three members of the old House and one former member, Cecil McFee, sought re-election and of these 19 were successful, including four of the five MHK members of Executive Council, Anderson, Edward Kerruish, Kneale and Percy Radcliffe. Vereker lost his seat in Castletown. McFee, retiring MLC and chair of the Health Services Board, narrowly failed to recapture his old seat in Rushen. McFee's defeat and the poor performance of the MLP in its traditional stronghold of South Douglas, where Albert Corkish lost his seat, was further evidence of the Party's decline since 1962; as in 1966 it emerged with only two MHKs. Both were new to the House, W. Alexander Moore, a 59-year-old lido manager and future member of Executive Council, winning in North Douglas, and Edmund Ranson, a 68-year-old retired coach operator, winning a seat in Middle on his fourth attempt. None of the three Mec Vannin candidates were successful. Two of the five new members were women, Elspeth C. Quayle and Katharine E. Cowin, bringing female membership of the House to three. Following the election of Kneale to the Legislative Council in 1974, the success of Betty Q. Hansen in West Douglas brought that membership to four. The other three by-elections between 1971 and 1976 had the effect of doubling MLP representation and bringing into the House three future members of Executive Council; in October 1974 the MLP recaptured a seat in South Douglas through the candidature of E. Matthew Ward, a 62-year-old retired Post Office engineer; the by-election in Rushen in December 1974, which followed the elevation of Simcocks to the Legislative Council, was won by 37-year-old farmer and auctioneer, Noel Q. Cringle, after a close two-way battle with MLP candidate, Edmund G. Lowey; the following December, Lowey, a 37-year-old setter operator with the Ronaldsway Aircraft Company, gave Rushen its first MLP member since the elevation of McFee to the Legislative Council in 1962.

The five years from 1971 to 1976 were of major constitutional significance. Tynwald formally accepted the special relationship with the European Communities provided under Protocol 3 to the Treaty of Accession. The Isle of Man Constitution (Amendment) Act 1975 removed the First Deemster from the Legislative Council and Tynwald. The Governor's Financial and Judicial Functions (Transfer) Act 1976 was the first of a series of measures emanating from the work of the select committee chaired by Speaker Kerruish. The Representation of the People (Amendment) Act 1976 saw the introduction of election deposits and a residential qualification for candidates standing for the House of Keys. While Manx welfare policies continued to follow those of the UK, this period did see some of the specific improvements sought during the election campaign. In 1974 levels of supplementary benefit were increased above UK levels to compensate for the higher cost of living in the Island. Tynwald approved funding for improvements in secondary school provision and teachers' pay and in 1974 agreed to a phasing out of the education rate. Funding was also agreed for the development of facilities for geriatric patients at Noble's Hospital. The Housing Improvement Act 1975 provided for higher levels of improvement grants for both urban and rural housing and, much to the delight of MLP members, the Health and Safety at Work Act 1977 passed through both branches before the election in November 1976.

Economic policy after 1971 was increasingly interventionist, although not all proposals for intervention were successful. The powers of government to control and regulate the economy were increased by such measures as the General Control of the Economy Act 1974, the Land Speculation Tax Act 1974 and the Banking Act 1975. Attempts were made to control the influx of new residents, but these were first watered down in the House of Keys and then defeated in the Legislative Council. The Town and Country Planning (General Development) Order 1974 provided that all development of land should have LGB approval and the Board continued with the preparation of an all-Island development plan. Major development projects were financed, including the Chester Street/Wellington Square development, new central government offices, new fire brigade headquarters and new police headquarters in Douglas and the South Ramsey Development. Tynwald's commitment to the tourist industry was reflected in support for the rebuilding of Summerland after the fire in 1973, progressively higher levels of funding for improvements to tourist accommodation, the compulsory registration and grading of such accommodation and measures to safeguard the lifeline provided by the Isle of Man Steam Packet Company, most notably the provision of loans, the purchase of shares and subsidies for travel in May and September. Tynwald also subsidised local passenger transport. Finally, Tynwald considered proposals by the Liquor Licensing

Commission to extend public house opening hours, but the branches failed to reach agreement before the 1976 election.

Although the 1976 election saw a confrontation between the defenders of government policy, led by the chair of Executive Council, Percy Radcliffe, and critics, including several Independents and the ten Mec Vannin candidates, the areas of disagreement were far less than was suggested by the language of the campaign. While Mec Vannin adopted the most extreme position on the constitution, there was general support among other candidates for Tynwald's ongoing campaign to maximise the Island's constitutional autonomy. Mec Vannin campaigned for the direct election of the Legislative Council, referenda on major policy and, in common with several Independents, more open and accountable government. For most candidates electoral reform was not an issue, but Mec Vannin demanded proportional representation, redistribution and single member constituencies. Equally controversial were proposals under discussion for the regionalisation of Manx local government, most raising the issue choosing to defend the status quo. As in other elections since the war, there was a consensus on most welfare issues, a better deal for pensioners, better standards and new investment in education, health and housing and measures to enable more people to gain permanent employment. Mec Vannin and a few Independents pressed for Manx or Celtic Studies to be made part of the educational curriculum. On employment the two political parties advocated more controversial policies, both supporting a national minimum wage and the MLP seeking to emulate the UK with legislation on redundancy payments, unfair dismissal and equal pay.

With unemployment rising, inflation high and eve-of-election reports by PA Management Consultants on the economy (1975) and the Common Purse (1976), the major issues in the election were economic. The campaign produced the usual mixture of consensus and controversy, virtual agreement over the need for state intervention and control, but conflict over important detail. Candidates wanted to see a more self-sufficient and revitalised agricultural sector, benefitting from support equivalent to that available in the UK, and a better deal for Manx fishing, several stressing the need for an extension of Manx territorial waters from three to 12 miles. Most also accepted the need for state support to the tourist industry, but there were strong differences of opinion over the closure of the Laxey-Ramsey service by the MER, over whether public transport should be subsidised or nationalised, and over value-added tax, several seeing selective zero rating or abrogation from the Common Purse a potentially powerful fillip to tourism. The success of the Island in attracting new residents and new industry persuaded many candidates to support established policies, but they were opposed by a substantial group, including Mec Vannin, who pressed for immigration controls and a more selective encouragement of light industry. There was also conflict over the emergence of the Island as an offshore financial centre, with some anxious to see further state encouragement of the sector and others warning of the dangers for the Island of undue dependence on it. Not surprisingly, given the lack of progress in implementing the recommendations of the 1972 Liquor Licensing Commission, several candidates reiterated demands for a liberalisation of the Island's licensing laws, including Sunday opening in winter.

For the first time in the twentieth century law and order became an issue for almost all candidates. While there were some demands for improved policing, the key issue arose from Tyrer's petition to the European Commission on Human Rights alleging that the birch was a degrading form of punishment. Most candidates simply declared their support for the birch, both as a punishment and a deterrent, but Mec Vannin argued for an independent investigation into the effects of its use. Equally novel was the scale of demand for conservation measures and the preservation of the Island's heritage; a questionnaire to all candidates from the Society for the Preservation of Manx Countryside revealed overwhelming support for each of 20 propositions, although whether most would have raised and supported these independently is doubtful.[16]

Despite the introduction of £100 election deposits, there was a record 71 candidates in the 1976 election and contests in every constituency.[17] There were 10 Mec Vannin candidates, standing on a common manifesto in constituencies across the Island, four MLP candidates seeking election in two of the Douglas constituencies, Middle and Rushen, and 57 Independents. Nineteen members sought re-election, of whom 12 were successful, including three of the four MLP candidates—Ted Ranson was defeated in Middle—nine Independents and each of the MHK members of the Executive Council, Anderson, Creer, Irving, MacDonald and Percy Radcliffe. Following the election, Charles Kerruish was elected Speaker for a fourth term.

With a 50 per cent turnover of members, the level of continuity between the old House and the new was the lowest since 1946, added to which four of the 12 who were re-elected had only been MHKs for less than two years. As in 1919 and 1946 the scale of the turnover between October 1974 and November 1976 created opportunities for relatively inexperienced members to make their mark quickly. In the course of the next 10 years three of the four by-election winners of 1974 and 1975, Cringle, Ward and Lowey, and five new MHKs were elected to the Executive Council; the new members were Arnold A. Callin, the 52-year-old secretary and general manager of Isle of Man Farms Ltd, who topped the poll in Middle, Dominic F. K. Delaney, a 33-year-old company director and public relations consultant, who won the seven-way contest in East Douglas, Edgar J. Mann, a 50-year-old general practitioner who joined the Speaker in representing Garff, J. Norman Radcliffe, a 45-year-old farmer who was runner up to his namesake, Percy Radcliffe, in Ayre and Miles Walker, a 36-year-old farmer who came second to the MLP candidate, Eddie Lowey, in Rushen. Particularly rapid progress was made by Cringle who joined the Executive Council in December 1978, Mann who became a member in February 1980 and Walker and Ward who were elected in January 1982.

The performance of the two political parties contrasted sharply. The MLP was an established party that had undergone decline and recognised its weakness by fielding only four candidates, fewer than at any election since its formation in 1918. Each of the four were sitting members, of whom three were successful and well ahead of their rivals. They probably owed their success as much to their personality and performance as to their membership of the Party. Mec Vannin, by contrast, was a relatively new political organisation, which started life in 1964 as a pressure group. It fielded candidates on an Island-wide basis and a common manifesto for the first time in 1976. One out of the 10 candidates was successful, Peter A. Craine, a 39-year-old master baker, winning a seat in South Douglas. Two others were within striking distance of victory, Charles H. Faragher, a 25-year-old hotelier coming a creditable fourth in Rushen and Allan R. Bell, a 29-year-old retailer, just 42 votes short of victory in a 10-way contest in Ramsey. Craine's election was to be Mec Vannin's first and only success in elections for the House of Keys and even that was short-lived. Divisions within the Party in 1977 led to the creation of a separate Manx National Party (MNP) with Craine becoming its solitary MHK. The failure of Mec Vannin's single candidate in the 1981 election convinced it to revert to its earlier role as a pressure group. The life of the MNP as a parliamentary party was also short-lived; although Audrey Ainsworth came within seven votes of victory in the North Douglas by-election in December 1978, the defeat of both Ainsworth and Craine in 1981 marked the end of the Party. The failure of Mec Vannin and the MNP was only partly the result of divisions in the nationalist movement. Far more important was the fact that their policies were not radically different from those advocated by other candidates save in respect of their demands for full independence. Even on the independence issue other candidates were united in seeking to maximise the Island's autonomy and welfare; in their own way many were as nationalist as their Mec Vannin challengers. As with the MLP the level of support for Mec Vannin candidates was probably as much the result of candidate personality as of party ideology, a speculation borne out by the widely different support given to the Party's candidates in the two constituencies where it fielded two candidates. It is worth noting that two of the Party's candidates in 1976 did go on to become MHKs as Independents, Faragher in 1982 and Bell in 1984, Bell going on to serve as a minister from 1986.

There were three by-elections between 1976 and 1981, following the elevation of Alex Moore, Roy MacDonald and Percy Radcliffe to the Executive Council. They saw the election of two future members of the Executive Council/Council of Ministers; David L. Moore, a 37-year-old psychologist and son of the former member for Peel, George Moore, replaced MacDonald in Peel in December 1978; Clare Christian, a 34-year-old housewife and daughter of the Speaker, captured the Ayre seat vacated by Radcliffe in March 1980; and in North Douglas in December 1978, MLP candidate, G. Arthur Quinney, a 60-year-old trade union official, scraped home by seven votes over the MNP candidate, showing that even the safest of the MLP's seats was vulnerable.

During the five years from 1976 to 1981 constitutional development was given an extremely high priority. Tynwald persisted with its struggle to maximise the Island's autonomy in the face of international pressures, while legislation reduced the delaying powers of the Legislative Council, provided for the further transfer of gubernatorial functions and empowered Tynwald to nominate and elect the chair of Executive Council. Preliminary steps were also taken towards a rationalisation of the board system. The campaign for fairer electoral representation received the support of the authoritative Butler Commission, but legislation to give effect to its recommendations was rejected by the House of Keys. No progress was made with the regionalisation of local government.

Welfare policies, which remained broadly in line with those of the UK, reflected the priorities identified during the election, with investment in residential homes for the elderly, schools, primary health care centres and extensions to Ballamona and Ramsey Cottage Hospitals. Opportunities for permanent employment were enhanced both generally by government investment in support of the economy and more particularly by the creation of a register of vacancies, the introduction of new apprenticeship schemes and amendments to the Control of Employment Acts. The Contracts of Employment Act 1981 marked the successful conclusion of a lengthy campaign by MLP members to bring the Island into line with the UK in requiring contracts of employment.

Tynwald supported an interventionist economic policy and approved a massive programme of support for the Manx economy, facilitating development by means of legislation and regulation and providing unprecedented levels of financial assistance for infrastructural and sectoral development. It continued the long and tortuous process of establishing a planning blueprint for the development of the Island and, although it was June 1982 before the Development Plan finally received approval, this period saw prolonged consultations, a public inquiry into the draft plan and legislation, the Town and Country Planning Act 1981, to facilitate its eventual implementation. It agreed in 1979 to maintain support for agriculture and fisheries on a similar basis to the UK. Members welcomed the Lieutenant-Governor's announcement in June 1981 that the UK planned to extend its territorial waters to 12 miles and that this would pave the way for a similar extension of Manx waters. Tourism was assisted by investment in amenities, improvements to tourist accommodation, a range of events associated with the celebration of Tynwald's Millennium, the public ownership of local passenger transport and the promotion of easier access to and from the Island, notably through loans to the

Members of Tynwald outside Government House on the occasion of Tynwald's Millennium, July 1979. On the front row the Queen and the Duke of Edinburgh are sitting with the Governor and Deputy Governor and members of the Legislative Council; behind, the Speaker is at the centre of the middle row with representatives of the six sheading constituencies; the back row has the representatives of the four towns and the second member for Garff. Front row, from left to right: A. H. Simcocks, R. E. S. Kerruish, R. MacDonald, J. A. C. K. Nivison, the Right Reverend V. S. Nicholls (Lord Bishop), Sir John Paul (Lieutenant-Governor), Her Majesty Queen Elizabeth II, His Royal Highness Prince Philip, R. K. Eason (First Deemster and Deputy Governor), J. W. Corrin (Attorney General), Sir John Bolton, G. V. H. Kneale, W. A. Moore, G. T. Crellin and T. A. Bawden (Clerk of the Legislative Council); middle row: R. S. Caine (Tynwald Messenger), P. Radcliffe and J. N. Radcliffe (Ayre), J. J. Radcliffe (Michael), W. K. Quirk and R. J. G. Anderson (Glenfaba), R. B. M. Quayle (Clerk of Tynwald), Sir Charles Kerruish (Speaker and member for Garff), the Reverend J. Wilson (Chaplain of the House of Keys), A. A. Callin, R. L. Watterson and J. R. Creer (Middle), E. G. Lowey, M. R. Walker and N. Q. Cringle (Rushen) and R. H. Clarke (Tynwald Messenger); back row: G. A. Quinney (North Douglas), E. C. Irving and D. F. K. Delaney (East Douglas), E. M. Ward and P. A. Craine (South Douglas), D. L. Moore (Peel), F. Joughin (Tynwald Messenger), J. J. Christian and G. C. Swales (Ramsey), B. Q. Hanson and T. E. Kermeen (West Douglas), E. C. Quayle (Castletown) and E. J. Mann (Garff).

Isle of Man Steam Packet Company and Douglas Harbour improvement works. Encouragement for light industry was given through rapidly rising levels of grant aid and loans. Far from discouraging the financial sector as some candidates had suggested, such measures as the Banking Act 1977, the Industrial and Building Societies Act 1979, the Usury Acts (Repeal) Act 1979, the Money Lenders (Amendment) Act 1979 and the Companies Act 1982 were designed to facilitate and regulate its development. Public projects commenced during this period included new headquarters for the Isle of Man Post Office, shore-based facilities for a roll on/roll off linkspan unit, the Douglas Harbour breakwater scheme and the Sulby reservoir. There was also action in each of the areas of highest controversy during the election. Subsidies for local passenger transport were increased, the Laxey-Ramsey stretch of the MER reopened and the steam railway and buses taken into public ownership. Negotiations with the UK led to the replacement of the Common Purse Agreement by the Customs and Excise Agreement in 1979, albeit without any new variations from UK levels of indirect taxation. A select committee of Tynwald recommended the introduction of statutory controls of immigration so that they would be available if needed. Considerable energy was expended on the issue of judicial corporal punishment following the 1978 decision of the European Court of Human Rights, but to no real avail. Finally, after twice being rejected by the Legislative Council, the Licensing (Sunday Opening) Act 1981 provided for the opening of public houses on Sundays in winter.

## Expansion of the Welfare State

Although there were differences between the two major UK parties over both principle and the detail of policy, there were important areas of bipartisan agreement and a common commitment to improving services. The end result was that successive governments presided over a steady increase in welfare spending. For the most part the Isle of Man chose to follow the UK. There were important differences of detail in the way particular services were developed, but in each of social security, education, health and housing a policy of expansion prevailed.

In the case of social security there were few differences even of detail, save in the field of noncontributory benefits. Although there were periodic expressions of concern at the lack of any real opportunity for the Island to influence policy, the benefits of research, development, legislative and regulatory expertise and above all reciprocity were generally seen to outweigh this cost.[18] This was certainly the view of Jack Nivison, the highly respected chair of the Board of Social Services/Social Security from 1951 to 1976. Notwithstanding their controversial nature, the Board under both Nivison and his successor Noel Cringle advised Tynwald to keep strictly in line with the major changes in UK provision insofar as contributory schemes were concerned.[19] Changes to contributions and associated benefits came into effect simultaneously with the UK, including the major increases introduced by the Labour Government on coming to office in 1964 and 1974 and the subsequent linking between 1975 and 1980 of pensions and other long-term benefits with the more beneficial of movements in retail prices or average earnings and short-term benefits with retail prices; in 1980 the Island followed the Conservative Government's decision to upgrade benefits solely by reference to retail prices. In 1961 the Island emulated the Conservative Government in providing for graduated additions to retirement pensions in return for earnings-related contributions. In 1966 it adopted the Labour Government's scheme for paying earnings-related supplements with employment and sickness benefits in return for graduated contributions. In 1975 it followed the Labour Government in replacing the 1961 graduated pension scheme with a fully earnings-related scheme and in 1978 adopted UK modifications to that scheme.

The position regarding noncontributory benefits was different, at least in respect of those that were means tested. Here the absence of the constraints of reciprocal agreements left room for local discretion. For the most part the Island still ended up following the UK, but after an interval of years and an evaluation of UK experience in relation to Manx needs. Thus the Labour Government's introduction of supplementary benefit in place of national assistance grants in 1966 was not followed until 1970.[20] Under this scheme access to financial benefit became a right once individuals had satisfied the prevailing means test; in the case of the Isle of Man there was also a five-year residential qualification and this was increased to 10 years in 1975. In a similar way, the Conservative Government's family income supplement scheme, initiated in 1971 to help poor families, was not taken up until 1975.[21] By contrast, Labour's replacement in 1977 of family allowances, which were payable only to second and subsequent children, by child benefit, payable to mothers in respect of every child, came into effect simultaneously in the Isle of Man. As with family allowances the new benefit was not means tested and was the subject of a reciprocal agreement with the UK.[22] The only significant independent initiative was the 1974 decision to increase supplementary benefit above UK levels to compensate for higher costs of living; repeated demands had been made for a cost-of-living supplement for all pensioners, but, on the advice of the Finance Board, Tynwald followed the precedent set with national assistance between 1954 and 1961 and targeted an extra cost-of-living increase for those most in need.[23]

Total revenue spending by Tynwald on social security and related welfare services for the elderly and infirm rose steadily from £486,824 in 1957/58 to £1,758,772 in 1973/74 before rising sharply to £8,473,562 in 1980/81. This represented an increase in real terms of just over 200 per cent, attributable partly to enhanced standards of service and partly to the rise in the Island's population as a whole and the numbers of pensioners and children in particular.[24] Capital spending on residential accommodation for the elderly and infirm also increased towards the end of this period with major investment in new residential homes in Victoria Road, Douglas and South Ramsey. After modest levels of spending between 1962/63 and 1975/76, a sum of £477,062 over the 14-year period, capital spending by the Board in the five years up to and including 1980/81 totalled £1,370,707.

Improvements in the quality of service were also evident in the field of education. In the UK both Conservative and Labour Governments expanded and improved their education service.[25] Education was increasingly seen as an economic investment and the means of achieving a fairer society. Spending on education increased dramatically with investment in building programmes and facilities, more and better paid and trained teachers and greatly enhanced opportunities for higher education and training. With an education system closely integrated with that of England, the Isle of Man willingly accepted the challenge of expansion and qualitative improvement.[26] School buildings were extended and modernised and new schools built to meet rising demand and UK standards; improvements in the numbers, training and pay of teachers mirrored those of the UK; grant aid for education was maintained at or above UK levels and opportunities for post-secondary education were improved with investment in training, a new college of further education and support for Manx students to attend British institutions of higher education.

In one important area, that of raising the school leaving age to 16, the Island chose not to follow the UK lead, at least not until 1987. The idea had been under discussion since 1944 and Tynwald actually agreed in principle to the change on 13 December 1967.[27] Indeed, this agreement was followed by the Education (Compulsory School Age) Act 1971,[28] enabling the change to be introduced once an 'appointed day' had been decided. Both the 1967 resolution and the legislation had been strongly opposed on grounds of cost, lack of preparedness and the denial of choice to the group of children concerned.[29] Following the general election in 1971 the minority became a majority. Although the first attempt by the Board of Education to set the appointed day as 1 September 1974 failed to win the necessary approval of the Finance Board,[30] it was Tynwald that rejected the second attempt in April 1973, the motion failing in the Keys by nine votes to 13 and succeeding in the Council only because of the casting vote of the Lieutenant-Governor.[31]

Tynwald also turned its attention to two long-standing issues that were not UK-related. Both concerned the extent of Tynwald's responsibility in the field of education. Since 1920 responsibility for Manx education had been shared by a council or board responsible to Tynwald and the directly elected Authority, a duality of control that had led to conflict over policy, duplication of effort and debates about their respective mandates and accountability. After several unsuccessful attempts to address this problem, the Education Act 1968 provided for the merger of the two authorities.[32] A new board of education was established with five members of Tynwald and 24 elected representatives, the former with a built-in majority on the Board's Finance and Executive Committee as a means of retaining for Tynwald the financial control previously exercised by the old Board. Both outgoing authorities supported the change, and although a minority in the Keys would have preferred a smaller board with one elected member for each of the Island's 13 constituencies, the general reaction in Tynwald was favourable.[33]

Much more controversial was the campaign between 1962 and 1974 by the Board of Education and its chairman until 1971, Victor Kneale, to abolish the education rate, which was seen as a regressive tax on property and an inappropriate vehicle for funding a rapidly growing national service. Eventually in 1971, following yet another rejection of abolition by a clear majority in both chambers,[34] Tynwald agreed to stabilise the rate for a period of five years in recognition of the unfair burden the escalating education budget was placing on some ratepayers.[35] At the time approximately 25 per cent of net expenditure on education was rate-borne, the balance being paid as grants from the General Revenue. Two further attempts at abolition were made by Kneale in 1973 and 1974, by which time the share of grant-borne expenditure had risen to over 80 per cent and looked set to rise further as a consequence of stabilisation policy. The first was narrowly approved by the Keys but rejected by the Council.[36] The second was amended in favour of a phased abolition, in five equal stages commencing in 1975/76, and carried by an overwhelming majority.[37] Since 1980 the entire education budget has been funded by Tynwald.

Revenue spending by Tynwald on education increased steadily but substantially from £338,203 in 1957/58 to £1,977,248 in 1973/74, before rising rapidly to £11,504,466 in 1980/81, a real increase over the period as a whole of 487 per cent. Simultaneously, the Island embarked on a major capital building programme. After relatively modest expenditure between 1958 and 1968, a total of £419,647 including 75 per cent of the cost of the new Castle Rushen High School, the next 13 years saw extremely high levels, a total of £8,796,514 covering a rescheduling of Education Authority debt, the full cost of a series of school extensions and improvements, new schools including the Queen Elizabeth II High School at Peel and a new college of further education in Douglas. While the increases in revenue and capital spending have to be seen in the context of rising school rolls and the declining share of rate-borne funding after 1971, the main factors were undoubtedly the expansion and improvement of the service.

There was a similar story of expansion in the field of public health. While the environmental health activities of the LGB and local authorities and the health screening and treatment work of the School Medical Service remained crucial if relatively inexpensive components of the public health services, the critical changes in this period concerned the Manx NHS. In the UK both Conservative and Labour Governments pursued a policy of expansion, providing funds for new and improved hospitals, more expensive drugs, enhanced local authority welfare services and better pay and conditions for health service workers. While economic difficulties and competing priorities limited the extent of growth, disputes with consultants, junior doctors, GPs and nurses ultimately forced successive governments to commit funds well in excess of what was originally planned.[38] Every attempt was made by the Island to keep abreast of mainland developments and, where necessary, provide Manx people with access to improved specialist services in the UK. The period saw improvements in hospital buildings and facilities, in the availability and pay of consultants, doctors and other health service workers, in the quality of general medical, pharmaceutical, dental and opthalmic services and in the provision of services that in the UK were the responsibility of local authorities, namely the ambulance service, maternity care, health visiting, home helps, care in the community for the physically and mentally disabled and the vaccination and immunisation service.[39] Although political separateness insulated the Manx NHS from many of the conflicts over pay and conditions that plagued the UK service, the Island accepted the main outcomes of such disputes and kept pay and conditions in line with the UK.

In one important area where Tynwald had decided not to follow the UK in 1948, a decade of experience brought about a change of heart. The 1948 Act had allowed the three voluntary hospitals to continue, with their own management committees but almost 100 per cent public funding. Difficulties experienced in devising a coherent hospital policy for the Island, the waste and duplication resulting from separate management and concerns about the lack of public accountability convinced the Health Services Board and most members of Tynwald that these hospitals should be transferred to the Board.[40] The National Health Service (Isle of Man) Act 1963 provided for this transfer, ending the voluntary status of Noble's Isle of Man Hospital, the Ramsey and District Cottage Hospital and the Jane Crookall Maternity Home.[41]

The 1963 Act also provided for the transfer of the functions of the LGB in relation to nursing to the Health Services Board, further integrating the political management of the Island's health and welfare services. The extent of that integration made much of the UK debate prior to and following the 1974 reorganisation of the NHS quite irrelevant to the Island. While in the UK the postwar reforms had left the three main arms of the service under separate management, in the Isle of Man a single Health Services Board was now responsible for the management of the entire hospital service, the general medical services and those health services that in the UK had remained the responsibility of local government. The Island was also able to use its special status to avoid the bitter conflict between the Labour Government and consultants over plans to outlaw private beds from public hospitals by choosing not to follow Parliament's short-lived National Health Services Act 1978.[42]

The Manx NHS remained the Island's most expensive service throughout this period, revenue spending increasing steadily during the 1960s and rapidly in the 1970s from £606,869 in 1957/58 to £1,353,942 in 1968/69 and £12,299,555 in 1980/81, a real increase for the whole period of 250 per cent. In parallel with this spending, work began on the hospital modernisation programme approved by Tynwald in 1956, the main part of which, a new wing and facilities for Noble's Hospital, had been completed by 1961. In the 10 years to March 1968 capital spending totalled £541,119, of which over two thirds was committed to the 1956 scheme. The next 13 years saw much higher levels of spending, a total of £3,593,533, on hospital improvements and extensions, including new psycho-geriatric and therapeutic community units at Ballamona Hospital and a new geriatric day hospital and ward at Noble's Hospital.

Although the LGB had reported in 1959 that the demand for housing had been substantially met, within a few years housing was back on the political agenda. On 19 March 1963 Tynwald accepted a report from the LGB which called for a major public sector building programme, including homes for the elderly, and legislation to encourage owners and tenants to renovate and modernise existing private properties.[43] Population growth, the age and facilities of existing dwellings, the aspirations of the Manx people for better standard accommodation, the particular needs of the elderly and the less well off and awareness of the policies of successive UK Governments combined to produce an expansionary state programme This aroused remarkably little conflict, whether in relation to public sector housing, the encouragement of home ownership or the control of rents in the private sector.

Public sector housing remained the responsibility of the LGB, acting on behalf of the Island's rural authorities, and those local authorities that had opted to provide a service since 1946. The funding arrangements agreed in 1946 continued until 1974, when Tynwald agreed to take on full responsibility for local authority housing deficiency payments in recognition of 'the urgent need' to accelerate the programme of public building.[44] Although the change made little difference to the rate of house building in the longer term, the removal of housing as a burden on the rates was widely welcomed. Between April 1961 and December 1981 9,249 new houses were built on the Island, of which 2,269 or 25 per cent were in the public sector. After almost no public building in the late 1950s and early 1960s, the 14-year period from April 1964 saw an average of 126 completions per year; the rate of building fell to less than half that level for the next three years before rising again to 138 completions in 1981.[45] Net revenue spending by Tynwald hit a postwar low between 1958 and 1967, before rising rapidly as a result of new investment and Tynwald's decision in 1974 to assume full responsibility for the deficiency payments on local authority housing. In 1958/59 the figure was £20,905 and remained around that level for the next five years, before escalating from £42,072 in 1968/69 to £562,963 by 1980/81, a real increase over the whole period of 372 per cent.[46]

In 1962 Tynwald approved two schemes for the encouragement of home ownership. The Housing Advances Scheme, based on well-established local authority schemes in the UK but quite novel in the Isle of Man, provided residents with up to 95 per cent mortgages on houses with a maximum value of £7,000.[47] In 1975 the maximum value was increased to £10,000 and preferential interest rates were introduced for those on low incomes.[48] Up to December 1978 when the scheme was replaced, 4,195 persons were assisted with loans.[49] The Building by Private Enterprise Scheme, a modified version of the postwar scheme that ran until 1954, was designed to help private individuals to build their own house with the help of grants covering 10 per cent of the costs, interest-free loans covering a further 10 per cent and low interest loans another 20 per cent. To be eligible the cost of the proposed house had to be between £2,000 and £5,000.[50] Between 1963 and 1978 when the scheme expired help was given to 998 persons.[51] In 1978 the two schemes were replaced by the House Purchase Scheme, increasing the maximum value of houses eligible from £10,000 to £15,000 and providing grants of up to £1,000 for low income first-time buyers. The maximum loan was increased in 1980 to £18,000. In the first three years of the new scheme help was given to 1,141 buyers, expenditure reaching a peak in 1980/81.[52] Between 1963 and March 1981 the three schemes provided £436,149 in grants and £37,141,236 in loans.[53] Throughout the period Tynwald retained the additional incentive to home ownership of 100 per cent mortgage interest tax relief.[54]

On a much smaller scale support was provided for home improvement in the private sector, initially under the Rural Housing Acts 1947–55[55] and subsequently, following similar UK initiatives, under the Urban Housing Improvement Act 1969[56] and the Housing Improvement Act 1975.[57] The latter brought together the rural and urban schemes under one legislative umbrella. The aim of the legislation was to provide grants and loans for home-owners to bring their dwellings into line with minimum standards. Between April 1958 and March 1981 the three schemes together provided £110,142 in grants and £513,000 in loans.[58]

The role of government in controlling house rents varied widely between public and private sectors. In consultation with the Island's housing authorities, the LGB determined rents in the public sector and from May 1971 operated a rent rebate scheme for tenants of modest means. In the private sector, however, government had very little involvement.[59] The Island had followed the UK in retaining and strengthening rent control immediately after the war, the Rent Restriction Act 1948 providing for both security of tenure and security against excessive rents.[60] In 1959 the decision not to renew the Rent Restriction Act was clearly influenced by the UK Rent Act of 1957 and was instrumental in removing security of tenure and rent control, save for the controls over the rents of furnished accommodation.[61] An attempt was made by MLP members to restore security of tenure and rent control in 1959, but their Rent Bill was defeated at second reading in the Keys by 14 votes to six on 7 April 1959.[62] Security from eviction without a court order was subsequently provided by the Landlord and Tenant (Miscellaneous Provisions) Act 1975,[63] but between 1959 and 1981 rent control was confined to furnished accommodation. Under the Furnished Houses (Rent Control) Act 1948 tenancy agreements could be referred to the Assessment Board for arbitration.[64] With private sector accommodation for rent in short supply and evidence of exorbitant rents being charged, in May 1981 the Assessment Board, chaired by MNP member Peter Craine, initiated legislation to extend the provisions of the 1948 Act to include unfurnished accommodation. After a smooth passage through both branches it became law as the Housing (Rent Control) Act 1981.[65]

An overriding consideration behind the public policies developed was the goal of full employment. The expansion of government activity and the economy generally in the 1960s and early 1970s brought the Island very close to this goal. Unemployment remained a problem but much less serious as more employment became available outside of the tourist sector. After 1974 the Island felt the effects of recession in the UK and beyond, unemployment reaching levels not experienced since the early 1960s. Employment Exchange data for January of each year reveal a steady decline in winter unemployment from 1,209 in 1960 to 461 in 1974, a rapid rise to 968 in 1977 and a fall to 646 in 1980 before rising to 1,020 in 1981. July data show that summer unemployment remained below 250 through the 1960s before rising to 547 in 1977; it returned to below 250 in Tynwald's millennial year before rising to 795 in 1981, the highest of the postwar period.[66] On the eve of the 1981 election unemployment was higher still and showed every sign of continuing to rise as the recession in the UK deepened. Even so, as the chair of the Board of Social Security, Noel Cringle, reminded Tynwald in October 1981, the offshore economy was faring much better than that of the UK; the September 1981 figures for the Isle of Man were 1,331 or 4.8 per cent of registered unemployed compared with 12.2 per cent for the UK.[67] An interesting aspect of the changes in unemployment figures after 1960 was the decline in the seasonal variation. While in 1960 the monthly unemployment rate ranged between 9.0 and 3.1 per cent, by 1964 the range had narrowed to 4.7 and 1.4 per cent. The much narrower range continued for the rest of this period, the 1978 figures of 3.8 to 1.5 per cent marking the lowest seasonal variation since the war.

To a significant extent employment policy reflected these trends. Winter works schemes were an important ingredient of policy until the late 1960s, reemerging at the height of recession in 1976/77 on the recommendations of the House of Keys Committee on Unemployment[68] and again in 1980/81 on the advice of Tynwald's Select Committee on Unemployment.[69] Both committees were chaired by Speaker Kerruish. In addition to winter work in the public sector, between 1958 and 1962 Tynwald funded the Private Enterprise Employment Scheme providing contributions to the wages of additional men taken on in the winter months (October to April inclusive). Similar incentives were made available under the 1958 Farm Labour Scheme and the 1962 Improvement of Tourist Accommodation Scheme. From 1958 onwards additional funding was provided for training and apprenticeships and 1965 saw the establishment of the much needed Youth Employment Service.[70] The downturn in the economy in the late 1970s resulted in similar initiatives, some building on existing government policy and others quite new. In 1977/78 the Board of Social Security gained Tynwald's approval for new apprenticeship schemes for young Manx people to become key workers in the manufacturing and service industries.[71] In February 1978 Tynwald accepted recommendations from the Keys' Committee on Unemployment for the maintenance by the Employment Exchange of a register of employment vacancies, the establishment of a job centre and the introduction of a special insurance credits register for persons over 58 wishing to take early retirement without losing insurance credit. Tynwald rejected the Committee's proposal for a new board of trade and employment, but did agree to give to the Board of Social Security the additional responsibility for coordinating and improving government employment policy.[72] On the recommendation of its own select committee in December 1980, Tynwald agreed to cover 50 per cent of the cost of additional private sector employment provided during the winter period. In April 1981 it accepted the Committee's recommendations for the Tourist Board and the Finance Board to devise ways of stimulating the tourist industry in 1981and 1982, for public construction work to be phased with periods of high unemployment and to be undertaken wherever possible with local labour, for better incentives for small businesses and for wider training opportunities. On 13 October 1981 the chair of Executive Council, Clifford Irving, reminded members of the contribution that all government spending makes to employment and gave assurances that action on the Committee's recommendations was under way: steps were being taken to stimulate the tourist industry, additional funding was being provided for winter work schemes, the Industrial Advisory Council and the Finance Board were preparing a much improved package of incentives for industry and the various boards had been asked to give preference to local contractors. The seriousness of Tynwald's response to rising unemployment was shown by the supplementary votes for the winter job creation programmes in 1980/81 and 1981/82; an initial vote of £100,000 for this purpose in 1980 was subsequently increased to £150,000 and that of £150,000 in 1981 to £500,000.[73]

In tandem with measures to address unemployment came modifications to the legislation giving preferential treatment to resident workers. The Employment Act 1954 had enabled the Island to give preferential treatment to resident male workers. The special terms negotiated for the Island when the UK joined the EEC left the Island free to regulate the movement of labour. Immediately following the successful outcome of those negotiations, a review of the 1954 Act led to new legislation. The Control of Employment Act 1975 extended the work permit system to include female workers and the self-employed and changed the residential qualification for Isle of Man worker status from five to 10 years.[74] Exempted employments were unchanged. However, the rapid rise in year-round unemployment after 1975 convinced Tynwald of the need to limit the exemption in respect of temporary employment. On 16 November 1977, rather controversially outside of Tynwald but without debate or division inside, the exemption in respect of temporary employment was reduced from two weeks to three days.[75]

One final strand of employment policy was a series of measures to improve the conditions of those fortunate enough to be in employment. In the UK the Labour Governments of 1964–70 and 1974–79 were responsible for a raft of employment legislation, providing for redundancy payments (1965), equal pay for equal work (1970), contracts of employment (1972), health and safety at work (1974), protection against unfair dismissal (1978) and protection against sexual and racial discrimination (1975 and 1976). With the notable exception of the Health and Safety at Work Act 1974, there was initially little enthusiasm for these measures. There was no attempt during the 1970s to follow the three equal opportunity measures. Bills introduced by MLP members in 1970 to provide for contracts of employment and redundancy payments were effectively killed by the approval of hostile amendments.[76] However, following the general election of 1976 a number of progressive measures were approved. Promoted by the LGB, the Health and Safety at Work Act 1977 was an enabling measure, empowering the LGB to bring forward for approval by Tynwald such parts of the UK Act and subordinate legislation as were deemed appropriate for the Isle of Man. Broadly welcomed, the aim of the legislation was to subject the health, safety and welfare of all people at work to a comprehensive system of control, inspection and enforcement.[77] Following negotiations between public sector employers and trade unions, in July 1977 Tynwald approved the Isle of Man Public Service Manual Workers Superannuation Scheme, whereby manual workers would contribute five per cent of their pay in return for superannuation benefits. After lengthy discussions between the Board of Social Security and representatives of employers and the unions, legislation was initated by the Board in 1980 requiring employers to provide employees with contracts of employment and specifying minimum periods of notice. On the basis of those discussions the idea of more inclusive legislation covering redundancy payments and protection against unfair dismissal was rejected. The possibility of more inclusive legislation was also considered and rejected by a committee of the House set up to report on the Bill.[78] The end result was the Contracts of Employment Act 1981, modelled closely on Parliament's Act of 1972 as amended in 1975.[79] In November 1980 MLP member Arthur Quinney was given leave to introduce a private member's bill to protect employees against unfair dismissal, but no progress was made with the legislation before the dissolution of the House in October 1981.

## *Increased State Intervention and Support for the Economy*

Faced with declining population and undue dependence on tourism, members of Tynwald set about using their newly acquired political autonomy to create an economic environment that was more conducive to economic growth and diversification. A combination of internal decision-making and fortuitous external developments helped to transform the economy. Internally, the expansion of welfare provision brought about huge increases in revenue spending and unprecedented levels of investment in buildings and facilities. Tynwald also provided generous financial support for public buildings and major town developments. Infrastructural investment on harbours, highways and local authority roads remained at a high level, much of it tourist inspired but of value to the economy as a whole. The Island invested heavily in its traditional industries, transport and the public utilities. The decision to abolish surtax in 1961 marked the beginning of a series of initiatives designed to attract new residents, new industries and new wealth and to accelerate the process of economic diversification. Externally, the reduced scope of the sterling area and the negotiation of special status in relation to the EEC left the Island well placed to take further advantage of its growing reputation as a low tax centre. With economic growth and diversification under way, Tynwald had to respond to demands for measures to mitigate the less desirable side effects of rapid development.

Before considering the detail, reference should be made to two ingredients that were vital to the overall strategy adopted, the commitment of the Island's leaders to intervention for development and the adoption of a radically new approach to the funding of capital projects. Both were illustrated in January 1963 when Tynwald agreed to support a 14-point Development Plan.[80] Garvey first suggested the idea of a development plan in 1959 and, with the help of Executive Council and boards of Tynwald, a plan was prepared and presented to Tynwald, which agreed in principle to accept each of 14 development projects on the understanding that they would be funded through borrowing. These included legislation to facilitate the private development of a casino, completion of the Douglas Sea Terminal, contributions to the Summerland complex, the South Ramsey Development, funding for hotels and swimming pools and new public buildings. Over the next 18 years a rolling programme of major development projects was approved by Tynwald, contributing to very high levels of capital investment. In 1962/63 the Island abandoned the practice of funding most capital development directly out of the Accumulated Fund and replaced it with a system of capital advances or borrowing from the Fund. In this way payment for developments was spread over a much longer period. The capital transactions account records a massive overall increase in capital advances from £827,118 in 1962/63 to £19,495,418 in 1980/81, a real increase of 355 per cent. Out of a total investment in the 19-year period of just over

£100 million, almost 87 per cent was committed in the 10 years from April 1971 and 54 per cent in the last five of those years, a reflection partly of the high rate of inflation and partly of the unprecedented level of government intervention in the economy and society following the elections of 1971 and 1976.

Town developments and public buildings accounted for a significant portion of this capital investment. Two projects were concerned with the infrastructure and development of the Island's major towns, the South Ramsey Development from the mid-1960s and the Chester Street/Wellington Square area of Douglas from 1975/76. The former scheme, developed in conjunction with the Ramsey Commissioners and private enterprise, provided Ramsey with a new swimming pool and restaurant, a modern aparthotel, housing, shops, parking facilities and an area for light industry. The latter, developed in partnership with Douglas Corporation, provided a multistorey car park and accommodation for a supermarket and restaurant. During the 1970s and early 1980s Tynwald funded four major government building projects at a cost of £4.2 million, new central government offices opening in 1975, new fire service headquarters in 1977, new police headquarters in 1979 and new headquarters for the Isle of Man Post Office in 1983.

Economic support for agriculture came in the form of new legislation, a series of schemes to improve the state of Manx agriculture and a programme of subsidies broadly in line with the UK. The prime mover in this sector was the Board of Agriculture and Fisheries, although there were repeated questions and comments from other members of Tynwald seeking reassurances that the support available for Manx farmers was equivalent to that available in the UK. Legislation promoted by the Board was primarily concerned with improving the state of Manx agriculture. The Agricultural Credits Act 1966 was the latest in a series of measures going back to 1924 providing for loans to farmers for the improvement of agricultural holdings.[81] The Agriculture and Horticulture Act 1966 enabled the Island to follow the UK in fixing minimum prices for imports and imposing levies on imports below the fixed prices, with a view to reducing expenditure on agricultural support and promoting a more stable market for agricultural and horticultural products.[82] The Agricultural Holdings Act 1969, the product of many years' negotiations between the Board and agricultural interests, provided tenant farmers with security of tenure.[83] The Agriculture (Safety, Health and Welfare Provision) Act 1974 was a much needed health and safety at work measure, belatedly bringing the Island into line with the UK Act of 1956.[84] In parallel with these legislative initiatives, Tynwald approved direct financial support in the form of apprenticeship schemes, farm purchase and improvement schemes, grants and loans to the various marketing associations and investment in the building and subsequent upgrading of a central abattoir. It also kept repeating its support for the maintenance of government assistance to Manx agriculture and fishing at UK levels, irrespective of whether such assistance emanated from the UK or Europe. This policy was formally reiterated in November 1959 on the occasion of Tynwald's approval in principle of the establishment of a European Free Trade Association, in May 1963 during a debate on agricultural marketing, in February 1974 in reply to a question by the Speaker after UK entry into the EEC and in February 1979 in an agricultural and fishing policy resolution.[85] In the case of fishing support was given under a series of herring and white fish subsidy schemes and in the form of grants and loans for the purchase of fishing boats. Legislation in 1963 and 1964 increased the powers of the Board of Agriculture and Fisheries to control fishing in Manx territorial waters.[86] Following the UK's participation in the European

Fisheries Conference, Parliament's Fishery Limits Act 1964 extended the fishery limits surrounding the UK and Islands from three nautical miles to 12, with the six inner miles exclusive to the UK and Islands and the six outer miles open by order to other countries. However, the UK Act did not provide for an extension of UK or Manx territorial waters and the area within which the Manx Board had exclusive rights remained three nautical miles.[87] When in 1981 the UK announced that it intended to extend UK territorial waters from three to 12 miles, Tynwald readily supported the recommendation of its Constitutional Issues Committee for an equivalent extension for the Isle of Man.[88] Total expenditure on agriculture and fisheries fell in real terms during this period. This was not so much the result of specific Manx initiatives as of the commitment to follow the UK. Initially the result was a continuing increase in spending from £218,918 in 1957/58 to £604,007 in 1961/62. Thereafter, while there were major fluctuations in spending, the overall trend in real terms was one of major decline. The 1980/81 figure of £1,887,073 represented a real reduction over 1961/62 of almost 42 per cent. Capital advances to the Board in the 11 years up to and including 1972/73 totalled £587,208; in the eight inflationary years following UK entry into the EEC the total was £3,087,719, a reflection perhaps of the overriding need for the industry to remain competitive. The advances were used primarily to fund loans for farm improvement and, with the introduction of the Agricultural Holdings (Loans) Scheme in 1978, for the purchase of farmland by tenants and young people wishing to enter the industry; between May 1978 and October 1981 the mortgage scheme alone accounted for loans to 36 applicants totalling £1,340,000.[89]

Competition also lay at the heart of policy on tourism, where the Island was less constrained by UK policy save in respect of indirect taxation and strived to stem the decline of what was still seen as the Island's most important industry. The importance of the industry was reflected in the priority given to implementing the recommendations of the 1955 Visiting Industry Commission and the 1970 Tourist Industry Commission, which helped to set the agenda for higher levels of state intervention in the industry. Tynwald paved the way for action by approving the necessary legislation and funding. Within Tynwald the lead players were the members of the Executive Council, the Finance Board, the Tourist Board and the Steering Committee on Transport, especially the chairs of those bodies. Particular reference should be made to the three individuals who chaired the Tourist Board, James Cain (1958–62), William Quayle (1962–71) and Clifford Irving (1971–81), and to two members of Tynwald who had been members of the Visiting Industry Commission in 1955, Charles Kerruish and Jack Nivison. Cain was the first Tourist Board chair to serve on Executive Council and both of his successors were members, Irving becoming chair of the Executive Council from 1977 to 1981, a reflection not only of his standing in the estimation of colleagues but also of the political importance of the industry. Kerruish was chair of the Executive Council associated with the 1963 Development Plan and an effective participant in tourist-related debates throughout the period. Nivison was a member of both the 1955 and the 1970 Commissions, a member of the Tourist Board from 1962 onwards and chair of the Steering Committee on Transport from its establishment in 1974 until 1981. The detail of the many initiatives taken is beyond the scope of this study; it will suffice to comment briefly on four areas of intervention, investment in tourist attractions, improvements in tourist accommodation, the enhanced role and funding of the Tourist Board and other boards with a tourist remit and the high priority given to transport both to and from and within the Island.

The poor state of the Manx economy in the late 1950s and early 1960s, the Visiting Industry Commission's recommendations and Garvey's belief in development planning persuaded Tynwald to support a series of projects designed to make the Island a more attractive resort. These involved cooperation with both the private sector and local authorities. Where state funding was involved it was provided through borrowing. The most controversial initiative was the introduction of legislation to facilitate the private development of a casino. The Visiting Industry Commission had recommended such a development in 1955, but government attempts at implementation before the 1962 general election foundered in the Legislative Council.[90] Candidates in the election were divided on the issue, but after the election a slender majority in both branches supported the enabling legislation. The Gaming, Betting and Lotteries (Casino) Act 1962 paved the way for the development of a casino and hotel,[91] the hotel being one of several to benefit from loans and grants made under the 1962 Tourist Accommodation Improvement Scheme. Equally controversial were the moves to liberalise the Island's licensing laws by providing for the opening of public houses and the sale of alcohol in hotels and clubs on Sundays. Recommended by the Visiting Industry Commission in 1955, Tynwald's immediate reaction had been to reject the idea, but supporters of the industry kept the issue alive. Following the defeat of a bill in the Keys in 1959, the Licensing (Miscellaneous Provisions) Act 1960 provided for Sunday opening on an experimental basis during the summer of 1960.[92] It was subsequently extended by resolution of Tynwald, the majority of members agreeing that the innovation was helpful to the tourist industry.[93] Thereafter, controversy centred on moves to introduce Sunday opening out of season; after several unsuccessful attempts, this was delivered by the Licensing (Sunday Opening) Act 1979.[94]

Support for the ongoing development of the casino complex was given by Tynwald as part of the 1963 Development Plan. Presented to Tynwald in January 1963 by the chair of Executive Council, Speaker Kerruish, this 14-point plan was accepted by the overwhelming majority of members. It was dominated by tourist projects and more were added in later years. The result was a series of major investments in the industry, including substantial grants to Douglas Corporation for the Derby Castle Development Scheme (Summerland) both before and after its destruction by fire in 1973, support for local authority swimming pools in Castletown, Douglas and Ramsey, the latter as part of the South Ramsey Development Scheme which also included funding for a new hotel, the purchase of the Ballaugh Curraghs and the development on site of the Wildlife Park between 1963 and 1966, the purchase of the Laxey Wheel in 1965, the Gaiety Theatre in 1971 and Glen Wyllin in 1978, and the funding of the celebration of the Millennium of Tynwald in 1977/79.[95]

The Island's success as a resort depended heavily on the availability and quality of tourist accommodation. Tynwald had been providing modest levels of assistance for the improvement of such accommodation since 1954, but not on the scale made available after 1957. The Tourist Accommodation Act 1957, the Tourist Premises Improvement Acts of 1961, 1963, 1969, 1974, 1976 and 1977 and associated improvement schemes enabled Tynwald to offer increasingly generous assistance in the form of guaranteed loans and grants to established hoteliers and boarding house keepers and to companies embarking on major new developments, extensions or renovations.[96] After an initial burst of lending in the three years following the 1961 Act, applications and loans remained at a low level until 1974. In the seven years from 1974/75 to 1980/81 the Local Government Board approved £3,052,020 in loans and £1,179,390 in grants for new projects and

Tourist Board members and Secretary, December 1971. Following the report of the Visiting Industry Commission in 1955 and the Tourist (Isle of Man) Act 1958, the Isle of Man Tourist Board enjoyed greatly increased powers to protect and promote the Island's ailing tourist industry. The 1971 Board included Clifford Irving and Jack Nivison, who had been to the forefront of the battle to regenerate the tourist industry since its demise in the 1950s. From left to right the picture shows John Bell, Jack Nivison (Vice Chair), John Clucas, Clifford Irving (Chair), Len Bond (Secretary) and Gordon Howarth.

improvement purposes, a clear indication of Tynwald's growing concern to promote the industry in the years immediately prior to and following Tynwald's Millennium celebrations. When in 1967 the Grand Island Hotel near Ramsey and the Peveril Hotel in Douglas—both had taken out loans against the security of the accommodation—were declared bankrupt, they were taken temporarily into public ownership. New accommodation partly funded by Tynwald in this period ranged from a major hotel development in Ramsey and the Groudle holiday village self-catering complex to a camp site in the newly purchased Glen Wyllin. When the Visiting Industry Commission recommended the compulsory registration and grading of tourist accommodation as a means of raising the quality of accommodation and informing visitors about standards, it was a step too far for many members of Tynwald and the Tourist (Isle of Man) Act 1958 merely provided for a voluntary system. The ineffectiveness of this system persuaded Tynwald to pass the Tourist (Isle of Man) Act in 1961, which provided for the compulsory registration of accommodation.[97] Under both the voluntary and compulsory arrangements, registration could be turned down if, on inspection, the premises were deemed to be in a bad state of repair, failed to meet minimum standards of cleanliness, sanitation, ventilation or safety or were inadequate for the number of guests specified or if the business was being badly managed. In 1970 the Tourist Industry Commission strongly recommended the compulsory grading of accommodation, ushering in a lengthy round of negotiations between the Tourist Board and the trade. The Tourist Act 1975 was a compromise acceptable to the trade and Tynwald; it provided for the compulsory classification of accommodation and the voluntary grading of categories.[98]

Public investment in the tourist industry also increased as a result of a much more interventionist Tourist Board. Its role was greatly enhanced by the Tourist (Isle of Man) Act 1958, the strong leadership provided by Quayle (a member from 1957 and chair from 1962 to 1971), Irving (a member from 1956 to 1962 and chair from 1972 to 1981) and Nivison (a member from 1962 to 1981), and the commitment of Tynwald to revitalise the industry. The new Board was to the fore in promoting action on the outstanding issues raised by the Visiting Industry Commission and assumed responsibility for advising Tynwald on the recommendations of the Tourist Industry Commission. The 1970 Commission's central recommendation, that Tynwald should recognise the pre-eminence of the industry in the Island's economy and invest in it, was carried forward by the Board with respect to accommodation, amenities, transport and marketing. In 1971 the Board obtained approval for the appointment of its first marketing officer. The Tourist Board also led a lengthy campaign to free the industry and the Island from the constraints imposed by the Common Purse Agreement; however, despite reviews by the Finance Board in 1966 opposing abrogation, by PA Management Consultants in 1975 recommending abrogation and by a select committee of Tynwald from 1977 to 1981, only limited progress was made. The 1979 Customs and Excise Agreement, which resulted from the Select Committee's negotiations with the UK, was explained in Tynwald by Percy Radcliffe as 'a stepping stone' towards the Island taking complete control of indirect taxation, but did not deliver either the zero VAT rating that had been requested by the industry or any immediate prospect of lower duties to attract more tourists.[99] Revenue spending by the Tourist Board increased steadily from £88,000 in 1957/58 to £221,411 in 1970/71 before rising rapidly to £1,656,583 in 1980/81, a real increase over 1957/58 of 225 per cent.

Tourism was also the *raison d'être* of spending by other boards of Tynwald. Much of the work of the Forestry, Mines and Lands Board and the Manx Museum and National Trust was tourist related. The former remained responsible for the care, maintenance and control of the national glens, and some 20,000 acres of open hill land. By 1958 the Board was responsible for Ballaglass Glen, Colby Glen, Dhoon Glen, Glen Helen, Laxey Glen, Molly Quirk's Glen/Bibaloe Walk and Tholt-y-Will. Between 1958 and 1981 a further 10 glens were acquired as a result of a gift to the nation by private individuals, purchases by the Board and leasing from local authorities: Ballure Walk, Bishopscourt Glen, Elfin Glen, Glen Maye, Glen Mooar, Glen Wyllin, Groudle Glen, Lhergy Frissell, Port Soderick and Silverdale.[100] Revenue spending by the Board increased from £47,500 in 1957/58 to £428,299 in 1980/81, a real increase of 56 per cent. The responsibilities of the latter included the the various branches of the Manx Museum, the Island's principal ancient monuments and the lands of the Manx National Trust. The 1970s saw the expansion of the site and facilities at Crellin's Hill in Douglas and the development of the Grove Agricultural Museum in Ramsey. Revenue spending increased from £10,060 in 1957/58 to £222,105 in 1980/81, a real increase of 281 per cent.

The role of government in facilitating and providing transport was also crucial in the protection and promotion of tourism. Certainly transport served the needs of residents as well as visitors and of other industries as well as tourism, but the impetus for many of the measures and much of the investment came from tourism. Even though the measures included subsidies and public ownership, most were approved in Tynwald without major dissent. A major problem facing Tynwald was the fragmentation of responsibility between several boards, Douglas Corporation and the private sector, notably Isle of Man Road Services Ltd, the Isle of Man Steam Packet Company and various airlines. The 1966 Commission on Transport, chaired by Hubert Radcliffe, recommended the formation of a single transport board as a means of overcoming the fragmentation of control, public ownership of the Island's rail and bus services and the purchase of a controlling interest in the Isle of Man Steam Packet Company, but little immediate progress was made.[101] In May 1974, eight years after the Commission reported, Tynwald appointed a Steering Committee on Transport, comprising a member of each of the Airports, Harbour, Highway and Transport and Finance Boards and Jack Nivison, Vice Chair of the Tourist Board, who chaired the Committee from its inception until 1981. The Steering Committee was the driving force behind a series of major initiatives between May 1974 and the election in November 1981.

Access to the Island was promoted by investment in harbours, notably the provision in Douglas of the Sea Terminal in the 1960s and roll on/roll off facilities in the late 1970s. In November 1979 Tynwald approved a major harbour improvement scheme, involving the protection of the 100-year-old Battery Pier and its extension seawards by means of a breakwater. Although the scheme was under way by 1981, only the first £500,000 of an estimated £8.9 million had been expended by March of that year.[102] Between 1958/59 and 1969/70 net revenue spending by the Harbour Board fluctuated between £25,207 and £99,552 before rising rapidly from £111,825 in 1970/71 to £788,483 in 1980/81, a real increase over the 10-year period of 96 per cent. Capital spending by the Board between 1962/3 and 1980/81 totalled £2,094,366, of which 65 per cent was committed in the last four years. Tynwald also committed funds to safeguard services by the Steam Packet. With effect from 1969/70 the Llandudno service was subsidised by an annual grant towards the upkeep of Llandudno Pier. Between 1971 and 1978 loans totalling £2.75 million were provided to the Steam Packet Company for the reconstruction of the Princes Landing Stage in Liverpool to safeguard the Liverpool service. From September 1972 onwards the Isle of Man Government became a major shareholder in the Company to protect the Island from a harmful takeover and from 1974 Tynwald subsidised Steam Packet fares in May and September of each year as a means of promoting a longer tourist season. Access by air also depended on public subsidy. Net revenue spending by the Airports Board, including charges on loans incurred to pay for improvements to the airport, fluctuated widely. After an average subsidy of £88,690 in the 10 years from 1957/58, the level of support rose sharply from £107,493 in 1967/68 to £451,869 in 1975/76 before falling equally sharply to the first ever profit of £38,977 in 1978/79 and a small deficit of £13,174 in 1979/80; with the celebrations of Tynwald's Millennium over, the level of subsidy in 1980/81 was £299,903. Capital spending in this period was low, save for investment in radar facilities in 1965/67 and a runway extension in 1969/72.

Responsibility for the Island's roads was shared by the Highway and Transport Board and six local authorities, with Tynwald meeting the most of the costs. In March 1980 Tynwald approved a resolution moved by Victor Kneale asking the Board to introduce legislation for the abolition of the highways rate and the transfer of responsibility for all the Island's roads to the Board.[103] The Highways (Transfer) Act 1981 was an enabling measure, providing for that transfer to take place by order of the Board when it had the capacity and finance to undertake the responsibility—five of the transfers were completed during 1982/83 and the sixth, Port Erin, in April 1983.[104] Between 1958 and 1981 net revenue spending by Tynwald on highways fluctuated wildly, averaging £192,119 in the first 10 years before rising rapidly from £203,945 in 1967/68 to £1,827,920 in 1980/81. Capital spending fluctuated even more widely and totalled £1,553,784 over the 19 years from 1962/63, of which 38 per cent was committed at the time of the Millennium celebrations in 1979/80.

After 1974, Tynwald's acceptance of a series of recommendations by the Steering Committee on Transport brought public transport on the Island increasingly under public ownership and control. The fact that both Douglas Corporation and the private sector were finding it increasingly difficult to sustain economic bus services in the age of the motor car persuaded Tynwald to support the idea of an integrated national service. Already subsidising the bus/air terminal in Douglas (from 1966/67 onwards), the purchase of new buses and the operation of rural bus services (both from 1974/75), in October 1975 Tynwald agreed in principle to the purchase and amalgamation of the undertakings run by Douglas Corporation and Isle of Man Road Services Ltd. In spite of

Members of the Manx Electric Railway Board standing by one of the newly nationalised steam locomotives, April 1978. The Isle of Man Steam Railway was taken into public ownership in 1977 and placed under the control of the MER Board. From left to right are John Radcliffe, Peter Craine, W. Jackson (Chief Executive), Matty Ward and Roger Watterson.

reservations about nationalisation expressed by a minority of members, the resolution was approved without division. In July 1976 Tynwald approved the investment of £500,000 in Isle of Man National Transport Ltd, a private limited company with the Government as the sole shareholder, and the purchase by the new company of the two bus undertakings for the sum of £320,000.[105] Isle of Man National Transport Ltd was established in October 1976 and the commitment was to provide a subsidised service. In the first three full years after nationalisation, Tynwald funded deficits incurred by Isle of Man National Transport totalling £803,038.

Simultaneously with these moves, concern was being expressed over the gradual demise of the steam railway. Since the late 1950s services had been cut, winter services withdrawn and the lines to Peel and Ramsey closed. By the 1970s the remaining line to Port Erin was under threat. In 1977, after much heart searching and a period of guaranteeing the Isle of Man Railway Company against operating losses, Tynwald agreed by a substantial majority to bring the railway into public ownership for the sum of £250,000 as a means of preserving a unique tourist attraction.[106] Responsibility for the steam railway was vested in the Manx Electric Railway Board. It was well understood that it would be necessary to subsidise the service, as had been the case with the MER since 1957. The annual subsidy to the publicly owned railways increased from the £25,000 that had been agreed in 1957 to £127,529 in 1976/77 and, following the purchase of the steam railway, to £501,245 by 1980/81, a real increase over 1957/58 of 246 per cent. Following the nationalisation of the bus and railway services, the Steering Committee proposed the amalgamation of the bus and railway undertakings under the management of a single authority. This was accepted by Tynwald in March 1980 and implemented by the Isle of Man Passenger Transport Board Act 1982, which provided for the replacement of the MER Board by the Isle of Man Passenger Transport Board.[107]

Subsidies were also paid to the public utilities, electricity and water, although not on the scale of the immediate postwar period. Both remained in public ownership. For most of the period the Isle of Man Electricity Board provided a strictly commercial service, the only exception being subsidies for the farm extension scheme until the mid-1960s and interest-free loans for hydroelectric schemes at Bloc Eary in 1977, above Kirk Michael in 1979 and as part of the Sulby Reservoir project in 1980.[108] The period also saw much closer cooperation between the Electricity Board and Douglas Corporation with the establishment of a joint advisory committee in 1958 and a joint authority in 1966.[109] In the case of water, subsidies were provided throughout the period, albeit on a small scale in relation to total spending, for such items as the augmentation of overall supplies, deficits incurred by Douglas Corporation in supplying rural areas outside the borough, exploratory work for the Sulby Reservoir and, from 1977/78, the payment of charges on loans made to the Water and Gas Authority for the erection of the Reservoir, at that time by far and away the most expensive public utilities project in the Island's history.[110] Under the Water Act 1972 the supply of water for the whole Island became the responsibility of the Isle of Man Water Authority, Douglas Corporation relinquishing the independent status it had enjoyed in respect of water supply since 1890.[111] In 1974 the Authority was renamed the Isle of Man Water and Gas Authority and given the additional responsibility for the newly acquired state gas industry.[112]

In the case of gas the role of government prior to this period had been one of regulation rather than ownership. Gas companies had been authorised to supply gas since the mid-nineteenth century. However, financial problems experienced by some of these companies led to their giving notice to the Government that they were unable to continue supplying gas. Once again Tynwald embarked on a programme of nationalisation, not out of ideological commitment but because of the failure of private enterprise. Between May 1965 and January 1967 Tynwald authorised the purchase of the undertakings of the Peel Gas Company, the Castletown Gas Works Company and the Port Erin and Port St Mary Gas Company as a means of ensuring that gas supplies were maintained. The total cost of the three undertakings was £56,522. Under the direction of the Gas Committee of Tynwald from 1967, the Isle of Man Gas Authority from 1972 and the Isle of Man Water and Gas Authority from 1974,[113] a major programme of investment was undertaken and a subsidised service provided to the south and west of the Island.[114] The rest of the Island continued to be serviced by the private sector.

Tynwald's willingness to take enterprises into public ownership in pursuit of the national interest was a remarkable feature of this period. Reference has already been made to the buses, the steam railway and gas, the purchase of tourist amenities such as the Gaiety Theatre and national glens, the temporary acquisition of hotels and the transfer to the Island of responsibility for the Post Office, but it is worth drawing these together with a miscellany of other purchases to show the surprising frequency with which Tynwald resorted to public ownership as the preferred solution to a variety of problems. In 1964 the Island agreed to purchase Jurby Airport from the UK for £133,000 for use both as a diversionary airfield and an industrial estate.[115] When later that year the UK decided to close the fish and oil meal factory in Peel that it had built in 1955 at a cost of £60,000, Tynwald agreed without division to purchase the factory for £4,000 in order to maintain facilities for processing fish and thereby encourage the landing of fish at the Island's ports.[116] Between 1965 and 1967 three gas undertakings were taken into public ownership. In April 1965 Tynwald approved a Tourist Board resolution calling for the purchase of Laxey Wheel in order to preserve it as a unique tourist attraction; the eventual cost was £4,035.[117] In 1968 the prospect of Manx Radio being owned and controlled from outside the Island persuaded Tynwald to approve its purchase for £50,000.[118] When in 1971 the Palace and Derby Castle Company decided that the Gaiety Theatre was no longer a viable concern, Tynwald agreed to purchase it for £41,000 in order to maintain a theatre for live entertainment during the summer and local productions during the winter.[119] In 1972 the Nunnery was purchased for the nation at a cost of £50,000, but in the absence of agreement on an appropriate public use it was subsequently sold to Robert Sangster on condition that the grounds be maintained as green belt.[120] Negotiations with the UK authorities led to the transfer of postal services to the Isle of Man Postal Authority in 1973. When in 1974 the Laxey Glen Flour Mills ran into economic difficulties, Tynwald approved an Executive Council proposal that the mills be purchased from R. G. Corlett Ltd for the sum of £65,000. The rationale for the decision was the maintenance of an operating flour mill and a storage facility on the Island, the encouragement of local grain production and reduced dependence on the international market.[121] Between 1974 and 1981 the Government subscribed £300,000 of share capital to enable Laxey Glen Mills Ltd to operate and expand the public business.[122] In 1976 Bishopscourt was purchased for the nation at a cost of £70,000, but as with the Nunnery there was no agreement on an appropriate public use and, much to the chagrin of the Speaker and others who wanted to see the property transferred to the Manx Museum and National Trust, in 1979 Tynwald approved its sale to Joseph Fairhurst.[123] 1976 and 1977 saw the two bus undertakings and the steam railway taken into public ownership. Finally, on 10 separate occasions between 1958 and 1981, the Forestry Board was able to further its policy of taking national glens into public ownership, the final and most expensive purchase being that of Glen Wyllin in 1978 for £28,000.[124]

The decisive economic change was the management of the economy with the explicit purpose of attracting new residents, industry and wealth. In his first budget speech to Tynwald in June 1960, Sir Ronald Garvey announced that, in consultation with the Executive Council about development planning and in the light of proposals being made by the Income Tax Commission and B. A. Williams of Liverpool University, it had been agreed to prioritise the attraction of new residents, tourism and light industry.[125] This was achieved in two main ways, by establishing the Island as a low tax centre and providing additional incentives to invest in the Island. In 1956 Tynwald had supported a proposal from the Lieutenant-Governor to appoint an Income Tax Commission to review the Island's policy on direct taxation.[126] With four members of Tynwald and three income tax experts from the UK, initially under the chair of Deemster Cowley and, after his death in 1958, under John Bolton, the Commission paved the way for a radical shift in taxation policy. During the late 1950s there had been periodic calls from the financial and business communities for lower direct taxes to stimulate the economy. Clifford Irving, who was appointed to the Commission in 1960, persuaded members to investigate the abolition of surtax as a means of promoting the Manx economy. In January 1960 the Commission had reported against further tax concessions to industry on the grounds that there was little prospect that they would lead to better results, but following Irving's initiative devoted an entire report in May 1960 to justifying the abolition of surtax as a means of attracting well-to-do residents, investment in industry and generally 'strengthening the economy of the Isle of Man'.[127] On 21 June 1960 Tynwald accepted the Commission's recommendation after a strongly argued debate, by 15 votes to nine in the Keys and seven votes to one in the Legislative Council, with MLP members strongest in their opposition.[128] Surtax was formally abolished by the Income Tax (No. 2) Act 1960.[129] In 1960/61, the final year in which surtax was levied, the standard rate of income tax was 22.5 per cent and surtax, paid in addition to income tax on income over £2,500, was charged on a progressive 10-point scale ranging from 3.75 to 37.5 per cent on income over £20,000.[130] The revenue from surtax in 1960/61 was £120,694 or 13.5 per cent of total revenue from direct taxation. Between 1961 and 1981 the policy of low direct taxation continued, the standard rate being lowered to 21 per cent by 1980/81.[131]

The Island's policy on diversification was further informed by the reports of three major economic surveys. The 1960 Report by B. A. Williams of Liverpool University[132] resulted in the establishment in April 1961 of the Industrial Advisory Council and an Industrial Office, the former with the task of advising Tynwald on industrial policy and the latter responsibility for implementation. It also persuaded Tynwald to fund a more generous package of incentives for both existing and new industry. Priority would be given to established Manx industries, providing work for the unemployed and attracting new industry that was compatible with the preservation of the Island as a holiday resort. In addition to the benefits of low income tax and the absence of surtax and company taxation, the Industrial Office was able to offer prospective investors grants and loans for the acquisition of property, the erection or improvement of factories and workshops, the purchase of plant and machinery, housing for workers and the cost of training personnel.[133] Between 1962/63 and 1972/73 Tynwald provided £244,342 in grants, £397,830 in loans and £628,578 for the purchase, erection and repair of buildings, a

Industrial Advisory Council, January 1964. Concerned at the lack of progress during the 1950s in attracting new industry, in 1961 Tynwald established an Industrial Advisory Council and an Industrial Office to promote the policy of diversification. From left to right those sitting are Sir Ralph Stevenson (MLC and Chair), J. Stanley Kermode, A. E. Costain and James M. Cain (MHK); those standing are J. Nelson Bates, Maurice Kelly (Secretary), R.P. Kelly (civil servant) and J. Hinton.

total aid package of £1,270,750. The success of the policy was limited by housing and labour shortages and competition from the UK development areas. Even so, existing firms did expand, new firms were attracted to the Island and between the censuses of April 1961 and April 1971 the number of people employed in manufacturing rose from 2,189 to 3,111 and the percentage of the total workforce from 11 to 13 per cent.[134]

Following the 1971 Report by PA International Management Consultants,[135] Tynwald appointed a firm of development consultants, Polecon Company Ltd, to advise on industrial development. The result, approved by the Industrial Advisory Council and the Finance Board, was one of the most generous packages of incentives available in the Western world. Commencing in January 1973 the package comprised investment grants of up to 40 per cent towards the cost of new buildings, plant and machinery, first year grants of up to 40 per cent of nonrecurring initial expenditure, transfer grants of up to 40 per cent, training grants of up to 50 per cent to employers operating an approved training scheme, loans of up to 50 per cent of the venture's working capital requirement,

Sir Peter Stallard visiting Iloman Engineering factory in Onchan, 14 December 1966. This was one of the first new factories to be built with the help of government support following the establishment of the Industrial Advisory Council.

sites zoned for industrial development, depreciation allowances and the taxation of profits solely at the standard rate of income tax.[136] In the eight years from 1973/74 the development of manufacturing industry really gathered momentum, helped by £4,731,606 of government financial assistance, £3,134,644 in grants, £1,384,669 in loans and £212,293 towards the purchase of sites and the erection of buildings.[137] Between the 1971 and 1981 censuses the number of full-time employees in manufacturing increased from 3,111 to 3,467, from 13 to 15 per cent of an expanding workforce.[138]

The main recommendation of the 1975 Report by PA International was that the Island should reduce its dependence on the UK.[139] While Tynwald's response was varied, including attempts to attract European investment and find new markets for Manx goods, the replacement of the Common Purse by the Customs and Excise Agreement and the serious marketing of the Island as a resort in Europe, the most important changes related to the financial sector. The Island's position as a low tax centre had been greatly enhanced by the ending of the sterling area in 1972. This had left the Isle of Man and the Channel Islands as virtually the only scheduled sterling territories outside the UK, giving them considerable investment appeal. Between 1975 and 1981 the Finance Board initiated a programme of legislation that was to provide the basis for the rapid expansion of the financial sector. The Banking Acts of 1975 and 1977 were designed to create a more favourable environment for the international banking community[140] and resulted in the incorporation of several new banks, a development accelerated by the UK's abolition of exchange controls in 1979.[141] After unsuccessful attempts in 1962, 1964 and 1973, the Usury (Repeal) Act 1979 abolished the centuries' old practice of fixing maximum rates of interest on borrowing by Act of Tynwald, removing a long-standing obstacle to investment in the Isle of Man.[142] The Industrial and Building Societies Act 1979 was passed to attract building societies to the Island.[143] The Exempt Insurance Companies Act 1981 provided for the profits and income of certain insurance companies to be exempt from tax, the first in a series of steps designed to develop the Island as an insurance centre.[144] The Companies Act 1982, which was approved by the Branches before the general election in November 1981, provided for important modifications to company law, increasing governmental control over the financial sector with a view to ensuring its future integrity and reputation.[145] Between 1961 and 1981 the numbers employed in insurance, banking, finance and business services more than tripled from 370 to 1,515, from 1.9 to 5.8 per cent of the total workforce.[146]

These policies on taxation and diversification were the decisive factors behind the remarkable transformation of the Manx economy that occurred after 1961. In the 20 years from 1961 the population increased by 37 per cent from 48,133 to 66,101.[147] The same period saw 19,359 new residents, including 2,092 Manx persons returning to the Island,[148] and a 36 per cent rise in the number of persons in employment from 18,999 to 25,864.[149] Between 1960/61 and 1980/81 the revenue from income tax (and surtax in 1960/61) increased from £896,337 to £23,054,000, a real rise of 361 per cent. Although national income data are not available for the whole of this period, the total income generated from Manx sources rose from £31,109,000 in 1969/70 to £161,502,000 in 1980/81, a real increase of 32 per cent. Much of that increase was attributable to the financial sector, whose share almost doubled from 12 to 23 per cent. By 1980/81 the sectoral composition of national income revealed an Island no longer dominated by tourism, the three major sectors—finance, manufacturing and tourism—accounting for 23, 15 and 10 per cent respectively.[150]

While the economic growth detailed here was broadly welcomed in the Island, it did bring with it social tensions and demands for government action to mitigate its worst effects. With buoyant sources of revenue at its disposal, it was not too difficult for Tynwald to respond to the increased calls being made on the services provided by the welfare state, but responding to the perceived threats posed to the wellbeing and culture of the indigenous population and the Manx environment was an altogether more difficult and controversial proposition. For those expressing concern over these related issues, the central demands were for immigration control and more effective land use planning. In November 1972 Tynwald responded to the demands for immigration control by appointing a select committee to report on the Island's new residents policy. Chaired by Edward Kerruish, the Committee recommended a licensing sytem with new residents being required to meet agreed criteria and make an investment in government securities in order to qualify for a license.[151] Although Tynwald narrowly approved the Committee's central recommendations in May 1973, the resultant Registration of

Victory House, Prospect Hill, September 1974. With government encouragement the 1970s saw growth in the Island's financial sector. Much of the initial expansion was accommodated in existing or extended buildings, but some new buildings, including Victory House, were opened as the industry embarked on a programme of growth that was to accelerate and become the outstanding feature of the Manx economy in the 1980s and 1990s.

Residents Bill was first emasculated by the House and then defeated in the Legislative Council. By the time the Bill left the House in October 1974 it merely provided for the maintenance of a register of residents; after a lengthy delay, the Legislative Council rejected the central clause of the truncated Bill, seeing no good reason for maintaining such a register, and the Bill fell.[152] Following renewed demands for immigration control during the 1976 general election and with population projections pointing to a population of 94,000 by the year 2000, in January 1979 Tynwald appointed a select committee to report on population growth and the control of immigration. This Committee, chaired by Clifford Irving, reported in April 1980. It argued that population policy should be informed by the twin objectives of preserving the quality of life and increasing the standard of living, and saw a population of 75,000 as compatible with those objectives, a ceiling not likely to be reached before the turn of the century. The Committee recommended the establishment of a register of all residents and machinery to enable Tynwald to control immigration should such control prove necessary, and the introduction of strict control of all land use by means of an all-Island development plan and firm planning decisions.[153] In marked contrast with 1973, the proposals were approved in April 1980 by an overwhelming majority of members, 20 votes to two in the House and eight votes to one in the Council. As part of the same resolution it was also agreed to make the Select Committee a standing committee of Tynwald, in anticipation perhaps of the long struggle that lay ahead in respect of the legislation to control immigration.

Progress with land use planning following the 1980 resolution was less problematic. Here most of the long struggle had preceded the resolution. On 8 July 1970 Tynwald asked the LGB to submit a development plan for its consideration by the following July.[154] At the time the Board maintained 'a rough guide' to land use planning and the request was for this to be upgraded to a legally binding development plan. During the debate concerns were expressed about the piecemeal approach to planning that had predominated since the 1930s and the considerable pressures on the countryside caused by new residential and industrial developments. The Draft Development Plan was duly laid before Tynwald in July 1971 and the following October Tynwald instructed the Board to prepare the Provisional Order needed under the Town and Country Planning Acts for the Plan to have statutory force.[155] Although the Draft Plan was not at this stage legally binding, it did become a general guide to planning policy. It took a decade of controversy, consultations, amendments to planning law, a public inquiry and much redrafting before the Plan eventually came into force in August 1982 under the Isle of Man Planning Scheme (Development Plan) Order 1982. This provisional Order was approved by Tynwald on 15 June 1982 with just four MHKs dissenting.[156]

Orry Williams demonstrating on Tynwald Hill, July 1976. Williams was one of a group of demonstrators protesting about low taxation and the adverse impact of the arrival of new residents on culture, employment, housing and the environment.

# Manx Finances 1958–81

Although the removal of UK Treasury control, the establishment of a Finance Board and a Tynwald anxious to assert its authority did lead to important changes in Manx budgetary policy, they did not lead to any immediate diminution of UK influence over spending on key services or indirect taxation. The Island continued to harmonise policy with the UK in such high-spending areas as police, agriculture, education, health and social security. These alone accounted for almost 70 per cent of total revenue spending in 1980/81 and much other expenditure was still committed under legislation adapted from the UK. Under the Contribution Act 1956 Tynwald paid to the UK Treasury a contribution in respect of defence and common services. This was maintained at five per cent of net Common Purse receipts until 1979 when, following consultations with the UK authorities, it was reduced to 2.5 per cent. The UK opposed the reduction but recognised that under the 1956 Act Tynwald was free to decide. However, the main reason for the percentage reduction was the large increase in the actual contribution during the 1970s, from £224,671 in 1969/70 to £716,377 in 1977/78, as a direct result of UK policy on indirect taxation.[157]

On the revenue side, UK influence over indirect taxation remained almost total. With the exception of duties on beer, levels of taxation were kept in line with the UK. By the time the Common Purse Agreement gave way to the Customs and Excise Agreement in October 1979, it had been modified to include pool-betting duty in 1961, the Continental Shelf Agreement in 1966 and value-added tax (VAT) when it replaced purchase tax on UK entry to the EEC in 1973.[158] When the Conservative Government increased VAT from eight to 15 per cent in June 1979, the Island had automatically followed suit, highlighting for critics of the Common Purse the Island's unhealthy dependence on the UK. Notwithstanding the criticisms, at the same sitting of Tynwald on 10 July 1979, it was agreed by 18 votes to three in the Keys and by seven votes to two in the Council to accept the draft Customs and Excise Agreement, whereby the Island agreed, for the time being at least, not to introduce fresh differences in indirect taxation. Between 1957/58 and 1978/79 the revenue from indirect taxation increased from £2,402,760 to £18,393,920, before jumping to £24,737,847 in 1979/80 and £29,306,294 in 1980/81, the first full year with VAT at 15 per cent. In 1957/58 the proportion of this revenue attributable to the Common Purse, and therefore directly determined by the UK Chancellor, was 92 per cent; in 1980/81 the proportion of the much larger total was 95.4 per cent. Despite a real increase in the revenue from indirect taxation of 110 per cent, there was a further decline over the period in its share of total revenue from 60 per cent to 50.7 per cent. The main reason for the decline, which would have been higher still but for the increase in VAT rates in 1979, was the massive increase in the revenue from income tax whose share rose from 30.3 per cent in 1957/58 (including revenue from surtax) to 39.6 per cent in 1980/81. The revenue from income tax ceased to be earmarked for specific purposes in 1958 and became part of the General Revenue.

Devolution in 1958 did not usher in an immediate increase in the real level of spending. On the contrary economic and demographic circumstances combined to limit the postwar expansion. After the constitutional changes of 1958 the real level of spending fell below the postwar high of 1957/58 for seven out of the next eight years (1961/62 being the exception), before rising steadily for the rest of the period. Changes in the level of expenditure are summarised in Table 7.1. Taking the period as a whole expenditure rose from £4,137,228 in 1957/58 to £52,086,404 in 1980/81, a real increase of 117 per cent.

**Table 7.1. Central Government Spending 1958/59 to 1980/81**

| Financial Year up to 31 March | Total Expenditure £ | Expenditure at 2000 Prices £ |
|---|---|---|
| 1959 | 3,970,994 | 54,204,068 |
| 1960 | 3,857,992 | 52,950,940 |
| 1961 | 4,129,246 | 55,166,726 |
| 1962 | 4,829,011 | 61,878,946 |
| 1963 | 3,979,001 | 49,415,213 |
| 1964 | 3,966,774 | 48,561,247 |
| 1965 | 4,232,278 | 49,593,833 |
| 1966 | 5,071,484 | 56,988,265 |
| 1967 | 5,595,295 | 60,753,713 |
| 1968 | 5,840,205 | 61,345,513 |
| 1969 | 6,605,914 | 65,286,248 |
| 1970 | 6,820,647 | 64,114,081 |
| 1971 | 7,993,056 | 69,083,983 |
| 1972 | 9,116,607 | 73,242,820 |
| 1973 | 10,080,789 | 74,870,019 |
| 1974 | 11,624,339 | 76,069,674 |
| 1975 | 16,126,145 | 87,113,435 |
| 1976 | 21,544,907 | 96,047,195 |
| 1977 | 24,391,003 | 95,295,648 |
| 1978 | 27,772,294 | 98,647,188 |
| 1979 | 32,716,690 | 106,067,500* |
| 1980 | 41,594,627 | 111,390,410 |
| 1981 | 52,086,404 | 124,851,110 |

\* (to nearest £10)

The sources of the raw expenditure data were the *Accounts of the Government Treasurer* from 1958/59 to 1980/81. The level of spending at 2000 prices was calculated with the help of the Price Index supplied by Martin Caley of the Economic Affairs Division of the Manx Treasury. The real expenditure figures should be treated with caution as they are derived with the help of an index designed for a different purpose.

To avoid double counting, expenditure facilitated by borrowing is not included in the raw totals, which are:

i)   1958/59 to 1961/62 The sum of expenditure from the General Revenue Account, the Income Tax Fund and the Accumulated Fund.

ii)  1962/63 to 1980/81 Total expenditure from the General Revenue Account.

# *Notes*

1   *Statutes*, xxi, pp. 161–64.
2   The Select Committee on the Representation of the People Acts 1951–61 was proposed by R. C. Stephen and chaired initially by Deemster MacPherson and subsequently by Deemster Moore; see 81 *Manx Deb.*, 21 January 1964, pp. 398–434.
3   See 85 *Manx Deb.*, 28 November 1967, p. 388, 86 *Manx Deb.*, 11 March 1969, pp. 1183–95 and 1206–08 and 29 April 1969, pp. 1561–63.
4   *Acts of Tynwald 1971*, pp. 21–26.
5   See 81 *Manx Deb.*, 21 January 1964, pp. 398–434, where the voting was 10 to 12 in the Keys and eight to three in the Council; 88 *Manx Deb.*, 4 May 1971, pp. K481–85 where the voting on the third reading of the Bill was 12 in favour and 10 against, just one vote short of the 13 required to pass at third reading; and 93 *Manx Deb.*, 7 October 1975, p. C22 and 25 November 1975, pp. K121–28.
6   *Acts of Tynwald, 1976*, pp. 21–26; see also 93 *Manx Deb.*, 7 October 1975, p. C19.
7   See 88 *Manx Deb.*, 18 November 1970, pp. T193–214, 89 *Manx Deb.*, 20 October 1971, pp. T168–76, 94 *Manx Deb.*, 22 March 1977, pp. T587–601 and 724–29, and 96 *Manx Deb.*, 20 June 1979, pp. T887–903.
8   *Report of the Commission on the Representation of the People Acts*, 26 March 1980 (Douglas, 1980).
9   See 97 *Manx Deb.*, 22 April 1980, pp. T906–42, 17 June 1980, pp. T1240–61 and 9 July 1980, p. T1308.
10  See 98 *Manx Deb.*, 16 December 1980, pp. K207–26 and 3 February 1981, pp. K318–33.
11  See 77 *Manx Deb.*, 19 January 1960, pp. 257–62 and 263–65; see also G. N. Kniveton (ed.), *A Chronicle of the Twentieth Century: The Manx Experience*, vol. 2: 1951–2000 (Douglas, 2000), p. 53.
12  *Statutes*, xix, pp. 336–37.
13  See 79 *Manx Deb.*, 13 February 1962, p. 567.
14  Effected by the Representation of the People Act 1966; *Statutes*, xx, pp. 76–85.
15  See 88 *Manx Deb.*, 5 July 1971, p. T1048. The petition was presented by Millicent Faragher and other women, who had been campaigning for the abolition of corporal punishment, but did not attract any support in Tynwald. For further details, see Angela Kneale, *Against Birching: Judicial Corporal Punishment in the Isle of Man* (London, 1973).
16  Candidates were asked if they supported the preservation of the green belt, the creation of an Ayres National Park, no sale of government land without public consultation, a coastal footpath, the full restoration of land following mining, early consultations on the all-Island development plan, the listing and protection of historic buildings, the preservation of Bishopscourt for the nation, no residential development on Douglas Head, the maintenance of public access to beaches, the restoration of MER services and the Steam Railway from Douglas to Port Erin, the use of the railway track from St Johns to Ramsey as a public footpath, immigration control, the establishment of a board of environment and the acquisition by the Manx National Trust of areas of natural beauty; see *Isle of Man Examiner*, 12 November 1976.
17  For a more detailed discussion of selected aspects of the election, see the author's *Devolution at Work: A Case Study of the Isle of Man* (Farnborough, Hampshire, 1979), pp. 79–93.
18  Following a resolution of Tynwald on 15 April 1975 there was an investigation into the case for maintaining reciprocity. The outcome was the renewal of the Island's reciprocal agreement with the UK in 1978, replacing that of 1948; see 92 *Manx Deb.*, 15 April 1975, pp. T907–16 and 95 *Manx Deb.*, 21 February 1978, p. T145.
19  Nicholas Timmins, *The Five Giants: A Biography of the Welfare State* (London, 1996) provides an excellent analysis of the politics of social security in the UK during this period. For details of developments in the Island, see the 29th, 30th, 31st, 32nd and 33rd *Reports of the Board of Social Services* for the period between 1958 and 1969; *Isle of Man Social Security. Report of the*

*Government Actuary ... as at 31 March 1977* (Douglas, 1980), covering the period from 1964 to 1977; and *Isle of Man National Insurance Fund. Report of the Government Actuary on the operation of the Social Security Acts in the Isle of Man in the period from 1 April 1977 to 31 March 1982* (Douglas, 1984).

20   Under Part II of the Isle of Man Board of Social Security Act 1970; *Statutes*, xxi, pp. 395–427. Between 1970 and 1974 the level of supplementary benefit was uprated in line with the UK.

21   By means of the Family Income Supplements (Isle of Man) Act 1975; *Acts of Tynwald 1975*, pp. 3–22. Prior to the 1980s the rates of benefit were kept in line with the UK.

22   See the Social Security Legislation (Application) (Child Benefit) Order 1976, approved by Tynwald in January 1977; 94 *Manx Deb.*, 18 January 1977, p. T276.

23   See 91 *Manx Deb.*, 9 April 1974, pp. T708–09.

24   The number of retirement pensions in payment increased from 6,709 in the year ended 31 March 1958 to 13,865 in the year ended 31 March 1981; the equivalent figures for numbers in receipt of family allowance/child benefit were 2,996 and 7,530; the total number of insured persons rose from 21,915 to 25,541 between 1958 and 1981. See *Twenty Ninth Report of the Isle of Man Board of Social Services covering the Period from 1 April 1954 to 31 March 1961* (Douglas, 1962); *Isle of Man Digest of Economic and Social Statistics 1982/83*, p. O9 and *Isle of Man National Insurance Fund. Report by the Government Actuary on the Operation of the Social Security Acts in the Isle of Man in the period 1 April 1977 to 31 March 1982* (Douglas, 1984), para. 6.3.

25   For a discussion of policy in the UK, see Timmins, *Five Giants*, Parts III and IV.

26   For a detailed discussion, see Hinton Bird, *An Island that Led: The History of Manx Education*, vol. 2 (Port St Mary, 1995), pp. 235–90.

27   85 *Manx Deb.*, 13 December 1967, pp. 468–513.

28   *Acts of Tynwald 1971*, pp. 639–42.

29   See 85 *Manx Deb.*, 13 December 1967, pp. 468–513 and 88 *Manx Deb.*, 27 April 1971, pp. K473–80 and 11 May 1971, pp. K543–58.

30   90 *Manx Deb.*, 13 December 1972, pp. T222–23.

31   90 *Manx Deb.*, 17 April 1973, pp. T824–41.

32   *Statutes*, xx, pp. 482–501.

33   For the views of members of the Keys, see 85 *Manx Deb.*, 23 January 1968, pp. 694–710 and 30 January 1968, pp. 721–26; for those of members of the Legislative Council, see 6 February 1968, p. 771 and 5 March 1968, p. 1028.

34   See 88 *Manx Deb.*, 17 February 1971, pp. T507–36.

35   88 *Manx Deb.*, 16 March 1971, pp. T555–67. The resolution was only carried in the Legislative Council with the casting vote of the Lieutenant-Governor.

36   90 *Manx Deb.*, 21 February 1973, pp. T478–507.

37   91 *Manx Deb.*, 19 March 1974, pp. T485–503.

38   For a discussion of the politics of the UK service, see Timmins, *Five Giants*, Parts III and IV.

39   Expenditure on the services provided under Part III of the 1948 Act increased from £32,035 in 1958/59 to £708,253 in 1980/81; see 75 *Manx Deb.*, 16 April 1958, p. 773 and *Isle of Man Digest of Economic and Social Statistics 1985*, p. O6

40   The progress of the legislation was interrupted by the 1962 general election, but this was in no way due to opposition to the main aims of the legislation; see 79 *Manx Deb.*, 31 October 1961, pp. 162–66 and 80 *Manx Deb.*, 6 November 1962, pp. 132–58 and 5 March 1963, pp. 753–62.

41   *Statutes*, xix, pp. 1173–206.

42   For a discussion of the conflict, see Timmins, *Five Giants*, pp. 330–41.

43   See 80 *Manx Deb.*, 19 March 1963, pp. 808–38.

44   91 *Manx Deb.*, 9 July 1974, pp. T1003–12.

45   Isle of Man Government, *Digest of Economic and Social Statistics 1996* (Douglas, 1997), Table 12.1.

46  Data derived from the *Accounts of the Government Treasurer* by adding the total net expenditure by the LGB on housing and the cost of deficiency payments in respect of local authority housing.

47  79 *Manx Deb.*, 10 July 1962, pp. 1401–17.

48  92 *Manx Deb.*, 21 January 1975, pp. T493–95.

49  *Housing. Report of the Local Government Board*, 4 June 1971, p. 7 and *Isle of Man Digest of Economic and Social Statistics 1980* (Douglas, 1980), p. 120.

50  79 *Manx Deb.*, 10 July 1962, pp. 1417–28.

51  See *Isle of Man Digest of Economic and Social Statistics 1980*, p. 121.

52  96 *Manx Deb.*, 12 December 1978, pp. T278–86 and *Isle of Man Digest of Economic and Social Statistics 1982–83*, (Douglas, 1983), p. H8.

53  Calculated with the help of *Housing. Report of the Local Government Board*, 4 June 1971, pp. 7–8 and the *Accounts of the Government Treasurer* for the period 1971–81.

54  Between 1927 and 1966 such relief was set against income payable in respect of the gross value of residential property. Although in 1966 such income ceased to be income for income tax purposes, Section 2b of the Income Tax Act 1966 (*Statutes*, xvi, pp. 383–462) provided for the retention of mortgage interest tax relief.

55  The main Acts were passed in 1947 and 1949, *Statutes*, xvi, pp. 636–51 and xvii, pp. 810–12.

56  *Statutes*, xxi, pp. 29–40.

57  *Acts of Tynwald 1975*, pp. 265–89.

58  Calculated with the help of the *Annual Report of the Isle of Man Local Government Board for the Year ended 31 March 1959* (Douglas, 1960), *Housing. Report of the Local Government Board*, 4 June 1971, p. 11 and the *Accounts of the Government Treasurer* for the period 1971–81.

59  See *Housing. Report of the Local Government Board*, 4 June 1971, pp. 17–18 and Appendix J; see also *Isle of Man Local Government Board Report to Tynwald on Housing*, 2 November 1984, p. 13.

60  *Statutes*, pp. 51–76.

61  See 76 *Manx Deb.*, 17 February 1959, p. 415.

62  76 *Manx Deb.*, 7 April 1959, pp. 689–700.

63  *Acts of Tynwald 1976*, pp. 121–30.

64  *Statutes*, xvii, pp. 190–97.

65  *Acts of Tynwald 1981*, pp. 507–10.

66  See *Isle of Man Digest of Economic and Social Statistics 1982–83* (Douglas, 1983), p. D9.

67  See 99 *Manx Deb.*, 13 October 1981, pp. T47–50. Cringle also pointed out that the Manx figures were better than for any region or nation of the UK.

68  See *Report of the House of Keys Committee on the Unemployment Situation*, 12 January 1977.

69  *First Interim Report of the Select Committee of Tynwald on Unemployment*, 5 December 1980, *Second Interim Report of the Select Committee of Tynwald on Unemployment*, 3 April 1981 and *Final Report of the Select Committee of Tynwald on Unemployment*, 31 October 1981; see also 98 *Manx Deb.*, 9 December 1980, pp. T371–406 and 14 April 1981, pp. T1062–85 and 99 *Manx Deb.*, 13 October 1981, pp. T18–23.

70  For details of these schemes, see the *Bi-annual Reports of the Industrial Advisory Council* for the period.

71  See *Report of the House of Keys on the Unemployment Situation*, 12 January 1977 (Douglas, 1977) and 95 *Manx Deb.*, 13 December 1977, pp. T306–08 and 21 February 1978, p. T415; 97 *Manx Deb.*, 23 April 1980, pp. T992–93.

72  See 94 *Manx Deb.*, 15 February 1977, pp. T326–44 and 95 *Manx Deb.*, 21 February 1978, pp. T382–401.

73  See 98 *Manx Deb.*, 9 December 1980, p. T428; 99 *Manx Deb.*, 13 and 14 October 1981, pp. T54–73, 84–96 and 97–105.

74  *Acts of Tynwald 1975*, pp. 233–45.

75  95 *Manx Deb.*, 16 November 1977, p. 1244.

76  See 88 *Manx Deb.*, 3 November 1970, pp. K30–38 and 41–43.

77  *Acts of Tynwald 1977–78*, pp. 3–5.
78  See 98 *Manx Deb.*, 11 November 1980, pp. K55–108 and 26 May 1981, pp. K769–87.
79  *Acts of Tynwald 1981*, pp. 445–55.
80  See 80 *Manx Deb.*, 15 January 1963, pp. 386–87 and 378–439.
81  *Statutes*, xx, p. 201.
82  *Statutes*, xx, pp. 7–11.
83  *Statutes*, xxi, pp. 134–60.
84  *Acts of Tynwald 1974*, pp. 289–304.
85  See 77 *Manx Deb.*, 10 November 1959, pp. 94–104; 80 *Manx Deb.*, 22 May 1963, pp. 1282–302, 91 *Manx Deb.*, 19 February 1974, pp. T338–42; and 96 *Manx Deb.*, 21 February 1979, pp. T441–69.
86  The Fishery Acts 1963 and 1964; *Statutes*, xix, pp. 853–58 and 1280–88. The powers of the Board were also increased in respect of inland waters by the Inland Fisheries Act 1976; *Acts of Tynwald 1976*, pp. 541–89.
87  See 82 *Manx Deb.*, 8 December 1964, pp. 393–94.
88  See 98 *Manx Deb.*, 16 June 1981, p. T1272 and 14 July 1981, pp. T1499–517 and 1531–42.
89  See 99 *Manx Deb.*, 14 October 1981, pp. T105–17.
90  In the Keys the third reading was carried by 14 votes to 10. The Legislative Council did not reject the Bill, but postponed a decision on it until after the forthcoming election; see 78 *Manx Deb.*, 30 June 1961, pp. 2023–53 and 25 July 1961, pp. 2189–206.
91  *Statutes*, xix, pp. 708–24.
92  The Licensing Bill 1959 was passed by the Legislative Council, but defeated at second reading in the Keys following a tied vote, the Speaker using his casting vote to support the status quo; see 76 *Manx Deb.*, 7 April 1959, pp. 663–89. The following year the House approved experimental reform by 15 votes to eight at second reading and 15 votes to nine at third reading and the Bill had a smooth passage in the Legislative Council; see 77 *Manx Deb.*, 29 March 1960, pp. 708–46 and 5 April 1960, p. 796. For details of the Act, see *Statutes*, xix, pp. 40–47.
93  See 78 *Manx Deb.*, 20 December 1960, pp. 555–59 and 79 *Manx Deb.*, 22 November 1961, pp. 324–28.
94  See *Acts of Tynwald 1979*, pp. 85–92. Licensing bills to provide for the sale of alcohol in clubs throughout the year were defeated in 1968, 1969 and 1970, on the first two occasions by the Legislative Council and on the third by the House of Keys. The more broadly based Licensing (Sunday Opening) Act 1979 only became law under the terms of the Isle of Man Constitution Acts after being rejected by the Legislative Council in December 1977 and October 1978; see 96 *Manx Deb.*, 22 October 1978 and 9 January 1979, pp. K14 and C46–50.
95  For details of expenditure incurred, see *Accounts of the Government Treasurer* for the years in question.
96  *Statutes*, xviii, pp. 904–09; xix, pp. 522–32 and 851–53; xxi, pp. 41–43; *Acts of Tynwald 1974*, pp. 237–46; *Acts of Tynwald 1976*, pp. 249–52 and *Acts of Tynwald 1977*, pp. 55–64.
97  *Statutes*, xix, pp. 503–22.
98  *Acts of Tynwald 1975*, pp. 181–96.
99  See 96 *Manx Deb.*, 10 July 1979, pp. T960–77 and 98 *Manx Deb.*, 14 July 1981, pp. T1542–44.
100 Six were purchased: Glen Mooar in 1958/60 for £200, Glen Maye in 1959/60 for £1,500, Silverdale in 1959/62 for £2,900, Elfin Glen in 1962/64 for £3,850, Bishopscourt Glen in 1963/64 for £400 and Glen Wyllin in 1977/78 for £28,000; see *Reports of the Forestry, Mines and Lands Board* for the period. Ballure Walk was a gift to the nation from J. H. Murray in 1960; see 78 *Manx Deb.*, 22 March 1961, p. 1187. Lhergy Frissell was leased from the Ramsey Commissioners in 1972 and Groudle Glen from the Onchan Commissioners in 1975; see 89 *Manx Deb.*, 20 June 1972, pp. T907–08 and 91 *Manx Deb.*, 21 October 1975, pp. T51–52. Port Soderick was acquired from Douglas Corporation for a nominal fee in 1975

(thanks are due to Robin Pollard, Chief Forestry Officer, for the information regarding Port Soderick; in a letter to the author, dated 12 April 2000).

101 The Commission was appointed following an initiative by the Executive Council. It reported a few months before the election in 1966; see *Report of the Transport Commission*, May 1966 (Douglas, 1966) and 83 *Manx Deb.*, 22 June 1966, pp. 1785–814.

102 See 99 *Manx Deb.*, 16 December 1981, p. T322.

103 See 97 *Manx Deb.*, 25 March 1980, pp. T809–14.

104 *Acts of Tynwald 1981*, pp. 57–62.

105 See 93 *Manx Deb.*, 22 October 1975, pp. T110–28 and 7 July 1976, pp. T1020–46.

106 95 *Manx Deb.*, 19 October 1977, pp. T71–90.

107 Following acceptance of the Steering Committee recommendation the first step towards amalgamation was to appoint MER Board members as directors of Isle of Man National Transport Ltd pending the legislation providing for the Isle of Man Passenger Transport Board; see *Acts of Tynwald 1982*, pp. 81–112.

108 For details of expenditure incurred, see *Accounts of the Government Treasurer* for the period in question.

109 Under the Joint Electricity Authority Act 1966, *Statutes*, xx, pp. 50–55.

110 For details of the expenditure incurred, see *Accounts of the Government Treasurer* for the period.

111 *Acts of Tynwald 1972*, pp. 21–97.

112 Under the Water and Gas Act 1974, *Acts of Tynwald 1974*, pp. 9–19.

113 See 84 *Manx Deb.*, 28 February and 16 April 1967, pp. 699–704 and 1151–54 regarding the appointment of the Committee; *Acts of Tynwald 1972*, pp. 147–66 regarding the establishment of the Gas Authority and *Acts of Tynwald 1974*, pp. 9–19 regarding the Isle of Man Water and Gas Authority.

114 For details of expenditure incurred, see *Accounts of the Government Treasurer* for the period in question.

115 See 80 *Manx Deb.*, 15 January and 9 April 1963, pp. 386 and 959–60; 81 *Manx Deb.*, 10 December 1963 and 18 February 1964, pp. 285–87 and 537–44. The Executive Council resolution in favour of purchase was carried without division on 18 February 1964.

116 See 82 *Manx Deb.*, 21 October 1964, pp. 81–83.

117 See 82 *Manx Deb.*, 14 April 1965, pp. 1105–10.

118 See 85 *Manx Deb.*, 17 January 1968, pp. 626–56.

119 See 88 *Manx Deb.*, 16 February 1971, pp. T401–10.

120 This was one of the few purchases to arouse serious opposition, the resolution being carried in the Keys by 12 votes to nine and in the Council only with the casting vote of the Lieutenant-Governor; see 90 *Manx Deb.*, 12 December 1972, pp. T173–79. The sale to Sangster for £105,000 was almost as controversial with many in the House supporting the Speaker's view that the property be transferred to the Manx Museum and National Trust and maintained for cultural and tourist purposes; 93 *Manx Deb.*, 9 December 1975, pp. T252–57.

121 See 91 *Manx Deb.*, 9 April 1974, pp. T641–69.

122 See 91 *Manx Deb.*, 9 July 1974, pp. T1001–02; 93 *Manx Deb.*, 6 July 1976, pp. T976–78 and 97 *Manx Deb.*, 16 October 1979, pp. T60–65.

123 The purchase was approved by 17 votes to six in the Keys and unanimously in the Council; see 93 *Manx Deb.*, 6 July 1976. The sale proved altogether more controversial but was eventually approved by by 11 votes to eight in the House and six votes to one in the Council; see 95 *Manx Deb.*, 22 February 1978, pp. T443–60 and 96 *Manx Deb.*, 10 April 1979, pp. T718–24.

124 See 95 *Manx Deb.*, 11 July 1978, pp. T970–73.

125 See 77 *Manx Deb.*, 21 June 1960, pp. 1261–65; see also Kniveton, *Chronicle of the Twentieth Century*, vol. 2, p. 61, for details of a brochure produced by the Permanent Residents Committee of the Tourist Board to promote the Island to potential new residents.

126 74 *Manx Deb.*, 18 November 1956, pp. 25–26.

127 See *Fifth Interim Report of the Income Tax Commission*, 28 January 1960, p. 6 and *Sixth Interim*

*Report of the Income Tax Commission*, 25 May 1960. In an interview with the author on 1 February 2000, Clifford Irving recounted how, following consultations with businessmen friends, he had proposed abolition at the first meeting of the Commission he attended and how, after initial reluctance to discuss the proposition, the Commission had investigated it and endorsed the stategy adopted by Guernsey in 1954.

128  *77 Manx Deb.*, 21 June 1960, pp. 1279–303.

129  *Statutes*, xix, pp. 115–16.

130  *77 Manx Deb.*, 22 June 1960, pp. 1306–26.

131  *97 Manx Deb.*, 27 May 1980, p. T1094.

132  *Report of the Isle of Man Industrial Survey 31 May 1960* (Liverpool, 1960).

133  See *Report of the Industrial Advisory Council*, 30 October 1961.

134  Isle of Man Government, *Digest of Economic and Social Statistics 1996* (Douglas, 1997), Table 3.3.

135  *An Economic Appreciation of the Isle of Man* (London, 1971).

136  See *Twenty Fourth Bi-annual Report of the Industrial Advisory Council*, 30 April 1973 (Douglas, 1973) and *Isle of Man Digest of Statistics 1982–83*, (Douglas, 1983), Section I, pp. 1–5.

137  *Isle of Man Digest of Statistics 1982–83*, Section I, pp. 5–6.

138  Isle of Man Government, *Digest of Economic and Social Statistics 1996* (Douglas, 1996), Table 3.3.

139  *Economic Survey of the Isle of Man* (London, 1975).

140  *Acts of Tynwald 1975*, pp. 67–77 and *Acts of Tynwald 1977*, pp. 7–9.

141  See Sue Stuart, *Offshore Finance Handbook: Isle of Man 1996–97* (Narberth, Pembrokeshire, 1996), p. 28.

142  *Acts of Tynwald 1979*, pp. 155–58.

143  *Acts of Tynwald 1979*, pp. 149–54. Although building societies had been legally free to operate in the Island since 1892, they had not in fact established in the Island. This was partly due to the fact that UK societies were not legally allowed to lend money outside the UK and partly the result of the restrictions on interest rates imposed under the Usury Acts.

144  *Acts of Tynwald 1981*, pp. 169–78.

145  See *Acts of Tynwald 1982*, pp. 13–79.

146  Isle of Man Government, *Digest of Economic and Social Statistics 1996*, Table 3.3.

147  Isle of Man Government, *Digest of Economic and Social Statistics 1996*, Table 2.3.

148  *Isle of Man 1981 Census Report* (Douglas, 1982), Part 1, Tables 6 and 7, pp. 6–7.

149  Isle of Man Government, *Digest of Economic and Social Statistics 1996*, Table 3.3.

150  For details of national income data for this period, see *Isle of Man Digest of Economic and Social Statistics 1982–83*, pp. B6–7.

151  See *90 Manx Deb.*, 21 November 1972, pp. T99–118 and 120–30 and 16 May 1973, pp. T927–80.

152  See *92 Manx Deb.*, 22 October 1974, pp. K12–24 and 1 July 1975, pp. C332–38; *93 Manx Deb.*, 4 November 1975, pp. C38–45.

153  See *96 Manx Deb.*, 16 January 1979, pp. T362–63 and *97 Manx Deb.*, 22 and 23 April 1980, pp. T942–79.

154  See *87 Manx Deb.*, 7 and 8 July 1970, pp. 1921–26 and 1949–65.

155  See *89 Manx Deb.*, 20 October 1971, pp. T147–53.

156  Moving acceptance of the Order the chair of the LGB, Miles Walker, provided a useful history of its development between 1971 and 1982; see *99 Manx Deb.*, 15 June 1982, pp. T973–77 and 1000–11.

157  See *96 Manx Deb.*, 21 November 1978, pp. T168–74. Although the increase quoted by the chair of the Finance Board, Percy Radcliffe, was a large one in cash terms, the real increase was only just over 20 per cent.

158  See Kermode, *Devolution at Work*, pp. 119–20.

# CHAPTER EIGHT

# The Advent of Ministerial Government 1981–2000

Constitutionally the final decades of the century were characterised by four main developments. First, the Island continued to campaign for greater autonomy from the UK, but in a climate where international agreements and European as well as UK authorities visibly limited the real room for manoeuvre. Second, there was a lengthy but largely unproductive campaign for the further democratisation of Tynwald. Third, the search for a stronger executive and a rationalisation of the Island's unwieldy board system led to the establishment of a ministerial system of government. Fourth, tensions between the authority of the new executive and Tynwald led to demands for the more effective accountability of government to Tynwald.

After 1981 political leadership was provided mainly by the chair and members of the Executive Council and, after 1986, by the Chief Minister and Ministers. The Lieutenant-Governors retained few political powers with the result that the incumbents—Sir Nigel Cecil (1980–85), Sir Laurence New (1985–90), Sir Laurence Jones (1990–95) and Sir Timothy Daunt (1995–2000)—were no longer numbered among the Island's political leaders.[1] Members of Tynwald outside the Executive Council or the Council of Ministers were still able to pursue their own initiatives and influence votes, but a combination of constitutional and political developments meant that the prospects of successful initiatives were limited unless supported in some measure by the leadership. That leadership continued to be recruited from both branches of Tynwald, but with the Keys increasingly predominant. Between 1981 and 1986 the leadership of the Executive Council was provided by Percy Radcliffe (1981–85) and Edgar Mann (1985–86), both MLCs chosen by Tynwald as the best man for the job. Their successors, Miles Walker (1986–96) and Donald Gelling (1996–) were both MHKs. Others recruited from the Legislative Council (the dates in brackets refer to the term served on the executive bodies) were for the most part elder statesmen first elected as MHKs in the 1960s and mid-1970s—Edward Kerruish (1978–85), Roy MacDonald (1982–85), Ian Anderson (1984–88), Arnold Callin (1985–95), Edmund Lowey (1985–96) and Norman Radcliffe (1985–86). Edgar Mann was also an MLC member of the Council of Ministers between 1996 and 1999. The one exception was Clare Christian (1996–), who was first elected to the Keys in 1980. Although a nonvoting member of Tynwald, reference should also be made to the Attorney Generals of this period—T. William Cain (1980–93), John M. Kerruish (1993–97) and William J. H. Corlett (1998–)—who remained influential, advising the Government and in attendance at meetings of the Executive Council/Council of Ministers.

Twenty-five MHKs served on the Executive Council/Council of Ministers between November 1981 and the turn of the century. Of these six were first elected to the House before 1981: Edgar Mann (1980–85), Victor Kneale (1982–90), Miles Walker (1982–96), Matthew Ward (1982–85), Noel Cringle (1982–86 and 1996), David Moore (1985–86) and Dominic Delaney (1986–89). Fourteen were first elected during the 1980s: Allan Bell (1986–94 and 1996–), J. Anthony Brown (1986–), J. David Q. Cannan (1986–89), Donald G. Maddrell (1986–88), Donald J. Gelling (1988–), Bernard May (1988–96), James C. Cain (1989–91), David North (1989–), L. Ronald Cretney (1990–91), John Corrin (1991–96), Hazel Hannan (1991–99), David C. Cretney (1996–), R. Edgar Quine (1996–99) and Walter A. Gilbey (1999–). The remaining four first became MHKs in the 1990s: Terry R. A. Groves (1994–96), Richard K. Corkill (1995–), Alexander F. Downie (1998–) and Stephen C. Rodan (1999–). In the case of the House of Keys reference should also be made to the office of Speaker. Although the incumbents of this period did not enjoy the executive roles of some of their predecessors, they were still politicians of some distinction. Sir Charles Kerruish, first elected Speaker in 1962, continued to hold the office until 1990 when he became the first Manx President of Tynwald, a post he held until his retirement from politics in April 2000. The successors of this 'absolutely outstanding Manxman and politician'[2] were Victor Kneale until his retirement from politics in 1991, James Cain until his defeat in the general election of 1996 and Noel Cringle until his election as President of Tynwald in April 2000.

The politics of Tynwald continued to be dominated by Independent members, the

Sir Nigel Cecil, Lieutenant-Governor 1980–85, signifying the Royal Assent to Manx legislation, June 1982. The photograph shows the first exercise of the authority since it was delegated to the Lieutenant-Governor in 1981. From left to right those in attendance are Peter Hulme, Government Secretary, Robert Quayle, Clerk of Tynwald, Sir Charles Kerruish, Speaker of the House of Keys, Percy Radcliffe, Chair of Executive Council 1981–85, Jack Nivison, President of the Legislative Council, William Cain, Attorney General and Arthur Bawden, Clerk to the Legislative Council.

small MLP the only organised political party with representation in Tynwald throughout this period. However, with the establishment of a full ministerial system in 1988, certain critics of government started thinking of operating as an organised parliamentary opposition. After the 1991 election and the defeat of Edgar Mann in the election for Chief Minister, five MHKs agreed to form the Alternative Policy Group (APG) under Mann's leadership. The other founding members were David Cannan and Dominic Delaney, both ministers until 1989, Edgar Quine and Adrian Duggan. Initially the APG refused to accept any office under Miles Walker and worked as an organised opposition pressing for greater autonomy for the Island, more accountable government, a higher priority to economic development and abrogation of the Customs and Excise Agreement (CEA). On many issues there was common ground between the Government and the APG and in May 1993 Mann and Duggan accepted membership of the Departments of Industry and Home Affairs, thus relinquishing a strictly opposition role. In November 1996 APG members, still without an extraparliamentary organisation, contested and won six seats in the general election under the leadership of Edgar Quine; each stood as an Independent supporting APG core policies. With Delaney and Mann in the Legislative Council, this brought the group's representation in Tynwald to eight. Following the election each accepted office under Gelling, Mann and Quine as ministers. In 1998 the group changed its name to the Alliance for Progressive Government. In 1999 the APG ceased to be represented on the Council of Ministers, but continued to participate in government as members of various departments.

Sir Laurence New, Lieutenant-Governor 1985–90, being welcomed to the Island on 16 September 1985. From left to right are William Cain, Attorney General, Deemster Jack Corrin, Edgar Mann, chair of the Executive Council, Deemster Arthur Luft, Sir Laurence New, Sir Charles Kerruish, Speaker of the House of Keys, Jack Nivison, President of the Legislative Council, and Bishop Attwell.

## *Devolution in an International Context*

In the aftermath of its frustrations over judicial corporal punishment Tynwald resolved unanimously in July 1981 to pursue the constitutional objective of 'more complete self-government'.[3] It subsequently endorsed a series of resolutions and reports, which reiterated and expanded upon that fundamental goal—on 26 February 1986 it approved a resolution moved by Speaker Kerruish and in May 1991, November 1993 and February 1996 endorsed more detailed reports by the Council of Ministers.[4] In June 1999 a report prepared by the Council of Ministers for the House of Keys stressed that responses to international developments likely to affect the Isle of Man would be informed by three commitments, to 'more complete self-government', the pursuit of economic growth with the Island's tax regime as a central component and adherence to international standards.[5] Following an investigation into the implications of full independence by the Council of Ministers in November 2000, Tynwald accepted, by 21 votes to one in the Keys and unanimously in the Legislative Council, that there was 'insufficient advantage' in seeking independence at present and that policy on constitutional development should be to promote and defend vigorously the Island's domestic autonomy and extend the Isle of Man's influence over external issues affecting the Island.[6]

Despite the special relationship the Island enjoys with both the UK and the EC/EU, the Island has found itself increasingly influenced by and vulnerable to events in Europe. While formally and perhaps symbolically considerable progress was made towards the constitutional objective of 'more complete self-government', in practice almost every devolutionary advance, save for those involving further transfers of gubernatorial power, was qualified by international obligation. After 1981 the struggle took three main forms, the negotiation of Tynwald's rights in areas previously occupied by the UK, the transfer of power from the Lieutenant-Governor and the 'Governor in Council', and monitoring and responding to international developments likely to affect the Island's interests.

Demands for the transfer of powers and responsibilities from the UK were modest, a reflection of past successes and the lack of support for full independence from the UK. The aim was to bring to an end a colonial-style situation where the Island was subject to legislation without representation. For the most part Manx demands were successful, if on occasions only after protracted negotiations and compromise. The UK authorities were willing to accede to the Island's request for primary legislation in Tynwald to replace the extension of UK legislation by order in council. In some cases this simply involved Tynwald introducing legislation modelled on that of the UK and honouring relevant international agreements. Thus the Data Protection Act 1986 was a direct copy of UK legislation and honoured the 1981 Council of Europe Convention on Data Protection.[7] The Airports and Civil Aviation Act 1987 empowered the Isle of Man Government to apply by order certain UK civil aviation legislation,[8] following the model already adopted in the fields of customs and excise, social security, medicine and merchant shipping safety, whereby Manx Departments were empowered but not obliged to adopt UK measures. The Prevention of Terrorism Act 1990 brought the Island into line with UK legislation.[9] The Copyright Act 1991and the Design Rights Act 1991 were both modelled on UK legislation, the Island's real room for independent action being limited by bilateral agreements with the UK and international conventions.[10] The Maritime Security Act 1995 was also a copy of UK legislation, giving lawful effect to international conventions on maritime safety.[11] In a handful of other cases, involving judicial appointments, merchant shipping, telecommunications and the Island's territorial sea, legislation in Tynwald reflected a more significant devolution of power and will be considered in more detail.

Based on a recommendation of the Select Committee on the Governor's Powers and Duties, the Justices Act 1983 provided for the appointment of JPs to be made by the Lieutenant-Governor instead of by the Lord Chancellor on his advice.[12] However, while the Home Office was happy to accept this legislation, it was not willing to accede to Tynwald's requests in 1996 and 1999 for the Attorney General to be appointed by the Council of Ministers rather than by the Crown because of his continuing role as advisor to the Crown.[13] Neither was it willing to act on the recommendation of Tynwald in February 2000 that 'future Lieutenant-Governors should preferably be Manx persons or persons of Manx descent',[14] choosing to appoint the 58-year-old Air Marshal Ian MacFadyen as successor to Sir Timothy Daunt in preference to His Honour Jack Corrin, a Manx applicant for the post who had been the Island's First Deemster and Deputy Governor from 1988 to 1998.[15]

In the case of merchant shipping Tynwald continued the process started in 1979 of facilitating the development of the Island as a merchant shipping management centre meeting the highest international standards. Whereas before 1984 the Island's shipping register was obliged to accept all British vessels regardless of condition or type, the Merchant Shipping (Registration) Act 1984 empowered the Harbour Board to decide which British ships should be registered, enabling the Board to exclude ships not managed from the Isle of Man, ships with dangerous cargoes and ships not meeting international safety standards, and to appoint a marine surveyor or surveyors to enable it to discharge the Island's international obligations under a series of safety conventions. The Merchant Shipping Registration Act 1991 replaced a series of UK Acts going back to 1894 and consolidated their provisions with more recent Manx legislation into a single measure.[16]

The Telecommunications Act 1984 empowered the Governor in Council to licence telecommunication services in the Isle of Man. Prior to 1984 such services were governed by UK legislation and provided by the publicly owned British Telecom. Having turned down the opportunity of taking over responsibility for telecommunications in 1972, an initiative in Tynwald by Speaker Kerruish in October 1980 resulted in the Executive Council being asked to explore the possibility of the Island taking over and operating the service.[17] During the protracted negotiations which followed, British Telecom was privatised, opening the way for a transfer of legislative responsibility for telecommunications without the considerable financial burden of ownership and development. Following the privatisation of BT in 1984, it fell to the Governor in Council under the new Act to decide who should provide a Manx service. After exploring the relative merits of continuing with BT or offering the licence to Cable and Wireless, on 19 February 1986 Tynwald gave its unanimous backing to the grant of the licence to Manx Telecom Ltd, a wholly owned subsidiary of BT, subject to agreement between the Governor in Council and BT over terms and conditions. On 16 July 1986 Tynwald approved the terms negotiated, by 20 votes to one in the Keys and unanimously in the Legislative Council; the agreement provided *inter alia* for the payment of license fees including an initial fee of £7.5 million, the local regulation of the prices to be charged and a detailed modernisation programme. Although the UK remained responsible for international aspects of telecommunications, members of Tynwald were well pleased with what had been negotiated as a result of the Government's new licencing powers.[18]

When in 1981 Tynwald was informed by Lieutenant-Governor Cecil that the UK planned to introduce legislation to extend its territorial sea from three to 12 nautical miles and that the way would be open for similar legislation relating to the Isle of Man, little did anyone realise that a full 10 years would elapse before the actual extension of Manx territorial waters.[19] For the Isle of Man the importance of such an extension was in relation to fishing and potential mineral exploitation. However, the UK's own legislation was not in place until 1987 and the ensuing negotiations with the Island ran into difficulties over both fishing and mineral rights, the UK anxious to safeguard the interests of UK fishermen and the National Coal Board unwilling to relinquish rights to coal reserves in the new area. Although the deal presented by Chief Minister Walker to Tynwald in July 1991 was very much a compromise, it went a long way towards meeting Tynwald's aspirations, providing for the extension of Manx territorial waters to 12 miles, the transfer of rights to oil and gas (but not coal) free of charge, the transfer of all other rights to the seabed for the sum of £800,000 and the extension of Manx jurisdiction over fisheries, subject to UK approval of bylaws regulating fishing in the extended area. The deal was accepted by 16 votes to eight in the Keys and by eight votes to one in the Legislative Council, opponents being critical of the qualified control over fishing, the exclusion of coal and the fact that the Island was being charged for seabed rights.[20] Following Tynwald's acceptance of the deal, Parliament's Territorial Sea Act 1987 was extended to the Island by order in council simultaneously with the passing by Tynwald of the Territorial Sea (Consequential Provisions) Act 1991.[21] The former provided for the actual extension of Manx territorial waters on 2 September 1991, while the latter amended existing legislation referring to the territorial sea, vested in the Department of Industry the ownership of minerals other than coal under the extended territorial sea, made the Department of Highways, Ports and Properties the landowner of the seabed and amended the Island's sea fisheries legislation. Following the privatisation of the UK coal industry in 1994, a further agreement was negotiated for the Island to pay £10,000 for the rights to coal in the extended territorial waters; the Territorial Sea (Rights to Coal) Act 1996 vested these rights in the Manx Department of Industry.[22]

In the case of wireless telegraphy the Island was unsuccessful in securing a devolution of authority, the UK insisting on retaining the responsibility for allocating frequencies and determining transmitting power. The Island's long-running campaign for freedom to legislate in this area was resuscitated in 1986 but to no avail, the UK still insisting that wireless telegraphy transcended the boundaries of the Isle of Man.[23] Between the inception of the Manx campaign in 1962 and 1996 the UK authorities also refused to approve requests for a long-wave frequency or any increase in the transmitting power of Manx Radio beyond what was necessary to provide reasonable all-Island coverage. It came as something of a surprise therefore, when an application by the Isle of Man Broadcasting Commission in 1996 for the allocation of an unused long-wave frequency resulted in it being offered to the Island. In April 1998 the Radio Communications Agency of the UK Department of Trade and Industry informed the Commission that international clearance had been obtained for the frequency to be assigned to the Island for use at a strength sufficient to reach much of the UK, Ireland and northern Europe. On 21 April 1999 Tynwald accepted without division a resolution approving the award of a provisional licence for a new commercial radio station to a private company, the Isle of Man Broadcasting Company Ltd, a full licence being conditional on satisfying the Broadcasting Commission on technicalities of the proposed operation and obtaining planning permission. Although the first attempt to obtain planning permission for the construction of a transmitting station at Cranstal in Bride was unsuccessful, the licence agreement still holds out the prospect of an additional radio station without public subsidy, fee income over the period of the licence and a programme service presenting the Isle of Man in a favourable light.[24]

The moves taken to transfer powers from the Lieutenant-Governor and the Governor in Council to bodies responsible to Tynwald were much less controversial and continued a process begun in 1961. Twenty years later the most important powers had been transferred, but some remained and some had merely been transferred to the Governor in Council, moreover, constitutionally the Executive Council was still advisory to the Lieutenant-Governor. For the leaders of Tynwald the exercise of power by an externally appointed colonial official was incompatible with their search for 'more complete self-government' and a series of initiatives was taken to modify the Lieutenant-Governor's institutional role and transfer most of his residual powers. They followed recommendations of the Constitutional and External Relations Committee of the Executive Council/Council of Ministers, chaired by the Chief Minister, their endorsement by Council and subsequent approval by Tynwald.

The first changes came in the wake of the reorganisation of government into departments. The Government Departments Act 1987 and the Statutory Boards Act 1987 empowered the Governor in Council to transfer by order Governor in Council functions to a department or statutory board; several such functions under 30 Acts of Tynwald were transferred by the Transfer of Functions (Governor in Council) Order 1988, which was approved without debate or division in Tynwald on 16 March 1988.[25] The second group of changes, in 1990, concerned the Lieutenant-Governor's institutional role. An Executive Council report to Tynwald in April 1989 recommended that Tynwald elect its own President from among the members of the Legislative Council and that, if the Report's main recommendation to replace the Executive Council by a Council of Ministers was accepted, the Lieutenant-Governor should lose his right to attend and participate in the deliberations of the Council. Tynwald accepted the recommendations on 16 May 1989 by 14 votes to eight in the Keys and six votes to two in the Legislative Council.[26] Opponents were especially critical of the proposal that candidates for the presidency of Tynwald should be MLCs. Two pieces of legislation followed. During the passage of the Constitution Bill, Victor Kneale successfully moved an amendment providing for the President of Tynwald to be elected from among the MHKs and the indirectly elected MLCs and for the successful candidate to serve both as President of Tynwald and the Legislative Council. The Constitution Act 1990 provided for the election of the President of Tynwald as proposed by Kneale and for the Lieutenant-Governor's role as President to be confined to the annual Tynwald at St Johns.[27] The Council of Ministers Act 1990 repealed the legislation relating to the Executive Council and made no equivalent provision for the Lieutenant-Governor to attend and participate in meetings of the Council of Ministers.[28]

Between 1991 and 1993 a third group of changes provided for the transfer of most of the residual functions of the Lieutenant-Governor and the Governor in Council covered by Manx legislation and no longer deemed appropriate to his position. A detailed report, proposing the transfer by order of almost 200 functions of the Governor in Council and the introduction of legislation for the transfer of over 100 functions of the Lieutenant-Governor, was presented to Tynwald and accepted without division on

19 June 1991.[29] The former was effected by the Transfer of Functions (Governor in Council) Order 1991, which was approved by Tynwald without division on 19 January 1991,[30] and the latter by the equally uncontroversial Transfer of Governor's Functions Act 1992.[31] The Lieutenant-Governor's functions in relation to the police were dealt with by separate legislation and, as with the Police (Amendment) Act 1980, this proved much more controversial. Under the 1980 Act, as amended, responsibility for the police was shared between the Governor in Council and the Department of Home Affairs. The Police Act 1993 provided for most of the Governor in Council functions to be transferred to the Department and certain reserve functions to the Council of Ministers, but it only became law after the narrow defeat by 11 votes to 12 of an amendment moved by Edgar Quine, requiring the Minister of Home Affairs to exercise his duties on the advice of a Police Committee comprising the Minister, a second member of the Department, two other MHKs and two JPs; as in 1980 the proposal for a more democratic devolution of responsibility was defeated.[32]

Later in 1993 the Council of Ministers and Tynwald endorsed a report by the Constitutional and External Relations Committee[33] in which members saw the Lieutenant-Governor's remaining functions under Acts of Tynwald as 'appropriate to his position' as representative of a constitutional monarch. The Committee concluded that 'the process has reached a point where it is difficult to see what further powers could with advantage be transferred.' It saw little scope for change in the Lieutenant-Governor's role in advising or acting for the Crown on Crown appointments, the Royal Assent to Manx legislation and the prerogative of mercy. It noted that the Lieutenant-Governor already acted on local advice with respect to Crown appointments, that as long as it remained responsible for the good government of the Island the UK was bound to resist suggestions that Tynwald rather the Privy Council advise on the Royal Assent and that it was quite proper for the Queen's representative on the Island to exercise the Royal prerogative of mercy.

After 1981 international developments, especially in Europe, assumed centre stage in Manx politics. Although the UK remained responsible for the international relations of the Isle of Man, it did not require the Island to sign up to the same level of international cooperation. Protocol 3 provided the outstanding example of the Island pursuing a less integrationist path. In many other areas the expectation was that the Island would follow the UK and, after consultations, the insular authorities usually supported the extension of international agreements to the Island. The overriding concern of the Manx authorities was to ensure that international action did not jeopardise the autonomy that underpinned the Island's economic success. Of course it was not always possible to predict the consequences of signing up to agreements, as the Island found to its cost over commercial broadcasting in 1967 and judicial corporal punishment in 1978. After 1981 there were further examples of the UK expecting or requiring action by the Island because of international commitments and pressures. In most cases the Island was willing to cooperate, but in a few there were tensions between a UK responsible for the Island's international relations and the insular authorities jealously guarding their right to domestic self-government.

Although the development of the EC continued to have a major impact on Manx policy making, successive reports by the Executive Council and the Council of Ministers drew similar conclusions to the 1981 Select Committee on the Common Market regarding the value of the special relationship.[34] The Government's 1999 Policy Review stated that 'the terms of Protocol 3 constitute the most appropriate relationship between the Isle of Man and the EU'.[35] The commitments made by the UK to the enlargement of the EC/EU in 1981 (Greece), 1985 (Spain and Portugal) and 1995 (Austria, Finland and Sweden), the Single European Market in 1992, the European Union and the European Economic Area Agreement (EEAA) in 1994 and the further development of the EU following the Treaty of Amsterdam in 1998 were each incorporated into Manx law by means of amendments to the European Communities Act 1973; each received a smooth passage through the branches following assurances from the Executive Council/Council of Ministers that the developments in question did not involve any amendment to Protocol 3. Between 1981 and 1995 the market to which Manx goods enjoyed free access expanded to include six new member states and, under the EEAA, the remaining members of the European Free Trade Association. Through the 1979 Customs and Excise Agreement with the UK, the Island remained subject to European directives on VAT and, when the Agreement was amended to enable the Island to charge a 5 per cent rate of VAT on holiday accommodation and related services from 1994 and home repairs and renovation from 2000, the variation agreed with the UK complied with the relevant European directive.[36]

Manx agriculture was more heavily affected by European policy than any other industry. The special trade regime established in 1973 and the regulations associated with that trade became more and more embracing. The extent of regulatory control was evident over the timing and development of the Island's new meat plant in the early 1990s and its response to the bovine spongiform encephalopathy (BSE) crisis, especially following the EU ban on British beef between 1996 and 1999. In addition to satisfying relevant European regulations, the Island felt obliged to keep its economic support for agriculture and fisheries broadly in line with the UK so that the Manx industry could compete on even terms. In one important area Protocol 3 was successfully exploited to assist Manx agriculture. Faced with a threat to insular meat production by cheap European imports, in 1982 the Island obtained approval under Article 5 for import controls to protect local meat products and such controls have remained in force since with the sanction of the Council of the EU.[37]

For areas other than customs and agriculture, the application of European policies was a matter of choice. This was made very clear by the European Court in the case of *The Department of Health and Social Security v. Barr and Montrose Holdings Limited* in 1991; this involved a challenge to the Island's work permit legislation on grounds of incompatibility with Article 4 of Protocol 3, which required the equal treatment of all European persons. The European Court made it clear that Manx policies must be applied in a nondiscriminatory way, that a work permit system was in order so long as there was no discrimination in favour of particular nationality groups and that there should be no creeping application of EC law against the intentions of the framers of Protocol 3.[38] In practice, there has been a growing tendency for the Island to accept EC/EU policies in the same way as it has traditionally modelled much of its legislation on that of the UK. During a debate on the implications of the Single European Market in June 1990, Chief Minister Walker stressed that the Island ignored European developments at its peril:

> Increasingly in the future, if we want to trade with the United Kingdom or any other country in the Community, we will have to supply goods and components and services to satisfy agreed European standards. Increasingly health, safety and environmental standards will be dictated for Europe and will undoubtedly be imported. The European bathing waters directive is perhaps a good example of a European environmental standard that we have adopted as one of our policies.[39]

Sir Laurence Jones, Lieutenant-Governor 1990–95, swearing in Miles Walker for a second term as Chief Minister, December 1991. Miles Walker, MHK for Rushen from 1976, served on the Executive Council while chair of the Local Government Board 1982–86 and as the Island's first Chief Minister 1986–96.

Sir Timothy Daunt, Lieutenant-Governor 1995–2000, swearing in two new ministers, April 2000. The picture shows, from left to right, Donald Gelling, Chief Minister, Alex Downie, Minister for Agriculture, Fisheries and Forestry, Stephen Rodan, Minister for Education, and the Lieutenant-Governor.

Shortly after this debate the European Communities (Amendment) Act 1991 empowered the Governor in Council to apply by order any European legislation that would not otherwise apply, a reflection of the frequency with which the Island turned to the EC as a source of policy. Under the European Communities (Amendment) Act 2000 the power was transferred from the Governor in Council to the Council of Ministers.[40]

The Isle of Man might not have always liked the detail of the European policies it had to or chose to apply, but recognised that, if it was to meet the rising expectations for high standard public services and remain competitive in its main market, it could not afford to fall behind the UK and Europe. At the same time the Island remained vulnerable to the collective action of its larger and more populous neighbours who determined the detail and implementation of the international agreements which apply to the Island. Some conflict between Manx and UK or European interests was inevitable, the more so as collective action impinged on the Island's freedom to protect what it regarded as most dear. The circumstances surrounding Tynwald's legalisation of homosexuality between consenting adults in private in 1992, the Home Office review of financial regulation in the Crown dependencies in 1998 and proposals towards the end of the century for international action by the EU and the Organisation for Economic Cooperation and Development (OECD) against business tax regimes which distort fair competition provided evidence of both conflict and vulnerability.

The controversy over homosexuality arose following the judgement of the European Court of Human Rights in the case of *Dudgeon v. UK* in 1982 that Northern Ireland's law against homosexual acts in private between consenting adults contravened the right to privacy under Article 8 of the European Convention on Human Rights. Immediately the Home Office informed the Island that Manx law should be changed to ensure compliance with the Convention. Still bristling over the Court's decision on judicial corporal punishment in 1978, Tynwald was initially unwilling to embark on the extremely unpopular road to decriminalisation. It had denied the right of individual petition to the European Commission on Human Rights since 1976 and in February 1986 carried an Executive Council resolution opposing the restoration of that right by 11 votes to nine in the Keys and five votes to two in the Legislative Council.[41] The chair of Executive Council, Edgar Mann, justified the resolution by reference to the strength of feeling among members of Tynwald and the public in support of Manx law in such areas as homosexuality, the importance of allowing Tynwald to debate reform at an appropriate time after the general election and the advisability in the meantime of avoiding the embarrassment of an individual petition.

Following the 1986 election, Speaker Kerruish reopened the question with a resolution seeking the restoration of the right of individual petition, arguing that it was wrong to deny a general right because of frustration over the Tyrer case. Chief Minister Walker agreed, but persuaded Tynwald to defer consideration until a Sexual Offences Bill had been introduced and debated.[42] Thus began a bitter five-year debate between those anxious to honour the Island's international obligations and avoid the humiliation of reform being imposed by the UK and the principled opponents of reform, who supported the existing law, were sure that their views represented the vast majority of the Manx people and believed that it was a matter for Tynwald not international decision making.

The battle commenced in May 1987 when, by a 12 to 11 majority, the Keys approved a resolution by Brigadier Butler asking the Executive Council not to include decriminalisation in the forthcoming Sexual Offences Bill.[43] Accordingly when the legislation to update the Sexual Offences Act 1967 came before the House in December 1987 there was no such provision. After giving the Bill a second reading, the House agreed to a resolution by Walker referring the Bill and proposed amendments to a select committee. In March 1988, the Select Committee, chaired by Edgar Quine, a strong opponent of decriminalisation, recommended many changes to improve the Bill, but felt that any relaxation of the law on homosexuality would be unacceptable to the Manx people. All but two principled supporters of decriminalisation accepted the Committee's recommendations, but only after the defeat of an attempt by Walker to provide for decriminalisation.[44] The far-reaching changes agreed necessitated the preparation of a revised bill.

By the time the new Sexual Offences Bill was published in 1990, the Executive Council had decided, on the advice of the Home Office, to incorporate clauses providing for decriminalisation along the lines deemed necessary for compliance with the European Convention. In reply to questions in Tynwald on 20 March 1990, the Chief Minister explained that 'either we can change the law ourselves or have change imposed upon us', quoting from a Home Office letter saying that if Jersey and the Isle of Man did not take steps to amend their law 'the UK will have to legislate for them'.[45] Despite this very clear message and advice from the Chief Minister that the Island could not be 'a fair weather signatory to an international convention', a majority in both the House and Legislative Council voted to exclude what they saw as 'the offending clauses'. When a select committee of the House, chaired by Donald Gelling, reported in favour of the existing law, the House approved the Committee's recommendations by 15 votes to eight and proceeded to pass the Bill without the controversial clauses.[46] The Legislative Council did likewise, rejecting moves by Clifford Irving and Eddie Lowey to reinstate the clauses by four votes to five; however, two minor amendments were approved and by the time the Bill had received its third reading on 21 June 1991, there was no time for the House to consider them before the general election.[47]

It fell to the new House to take the Bill as approved by the Legislative Council through all its stages, providing Walker with a further opportunity to have the Bill amended to meet international obligations. On 31 March 1992 the House agreed by 13 votes to 11 to support decriminalisation, the decisive factor being the support of each of the five new MHKs.[48] The Legislative Council reluctantly fell in line, unwilling to challenge the decision of the newly elected House[49] and the Bill became law as the Sexual Offences Act 1992.[50] Even though few members of Tynwald were principled supporters of decriminalisation, a majority of both branches were eventually willing to comply with international obligations. The Island only narrowly avoided a repeat of the experience in 1967 when the UK carried out its threat of legislating for the Island against the expressed wishes of Tynwald.

Shortly after the Sexual Offences Act became law, Tynwald agreed without division to request the restoration of the right of individual petition.[51] It also approved a resolution by Peter Karran for the appointment of a select committee to investigate the desirability of incorporating a Bill of Rights into Manx law.[52] In December 1995 Tynwald accepted the recommendation of the Select Committee, chaired by ex-Deemster Arthur Luft, to await the outcome of UK legislation.[53] The UK Human Rights Act 1998, which incorporated into UK law the European Convention of Human Rights, provided the basis of the Manx Human Rights Act 2001.[54] The uncertainty of judicial interpretation in the light of changing attitudes and values will remain, as too will the ultimate right of individual petition to Europe, but the initial right to seek redress in the

Manx courts will not only be more direct and less expensive, but also more appropriate to an Island committed to 'more complete self-government'.

The unilateral initiative by the Labour Home Secretary, Jack Straw, on 20 January 1998 to institute a review of the quality of the regulation of the financial sectors of the Crown dependencies was another reminder of the ultimate responsibility of the UK for the international relations and good government of the Isle of Man. In this case there was no actual threat of UK legislation, but an implied one should the Island be found wanting or resistant to the changes necessary to meet the highest international standards. The immediate background to the appointment of Andrew Edwards to carry out the review with the insular authorities was the concern of various international organisations, including the G7 group of industrial countries and the EU, that offshore financial centres in the Caribbean and the Crown Dependencies were being used for international criminal purposes such as money laundering, tax evasion and drug trafficking. The terms of reference for the review reflected this international concern by focusing on three areas where shortcomings might prejudice the UK's own commitment to combatting international financial crime and damage the reputations of both the Crown dependencies and the UK itself: the quality of financial regulation and international collaboration, the deterrence, investigation and punishment of financial crime and the registration of companies.

Reporting in November 1998,[55] Edwards concluded that practice in each of these areas was for the most part satisfactory and that the islands were 'clearly in the top division of offshore financial centres'.[56] There was room for improvements, but some of these were already being progressed and the islands had indicated their willingness to introduce other remedial measures. On financial regulation, Edwards noted that the Isle of Man already complied with international and EU standards, that it was a member of international groups concerned with standards—the Offshore Group of Banking Supervisors, sponsored by the Basle Committee on Banking Supervision, the International Organisation of Securities Commission, the Contact Group on the Supervision of Collective Investment Funds, the International Association of Insurance Supervisors, the Offshore Group of Insurance Supervisors, the Egmont Group of professionals from national crime intelligence and investigation units and the International Group of Insurance Fraud Agencies—and that the Island had willingly subjected its regulatory standards to international evaluation. Edwards concluded that the Island had in place and was further developing a 'considerable arsenal' of measures to combat financial crime, including money laundering, tax evasion and fraud and that it had complied with the 40 recommendations in this area made in 1996 by the G7 Financial Action Task Force. Edwards reserved his main criticisms for supervision of company registration and administration, recommending the reform of company legislation to prevent the use of nonresident companies for disreputable purposes, by requiring the vetting of company registrations, the confidential disclosure of beneficial ownership, the production of audited accounts in accordance with EU standards and by abolishing locally incorporated nonresident companies that were managed and controlled from outside the Island and not liable to insular taxation save for an annual duty of £750. The Council of Ministers published a very positive response to the Review in April 1999, reaffirming its commitment to improve the regulation of companies and corporate service providers and imposing a moratorium on new nonresident duty companies as a prelude to the abolition of existing ones.[57] Important legislation followed, the Companies (Transfer of Functions) Act 2000, which gave the Financial

Services Commission responsibility for the regulation of companies, and the Corporate Service Providers Act 2000, which empowered the FSC to regulate providers of services to companies registered in the Isle of Man.[58] The Review's endorsement of the quality of the Island's regulatory regime and the Island's positive response to proposals for its improvement removed any need in this case for the UK authorities to impose their will on the Island.

While the successful exploitation of international financial markets during the 1990s earned the Island unprecedented levels of income, critics in the EU and the OECD saw the Isle of Man as one of a number of centres diverting business from onshore jurisdictions by means of preferential tax regimes. Right from the establishment of the EEC there was talk about the harmonisation of taxation as a necessary ingredient for genuinely free and fair competition and, while some progress towards this goal was made with respect to indirect taxation, member states proved unwilling to equalise either indirect or direct tax rates. Towards the end of the century there was a growing concern on the part of EU and OECD members that fiscal policies sustaining centres of international finance, both onshore and offshore, were a major impediment to free and fair competition. Such members argued for the application of agreed principles to reduce distortions in the competition between financial centres caused by widely differing levels of taxation on companies and capital. In 1998 their concerns led to proposals by the EU for a withholding tax on cross-border savings and official investigations by both the EU and the OECD into ways of curbing practices that distort competition. For the Isle of Man the central questions were the nature of any resulting agreements and the extent to which they would apply to the Isle of Man.

In 1998 the EU began debating a draft directive on cross-border savings, requiring member states to impose a 20 per cent withholding tax on all interest earned on cross-border investments or inform nonresidents' home state tax authorities about the interest earned on investments. Some EU members wanted to see the directive apply to both member states and their dependent territories, impossible without pressure of the sort applied by the UK over sexual offences or formal amendment to Protocol 3. Although most members supported the proposal as a means of preventing legal tax avoidance, the UK opposed the withholding tax because of the damage it would do to London's lucrative Eurobond market and pressed for agreement on the exchange of information part of the draft directive. In June 2000, after a series of unsuccessful summits and still without the support of Austria, EU members pledged their support for an exchange of information directive on the savings of nonresidents.[59] By then the UK had already given the Isle of Man notice that it wished to renegotiate the 1955 Double Taxation Agreement (DTA) with the primary aim of securing greater exchange of information.[60] The insular authorities too had recognised that cooperation on this front was absolutely essential if the Island was to safeguard its reputation as an international financial centre and both the Council of Ministers and Tynwald, through its Standing Committee on Economic Initiatives, were in the process of considering the best course of action to meet international pressures while safeguarding Manx interests.[61] Although under Protocol 3 a directive on exchange of information could not be imposed on the Island, Manx politicians were very aware that pressure from the Home Office and the international community to support a policy designed to combat unfair practices would be hard to resist.

While the withholding tax/exchange of information agreement was still being debated, in December 1998 the European Commission initiated plans for an EU code of conduct on business taxation with the aim of curbing practices that were distorting competition. The proposal was investigated by a Council of Economic and Finance Ministers (ECOFIN Council) working party under the chair of the UK Paymaster General, Dawn Primarolo, and, although the Isle of Man stressed that the EU had no jurisdiction over Manx fiscal policy, it was included in the investigation. The Working Party reported to the ECOFIN Council in November 1999 with an evaluation of business taxation in both member states and their dependent territories and recommendations for a code of conduct.[62] Six aspects of business taxation in the Isle of Man were deemed to be harmful: low taxation of international business companies, exemption from tax of nonresident companies, exemption from tax of the profits of insurance companies arising on risks outside the Island, tax holidays for industry, management charge tax deductions against international loan business profits and exemption from income tax for profits arising from offshore banking.[63] The recommended code of conduct was to include a commitment by members not to introduce new measures that were harmful, to eliminate harmful practices as soon as possible, to ensure that tax measures in support of the economy of particular regions did not undermine the integrity of the internal market, to recognise the fundamental importance of anti-abuse provisions in tax laws and double taxation agreements and to promote the abolition of harmful taxation in dependent territories outside of the EU 'within the framework of their constitutional arrangements'.[64] When the ECOFIN Council decided to publish the Report in February 2000, it did so without taking a position on its content, a reflection of the considerable obstacles in the way of international agreement. Subsequently the Home Office Minister, Lord Bassam, made it clear that the UK Government supported the work of the Code of Conduct Group and, in the event of EU agreement, would work closely with the Crown dependencies 'to achieve our objectives through the usual methods of discussion and negotiation'.[65]

A parallel investigation into preferential business tax regimes, launched by the OECD in 1998 with the Isle of Man one of 47 international financial centres to be investigated, proved much more immediate in its impact, pressurising the Island and other financial centres to modify their tax regimes to comply with international standards. In April 2000 an OECD report calling on banks to provide other countries' tax authorities access to accounts in pursuit of particular tax evasion inquiries received the backing of each of the 29 OECD members. At the same time the OECD Tax Forum opened a dialogue with governments in the various financial centres, including the Isle of Man, with the aim of persuading them to eliminate the harmful aspects of their tax regimes such as selective exemption from taxation, nonresident companies, the lack of transparency in the operation of tax regimes and the absence of effective exchange of information. In June 2000 an OECD report listed 35 jurisdictions, including the Isle of Man, that were regarded as 'tax havens' and warned that centres refusing to modify their preferential tax regimes by July 2001 faced the risk of defensive sanctions by OECD members—the termination of double taxation agreements, isolation for financial purposes and, in the case of Caribbean territories, a cut in their aid budgets.[66]

The Island's first line of action was to demonstrate to the international community the validity of its claim to be a reputable and responsible jurisdiction, already evidenced during and in response to the Edwards Review. The second was to recognise the need for compromise, while safeguarding the Island's autonomy and economic interests.[67] Accordingly an ongoing review of the Island's tax regime was broadened to include consideration of criticisms by the EU and the OECD. The outcome of this review, first announced in Tynwald on 20 June 2000, spelled out in the Government's Policy Review 2000 and endorsed—with only a single voice of dissent—by Tynwald on 18 October 2000, was a radical new taxation strategy, designed both to reduce the burden of taxation on individuals and companies—further reference will be made to the redistributive and promotional aspects of the strategy in Chapter Nine—and to meet head on the concerns of the Island's international critics.[68] Opening the October debate in Tynwald, the Treasury Minister saw the new strategy as being consistent with OECD principles and detailed four important policy commitments that were being made in response to international concerns. First, the Island was willing to negotiate an updated DTA with the UK so that business could be undertaken and information exchanged in accordance with internationally agreed standards. Second, the concern of the OECD that there should be greater transparency in the operation of the tax regime will be met by requiring all companies to file details of beneficial ownership and annual accounts and by ending the secrecy surrounding the taxation of specific companies. Third, ring fencing, whereby enterprises such as insurance and shipping management companies engaged in purely international business enjoy preferential tax status, will be lifted so as to end discrimination between businesses of a like nature; for this group of businesses the intention is to replace tax exemption with a zero rate of taxation. Finally, the preferential tax status of nonresident duty companies, international companies and exempt companies other than those engaged in insurance, shipping management and fund management will either be terminated or, in the case of the latter category, be subject to further discussions with the OECD regarding changes necessary to make them internationally acceptable.[69] A detailed report by the Council of Ministers on the new tax strategy and the OECD, including a schedule of commitments to meet OECD criticisms and escape condemnation as a 'tax haven' was endorsed by Tynwald on 12 December 2000. The endorsement followed assurances by Corkill that the Island's cooperation with the OECD was contingent on the changes being embraced by OECD members 'on a level playing field basis as new international standards'.[70] As a direct result of these commitments, in February 2001 the OECD Tax Forum informed the Island that it would not be included on the list of uncooperative 'tax havens' to be published in July 2001.[71]

At the time of writing the final outcomes of negotiations with the UK on exchange of information and the OECD on harmful tax competion are not known, but the experience of the last two years has already shown very clearly the vulnerability of the Island to international pressures. The Island was obliged to engage in a damage limitation exercise but, with the support of Tynwald and the business community, was able to do so in a relatively painless way.

## *Towards a More Democratic Tynwald?*

The period after the 1981 general election saw very little constitutional change relating directly to the Island's parliamentary institutions. With the exception of Tynwald's reduced role in selecting members of the executive and changes to the presidency of Tynwald and the Legislative Council, which will be discussed below, the positions of Tynwald and the two branches were unchanged. The relative absence of change was not the result of any consensus about the status quo; on the contrary, conflict both within and between the branches of Tynwald was a perennial feature of debate. The constitutional authority of the indirectly elected Legislative Council lay at the heart of that debate. Critics questioned the need for a second chamber in such a small island and whether ex officio and indirectly elected members were appropriate in an otherwise democratic state. For advocates of a more democratic Tynwald the choice was between direct election of the Legislative Council or further reductions in its powers so that it could not defeat the wishes of the elected chamber; for a small minority the best solution was abolition and the adoption of a unicameral legislature.

Proposals for the direct election of a majority of MLCs have been made on and off since the Keys' petition in 1907. The renewed interest in reform since 1981 owed much to the energy and drive of Victor Kneale, one of the very few Manx politicians to have gained re-election to the House after a period of service in the Legislative Council. He believed that direct election would make all Tynwald's decision makers directly accountable to the people, obviate the need for by-elections to replace the MHKs elected to the Legislative Council, overcome the difficulties in finding nominees who are willing to serve and capable of attracting majority support, and reduce delays in progressing legislation by allowing government bills to be introduced in either branch. Kneale first proposed reform when an MLC by moving a declaratory resolution in Tynwald in June 1981, calling for the popular election of the Legislative Council from four regional constituencies, voting in Tynwald as a single body and the election of all board and committee chairs on the basis of the best person for the job. On that occasion the idea of popular election was rejected unanimously by a House anxious to retain its recently gained pre-eminence in Tynwald and by five votes to two in the Legislative Council.[72] After the election, in which he was returned to the Keys, Kneale introduced a private member's bill for a directly elected Legislative Council with one member representing each of nine districts. After the second reading in May 1982, the Bill was referred to a select committee already established under his chair to report on the Representation of the People (Redistribution of Seats) Bill.[73] On the recommendation of the Select Committee, Kneale's two bills were discharged in favour of a more radical proposal for the direct election of 33 members of Tynwald from 16 multimember constituencies and their subsequent division into two branches. This approach, similar to prevailing practice in the Norwegian Storting, was the brainchild of Select Committee member, Eddie Lowey. The new Representation of the People Bill, which would have also removed the voting rights of the Lord Bishop, was approved by 17 votes to seven at the second reading and by 15 votes to nine at the third. Feeling that its own reform and redistribution should be kept separate, the Legislative Council approved a much truncated bill simply providing for the redistribution of seats into 12 new two-member constituencies. As the branches were unable to agree the Bill fell.[74]

Kneale's third attempt at extending the principle of direct election to the Legislative Council came in 1987/88. The Representation of the People (Election of Tynwald) Bill was modelled on that of 1983/84 with respect to direct election, but also provided for Tynwald to vote on all matters as one body and for conflicts between the branches over legislation to be resolved by a joint vote; it met a similar fate, except that this time defeat was at the hands of a 12 votes to nine majority in the Keys. Members felt that such change was unnecessary, that the time was not ripe given the recent introduction of the ministerial system and that a prerequisite was to investigate whether the Island really needed a second chamber.[75] A fourth private member's bill in 1990, similar to that of 1987/88, received a second reading in the Keys by 13 votes to eight; it was referred to a select committee, but the Committee failed to report before the dissolution of the House in 1991.[76] Although Kneale retired from politics in 1991, his contribution to the debate continued both through the Manx press and in evidence to a select committee established by the House of Keys in 1997.

With the passing of the Isle of Man Constitution Act 1978, there was broad agreement with the principle of bicameralism and the respective powers of the two chambers, both sitting separately for legislative purposes and together in Tynwald. No serious consideration was given to the unicameral alternative until the 1990s, which saw investigations by a select committee of Tynwald between 1992 and 1994 and by a select committee of the House of Keys between 1997 and 1999. The Tynwald Committee was established in November 1992 following an initiative by Speaker Cain, who supported a directly elected second chamber, but felt that such a change should only be considered after a full investigation into the role of the Council.[77] The Committee, chaired by the Speaker and with Noel Cringle, Richard Corkill, Clifford Irving and Edgar Mann as members, reported in June 1994, recommending the retention of the Legislative Council and a package of reforms involving minimal change.[78] Edgar Quine, representing the view of the five members of the Alternative Policy Group, and Peter Karran pressed the case for abolition on the grounds that the Legislative Council was both unnecessary in such a small island and undemocratic given its ex officio and indirectly elected membership. The Committee countered such arguments by reference to the general lack of support for such a radical move both inside and outside Tynwald, the useful role performed as a revising chamber and the checks and balances inherent in the Manx hybrid of two chambers meeting separately for legislative purposes but coming together to debate policy and finance. The Committee did recommend limiting the powers of MLCs in relation to the tabling of financial resolutions, but this and other minor changes fell with Tynwald's rejection of the overall package of reform. Prior to outright rejection, Tynwald did consider an amendment moved by Hazel Hannan to provide for the direct election of the Legislative Council, but it was defeated by 14 votes to nine in the House and five votes to two in the Council. The rejection of the overall package in July 1994 was because of a hostile vote by the Legislative Council, but the following November, with the branches voting together, it was defeated by 21 votes to 12, the result of an unholy alliance of MLCs opposed to losing power, supporters of democratisation and abolitionists.[79]

The Keys' Committee was established on 22 April 1997 following the approval without division of a resolution moved by Tony Brown, who felt that the House rather than Tynwald 'should determine whether or not it has an unelected body sitting in another place determining the future of the Isle of Man.'[80] This Committee's brief was to consider the role, constitution and method of electing the Legislative Council. Edgar Quine, a supporter of abolition, was the unanimous choice for chair by the other members, Brenda Cannell, Speaker Cringle, David Cretney and Steve Rodan. The Committee considered the possibility of abolition and a range of options limiting the powers of the Council to make its continued existence compatible with a democratic system. It reported in June 1999, concluding that the difficulties associated with abolition, in particular the fact that there would be fewer members to hold government appointments and serve on committees and a consequential increase in workload for MHKs, were such as to make it politically impractical and that, in preference to alternative models involving a reduction in its powers, the Legislative Council should become a constituent part of a directly elected Tynwald. In the event of direct election proving politically unacceptable, the Committee proposed a major reduction in the powers of the Legislative Council, by making the selection of chief minister exclusively a matter for the Keys, rendering MLCs ineligible to serve on the Council of Ministers and

Left: Sir Charles Kerruish, first Manx President of Tynwald 1990–2000. Kerruish was the outstanding politician of the postwar period, MHK for Garff (1946–90), a member of the Executive Council (1955–68 and chair 1962–67), and Speaker of the House of Keys from 1962 until 1990 when he succeeded Sir Laurence New as President of Tynwald, a post he held until retiring from politics in April 2000.

Right: Edgar Mann, Chair of the Executive Council 1985–86, at the launch of the Manx Shipping Register in London in January 1986. Despite being a new resident to the Island in 1973, Mann was successful in gaining election to the Keys in 1976 and quickly went on to achieve high office, becoming chair of the Board of Agriculture and Fisheries in 1980, chair of the Finance Board in 1981 and chair of Executive Council 1985.

ending their capacity to table or vote on financial resolutions.[81] Kneale submitted evidence to the Committee and was clearly influential in shaping the Committee's thinking. As with Kneale's earlier scheme, that of the Committee involved a directly elected Tynwald, the subdivision of Tynwald into two legislative committees called the Legislative Council and the House of Keys and a return to equal bicameralism by providing for the resolution of interbranch conflict over legislation to be resolved by Tynwald voting as one body and for all parliamentary business other than legislation to be determined by a majority of the elected members of Tynwald present voting as one body. The House approved the Committee's recommendations on 26 October 1999 by the barest of majorities; while there was a 20 to four vote in favour of the principle of direct election, the decision in favour of the particular scheme put forward by the Committee required the casting vote of the Speaker following a tied vote.[82]

The Legislative Council, angry that its future should have been the subject of an investigation by the Keys rather than by Tynwald and concerned at the prospect of emasculation without direct election, accepted the principle of democratisation and, in advance of any discussion of the Keys' proposals in Tynwald, took the unusual step of promoting constitutional legislation. The Constitution Bill 1999 aimed to provide for a

Senate, comprising the President of Tynwald, the Attorney General and the Lord Bishop and eight directly elected members, chosen by the registered electors of five regional constituencies midterm between general elections for the House of Keys. After a speedy passage through the Legislative Council, in February 2000 it was rejected by the Keys by 19 votes to five. Although the House was divided on the question of reform, a directly elected Senate capable of challenging the supremecy of the House was quite out of the question.[83]

The following month Tynwald agreed, by 17 votes to five in the Keys and unanimously in the Legislative Council, to call on the Council of Ministers to prepare legislation for the direct election of the Legislative Council.[84] The resolution made no reference to the direct election of Tynwald that had been so narrowly approved by the House or to any alternative means of delivering democratisation. The Council of Ministers set up a committee to consider the matter, but before it could report, on 30 May 2000 a private member's bill was introduced into the House by Geoffrey Cannell. The main objects of the Constitution Bill 2000, broadly based on Kneale's earlier proposals and the Keys' Select Committee Report, were to provide for the direct election of 33 of the 35 members of Tynwald, the subdivision of Tynwald into an 11-member Legislative Council and a 24-member House of Keys for legislative purposes, the restoration of equal bicameralism and for all voting in Tynwald, including any votes to resolve legislative conflicts between the branches, to be as one body. After a successful second reading on 21 June 2000 by 14 votes to eight and reference to a select committee at the clauses stage on 24 October 2000, the Bill eventually met a fate similar to those of Kneale, being withdrawn by Cannell after the defeat of the integral first clause by 15 votes to eight on 23 January 2001.[85] Opposition came from supporters of the status quo and the alternatives of a reduction in the powers of the Legislative Council or a unicameral legislature, several seeing the combination of direct election and equal bicameralism as a threat to the hard-won supremecy of the House.

## The Transition to Ministerial Government

The period between 1981 and 1990 saw a major transformation of the Manx governmental system. A relatively weak central executive, led by the chair of Executive Council, and a fragmented board system gave way to a powerful Council of Ministers, under the leadership of a chief minister, and nine departments. The period opened in November 1981 with Tynwald's first election of the chair of Executive Council under the Constitution (Amendment) Act 1981, an important landmark in the history of legislative-executive relations in the Isle of Man. Subsequent changes were the result of the interaction between two select committees of Tynwald, the Select Committee on the Responsibilities of Boards of Tynwald and the Select Committee on Constitutional Issues, and individual members of Tynwald. Talk of a ministerial system predated the 1981 election—Bert Stephen and Howard Simcocks advocated such a system during the 1962 general election—but no formal proposals were made. In November 1980 when Tynwald agreed to an investigation of the board system, Dominic Delaney, who seconded the Speaker's successful amendment expanding the scope of the Select Committee's investigation, anticipated the development of a ministerial system, and during the 1981 election Sir Charles Kerruish argued for such a reform as a means of streamlining government and making more efficient and effective use of the time of members of Tynwald.[86] Although the Speaker was still a leading advocate of change, he was not a member of either of the select committees, from which the real impetus for reform emerged.

The Select Committee on the Responsibilities of Boards of Tynwald, under the chair of MLC member Jack Nivison, had already agreed before the election that its goal should be to replace the existing board system with an efficient, streamlined and better coordinated system of administration. When the Committee was reconstituted after the election, Nivison retained the chair and continued to strive for this goal with the support of the new membership, Percy Radcliffe, Eddie Lowey, Roy MacDonald, John J. Radcliffe and Matty Ward. When Nivison himself proposed a ministerial approach in November 1982, members accepted that, while the amalgamation of boards was well within the Committee's terms of reference, the issues of central direction and coordination and the possibility of achieving these through a ministerial system involved much wider constitutional considerations that should be considered jointly with the Constitutional Issues Committee. Eventually it was agreed that the latter Committee, chaired by Percy Radcliffe and with Charles Cain, Eddie Kerruish, Victor Kneale, Edgar Mann and David Moore as members, should take the proposal forward and report to Tynwald. The Report of the Constitutional Issues Committee, dated 14 April 1983, was presented to Tynwald by Radcliffe in June 1983.[87]

He explained the 'radical' proposals by reference to the need to rationalise and modernise government by moving away from a committee system of government more associated with local than national government, empowering the Executive Council to lead and coordinate government activity and bringing to an end the position where principal agencies of government could be excluded from Executive Council—at the time Agriculture and Fisheries, Health, Tourism and Social Security were among the boards not represented on Executive Council. The main proposals were for a chief minister elected by Tynwald, a cabinet of eight ministers chosen by the chief minister but with the approval of Tynwald and collectively responsible for the government of the Island, a ministerial system with ministers individually responsible for departments and a statutory requirement for the chief minister to resign in the event of losing the confidence of Tynwald. The division of responsibilities between the eight ministries was to be the subject of a further report by the Boards' Responsibilities Committee. These proposals were accepted by the narrowest of majorities, the House of Keys supporting them by 12 votes to nine and Lieutenant-Governor using his casting vote to bring the Legislative Council into line with the elected chamber. Several members opposed the resolution on the grounds that much more work was needed on the detail of the proposals before it was possible to make an informed decision. Others were unhappy with the proposed transfer of the power of selection of members of the Executive Council from Tynwald to the chief minister. Miles Walker, who would later become the Island's first chief minister, was among those who objected to this transfer of power, although he did support the proposals overall.

Although Tynwald had directed the Boards' Responsibilities Committee to come forward with detailed proposals for a rationalisation of the Island's boards into departments, it was a joint report with the Constitutional Issues Committee that was presented to Tynwald by the chair of Executive Council in February 1984. Radcliffe was now chair of both Committees and the signatories included four other members of Executive Council.[88] The Joint Report envisaged a phased movement towards ministerial government, with the amalgamation of boards into eight departments by

December 1984, a nine-member Executive Council comprising a chair and the chairs of the departmental boards from January 1985 and a full ministerial system after the 1986 election.[89] The Report was rejected, with only seven votes in favour and 16 against in the Keys and two in favour and five against in the Council, a major setback for the reformists.[90] Apart from the signatories, only two members supported the proposals. The opponents were a mixture of those who saw no justification for change and those who felt they were being asked to move too quickly or too slowly; many continued to support the principle of change but not the particular details proposed.

The following month, anxious for some progress, Speaker Kerruish moved the introduction of legislation to provide for an Executive Council with a mixture of members nominated by the chair and ex officio members representing four major boards. On behalf of the Constitutional Issues Committee, Radcliffe moved an amendment replacing the entire resolution with one to accept a report prepared by the Committee, in response partly to the Speaker's proposal and partly to the desire of most members to move more slowly than had been contemplated in the Joint Report. The Fourth Interim Report of the Committee proposed that the chair of Executive Council continue to be elected by Tynwald, that the other members be the persons selected by Tynwald to chair the eight main unreformed boards (the Agriculture and Fisheries, Education, Finance, Health, Home Affairs, Industry, Local Government and Tourist Boards), that the requirement that each of the branches have a particular number of representatives on Executive Council be dropped in favour of selecting 'the best man for the job' and that the legislation should specify the right of Tynwald to pass a motion of no confidence in the Executive Council. No change was proposed to the method of electing the chair of Executive Council, to his position as ex officio chair of the Selection Committee or to the functions of Executive Council. The amendment was carried by 14 votes to nine in the House and by eight votes to one in the Council and the motion as amended by 16 to seven and eight to one, paving the way for the Constitution (Executive Council) Act 1984.[91] The legislation had a smooth passage through the branches, the only divisions being over the inclusion of a ninth board and the nomenclature of members of Executive Council. Clare Christian's proposal to include the Board of Social Security was carried in the Keys but reversed in the Legislative Council and David Cannan's attempt to rename the chair and members the chief minister and ministers was defeated in the Keys.[92] The Act, an extremely modest reform compared to the proposals approved in June 1983, guaranteed that in future the eight main boards would be represented on Executive Council but did not really advance the cause of ministerial government.

The first real advance came with the amalgamation of boards into nine departments between 1985 and 1987. At the sitting of Tynwald in March 1984, Speaker Kerruish successfully moved that the Finance Board be converted into a statutory board under the Boards of Tynwald Act 1952 and that consideration be given to placing the new board in charge of the Treasury.[93] This led to the Treasury Act 1985, under which a new board called the Treasury took over the responsibilities of the Finance Board, the Treasury and the Assessment Board.[94] Between October 1985 and February 1986 Tynwald accepted without division three further reports from the Select Committee on Boards' Responsibilities, each presented by Edgar Mann, the new chair of the Committee following election as chair of Executive Council in March 1985. In October 1985 it accepted the principle of amalgamating the various boards into nine departments rather than the eight proposed in 1984, while recognising that more work was required on the detail of six of the proposals. In February 1986 it approved of a Department of Education taking over the functions of the Board of Education and in March 1986 it went along with the fine detail regarding the other five departments.[95] The new departments came into being between January 1986 and September 1987, partly through primary legislation and partly through orders made by the Governor in Council under the Statutory Bodies (Transfer of Functions) Act 1969, which had been amended in 1983 to allow the creation of new statutory bodies as well as the transfer of functions between existing bodies.[96]

The Treasury Act came into force on 2 December 1985. The Department of Health and Social Security was established under the Health and Social Security Act 1986, bringing together the Health and Social Security Boards and transferring responsibility for the School Medical Service from Education and child welfare from the LGB. The Department commenced operations on 1 April 1986. Later the same month, four orders were approved by Tynwald creating the Department of Agriculture, Fisheries and Forestry (DAFF) in place of the Board of Agriculture and Fisheries and the Forestry, Mines and Land Board, the Department of Home Affairs in the place of the Home Affairs Board, the Department of Industry in place of the Industry Board and the Department of Tourism and Transport (DTT) in the place of the Tourist and Passenger Transport Boards.[97] In May 1986 two further orders were approved creating the Department of Highways, Ports and Properties (DHPP) which replaced the Airports Board, the Harbour Board, the Highway and Transport Board and the Government Property Trustees, and the Department of Local Government and the Environment (DOLGE) replacing the LGB.[98] Finally, legislation was passed to effect the changes with respect to education. The Education Act 1986 provided, with effect from 1 September 1987, for a Department of Education, taking over most of the functions of the Board of Education, and a directly elected board of education relegated to an essentially advisory role.[99]

The new departments were still technically boards, albeit with fewer members than most of the boards they replaced, but not for long. A series of parallel moves paved the way for a ministerial system in 1988. The spur to this further reform came at the January sitting of Tynwald in 1985. Speaker Kerruish moved that legislation be introduced to enable the chair of Executive Council to appoint the chairs of the new boards and this was carried with an amendment proposed by Jack Nivison requiring the appointments to be approved by Tynwald.[100] The following day Dominic Delaney proposed that the Standing Orders Committee be asked to report on the method of electing both chairs and members of boards; Tynwald accepted the proposal but with an amendment moved by Percy Radcliffe asking the Constitutional Issues Committee to do the reporting.[101] In March 1985 the Committee's recommendations were accepted by Tynwald without division.[102] Under the agreed proposals the Executive Council would consist of a chief minister elected by Tynwald for a period of five years and a team of ministers selected by the chief minister for three years but subject to the approval of Tynwald for the team as a whole. The ministers were to be the chairs of the departments emerging from the process of amalgamation. The nonministerial members of departments were to be nominated by the Chief Minister following consultation with the Executive Council and approved by Tynwald. The Constitution (Executive Council) (Amendment) Act 1986, which had a smooth passage through the branches, gave effect to these recommendations, providing for a significant enhancement of the constitutional authority of the leader of the Executive Council and bringing into Executive Council the chairs of the nine new departments.[103] However, despite the ministerial nomenclature, ministers under the 1986 Act were not individually responsible for their departments, which were still technically boards with a collective responsibility to Tynwald.

On 10 July 1985, well before this legislation was implemented in December 1986, two relatively new MHKs, Allan Bell and Tony Brown, had asked Tynwald to reaffirm its support for a full ministerial system. An attempt by the Speaker to persuade Tynwald to legislate before the 1986 election was defeated without a division and Tynwald agreed, by 23 votes to one in the Keys and eight to one in the Council, to direct the Executive Council in conjunction with the Constitutional Issues Committee to bring forward recommendations, accepting that the necessary legislation would not be introduced until after the election.[104] The result was the Government Departments Act 1987 which came into operation on 1 February 1988.[105] It confirmed the nine department structure, while empowering the Governor in Council by order and with the approval of Tynwald to make changes either by creating or dissolving departments or transferring functions between departments. Each department formally replaced the relevant board as a body corporate with a minister and one or more other members of Tynwald, the nonministerial appointments ceasing to be subject to the approval of Tynwald despite a tied vote on Edgar Quine's amendment to restore the role of Tynwald.[106] Ministers became individually responsible for their department and for departmental decisions, bringing to an end the collective responsibility associated with boards. Finally, the Governor in Council was formally empowered to give departments directions 'in relation to any matter which appears to the Governor in Council to affect the public interest' and required departments to comply with such directions. Building on the foundations provided by earlier measures regarding the membership of Executive Council and the amalgamation of boards, the Act provided for the most far-reaching changes in the Manx governmental system since the transfer of executive power from the Lieutenant-Governor: the end of the board system, the introduction of individual ministerial responsibility and a formal recognition of the growing authority of Executive Council vis-à-vis the several departments.

Simultaneously with this legislation, Tynwald passed the Statutory Boards Act 1987, providing a single legislative framework for a group of statutory authorities which it was felt should be independent of the ministerial system on account of their regulatory or commercial responsibilites.[107] The Act, which also came into effect on 1 February 1988, provided for seven statutory boards, the Board of Consumer Affairs, the Financial Supervision Commission (FSC), the Insurance Authority, the Isle of Man Post Office Authority, the Isle of Man Water Authority, the Manx Electricity Authority and the Telecommunications Commission. The Governor in Council was given powers to create, dissolve or modify the functions of such authorities, by order and with the approval of Tynwald.

Since 1988 subordinate legislation has been used to effect a number of changes both to the structure of departments and statutory boards and to their respective functions. While the detail of these changes is beyond the scope of this study, brief reference should be made to those involving the creation of new departments and statutory boards and name changes reflecting changes in responsibility.[108] The Telecommunications Commission was replaced by the Communications Commission in April 1989. The DTT became the Department of Tourism, Leisure and Transport (DTLT) in October 1990, a reflection of the increased importance attached to the development of leisure facilities for residents as well as visitors. The Isle of Man Post Office Authority was renamed the Isle of Man Post Office in February 1994. In January

1995 the creation of a Department of Transport in place of the DHPP also led to the DTLT becoming the Department of Tourism and Leisure (DTL) and DOLGE assuming responsibility for government properties. In July 1996 the Department of Industry was renamed the Department of Trade and Industry. 1996 also saw the formation of a new statutory board, the Tourism Registration and Grading Commission. In January 1997 the Insurance Authority was replaced by the Insurance and Pensions Authority (IPA) and finally in 1998 the Board of Consumer Affairs was replaced by the Office of Fair Trading.

It was a reflection of the growth in the power of the executive authority at the expense of Tynwald that the proposals for the 1987 constitutional legislation were made by the Executive Council and not a committee of Tynwald. This was also true of the next stage in the development process, the Council of Ministers Act 1990. Not only were the proposals made by the Executive Council, but when they were presented to Tynwald in May 1989, an attempt by the Speaker to have them referred to a select committee of Tynwald was unsuccessful in both branches. In September 1988 the Executive Council had appointed a Constitutional and External Relations Committee under the chair of the Chief Minister, Miles Walker. It came forward with proposals, which were endorsed by the Executive Council, for legislation to be introduced establishing a Council of Ministers as the central executive authority in the Isle of Man and giving the Chief Minister the right to hire and fire 'such ministers as he may determine' without reference to Tynwald.[109] The recommendations were approved by 14 votes to eight in the Keys and six votes to two in the Legislative Council, but in the face of strong opposition from Edgar Quine who saw them as an unwarranted erosion of Tynwald's authority and Manx democracy.[110] The Council of Ministers Act 1990 came into effect on 1 October 1990,[111] but only after a stormy passage in the House of Keys.[112] The Act reconstituted the Executive Council as the Council of Ministers with the Chief Minister chosen by Tynwald in an open vote and nine ministers chosen and assigned by the Chief Minister without reference to Tynwald. An attempt by Quine to have the Chief Minister chosen by the House of Keys rather than Tynwald was defeated by 15 votes to nine, but a successful amendment by Adrian Duggan reduced the maximum number of ministers that could be appointed from 10 to the current actual figure of nine. Under normal circumstances the Chief Minister was to hold office for five years until the election of a successor or re-election following the next general election. However, if an absolute majority of the voting membership of Tynwald supported a motion of no confidence, both the Chief Minister and ministers would have to resign. Otherwise ministers were to hold office during the pleasure of the Chief Minister. The Council of Ministers inherited the authority given to the Executive Council under the Government Departments Act 1987 but without the formal constraint of being advisory to the Lieutenant-Governor.

The most controversial aspect of the 1990 Act was the Chief Minister's right to hire and fire without reference to Tynwald. Following the 1991 general election, the newly established Alternative Policy Group and Noel Cringle, who had been returned to the House after a five-year absence, campaigned for the restoration of Tynwald's authority. It was argued that, in the absence of a party system, no one member of Tynwald could possibly claim to represent the people of the Island and that steps should be taken to require candidates for the post of Chief Minister to issue a manifesto before Tynwald was asked to vote and to restore to Tynwald the power to approve the Chief Minister's choice of cabinet. Until the appointment in 1998 of a select committee of Tynwald to review the ministerial system, it was left to private members to to take the initiative. One private member's bill received an easy passage through the branches to

Members of the Alternative Policy Group, January 1992. The formation of this parliamentary opposition group was the result of policy differences between Chief Minister Walker and supporters of Edgar Mann in the chief ministerial election of 1991. From left to right are Adrian Duggan, David Cannan, Edgar Mann, Dominic Delaney and Edgar Quine.

become the Council of Ministers (Amendment) Act 1994.[113] Initiated by APG member, Edgar Quine, it required the proposers of candidates for the post of Chief Minister to give seven days' notice in writing of their nomination and the candidates to circulate members of Tynwald with a written statement of policy commitments. Three bills introduced by Noel Cringle with the aim of restoring Tynwald's right to approve the Chief Minister's team were much more controversial and met with defeat in the Keys, in June 1992, February 1994 and January 1996.[114] On the first two occasions each of the eight MHK ministers opposed the change; in 1996 only six were opposed, Cringle having become a minister and David North joining the support group. In February 1998 Tynwald approved a resolution moved by MLP member, Peter Karran, for the appointment of a select committee to review the ministerial system. The Select Committee, chaired by the new Speaker of the House, Noel Cringle, reported in favour of the restoration of Tynwald's power and in November 1999, Tynwald accepted this and other recommendations by 17 votes to six in the Keys and five votes to two in the Legislative Council.[115] Six ministers, including Chief Minister Gelling, who had opposed the earlier initiatives by Cringle, supported the recommendation. Notwithstanding this support, when Government legislation to democratise the process of cabinet selection was introduced in April 2001, it met a similar fate to earlier attempts at reform—after the second reading, opponents of the Council of Ministers Amendment Bill were successful in moving the adjournment of the clauses stage 'sine die'.[116]

## Executive Power and Political Accountability

So far this chapter has focused on constitutional change. What of political reality? How significant were the constitutional changes in relation to Tynwald's choice of executive, the selection and accountability of the Manx cabinet and individual ministers and the general operation of the governmental system? There were five elections in this period for the post of chair of Executive Council or chief minister and only minor changes to the method of election. The first four involved Tynwald choosing between personalities with experience and known records but no formal policy statements, whereas in 1996 the choice was between personalities and policy statements. In practice the difference was not very marked. On each occasion the successful candidates were senior politicians whose policy commitments were well known. Each was closely involved with the outgoing administration, three of the four having been chair of the Finance Board or Treasury Minister immediately prior to election. In each case but that of March 1985, the selection took place following a general election in which candidates had made clear their stand on government policy. This was especially true in 1991 and 1996 when the successful contestants had pledged their support for the programmes detailed in the outgoing Government's *Policy Report 1991* and *Annual Review of Policies and Programmes 1996*. Policy commitments by the candidates were not markedly dissimilar and even in 1996 when one of the candidates was openly associated with an opposition grouping inside Tynwald, the APG, the circulated policy statements of the two candidates revealed significant common ground, some differences of emphasis and few major policy differences.

In 1981 Irving's defeat in the preceding general election obliged Tynwald to look for a new chair of Executive Council. There were four nominations, Ian Anderson, Noel Cringle, Edgar Mann and, after a fourth inconclusive ballot, Percy Radcliffe, who had just been elected to the Legislative Council. Each had been a member of the previous administration. On the seventh ballot Radcliffe was elected with 18 votes to Mann's 14.[117] He was by far the most experienced candidate, having already served as chair from 1972 to 1976 and as chair of the Finance Board during the Irving administration from 1976 to 1981. When Radcliffe retired in 1985, there was a four-way contest between Sir Charles Kerruish, who had resigned as Speaker to allow his name to go forward, Edgar Mann, recently elected to the Legislative Council, David Moore and Miles Walker. Mann was successful on the third ballot with 15 votes to Kerruish's 11.[118] He had been chair of the Finance Board under Radcliffe, although it is worth noting that his main rival also had a wealth of executive experience including a controversial stint as the first chair of Executive Council between 1962 and 1967. Immediately following Mann's election, Kerruish was re-elected Speaker. Mann decided in 1986 that it was inappropriate for the chair of Executive Council to sit in the Legislative Council and resigned to contest the election in his old constituency of Garff. His defeat by Sir Charles Kerruish in what was now a single seat constituency paved the way for the election of Miles Walker unopposed.[119] An MHK, he had been a member of the Executive Council since 1982, serving as chair of the LGB in both the Radcliffe and Mann administrations; faced with a seamen's strike immediately following the general election and in the absence of Mann, the outgoing Executive Council elected him Acting Chair and his leadership during the first few days of the dispute made him seem a natural choice to succeed Dr Mann. In 1991 Walker was re-elected in a two-way contest against Mann, who had returned to the Keys as the member for Garff in 1990. In the initial secret ballot 23 votes were cast for Walker and 10 for Mann. This ballot was followed by an open vote for Walker as chief minister, in which there were 27 votes in favour and six against.[120] It was in the aftermath of defeat that Mann decided with four others who had opposed Walker's re-election to establish the APG. In 1996 Walker let it be known that he did not wish to stand for a third term, leaving the way open for his Treasury Minister, Donald Gelling, to contest the election against the APG candidate, Edgar Quine, an MHK with a background in the Royal Hong Kong Police but no ministerial experience. The result in an open ballot was 22 votes to 10 in favour of Gelling.[121]

Although the constitutional changes regarding the selection of the other members of the executive team were quite radical, the increase in the leader's freedom to choose his own team was constrained by political considerations. Only 30 other members of Tynwald were eligible for selection, an extremely small pool compared with many legislatures. Independently of the changing statutory provision in relation to the representation of the branches, there has been a general recognition that, while the House should provide most members, the best person for a particular appointment may be in the Legislative Council. The experience and ability of certain members made their selection a foregone conclusion and conversely the inexperience of other members placed them outside of the frame. Members of a team have to able to work together and on occasions a clash of personalities limited the discretion available. The selector(s) had to strive for a balance between the regions and constituencies of the Island. Last and by no means least, they were concerned to maintain the Island's tradition of coalition and consensus government.

In 1981 Radcliffe could only influence the selection of his team through his role as ex officio chair of the Selection Committee. He clearly used that influence in gaining Tynwald's support for the election of his two main rivals to the ex officio positions on Executive Council, Mann as chair of the Finance Board and Anderson the Home Affairs Board.[122] Beyond that he was able to influence the selection of other chairs of boards, but it was left to the branches to nominate the other five members for the approval of Tynwald. As an MLC he supported the nomination of the only two board chairs who were members of the Legislative Council, Eddie Kerruish, chair of the Industry Board, and Roy MacDonald, chair of the Harbour Board, but had no say over the Keys' selection of Victor Kneale, chair of the Education Board, Miles Walker, chair of the LGB and Matty Ward, the MLP chair of the Forestry, Mines and Land Board.[123] In the Keys the chairs of other major boards, including John J. Radcliffe at Agriculture and Fisheries, Arnold Callin at Health, Noel Cringle at Social Security and Eddie Lowey at the Tourist Board were also nominated, but there were only three positions to be filled. The voting in the House was illustrative of the problems of reaching agreement using this method of selection; the choice of the three members involved nine nominations and 11 ballots, Kneale and Ward achieving the necessary majority on the eighth ballot and Walker not until the eleventh ballot. In Tynwald each of the five nominees were elected with comfortable majorities.

There were two changes in the membership of the Executive Council under Radcliffe. When Anderson was elected to the Legislative Council in 1982, Noel Cringle became chair of the Home Affairs Board on the recommendation of the Selection Committee.[124] The second change came two years later, when midterm elections were due for all the chairs of boards save for the Finance Board. Insofar as seven of the positions were concerned Tynwald was now being asked to elect members to become ex officio members of the Executive Council with effect from 15 January 1985. Two changes in personnel were necessary because of the increase in the size of the Council and the pending retirement from politics of Eddie Kerruish; others were likely because of the inclusion of chairs of boards excluded by the decisions of the branches in 1981. As chair of the Selection Committee Radcliffe might have been expected to wield greater influence than in 1981, but events proved that the approval of Tynwald on such matters can never be taken for granted. The Selection Committee, whose nominations were presumably made with Radcliffe's blessing, recommended a major reshuffle with Cringle staying at Home Affairs and Kneale at Education, Walker moving to Industry and four new members. Kneale, who was not a member of the Selection Committee, orchestrated a successful campaign to re-elect, wherever possible, existing chairs of boards for the rest of the term and express confidence in the existing administration. The result was that Tynwald accepted just four out of the seven Selection Committee recommendations. Cringle and Kneale retained their existing portfolios as too did Norman Radcliffe at Agriculture and Fisheries and Lowey at the Tourist Board; it was agreed that Walker remain at Local Government, leaving Industry free for the return of Anderson to the Executive Council; finally it was decided that Callin should stay at Health in preference to Clare Christian. MacDonald and Ward retained their positions as chairs of the Harbour and Forestry, Mines and Land Boards, but lost their seats on the Executive Council.[125] The overall result was the election of three sitting members, the return of a former member and three completely new members. The Executive Council now comprised three MLCs, including the chair, and six MHKs. Politically it remained a broad coalition including both conservatives like Percy Radcliffe himself and MLP member, Lowey.

If Radcliffe's room for manoeuvre was limited, in March 1985 Mann's was even more so. In effect he inherited a team. The only elections he could influence through the Selection Committee were for his own replacement as chair of the Finance Board and the filling of the vacancies at Health and Agriculture and Fisheries following the election of

Callin and Norman Radcliffe to the Legislative Council. In the event Tynwald accepted the nomination of existing Finance Board member, David Moore, to chair the Finance Board and approved the re-election of Callin and Radcliffe, tilting the balance of membership in favour of the Legislative Council with the chair and four members.[126] There were no other changes until after the 1986 election.

Constitutionally Walker had much greater freedom than his predecessors, but was very aware of the difficulty of persuading the voting members of Tynwald to accept nine of their number for membership of the Executive Council. His proposals for the initial three-year term followed individual consultations with members and involved major change. Some change was necessary as a result of his own elevation to high office, the defeat of Cringle and Mann in the general election, Moore's retirement from politics, the inception of the new departmental structure and the associated increase in the size of the ministerial team. Walker explained his selection in terms of the interests, qualities and experience of members, the need to redress the balance of membership in favour of the House and his belief in consensus government. In terms of personnel his proposal was for a combination of continuity and change, for a broadly based coalition with four other members of the outgoing team, including three MLCs, and five new members from the Keys. Of the former group Anderson and Kneale were to stay at Industry and Education, while Callin and Lowey were to move from Health to the DHPP and from Tourism to Home Affairs. The proposal in relation to new members was for Allan Bell to take on Tourism and Leisure, Tony Brown, Health and Social Security, David Cannan, the Treasury, Dominic Delaney, Local Government and the Environment and Donald Maddrell, Agriculture, Fisheries and Forestry. Under standing orders no discussion on the proposal was permitted. The team was accepted by 18 votes to 14, just one vote above the absolute majority of the members of Tynwald present and eligible to vote and a clear indication of dissatisfaction with at least some members of the team.

Between 1986 and 1991 there were three opportunities for Walker to make adjustments to his team. The first, in April 1988, followed the election of Anderson to succeed Nivison as President of the Legislative Council and the death of Maddrell. Walker's nomination of businessman, Walter Gilbey, to replace Anderson at the Department of Industry was defeated in Tynwald on 20 April 1988 by 18 votes to 13. The following week and with two posts to fill after the sudden death of the Minister of Agriculture, Fisheries and Forestry, the nomination of MLP member, Bernie May, to replace Anderson was accepted by 20 votes to 10 and that of Donald Gelling to replace Maddrell by 19 votes to 11.[127] Both were comparative newcomers to Tynwald, May having been in the Keys since 1985 and Gelling since 1986. The second opportunity was presented by the midterm review in December 1989. Following consultations with all members of Tynwald, Walker explained to Tynwald that it was 'eminently clear' that Tynwald support for the Council with the current membership would not be forthcoming and that the reshuffle he was proposing was the result of widespread dissatisfaction. Walker referred to the dilemma facing him during a later debate on Tynwald's role in the selection process:

> I canvassed the views of members very carefully on that occasion because I thought it was important not to have individual nominations made across the floor of the House and I found there were just two combinations of members that would have found overall support ... I can say that only one of those combinations was acceptable to me as Chief Minister and it was approved by one vote, one vote. Any other combination of members apart from one that would not have been acceptable to me would not

have received approval and we would have gone through that rather miserable experience of nominating one member after another … and goodness knows what concern and unrest that would have caused.[128]

The package presented involved the removal of two members, the transfer of another two and the introduction of two new members. One of the two to be removed, Dominic Delaney, had already indicated to Walker his unwillingness to serve beyond December 1989 unless steps were taken to discipline MLP members of the cabinet for breaches in collective responsibility.[129] The other, David Cannan, had simply alienated too many colleagues.[130] Cannan at the Treasury and Delaney at DOLGE were to be replaced by existing members, Gelling and Brown. They in turn were to be replaced at the DAFF and the DHSS by David North, first elected to the House in 1988, and Jim Cain, who had been an MHK since 1986. The new team was narrowly approved by 17 votes to 16.[131] The removal of Cannan and Delaney was widely seen to be about conflicting personalities rather than policy or performance. The *Manx Independent* believed the two had much in common, 'a troublesome backbench past, formidable energy, total commitment, a bruising political style and an overwhelming desire to be popular with their constituents', adding that the backbenches now had 'two expert boat-rockers'.[132] The final opportunity came in October 1990 following the election of Kneale as Speaker of the House of Keys. Under the Council of Ministers Act 1990 Walker no longer required the approval of Tynwald and appointed Ron Cretney as Minister of Education for the year leading up to the general election.[133] Cretney was a retired headmaster who had been elected to the House in 1989 and was already a member of the Department.

Walker's second administration commenced with a major cabinet reshuffle. Although he no longer needed the formal approval of Tynwald he was well aware of the dangers of confidence motions should he, the team or individual ministers lose the confidence of Tynwald. He asked his rival and critic if he would be willing to serve, but Mann declined because of the depth of their differences over policy.[134] With Mann out of the reckoning, Walker opted for maximum continuity of personnel. He was obliged to replace Education Minister Cretney who had decided not to seek re-election to the House and DHSS Minister Cain who had been elected Speaker of the House. Three members of the outgoing team, Gelling, Brown and Bell, retained their portfolios although in Bell's case he was given responsibility for both Tourism and Leisure and Industry. Three of the other four continuing members were transferred to new departments, Callin to Home Affairs, May to the DHSS and North to the DHPP; Lowey became Minister without Portfolio. The two new ministers, John Corrin and Hazel Hannan, were appointed to the DAFF and Education respectively.[135] Lowey's appointment was to enable him to undertake preparatory work for the creation of a Department of Transport and when the initial work was completed in October 1992 he was appointed Minister of Industry, thus relieving Bell of the dual responsibility that he had accepted for nearly a year.[136] The new Council of Ministers comprised two MLCs and eight MHKs.

Between October 1992 and November 1996 the Chief Minister's team was changed on five separate occasions, twice because of a rising tide of criticism directed towards individual ministers and once each following the creation of the Department of Transport, the retirement of a minister and the resignation of a minister. In October 1994 Bell's offer of resignation was accepted by Walker after prolonged criticism from Tynwald over a series of misadventures in the DTLT, the loss of public money in abortive attempts to create a replica of the Bounty and to set up a bowling alley in Nobles Park and, most seriously, expenditure by a civil servant in excess of what had been approved by Tynwald on a new motor racing circuit at Jurby airfield.[137] Bell was replaced by Brown, and Terry Groves, first elected to the House in 1991, appointed Minister of Local Government and the Environment.[138] The second change in January 1995 merely involved a change of responsibility, North becoming Minister of the new Department of Transport instead of Highways, Ports and Properties and Brown, Minister of Tourism and Leisure instead of Tourism, Leisure and Transport. Third, following Callin's decision not to seek re-election to the Legislative Council in February 1995, Walker appointed Richard Corkill as Minister of Home Affairs; first elected to the Keys in 1991 and already a member of the Department, he was able to assume this responsibility with minimum disruption to the rest of the Council.[139] The fourth change involved the forced resignation of the Minister of Agriculture, John Corrin. He had already been the target of an unsuccessful motion of no confidence in April 1994, when APG members criticised him for mismanaging the relocation of a sea-lion pup from the Wildlife Park amid embarrassing publicity for the Island, for failure to improve the condition of the Park, for poor management of the introduction of the Island's expensive new meat plant and for an abrasive style.[140] On that occasion Walker defended Corrin, but in December the following year he called for Corrin's resignation for undermining a fellow minister. Corrin had placed a resolution before Tynwald calling for the appointment of a select committee to investigate ways of improving government support for the elderly in residential care; Walker interpreted the resolution as a motion of no confidence in Bernie May and a matter that should have been raised with the DHSS Minister and the full Council. As with Bell in 1994 a history of criticism rather than the single incident led to the resignation.[141] The vacancy was filled by transferring Hannan from Education and inviting former Executive Council member, Noel Cringle, to become Minister of Education.[142] The final change involved a minister resigning on principle. In July 1996 Lowey, MLP member and the sole remaining MLC, resigned in protest over the introduction of the job seeker's allowance, promoted on behalf of the Council of Ministers by DHSS Minister May, also a member of the MLP. After this unsolicited resignation the Chief Minister himself took over the Industry portfolio, pending a successful invitation to Allan Bell to rejoin the Council in August 1996.[143]

Gelling too benefitted from the freedom to select his team without the formal approval of Tynwald, but politically was initially constrained by his desire for a coalition involving the APG and later by critically motivated motions of confidence both in his team and individual ministers. With the resignation of Miles Walker, his own election as Chief Minister, the defeat of May and Groves in the general election and the election of Cringle as Speaker of the House of Keys, at least four new appointments were necessary. The success of APG members in winning six seats in the general election and the fact that a third of Tynwald had supported the APG candidate for chief minister provided additional food for thought for a leader committed to consensus government. After consultations spread over two days, he announced the formation of a government with five other members from the previous administration and four new members, including two from the APG and one from the MLP; two of the new members were MLCs. Continuity was less evident in the assignment to departments. Hazel Hannan, only appointed to the DAFF a year earlier, was asked to continue, but elsewhere there was change. Bell moved from Trade and Industry to Home Affairs, North from Transport to Trade and Industry, Brown from Tourism and Leisure to Transport and Corkill from Home Affairs to the Treasury. The two new MLC members were both experienced politicians, Clare Christian at Health and Social Security having previously served as chair of the old Board of Social Security and as a member of the Department, and Edgar Mann at Education. The most significant aspect of Mann's appointment and that of Edgar Quine to DOLGE was the fact that they were the members of the APG. During the negotiations that preceded Gelling's announcement, Quine had pressed unsuccessfully for a third APG member and insisted on continuing the struggle for a reform of the ministerial system and an independent review of the Customs and Excise Agreement. The fourth new member, filling the party political gap left by May and accepting responsibility for the DTL, was David Cretney, an existing member of the Department and one of Tynwald's three MLP members.[144]

Given the personality and policy differences of the members, in particular the hostility of a minority of members to the inclusion of the APG, there was every prospect of internal conflict. At the December Tynwald in 1998, Quine moved a two-part resolution seeking the suspension of standing orders to enable members to vote by secret ballot on a motion of confidence in the nine members of the Gelling team.[145] He justified the resolution by reference to the APG policy of restoring to Tynwald the right to approve the Chief Minister's ministerial team. Despite the constitutional change in 1990, Gelling was placed in a very similar position to that which had confronted Walker in 1989 and the events which unfolded obliged him to make changes to his team in order to retain the support of Tynwald. David Cannan, in open disagreement with Quine, moved a procedural motion with a view to a separate vote being taken on secrecy of ballot and on each of the nine named ministers. Tynwald agreed without division to a separate vote on secrecy of ballot, but rejected the proposal to replace the general confidence motion by nine individual ones by 14 votes to 10 in the Keys and unanimously in the Legislative Council. Following voting on the procedural motion, Tynwald refused to suspend standing orders to allow secrecy of ballot and proceeded to debate the confidence motion. During the debate Gelling reiterated his belief in consensus government despite the difficulties involved and urged members to support his team. The motion was carried by 13 votes to 10 in the Keys and five to four in the Legislative Council. The outstanding feature of the open voting was the opposition of the two APG ministers to the motion that one of them had moved. They were not asked to resign and did not offer to do so, but their open refusal to express confidence in a team of which they were members and the fact that they were supported by 12 other members put pressure on the Chief Minister to consider a midterm reshuffle.

Matters came to a head the following January in the House of Keys when Cannan moved the suspension of standing orders to allow the House to vote by secret ballot on nine motions of confidence.[146] He referred to 'a crescendo' of discontent with over half the House having expressed the need for change during the debates and votes on the general confidence motion. Alex Downie, acknowledging the need for change, moved an adjournment to 27 April 1999 to allow the Chief Minister time to respond to the message of the House. Gelling promised to respond by April, saying that he was not willing to continue with 'this incessant niggling and stress', which was in danger of prejudicing the 'absolutely superb' state of the Manx economy and the stability of Manx government. On 27 April 1999 Gelling returned to the House to announce his decision, which can hardly have been what the APG had in mind the previous December.[147] He had consulted with all members of Tynwald, found a high level of satisfaction with most of the team and hoped that, with the two changes he was announcing, that it would be accepted as a whole. The problem for Gelling was that the consultations revealed a lack of agreement over the changes desired, some wanting the removal of the APG from the Council of Ministers, the APG the replacement of their chief critics in the Council, Tony Brown and Hazel Hannan and others an end to the practice of appointing MLCs to key ministries. Given his continuing commitment to consensus politics, there was limited room for manoeuvre and the decision to replace one APG member and one other was a delicate balancing act. Alex Downie was appointed Minister of Agriculture, Fisheries and Forestry in place of Hazel Hannan and Steve Rodan as Minister of Education in place of APG member, Edgar Mann.

As with Walker's decisions to drop Cannan and Delaney in 1989, the removal of Hannan and Mann seems to have been a response to political pressure for change rather than the result of any differences of opinion with the Chief Minister over policy or performance. The decision to replace Mann was relatively easy: his term of office as an MLC had less than a year to run and he had offered to resign if he could remain a member of the Department to see through a number of new initiatives. Mann even suggested Rodan as a possible successor.[148] The reason for replacing Hannan was much less clear, a response by Gelling to APG critics reflecting a determination to keep the APG on board.[149] Gelling stressed that as far as he was concerned 'the team stands or falls together'.[150] Although there was no vote on the new appointments, not all members were satisfied. There were two main reasons for continuing dissatisfaction. The first was the fact that the DHSS minister, whose Department was responsible for over 40 per cent of total government spending, was still an MLC rather than a member of the elected chamber. In reply to questioning by Cannan about his decision not to appoint an MHK to the DHSS, Gelling explained that the present appointment was constitutionally proper and that the incumbent, Clare Christian, was doing 'sterling work'. Although Cannan then withdrew the nine confidence motions, he insisted that the Council of Ministers still did not reflect the will of the House. For Edgar Quine and the APG, the removal of an APG member without replacement by another breached the Group's understanding of the agreement reached with Gelling in 1996 that the APG should be represented by two Ministers and he became the second minister to submit an unsolicited resignation.[151] Walter Gilbey, MHK, was appointed as Minister of Local Government and the Environment on 12 May 1999.[152] APG members, including Mann and Quine, continued to serve as departmental members, but the largest organised group in Tynwald with six MHKs and three MLCs was no longer represented on the Council of Ministers.

It is impossible to predict the political consequences of Tynwald's decision in November 1999 in favour of restoring Tynwald's right to approve the Chief Minister's team. The necessary legislation has to be approved and that is by no means assured. If it is eventually passed, recent political history suggests a real possibility of Tynwald failing to approve teams en bloc and having to vote on individual nominations unless there is a renewed commitment to a comprehensive coalition at ministerial level.

The arguments concerning the respective roles of executive leader and Tynwald in selecting ministers were part of a wider debate concerning the respective roles of the executive and Tynwald, with the former visibly expanding at the expense of the latter. The emergence of a more prominent executive leader after 1981 was only partly the result of the increase in their powers of patronage. Each of the four leaders benefitted from being elected by Tynwald and held office without portfolio, leaving them free to stand above the sectional interests of boards and departments, provide general direction and coordination and chair the major policy committees. Each came to be regarded as chief government spokesman, answerable inside and outside Tynwald for central government policy. Radcliffe and Mann were responsible for the first real exercise in policy planning, the Policy Planning Programme of 1982 detailing a broad five-year strategy for the Island and gaining acceptance in Tynwald without division.[153] Immediately following his election as Chief Minister, Walker declared his intention to present to Tynwald for approval a detailed policy statement and the result was a series of annual policy reviews that combined reporting to Tynwald on performance with policy and financial planning. Gelling continued the practice. The fact that these documents and the associated budgets were approved either without division or by substantial majorities gave an added legitimacy to the leadership of Walker and Gelling. Both Radcliffe and Mann were elected to chair major policy committees of Tynwald, on constitutional issues, the responsibilities of boards of Tynwald, the common purse, transport, population growth and immigration and, in Mann's case, energy and the structure of local government too. They also chaired important policy committees of the Executive Council, an increasingly important source of policy as was evidenced by the work of the Policy Planning Committee in preparing the Policy Planning Programme of 1982. Both were determined to see the Executive Council play a leading role.

Left: Jack Nivison, first Manx President of the Legislative Council 1980–88. A member of Tynwald from 1948 until 1988, Nivison was one of the most effective politicians of his generation. He chaired the Board of Social Security 1951–76 and was also at the forefront of debates about tourism, transport and constitutional reform. He joined the Legislative Council in 1962 and succeeded Sir John Paul as chair in 1980. He retired from politics in 1988.

Right: Noel Cringle, SHK 1996–2000. Cringle entered the Keys in 1974 and very quickly achieved high executive office, becoming chair of the Board of Social Security in 1976 and the Home Affairs Board in 1982. Following defeat in the 1986 general election, he returned to the Keys in 1991, became Minister of Education in 1995 and Speaker in 1996. He resigned in April 2000 on being elected to succeed Sir Charles Kerruish as President of Tynwald.

However, it was Walker who took the most significant steps to make the Executive Council the generating force for policy planning and development. In Tynwald on 20 January 1987 he moved the discharge of seven select committees of Tynwald as part of a general strategy of transferring responsibility for initiating policy to the Executive Council. The resolution to dispense with the Select Committees on Constitutional Issues, the Responsibilities of Boards of Tynwald, the Common Purse, Energy, Transport, Trade Union Legislation and the Structure of Local Government was agreed without division.[154] Tynwald's committees were replaced by equivalent committees of the Executive Council. While Tynwald continued to appoint select committees after 1987, many of the attempts to do so resulted in ministers successfully moving amendments to refer the matter in question to the Executive Council or, after 1990, to the Council of Ministers. A similar shift was seen with regard to the conduct of external relations. Under Radcliffe and Mann the Tynwald members of the Standing Committee on the Common Interests of the Isle of Man and the UK were the chair of Executive Council, the chair of the Finance Board and a third nominee of the Executive Council. Under Walker, with the full support of the Home Office, the Committee was disbanded in favour of intergovernmental meetings and negotiations and appropriate reporting to Tynwald.[155]

In keeping with the declared intentions of the leaders, the Executive Council and the Council of Ministers did become the major source of policy. Much of the detailed work was still left to the departments, but major policy emanating from the departments had to have clearance from the collective leadership and general strategy and policy and expenditure priorities were presented to Tynwald on behalf of that leadership. The development of a stronger central executive was due partly to the constitutional changes between 1981 and 1987, partly to its success in presenting a united front in Tynwald and partly to Tynwald's overwhelming support for the development. The constitutional changes provided for a more inclusive and powerful Executive Council than was possible under the board system, but it did not guarantee unity of purpose or strength in Tynwald. In the Isle of Man there was no party discipline to cement the relationship between members of the executive and a majority in Tynwald, but there were alternative ways of sustaining both unity of purpose in the executive and majority support in Tynwald. Collective responsibility was an aspiration of Manx politicians long before the advent of ministerial government in 1987. Postwar Manx politics revealed a high level of consensus with regard to fundamental issues and policies, so that politicians recruited to leadership did not find it difficult to find common ground and majority support in Tynwald. Of course there were occasions when consensus proved elusive because of strongly held differences of opinion, electoral commitments, constituency interests and conflicts of personality, but the publicity given to such occasions should not lead to an exaggeration of conflict overall. Even without a formal agreement on collective responsibility, there was a relatively high level of discipline and unity on the part of members of the Radcliffe and Mann cabinets, which in turn increased the likelihood of Tynwald accepting their lead.

With the removal of the final constitutional obstacles in the way of unity in 1986 and 1987, there was a demand by Tynwald for the formal application of the convention of collective responsibility. The debate on the subject in February 1989 provided insights into the practice of the Executive Council in the early years of Walker's administration.[156] Phil Kermode, a nonmember who moved the resolution, expressed concern at the frequency with which ministers disagreed in Tynwald, but his seconder, Clifford Irving, believed ministers were showing a sense of collective responsibility. Victor Kneale suggested that it was 'wishful thinking' to imagine that 10 ministers could agree to follow a common line on all issues regardless of political background, election promises, issues of conscience and constituency interests. Chief Minister Walker spoke of 'a growing togetherness', but that ministers did not have the party bonds of their counterparts in the UK. He felt that, given the limited pool of potential members, it would be unwise to insist on resignations whenever individuals opposed a policy. If the disagreement was over a major plank of government policy, resignation would be expected, but if it was not, and the member concerned had good reason for opposition and remained willing to support other policies, he would not insist on resignation. Treasury Minister Cannan was of the opinion that the doctrine was 'fit, well and thriving'. Kermode's resolution was carried by 22 votes to one in the Keys and unanimously in the Legislative Council. Following Tynwald's decision formal guidelines on collective responsibility were agreed by the Council of Ministers.[157] Under these guidelines a minister may argue against any proposal in the Council of Ministers, but once a policy has been agreed must be prepared to support it both inside and outside of Tynwald. It is deemed unacceptable for ministers to ask other ministers questions for oral or written answer in Tynwald or the branches. Ministers are expected to support the Council in votes on the annual policy review, the budget, motions promoted by the Council or departments and any legislation promoted by the Council. In the event of being unable to accept a policy, the minister should resign unless there are exceptional circumstances involving matters of conscience, constituency interests, inconsequential matters or where ministers have entered the Council with strongly held views and a publicly declared position.

In 1999 the Select Committee on Ministerial Government reviewed the convention of collective responsibility as it had applied over the preceding decade and concluded that because of the exceptions, especially those relating to previously declared positions and constituency interests, it has 'rather a weak application in the Isle of Man'.[158] However, such a conclusion seems to exaggerate the frequency with which consequential exceptions to the convention occur. In the first two years under Gelling's leadership, when members of the Council of Ministers included Independents of varying political persuasions and APG and MLP members, there were 466 motions promoted by the Government in Tynwald and the branches and only 29 instances of ministers voting against. Commenting on these figures in an answer to a question in Tynwald by Eddie Lowey, Gelling stressed that such voting was infrequent and almost always within the agreed guidelines on collective responsibility.[159]

The Council of Ministers was unable to get its way without the support of Tynwald. Unity of purpose and discipline may have helped to generate the majorities required in the Legislative Council, the House of Keys and Tynwald for policy proposals, but ultimate success depended on the support of nonministerial members. The fact that this was usually forthcoming was due to the quality of what was on offer, the fact that some nonministerial members had been involved in the development of particular policies through membership of boards or departments and committees of the Council of Ministers and the extent of consensus politics. It may also have been because of the superiority of the sources of information and policy research available to the Council of Ministers.

One important reaction on the part of nonministerial members of Tynwald to the growth in executive power since 1981 has been to try and improve the effectiveness of

Tynwald in holding ministers accountable for the policies they promote, partly through traditional means such as question time, contributions to debate on government policy and finance, declaratory resolutions and private members' bills, and partly by means of three new committees established to scrutinise aspects of government policy. The first of these committees was the result of a private initiative in Tynwald by a member of the Executive Council. In July 1982 Roy MacDonald moved the appointment of a select committee to report on the desirability of establishing a public accounts committee. The proposal was agreed without division and a committee appointed with MacDonald, Callin and Mann as members.[160] In November 1982 Tynwald accepted the Select Committee's recommendations for a committee with the freedom to scrutinise public expenditure accounts in order to identify waste and ensure value for money. The Standing Committee on Public Accounts was established under the chair of Speaker Kerruish on 22 March 1983,[161] a position he held until his election as President of Tynwald in 1990. His successors were also Speakers of the House of Keys until 1997, when revised standing orders prevented the presiding officers of the branches being elected as chair. In addition to reports of its own choosing the PAC was also asked by Tynwald to report on particular subjects. As with its UK namesake the focus on accounts meant that it could only scrutinise expenditure after it had occurred and, while lessons were learned from experience, a more effective scrutiny necessitated a wider remit for the Committee.

In January 1992, Edgar Quine, concerned about the absence of adequate checks and balances within the ministerial system, proposed to Tynwald the establishment of a select committee to report on ways of providing for the more effective scrutiny of government policies and activities. Tynwald approved the resolution without division.[162] The Select Committee, chaired by Speaker Cain and with Quine as one of the five members, reported in December 1992 with an evaluation of existing methods of scrutiny and proposals for reform.[163] It concluded that question time, debates on government policy and finance and meetings to consider the summaries of Council of Ministers proceedings were valuable mechanisms, but that they tended to focus randomly on issues of immediate political concern at the expense of a more systematic scrutiny. The contribution of the PAC was useful but limited by the obligation to look at matters retrospectively. Ad hoc select committees served well for particular purposes. It recommended a modification to the remit of the PAC to allow the selective examination of estimates and the establishment of a new standing committee with responsibility for scrutinising delegated and EC legislation prior to approval by Tynwald. Tynwald approved the recommendations without division in March 1993, but they were not implemented immediately because of a general government embargo on the appointment of new personnel. When, in July 1993, the Speaker moved the approval of £13,250 for additional staff in the Clerk of Tynwald's Office in the financial year ending 31 March 1994, the resolution was defeated on the advice of the Council of Ministers.[164] The matter rested there until April 1996, when Quine moved the extension of the remit of the PAC as recommended nearly three years earlier. The proposal was approved without division and the Committee was immediately renamed the Expenditure and Public Accounts Committee (EPAC). Following the general election, Sir Miles Walker, freshly knighted in the New Year Honours for services to the Isle of Man, was elected chair of the EPAC. Since 1987 the entire membership of the PAC and the EPAC has been nonministerial, although when first established there were two members of Executive Council on the PAC.

The campaign by nonministerial members of Tynwald for additional checks on the policies of the Council of Ministers continued after the 1996 general election and two further parliamentary committees were established. Both emerged in response to perceived threats to the Island's constitutional autonomy by international developments. The Standing Committee on Constitutional Matters was set up following a successful initiative by MLP member, Eddie Lowey. The debate on Lowey's resolution on 19 March 1997 revealed some of the tensions between the Council of Ministers and Tynwald over constitutional policy making.[165] With the disbandment of the Constitutional Issues Committee in 1987, major constitutional initiatives had become the responsibility of the Executive Council or private members. Lowey felt that the time was ripe for a new look at the Island's constitutional position with independence as a possible goal and was emphatic that the responsibility for initiating policy should be returned to Tynwald. His proposal was for a five-member standing committee to consider and report on important constitutional matters. Chief Minister Gelling disagreed, arguing that the Constitutional and External Relations Committee of the Council of Ministers was already performing the task on behalf of the Council of Ministers and Tynwald. He moved an amendment restricting the role of the committee to considering and reporting on the constitutional policies of the Council of Ministers. David Cannan moved a further amendment incorporating Gelling's proposal and adding the proviso that members should not also be members of the Constitutional and External Relations Committee. Cannan's amendment was carried by 15 votes to five in the Keys and five votes to two in the Legislative Council. Cannan became the first chair of the new committee and Lowey a member and it very quickly became clear that the agreed terms of reference were not nearly as restrictive as Gelling had intended. The Committee agreed that its first major task would be to inquire generally into the constitutional status of the Isle of Man in relation to the UK. It appointed a Scottish advocate and former UK Lord Chancellor (1987–97), Lord Mackay of Clashfern, to act as advisor to the inquiry and, while it initially planned to report to Tynwald in 2000, due to pressure of business on members it now seems unlikely to complete its investigations before the general election in November 2001.

The Standing Committee on Economic Initiatives was set up in July 1999 to monitor and consider economic, fiscal and monetary initiatives of the EU, other international agencies and individual states that might affect the Isle of Man.[166] Moving the resolution for the establishment of the five-member committee, Edgar Quine, who had just resigned from the Council of Ministers, believed that such monitoring should no longer be the exclusive prerogative of the Council of Ministers and that Tynwald itself had an obligation to scrutinise external policy developments likely to affect the Island. The Chief Minister warned against the dangers of unnecessary duplication of effort, but supported the idea in principle. He moved an amendment requiring the standing committee to report each July and at such other times as it deemed appropriate. The amendment and the amended resolution were carried without division and the Committee established. Members of the Constitutional and External Relations Committee were not precluded from membership and the first chair, Speaker Cringle, and one other member, Sir Miles Walker, were also members of that Committee. The Standing Committee's first major investigation, to which reference has already been made, was into double taxation agreements and the exchange of information.[167]

The search on the part of nonministerial members for more effective scrutiny of the work of government is hampered by their participation in the work of government and by the lack of time and resources allocated to the scrutiny function. The small size of the legislature makes it impossible to sustain the numerical ratio between government and backbenchers that obtains elsewhere. Indeed, when the Island moved from a board system to a ministerial system, the practice of involving nearly all the elected and indirectly elected members of Tynwald in the work of government was retained, making genuinely independent scrutiny extremely difficult. The independent resources available to the Office of the Clerk of Tynwald to support members in the performance of their parliamentary duties are dwarfed by those available to the Government.

At the opening of the twenty-first century the debate over the respective roles of the Council of Ministers and Tynwald continued. While the balance of power may seem to favour the Council, the political reality is of a much more effective system of checks and balances than critics would have us believe. The Chief Minister is elected by and has to retain the confidence of Tynwald. To date there have been no no confidence motions directed against a chief minister, but the Council of Ministers Act 1990 does provide for such an eventuality and requires the Chief Minister to resign if at least 17 members of Tynwald voting as one body resolve that they have no confidence in the Council of Ministers. Although the Chief Minister no longer needs the approval of Tynwald for members of the Council of Ministers, the motions of confidence directed at Gelling's team and individual ministers in December 1998 and January 1999 were useful reminders of the ultimate authority of Tynwald; moreover, Tynwald is committed to a formal restoration of its rights in this area. The Council of Ministers is a parliamentary executive with a collective obligation and interest in formulating policy that will be acceptable to themselves, the rest of Tynwald and the Manx people. To be successful government resolutions and legislation must attract majority support and such support may be withheld or made conditional. There is no party system in the Isle of Man and no disciplined majority to ease the passage of government proposals. The fact that most do attract majority support should not detract from the importance of the formal requirement for such support. The real authority of Tynwald is shown every time its support is required and not just when it refuses support or makes it conditional on the acceptance of amendments.

## Notes

1  For a discussion of these four Lieutenant-Governors, see Derek Winterbottom, *Governors of the Isle of Man since 1765* (Douglas, 1999), Part 8, pp. 247–65.
2  Speaker Cringle paying a tribute to Sir Charles on his retirement; for further details, see 117 *Manx Deb.*, 11 April 2000, pp. T649–54; see also G. N. Kniveton (ed.), *A Chronicle of the Twentieth Century: The Manx Experience*, vol. 2: 1951–2000 (Douglas, 2000), p. 279.
3  See 98 *Manx Deb.*, 14 July 1981, pp. T1499–517 and 1531–42.
4  See 103 *Manx Deb.*, 26 February 1986, pp. 1273–84; *Interim Report on Future Constitutional Objectives: A Report by the Council of Ministers*, April 1991 and 108 *Manx Deb.*, 21 May 1991, pp. T1767–82; *Second Interim Report on Future Constitutional Objectives ...*, October 1993 and 111 *Manx Deb.*, 10 November 1993; *Third Interim Report on Future Constitutional Objectives ...*, December 1995 and 113 *Manx Deb.*, 20 February 1996, pp. T489–97.
5  *Developments within the European Union and Other International Bodies which have Potential Economic Implications for the Island: Interim Report by the Council of Ministers*, June 1999, Appendix 1, p. 23 and 116 *Manx Deb.*, 22 June 1999, pp. K477–96.
6  See *Fourth Interim Report on Future Constitutional Objectives: the Implications of Independence.*

*A Report by the Council of Ministers*, November 2000 and 118 *Manx Deb.*, 22 November 2000, pp. T298–317.

7   See *Acts of Tynwald 1986*, pp. 707–54.

8   See *Acts of Tynwald 1987*, pp. 169–84.

9   See *Acts of Tynwald 1990*, pp. 559–618.

10  See *Acts of Tynwald 1991*, pp. 157–323 and 327–65.

11  See *Acts of Tynwald 1995*, pp. 75–101.

12  Under UK legislation dating back to 1835; see *Acts of Tynwald 1983*, pp. 339–43.

13  Tynwald approved a recommendation from the Council of Ministers on 20 February 1996; see *Third Interim Report on Future Constitutional Objectives: A Report by the Council of Ministers*, December 1995; this report was an endorsement of the Council's Constitutional and External Relations Committee chaired by the Chief Minister, Miles Walker; see also 113 *Manx Deb.*, 20 February 1996, pp. 489–97. Following concerns expressed in Tynwald over the way in which the Edwards Review of Financial Regulation in the Crown Dependencies had been communicated to the Isle of Man—the Attorney General was one of four officials to learn of the decision before the Chief Minister—on 19 January 1999 Tynwald gave overwhelming backing to a Council of Ministers Report reiterating the view that the Attorney General should be an Isle of Man Government appointment; see 116 *Manx Deb.*, 19 January 1999, pp. 421–29.

14  See 117 *Manx Deb.*, 16 February 2000, pp. T512–14.

15  On this occasion the Home Office chose to advertise the vacancy and invited the Chief Minister to serve on the appointment committee which advised the Home Secretary. Following MacFadyen's appointment Tynwald expressed regret at the decision and, following a report by its Standing Committee on Constitutional Matters, agreed to seek an inter-governmental review of the appointment procedure; see 117 *Manx Deb.*, 12 July 2000, pp. T1019–31, *Report of the Standing Committee on Constitutional Matters: The Appointment Process of the Lieutenant-Governor of the Isle of Man*, March 2001 and 118 *Manx Deb.*, 20–21 March 2001, pp. T663 et seq.

16  See *Acts of Tynwald 1984*, pp. 417–19 and *Acts of Tynwald 1991*, pp. 593–661.

17  The Speaker's proposal was for an investigation by a select committee, but Tynwald accepted an amendment by Victor Kneale to refer the matter to the Executive Council; see 98 *Manx Deb.*, 22 October 1980, pp. T133–55.

18  For details, see 103 *Manx Deb.*, 19 February 1986, pp. 1111–91 and 16 July 1986, pp. 2419–33.

19  For a discussion of the background and detail of the extension, see T. W. Cain, 'The Extension of the Territorial Sea', 15 *MLB* (1 June 1990–10 November 1990), pp. 87–97.

20  See 107 *Manx Deb.*, 11 July 1990, pp. T2133–94.

21  See *Acts of Tynwald 1991*, pp. 145–54.

22  See *Acts of Tynwald 1996*, pp. 499–500.

23  See 103 *Manx Deb.*, 26 February 1986, pp. T1273–84.

24  For the debate leading to the approval of the provisional licence, see 116 *Manx Deb.*, 21 April 1999, pp. 766–75; for details of the failure of the first attempt to obtain planning permission, see *Town and Country Planning Acts 1934–99: Report of an Enquiry into a Planning Application for Full Planning Permission for the Construction of a Long Wave Transmitter Station and Associated Vehicular Access at Ballafayle, Cranstal, Bride*, 28 December 2000 and 118 *Manx Deb.*, 20 February 2001 (forthcoming).

25  See *Acts of Tynwald 1987*, pp. 265–83 and 287–305 and 105 *Manx Deb.*, 16 March 1988, p. T1097.

26  See *Aspects of the Constitution of the Isle of Man. The Position of the Governor and the Development of a Council of Ministers. A Report by Executive Council*, April 1989; 106 *Manx Deb.*, 16 May 1989, pp. T1669–724.

27  See *Acts of Tynwald 1990*, pp. 165–73. The Kneale amendment was carried in the Keys by 17

votes to six; 107 *Manx Deb.*, 28 November 1989, pp. K425–63. Following a review by the Constitutional and External Relations Committee of the Council of Ministers, on 19 June 2001 Tynwald accepted recommendations from the Council of Ministers that the Lieutenant-Governor continue to preside over the Tynwald Day ceremony, but that legislation be introduced to enable the President of Tynwald to preside over the sitting of Tynwald in the church at St Johns; see *Second Report on Presidence at the Tynwald Ceremony: A Report by the Council of Ministers*, May 2001 and 118 *Manx Deb.*, 19 June 2001 (forthcoming).

28  *Acts of Tynwald 1990*, pp. 139–50.

29  See *Transfer of the Governor and Governor in Council Functions: A Report by the Council of Ministers*, May 1991 and 108 *Manx Deb.*, 19 June 1991, pp. 2017–23. Appendix 1 to the Report details the proposed transfer of gubernatorial functions and Appendix 2 the Governor in Council functions.

30  See 108 *Manx Deb.*, 19 June 1991, pp. 2017–23.

31  See *Acts of Tynwald 1991*, pp. 241–49.

32  See *Acts of Tynwald 1993*, pp. 121–39 and 110 *Manx Deb.*, 2 March 1993, pp. K253–88.

33  See *Second Interim Report on Future Constitutional Objectives: A Report by the Council of Ministers*, October 1993 and 111 *Manx Deb.*, 16 November 1993, pp. 125–40. Tynwald's endorsement of the Report was by 22 votes to one in the Keys and unanimously in the Legislative Council.

34  See *Report by Executive Council on the Implications of the European Community Proposals for Completing the Internal Market in 1992*, May 1990, *The European Community: Political, Economic and Monetary Union, A Report by the Council of Ministers*, April 1992, *The Treaty on European Union and the European Economic Area Agreement. A Report by the Council of Ministers*, November 1993 and *The Treaty of Amsterdam. A Report by the Council of Ministers*, March 1998.

35  Isle of Man Government, *Policy Review 1999*, vol. 1, para. 5.3.

36  See T. W. Cain, 'The Isle of Man and the European Union', 27 *MLB* (1 July 1996–31 December 1996), p. 68 and 117 *Manx Deb.*, 15 February 2000, p. T418.

37  Cain, 'The Isle of Man and the European Union', p. 73.

38  Cain, 'The Isle of Man and the European Union', p. 73.

39  See 107 *Manx Deb.*, 20 June 1990, pp. T1903–04.

40  See *Acts of Tynwald 1991*, pp. 1–5 and *Acts of Tynwald 2000*, pp. 127–28.

41  See 103 *Manx Deb.*, 26 February 1986, pp. 1284–325.

42  See 104 *Manx Deb.*, 24 March 1987, pp. T896–917. The amendment was carried by 19 votes to five in the Keys and unanimously in the Legislative Council.

43  See 104 *Manx Deb.*, 5 May 1987, pp. K421–66.

44  See 105 *Manx Deb.*, 22 March 1988, pp. K626–69.

45  See 107 *Manx Deb.*, 20 March 1990, pp. T1110–17.

46  See 108 *Manx Deb.*, 26–27 March 1991, pp. K1273–85.

47  See 108 *Manx Deb.*, 28 May 1991, pp. C413–22.

48  See 109 *Manx Deb.*, 31 March 1992, pp. K135–71.

49  See 109 *Manx Deb.*, 26 May 1992, pp. C71–77.

50  *Acts of Tynwald 1992*, pp. 183–205. The 1992 Act decriminalised such activity between consenting adults aged 21 or over; the Criminal Justice Amendment Act 2001 reduced the age of consent to 18.

51  See 110 *Manx Deb.*, 17 November 1992, p. T201.

52  See 110 *Manx Deb.*, 8 July 1993, pp. T712–18. The resolution was carried by 20 votes to three in the Keys and five votes to three in the Council.

53  See 113 *Manx Deb.*, 12 December 1995, pp. T338–53. The resolution was accepted by 17 votes to six in the Keys and eight votes to one in the Council.

54  *Acts of Tynwald 2001*, pp. 3–24.

55  *Review of Financial Regulation in the Crown Dependencies: A Report*, Cm. 4109–1 and Cm.

4109–4 (November 1998); the first of these volumes constitutes the report by Edwards, the second a professional guide to the financial sector in the Isle of Man prepared by the Island authorities in consultation with Edwards.

56  Cm. 4109, p. x, s. 10.

57  *Isle of Man Government Response to the Review of Financial Regulation in the Crown Dependencies*, March 1999.

58  See *Acts of Tynwald 2000*, pp. 27–43 and 155–94.

59  See *The Guardian*, 21 June 2000, p. 12.

60  See *First Report of the Standing Committee on Economic Initiatives 2000/2001: Double Taxation Agreements and Exchange of Information*, September 2000, pp. 1–2.

61  *First Report of the Standing Committee on Economic Initiatives 2000/2001: Double Taxation Agreements and Exchange of Information*, pp. 1–34. The Committee recommended the Government to consider addressing the exchange of information issue through a multilateral agreement or as part of a bilateral double taxation agreement and that any agreement should be subject to the approval of Tynwald; Tynwald accepted these and other recommendations on 22 November 2000; see 118 *Manx Deb.*, 22 November 2000, pp. T318–19.

62  See *European Union Code of Conduct (Business Taxation) Report*, 29 November 1999.

63  *European Union Code of Conduct (Business Taxation) Report*, pp. 177–78 and 248–49.

64  *European Union Code of Conduct (Business Taxation) Report*, pp. 177–78 and 248–49.

65  In reply to a question in the House of Lords; 611 *House of Lords Deb.*, no. 70, 5 April 2000, cols. 1295–97.

66  See *The Organisation For Economic Cooperation and Development: Harmful Tax Competition. A Report by the Council of Ministers*, November 2000, Appendix 4.

67  Early evidence of this was seen in the comments of Richard Corkill during his budget speech in 2000; 117 *Manx Deb.*, 15 February 2000, p. T416. Similar comments about the need to compromise were made by the Chief Minister in reply to a question by David Cannan on 21 March 2000; see 117 *Manx Deb.*, 21 March 2000, pp. T541–42.

68  See 117 *Manx Deb.*, 20 June 2000, pp. T792–97, Isle of Man Government, *Policy Review 2000*, vol. 1, pp. 21–26 and 118 *Manx Deb.*, 18 October 2000, pp. T73–93.

69  118 *Manx Deb.*, 18 October 2000, pp. T75–76.

70  See *The Organisation for Cooperation and Development: Harmful Tax Competition. A Report by the Council of Ministers*, November 2000 and 118 *Manx Deb.*, 12 December 2000, pp. T389–99.

71  See *Isle of Man Examiner Business News*, 13 February 2001, where the letter signed by Bruno Gibert, the Co-Chair of the Tax Forum, is printed in full.

72  The clauses relating to voting in Tynwald and the selection of board and committee chairs were accepted, but there was no time for legislation prior to the general election; see 98 *Manx Deb.*, 16 June 1981, pp. T1293–346.

73  See 99 *Manx Deb.*, 4 May 1982, pp. K470–71.

74  See 101 *Manx Deb.*, 8 November 1983, pp. K18–83, 22 November 1983, pp. K94–139, 6 December 1983, pp. K174–200, 15 June 1984, pp. C571–96 and 26 June 1984, pp. K871–76.

75  See 105 *Manx Deb.*, 29 March 1988, pp. K691–716.

76  See 107 *Manx Deb.*, 8 May 1990, pp. K1292–302 and *Report of the Select Committee on the Legislative Council*, June 1999, Appendix A, where Kneale provides in evidence to the Committee a useful summary of his attempts at reform.

77  See 110 *Manx Deb.*, 22 October 1992, pp. T148–49 and 18 November 1992, pp. T221–27.

78  *Report of the Select Committee on the Functions, and Procedure for Election, of the Legislative Council*, June 1994. In separate interviews with the author during February 2000 the members explained the lack of major recommendations on the conflict between members.

79  The initial voting was 13 to 10 in favour in the Keys and one to eight against in the Council; see 11 *Manx Deb.*, 13 July 1994, pp. T762–99 and 112 *Manx Deb.*, 15 November 1994, pp. T167–76.

80  See 114 *Manx Deb.*, 22 April 1997, pp. 118–25.

81  See *Interim Report of the Select Committee on the Legislative Council*, February 1998 and *Report of the Select Committee on the Legislative Council*, June 1999.

82  See 117 *Manx Deb.*, 26 October 1999, pp. K6–23.

83  See 117 *Manx Deb.*, 1 February 2000, pp. K306–19.

84  See 117 *Manx Deb.*, 21 March 2000, pp. T553–62.

85  See 117 *Manx Deb.*, 27 June 2000, pp. K743–50 and 118 *Manx Deb.*, 24 October and 5 December 2000 and 23 January 2001, pp. K25–34.

86  See *Isle of Man Examiner*, 18 September 1981.

87  The detail which follows is taken from the *Third Interim Report of the Select Committee on Constitutional Issues*, 11 April 1983 and Tynwald's debate on the Report, 101 *Manx Deb.*, 21 June 1983, pp. T1109–31 and 1180–201.

88  The Report was signed by Radcliffe and seven other members of the two Committees: Edgar Mann, who had also become a member of both Committees, Miles Walker and Tony Brown from the Boards' Responsibilities Committee and Charles Cain, Noel Cringle, David Moore and Eddie Kerruish from the Constitutional Issues Committee. The other members of Executive Council were Cringle, Mann, Kerruish and Walker.

89  See *Joint Report of the Select Committees on the Responsibilities of Boards of Tynwald etc. and on Constitutional Issues*, 26 January 1984.

90  See 101 *Manx Deb.*, 21 February 1984, pp. T767–82 and 784–812.

91  See *Fourth Interim Report of the Select Committee of Tynwald on Constitutional Issues*, 5 March 1984; 101 *Manx Deb.*, 28 March 1984, pp. T1204–25 and *Acts of Tynwald 1984*, pp. 565–70.

92  See 102 *Manx Deb.*, 30 October 1984, pp. K3–38 and 13 November 1984, pp. C22–53 and K216–19.

93  See 101 *Manx Deb.*, 28 March 1984, pp. T1225–28.

94  *Acts of Tynwald 1984*, pp. 513–56.

95  *Second Interim Report of the Select Committee of Tynwald on the Responsibilities of Boards of Tynwald etc.*, 30 September 1985, *Third Interim Report ...*, 22 January 1986 and *Fourth Interim Report ...*, 26 February 1986; and 103 *Manx Deb.*, 16 October 1985, pp. T119–69, 19 February 1986, pp. T1191–212 and 25 March 1986, pp. T1604–17.

96  By Section 1 of the Statute Law Revision Act 1983, *Acts of Tynwald 1983*, pp. 107–09.

97  See 103 *Manx Deb.*, 15 April 1986, pp. 1711–12.

98  See 103 *Manx Deb.*, 28 May 1986, pp. T2032–35.

99  *Acts of Tynwald 1986*, pp. 689–97.

100 See 102 *Manx Deb.*, 15 January 1985, pp. T814–31.

101 See 102 *Manx Deb.*, 16 January 1985, pp. T892–95.

102 See 102 *Manx Deb.*, 20 March 1985, pp. T1584–94.

103 *Acts of Tynwald 1986*, pp. 757–67.

104 See 102 *Manx Deb.*, 10 July 1985, pp. T2344–63.

105 *Acts of Tynwald 1987*, pp. 265–83.

106 See 104 *Manx Deb.*, 26 May 1987, p. K569. Voting on the amendment was 11 votes to 11, the clause removing Tynwald's power then being passed by 13 votes to nine.

107 *Acts of Tynwald 1987*, pp. 287–305.

108 A useful summary of the development of the departments and statutory boards together with the changes between 1988 and 1996 is to be found in K. F. W. Gumbley, 'Government Departments and Statutory Boards', 10 *MLB* (1 December 1987–31 May 1988), pp. 61–67 and 'Government Departments and Statutory Boards. An Update', 28 *MLB* (1 January 1997–30 June 1997), pp. 95–96; see also Isle of Man Office of Fair Trading Order 1998, Statutory Document No. 579/98. There are plans to establish a Waste Disposal Board with effect from 1 April 2002; see 117 *Manx Deb.*, 20 June 2000, pp. T773–74.

109 See *Aspects of the Constitution of the Isle of Man. The Position of the Governor and the Development of a Council of Ministers. A Report by Executive Council*, April 1989.

110 See 106 *Manx Deb.*, 16 May 1989, pp. T1669–724.

111 *Acts of Tynwald 1990*, pp. 139–50.

112 See 107 *Manx Deb.*, 7 and 14 November 1989, pp. K171–50 and 251–67.

113 *Acts of Tynwald 1994*, pp. 51–52.

114 The 1992 Bill was lost at the third reading with 11 votes in favour and 12 against; see 109 *Manx Deb.*, 30 June 1992, pp. K383–90. The 1994 attempt failed at the clauses stage when the central clause was defeated with only 10 votes in favour and 13 against; see 111 *Manx Deb.*, 23 January and 1 February 1994, pp. K157–72 and 193–202. The third attempt failed at the same stage and by a similar margin of 10 votes to 12; see 113 *Manx Deb.*, 30 January 1996, pp. K155–210.

115 See *Report of the Select Committee on Ministerial Government*, September 1999, Sections 7 and 9.4, and 117 *Manx Deb.*, 16 November 1999, pp. T179–200. The Council of Ministers was divided on the proposal, with Bell, Cretney, Downie, Gelling, North and Rodan in favour and Brown, Corkill, Christian and Gilbey opposed.

116 The voting on the adjournment motion was 15 to seven with the Council of Ministers once again divided, Bell, Brown, Corkill, Gelling and Gilbey in favour and Cretney, North and Rodan opposed; see 118 *Manx Deb.*, 22 May 2001 (forthcoming).

117 See 99 *Manx Deb.*, 24 November 1981, pp. 235–37.

118 See 102 *Manx Deb.*, 6 March 1985, pp. T1377–86.

119 See 104 *Manx Deb.*, 9 December 1986, pp. T204–06.

120 See 109 *Manx Deb.*, 10 December 1991, pp. T2–4.

121 See 114 *Manx Deb.*, 3 December 1996, pp. T2–5.

122 See 99 *Manx Deb.*, 24 November 1981, pp. T235–37.

123 See 99 *Manx Deb.*, 15 December 1981, p. C101 and 22 December 1981, pp. K69–74.

124 See 100 *Manx Deb.*, 14 December 1982, pp. T295–99.

125 See 102 *Manx Deb.*, 12 December 1984, pp. T689–95.

126 See 102 *Manx Deb.*, 20 March 1985, pp. T1613–14.

127 See 105 *Manx Deb.*, 20 and 27 April 1988, pp. T1280–81 and 1320–24.

128 During the debate on Cringle's 1992 attempt to reinstate Tynwald's power of approval; see 109 *Manx Deb.*, 30 June 1992, p. T388.

129 Information given by Delaney in an interview with the author on 10 February 2000 and confirmed by Walker in an interview on 4 February 2000.

130 Information given by Walker in an interview with the author on 4 February 2000.

131 See 107 *Manx Deb.*, 19 December 1989, pp. T639–43.

132 22 December 1986, p. 6.

133 *Assignment of Ministers Notice*, 29 October 1990

134 Information provided by Miles Walker in an interview with the author on 4 February 2000.

135 *Assignment of Ministers Instrument 1991*, GC 424/91, 18 December 1991.

136 *Assignment of Ministers Instrument 1992*, GC 399/92, 13 October 1992.

137 Information regarding the offer of resignation was given in an interview with the author on 11 February 2000; see also *Isle of Man Examiner*, 11 October 1994 and *Manx Independent*, 14 October 1994. For details of the particular incidents, see *Special Report of the Standing Committee of Public Accounts on the Project to build a Replica of HMS Bounty*, 16 June 1989 and 106 *Manx Deb.*, 12 July 1989, pp. T2113–57; *Special Report of the Standing Committee of Public Accounts on the Nobles Park Bowling Complex* and the debate of the Report in Tynwald, 112 *Manx Deb.*, 22 February 1995, pp. T425–36.

138 *Assignment of Ministers Instrument 1994*, GC 27/94, 11 October 1994.

139 *Assignment of Ministers Instrument 1995*, GC 8/95, 13 March 1995.

140 See 111 *Manx Deb.*, 26 April 1994, pp. K379–48.

141 See *Isle of Man Examiner*, 12 December 1995, p. 5 and 113 *Manx Deb.*, 12 December 1995, pp. T370–82.

142 *Assignment of Ministers Instrument (No. 2) 1995*, GC 43/95, 14 December 1995.

143 *Assignment of Ministers Instruments 1996 and (No. 2) 1996*, GC 32/96, 18 July 1996 and GC 34/96, 6 August 1996.

144 *Assignment of Ministers Instrument (No. 3) 1996*, GC 48/96, 6 December 1996.

145 See 116 *Manx Deb.*, 16 December 1998, pp. T345–75.

146 See 116 *Manx Deb.*, 26 January 1999, pp. K230–38.

147 See 116 *Manx Deb.*, 27 April 1999, pp. K394–96 and *Assignment of Ministers Instrument 1999*, GC 16/99, 27 April 1999.

148 Information given by Mann during an interview with the author on 3 February 2000.

149 For a discussion of the background to these two resignations, see *Manx Independent*, 30 April 1999, p. 2.

150 See 116 *Manx Deb.*, 27 April 1999, pp. K394–97.

151 See *Manx Independent*, 14 May 1999, p. 2.

152 *Assignment of Ministers Instrument 1999*, 12 May 1999, GC 20/99.

153 See 100 *Manx Deb.*, 16–17 November 1982, pp. T174–216.

154 See 104 *Manx Deb.*, 20 January 1987, pp. T356–62.

155 Walker believed that the Standing Committee meetings had ceased to be effective for the Isle of Man and that experience after disbandment had shown that ad hoc meetings involving interested parties were far more effective; in an interview with the author on 18 October 2000.

156 See 106 *Manx Deb.*, 22 February 1989, pp. T1022–47.

157 The latest version of these guidelines was issued in 1996; see Council of Ministers, *Notes for Ministers*, October 1996, Appendix 2.

158 See *Report of the Select Committee on Ministerial Government*, September 1999, pp. 17–23.

159 Such statistics do not take account of ministerial absences when crucial votes take place; see 116 *Manx Deb.*, 15 December 1998, p. T278.

160 See 99 *Manx Deb.*, 13 July 1982, pp. T1092–93.

161 See 100 *Manx Deb.*, 17 November 1982, pp. T228–38.

162 See 109 *Manx Deb.*, 23 January 1992, pp. T149–62.

163 For details of the Report and Tynwald's debate, see 110 *Manx Deb.*, 15 December 1992, pp. T278–81 and 16 March 1993, pp. T442–49.

164 See 110 *Manx Deb.*, 8 July 1993, pp. T710–18. The voting was seven to 16 against in the Keys and four to four in the Legislative Council with the President's casting vote in favour.

165 See 114 *Manx Deb.*, 19 March 1997, pp. T319–32.

166 See 116 *Manx Deb.*, 14 July 1999, pp. T1065–71.

167 See *First Report of the Standing Committee on Economic Initiatives 2000/2001: Double Taxation Agreements and Exchange of Information*, September 2000 and 118 *Manx Deb.*, 22 November 2000, pp. T318–19.

# CHAPTER NINE

# Towards a Prosperous and Caring Society 1981–2000

Politically the Island retained close ties with the UK and this was reflected in the continuing influence of UK policies in several major policy areas, notably law and order, welfare, agriculture and indirect taxation. Interestingly, however, many of the more radical policies of the Thatcher and Major Governments with their emphasis on a free market, privatisation and deregulation were either resisted or ignored, successive governments persisting with the welfare state, retaining a strong public sector and maintaining substantial programmes of public support for the private sector. The Island had the constitutional authority to pursue a different line and the successful use of that authority during the 1960s and 1970s meant that it could also afford to be different. Uninterrupted economic growth between 1983 and the turn of the century brought with it the buoyant revenues necessary to meet the demands of a steadily growing population for better public services and expensive infrastructural investment and economic policies to facilitate sustainable growth. Sustainability was possible in large part because of the Island's success as an international financial centre, a success which not only demonstrated the immense economic importance of a high level of constitutional autonomy, but also its vulnerability to any loss of autonomy that might result from allegations of unfair competition by the UK or the international community.

## *The Elections of 1981, 1986, 1991 and 1996*

The debate over electoral reform in this period centred on the search for a fairer system of electing members of the House. The outcome was changes in the method of election in 1982, 1990 and 1995, a redistribution of seats in 1985 and the introduction of a residential qualification for candidates, the abolition of election deposits and provision for proxy voting for electors in 1995. The impetus for change was for the most part provided by private members, notably Victor Kneale, although the consolidation and amendment of legislation in 1995 was the result of work by the Election Committee of the Council of Ministers.

The introduction of STV had been recommended by the Butler Commission in 1980, but the attempt to implement the recommendation in 1981 had foundered in the Keys. In 1982 Kneale introduced a private member's bill similar to that defeated in 1981 except that it did not allow plumping; electors were required to indicate both first and alternative preferences. It had a relatively easy passage through the branches[1] and became

**Figure 9.1. House of Keys Constituency Boundaries, 1985**

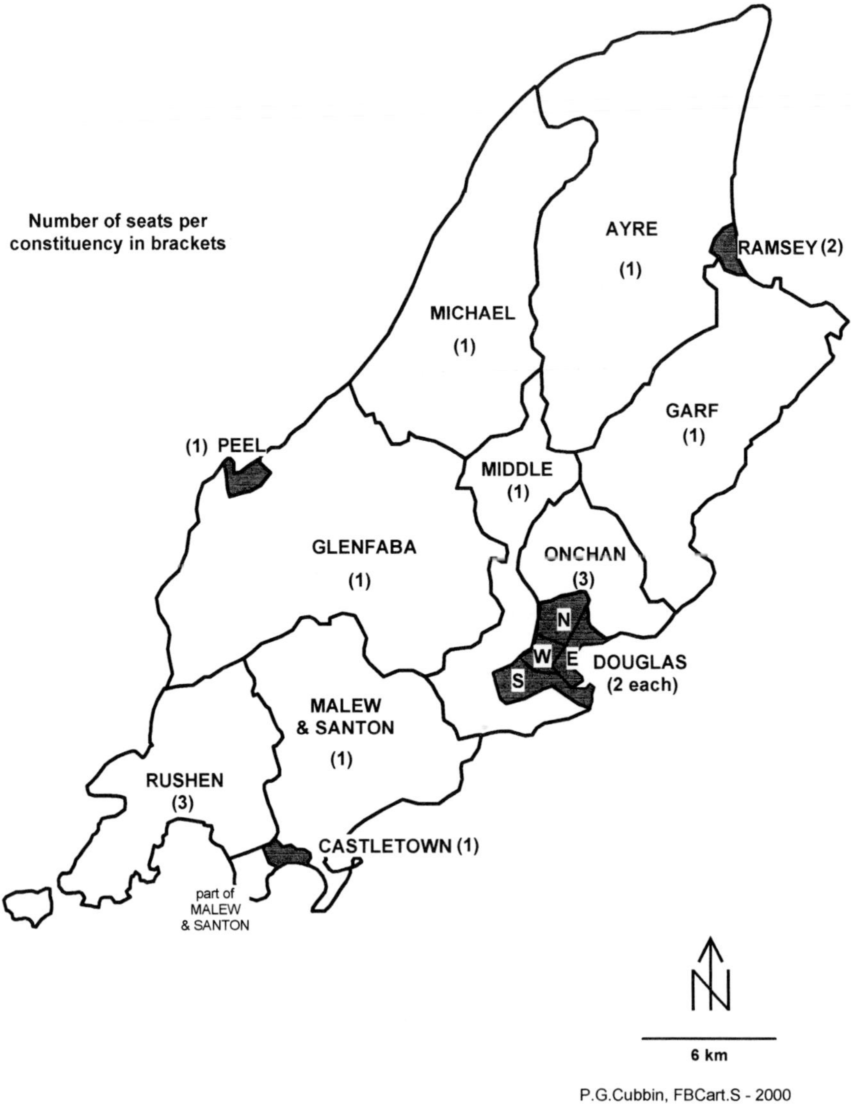

Number of seats per
constituency in brackets

AYRE
(1)

RAMSEY (2)

MICHAEL
(1)

GARF
(1)

(1) PEEL

MIDDLE
(1)

GLENFABA
(1)

ONCHAN
(3)

N
W  E
S

DOUGLAS
(2 each)

MALEW
& SANTON
(1)

RUSHEN
(3)

CASTLETOWN (1)

part of
MALEW
& SANTON

6 km

P.G.Cubbin, FBCart.S - 2000

law as the Representation of the People (Preferential Voting) Act 1982.[2] An attempt by David Cannan in 1988 to revert to the simple plurality system, in the light of experience in the general election in 1986, was narrowly defeated at third reading.[3] However, just before the second election under STV, Dominic Delaney was successful in promoting legislation to allow plumping; under the Representation of the People Act 1990 the registration of alternative preferences became optional.[4] During and after the 1991 general election STV was subject to mounting criticism. In January 1994 Tynwald approved a resolution moved by David Corlett declaring that STV was inappropriate for the Island; it was carried by 15 votes to seven in the Keys and unanimously in the

Legislative Council.[5] Corlett condemned STV as unpopular, misunderstood and mathematically complicated and sought a return to the first-past-the-post system. He achieved this goal by moving a successful amendment to the consolidation legislation being promoted by the Council of Ministers and which became law as the Representation of the People Act 1995.[6] As a result the Island returned to the inequality of voting opportunities associated with the mixture of single, two- and three-member constituencies, with each voter having as many votes as there were seats in the constituency.

While the legislation providing for STV was still under discussion, Kneale introduced another private member's bill to provide for a redistribution of seats and 12 two-member constituencies, a slightly modified version of one of the Butler Commission proposals. Kneale aimed to combine roughly equal numbers of electors per seat and equality of voting rights. The Bill received a second reading in April 1982 and was referred to a select committee,[7] whereupon progress was delayed by the Committee's recommendation to incorporate redistribution into a much more radical measure providing for the direct election of Tynwald. When that reform was rejected by the Legislative Council in June 1994, Kneale returned to separate legislation for the Keys, but with modifications to the 1982 scheme to take account of criticisms of its unnecessary departures from traditional constituencies. The Bill had a smooth passage through the branches and the result was the Representation of the People Act 1985, providing for rough equality of voters per seat, but not the equality of voting rights aimed for in 1982.[8] The new distribution between eight single, five two- and two three-member constituencies is shown in Figure 9.1.[9]

Over the next 15 years other attempts to deliver equality of voting rights by means of 24 single member constituencies foundered on the rocks of tradition. Cannan's attempt in 1987/88 to abolish STV included such provision, but fell at third reading. Dominic Delaney tried in 1989/90, but the clause providing for single member constituencies was decisively rejected.[10] When the Election Committee of the Council of Ministers, chaired by Speaker Cain, recommended this reform in Tynwald in 1993, it was rejected by both branches.[11] A further attempt by Cannan was defeated in March 1994, as too was an amendment by Edgar Mann to the Representation of the People Bill in January 1995.[12] Immediately following Mann's failure and the subsequent success of Corlett in removing all reference to STV from the Bill, Hazel Hannan made two attempts to have standing orders suspended to allow the House to reconsider its position on constituencies in the light of the decision on the voting system; both failed to obtain the necessary two thirds majority.[13] A firm believer in equality of voting rights, Hannan then made two attempts to achieve this by restricting voters in the Island's multimember constituencies to a single vote. However, such was the strength of feeling in those constituencies that in March 1996 Hannan was even refused leave to introduce a private member's bill for the purpose—all but two of the 12 objectors represented two- or three-member constituencies.[14] After the general election in 1996, she was given leave to introduce a bill but it met with an overwhelming defeat at second reading by 18 votes to five—apart from Hannan, only four MHKs were prepared to support the implementation of the principle of one person one vote, Cannan and Brown, two other representatives of single member constituencies, and Cretney and Karran, the two MLP members of the House.[15]

Recession and rising unemployment provided the economic setting for the 1981 general election. Constitutionally the main issue was how best to secure maximum control over the Island's internal affairs. While a few candidates, including three nationalists, advocated full independence and some pointed to areas such as judicial corporal punishment, broadcasting, fishing rights and indirect taxation where Manx autonomy needed strengthening, most talked rather vaguely of their support for internal self-government. Other constitutional issues attracted little attention. A handful of reformers, including Noel Cringle and Sir Charles Kerruish, pressed the case for a stronger Executive Council and a streamlined board system and others, notably Victor Kneale, argued for the direct election of the Legislative Council, but the election campaign gave little inkling of the major constitutional debates that were to dominate the next term of Tynwald. Electoral reform was also a minority interest, only the MLP, Mec Vannin and a few Independents, notably Jim Cain, Dominic Delaney and Miles Walker, pressing for action to implement the recommendations of the Butler Commission. The structures, functions and funding of local government also attracted the attention of reformers, with calls by the MLP and others for fewer stronger local authorities and demands, especially from the Douglas constituencies, for the abolition of the domestic rate or the equalisation of the rate burden across local authorities; these proposals provoked strong defensive reactions from the rural constituencies in support of the status quo.

There was general support for the retention and selective strengthening of the welfare state and relatively little conflict even over details. The outstanding welfare issue was unemployment, which had risen steadily from 2.3 per cent in October 1979 to 5.7 per cent on the eve of the election. No serious candidate could afford to ignore the issue and there were widespread demands for special public works schemes, extended training opportunities, increased investment in housing, tourism and industry and tighter work permit controls. The three MLP candidates also campaigned for legislation to provide for redundancy payments, protection against unfair dismissal and the abolition of sexual discrimination at work. Gainful employment was also seen by the MLP as a prerequisite for law and order, one of the central issues of the campaign. For most, however, law and order was primarily a matter of additional resources for the police service and taking the necessary steps to restore the Island's right to use the birch as a deterrent and punishment for crimes of violence.

The major sources of conflict were aspects of economic policy. While there was a consensus in favour of low direct taxation, candidates were divided over whether to retain, amend or abrogate the Customs and Excise Agreement. While there was acceptance of the need for value for money investment in agriculture, fishing, tourism and light industry and the further encouragement of the financial sector, there were major differences of opinion over the high levels of spending approved by Tynwald on capital projects such as the Sulby Reservoir and the Douglas Breakwater. There was recognition of the value of new residents to the economy, but a minority were convinced of the need to limit new immigration to safeguard the Manx environment, culture and heritage.

There were 54 candidates in the 1981 election and contests in each of the 13 constituencies. There were three MLP candidates, two MNP, one Mec Vannin and 48 Independents, one of whom was Independent Labour. Twenty retiring members and two former members sought re-election; 17 were successful including the MLP candidates, Kneale and 13 other Independents. Of the five MHK members of the Executive Council, Creer did not seek re-election, Irving was defeated in West Douglas, Anderson and Mann topped the polls in Glenfaba and Garff respectively and Cringle came a comfortable third to hold his seat in Rushen. The defeat of Irving, the 67-year-old chair of Executive Council and the Tourist Board, was the result of an unwise decision to switch from the constituency of East Douglas which he had represented since 1966 to that of West Douglas which he had represented between 1956 and 1962, the competition in West Douglas and his independent stand in support of the abolition of corporal punishment. The five-way contest was won by Kneale, the former MHK who had topped the poll in West Douglas so convincingly in 1966 and 1971 and had been nursing the constituency over a period of two years in preparation for a return to the Keys. Betty Hanson, a popular sitting member and the outgoing chair of the Board of Education, pushed Irving into third place.

The election was dominated by Independents. Neither the MLP nor the two nationalist organisations had the capacity or commitment to field anything approaching an Island-wide slate of candidates. The MLP with three candidates in North Douglas, South Douglas and Rushen contested fewer seats than at any election since 1918. The divided nationalist movement also fought three seats, the MNP in North Douglas and South Douglas and Mec Vannin in Peel, a far cry from the 10 candidates fielded by the undivided movement in 1976. As in 1976 the contrast in the performance of the MLP and the nationalists was very marked. The MLP held the three seats they contested, Quinney and Ward successful in seeing off the MNP challenge in Douglas and Lowey topping the poll in Rushen. The nationalists, including sitting MNP member, Peter Craine, were defeated, bringing to an end attempts to achieve nationalist goals by electoral means, at least for the rest of the twentieth century. Between 1981 and 1986 the MLP remained an influential minority grouping in Tynwald, its fortunes and personnel changing as a result of elevations to the Legislative Council and the death in 1985 of Arthur Quinney. On the elevation of Eddie Lowey to the Legislative Council, the Party lost its Rushen seat in December 1982 to a former Mec Vannin member, Charles H. Faragher. On Quinney's death, Bernard May, a 43-year-old taxi driver, retained the North Douglas seat for the Party in March 1985. The following month the MLP won two further by-elections caused by elevations to the Legislative Council, Peter Karran, a 24-year-old youth worker, replacing Independent, Arnold Callin, in Middle and David Cretney, a 31-year-old shop manager, taking over from Matty Ward in South Douglas.

With seven new members and the re-election of Kneale, the percentage turnover resulting from the general election was modest by comparison with 1976. However, within four years a combination of seven elevations to the Legislative Council, three deaths and one resignation paved the way for the election of a further 10 new members and the re-election of Clifford Irving. Once again there were opportunities for relatively inexperienced members to achieve high executive office quickly. Two of the 1981 intake and three of the subsequent by-election winners joined the Executive Council within five years of their initial election; two other by-election winners became members of the Council of Ministers after a much longer political apprenticeship. The two elected in 1981 were Tony Brown, a 31-year-old electrical contractor, who won nearly 65 per cent of the vote in Castletown, and Donald Maddrell, a 62-year-old engineering executive who came a close second to Callin in a nine-way contest in Middle. Both joined the Walker administration at its inception in 1986. The by-election victors were David Cannan, a 46-year-old businessman who won the Michael seat in November 1982 following the death of John J. Radcliffe, Walter Gilbey, a 47-year-old merchant banker who won a seat in Glenfaba in November 1982 on Anderson's elevation to the Legislative Council, Allan Bell, a 37-year-old retailer and former Mec Vannin member

Left: David Cannan, MHK for Michael and Treasury Minister 1986–89, December 1987. Cannan followed in the footsteps of his grandfather by becoming MHK for Michael in 1982. Four years later he was appointed by Walker for a three-year term as the Island's first Treasury Minister. He was not reappointed in 1989 and returned to the backbenches until April 2000 when he succeeded Noel Cringle as Speaker of the House.

Right: Richard Corkill, MHK for Onchan and Home Affairs Minister 1993–96, September 1996. First elected to the Keys in 1991, Corkill was quickly rewarded with high office, becoming Minister for Home Affairs under Walker in 1993 and succeeding Gelling as Treasury Minister after the general election in 1996. In the background to the portrait are the old Government Office and the church now used as offices by the Royal Skandia Life Assurance Company.

who won a seat in Ramsey in November 1984 after the resignation of Hugo Teare, Bernard May in March 1985 and David Cretney in April 1985. Cannan and Bell joined the first Walker administration in 1986 and May followed in 1988; Cretney became a member of the Gelling team in 1996 and Gilbey in 1999.

Even though the chairs of the Executive Council between 1981 and 1986 were MLCs, who owed their position to Tynwald rather than the electorate, the strong relationship between elections and policy continued. Tynwald supported policies aimed at maximising internal self-government. The leading advocates of constitutional reform were successful in persuading colleagues to accept a strengthening of the Executive Council and a streamlining of the board system, but not in progressing towards a full ministerial system before the 1986 election. The case for the direct election of the Legislative Council or the whole of Tynwald was vetoed by the Legislative Council. Electoral reform was agreed with legislation providing for STV in 1982 and a redistribution of seats in 1985. Local government was the subject of investigations by select committees of Tynwald on domestic rating and the structure of local government, but very little was achieved by the supporters of reform. Despite a decision of Tynwald in 1980 in favour of the abolition of the domestic rate, the economic circumstances of the early 1980s effectively precluded implementation. The only positive outcome of the debate on local government structure was the Onchan District Act 1986, providing for

Left: Victor Kneale, SHK 1990–91. Kneale became Speaker towards the end of a political career that began with election to the Education Authority in 1951. He was a member of Tynwald 1962–91 and the Executive Council 1970–74 and 1982–90, and is best remembered as a committed constitutional and educational reformer, serving on several constitutional committees, chairing the Board of Education 1962–72 and 1981–86 and going on to become the Island's first Minister of Education 1986–90. He retired from politics in 1991.

Right: James C. Cain, SHK 1991–96. When Cain entered the Keys in 1986, he was following the example of two grandfathers, Richard Cain and Arthur Crookall, his father, James, and his uncle, Harold. After serving as Minister for Health and Social Security from 1989 until 1991, he succeeded Kneale as Speaker, a position he held until his defeat in the general election in 1996.

the amalgamation of Onchan Parish and Onchan Village District, a measure promoted by the two authorities concerned.[16] It reduced the number of local authorities from 26 to 25, Douglas and three other towns, five village districts, including Onchan, and 16 parishes.

Policy objectives for the five-year term were accepted in November 1982, the commitments to constitutional autonomy, increased governmental efficiency and the use of resources to increase employment, the standard of living and the quality of life reflecting the electoral consensus on these 'apple pie' issues. The capacity of government to deliver improved services and better support for the economy was constrained by the recession. The needs of those on low incomes and employment-generating investment were prioritised. While mainstream social security benefits were upgraded in line with the UK, selected supplementary benefits were raised above UK levels to help those in greatest need. There were no real increases in the funding of the education and health services until 1985/86, when both also benefitted from new capital investment. In the case of education, Tynwald's commitment in 1983 to raise the school leaving age to 16 with effect from September 1985 provided the rationale for most of the new spending. Investment in new public sector housing was stopped and funds for house purchase and improvement reduced and targeted towards the lower income groups. Electoral demands to address year-round unemployment and its rise from 5.8 per cent in

November 1981 to a high of 9.1 per cent in January 1986 kept the problem high on the political agenda. Budgets targeted low income groups by increasing tax allowances, prioritising work creation and training schemes, enhancing unemployment benefit and investing in tourism and other industries capable of generating employment. In parallel, new measures were introduced to stimulate further the growth of the financial sector. The MLP was no longer alone in seeking modern employment legislation. Although no progress was made with legislation to outlaw sex discrimination in employment, two important government measures were passed, the Trade Disputes Act 1985 and the Employment Act 1986, and a third to provide for redundancy payments narrowly defeated in the Keys in May 1986.

The law and order services were prioritised for growth during the recession with increases in police establishment and new capital investment in the prison service. In October 1982 Tynwald reiterated its commitment to judicial corporal punishment as an integral component of Manx law, but without any real prospect of implemention by a judiciary bound by the 1978 decision of the European Court of Human Rights. The issue of immigration was investigated by a committee of Tynwald and its report in favour of continuing to attract new economically active residents accepted. Critics of the CEA made every effort to have the Agreement modified or terminated, but without success in the face of UK opposition to a reduction in VAT on nonexportable services and the advice of the Select Committee on the Common Purse not to seek any other change in the prevailing economic circumstances and certainly not before the 1986 election.

By the time the election took place in November 1986, economic recovery was well under way and, although unemployment remained high at 8.1 per cent, the general economic outlook was healthy. With major reforms in place or due to be implemented after the election, there was a virtual moratorium on constitutional debate. A few candidates continued to press for greater autonomy, Kneale renewed his campaign for a directly elected Tynwald and Cannan promised to introduce legislation to abolish STV. The unresolved issues of local government structure and finance received another airing with similar divisions to those expressed during the 1981 election.

There were calls for more effective strategic planning in government. As in previous elections there was a consensus in support of the welfare state and no hint of any Thatcherite challenge to the principles which had sustained it since the 1940s. There was particularly strong support for a better deal for the elderly through higher pensions, sheltered accommodation and improved health care facilities, for a higher priority to be accorded to education, health and housing after the lean years of recession and for the provision of all-weather sports facilities. As in 1981, most candidates promised to fight unemployment, advocating both short-term relief measures and policies for sustainable long-term employment. Long-standing MLP policies in support of legislation for redundancy payments and better protection against unfair dismissal attracted widespread support and a small number of candidates advocated a guaranteed minimum wage. Law and order as an issue loomed larger than at any previous election, with demands for community policing, tougher penalties and extra police and equipment. Few candidates raised the question of homosexual law reform, although when asked for their views all but a handful were opposed to decriminalisation.

Candidates were agreed on the importance of investing in the diversification and growth of the Manx economy. Pledges were made to try and ensure that agricultural support was kept in line with the UK, to press the UK for the promised extension of Manx territorial waters, to promote the more effective planning of investment in the tourist industry, with heritage as a particular focus, to support enhanced incentives for new and existing industry and, in the aftermath of the 1982 collapse of the Savings and Investment Bank (SIB), to prioritise the rigorous regulation of the rapidly growing financial sector. There was almost no reference to earlier concerns about immigration, although many qualified their support for economic growth by reference to the need to safeguard the environment. Several candidates protested against the continued operation of the British Nuclear Fuels plant at Sellafield in Cumbria, while others demanded assurances from the UK that all radioactive discharges from the plant into the Irish Sea would be stopped. Eve-of-election reports by Tynwald's Select Committee on the Common Purse and the Manx Consultancy Group on behalf of the Isle of Man Chamber of Commerce made the CEA a central issue in the election, with candidates evenly divided between those advocating further analysis, retention or abrogation. A decline in the quality of shipping services to and from the Island following the 1985 merger of the Isle of Man Steam Packet Company and Sealink (Isle of Man) Ltd opened up a serious debate over the role of government in this area. Sir Charles Kerruish was pre-eminent among a small number to advocate public ownership; others pressed for public ownership of the linkspans used by shipping and the negotiation of user agreements to achieve control over the standard of services provided by the private sector. Surprisingly perhaps, given the privatisation policies of the Thatcher Government in the UK, there were no demands for pruning the Manx public sector.

The 1986 election was the first to be held using STV and the 1985 distribution of seats into 15 constituencies. There were 74 candidates and contests in 14 of the 15 constituencies, Walter Gilbey being returned unopposed in the new single seat constituency of Glenfaba. There were 63 Independents and 11 party candidates, six representing the MLP and five the newly established Manx Democratic Party (MDP). The MLP defended three seats in the 'Greater Douglas' area and sought to reestablish itself in Peel and Rushen. The common part of the six candidates' manifestos was not noticeably different from those of the more progressive Independents, but they were distinctive in their emphasis on employment and housing issues and their support for the CEA. The MDP contested seats in Ayre, Douglas East, Onchan, Ramsey and Rushen on a joint manifesto critical of the lack of unity in government and promising to operate as a disciplined team if elected; in other respects the manifesto was not particularly distinctive, save for commitment to a guaranteed minimum wage and abrogation of the CEA. Eighteen retiring members and three former members sought re-election, including three of the four MHK members of the Executive Council, Noel Cringle, Victor Kneale and Miles Walker, and one MLC member, Edgar Mann, who resigned from the Legislative Council to seek re-election to the House. Treasury leader, David Moore, did not seek re-election. Thirteen of the retiring members were successful, but only Kneale and Walker from the Executive Council. Mann, who was expected to continue as chair of the Executive Council if elected, was defeated by Sir Charles Kerruish in Garff. Under the 1985 redistribution, Garff was now a single member constituency and one of the two eminent politicians contesting the constituency was certain to fail. Cringle, the outgoing chair of the Home Affairs Board, was squeezed into fourth place in an 11-sided contest in Rushen. The 11 new MHKs included five future members of the Executive Council/Council of Ministers. Donald Gelling, a 48-year-old general manager of an agricultural and industrial machinery retail outlet, was successful in the new constituency of Malew and Santon and joined the Walker cabinet in 1988; Jim Cain, a 59-year-old chartered accountant, topped the poll in Douglas West and became a member in 1989; John Corrin, a 52-year-old retired trade union official, who came third in Rushen, and Hazel Hannan, a 42-year-old state registered nurse and former member of Mec Vannin, who won a nine-way contest in Peel, joined Walker's second administration in 1991; Edgar Quine, a 52-year-old retired police officer who defeated the sitting candidate, Clare Christian, in Ayre, became a member of Gelling's team in 1996.

The fate of the two political parties contrasted sharply. The MLP won three of the six seats it contested, the three retiring members, Cretney, May and Karran winning comfortably in the two Douglas seats and the new three-member constituency of Onchan. It remained a party of the 'Greater Douglas' area. The MDP candidates suffered the most convincing of defeats, although it is worth noting that Richard C. Leventhorpe, a 59-year-old director of several agricultural businesses who resigned as leader of the Party to contest the election as an Independent, was successful in Onchan. The Party quickly disappeared from the Manx political scene.

What was the impact of the new electoral system on the results? STV certainly provided a fairer system. Each voter had a single transferable vote regardless of the number of seats in the constituency. Where candidates attracted fewer first preference votes than the quota they were only elected if supported by voters' alternative

The Chief Minister, Miles Walker, with the Executive Council, December 1986. A member of Executive Council 1982–86 and Chief Minister 1986–96, Miles Walker was the fourth farmer to become chair of Executive Council since 1962. The members on the front row, from left to right, are Ian Anderson (Industry), Miles Walker (Chief Minister), Allan Bell (Tourism and Transport) and Victor Kneale (Education); those on the back row are Eddie Lowey (Home Affairs), Don Maddrell (Agriculture, Fisheries and Forestry), Arnold Callin (Highways, Ports and Properties), Tony Brown (Health and Social Security), Dominic Delaney (Local Government and the Environment) and David Cannan (Treasury).

preferences. One candidate was elected unopposed and 12 others achieved the necessary quota of first preference votes to be declared elected after the first count. Of the remaining 11, four were elected after a second count, one after a third, two after a fifth, two after a seventh and two after an eighth count. Interestingly, in every case, the one, two or three candidates with the most first preference votes were elected, leading some critics to argue that the results would have been identical under the old system. While that may have been true of the eight single member constituencies, it is impossible to be sure in the case of the seven constituencies where the electorate would have had two or three votes.

The turnover of membership in the House during the 1980s continued apace. With seven new MHKs in 1981, 11 between 1981 and 1986 and a further 11 in 1986, only Miles Walker and Dominic Delaney, first elected in 1976, had been members for more than five years. The new term brought considerably fewer changes with only three by-elections. Ronald Cretney, a 64-year-old retired headmaster, won a seat in Onchan in April 1988 following the elevation of Donald Maddrell to the Legislative Council; David North, a 46-year-old businessman, won in Middle in June 1988 after the elevation of Brian Barton, and Edgar Mann was returned to the House in September 1990 as the member for Garff following the election of the Speaker as President of Tynwald. Each of the three subsequently became members of the Executive Council/Council of Ministers, North following Walker's reshuffle in December 1989, Cretney as Minister of Education following Kneale's election as Speaker in 1990 and Mann returning to government as Gelling's Minister of Education in 1996.

After the general election, progress towards Island self-government was uneven. The establishment of a full ministerial system in 1988 and the Council of Ministers in 1990, the replacement of the Lieutenant-Governor as President of Tynwald in 1990 and the further transfer of gubernatorial powers in 1991 each accorded with Tynwald's declared goal, but the belated and conditional extension of Manx territorial waters in 1991 and the controversy over the law on homosexuality were important reminders of the UK's continuing responsibility for the Island. Private members' initiatives for the direct election of the Legislative Council or Tynwald were unsuccessful, as too were moves for the abolition of STV and the introduction of 24 single-member constituencies. With the disbandment of the Select Committee on the Structure of Local Government in January 1987, the responsibility for initiating local government reform passed from Tynwald to the Executive Council; DOLGE embarked on a review of structures, functions and finance, but no proposals were made until after the 1991 election. In the meantime, a second voluntary initiative by two local authorities had the effect of reducing the number of local authorities to 24 and the number of parishes to 15, the Michael District Act 1989 providing for the amalgamation of Michael Parish and Michael Village District.[17]

Chief Minister Walker responded to demands for more effective policy planning by initiating an annual series of policy reports. The first of these, *The Development of a Prosperous and Caring Society* (October 1987) and the four that followed reflected electoral support for a strong welfare state and public investment in economic growth. Moreover, successive budgets demonstrated that the Island now had both the commitment and the capacity to deliver additional social security benefits for those on low incomes, enhanced budgets for the welfare services and new investment in the Manx economy. The overall burden of direct taxation was reduced by the introduction of a new standard rate of 15 per cent in 1988 and successive increases in tax allowances. Where the Island had discretion outside of the reciprocal agreements with the UK, it was used to provide higher benefits for those in need. Capital spending on hospitals, education, housing and public health were prioritised after a period of low investment. Education, training and public works investment were simultaneously targeted at the problem of unemployment, which fell rapidly from 8.1 per cent in November 1986 to 1.8 per cent in November 1989 before rising again to 3.8 per cent in November 1991. Employment law was radically reformed with the passing of the Redundancy Payments Act 1990, the Employment Act 1991 and the Trade Unions Act 1991. Expenditure on law and order was increased in real terms by 41 per cent over the five-year term, with particular attention being given to the drugs problem through education, social service, policing and legislation to combat dealing.

Additional subsidies and assistance were provided for the depressed agricultural and fishing industries, albeit within the constraints imposed by the EC. Tourism benefitted from new investment in infrastructure, accommodation, amenities, transport and marketing, as well as from the new focus on all-weather leisure facilities for both residents and tourists. The Island continued to offer an extremely competitive package of incentives for new and existing industry. While the growth of the financial sector was still encouraged, the Government responded to electoral and business concerns with measures to provide for the regulation of the industry to UK and international standards. Although the CEA was unchanged, attempts were made to negotiate special VAT treatment for tourist accommodation. Candidates' concerns over the Island's vulnerability to any deterioration in the quality of shipping services led to prolonged investigations and acceptance by Tynwald in June 1991 of the principle of public ownership of the linkspans in Douglas Harbour and an exclusive user agreement as a means of guaranteeing the quality of shipping services. Electoral disquiet about the adverse consequences of economic growth were reflected in policies on immigration and environmental protection. Proposals for governmental reserve powers to introduce residence controls were approved by Tynwald in July 1989, although legislation was not passed before the general election. Environmental protection became a prime consideration in policy making, planning policy seeking to balance the needs of development with those of conservation, the Government's capital investment programme prioritising environmental health and the concerns over Sellafield being raised with the UK at successive intergovernmental meetings.

The background to the 1991 election was a healthy economy, a slight rise in unemployment as the Island felt the impact of a downturn in the UK economy and warnings from Treasury Minister Gelling about the need to avoid profligate spending and prioritise projects capable of generating the growth required to fund social improvements. During the election campaign most candidates seemed satisfied with the constitutional status quo; minorities called for reforms of the ministerial system to increase the accountability of the Chief Minister and the Council of Ministers to Tynwald, more open government, the restoration of the first-past-the-post electoral system, the rationalisation of the Island's antiquated local government structure and the equalisation of domestic rates. As in previous postwar elections there was a consensus in support of 'the caring society'. There were demands for enhanced social security benefits for pensioners, including the upgrading of pensions in line with average earnings, concessionary travel and a cost-of-living supplement. Candidates wanted quality welfare services and gave particular attention to preschool and postschool education, community health centres and the redevelopment of Noble's Hospital, housing for the elderly and first-time buyers, and leisure and recreation facilities. With low unemployment and new employment legislation on the statute book, little reference was made to employment issues; a few pressed for legislation prohibiting sex discrimination in employment and providing for a statutory minimum wage. Law and order was a central issue, candidates variously advocating more emphasis on education and the prevention of crime, community policing, increased manpower especially in the drugs squad and tougher penalties. The big new law and order issue for 1991 was the proposed decriminalisation of homosexual practice in private between consenting adults, with a clear majority promising to oppose forthcoming legislation. A few candidates pressed for the legalisation of abortion on health grounds.

There was general agreement with government economic policy, including the maintenance of support for the agricultural and fishing industries, value-for-money investment in tourism and Manx heritage, the attraction and retention of high value-added industries and the imperative of high standards of regulation in the financial sector. Set against this general support, there was some criticism of the high level of capital spending, the lack of progress in renegotiating the CEA and undue dependence on the financial sector. Notwithstanding the wave of privatisations in the UK during the 1980s, only two candidates suggested that the Island should follow suit. A few candidates pressed for the introduction of the promised legislation to control immigration through residence controls. Environmental protection was prioritised by several candidates, who variously argued for policies to promote a healthy environment, clean air, the use of renewable sources of energy, an integrated public transport system and the closure of Sellafield. Opinion was divided over the Government's two expensive environmental health projects; a clear majority favoured the Island-wide sewage disposal scheme, the Integration and Recycling of the Island's Sewage (IRIS); however, candidates were far less sure about the proposed incineration of refuse, alternative schemes involving landfill and recycling attracting as much support as the incinerator.

There were 73 candidates in the 1991 election and contests in 13 of the 15 constituencies, Tony Brown and Edgar Quine being unopposed in Castletown and Ayre respectively. There were 68 Independents and five party candidates. The three sitting MLP members defended their seats in Douglas and Onchan on manifestos that were scarcely distinguishable from those of progressive Independents. The Manx Green Party fielded two candidates, in Douglas North and Rushen, and campaigned on a distinctively 'green' manifesto, pressing for community to be at the heart of policies on welfare and for environmental considerations to inform all economic policy. Twenty retiring and four former members sought re-election, including seven of the eight MHK members of the Council of Ministers, Bell, Brown, Cain, Gelling, May, North and Walker; only Ronald Cretney did not seek re-election.

Eighteen retiring members and one former member, Noel Cringle, were successful. All but three were Independents. Each of the ministers was returned, Brown unopposed, Gelling and North comfortable winners in their single-member constituencies and Bell, Cain, May and Walker topping the poll in their respective two- or three-member constituencies. The MLP candidates, Cretney, Karran and May were also returned at the top of the polls in Douglas South, Onchan and Douglas North respectively. By contrast the Green Party candidates both lost their deposits. There were five new faces, including three who have since served on the Council of Ministers. Richard Corkill, a 40-year-old pharmacist, was successful in Onchan and joined the Council of Ministers in 1995; Terry Groves, a 45-year-old estate agent and businessman, won a seat in Ramsey and became a member of the Council of Ministers in 1994; Alex Downie, a 46-year-old businessman, gained a seat in Douglas West and joined Gelling's team in 1999. As in 1986 the successful candidates in the 13 contested constituencies were those with the most first preference votes, 10 achieving the quota necessary to be declared elected on the first count, three after a second count, one after a third, four after a fourth, two after a fifth, one after a sixth and one after a tenth count. Following the election Jim Cain was elected by the House to succeed Kneale as Speaker.

The 25 per cent turnover of membership of the House was the lowest since 1971. Moreover, as with the preceding five years, the number of by-elections between 1991 and 1996 was low. There were four, the last elections to be held under the STV system and each was won by an Independent. One of these, Stephen Rodan, a 41-year-old chemist, was elected in May 1995 as the representative for Garff in succession to Edgar Mann on his second elevation to the Legislative Council; four years later, in April 1999, he also succeeded Mann as Minister of Education in the Gelling cabinet.

The second Walker administration saw further progress towards Island self-government with the transfer of gubernatorial powers in 1992 and 1993, but considerable resentment over being virtually forced to decriminalise homosexual activity in private between consenting adults. It also saw unsuccessful attempts to instigate a review of the ministerial system, to make the Chief Minister's selection of ministers subject to the approval of Tynwald and to reform the Legislative Council. However, some progress was made towards more open and accountable government with the publication in July 1993 of a Council of Ministers directive for the 'reasonable' discharge of information to members of Tynwald and an enhancement of the role of Tynwald's Public Accounts Committee. Local government reform was the subject of extensive consultations with interested parties and a series of DOLGE reports proposing fewer local authorities with additional functions, but the final report was merely received by Tynwald in June 1994 and no programme of reform agreed.[18]

Most of the other issues raised in the election were reflected in the increasingly detailed annual policy reports, which restated the overall goal laid down in *The Development of a Prosperous and Caring Society* of October 1987. The 'caring' approach adopted in successive budgets provided for a sharing of the fruits of economic growth, with real increases in income tax allowances, more generous social security benefits than in the UK, a range of special provisions for persons on low incomes, higher levels of revenue and capital spending on all branches of education, hospitals and community health centres, public sector housing and support for first-time buyers, environmental health schemes, notably the multimillion pound IRIS, and the relief of unemployment. The Government promised to introduce an Employment (Sex Discrimination) Bill in the next Tynwald. Law and order received the high priority demanded during the election. Tougher penalties were provided by the Criminal Justice (Penalties etc.) Act 1993, the Custody Act 1995 and the Drug Trafficking Act 1996; in July 1994 Tynwald approved a major Home Affairs report on drug abuse; in January 1995, it appointed a select committee to examine law and order issues; the following July it approved a Home Affairs report on policing and in July 1996 it agreed to adopt all 31 recommendations of the Select Committee on Law and Order.[19] In a slightly different vein the Sexual Offences Act 1992 decriminalised homosexual practice in private between consenting adults and the Termination of Pregnancy (Medical Defences) Act 1995 legalised abortion.[20]

Public investment in the economy remained a government priority. Every industry benefitted directly or indirectly, agriculture and fishing from similar levels of support to the UK, tourism from the lowering of VAT on holiday accommodation and the funding, on an unprecedented scale, of events, amenities and improvements to accommodation, light industry from increased grant aid, the financial sector from a series of legislative measures designed to enhance its competitiveness, and the commercial public sector from continuing commitment and funding. Although legislation to provide reserve powers to control the influx of new residents was initially promised for introduction during 1995/96, consultations with the Home Office over the relationship between what was being proposed and general immigration law precluded progress prior to the 1996 general election.

The final general election of the twentieth century in November 1996 took place against a backdrop of unprecedented economic health; real national income and Treasury receipts were at record levels, the rate of economic growth was six per cent and both inflation and unemployment below three per cent. Moreover, prospects were generally regarded as good and the election campaign reflected this. Constitutional autonomy was seen as the source of economic prosperity and there was general support for the maximisation of control over domestic matters. There was support for the ministerial system, but continuing demands by a minority, including APG candidates, for the appointment of ministers to be subject to the approval of Tynwald and for better means of holding government accountable to Tynwald. A handful of candidates used the accountability argument to justify the democratisation of the Legislative Council. Few candidates mourned the demise of STV in 1995 and electoral reform as a campaign issue virtually disappeared. Local government reform was very much a live issue, with opinion divided over proposals for the amalgamation of urban and rural constituencies.

The postwar consensus in support of a strong welfare state was very much in evidence. Candidates pressed for the upgrading of old age pensions in line with average earnings, increases in supplementary benefits, improved facilities for the elderly and extra investment in education at all levels, the health service, housing and employment. The one welfare issue which split candidates was the DHSS proposal for the much needed new hospital to be built on a greenfield site with funding out of the Manx National Insurance Fund; ministers were the leading supporters and APG members the most vociferous opponents. Employment attracted very little attention, although a few argued for a statutory minimum wage. Environmental health projects, for refuse and sewage disposal, were the source of similar conflict and environmental issues generally received more coverage than at any previous election, with demands for sustainable energy policies, clean air, protection of the green belt and inner-city regeneration, the encouragement of public transport and the closure of Sellafield. Candidates wanted a high priority to be given to law and order and variously advocated crime prevention, community policing and increases in police establishment. In stark contrast to elections at the start of the century there was almost no reference to licensing and the associated question of Sunday opening.

The economic policy debate saw the usual mixture of consensus and conflict. There was general support for public investment in Manx industries, but some criticism of wasteful spending. There was almost universal backing for low taxation, but division over the CEA with the APG in particular seeking a full inquiry into the Agreement. Many welcomed the recently negotiated user agreement with the Steam Packet Company, but the APG advocated the alternative of franchising as a means of securing public control over service standards. While there were renewed demands for reserve powers should they be needed to control the influx of new residents, a minority wanted the immediate implementation of such controls. Even after 17 years of privatisation activity in the UK, there was no electoral challenge to the retention of a strong public sector and specific regret by the APG that there should have been an attempt by the Council of Ministers to privatise Manx Radio.

The 1996 election marked a return to the first-past-the-post electoral system and unequal voting rights; thus, of the 52,802 registered electors, 34.4 per cent in the eight single-member constituencies had a single vote, 41.4 per cent in the five two-member constituencies had two votes and 24.2 per cent in the two three-member constituencies had three votes. There were 52 candidates and contests in 14 out of the 15 constituencies, Donald Gelling being elected unopposed in Malew and Santon. These included 48 Independents and four MLP candidates. Six of the Independents pledged to support the 'alternative' policies of the APG, in particular the redress of the imbalance between the Council of Ministers and Tynwald following the development of the ministerial system. Four were seeking re-election, David Cannan in Michael, Adrian Duggan in Douglas South, the Group's leader, Edgar Quine, in Ayre and Ray Kniveton in Onchan; Brenda Cannell in Douglas East and Leonard Singer in Ramsey were contesting the election for the first time. Three of the Labour Party candidates were official MLP, Alan Cowley and David Cretney in Douglas South and Peter Karran in Onchan. Because of his central role as DHSS Minister in introducing the job seeker's allowance, the MLP refused to sponsor Bernard May and he stood as the Willaston and District Labour Party candidate in Douglas North. Twenty-three retiring members of the House sought re-election, including all 10 members of the Council of Ministers, Bell, Brown, Corkill, Cringle, Gelling, Groves, Hannan, May, North and Walker.

Nineteen of the retiring members were successful, including all but two of the ministerial team. The seven successful ministers who faced a contest won comfortable majorities, Walker topping the poll in Rushen. Groves, the outgoing DOLGE Minister, came last in a three-cornered fight in Ramsey, a reflection perhaps of the strength of the opposition, the fact that he was not a resident of Ramsey and the manner in which he had exercised responsibility for the Government's highly controversial waste disposal strategy. DHSS Minister May came a poor third in Douglas North, almost certainly the result of his association with the job seeker's allowance, the resultant split in the MLP and the groundswell of opposition to the siting and method of funding of the Island's new hospital. Groves and May were not the only establishment figures to suffer defeat, Jim Cain becoming the second Speaker since the war to lose his seat while in office. Following Cain's defeat, Noel Cringle was elected Speaker. With the defeat of May, MLP representation in the House was reduced to two, Cretney and Karran topping the polls in their respective constituencies well ahead of their nearest rivals. There was one MLP member, Eddie Lowey, in the Legislative Council. Each of the six APG Independents were successful, Cannan and Quine comfortable winners and Singer, facing competition from two ministers, topping the poll in Ramsey. There were two APG supporters, Dominic Delaney and Edgar Mann, in the Legislative Council. All eight APG members of Tynwald were representatives or former representatives of constituencies in the Douglas-Onchan area or the north of the Island. The very different results of the two MLP candidates in Douglas South were a reminder of the limited appeal of political parties in the Isle of Man and the importance of other factors such as records of achievement and personality—while Cretney with 2,061 votes won 78 per cent of the vote, fellow party member, Cowley polled only 247 votes or nine per cent of the vote. The appeal of both the MLP and the APG to the electorate was probably more to do with alternative personalities than alternative policies.

The turnover of membership was again low. Just five new members joined the House. Between November 1996 and July 2001 there were three by-elections, two caused by the elevation to the Legislative Council of relatively new members of the House, APG supporter, Ray Kniveton, first elected in 1995, and Alan Crowe, one of the new intake in 1996; the third resulted from Noel Cringle's election as the President of Tynwald in April 2000. In May 1998 Independent Geoffrey T. Cannell, a 55-year-old broadcaster and journalist, replaced Kniveton in Onchan, narrowly defeating APG candidate, David Quirk. In July 1998 the APG compensated for their loss in Onchan by gaining a seat in Douglas North; R. William Henderson, a 36-year-old night hospital manager, won the seat in a five-way contest, narrowly defeating an MLP-sponsored attempt by Bernie May to return to the House. With the elevation of Kniveton and the election of Henderson, APG representation in Tynwald increased to nine, although within a matter of months divisions within the Group had led to the resignation of David Cannan (December 1998) and Ray Kniveton (April 2000). In the Rushen by-election in June 2000, Independent John Rimington, a 47-year-old landscape gardener and supply teacher, proved a clear winner in a seven-way contest in which the APG candidate came a poor sixth.

The Chief Minister, Donald Gelling, with the Council of Ministers, December 1996. Donald Gelling, MHK for Malew and Santon from 1986, Minister of Agriculture 1988–89 and Treasury Minister 1989–96, succeeded Walker as Chief Minister after the general election in 1996. The seated members, from left to right, are Edgar Mann (Education), David North (Trade and Industry), Donald Gelling (Chief Minister), Tony Brown (Transport) and Edgar Quine (Local Government and the Environment); the standing members are Allan Bell (Home Affairs), Clare Christian (Health and Social Security), Richard Corkill (Treasury), David Cretney (Tourism and Leisure) and Hazel Hannan (Agriculture, Fisheries and Forestry).

Continuity of policy was the hallmark of the new regime, adopting the pre-election *Annual Review of Policies and Programmes 1996* as a framework for government. Gelling's commitment to consensus politics provided the essential background to policy making. There were no further changes in the Island's constitutional relationship with either the UK or the EU, but a determination in Tynwald to defend hard-won constitutional rights in the face of external threats. Supporters of direct election of the Legislative Council were successful in promoting a major review of the Island's second chamber by a select committee of the House of Keys, but unsuccessful in promoting legislation to provide for a directly elected Tynwald. Advocates of measures to improve the accountability of government persuaded Tynwald to set up two new standing committees of Tynwald and to approve the recommendations of the Select Committee on Ministerial Government. An attempt by Hazel Hannan to reform Manx electoral law and provide for one person one vote was defeated at second reading. A further round of consultations and debate on local government reform ended in failure with the Council of Ministers refusing even to attempt to impose a solution on local authorities opposed to the changes proposed; however, in December 1999 Tynwald agreed to appoint a select committee to reconsider the options for reform thus keeping alive what must surely be the longest running debate of the twentieth century.[21]

The Policy Reviews of 1998, 1999 and 2000 and the related budgets incorporated action or proposed action on most of the other issues raised in the election and were approved in Tynwald without dissent or with just a single dissenting voice. The Government had the financial resources with which to respond to electoral shopping lists; nowhere was this more evident than with respect to welfare policies. As well as funding real increases in social security provision, high levels of investment in education, the health service, housing and environmental health were prioritised, the main points of controversy being those raised during the election with regard to the Government's major capital projects, the new hospital, IRIS and the incinerator. Despite an adverse report by a select committee, in February 1999 Tynwald accepted the principle of a statutory minimum wage and proceeded to pass the necessary enabling legislation in 2001. The response to law and order concerns included legislation to increase police powers, the implementation of the recommendations of the Select Committee on Law and Order, the approval in March 1999 of a five-year drugs strategy and in January 2000 of a five-year alcohol strategy, and increased revenue and capital spending on the law and order services. Although not in response to electoral demands, the new century saw legislation providing for the deregulation of shop opening and licensing hours, the Shop Hours Act 2000 and the Licensing Act 2001.[22]

Continuity of economic policy was generally accepted. Agricultural support mirrored that of the UK with the BSE crisis necessitating a temporary increase in the level of subsidy. Ongoing investment in the tourist industry was supplemented by major new commitments such as the acquisition of Rushen Abbey and the Villa Marina and the promise of support for the development of marinas in Ramsey and Port St Mary. Industrial diversification was promoted, the film industry and e-commerce being the latest beneficiaries of investment. Commitment to the financial sector was reflected in further supportive legislation and, in the wake of the Edwards Review, a determination to show that the sector was regulated to the highest international standards. Low direct taxation and the retention of the CEA remained the main platforms of fiscal policy with the new century seeing the approval by Tynwald of a radical three-year plan for further reductions in income tax. The long-awaited Residence Act became law in 2001. Major investment in public sector commercial services was approved by the responsible statutory boards and Tynwald, with environmental factors a major consideration in relation to water supply, energy and transport.

## A Caring Society: the Persistence of the Welfare State

*The Development of a Prosperous and Caring Society* encapsulated the main policy commitments of government both before and after its publication in October 1987, the promotion of growth to provide increased prosperity and some sharing of that prosperity through lower taxation on incomes and improvements to welfare services. Although recession in the early 1980s limited the capacity of the Radcliffe administration to deliver on these commitments, between the mid-1980s and the turn of the century considerable progress was made. Low taxation, previously primarily associated with the encouragement of new residents and investment, became an important vehicle for assisting people on low incomes. Welfare services, under attack in the UK from a Conservative Government determined to scale down the role of the state, were protected and strengthened in the Isle of Man.

Between 1981 and 1988 the standard rate of income tax was fixed at 20 per cent, but in his 1998 budget David Cannan announced a two-rate structure with the higher rate of 20 per cent applying to all company profits, the income of nonresidents and the taxable income of residents in excess of £6,000, and a standard rate of 15 per cent on the taxable income of residents up to £6,000.[23] Cannan's successors at the Treasury retained the two rates; up to the end of 1999/2000 the only changes were to the standard rate which was reduced to 14 per cent in February 2000, to the threshold at which residents pay the higher rate, which in the same budget was set at £10,000, and the provisions in Corkill's 1999 and 2000 budgets applying the standard rate initially to the first £100,000 of profits earned by trading companies and subsequently to the first £125,000, in effect relieving 80 per cent of trading companies from the higher rate.[24] In parallel with lower rates of taxation, there were substantial real increases in the value of income tax allowances. Comparisons between the early 1980s and the later period are difficult because of a major simplification of the system of allowances announced in Moore's second budget in 1986. That budget increased the single person's allowance to £3,200, the married couple's allowance to £4,800, but with a commitment to making the allowance double that of the single person's, and the additional single parent's allowance to £670, the new allowances had the effect of removing some 3,000 persons from the tax net.[25] Under Cannan, Gelling and Corkill each of these allowances was raised well above the rate of inflation. The married couple's allowance became double that of the single person's in 1989/90. By the time of Corkill's fourth budget in 2000 the actual values of the three main allowances had risen to £7,535, £15,070 and £5,160, an increase in real terms over 1986 of 35, 80 and 342 per cent respectively, with the result that by the turn of the century a third of all persons within the income tax system were no longer paying tax.[26]

Corkill's announcement in June 2000 of plans to introduce the most radical change in direct taxation since the abolition of surtax in 1960 heralded a three-year programme of reductions in the burden of taxation on individuals and the introduction of a new mechanism for the redistribution of wealth towards those on low incomes; assuming the continuing buoyancy of the Manx economy, the plan is to lower the standard rate of income tax to 10 per cent and the higher rate to 15 per cent and to top up benefits for those on low incomes by means of a refundable tax credit system.[27] The first phase of the strategy formed the centrepiece of Corkill's budget in February 2001; with effect from April 2001 the standard and higher rates of income tax were lowered to 12 and 18 per cent respectively and, while the threshold at which individuals pay the higher rate remained at £10,000, for trading companies it was increased from £125,000 to £500,000.[28] As in 1960 the assumption behind the new strategy is that the increase in income derived from new residents and business will be sufficient to fund the general reduction in the level of taxation.[29]

Insofar as social security policy is concerned, reciprocity with the UK continued to provide the basis of the Manx system, but an increasingly important feature of the 1980s and 1990s was the exercise of local discretion in respect of supplementary schemes that were not subject to reciprocity. Most of the changes were agreed without division or with very little dissent. UK legislation provided the basis of the changes that were deemed necessary to preserve reciprocity. In March 1987 Tynwald approved the Social Security Legislation (Application) Order 1987 applying parts of the UK Social Security Act 1986 to the Island. The UK Act provided for modifications to the State Earnings Related Pension Scheme, the encouragement of personal and occupational pension schemes, the replacement of family income supplement, supplementary benefit and housing benefit by income support, and the introduction of statutory maternity pay. The Manx Order followed the UK save with respect to income support and statutory maternity pay; the Island chose to retain family income supplement and supplementary benefit, and opted to increase maternity allowances rather than adopt statutory maternity pay.[30]

In July 1996 Tynwald approved a package of orders extending and adapting the Job Seeker's Act 1995 to the Isle of Man and providing for a distinctively Manx job seeker's enhanced allowance scheme. The UK measure consolidated unemployment benefit and income support into a single job seeker's allowance (JSA), comprising a contribution-based allowance payable for six months and an income-based allowance payable after six months. Controversially it reduced the period for which benefit was paid to the unemployed from twelve to six months and introduced means testing for subsequent benefit. The Island was obliged to follow the UK with regard to the contribution-based component in order to maintain reciprocity, but was able to do so in conjunction with a measure to prevent any deterioration of provision. The Island's earlier decision to retain supplementary benefit, which was not the subject of a reciprocal agreement, meant that it was able to determine its own level of income support. The DHSS Minister and MLP member, Bernie May, felt able to recommend acceptance only because of these two mitigating factors. May argued that 85 per cent of those claiming unemployment benefit in the Isle of Man would not be affected by the income-based element of the UK scheme on account of being in receipt of supplementary benefit. For the other 15 per cent it was proposed to extend the period during which benefits could be claimed under the Island's Enhanced Unemployment Benefit Scheme from three to twelve months, so that no one would suffer the loss of six months' benefit. After a seven-hour debate, the package was approved by 15 votes to eight in the Keys and six votes to two in the Legislative Council, the main opposition coming from the APG and the other members of the MLP. Eddie Lowey, the Minister for Industry, resigned from the Council of Ministers in protest against the adoption of a measure which he believed was designed to force the unemployed into low-paid work. The package came into effect in October

1996, payments of the Job Seeker's Contribution Based Allowance being kept in line with the UK and those of the Job Seeker's Income Based Allowance and the Job Seeker's Enhanced Allowance the subject of local budgetary decision making.[31]

The Pensions Act 1995 (Application) Order 1997 providing for the Island to follow the UK in equalising the pension age at 65 in 2010 was much less controversial and was carried by 20 votes to two in the Keys and seven to one in the Legislative Council.[32]

The Social Security Legislation (Application) (No. 3) Order 1999, based on the extremely controversial UK measure introduced by the Labour Government, changed the additional child benefit payable to lone parents from a universal cash payment to a means tested benefit, bringing lone parents into line with two-parent families. As with the JSA, approval in Tynwald was eased by steps to mitigate the worst effects of the proposed change. DHSS Minister, Clare Christian, explained that lone parents in receipt of supplementary benefit or the job seeker's allowance would be protected by the inclusion of a family premium component in those benefit payments. The Order was approved by 17 votes to five in the Keys and six votes to three in the Legislative Council, the main opposition coming from the APG whose members objected to the introduction of means testing.[33]

The Island's exercise of discretion with respect to income-based benefits and certain universal benefits was an outstanding feature of social security policy in this period. The Island's supplementary benefits were slightly higher than the UK in 1981 and between November 1981 and the end of the century the gap between the Island and the UK widened as the Manx Government responded to demands for measures to help those on lower incomes. In 1983 a 50 per cent increase in the Christmas bonus for pensioners and persons in receipt of supplementary benefit to £15 was the first in a series taking it to £75 by 1999, well above the UK level of £10. An Executive Council investigation into the position of people on low income reported in 1984 that supplementary benefits were already 15 per cent above UK levels and recommended a substantial addition to Family Income Supplement to help with the cost of housing and an extension of the scheme to include married couples without children. The recommendations were approved without division and the ensuing Family Income Supplement Act 1985 had an easy passage through the branches of Tynwald.[34] Following a DHSS review of social security in 1988, Tynwald approved a package of proposals, including a 10 per cent increase in supplementary benefit, double the rate of inflation, and free prescriptions for pensioners, the disabled, the unemployed and recipients of supplementary benefit.[35]

1988 saw the first of several enhancements above UK levels to universal social security benefits. Child benefit, which had been kept in line with the UK since introduction in 1977, was restructured to reflect the increased costs of children as they progressed through the educational system and to encourage older children to stay in full-time education. With UK child benefit frozen at the single rate of £7.25 per week, in April 1988 Tynwald accepted separate rates of £7.55 for children under 16 and £12.50 for children in education over 16 and under 19.[36] The following year—and with the UK rate still frozen—a three-rate structure was adopted with rates of £8 for preschool children, £8.75 for schoolchildren under 16 and £14 for schoolchildren over 16 but under 19.[37] In subsequent years the Island increased its three rates in line with or above the rate of inflation and in 2001/02 they were £17.55, £17.55 and £25.80 respectively.[38]

In July 1990 the Retirement Pension (Premium) Scheme provided for an additional pension of £7.50 to pensioners over 75. During the debate which led to the acceptance without division of this purely local initiative, DHSS Minister Jim Cain announced plans to commission an independent review of Manx social security.[39] When, in 1991, VAT was increased from 15 to 17.5 per cent, steps were taken to compensate those on low incomes by above inflation increases in income-based benefits and a widening of access to supplementary benefit by increasing the disregard of savings from £10,000 to £15,000.[40] A second local initiative in relation to pensions came as a result of the independent review undertaken for the DHSS by Derek Chislett of the UK Department of Health and Social Security. While supporting the retention of reciprocal arrangements with the UK, Chislett recommended the use of surplus moneys in the Manx National Insurance Fund to restore the link between pensions and average earnings that had been broken by the Conservative Government in 1980, to give pensioners a share of the prosperity of the Island and to reduce their dependence on means tested benefits. In October 1992 Tynwald approved without division the Pensions Supplement Scheme for the benefit of pensioners who were resident on the Island and had contributed to the Manx National Insurance Fund for at least 10 years; initially the pensions supplement was fixed at £5 per week for single pensioners and was to be uprated annually by the difference between increases in retail prices and average earnings.[41] When VAT was levied on domestic fuel at the rate of 8 per cent in March 1994, one of several measures introduced to mitigate the effects on the cost of living for the elderly and others on low incomes was an immediate increase of 15 per cent in the pension supplement, above inflation increases in supplementary benefit, weekly winter heating allowances (paid from January to the first week of April each year regardless of the weather) and the Christmas bonus, and an increase in the savings disregard for access to supplementary benefit to £20,000.[42] In the following year's budget, Gelling announced a 40 per cent increase in the pensions supplement from £5.75 to £8.05. Despite this rise, further increases were demanded by the APG who wanted to see full compensation for the temporary break in the link between pensions and average earnings between 1980 and 1993. In April 1997, as a direct result of a postelection initiative by APG members, Tynwald approved without division a DHSS resolution raising the pensions supplement from the £9.35 to £13.[43] With the Manx economy booming and in the face of continuing pressures on government for more generous provision for pensioners, in November 2000 Tynwald approved a further DHSS resolution, providing for the pension supplement to be set at 50 per cent of the basic pension with effect from April 2001. The resolution paved the way for a rise in the basic pension in line with the UK from £67.50 to £72.50 and a virtual doubling of the pensions supplement from £18.70 to £36.25.[44] The combination of a basic pension uprated in line with the UK, a supplement set at 50 per cent of the basic pension and for those over 75 a pensions premium contrasts very sharply with provision in the UK where, despite a Labour Government since 1997, there was no renewal of the link with average earnings.

Finally, the Government responded to the problem of homeowners being excluded from supplementary allowances on entering long-term residential care because of the value of their home pushing their savings above the £20,000 limit. In July 1999 Tynwald approved an amendment to the supplementary benefit regulations, excluding the value of a dwelling house, but not the income received from it, from the definition of capital resources of those in long-term residential care.[45]

Total revenue spending on social security and related social services rose steadily from £8,473,562 in 1980/81 to £52,525,113 in 1999/2000, a real increase of 159 per cent that can be attributed to the widening of access to benefits, population growth, the enhancement of benefits and better quality social services.[46] Capital spending on social services during this period totalled £6,205,655, of which more than 80 per cent was committed in the 10 years to March 2000 as part of the 1991 strategy for health and community services; most of the expenditure in the early 1980s was on residential accommodation for the elderly and infirm; there was no capital spending between 1983/84 and 1986/87 and from 1988/89 onwards the expenditure priority was community homes for the mentally and physically disabled and for people with learning difficulties.

The mainstream education service was also heavily influenced by the UK, although there was no slavish emulation of UK policies. The Board of Education and, after 1987, the Department of Education were committed to the provision of high quality education for all the people of the Island and their policies in response to UK developments, additional student numbers and a growth in the demand for education were for the most part accepted in Tynwald without controversy. The period saw a widening of access to education, involving better state provision for preschool education, the raising of the school leaving age to 16, the encouragement of children to stay in education after the age of 16 and increased investment in postschool education.

As early as 1973 the Board of Education had modified its entry policy to allow children to start school at the beginning of the year in which they were five and this was seen as a first step towards providing nursery education fom the age of three. However, apart from the opening of a nursery class in the new school at Jurby in 1983, no further progress was made until the 1990s. A Department of Education survey of nursery provision in 1993 led to the opening of a preschool unit at Pulrose and a commitment by the Government to expand nursery provision as resources became available.[47] By 1999 there were nursery classes at Jurby, Pulrose and three other schools in the Douglas area and plans for provision in Castletown, Peel and Ramsey.[48]

A major expansion of secondary education resulted from the raising of the school leaving age to 16, the encouragement of children to stay at school after 16 and an increase in the school age population. Enabling legislation for raising the school leaving age had been passed in 1971, but the policy was not implemented during the 1970s despite the best efforts of the Board of Education and its chair, Victor Kneale. By 1981 over 70 per cent of children were staying at school beyond the compulsory age of 15, but in contrast to the UK there was no compulsion. In November 1982 Tynwald supported implementation as one of the Government's policy objectives and, with the necessary investment in accommodation and facilities either in place or under way, in February 1985 approved 1 September 1986 as the appointed day by 17 votes to six in the Keys and eight votes to one in the Legislative Council.[49] The next major landmark was the substantial increase in child benefit, announced in the 1988 budget for children in the 16–19 age group who were still in full-time education. This was followed in the 1990s by major investment in secondary education and by the end of the century the proportion of the 16–19 age group in full-time education was over 40 per cent.[50]

In common with successive UK Governments, the Island also expanded its provision for postschool education, although without following the Conservative Government in 1990 in replacing student grants by loans or the Labour Government in 1997 in requiring the part-payment of fees by students. The number of students attending the Isle of Man College, for both further and, from 1996, higher education, increased by almost 177 per cent from 3,656 in 1980/81 to 10,124 in 1999/2000 and

Minister of Education, Victor Kneale, opening the Victor Kneale Wing of the College of Further Education, May 1988. The College of Education was formed in 1972 and moved into a new building in 1975. It was renamed the Isle of Man College in 1990. Victor Kneale was closely involved with education throughout his political career, having been a member of the Education Authority before entering the Keys in 1962, chair of the Board of Education (1962–72 and 1981–86) and Minister of Education (1986–90).

the number receiving grants for full-time study in further and higher education rose by 128 per cent from 497 in 1980/81 to 1,132 in 1999/2000.[51] Following a feasibility study by the Isle of Man Government, the turn of the century saw the establishment of the Island's first specialist institution of higher education, the International Business School. Although a private company, the IBS commenced operations during the summer of 2000 with initial funding by the Department of Education, pending development into a largely self-financing institution.[52]

The Manx educational curriculum continued to be heavily influenced by UK policy. The national curriculum, introduced in the UK under the Education Reform Act 1988, was phased into Manx schools between 1989 and 1997 according to the same time frame as adopted for English schools. Although it was modified to allow space for the appropriate development of local studies, it was felt that the Island could not afford to place its own students at a disadvantage compared with their counterparts on the mainland.[53] Most of the vocational programmes offered by the Isle of Man College were either dictated by professional bodies in the UK or controlled by them. Until 1996 Manx students seeking degree-level education were obliged to undertake study off the Island or by distance learning. The Isle of Man College's venture into degree-level education from 1996 was as an associate college of the University of Liverpool;[54] the IBS plans to offer courses validated by universities in Liverpool and elsewhere in the UK.

The performance of schools was internally monitored using the same criteria and methods as those adopted by UK inspectors. The Island continued to pay for external inspections of schools by Her Majesty's Inspectorate until 1993 and by the UK Office for Standards in Education after 1993. The academic performance of pupils and schools was measured by the results gained in UK examinations and was generally reported to be well above the English average.[55] Further and higher education was also subject to external inspection and control.

Revenue spending on education rose steadily from £11,504,466 in 1980/81 to £30,423,310 in 1990/91 and thereafter more rapidly to £54,999,990 by 1999/2000, an increase in real terms over the whole period of 100 per cent. This increase, modest by comparison with the 1970s but from a much higher base, was the result of educational expansion, higher standards of provision, including accommodation and facilities both for general and special needs and the practice of increasing the pay of teachers in line with the UK. Capital spending over the 19 years to 1999/2000 totalled £50,188,636, of which over three quarters were committed during the economically buoyant 1990s. The relatively low level of investment in the 1980s included expenditure on new primary schools in Jurby, Marown and Foxdale, the reorganisation of secondary schools in the Eastern District and a major extension to the Isle of Man College. The high level of spending in the 1990s included new primary schools in Douglas and Port St Mary and major extensions to secondary schools to accommodate expansion, including the provision of purpose-built post-16 suites in four of the Island's five secondary schools.[56]

Growing public concern, the demands of public health professionals, pressure from within Tynwald and the adoption of higher standards in the UK and Europe guaranteed a high priority being accorded to public health. In March 1982, acting on the recommendations of its Select Committee on the Rating of Domestic Property, Tynwald agreed that central government should assume full responsibility for the funding of public health.[57] The Select Committee saw public health as an essential common service, the growing costs of which should be borne out of general revenue. Local authorities continued to share responsibility for such functions as waste management and sewerage, but were increasingly little more than agents of central government. Much of the routine public health work of the LGB and, after 1986, DOLGE attracted little political debate, but environmental pollution and the related issues of waste management and sewage disposal did feature prominently on Tynwald's agenda. In each case the Island came under pressure to meet the highest international standards of environmental protection.

Environmental pollution was the subject of legislation in 1983, 1990, 1993 and 2000. The Marine Pollution Act 1983 paved the way for the Island to ratify the 1974 Convention for the Prevention of Marine Pollution and empowered the LGB to control the discharge of inorganic pollutants into the sea.[58] Although it had a smooth passage through Tynwald, during the second reading in the Keys several speakers expressed concern that it did nothing to prevent or control the most prevalent source of pollution of Manx waters and beaches, namely the discharge of untreated sewage directly into the sea. The chair of the LGB, Miles Walker, acknowledged the problem, but feared that the cost of treating all sewage inland would be 'absolutely horrendous'.[59] The issue of environmental pollution was also at the heart of the debates leading to the Public Health Act 1990.[60] The aim of the Act was to consolidate and update public health legislation and provide a more effective framework for environmental protection, including an enhancement of the powers of DOLGE with respect to waste disposal. The Water Pollution Act 1993 made comprehensive provision for the control of pollution in the sea and inland waters in line with UK and European standards, empowering

DOLGE to set water quality objectives and making it an offence, save for licensed discharges, to pollute controlled waters.[61] The Public Health (Amendment) Act 2000 increased the powers of government with respect to the regulation of waste disposal.[62] The Acts of 1990, 1993 and 2000 provided a framework within which government sought to address the long-standing problems of waste and sewage disposal.

Waste disposal methods concerned Manx politicians long before 1990. As early as July 1979 the environmental problems associated with the use of landfill persuaded Tynwald to investigate the alternative of incineration with waste heat recovery. In October 1979 an LGB report to Tynwald in favour of incineration was approved without division,[63] but progress with finding a site was delayed by the general election of 1981. In July 1982 a second LGB report advocating incineration was accepted by 18 votes to six in the Keys and five votes to three in the Legislative Council.[64] In June 1984 Tynwald supported a change of heart by the LGB and narrowly agreed, by 12 votes to 10 in the Keys and six votes to two in the Legislative Council, to abandon incineration in favour of medium density baling.[65] Following a further reconsideration and a fourth government report, in February 1988 Tynwald agreed to return to the 1979 policy of incineration by 18 votes to six in the Keys and seven votes to two in the Legislative Council.[66] A further review of methods because of the high cost of incineration led, in December 1990, to the acceptance, by 21 votes to two in the Keys and eight votes to one in the Legislative Council, of a package of methods, including waste prevention, recycling, the limited use of landfill and incineration with heat recovery.[67] The further development of this strategy was approved in February 1994 with only a single voice of dissent.[68] From that point the main problems were finding sites and obtaining planning permission for their development. There were periodic demands for yet another look at alternative strategies, but these were resisted by an overwhelming majority of members. A site for the incinerator at Richmond Hill in Braddan was eventually approved in October 1998 by 14 votes to five in the Keys and unanimously in the Council. Despite widespread criticism of the project on environmental and health grounds, on 18 October 2000 Tynwald approved, by 14 votes to eight in the Keys and by seven votes to one in the Council, the expenditure of a sum not exceeding £43,523,000 to build the 'energy from waste' incinerator; it is expected to be operational in 2003.[69]

An environmentally acceptable solution to the problem of sewage disposal proved even more expensive. Despite the concerns expressed during the passage of the Marine Pollution Act 1983, little was done to remedy the problems of water and beach pollution during the 1980s. Towards the end of the decade an interdepartmental sewerage and drainage working party, chaired by Jim Cain, persuaded Executive Council to adopt as objectives the EC bathing water quality standard for marine water and the UK Royal Commission 20/30 standard for the discharge of sewage.[70] The subsequent resolution in Tynwald, moved by Tony Brown, the Minister for Local Government and the Environment, and successfully amended by John Orme, laid the foundation for the most ambitious and expensive infrastructural project in the Island's history. In February 1991, following research by the Sewerage Waste Water Treatment Working Party, chaired by Orme, Tynwald accepted in principle and without division, a long-term strategy for the collection and treatment of sewage, involving the construction of a single sewage treatment plant for the whole of the Island, a 'pumped main' transfer system to connect local sewage collection systems to the plant and a 'wetlands' processing of treated sewage prior to final discharge into an inland water course.[71] The consensus behind the IRIS project when detailed planning started in 1991 was put to the test as estimated costs began to spiral. However, despite delays and attempts by APG members in April 1995 and MLP members in April 1997 to persuade Tynwald to explore alternatives to the all-Island project, both Government and most members of Tynwald continued to support IRIS, albeit as a longer term project than originally envisaged.[72]

Revenue spending on public health was modest by comparison with that on the health service, but there was a real increase as Tynwald accorded a higher priority to environmental issues. Spending by the LGB/DOLGE/Department of Transport on public health, including waste disposal, rose from £514,669 in 1981/82 to £2,446,350 in 1999/2000, a real increase of 98 per cent. Spending on sewage disposal, including grants to local authorities, rose from £244,606 in 1981/82 to £5,433,024 in 1999/2000, a real increase of 827 per cent. Capital spending between April 1981 and March 2000, mainly on waste disposal and civic amenity sites, preparations for the incinerator and sewage disposal, totalled £29,675,326, of which almost 70 per cent was spent over the five years from April 1995. The recent high level of spending is set to continue, with the Government committed to spending over £138 million on its waste management and sewage disposal strategies over the five years to March 2005.[73]

The Manx National Health Service retained its position as the Island's most expensive welfare service. Even so commitment to the service was underpinned by a consensus in Tynwald, as was evident in both branches during the passage of the National Health Service Act 2001, which consolidated and updated NHS legislation.[74] The Manx service continued to be heavily influenced by UK policy and standards, but, because of the small scale of operation, a distinctively local organisation and the economic capacity and political commitment to invest at a higher per capita rate than the UK, the Island was able to avoid some of the worst features of the UK service. The problems in the UK service caused by the remoteness of government, organisational instability, the introduction and removal of the internal market and the lack of investment were for the most part avoided by the judicious exercise of local discretion. In this period the most important exercise of discretion followed two independent inquiries into the Manx NHS by experts from the UK. The first, by P. Benner and N. J. B. Evans from the UK Department of Health and Social Security, was commissioned by the Health Services Board in 1985 and reported in March 1986, recommending the stronger management of hospitals by teams of professionals in place of the hospital management committees that had operated since 1948, steps to improve intra-organisational policy making and public relations, and a hospital modernisation programme concentrating acute medical services at Noble's and long-term care for the elderly and infirm at Ballamona and increasing the scope for the treatment of patients in the community.[75] Limited progress in implementing these recommendations, a catalogue of service delivery problems and allegations of decision making without consultation provided the background to demands for a new inquiry. In October 1987 Hazel Hannan moved a resolution in Tynwald calling for the appointment of a commission of inquiry into the health service. The resolution was carried by 16 votes to seven in the Keys and unanimously in the Council; of the 10 members of Executive Council all but Tony Brown, the DHSS Minister, voted for the resolution, a clear acknowledgement of the seriousness of the issues raised during the debate.[76] In August 1990 the Liverpool University Health Planning Consortium was commissioned to undertake a wide-ranging review of health promotion, treatment and care. It reported in April 1991, recommending a clear delineation of policy making and managerial responsibilities, a balance between health promotion and care, the development of community care centres and a rebuilding of Noble's Hospital.[77] Many of the 115 detailed recommendations were implemented by the DHSS during the 1990s, but for Tynwald the prime focus of debate was on the development of a general strategy for health care.[78]

The strategy was prepared by the Department under the leadership of Jim Cain who had been appointed DHSS Minister in December 1989. The Department was assisted by a team of professionals and academics under Ceri Davies, an assistant director of the DHSS in London. The team had access to the unpublished work of the Liverpool Consortium. *A Strategy for Health and Community Services in the Isle of Man* (May 1991) was presented to Tynwald by Cain in July 1991. The aim of the 10-year strategy was to develop a modern health care system that was fit for the twenty-first century and comparable with the best in the western world. The strategy comprised two main elements, the redevelopment of the Noble's site to provide a comprehensive range of acute services, including dedicated short stay facilities, a full range of beds for acute geriatric, psychiatric and severely mentally ill patients and provision for the treatment of private patients, and a complementary range of community services, including three community hospitals, community-based units for the mentally handicapped, the young chronically sick and physically disabled and residential and nursing homes in the public and private sectors for the long-term care of the elderly. The strategy was approved without division[79] and, subject to two important changes, provided the basis for the Island's health policy into the twenty-first century.

The first change concerned the location of the central hospital and followed a change of minister in December 1991 and a review of the relative merits of redeveloping Noble's or building a new acute services hospital on a greenfield site. Given the age of much of the Noble's Hospital, the high level of disruption anticipated to existing services by redevelopment on that site, parking problems and the fact that redevelopment would be almost as expensive as replacement, the departmental review came out strongly in support of a greenfield development. On 22 October 1992 May presented the case for change and obtained the unanimous approval of Tynwald for a new acute hospital at Ballamona in Braddan.[80] The second change related to the funding of the new hospital. When the strategy was first approved the understanding was that the capital costs would be met out of the consolidated loans fund and that the loan charges would be funded as usual out of the general revenue over a period of 30 years. In October 1994 May moved acceptance of the principle of transferring surplus moneys from the Manx National Insurance Fund into a hospital estate development fund with a view to investing the money and using the interest and capital to meet the loan charges. The resolution was approved by 18 votes to five in the Keys and unanimously in the Legislative Council, the sole opposition coming from the five APG members of the House who objected to the use of National Insurance Fund moneys for purposes other than social security payments.[81] In April 1995 Tynwald duly authorised the transfer of £44 million to the Hospital Estate Development Fund.[82] Faced with significant increases in the estimated costs of building the new hospital because of delays in obtaining planning permission, the Government took advantage of the buoyant economic conditions in the late 1990s to pay a further £12 million into the Fund from the general revenue.[83] Implementation of the modified strategy proved much more controversial, but, despite planning delays, rising costs, electoral concerns and APG criticisms of the site and method of funding, the building of the new hospital at Ballamona remained at the heart of government policy and is expected to be completed in 2002/03 at a total estimated cost of £111.7 million.[84]

Net revenue spending on the health service increased steadily during the 1980s

Clare Christian, MLC and DHSS Minister (1996–), with other members of the Council of Ministers and the Treasury on the site of the new hospital, 16 June 1999. The politically sensitive task of overseeing the development of the £111 million hospital from plan towards completion by 2003 fell to the Minister of Health and Social Security, Clare Christian. From left to right the front row comprises five members of the Council of Ministers, Stephen Rodan, Richard Corkill, Clare Christian, Tony Brown and Alex Downie; a sixth minister, Allan Bell, is standing behind Brown and Downie.

from £12,299,555 in 1980/81 to £35,299,410 in 1990/91, a real increase of 55 per cent, and rapidly during the 1990s to £64,934,837 in 1999/2000, a real increase over 1980/81 of 120 per cent. Capital spending between April 1981 and March 2000 totalled £59,992,464, mainly on new facilities for Noble's Hospital, upgrading the Ramsey Cottage Hospital as the Northern Community Hospital, the new general hospital and the early stages of the Southern Healthcare Development. That 19-year total will be dwarfed by the £90 million which the Government plans to spend on completion of the general hospital (£80 million) and the Central and Southern Community Hospitals over the five years to March 2005.

Whereas the Government's policies on health were of direct value to most of the Island's population, those on housing were targeted primarily at those unable to obtain satisfactory housing on the open market. For most of this period population increase, economic growth, higher average earnings, low interest rates and rising expectations created pressures on that market and ensured a high level of demand for continued state intervention in housing matters. Housing was rarely off the political agenda as the state performed its traditional roles of regulating housing development, providing public sector housing, encouraging home ownership and controlling rents. Policies were distinctively Manx and much less influenced by the UK than in earlier periods.

Housing development, whether in the public or private sectors, had to be accommodated within the residential zones detailed in the all-Island Development Plan, which was given statutory force in 1982, and the various local plans that were approved by Tynwald between 1988 and the turn of the century. The Town and Country Planning Act 1999 consolidated and updated the Island's statutory provisions relating to land use planning and development, and placed on government an obligation to prepare and maintain an all-Island development plan comprising a strategic plan and a number of area plans.[85] The real politics of housing development planning took place at the local level during the formulation and implementation of plans, with local community groups, building firms, local authorities and DOLGE playing an important role. Tynwald's debates on both the all-Island planning order in June 1982 and those providing for the approval of local plans came at the end of a long political process and were for the most part approved with little dissent.[86]

While a Conservative Government in the UK was denying funds to public sector housing and encouraging the sale of council houses, the Island's politicians maintained a commitment to public sector provision. Fewer new dwellings were completed than in the 1960s or 1970s, but existing stock was maintained and refurbished. A combination of almost no new building and rising demand during the 1980s led to pressure in Tynwald for a new housing strategy. The result was DOLGE's *Housing Report* of October 1990 and Tynwald's commitment to a five-year programme of building in November 1990.[87] There was a further period of almost no new building in 1995, 1996 and 1997.

Between 1981 and 1999 public sector stock increased by 18 per cent from 4,958 to 5,849 dwellings, bringing the public sector share of the total housing stock down to 17 per cent; just under 10 per cent of the 1999 total was sheltered housing for the elderly.[88] At the end of the twentieth century demand for public sector housing still exceeded supply, waiting lists reflecting a general demand for around 20 per cent more properties than were currently available and a particular demand for over 80 per cent more sheltered units. The Government responded with additional building from 1998, and, following DOLGE's *Housing Policy Review Report* in 1999, embarked on a five-year programme of facilitating the building of 2,000 new housing units, including 400 public sector units, 400 first-time buyer units on communal land and the public sector redevelopment of older estates such as Lower Pulrose.[89] Revenue spending by Tynwald on deficiency payments on LGB/DOLGE and local authority housing totalled £562,963 in 1980/81 and remained fairly stable during the 1980s, before rising as a result of new investment to £3,787,507 in 1992/93, falling and rising again to £4,072,346 in 1998/99 and then falling to £2,995,241 in 1999/2000, in real terms 119 per cent above the 1980/81 level of spending.

In tandem with this continuing commitment to the public sector were policies to encourage home ownership. The Island retained the general incentive of 100 per cent mortgage interest tax relief, but increasingly tailored its policies to help those on low incomes as rising prices put house purchase beyond their reach. Average house prices rose from £27,599 in 1981 to £142,218 in 2000, with particularly sharp increases in the late 1980s and the late 1990s, and by 115 per cent in real terms.[90] The Government's House Purchase Scheme was introduced in 1978 with the aim of helping low income groups with a 90 per cent mortgage on low cost housing. During the recession of the early 1980s the funding available under the Scheme was reduced and restricted to those on very low incomes. Such restrictions stayed in place until the Scheme was replaced in

1991, although upward adjustments were made to the maximum loan available, from £18,000 on houses with a maximum value of £20,000 in 1981 to £45,000 and £50,000 respectively in 1988. Following demands in Tynwald for more generous provision because of escalating house prices, a departmental review of policy proposed a new low cost home ownership scheme, which included an element of interest-free loan assistance. On 19 February 1991 Tynwald approved without division the House Purchase and Refurbishment Scheme 1991. Still targeted at low income families, especially first-time buyers anxious to get on the first rung of the housing ladder, the new Scheme retained the maximum loan of £45,000 but introduced an interest-free period of five years.[91] The Scheme lasted until 1999, by which time it was visibly failing to keep pace with the housing market. The late 1990s saw a rapid decline in the number of mortgage applications, not because of any decline in demand but because most houses were now priced well above the maximum qualifying level of £50,000. Responding to political pressure for a more realistic scheme, the Government proposed abandoning its policy of providing mortgages as a lender of last resort in favour of grant aid in support of applications for commercial mortgages. On 13 July 1999 Tynwald approved without division the House Purchase Assistance Scheme 1999, under which grants of up to £15,000 were to be made to help people earning less than £22,000 per annum obtain a mortgage on a house whose value did not exceed £75,000.[92] Between April 1981 and March 1999 a total of £69 million was made available in loans and £464,819 in grants to 2,688 applicants under the 1978 and 1991 schemes. In its first year, 1999/2000, the House Purchase Assistance Scheme provided 34 applicants with grants totalling £423,000.[93]

A second way of encouraging home ownership at a time of rising house prices was to intervene in the private sector market by commissioning and subsidising the building of housing for sale to first-time buyers. Such intervention occurred for the first time after the 1986 general election and again at the end of the century. In 1988 DOLGE initiated a number of first-time buyers' schemes involving the construction of dwellings on land already owned by the Department or the local housing authorities for sale to first-time buyers. Private sector companies built houses to government specifications and buyers received a public subsidy in the form of building land and infrastructure costs. Between August 1988 and December 1990 the schemes resulted in the construction and sale of 242 houses.[94] With first-time buyer access to the housing market increasingly problematic in the late 1990s, in May 1999 Tynwald endorsed the policy of DOLGE to work with the private sector to subsidise the development of a further 400 first-time buyer houses over the five years from 1999/2000.[95]

The third way of supporting home ownership was through loans and grants for bringing private sector homes up to minimum standards under the Housing Improvement Act 1975 and grant aid for both general home improvement and specific purposes such as thermal insulation and rewiring. The Residential Property Modernisation Scheme, approved by Tynwald in December 1981, enabled the LGB to make grants for residential property improvement and very quickly became the main source of government assistance.[96] It was replaced in February 1988 by the House Repair and Modernisation Scheme, under which grant aid was increased but restricted to lower income owners and occupiers.[97] Between April 1981 and March 1988 loans and grants were given to 72 applicants under the 1975 Act totalling £167,714 and £38,462 respectively; a further 3,717 applicants received just over £4 million in grant aid under the various repair and modernisation schemes running between April 1981 and March

1999.[98] In October 2000 these schemes were replaced by the House Improvement and Energy Conservation Scheme 2000, retaining grant assistance for roof insulation, rewiring and general home improvement but for the first time allowing grant aid for the provision of additional bedroom space.[99]

There were no major changes in government policy on rent control in this period. In the public sector rents were kept low through the housing deficiency payments made by the Government. Lower income tenants were also eligible for rent rebates. Without the benefit of either subsidies or a rent rebate scheme, rented housing in the private sector was much more expensive, although protection for tenants continued to be provided under the Housing (Rent Control) Acts 1948–81.

Employment policy in the last two decades of the century was marked by continuity in relation to the drive for full employment and by change with regard to the framework of employment law. The Government attempted to achieve full employment by encouraging sustainable economic growth and investing in infrastructure and the welfare services and by short-term measures for the relief of unemployment. It responded to increasingly vociferous local demands and external advice by modernising the Island's employment laws. In both areas the influence of the UK was immense, unemployment levels tending to reflect the changing fortunes of the UK economy and employment legislation belatedly following the example set by the UK in the 1960s and 1970s, while taking on board some of the restrictions on trade union rights subsequently imposed by the Thatcher Government in the 1980s.

Although the Island was unable to escape the impact of recession in the UK during the early 1980s and to a lesser extent in the early 1990s, for most of this period the Manx economy experienced economic growth and much lower levels of unemployment than the UK. Between July 1981 and January 1982 Manx unemployment more than doubled from 795 persons or 2.9 per cent to 1,617 persons or 5.9 per cent, out of an economically active population of 27,564. The five years that followed saw much higher unemployment, reaching 2,505 or 9.1 per cent in January 1986. After January 1987 unemployment fell rapidly and between April 1988 and December 1991 remained below four per cent. Unemployment rates rose slightly above the four per cent figure over the next four years before falling rapidly from 1,460 or 4.3 per cent in January 1996 to 233 or 0.6 per cent in December 1999, out of an estimated economically active population of 36,000. The decline in the seasonal variation, which had been evident since the early 1960s, continued during the 1980s and virtually disappeared during the 1990s. In all but three of the 18 years from 1982 the variation fell below the previous record of 2.3 per cent in 1978 and from 1988 it was consistently below 2 per cent.[100]

These unemployment statistics were highly sensitive politically and, even though the general economic policies of government were designed to promote economic growth and full employment, there were pressures both from Tynwald and economic interest groups for additional employment-specific measures. During the 1980s the Executive Council, under Radcliffe, Mann and Walker and with the full backing of Tynwald, was responsible for coordinating a series of initiatives involving education, training, job creation and job release. Encouragement was given to older children to stay on at school after the age of 15 and, with the raising of the school leaving age in 1986, after 16. There was increased investment in vocational training and retraining schemes. Those who registered unemployed received social security benefits at UK rates, but were not eligible for redundancy payments. In April 1986 Tynwald approved the Enhanced

Employment Benefit Scheme to compensate for the lack of redundancy payments. Where unemployment followed at least two years of employment, an additional weekly payment was to be made for up to 13 weeks at the same rate as the standard unemployment benefit (£30.45 in April 1986), the assumption being that most would find employment within three months.[101] The Island's traditional preference for work-based support rather than welfare benefits led to the funding of job creation schemes and, wherever possible, the phasing of government contracts to alleviate unemployment. Between 1981/82 and 1989/90 a total of £2,832,537 was committed to job creation schemes, the allocation declining rapidly after 1985/86 as unemployment levels fell. The Control of Employment Acts remained in place enabling priority to be given to Isle of Man workers. From 1983 a job release scheme, based on a similar UK scheme, allowed males who were nearing retirement age to leave employment early if the employer agreed to fill the vacancy with an unemployed person.[102] During the 1990s the commitment to education and training remained integral features of Manx policy. Government also responded to the increase in unemployment in the early part of the decade with a modest job creation programme and, from 1996 continued to invest in job creation on a small scale despite negligible unemployment overall. Expenditure on specific job creation measures between 1992/93 and 1999/2000 totalled £1,058,305, a figure dwarfed by expenditure on other policies that contributed towards the achievement of full employment.[103]

By comparison with the UK very little progress was made before 1981 in furnishing employees with employment protection. This was partly the result of the uncompromising stand taken by employers and partly because of their influence in Tynwald, where the campaigning of MLP members and trade unions initially met with a lukewarm response. The campaigning continued during the 1981 general election and paved the way for prolonged consultations between the Board of Social Security's Industrial Relations Committee and representatives of the two sides of industry. The Board's priorities were to improve the machinery for resolving industrial disputes and to work towards some sort of compromise on employment protection. The results were the Trade Disputes Act 1985 and the Employment Act 1986.

Underpinned by a tripartite agreement between government, employers and the unions, the Trade Disputes Act 1985 had a smooth passage through the branches and was welcomed by the labour movement as a major advance in industrial relations. Prior to 1985 the responsibility for enquiring into disputes, referring them for conciliation or arbitration and setting up courts of inquiry was vested in the Board of Social Security's Industrial Relations Committee, which had been set up to advise the Lieutenant-Governor in 1976 and which, in 1980, had inherited his powers under the Trade Disputes Act 1936. Manx trade unions were critical of this arrangement because of the Government's involvement in industrial disputes involving public sector workers. Public utility workers also resented the fact that the 1936 Act made it illegal for them to take strike action. The 1985 Act provided for the appointment of an industrial relations officer, who was to exercise his good offices to try and resolve disputes, and the establishment of an independent employment tribunal, to which unsettled disputes would be referred. The employment tribunal assumed responsibility for the powers under the 1936 Act previously exercised by by the Industrial Relations Committee. The Act also repealed the controversial Section 8 of the 1936 Act, which had made it illegal for public utility workers to resort to strike action during an industrial dispute.[104]

Employment protection was an altogether more controversial matter and centred on unfair dismissal and redundancy payments. The trade unions and the MLP wanted the full range of employment protection available to employees in the UK, especially protection against unfair dismissal, whereas the employers were broadly satisfied with the status quo and vehemently opposed to redundancy payments. The Employment Act 1986 was very much a compromise and a pale shadow of UK legislation, MLP attempts to bring the measure into line with the UK being defeated in the Keys.[105] Nevertheless, it was a first step towards protection against unfair dismissal. It gave employees the right to claim compensation if dismissed because of union membership or activity, pregnancy, infectious disease or reasonable absence from work. It also gave female employees the right to return to employment within seven weeks of a confinement.[106]

Redundancy payments courted even greater controversy. In February 1986 MLP members, Lowey and May, moved a resolution seeking support for the principle of redundancy payments. Although it was carried by 15 votes to five in the Keys and seven votes to one in the Legislative Council, when the enabling bill was debated by a full House three months later, it was defeated by 14 votes to 10.[107] Some of the opponents objected to the principle of redundancy payments, others felt that Tynwald's decision in April 1986 to enhance unemployment benefits for up to 13 weeks after redundancy removed the need for such payments and several believed that such a controversial measure should be deferred until after the general election. It was with the latter point in mind that the Government promised to reintroduce the legislation early in the new House.[108]

Thereafter electoral pressure, industrial unrest and external advice combined to bring about a radical change in government policy. During the election the case for better protection against unfair dismissal and redundancy payments attracted considerable support. John Corrin, the moderate leader of the Transport and General Workers' Union from 1979–86, was elected to the Keys and replaced by the more militant Bernard Moffatt. With the TGWU to the fore, the trade unions campaigned for improved pay, employment protection and statutory recognition. The bitter industrial disputes which followed helped to persuade both the Government and Tynwald of the need for fairer employment legislation.[109] In February 1988 the Executive Council commissioned Collinson Grant Consultants Ltd to advise the Island on changes to Manx employment law. Broadly speaking the advice was to bring Manx law into line with that of the UK. The Executive Council, also guided by its own Social Issues Committee, reported to Tynwald in April 1989. It recommended legislation to provide for redundancy payments, protection against unfair dismissal and the statutory recognition of trade unions, but felt that measures to prohibit sexual and racial discrimination in employment were unnecessary.[110] A resolution to accept these radical proposals was moved by Chief Minister Walker and approved without division.[111] The result was a package of three legislative measures that encountered very little opposition.

The Redundancy Payments Act 1990 provided employees with the right to redundancy payments after two years of continuous employment.[112] Fortuitously, it fell to the MLP Minister for Industry, Bernie May, to take the other two bills through the House. He referred to them as 'the most significant and major step forward in employment law' in the Island's history, bestowing as they did 'fundamental rights' on the working people of the Isle of Man.[113] Surprisingly, given the long history of conflict preceding the legislation, both bills received the unanimous support of the House of Keys and a smooth passage in the Legislative Council. The Employment Act 1991 reinforced the rights of employees to contracts of employment first granted 10 years earlier, prohibited action by employers either to penalise employees for union membership or activity or to require them to join a union, provided employees with the right to time off for reasonable purposes such as union activity, jury service and antenatal care, extended the period within which employees had the right to return to work after a confinement and conferred on employees of three months' standing the right not to be unfairly dismissed.[114] The Trade Unions Act 1991 required trade unions to register, conferred on them the legal status and immunities needed to carry out their work and required them to conduct their affairs in a reasonable manner.[115] The Act incorporated two important restrictions on trade unions, one derived from the UK and one adopted because of the Island's vulnerability to strike action on the part of those who are responsible for essential services. First, protection for organisers and participants in industrial action from civil and criminal proceedings did not extend to acts of violence or offences against property, to industrial action not endorsed by a ballot of members or to secondary industrial action. Second, the Governor in Council was empowered, subject to the approval of Tynwald, to designate the supply of particular goods and services as 'essential services' and to require those engaged in disputes in such services to continue negotiating and, in the event of a breakdown in negotiations, to submit to a court of inquiry, whose recommendations would be binding on both parties.

Although there were no other major changes to employment legislation in the 1990s, further consideration was given to the subjects of discrimination in employment and a minimum wage. Following a report by the Council of Ministers in September 1991, Tynwald accepted the principle of legislation based on the employment provisions of the UK Sex Discrimination and Equal Pay Acts of 1970.[116] Extensive consultations followed but, despite inclusion in the Government's programme of legislation from 1992/93, the Employment (Sex Discrimination) Act was not passed until 2000.[117] Investigations were also carried out into the question of racial discrimination and a commitment made in 1996 to legislation in 1998/99, but again the legislation was delayed and a more wide-ranging employment discrimination bill is now expected to be introduced in 2001/02.

The issue of a statutory minimum wage had been raised by a few candidates during the general elections in 1991 and 1996 and debate on the subject increased following the commitment of the UK Labour Party to a statutory minimum wage. In the Isle of Man an initiative by MLP members, Lowey and Karran, in January 1997 led to the appointment by Tynwald of a select committee to investigate the matter. Chaired by Pamela Crowe and with Lowey a member, the Committee concluded that there was no statistical evidence to warrant the bureaucratic imposition of a minimum wage in the Isle of Man and that the matter should be reconsidered by the Council of Ministers within two years. Both the Council of Ministers and Tynwald disagreed. On the recommendation of the Chief Minister, the Council of Ministers was asked to bring forward detailed proposals for a statutory minimum wage.[118] The Council of Ministers reported in September 1999, recommending that a Statutory Minimum Wage Bill be added to the Government's legislative programme. Despite Tynwald's approval in October 1999 being subject to the requirement that legislation be introduced into the Keys no later than May 2000, the enabling bill was not passed until 2001.[119]

## Public Investment for a Prosperous Society

The twin goals of Manx economic policy between 1981 and the end of the century were sustainable economic growth and further industrial diversification. The aim was to achieve a more prosperous society and raise per capita national income in the Island up to and, if possible, beyond UK levels. It is a measure of the success of the Island's policies that gross national product per capita increased from £3,017 in 1982/83 to £12,311 in 1998/99, a real increase of 108 per cent. Over the same period GNP per capita in the Isle of Man increased from 70 per cent of the UK figure to 97 per cent.[120] Such success owed much to the role of the state in support of the economy, through the funding of enhanced welfare provision, new buildings and unprecedented levels of investment in both public and private sector development. The overall scale of capital investment during the period was indicative of the positive role played by the state. Capital advances reached a record level of £25.4 million in 1981/82, fell well below that level during the recession of the 1980s, reaching a low of £10.7 million in 1985/86, and then climbed well above it throughout the 1990s to a new record height of £123.6 million in 1999/2000. Out of a total investment in the 19-year period of just over £574 million, over 70 per cent was committed in the 10 years from April 1990, a reflection of the end of recession and the enhanced capacity of government to intervene in the economy and society.

Public buildings accounted for a significant portion of this total. Reference has already been made to the investment in schools, hospitals, housing and community accommodation for the elderly and other special groups. The expanding role of government called for additional office accommodation and major investments included Markwell House, opened in 1986 at a cost of £2.7 million, Murray House, a new office block purchased in 1990/91 at a cost of £5.2 million, and Illiam Dhone House purchased in 1992/93 at a cost of £1.5 million. A new courthouse and registry, originally planned for the 1980s but postponed because of the recession, were built next to the main Government Offices in Douglas over the course of the 1990s at a total cost of £10.4 million. Expenditure of a further £6 million is anticipated over the next five years on plans to refurbish the old Government Office and General Registry site for use by the legislature and the Clerk of Tynwald's Office.[121] Tynwald also funded the building of an extra deck for the Chester Street car park in 1988/90, contributed £3.8 million towards the cost of a multistorey car park in Drumgold Street, Douglas in 1994/96 and is expected to provide £5.7 million over the next five years towards the cost of the redevelopment of Douglas Corporation's car park at Shaw's Brow.[122]

Manx agriculture and fisheries generated £3.7 million or 2.3 per cent of national income in 1981/82; by 1998/99 the national income contribution had risen to £11.8 million, a real increase of 53 per cent, but accounted for only one per cent of total national income, the result of the extraordinary growth of the financial sector.[123] Despite the declining percentage contribution to national income, successive governments continued to acknowledge the importance of these traditional private sector industries. When the ministerial system was established the Department of Agriculture, Fisheries and Forestry was accepted without question as one of the nine departments of state, necessary to continue the provision of a wide range of support without which the industries would have ceased to be viable. The cornerstone of Manx policy on agriculture and fisheries was to provide economic support on a similar basis to the UK. Tynwald's resolution to that effect in February 1979 was reaffirmed in November 1995, when Tynwald approved an APG resolution with only a single dissenting voice.[124]

Revenue spending on agriculture, fisheries and forestry increased steadily from £2,315,372 in 1980/81 to £4,479,662 in 1988/89, before rising rapidly to £11,135,795 in 1999/2000, a real increase over 1980/81 of just over 100 per cent; the much higher levels of support during the 1990s were in response to the BSE crisis and the depressed state of the agricultural industry. Agricultural support in the form of subsidies and grants accounted for the bulk of the Department's budget. Much lower sums were used to provide grant aid for the purchase and improvement of boats in the Island's fishing fleet and for the management of the publicly owned forests, hills and glens of the Island. Capital spending between 1981/82 and 1999/2000 totalled £20,624,594 and was made up of loans to farmers and fishermen and investment in capital projects. The latter included the funding of a new meat plant between 1992/93 and 1996/97 at a total cost of £6.6 million, new fishery protection vessels in 1986/87 and 1998/2000 and a forestry expansion programme from 1985/86 into the twenty-first century.

Tourism was another traditional industry which became increasingly dependent on government support for survival. It generated £16.6 million or 10.4 per cent of national income in 1981/82 and £46.3 million or 5 per cent in 1998/89, a real increase of 34 per cent.[125] That increase was in no small measure the result of direct government involvement in the industry and support for the private sector to respond to the challenges of international competition. Prior to the reorganisation of government in 1986/88 that support was provided through a number of boards, including the Tourist Board and the Passenger Transport Board. With the creation of departments the prime responsibility was centred in one of the nine departments, the Department of Tourism

Isle of Man Courts of Justice, Douglas. The new courthouse and the adjacent registries building were built during the 1990s at a total cost of £10.4 million. They were officially opened by Chief Minister Gelling on 16 June 1997.

National Sports Centre at Pulrose, Douglas. The main phases of this £22 million leisure complex were completed during the 1990s, the outdoor facilities in 1991, the pool and water complex and the main sports hall and health suite in 1998, and the final indoor facilities in 2000.

and Transport until October 1990, Tourism, Leisure and Transport until January 1995 and Tourism and Leisure after that date. Other departments were also involved, the Department of Agriculture, Fisheries and Forestry with the Wildlife Park (until its transfer to the DTLT in April 1994) and the national glens and mountains, the Department of Harbours, Ports and Properties and after 1995 the Department of Transport with transport infrastructure and development, and the Manx Museum and National Trust.

The Government's aim was to transform both the image and reality of the Island as a resort, from outmoded destination for the traditional family holiday to high quality attraction for special interest holidays and short breaks. By the 1990s 'a new tourism' had emerged from the collapse of the Island's traditional market, a transformation achieved by a more interventionist government, better marketing and a much improved and diversified product.[126] The final decades of the twentieth century saw the development of much closer links between government and the private sector in planning and marketing the industry, better exploitation of the Island's traditional attractions, natural assets and heritage, the involvement of government in the promotion and sale of package holidays and the direct provision of recreational and leisure facilities for both resident and tourist. The Island was also successful, after a long campaign, in persuading the UK authorities to accept a reduction in VAT on holiday accommodation. In Tynwald there was a broad consensus in favour of such developments, although there was no shortage of conflict over issues of detail especially concerning the respective roles of central and local government and a minority would have preferred to see full abrogation of the CEA.

Revenue spending by the Tourist Board and its successor departments on tourism and leisure increased from £1,656,583 in 1980/81 to £10,078,102 in 1999/2000, a real increase of 154 per cent that was in large measure due to the enhanced role of national government in providing leisure facilities. Funding for marketing, the regulation and improvement of holiday accommodation and the development of amenities and events such as the TT Races continued, but by the turn of the century as much was being spent by the Department's Leisure Division on such facilities as the National Sports Centre, the Gaiety Theatre, Summerland and the Wildlife Park. In June 1994 Tynwald agreed to commit an additional £800,000 per annum in support of the industry by lowering VAT on holiday accommodation from 17.5 to 5 per cent.[127] Capital spending during this period totalled £25.9 million, of which 85 per cent was committed between April 1990 and March 2000. During the 1980s tourist premises improvement and development loans accounted for most of the spending; in the 1990s the outstanding commitment was to the £20 million National Sports Centre.

All the indications are that the role of government will continue to grow, whether directly as a provider of entertainment and leisure services or indirectly as a facilitator of development. Three recent decisions of Tynwald certainly point in that direction. In February 1999 Tynwald authorised a full feasibility study into the establishment of a TT Museum in time for the centenary of the first TT races in 1907; in January 2001 Tynwald authorised the DTL to investigate further the option of developing the museum on the Summerland site in partnership with the private sector.[128] In May 1999, following the breakdown of negotiations with Douglas Borough Council over a joint project to refurbish the Villa Marina complex, Tynwald agreed with only one dissenting voice to acquire, manage and develop the complex for the nation. The Villa Marina Act 1999 vested the Villa Marina in the Department of Tourism and Leisure and refurbishment is now proceeding at an estimated total cost of £15.6 million over the five years from 2000/2001.[129] In October 1999 Tynwald approved without division the Western Swimming Pool Order 1999, providing for the establishment of a combination authority to build and operate a swimming pool in the Peel area. As with the earlier development of pools in Douglas, Ramsey and Castletown, the Government promised to contribute towards the funding of the development and to cover any deficiency payments; the pool is expected to be completed by January 2003.[130]

Manx heritage provided the focus for further public investment in the tourist industry. The Manx Museum and National Trust, operating under the name of Manx National Heritage from 1986, was the vehicle for a programme of investment that won for the Island's museums international acclaim. The Trust also retained responsibility for Manx National Trust (MNT) territories, castles and ancient monuments. This period saw important additions to MNT territories, including the transfer of the Calf of Man from the English National Trust in 1986 and the purchase of the Calf Sound for the nation in 1999 at a cost of £500,000, significant improvements in the presentation of Manx heritage and a major expansion of the Manx Museum. Net revenue spending reflected this expansion, rising steadily from £222,105 in 1980/81 to £758,643 in 1988/89 and rapidly to £3,514,205 in 1999/2000, a real increase for the period as a whole of 560 per cent. Capital spending totalled £11,358,119, of which the major portion was for museum developments, an extension to the central museum in Douglas between 1985/86 and 1989/90, and the £5.5 million Peel Heritage Centre (House of Mananan) between 1994/95 and the end of the century. In addition in April 1998, following protracted negotiations with the owner and a select committee investigation,

Tynwald agreed unanimously to acquire the site of the ruins of Rushen Abbey for the nation for the sum of £1.1 million; at the same time Tynwald authorised Manx National Heritage to improve, present and interpret the site at a cost not exceeding £1.2 million.[131]

Tourism and the Island generally depended on good transport. Responsibility was shared between the private and public sectors, private enterprise providing services to and from the Island, the public sector maintaining the airport and the seaports and operating the main transport services within the Island. There were demands for further public ownership and control as services to the Island proved vulnerable to strikes, mergers and the changing priorities of companies whose Manx services were just a small part of their total operation. In contrast with the UK there was no privatisation of the airport, the seaports or the public transport services. Political responsibility was shared by several boards until 1986/88 and by two departments thereafter, albeit with several changes in title and responsibility. For much of the period under discussion most off-Island transport services were in the hands of virtual monopoly providers, Manx Airlines and the Isle of Man Steam Packet Company, leaving the Island vulnerable to variations in the quality of company management, the uncertain impact of mergers and takeovers, industrial disputes and decisions taken for reasons other than the Manx national interest. In practice the close links between the Government and Manx Airlines after its formation in 1982 ensured the maintenance and development of services that were for the most part to the satisfaction of the Island. There were occasional questions in Tynwald, but little by way of serious criticism. The same could not be said of the Steam Packet Company, which was rarely off the agenda of Tynwald between the merger with Manxline, a subsidiary of Sealink UK, in 1985 and a high-powered select committee report in 1999.

The 1985 merger was necessitated by commercial considerations, essentially the conviction of both parties that there was insufficient business for two companies. At the time the Isle of Man Government owned 305,635 shares in the company and was obliged to express a view on the merger. In March 1985 Tynwald agreed to support the merger by 15 votes to two in the Keys and eight votes to one in the Legislative Council, but only after serious questioning regarding the long-term viability of the ferry services.[132] The new Isle of Man Steam Packet Company became a monopoly provider and owner of both the linkspans in Douglas Harbour. In February 1987 Speaker Kerruish moved a resolution in Tynwald seeking public ownership of the Company because of bad management and its adverse effects on the Manx economy. After a lengthy debate, Tynwald accepted an amendment by the Chief Minister proposing the appointment of international shipping consultants to advise on an appropriate strategy.[133] Before Wallem (Isle of Man) Ltd could report, a seven-week strike by the National Union of Seamen in 1988 showed just how vulnerable the Island could be to the decision-making of the new company and reinforced Tynwald's resolve to devise a means of securing the Island's interests more effectively.[134] The Wallem Report recommended rejection of public ownership in favour of a system of licensing sea routes as a means of controlling the standard of service. The Executive Council rejected this proposal and recommended instead the public ownership of the two linkspans and the negotiation of a user agreement as the means of controlling the quality of service. Executive Council also recommended the sale of the Government's shares, which had clearly failed to provide an effective means of control. In June 1988 Tynwald accepted these proposals by an overwhelming majority, but only after the defeat of an amendment by Edgar Quine in favour of the franchising or licensing alternative.[135] The Harbours (Amendment) Act 1989 empowered the Department of Harbours, Ports and Properties to negotiate agreements for the use of harbour facilities, to acquire by compulsory purchase private harbour facilities such as the linkspans and to authorise the establishment of privately operated marinas in Manx harbours.[136]

After lengthy negotiations and investment in a new linkbridge that was more suited to contemporary needs, a user agreement with the Steam Packet Company was approved by Tynwald in July 1995 by 15 votes to seven in the Keys and six votes to two in the Legislative Council.[137] Under the Linkbridge User Agreement the Company was granted the use of the linkbridge in return for guaranteed levels of service, including a minimum investment in the service of £20 million over 10 years. The Government gained the security of owning the linkbridge, the freedom to bring in alternative operators in the event of disrupted services and the ability to challenge fares and charges. In effect the Steam Packet Company was to provide a commercial service within a framework of standards and controls operated by the Department of Transport. When Sea Containers Ltd acquired control of the Company in 1996, the new owners agreed to honour the Agreement.[138] However, it was not long before the performance of Sea Containers Ltd was highlighting the limitations of the user agreement system. Concerns over the frequency and quality of the passenger service and the design of the new ship, the *Ben-my-Chree*, which was seen by many as a freight ship with a passenger facility, led to the appointment by Tynwald of an extraordinary select committee, extraordinary in that it included the Chief Minister, the Minister of Transport and the Minister of Tourism and Leisure sitting ex officio and three other members. Chaired by MLC George Waft, the Select Committee recommended the formation of a statutory Manx Transport Users Consultative Committee, which carriers would be required to consult on policy initiatives and which would have the responsibility to consider complaints about service provision. The recommendation was accepted by Tynwald without division in July 1999 and the necessary legislation promised for 2001/02.[139]

Responsibility for the Island's airport and harbours rested with the Airports and Harbour Boards until 1988 and the Department of Highways, Ports and Properties/Transport thereafter. They were operated on a commercial basis with Tynwald meeting any deficit. In the case of the airport at Ronaldsway the operation was in deficit for 10 of the 19 years and in credit for the other nine, with losses totalling £2,644,270 and profits £2,096,955; the highest deficit was £335,087 in 1984/85 and the highest profit £798,740 in 1995/96. Capital spending totalled £14,642,702 most of which was committed to the development of a new terminal complex and ensuring that facilities conformed with the latest international standards. In the case of harbours and associated services net revenue spending increased from £788,483 in 1980/81 to £3,177,889 in 1989/90 before falling to £1,415,389 in 1999/2000 as a result of increased revenue from harbour dues. Capital spending totalled £22,723,504 and was almost all spent on improvements to Douglas Harbour, a further £9.8 million on the Douglas Breakwater bringing the total cost to £10.3 million between 1980/81 and 1986/87, £4 million on the new linkbridge between 1993/94 and 1997/98 and £3 million on the Douglas Harbour Bridge and Inner Harbour in 1998/2000. Although falling well short of privatisation, in January 1998 Tynwald authorised DOLGE to grant an exclusive option to a private sector developer to progress a scheme for the regeneration of Ramsey Harbour involving the construction of a marina, a housing development and a mixed commercial and leisure facility; it was to involve a public/private partnership between the

Government, the Ramsey Commissioners and Dean and Dyball Developments Ltd. On 14 December 1999 Tynwald approved expenditure not exceeding £1.2 million and guaranteed a £4.2 million loan to facilitate this development.[140] The Policy Review 2000, which was approved by Tynwald on 17 October 2000, anticipated the planning and development of a yachting marina at Port St Mary by 2006 at an estimated cost of £6 million.[141]

By 1981 public transport services had been brought into public ownership and there was agreement in Tynwald to provide an integrated service under the control of a single authority, the Isle of Man Passenger Transport Board. Political responsibility was exercised initially by National Transport Ltd and the Railways Board, from 1983/84 by the Passenger Transport Board and after 1986 by the Public Transport Division of its successor departments, the Department of Tourism and Transport until 1990, Tourism, Leisure and Transport until 1995 and Tourism and Leisure after 1995. Compared with the 1970s there were few conflicts in Tynwald over general strategy. There was broad

Douglas Breakwater under construction during 1982. In November 1979 Tynwald approved a major harbour improvement scheme providing for the protection of the 100-year-old Battery Pier and its extension seawards by means of a breakwater. Work commenced in 1981 and was completed at a cost of £10.3 million in 1983. It was opened by Princess Alexandra in July 1983 and named the Princess Alexandra Pier in her honour.

agreement in Tynwald about keeping passenger transport in the public sector. Most recognised the importance for residents and visitors alike of maintaining an effective bus service, and the evident value of the Island's Victorian railways in attracting visitors brought to an end any serious consideration of closure. Most also accepted that the price of such a strategy was a level of subsidy far in excess of that envisaged at the point of nationalisation. The main reasons for increases in the level of subsidy were the determination of government to keep fares generally well below the economic rate and the increased availability of concessionary fares. The subsidy provided by Tynwald rose sharply from £893,645 in 1980/81 to £4,431,510 in 1991/92, levelled off during the mid-1990s and then increased slightly to £6,057,643 in 1999/2000, a real increase over 1980/81 of 183 per cent. Until the late 1990s most of the service's capital needs were met out of revenue and total capital spending over the 19-year period was only £4,733,793, including the purchase of the assets of National Transport Ltd for £275,565 in 1983/84 and the initial stages of the development of a £4 million bus maintenance facility from 1996/97. At the end of the century the low level of capital investment in the railways infrastructure gave serious cause for concern on health and safety grounds and the Department commissioned consultants to advise on the measures necessary to make the railway system sound for the twenty-first century. The Government's response at a time of unprecedented prosperity in the Island contrasted sharply with the policies of the 1970s, which had seen the temporary closure of both the steam railway and the Laxey to Ramsey section of the electric railway. The Policy Review 1999 anticipated a 12-year capital programme to upgrade the railways at an estimated cost of £12.2 million.[142]

With the UK Government ideologically committed to a wholesale programme of privatisation during the 1980s, it would have been surprising if the subject had not been raised in Tynwald. When it was raised, successive leaders stressed that individual cases would be considered on their merits and that there would be no dogmatic pursuit of privatisation. In fact there were only two cases where privatisation was accepted as appropriate for the Island. In the case of telecommunications private ownership was virtually a *fait accompli* by the time the Island assumed responsibility under the Telecommunications Act 1984, and the role of government became one of regulation and control through licensing. At the time of granting the license to Manx Telecom Ltd support in Tynwald for the private sector option was unanimous. In the case of gas, privatisation of the small unprofitable government undertakings was accepted without division in October 1983, well before privatisation in the UK and for unrelated reasons. Calor Gas Ltd, which had taken over the Ramsey Gas Company, approached the Government with a view to purchase, believing they could achieve economies of scale and offer an efficient service to most of the Island outside the Douglas area. The sale of the government undertakings for £350,000 was recommended to Tynwald by the Select Committee on Energy and supported by the MLP Chair of the Water and Gas Authority, Alex Moore.[143] The Government's role in relation to the gas industry, which did not include natural gas, reverted to one of regulation.

The other components of the commercial public sector included the three statutory boards with responsibility for the post office, electricity and water and two private limited companies with responsibility for Manx Radio and the Laxey Glen Flour Mills. Of these only the Isle of Man Post Office operated without subsidy and, through the success of its philatelic service, was able to make a small annual contribution to the general revenue.[144]

The Island's main source of energy during this period was diesel-generated electricity, provision of which remained in the public sector despite privatisation in the UK in 1990 and 1991 and a takeover bid by the newly privatised Scottish Power in 1992. In 1981 there were still two electricity undertakings in the Isle of Man, the Isle of Man Electricity Board and the Douglas Corporation Electricity Department. In November 1982 Tynwald requested the appointment of a commission to report on their amalgamation. Chaired by Percy Radcliffe, the Commission recommended the formation of an all-Island electricity authority, unencumbered by the debts of the predecessor authorities. In May 1983, Tynwald accepted the principle of amalgamation by 13 votes to 10 in the Keys and six votes to two in the Legislative Council, the main opposition coming from the Douglas members.[145] The Manx Electricity Authority (MEA) was duly established in July 1983 and placed on a more permanent footing by the Electricity Act 1984.[146] The role of government was primarily one of strategic direction and financial assistance. In the mid-1980s the Executive Council and Tynwald approved the MEA proposal to rebuild Pulrose Power Station as the most appropriate means of securing electricity supply into the mid-1990s, the alternative of a submarine cable having been rejected on grounds of cost, insecurity and weather.[147] In the early 1990s the MEA's plans to increase the Island's generating capacity by building a new power station at Peel were put on hold temporarily following receipt of an outline proposal from Scottish Power for the purchase of the MEA with a view to supplying the Island by submarine cable from Scotland. In May 1992 independent consultants, Merz and McLelland, recommended acceptance of the privatisation offer, but the Government was not convinced. A special committee of the Council of Ministers, chaired by Clifford Irving, recommended rejection of the offer and that the MEA be authorised to proceed with the Peel development. In January 1993 Tynwald accepted the recommendation without division, the general feeling being that it was not in the Island's interests to sacrifice control of the supply of electricity to an off-Island company.[148] The Irving Committee recognised the importance of broadening the base of supply beyond that of diesel-powered generation, but saw the way forward as one of partnership between the MEA and organisations capable of delivering submarine supplies by cable or pipeline. In November 1998 Tynwald accepted an MEA strategy based on such principles, involving the installation of a 40-megawatt cable to the Island in cooperation with National Grid PLC and a feasibility study into the importation of natural gas via the Bord Gas Eireann pipeline to fuel a gas-powered power station and a mains gas supply.[149] The submarine electricity cable linking the Island to the UK national grid, between Douglas Head and Bispham near Blackpool, was completed and handed over to the MEA in October 2000. Following an initial feasibility study and approval in principle in November 2000, in July 2001 Tynwald endorsed a DTI/MEA proposal to bring natural gas to the Island from a Bord Gas Eireann pipeline, both to fuel a gas-fired power station at Pulrose and provide a mains gas supply for consumers.[150] The MEA hopes to have the new power station in commercial use by December 2002.

Financial assistance to the MEA came in the form of loans and subsidies. Between 1981/82 and 1990/91 the industry benefitted from loans totalling £37.2 million, of which over £23 million was spent on rebuilding the Pulrose Power Station. The MEA was able to fund its own capital developments during the 1990s. Public subsidy was mainly in the form of debt relief. Interest-free loans to develop hydroelectric power had been approved in 1977, 1979 and 1980. When Tynwald agreed to the formation of the MEA in 1983, it also authorised a waiver of the accumulated debts of the predecessor authorities totalling £4.5 million.[151] When VAT was increased from 15 to 17.5 per cent

Peel Power Station. Two new electric power stations were built by the Manx Electricity Authority during the 10-year Walker Administration, one at Pulrose in Douglas opened in 1989 and the other at Peel opened in 1995. While both developments were controversial, the latter was especially so because of its proximity to the resort of Peel and a stretch of coastline of outstanding natural beauty. The Peel Power Station was opened by Chief Minister Walker in May 1995.

in 1991, Tynwald agreed to commit part of the proceeds to lowering the cost of living; one of the measures approved was the assumption of responsibility for £9 million of MEA debt. The MEA's investment in natural gas at the commencement of the twenty-first century is to be facilitated by a £185 million Treasury loan, approval for which was given in Tynwald in July 2001.[152]

Water supply, privatised in the UK between 1989 and 1992, remained in the public sector, the responsibility of the Water and Gas Authority until 1985 and the Water Authority thereafter. It too became a statutory board in 1988 and enjoyed similar operational freedom to the MEA. Major strategy and financial support were the main reasons for the involvement of Tynwald. The period opened with an ongoing commitment, made initially in November 1977, to build the £12.9 million Sulby Reservoir.[153] It closed in 1999/2000 with Tynwald approving a £75 million loan to the Water Authority to fund its 20-year strategy for renewing the Island's ageing water infrastructure. In June 1999 the first part of that strategy, the Authority's Business Plan 1999/2009, was accepted without division on the understanding that the total cost would be met without further public subsidy.[154] Previous investment in the industry had attracted public subsidy; between 1981/82 and 1999/2000 financial support for the industry was given by payment of loan charges on capital advances totalling £18,993,705. Two thirds of these loan charges were paid in the nine years from 1991/92 as a result of the 1991 budget decision to use part of the additional revenue derived from raising the level of VAT to write off the debts of the Water Authority, a total of £11.4 million incurred primarily by investment in the Sulby Reservoir.

Sulby Reservoir being filled during 1982. The initial commitment to build the reservoir was made by Tynwald in 1977. Work commenced in the upper Sulby valley in 1979 and was completed in 1982 at a cost of £12.9 million. It was opened by Princess Alexandra in July 1983.

Throughout this period Manx Radio was publicly owned. It was operated by Radio Manx Ltd, a private limited company with independent directors and the Government as the sole shareholder, under agreements negotiated on behalf of Tynwald. The operation was subsidised through the payment of an annual public service fee, which increased from £100,000 in 1981/82 to £227,933 in 1999/2000. The Government also provided modest capital advances for such items as a new transmitter and studio development. The only serious questioning of public ownership and subsidy came as a result of a proposal by VideoVision Broadcast (Isle of Man) Ltd in January 1992 to purchase 75 per cent of the shareholding and take over the running of the radio station without public subsidy. After considering the detailed business plans of both VideoVision and Radio Manx Ltd, in December 1992 the Council of Ministers recommended acceptance of the proposal, subject to public consultation and an independent professional appraisal.[155] The following January APG members, Edgar Mann and David Cannan, moved a resolution in Tynwald opposing the sale and pressing for a commitment to public service broadcasting; however, an amendment by Speaker Cain asking the Council of Ministers to commission an independent report on the options open to Tynwald was carried by 13 votes to 10 in the Keys and seven votes to two in the Legislative Council. The ministers present supported the amendment.[156] A committee of enquiry was duly established under the chair of R. Coles and, in a very full report, it recommended that Radio Manx Ltd remain in public ownership and that its public service output be protected by a 'promise of performance' charter laying down minimum programme requirements and the establishment of a trust to oversee the running of the station. The Council of Ministers recommended acceptance of these recommendations and in February 1994 Tynwald concurred without division.[157]

In the case of Laxey Glen Flour Mills privatisation was never a serious option, the only realistic alternative to public ownership being closure. The Government was the sole shareholder, provided the company with an annual subsidy on the local flour to be milled and covered the firm's losses in the eight years from 1983/84 by means of a deficiency grant of between £57,987 in 1985/86 and £258,940 in 1990/91. In 1987 the Government was faced with the choice of either allowing the business to close or increasing the share capital to enable the business to invest in essential modernisation. In December that year, Tynwald approved a proposal by Chief Minister Walker to increase the Government's shareholding from £300,000 to £750,000 by 23 votes to one in the Keys and unanimously in the Legislative Council.[158] Two years later further capital was needed to continue animal feed production, but on this occasion Walker explained to Tynwald that the capital injection required was unjustifiable and that the animal feed division of the business would close.[159] Although the next financial year Tynwald was asked to meet a record deficit of £258,940, on that occasion the Minister for Industry, Bernie May, assured members that the business was under new management, was working towards a new corporate plan and was confident of being able to operate and fund capital requirements without further grant aid. To judge by the annual reports presented to Tynwald during the 1990s that confidence seems to have been well founded.

Private sector manufacturing industry also received extensive financial support from the Government and remained a vital sector in the Manx economy. In 1981/82 the sector generated £22.8 million or 14.3 per cent of national income; the figures for 1998/99 were £82.7 million and nine per cent respectively, a real increase in the contribution to national income of 74 per cent.[160] The number of people employed in manufacturing remained fairly stable, rising from 3,467 (14 per cent of the workforce) in 1981 to 3,562 (10 per cent) in 1996. The continuing success of the sector, especially during the years of recession, was in no small part the result of a supportive government and a consensus in Tynwald in favour of that support. For the most part the story was one of continuity of policy, but with some new initiatives. The low tax regime initiated in the early 1960s continued to favour industrial development. The combination of low corporate taxation, generous capital allowances and low business rates, extremely low personal taxation and freedom from taxes on capital gains, wealth and inheritance made the Island extremely competitive. Between 1981 and 1999 the profits of trading companies were liable to income tax at the rate of 20 per cent; 1999 saw the introduction of the lower rate of 15 per cent on the first £100,000 of taxable income and 2000 a lowering and extension of that rate to 14 per cent on the first £125,000 of taxable income. In October 2000 the Treasury proposed, and Tynwald accepted, a taxation strategy which includes a phased lowering of the level of taxation on trading companies to 10 per cent. The first phase of the strategy was implemented with effect from April 2001 when the standard rate of income tax on trading companies was lowered to 12 per cent on the first £500,000 of taxable income and the higher rate on the balance to 18 per cent.[161] The generous package of investment incentives introduced in 1973 for both new and expanding companies was maintained and from 1986 companies were offered the alternative of applying for a tax holiday for up to five years.[162] In the 19 years from 1981/82 manufacturing industry was helped by a massive £75,674,692 of government assistance, of which 71 per cent was in grants, 17 per cent in loans and the balance for the purchase of industrial sites and the erection of buildings. The highest level of support was in the the early 1980s when the Government prioritised investment in manufacturing to counter the worst effects of the recession, a period that also saw the early development of the Isle of Man Freeport.[163]

The ongoing commitment to the diversification of the Manx economy, which had provided the rationale for the Freeport, also led to support for other industrial ventures, notably in shipping, film production and e-commerce. Changes to the legislation regulating merchant shipping in 1984 and 1991 and the active promotion of marine enterprises by the Government helped to build a successful shipping register and an industry employing around 500 people. By December 2000 a total of 215 merchant ships, 82 fishing boats and 425 yachts were registered in the Isle of Man with a gross tonnage of 5.25 million.[164] Consultations with representatives of the film industry from 1988 onwards led to the adoption of measures to promote a Manx film industry. In December 1988 Tynwald approved without division the Income Tax (Exempt Companies) Order extending the range of companies that were exempt from income tax to include those involved in film production.[165] In April 1995 Tynwald approved without division a transferable tax credit scheme specifically designed to encourage the production of films where at least 20 per cent of the total investment would be spent locally. Under the scheme, which ran until 1998/99, recipients of tax credit who were not liable to tax in the Isle of Man could transfer the tax benefits to local individuals or companies that did have tax liability.[166] In July 1997 the Government established the Isle of Man Film and Television Fund with the aim of promoting the development of the industry partly through loans and partly by means of postdated guarantees covering the investment in films by financial institutions. In the three years from its establishment in 1997/98 the Fund received grants from the DTI totalling £10 million and by the end of March 2000 had provided £8.7 million in loans and postdated guarantees.[167] In 2001 the Lough House Group received a grant of £700,000 from the DTI towards the cost of the Island's first purpose-built film studio. The combination of locational attraction, tax exemption, transferable tax credits, grants, loans and investment guarantees contributed towards the growth of a new industry, the real value of which to the Manx economy lay in the greatly enhanced level of local spending.[168]

Following investigations at the turn of the century into ways of ensuring that the Island was equipped to make the most of the potential of modern communications technology, Tynwald gave its wholehearted approval to a series of initiatives by the Council of Ministers.[169] The Electronic Transactions Act 2000 was promoted by the DTI to facilitate the use of electronic methods in business transactions. In his budget statement to Tynwald in February 2000, Richard Corkill announced the establishment of an E-Commerce/Communication and Information Technology Fund with an initial sum of £7 million and a further £7.5 million in 1999/2000, with the aim of providing funding for measures to equip the Island to make the most of the opportunities presented by modern communications technology, including Internet and related services in government, educational provision and training and the promotion of high value-added business. The following July Tynwald approved the Government's E-Commerce Strategy Report, the central features of which were the appointment of a director of e-commerce to take a lead in coordinating, mobilising and marketing the Island as an e-commerce centre and a proactive role by government in providing education and training, advice and financial support, modern telecommunications services and an environment generally attractive to e-commerce.[170] Announcing the transfer of a further £12 million to the E-Commerce/ICT Fund in February 2001, Corkill reported rapid progress in implementing the strategy, with the necessary leadership, legislation and resources in place to develop e-commerce 'to its full potential'.[171]

The outstanding instance of government-assisted economic diversification during this period was the financial sector. In 1981/82 it generated £34.96 million or 21.8 per cent of national income; by 1998/99 the figures were £396.79 million and 42 per cent, a real increase in income generated of 444 per cent. Employment in the sector increased from 1,515 or six per cent of the total workforce in 1981 to 5,941 or 18 per cent in 1996.[172] While the growth of the sector must be seen in the context of a favourable international environment, in particular the growth in international trade and personal wealth and the progressive dismantling of exchange controls, the vital factor was the ability of the Island's political leadership to exploit the opportunities presented, a point made forcibly with reference to the Isle of Man and the Channel Islands by the Edwards Review in 1998.[173] The judicious exercise of internal self-government enabled the Isle of Man to maintain a favourable tax regime, pass supportive legislation, regulate the sector to international standards, cooperate internationally in the prevention and punishment of financial crime and generally ensure that the Island remained an internationally competitive centre.

Chief Minister Walker opening Barclays International Private Banking Unit, Victoria Street, Douglas, May 1989. The final decades of the twentieth century saw a massive expansion of the Island's financial sector. The opening of this unit took place at the Bank's Head Office in Victoria Street, which had been opened by Jack Nivison in 1983, in the presence of the Head of Barclays, Eddie Shallcross, Treasury Minister, David Cannan, and other bank officials. Between 1987 and 1996, when the bank opened its Eagle Court premises in Circular Road, Douglas, the number of people employed by Barclays in the Isle of Man rose from 85 to 410.

The real attraction of the Isle of Man for the financial sector was the low taxation of companies. Already by 1981 the taxable income of resident companies was subject to tax at the relatively low level of 20 per cent (that of nonresident companies was liable to the same rate of tax but only on taxable income arising in the Island), and Tynwald had passed the Exempt Insurance Companies Act 1981, enabling resident insurance companies to be exempt from income tax in respect of business undertaken outside the Island. Between 1981 and the end of the century a series of measures made the Island even more attractive to financial companies. The Income Tax (Exempt Companies) Act 1984 made it possible for nonresident companies whose income came from outside the Island to be exempt from income tax under certain conditions.[174] The International Business Act 1994 replaced the 1984 Act, renamed the exempt companies 'international companies', gave them similar exemption from income tax and extended exemption to international limited partnerships.[175] The Limited Liability Companies Act 1996 created a new form of company where capital contributions were made by members or partners rather than through the issue of shares and provided for nonresident members or partners to be exempt from income tax.[176] The lowering of company taxation in 1999 and 2000 also applied to resident financial companies. These measures also had the effect of diversifying the financial sector. Other measures with such diversification as a goal included the Building Societies Act 1986, the Credit Unions Act 1993, the Trust Act 1995, the Insurance (Amendment) Act 1995, the Purpose Trusts Act 1996, the Limited Liability Companies (Amendment) Act 1999 and the Retirement Benefits Schemes Act 2000.[177]

Royal Bank House, Victoria Street, Douglas. The new Royal Bank of Scotland International building was opened by Viscount Younger of Lockie, chair of the RBS Group, in January 2000. The Chief Minister, Donald Gelling, was a guest of honour. Between the launch of RBSI in the Isle of Man in 1996 and the opening of Royal Bank House the number of employees working for the Group increased from 100 to 202.

In parallel with measures to make the Island economically attractive to financial institutions were others designed to regulate the sector to the highest international standards. The collapse of the Savings and Investment Bank in 1982 highlighted the need for more effective financial supervision and led directly to the establishment of the Financial Supervision Commission (FSC) by order in January 1983. The FSC was placed on a permanent footing under the Financial Supervision Commission Act 1984.[178] This was followed by a raft of other regulatory measures: the Banking (Amendment) Act 1986, the Building Societies Act 1986, the Insurance Act 1986, the Financial Supervision Act 1988, the Investment Business Act 1991, the Insurance Intermediaries (General Business) Act 1996, the Banking Act 1998 and the Corporate Service Providers Act 2000.[179] A further group of measures was designed to prevent, deter and punish financial crime and to assist other jurisdictions. These and associated regulations were largely based on UK legislation and accorded with international agreements in the repective areas. They included the Corruption Act 1986, the Summary Jurisdiction Act 1989, the Prevention of Terrorism Act 1990, the Criminal Justice Acts 1990 and 1991, the Drug Trafficking Act 1996, the Police Powers and Procedures Act 1998, the Criminal Justice (Money Laundering) Act 1998 and the Insider Dealing Act 1998.[180]

The driving force behind the regulatory and criminal legislation and associated regulations was the Manx Government's determination, in the aftermath of the Savings and Investment Bank debacle, to attract the right sort of business and project a favourable image to the international financial community. Considerable attention was given to marketing and public relations with the aim of portraying the Island as a centre meeting the highest international standards. Much of the criticism directed generally at offshore centres during the 1990s was successfully rebuffed in this way and when the UK instituted the Edwards Review the Island cooperated and emerged with flying colours, firmly located by Edwards in 'the top division of offshore centres'.[181] The Government responded positively to the Edwards Review, promising action to deal with warranted criticism, a renewed commitment to the development of a world-class international financial centre and a determination, with the help of specialist consultants, to support that development by projecting a strong and accurate image to the international community.[182] The Government was equally positive in its response to EU and OECD criticisms of the Island, embarking on a new taxation strategy both to remain competitive as an international financial centre and to remove from that regime the elements that were deemed 'harmful' by its international critics.

## *Manx Finances 1981–2000*

Notwithstanding progress towards internal self-government, the influence of the UK on Manx finances continued to be a central feature of both expenditure and taxation. A large percentage of total expenditure was accounted for by high spending areas such as health, social security, education, agriculture and law and order where the Island chose to follow UK policy. The extent of the influence diminished slightly as the Island opted to spend more per capita on its welfare services than the UK. Expenditure on defence and common services under the Contribution Act 1956 was maintained at the rate of 2.5 per cent of the net revenue from the CEA until 1991/92. The above inflation increases in VAT, in particular the UK decision in 1991 to increase VAT from 15 to 17.5 per cent, led to Manx demands for a break in the link between the contribution and indirect taxation. The UK accepted the Manx request for change and under the Isle of Man Contribution Agreement 1994 the Isle of Man agreed to pay £1.75 million in 1992/93 and 1993/94 compared with £1.9 million in 1991/92. In subsequent years the contribution was to be uprated in line with inflation.[183] Total revenue spending increased from £58,226,000 in 1980/81 to £127,676,000 in 1989/90 and £291,804,000 in 1999/2000, a real increase for the period as a whole of 109 per cent. Changes in the level of expenditure are summarised in Table 9.1.

The most controversial aspect of Manx finances after 1979 was the formal agreement with the UK in relation to indirect taxation. Under the Customs and Excise Agreement 1979 (CEA) the Island agreed to keep almost all indirect taxation in line with the UK in return for a net share of the joint revenues. Within Tynwald it was generally acknowledged that the lack of direct control over one of the two major sources of revenue undermined the Island's right to internal self-government. Critics demanded abrogation of the Agreement so that the Island could be master of its own destiny, but

**Table 9.1. Central Government Spending 1981/2 to 1999/2000**

| Financial Year up to 31 March | Total Expenditure £ | Expenditure at 2000 Prices £ |
|---|---|---|
| 1982 | 60,698,607 | 129,834,320* |
| 1983 | 70,365,963 | 141,787,410 |
| 1984 | 77,955,894 | 149,831,220 |
| 1985 | 83,516,417 | 149,577,900 |
| 1986 | 87,846,728 | 152,941,150 |
| 1987 | 87,411,235 | 146,850,870 |
| 1988 | 100,605,616 | 161,371,410 |
| 1989 | 109,417,910 | 165,330,460 |
| 1990 | 127,676,016 | 178,363,390 |
| 1991 | 150,918,665 | 195,439,670 |
| 1992 | 175,480,236 | 215,489,730 |
| 1993 | 187,537,493 | 224,669,910 |
| 1994 | 195,677,648 | 228,942,850 |
| 1995 | 195,971,090 | 222,427,180 |
| 1996 | 208,812,707 | 229,902,790 |
| 1997 | 226,539,514 | 243,756,510 |
| 1998 | 240,139,621 | 251,186,040 |
| 1999 | 265,373,543 | 272,273,250 |
| 2000 | 291,804,095 | 291,804,095 |

\*   (to nearest £10)

The sources of the raw expenditure data were the *Accounts of the Government Treasurer* from 1981/82 to 1985/86, the *Isle of Man Government Accounts* 1986/87 to 1998/99 and *Detailed Government Accounts* 1993/94 to 1999/2000. The level of spending at 2000 prices was calculated with the help of the Price Index supplied by Martin Caley of the Economic Affairs Division of the Manx Treasury. The real expenditure figures should be treated with caution as they are derived with the help of an index designed for a different purpose.

To avoid double counting, expenditure facilitated by borrowing is not included in the raw totals, which are total expenditure from the General Revenue Account.

during the 1980s most members of Tynwald were prepared to accept the advice of the Select Committee on the Common Purse in favour of retention. This was despite the refusal of the UK authorities to agree a reduction in VAT on nonexportable services. The formula for sharing joint revenues was believed to favour the Island and it was accepted that unplanned increases in the cost of living could be mitigated by judicious spending.[184] In October 1984 Tynwald agreed not to seek any alteration to the CEA before the general election in 1986 and asked the Executive Council to report on abrogation.[185] After a long delay and protracted negotiations with the UK, the Council of Ministers eventually reported to Tynwald in June 1994 that the UK was now willing to accommodate within the CEA limited flexibility in VAT rates on certain nonexportable services. Accordingly it recommended maintaining the Agreement and lowering VAT on tourist accommodation from 17.5 to 5 per cent at an estimated annual cost of £800,000. An APG attempt to delete all reference in the resolution to the maintenance of the CEA was defeated and the resolution was carried with just the five members of the APG opposed.[186] In March 2000 the Island was successful in negotiating a second reduction in VAT from 17.5 to 5 per cent, this time on repairs and renovations to private dwellings at an estimated cost of £2 million per annum.[187]

Between 1980/81 and 1999/2000 the revenue from indirect taxation rose steadily from £29.5 million to £183.3 million, a real increase of 159 per cent. The proportions of these totals attributable to equal duties under the CEA were 95.4 and 99.6 per cent respectively, the increase being the result of the tax on beer being made an equal duty from 1993/94. The percentage of total revenue derived from indirect taxation fell from around 50 per cent in the early 1980s to a low of 43 per cent in 1990/91 before rising to just over 50 per cent in the six years to 1999/2000. Conversely, the percentage of total revenue from income tax increased from just under 40 per cent in 1980/81 to a high of 53 per cent in 1990/91 before falling to between 42 and 47 per cent in the same six years. The retention of the CEA constitutes an integral element of the new taxation strategy approved by Tynwald in October 2000, providing a relatively secure source of income and underpinning the Island's ability to be flexible on direct taxation. The impact of the proposed reductions in income tax on revenue is uncertain, but as with the abolition of surtax in 1960 the anticipation is that total tax receipts will increase as a result of tax-induced growth in the level and quality of economic activity.[188]

# *Notes*

1   See 99 *Manx Deb.*, 23 March 1982, pp. K323–28, 30 March 1982, pp. K352–56 and 29 June 1982, pp. C296–306.
2   *Acts of Tynwald 1982*, pp. 299–312.
3   See 106 *Manx Deb.*, 8 November 1988, pp. K87–125 and 15 November 1988, pp. K135–37. With the voting on the third reading on 8 November 1988 tied at 12 votes to 12, Speaker Kerruish cast his vote in favour and it seemed as if the Bill had passed; however, the following week the Speaker informed the House that as the Bill had only been supported by 12 members on the third reading, one short of the necessary 13, it had in fact failed.
4   *Acts of Tynwald 1990*, pp. 377–80.
5   See 111 *Manx Deb.*, 18 January 1994, pp. T285–94.
6   See Section 47 of Schedule 2 to the Act, *Acts of Tynwald 1995*, pp. 273–358.
7   See 99 *Manx Deb.*, 27 April 1982, pp. K419–45.
8   *Acts of Tynwald 1985*, pp. 91–98.

9   Although nominally this distribution obtained for the rest of the twentieth century, Tynwald's approval of a town boundary extension for Ramsey in 1993 increased the size of the Ramsey constituency at the expense of the adjacent sheading constituencies.

10  The clause was rejected by 15 votes to nine; see 107 *Manx Deb.*, 6 March 1990, pp. K981–1019.

11  By 15 votes to eight in the Keys and by five votes to three in the Legislative Council; see 110 *Manx Deb.*, 16 March 1993, pp. T471–86.

12  The Cannan proposal was defeated by 14 to nine; see 11 *Manx Deb.*, 1 March 1994, pp. K290–96. The Mann proposal, in the form of an amendment to the Government's consolidation bill, was rejected by 13 votes to 10; see 112 *Manx Deb.*, 31 January 1995, pp. K313–56.

13  See 112 *Manx Deb.*, 31 January 1995, pp. K313–56 and 14 February 1995, pp. K415–24.

14  See 113 *Manx Deb.*, 5 March 1996, pp. K318–21.

15  See 115 *Manx Deb.*, 11 November 1997, pp. K106–12.

16  See *Acts of Tynwald 1986*, pp. 151–62.

17  See *Acts of Tynwald 1989*, pp. 99–105. Michael Village District was created following a resolution of Tynwald in July 1905.

18  See DOLGE, *Time for Change*, December 1991, *Time for Change: Interim Report*, December 1992, and *Time for Change: Final Report*, March 1994. A useful summary of the proposals and Tynwald's reactions to them is contained in DOLGE, *Securing a Future for Local Government*, October 1997.

19  See *Acts of Tynwald 1993*, pp. 259–71, *Acts of Tynwald 1995*, pp. 3–39 and *Acts of Tynwald 1996*, pp. 255–322; 11 *Manx Deb.*, 14 July 1994, pp. T817–31; 112 *Manx Deb.*, 18 January 1995, pp. T319–49 and 350–53; 112 *Manx Deb.*, 12 July 1995, pp. T846–58 and 113 *Manx Deb.*, 15 July 1996, pp. T1168–85.

20  See *Acts of Tynwald 1992*, pp. 183–95 and *Acts of Tynwald 1995*, pp. 361–67.

21  See 117 *Manx Deb.*, 14 December 1999, pp. T265–83.

22  See *Acts of Tynwald 2000*, pp. 89–106 and *Acts of Tynwald 2001* (forthcoming).

23  See 105 *Manx Deb.*, 19/20 April 1988, pp. T1115–88 and 1221–40.

24  See 116 *Manx Deb.*, 16 February 1999, pp. T441–48 and 117 *Manx Deb.*, 15 February 2000, pp. T456–57; see also Isle of Man Government, *The Isle of Man Budget 1999–2000* and *The Isle of Man Budget 2000–2001*.

25  See 103 *Manx Deb.*, 20 May 1986, pp. T1775–855.

26  See 117 *Manx Deb.*, 15 February 2000, pp. T415–21.

27  See 117 *Manx Deb.*, 20 June 2000, pp. T792–97, *Policy Review 2000*, vol. 1, pp. 20–26 and 118 *Manx Deb.*, 18 October 2000, pp. T73–93.

28  *Isle of Man Budget 2000–2001*, February 2001, pp. xiii-xiv; the three main personal income tax allowances were increased by 2.2 per cent in line with inflation to £7,700, £15,400 and £5,270 respectively; see also 118 *Manx Deb.*, 20 February 2001, pp. 464–506.

29  See 117 *Manx Deb.*, 20 June 2000, pp. T792–97, *Policy Review 2000*, vol. 1, pp. 19–26, and 118 *Manx Deb.*, 18 October 2000, pp. T73–92.

30  See 104 *Manx Deb.*, 24 March 1987, pp. T849–67 and 105 *Manx Deb.*, 17 May 1988, pp. T1405–09.

31  See 113 *Manx Deb.*, 10 July 1996, pp. T1018–54. The three new allowances replaced basic unemployment benefit, supplementary benefit for the unemployed and enhanced unemployment benefit.

32  See 115 *Manx Deb.*, 22 October 1997, pp. T78–94.

33  See 116 *Manx Deb.*, 16 May 1999, pp. T632–37.

34  See 102 *Manx Deb.*, 21 November 1986, pp. T492–508; *Acts of Tynwald 1985*, pp. 221–29.

35  See 106 *Manx Deb.*, 13 December 1988, pp. T565–73.

36  See 105 *Manx Deb.*, 19/20 April 1988, pp. T1115–88 and 1221–40.

37  See 106 *Manx Deb.*, 18 April 1989, pp. 1290–352.

38   The UK rate remained frozen until 1991/92 when separate rates were introduced for the eldest child and others. By the final year of Conservative rule the UK rates were £10.80 and £8.80 compared with £12.90, £13.65 and £21.30 in the Isle of Man. Even with the Labour Government's above inflation increases after 1997, Manx rates remained well above those of the UK; for comparative figures for the UK and IOM, see DHSS, *Record £142 Million Social Security Spending*, 20 February 2001 (Press Release), Appendix 2.

39   See 107 *Manx Deb.*, 10 July 1990, pp. T2128–30.

40   See 108 *Manx Deb.*, 16 April 1991, pp. T1400–508.

41   See 109 *Manx Deb.*, 19 May 1992, pp. T395–407 and 110 *Manx Deb.*, 21 October 1992, pp. T105–10.

42   See 111 *Manx Deb.*, 15 March 1994, pp. T402–42.

43   See 114 *Manx Deb.*, 15 April 1997, pp. T380–87 and 22 October 1997, p. T110.

44   See 118 *Manx Deb.*, 22 November 2000, pp. T273–86 and *The Isle of Man Budget 2001–2002*, February 2001, p. xi.

45   See 116 *Manx Deb.*, 13 July 1999, pp. T982–92.

46   Between 1981 and 2000 the total claims for payment of social security benefit increased by 32 per cent from 26,031 to 34,381; the most significant were for child benefit, where the number of families making claims rose by 33 per cent from 6,934 to 9,212, and retirement pensions, where the number of claimants was up by 9 per cent from 13,865 to 15,164. Over the same period the number of recipients of supplementary benefit increased from 2,138 to 4,789 in 1995 before falling to 3,361 in 2000, a two thirds increase over 1981. See *Isle of Man Digest of Economic and Social Statistics 1982–83*, p. O9 and *Isle of Man Digest of Economic and Social Statistics 2001*, Tables 10.1 and 10.2.

47   See Isle of Man Government, *Policy Report 1993*, p. 43.

48   See Isle of Man Government, *Policy Review 1999*, vol. 2, p. 8 and *Isle of Man Budget 2000–2001*, p. 26.

49   For details of the debate between 1982 and 1985, see 101 *Manx Deb.*, 16 November 1983, pp. 491–597 and 13 December 1983, pp. T543–63 and 102 *Manx Deb.*, 19 February 1985, pp. T1111–13.

50   See *Isle of Man Budget 1999–2000*, February 1999, p. 33.

51   See *Isle of Man Digest of Economic and Social Statistics 2001*, Tables 11.2 and 11.3.

52   See *Isle of Man Examiner*, 18 July and 22 August 2000; see also *Policy Review 2000*, vol. 2, p. 17.

53   See Isle of Man Government, *Policy Review 1989*, pp. 30–31.

54   See 114 *Manx Deb.*, 15 April 1997, pp. T354–59.

55   See for example the comparative figures for 1995–98 reported in the *Policy Review 1999*, pp. 10–11.

56   See 116 *Manx Deb.*, 20 April 1999, pp. T714–15 and 13 July 1999, pp. T966–69; see also *Policy Review 2000*, vol. 1, pp. 76–77 for details of the expenditure incurred and about longer term plans for investment in a similar suite for Ramsey Grammar School.

57   See 99 *Manx* Deb., 17 March 1982, pp. T700–18.

58   *Acts of Tynwald 1983*, pp. 269–73.

59   See 100 *Manx Deb.*, 21 December 1982, pp. K168–78.

60   *Acts of Tynwald 1990*, pp. 219–333.

61   *Acts of Tynwald 1993*, pp. 187–223.

62   *Acts of Tynwald 2000*, pp. 47–59.

63   See 97 *Manx Deb.*, 17 October 1979, pp. T129–43.

64   See 99 *Manx Deb.*, 13 July 1982, pp. T1069–90.

65   See 101 *Manx Deb.*, 19 June 1984, pp. T1483–524.

66   See 105 *Manx Deb.*, 23 February 1988, pp. T853–919.

67   See 108 *Manx Deb.*, 12 December 1990, pp. T811–65.

68   See 111 *Manx Deb.*, 16 February 1994, pp. T347–72.

69  See 118 *Manx Deb.*, 18 October 2000, pp. T93–144; see also Isle of Man Government, *Policy Review 2000*, vol. 1, pp. xvi and 80 and vol. 2, pp. 61–62.

70  See 107 *Manx Deb.*, 20 March 1990, pp. T1182–200.

71  See 108 *Manx Deb.*, 20 February 1991, pp. T1231–60.

72  See Isle of Man Government, *Policy Review 2000*, vol. 1, pp. 33–35 and 84.

73  Isle of Man Government, *Isle of Man Budget 2000–2001*, pp. 109, 113 and 118. The planned expenditure covers landfill site use until the incinerator is ready, landfill sites for municipal solid waste and incinerator arisings, the 'energy from waste' incinerator, civic amenity sites, a knackery for the disposal of animal remains, and the next stages of the IRIS masterplan and related local authority schemes.

74  *Acts of Tynwald 2001*, pp. 307–41. The Act retained much of the original 1948 Act, including the duty to provide a comprehensive service, but also provided for a more flexible committee structure, better regulation of the Service and the establishment of a medical complaints procedure.

75  See *Isle of Man Health Services Inquiry. Report to the Health Services Board*, March 1986.

76  See 107 *Manx Deb.*, 25 October 1987, pp. T303–68.

77  For details, see Liverpool University Planning Consortium, *Isle of Man Health Services Review*, April 1991, vol. 1, pp. 1–259.

78  See *Report of the Council of Ministers on the Review of the Isle of Man Health Services by the Liverpool Planning Consortium*, June 1993 and the Isle of Man Government, *Policy Reviews* 1991–2000.

79  See 108 *Manx Deb.*, 11 July 1991, pp. T2269–73.

80  See 110 *Manx Deb.*, 22 October 1992, pp. T111–27.

81  See 112 *Manx Deb.*, 20 October 1994, pp. T114–36.

82  See 112 *Manx Deb.*, 11 April 1995, pp. T569–95.

83  See *Isle of Man Budget 1998–99*, March 1999, p. vii. Delays in commencing the hospital meant there was enough money in the DHSS vote to cover loan charges up to 1998/99; the balance in the Fund on 31 March 2000, after one year's payment of loan charges, was £79.4 million, enough to meet the loan charges in respect of the new hospital for the foreseeable future; see *Detailed Government Accounts for the Year ended 31st March 2000*, p. 129.

84  See Isle of Man Government, *Policy Review 2000*, vol. 1, p. 78.

85  *Acts of Tynwald 1999*, pp. 125–87.

86  See for example the debates on the all-Island order in 1982 and the local plans for Ramsey and Douglas in 1988 and 1989 respectively; 99 *Manx Deb.*, 15 June 1982, pp. T973–1011 and 106 *Manx Deb.*, 13 December 1989, pp. T573–79 and 17 January 1989, pp. T714–36 and 749–85.

87  See 108 *Manx Deb.*, 20–21 November 1990, pp. T477–99 and 501–56; after a lengthy debate the recommendations were accepted by 22 votes to two in the Keys and unanimously in the Legislative Council.

88  See Isle of Man Treasury, *Digest of Economic and Social Statistics 2000*, Table 12.1 and DOLGE, *Housing Policy Review Report*, November 1999, Appendix 2A.

89  See DOLGE, *Housing Policy Review Report*, November 1999, pp. 15–16 and 22–23 and *Policy Review 2000*, vol. 2, pp. 63–67. DOLGE's first progress report on the five-year plan was published in Februay 2001, revealing that 433 new housing units were completed during 2000, of which 79 were in the public sector; see *Isle of Man Examiner*, 27 February 2001.

90  Isle of Man Treasury, *Digest of Economic and Social Statistics 2001*, Tables 12.3 and 12.4.

91  See DOLGE, *Housing Report*, October 1990 and 108 *Manx Deb.*, 19 February 1991, pp. T1072–85.

92  See 116 *Manx Deb.*, 13 July 1999, pp. T999–1008.

93  My thanks are due to R. B. Briercliffe of the Isle of Man Treasury for supplying these data.

94  My thanks are due to Peter Whiteway of DOLGE for help in compiling this figure; see also 106 *Manx Deb.*, 25 October 1988, pp. T248–65 and 13 December 1988, pp. T550–59;

108 *Manx Deb.*, 11 December 1990, pp. T737–38 and 109 *Manx Deb.*, 22 January 1992, pp. T102–07 and 133–48.

95  See 116 *Manx Deb.*, 18 May 1999, pp. T875–81; see also Isle of Man Government, *The Isle of Man Budget 2000–2001*, February 2000, p. 46. The Scheme was widened in July 2000 to help second-time buyers and thereby free up lower priced properties for first-time buyers; see 117 *Manx Deb.*, 11 July 2000, pp. T1990–1006.

96  See 99 *Manx Deb.*, 16 December 1981, pp. T382–83.

97  See 105 *Manx Deb.*, 17 February 1988, pp. T761–67.

98  These data were provided by the Isle of Man Treasury and the Department of Local Government and the Environment; thanks are due to R. B. Briarcliffe of the Treasury and T. P. Whiteway of DOLGE for supplying the information.

99  See 118 *Manx Deb.*, 19 October 2000, pp. T172–77

100  These unemployment figures were derived from monthly data furnished by the Economics Division of the Treasury; see also Isle of Man Treasury, *Digest of Economic and Social Statistics 2001*, Tables 3.5 and 3.6.

101  See 106 *Manx Deb.*, 15 April 1986, pp. T1696–710. With the introduction of the Job Seeker's Allowance in 1996, the period during which this benefit could be paid was extended from three to 12 months.

102  See 102 *Manx Deb.*, 14 December 1982, pp. T319–22.

103  102 *Manx Deb.*, 14 December 1982, pp. T319–22.

104  *Acts of Tynwald 1985*, pp. 211–18.

105  See 103 *Manx Deb.*, 4 February 1986, pp. K596–623.

106  *Acts of Tynwald 1986*, pp. 1139–58.

107  See 103 *Manx Deb.*, 26 February 1986, pp. T1242–71 and 27 May 1986, pp. K1261–81.

108  See 103 *Manx Deb.*, 26 October 1986, pp. T53–54.

109  For a discussion of the role of the unions during this period, see Robert Fyson, 'Labour History', in J. C. Belchem (ed.), *A New History of the Isle of Man: The Modern Period 1830–1999*, vol. 5 (Liverpool, 2000), pp. 307–09.

110  See *Law relating to Employment for the Isle of Man. A Report by Executive Council*, March 1988.

111  See 106 *Manx Deb.*, 25 April 1989, pp. T1528–48.

112  *Acts of Tynwald 1990*, pp. 481–555.

113  See 108 *Manx Deb.*, 4 December 1990, pp. K309–10.

114  *Acts of Tynwald 1991*, pp. 725–875.

115  *Acts of Tynwald 1991*, pp. 879–914.

116  See *Sexual Equality in Employment. A Report by the Council of Ministers*, September 1991 and 108 *Manx Deb.*, 16 October 1991, pp. T2635–44.

117  *Acts of Tynwald 2000*, pp. 263–300.

118  See 116 *Manx Deb.*, 23 February 1999, pp. T565–91. Gelling's amendment was carried by 21 votes to three in the Keys and unanimously in the Legislative Council.

119  See *A Statutory Minimum Wage. A Report by the Council of Ministers*, September 1999 and 117 *Manx Deb.*, 20 October 1999, pp. T134–46; see also *Acts of Tynwald 2001* (forthcoming). The legislation is due to take effect on 1 January 2002. On 13 July 2001 Tynwald approved regulations setting the minimum wage at £4.10; see *Isle of Man Examiner*, 17 July 2001 and 118 *Manx Deb.*, 13 July 2001 (forthcoming).

120  Isle of Man Government, *Isle of Man National Income 1998/99*, September 2000, Table 6 and Figure 1, pp. 8–9.

121  See *Policy Review 2000*, vol. 1, p. 80 and 117 *Manx Deb.*, 16 May 2000, pp. T685–89.

122  See *Policy Review 2000*, vol. 1, p. 84 and vol. 2, p. 67.

123  Isle of Man Government, *Digest of Economic and Social Statistics 1988*, Table 14.3, p. 139 and *Isle of Man National Income 1998/99*, p. 5.

124  See 113 *Manx Deb.*, 22–23 November 1995, pp. T280–303

125 Isle of Man Government, *Digest of Economic and Social Statistics 1988*, Table 14.3, p. 139 and *Isle of Man National Income 1998/99*, p. 5.

126 Isle of Man Department of Tourism and Leisure, *Tourism Strategy: Building for the Future* (undated, but published during the summer of 1999), p. 6.

127 See 111 *Manx Deb.*, 21 June 1994, pp. T620–42.; see also *Policy Review 2000*, vol. 1, p. 80.

128 See 116 *Manx Deb.*, 17 February 1999, pp. T548–63 and 118 *Manx Deb.*, 16 January 2001, pp. T439–47.

129 See 116 *Manx Deb.*, 18 May 1999, pp. T869–75, *Acts of Tynwald 1999*, pp. 235–37 and *Policy Review 2000*, vol. 1, p. 81 and vol. 2, p. 99.

130 See 117 *Manx Deb.*, 20 October 1999, pp. T110–11; see also *Isle of Man Examiner*, 21 November 2000 and 17 July 2001.

131 See 115 *Manx Deb.*, 28 April 1998, pp. T551–55.

132 See 102 *Manx Deb.*, 19 March 1985, pp. T1416–78.

133 See 104 *Manx Deb.*, 17 and 18 February 1987, pp. T468–80 and 496–540.

134 See 105 *Manx Deb.*, 16 February 1988, pp. T672–734.

135 See 105 *Manx Deb.*, 21 June 1988, pp. T1527–85.

136 *Acts of Tynwald 1989*, pp. 193–206.

137 See 112 *Manx Deb.*, 11 July 1995, pp. T798–833.

138 See 113 *Manx Deb.*, 16 April 1996, pp. T691–701.

139 See 116 *Manx Deb.*, 14 July 1999, pp. T1025–32 and Isle of Man Government, *Policy Review 2000*, vol. 1, p. 94. In the 1999 Policy Review the legislation had been promised for 2000/01, but a congested timetable obliged the Government to postpone its introduction.

140 See 117 *Manx Deb.*, 14 December 1999, pp. T245–50. The project has since met with massive opposition from the pressure group, Ramsey Against Insensitive Development, and many members of Tynwald, including the Ramsey MHKs. Although it is still backed by the Government and a majority of members in Tynwald, it suffered a major setback when, on 11 July 2001, a Government resolution, which would have provided for the transfer of development land necessary for the project from the Ramsey Commissioners to DOLGE, was defeated by an adverse vote in the Legislative Council; see *Isle of Man Examiner*, 17 July 2001 and 118 *Manx Deb.*, 11 July 2001 (forthcoming).

141 See *Policy Review 2000*, vol. 1, p. 84 and vol. 2, p. 129.

142 *Policy Review 2000.*, vol. 2, pp. 76–77; see also Isle of Man Government, *The Isle of Man Budget 2000/01*, February 2000, p. 110.

143 See 101 *Manx Deb.*, 25 October 1983, pp. T301–13.

144 This ranged from no contribution in 1983/84 and 1984/85 to a high of £650,000 in 1981/82; from 1994/95 to 1998/99 the annual contribution was £250,000, but increased to £500,000 in 1999/2000; see *Accounts of the Government Treasurer* for the period up to 1985/86, the *Isle of Man Government Accounts* for 1986/87 to 1992/93 and *Detailed Government Accounts* for 1993/94 to 1999/2000. The Authority was able to fund most of its capital needs without borrowing.

145 See 100 *Manx Deb.*, 17 May 1983, pp. T995–1033.

146 *Acts of Tynwald 1984*, pp. 83–114.

147 See 103 *Manx Deb.*, 17 June 1986, pp. T2174–204.

148 See Council of Ministers, *A Report on the Scottish Power Proposal and other Options by the Committee on Generating Options*, December 1992 and 110 *Manx Deb.*, 20 January 1993, pp. T357–66.

149 See 115 *Manx Deb.*, 21 January 1998, pp. T363–68 and 116 *Manx Deb.*, 18 November 1998, pp. T241–53.

150 See Department of Trade and Industry, *Report on the initial feasibility study on the importation of natural gas to the Island*, November 2000, and *Report on Proposals to Import Natural Gas …*, 31 May 2001; see also 118 *Manx Deb.*, 21 November 2000, pp. T240–52, and 20 June 2001 (forthcoming).

151 See 100 *Manx Deb.*, 17 May 1983, pp. T995–1033.

152 See 108 *Manx Deb.*, 16 April 1991, pp. T1400–508 and 118 *Manx Deb.*, 10 July 2001 (forthcoming).

153 See 95 *Manx Deb.*, 16 November 1977, pp. T246–50.

154 See 116 *Manx Deb.*, 15 June 1999, pp. T913–21.

155 See *The Future of Manx Radio. A Proposal by the Council of Ministers*, December 1992.

156 See 110 *Manx Deb.*, 20 January 1993, pp. T367–89.

157 See *Manx Radio. Report of the Committee of Inquiry into the Options for the Future of Manx Radio with Initial Responses and Proposals by the Council of Ministers*, January 1994 and 111 *Manx Deb.*, 16 February 1994, pp. T372–88. The detailed implementation of the recommendations was the subject of two further reports by the Council of Ministers, both of which were accepted in Tynwald without division; see *Report of the Council of Ministers on the Outstanding Recommendations of the Committee of Inquiry into the Options for the Future of Manx Radio*, June 1994 and 111 *Manx Deb.*, 12 July 1994, pp. T753–60; *Report of the Council of Ministers on the Manx Radio Trust*, March 1995 and 112 *Manx Deb.*, 22 March 1995, pp. T548–49.

158 See 105 *Manx Deb.*, 15 December 1987, pp. T433–69.

159 See 107 *Manx Deb.*, 12 December 1989, pp. T549–50.

160 Isle of Man Government, *Digest of Economic and Social Statistics 1988*, p. 139 and *Isle of Man National Income 1998/99*, p. 5.

161 See *Policy Review 2000*, vol. 1, pp. 21–26, 118 *Manx Deb.*, 18 October 2000, pp. T73–93 and *The Isle of Man Budget 2000–2001*, February 2001, p. xiii.

162 Under the Income Tax (Amendment) Act 1986, *Acts of Tynwald 1986*, pp. 607–38. For details of the incentives available at the end of the century, see Isle of Man Government Treasury, *Factfile: Isle of Man* (2000).

163 See Isle of Man Government, *Digest of Economic and Social Statistics* for 1988, 1992, 1994, 1999, 2000 and 2001.

164 Isle of Man Government, *Digest of Economic and Social Statistics 2001*, Table 13.7.

165 See 106 *Manx Deb.*, 13 December 1988, pp. T560–65.

166 See 112 *Manx Deb.*, 11 April 1995, pp. T597–602.

167 See Isle of Man Government, *Detailed Government Accounts for the Year ended 31 March 1999*, p. 135, and *Detailed Government Accounts for the Year ended 31 March 2000*, p. 135.

168 See 116 *Manx Deb.*, 25 May 1999, pp. K449–50.

169 For details of these initiatives and the ongoing e-commerce strategy, see *Policy Review 2000*, vol. 1, pp. 32 and 40–50.

170 See 117 *Manx Deb.*, 12 July 2000, pp. T959–76.

171 See 118 *Manx Deb.*, 20 February 2001, pp.

172 Isle of Man Government, *Digest of Economic and Social Statistics 1999*, Table 3.3.

173 See *Review of Financial Regulation in the Crown Dependencies: A Report*, Cm 4109–1, November 1998, p. ix.

174 *Acts of Tynwald 1984*, pp. 177–88.

175 *Acts of Tynwald 1994*, pp. 21–44.

176 *Acts of Tynwald 1996*, pp. 661–706.

177 See relevant annual volumes of *Acts of Tynwald*.

178 See 100 *Manx Deb.*, 18 January 1983, pp. T380–81 and *Acts of Tynwald 1984*, pp. 531–40.

179 See relevant volumes of *Acts of Tynwald*.

180 See relevant volumes of *Acts of Tynwald*.

181 Cm 4109-1, November 1998, p. x.

182 See Council of Ministers, *Isle of Man Government Response to the Review of Financial Regulation in the Crown Dependencies*, March 1999 and 116 *Manx Deb.*, 20 April 1999, pp. T741–52 and 27 April 1999, p. K393.

183 See 111 *Manx Deb.*, 18 June 1994, p. T245. After 1 April 1999 the Agreement was to be subject to review following six months' notice by either party.

184 See the debates on the Fourth and Fifth Interim Reports of the Select Committee; 99 *Manx Deb.*, 16 March 1982, pp. T556–58 and 19 May 1982, pp. T876–93; 100 *Manx Deb.*, 12 and 13 July 1983, pp. T1320–67.
185 See 102 *Manx Deb.*, 16 October 1984, pp. T45–91.
186 See 111 *Manx Deb.*, 21 June 1994, pp. T620–42.
187 See 117 *Manx Deb.*, 15 February 2000, p. T418 and the Value-Added Tax (Reduced Rate) Order 2000, which was laid before Tynwald on 21 March 2000.
188 See *Policy Review 2000*, vol. 1, pp. 21–26.

# CHAPTER TEN

# Conclusion

## *Constitutional Status*

The twentieth century saw major constitutional change in both the Island's relationship with the UK and the pattern of Island self-government. Change was for the most part gradual, reflecting the initial reluctance of the colonial power to loosen its grip on the Island and the constitutional conservatism of the majority in Tynwald. In 1900 the Island's relationship with the UK was essentially colonial with important executive and financial power in the hands of UK politicians at the Home Office and the Treasury and their appointees in Tynwald. In the course of the century, in response to major UK developments and Manx demands, the UK relaxed its control over Manx affairs and power was devolved to Tynwald, and within Tynwald to locally elected politicians. Although the process of decolonisation remained incomplete, with the UK retaining responsibility for the good government of the Island and its defence and international relations, most Manx politicians seemed happy to see these residual controls so long as they were exercised reasonably. Their greatest concern arose out of the ongoing tensions between the devolutionary process and international politics. In the latter half of the century international obligations increasingly limited the Island's room for manoeuvre and caused considerable frustration and anger when such obligations either prevented independent action by the Island, as over commercial broadcasting, or forced the Island to conform, as with respect to the laws on judicial corporal punishment and homosexuality. Whereas the sacrifice involved in these instances was very limited, the potential erosion of Tynwald's sovereignty as a result of the UK negotiating for membership of the European Communities prior to 1972, and the EU and other international organisations pressing at the end of the century for the elimination of fiscal practices in restraint of free trade, was considerable. When a special relationship was negotiated with the EEC in 1972 members of Tynwald heaved a collective sigh of relief, and the OECD's acceptance in 2001 of the Island's new taxation strategy as a constructive response to criticisms about harmful tax competition was equally welcomed. However, both threats to self-government provoked analysis of the constitutional options open to the Island should the unthinkable happen.

The contemporary debate has focused on two constitutional options, the status quo or complete independence. Both options are politically feasible, the UK having made clear on a number of occasions since the early 1970s that the Island has the right to self-determination. Both options also involve some degree of uncertainty. Whether constitutionally involved with or formally independent of the UK, a small offshore island like the Isle of Man will be vulnerable to the actions of its more powerful neighbour, whether acting alone or in concert with EU or other international partners. Current debate has also made very clear that independence is the contingency option. Certainly that was the distinct message conveyed by members and former members of the Executive Council/Council of Ministers when interviewed by the author in January and February 2000.[1] So what is it about the constitutional status quo that makes it so attractive and why is full independence an option to be held in reserve?

Politically the constitutional status quo has secured for the Island maximum political freedom with minimum insecurity. It has allowed the Island a system of representative local self-government, one of the mainstays of a democratic society. Devolution of power has freed the Island from the remoteness and bureaucracy involved in close control from Whitehall and facilitated popular access to and understanding of government. It has enabled the Island to benefit from a close relationship with the UK without necessarily being subject to policies designed for a very different public. Tynwald has been free to emulate the UK and benefit from the teething troubles experienced by the UK, to decide when to follow the UK, to adapt UK measures to meet local circumstances and to support bilateral agreements with the UK in such areas as social security and indirect taxation and international agreements in a wide range of areas where joint action with the UK is deemed appropriate. The real political value of the status quo has stemmed from the right to be different, without in any way jeopardising the advice and support available on a day-to-day basis from the UK. Although the residual controls exercised by the UK have occasionally caused resentment, most of the time the way in which they have been exercised has been welcomed. Crown appointments have been made by the Home Secretary, following consultations with the Council of Ministers in the case of the Lieutenant-Governor and on the advice of the Lieutenant-Governor in the case of the other appointments, he in turn acting on appropriate local advice. The Royal Assent to Manx legislation has invariably been given and, although the process can still result in delays and modifications to legislation, more often than not these have proved advantageous to the Island. In return for a financial contribution to the UK Exchequer, the detail of which has been subject to bilateral agreement since 1957, the UK has provided for the Island's defence and certain other common services, including international and diplomatic representation. Even in the field of international relations, international obligations have almost invariably been entered into by the UK with the full backing of Tynwald.

The efficient use of the right to domestic self-government has enabled Tynwald to safeguard and promote its economic interests and in doing so advance the general welfare of Manx society. Since the major devolution of power in 1958, Tynwald has been free to introduce measures to support its traditional industries, diversify the economy, redress population decline and imbalance and exploit a European market without being constrained by the full range of EU policies and regulations. Clearly the Island still has economic and social problems, but the true economic value of the constitutional status quo is that it provides the political machinery with which to tackle such problems. That it still has the will to tackle them is perhaps a reflection of the use to which the machinery of self-government has been put in the past. Other island groups that form part of the UK such as Orkney, Shetland and the Western Isles have every reason to be envious.

The major drawback to the current relationship with the UK is the lack of any constitutional or political guarantee that Manx rights will be observed. They are not entrenched in a written constitution and, theoretically at least, could be eroded or ignored by the UK. The argument of some Manx constitutional lawyers that the legislative authority of Tynwald does not derive from any grant of authority from the UK Parliament, but predates the Island's association with England and the UK and cannot legally be removed by the UK Parliament is an interesting one,[2] but ignores the political reality of colonial rule for much of the period after 1765, the very limited scope of legislation prior to that date, the immense scope of UK legislation that applied to the Island after that date, the importance of UK legislation in devolving power to Tynwald and the UK Parliament's right to legislate for the Isle of Man, a right that has been recognised in Manx law and acknowledged by every major report into the Manx constitution during the twentieth century. The question to which there is no clear answer is whether the Island could successfully challenge an attempt by the UK to reverse the process of devolution by reference to the historical origins of Tynwald's legislative authority, especially if the legislation were to be justified by reference to international obligation. To date there has been no serious suggestion of such action with regard to the Isle of Man. On the contrary, the UK authorities have repeatedly assured the Island, constitutional investigators and the UK Parliament that they respect the Island's autonomy as a Crown dependency and that they would only exercise the residual prerogative power of the Crown to intervene in the Island's domestic affairs in exceptional circumstances. Even so the fear in the Isle of Man is that international circumstances may result in some political bargain being struck by the UK in which Manx interests are sacrificed to UK and international interests and the autonomy of Tynwald eroded. If the UK were to embark on such a course of action and impose legislation or taxation without representation, it would almost certainly be challenged in the courts. The Island could seek a judicial review of UK actions either in the Manx courts or those of the UK, in which case it would be for the courts to pass judgement on what is and what is not domestic to the Island. There would be little point in petitioning the Privy Council and having their grievance heard, as in 1967, by the very UK ministers who were responsible for imposing UK policy on the Island. If a judicial challenge was successful, the Island might emerge constitutionally stronger, but would remain politically and economically vulnerable to international action of the sort threatened by the OECD. If it was unsuccessful, Tynwald would almost certainly want to explore in detail the contingency option of complete independence. This option was explored by the Constitutional and External Relations Committee of the Council of Ministers between 1990 and 1993 and rejected, Tynwald approving the Committee's recommendations with only a single dissenting voice.[3] A similar conclusion was drawn by that Committee after extensive consultations over a period of three-and-a-half years and endorsed by the Council of Ministers and Tynwald in November 2000; again Tynwald accepted the recommendation of the Council of Ministers with a solitary voice of dissent. Tynwald also agreed that the Island's policy on constitutional development should be advanced

> by promoting and defending vigorously the Island's autonomy in relation to its internal affairs and seeking to extend the Island's influence over external issues affecting the Island; by maintaining and extending the Island's direct representation at international bodies; but acknowledging the option of independence as a sovereign state, if circumstances were to change and if that were to be the wish of the people.[4]

Formally at least independence would end the uncertainties regarding the Island's constitutional relationship with the UK. The Island would be free to enact legislation without reference to the UK, subject to any international obligations entered into by

Tynwald, assume responsibility for its own defence and international relations and replace British with Manx citizenship. Crown appointments would be made and the royal assent to legislation given on the advice of the Isle of Man Government. The fiscal autonomy that is seen as a prerequisite for a prosperous society would be preserved. In practice, independence would usher in a period of immense uncertainty. A new relationship with the UK would have to be negotiated at a time when relations might have been soured by the events provoking Manx consideration of independence. The close relationship with the UK over policy making would be jeopardised and the Island might lose the access to day-to-day advice that is currently available to Manx Departments from their counterparts in the UK. Bilateral agreements would be either terminated or subject to renegotiation. International relations, consular services, defence and other common services, currently funded under the 1994 Contribution Agreement would have to be provided by the Island or paid for on an agency basis, assuming the UK was still willing to provide them. The Island would lose its advantageous status in relation to the EU and have to negotiate a new relationship in order to maintain free access to the European market. Such negotiations would have to be undertaken at a time of EU hostility towards the Island over its taxation policies. Some Manx residents would almost certainly lose their British citizenship and their right of access to the UK employment market. The real freedom to make the decisions necessary to preserve a strong financial centre and a prosperous and caring society would be greatly diluted by the Island's commitment to international standards, the need to avoid being portrayed as a pariah state and the capacity of more powerful neighbours to impose sanctions and discriminate against the Island. Whether or not the independence option is accepted will depend on Tynwald's perceptions of the relative disadvantage caused by any erosion of autonomy and loss of competitive advantage in the financial sector, the circumstances and terms of the independence settlement and the associated risks of economic and political instability. It will also depend on the views of the Manx people, whose own links with and experience of the UK might influence their decision in any referendum on the issue.[5]

## Democracy and Policy Making

Closely related to the moves made towards Island self-government were the steps taken to democratise Manx politics. The electoral franchise was extended and power transferred from the UK and Crown-appointed officials to the elected and indirectly members of Tynwald. After a long constitutional struggle the directly elected chamber became pre-eminent, ensuring a much stronger link between the electorate and policy making. That link may be further strengthened if legislation to provide for a directly elected Tynwald ever reaches the statute book. The link in the Isle of Man was never as strong as in the UK or other political systems where election manifestos of successful political parties provided the basis of policy development, but an important one nevertheless. Throughout the century electoral politics was dominated by Independents, successive attempts to break their stranglehold on Manx politics foundering on the rocks of individualism. Only the MLP achieved a modicum of long-term success in promoting a collectivist alternative, although when, in 1946, it tried to win a majority of seats it aroused massive opposition and suffered a resounding electoral defeat. In recent years MLP representation in the House of Keys has been limited to the Douglas-Onchan area and even there success can be attributed as much to the performance of individuals as that of the Party. No other political organisation came close to achieving recognition as a national party. Electoral majorities were achieved in support of particular issues, as with constitutional reform in the Raglan era, but not by organised political parties.

The establishment of a ministerial system in 1986/88 and the appointment of 10 members of Tynwald to be collectively responsible for the government of the Isle of Man introduced a new dimension into Manx politics, both in Tynwald and during elections. The presence of a more or less disciplined group accounting for nearly a third of the voting membership of Tynwald was bound to influence the behaviour of both members and nonmembers of the Council of Ministers, but the expectations of some commentators that the new system would lead like-minded individuals to form political parties in support of particular leaders and policies did not materialise. Neither chief ministers nor ministers showed any inclination to abandon their independence and even the six APG members contesting their first general election in 1996 did so as Independents supporting the core policies of the APG. In the two general elections to be held since the adoption of a full ministerial system, Independents accounted for all but three of the successful candidates and political parties or groupings of Independents targeted relatively few seats. In 1996 the MLP contested only four seats, clearly lacking the organisation and commitment to contest seats on an Island-wide basis. The Independents supporting APG core policies contested and won six seats. Since 1996 the APG has refined its statement of policies and in November 1999 gave limited circulation to a consultative policy paper in preparation for the general election in 2001.[6] However, it has an aging leadership and has been prone to division, David Cannan leaving the Group in 1998 and Ray Kniveton in 2000. Only time will tell whether the APG can achieve its goal of breaking the mould of Manx politics by becoming the first political group with an agreed manifesto and enough successful members to form a government. To do so it will have to convince the electorate that it has the leadership, organisation and programme to take the Island forward in the twenty-first century and persuade it to disregard the vigorous opposition that will be mounted against party government and the attraction of the individual personalities involved in that opposition. A high level of consensus about major policy, a strong tradition of coalition politics and a long-standing distrust of party politics may prove decisive in preserving the power of Independents in Manx politics.

## Increased State Intervention in Manx Society

In parallel with the progress towards Island self-government and a more democratic society, the century saw a massive increase in intervention by the state in response to social and economic problems. A comparison between the revenue expenditure by the Henniker administration in 1899/1900 and that of Gelling in 1999/2000 provides one measure of the radical change that occurred. In 1899/1900 total revenue spending was £86,411 or £4,668,873 at 2000 values; in 1999/2000 the total was £291,804,095, a massive 62.5-fold increase in real terms. While in 1899/1900 the only significant welfare spending by central government was on education, in 1999/2000 each of education, health, housing and social security accounted for major portions of the much higher level of expenditure. While in 1899/1900 there was almost no public ownership or expenditure in support of private sector, by the turn of the century the Island was supporting an extensive public sector and providing considerable assistance to the private sector through supportive legislation, fiscal policy, regulation and financial assistance.[7] While in 1901 there were 221 public sector employees working for either central government, mainly in connection with the law and order services, or the UK authorities, mainly the customs and postal services, by 2000 the approved staffing for Executive Government, the Departments and Statutory Boards totalled 6,968.[8]

The advent of ministerial government coincided with an unprecedented period of economic growth and economic prosperity. The boost to government revenues brought about by the post-1960 diversification of the economy and the rapid growth of the financial sector enabled the Walker and Gelling administrations to spend on law and order, the welfare state and the economy on a scale undreamt of by their predecessors. A strong financial sector became a pillar of the Manx economy, but it also became a source of weakness. Just as in the 1950s and 1960s the Manx economy was unduly dependent on tourism and proved vulnerable to foreign competition, the real danger at the beginning of the twenty-first century is of excessive dependence on a financial sector that is vulnerable not only to market change but also to international economic and political forces. One of the main challenges for Manx political leaders in the new century is to make further progress in diversifying the economy and to show good judgement in responding to any threats to the Island's right of domestic self-government. The intelligent exercise of that right has been and will continue to be fundamental in the preservation of a prosperous and caring society.

## *Notes*

1  Interviews were conducted with 29 members and former members of the Executive Council/Council of Ministers between 31 January and 12 February 2000.

2  See for example the advice given to Tynwald's Select Committee on Constitutional Issues in 1986; *Fifth Interim Report of the Select Committee on Constitutional Issues*, 26 June 1986 and 103 *Manx Deb.*, 15 July 1986, pp. T2370–87.

3  See *Second Interim Report on Future Constitutional Objectives. A Report by the Council of Ministers*, October 1993 and 111 *Manx Deb.*, 16 November 1993, pp. T125–40.

4  See *Fourth Interim Report on Future Constitutional Objectives: The Implications of Independence. A Report by the Council of Ministers*, November 2000 and 118 *Manx Deb.*, 22 November 2000, pp. T298–317.

5  In January 2000 the view of Chief Minister Gelling was that there would be no independence unless approved by the Manx electorate in a referendum; in an interview with the author on 31 January 2000.

6  See *Statement of Policies: Alliance for Progressive Government*, 15 April 1998 and *Consultative Paper issued by Alliance for Progressive Government*, 10 November 1999. Around 200 copies of the consultative document were distributed; of the 30 responses received most were broadly supportive of APG policies; see *Isle of Man Examiner*, 20 June 2000.

7  In February 2000 and 2001 a new format was adopted for the annual budget pink book and included a useful summary of the role of the various departments and statutory boards; see for example *The Isle of Man Budget 2001–2002*, February 2001.

8  For 1901, see *Census 1901 Islands in the British Seas* (London, 1903). For the figures in 2000, see *Policy Review 2000*, vol. 1, pp. 37–38 and vol. 2, pp. 106, 157, 169 and 176; for a detailed breakdown of the figures in September 2000, see the personnel budgets in *The Isle of Man Budget 2001–2002*, February 2001.

# Bibliography

Relatively few books have been written on either twentieth-century Manx political history or contemporary Manx politics. The purpose of this list is to draw the reader's attention to those books which the author has found useful. It is not by any means a comprehensive bibliography and does not try to duplicate the many references to articles, official reports and other publications referred to in the extensive endnotes in each chapter. Readers wanting more detailed references should consult the Manx Studies bibliography maintained by the Centre for Manx Studies at 6 Kingswood Grove, Douglas.

J. G. Beckerson, *Advertising the Island: The Isle of Man Official Board of Advertising 1894–1914* (MA thesis, University of East Anglia, 1996).

J. C. Belchem (ed.), *A New History of the Isle of Man: The Modern Period 1830–1999*, vol. 5 (Liverpool, 2000).

J. W. Birch, *The Isle of Man: A Study in Economic Geography* (Cambridge, 1975).

Hinton Bird, *An Island that Led: The History of Manx Education*, vol. 2 (Port St Mary, 1995).

T. W. Cain, 'The Isle of Man and the European Union', 27 *MLB* (1 July 1996–31 December 1996), pp. 65–76.

Connery Chappell, *Island of Barbed Wires: The Remarkable Story of World War Two Internment on the Isle of Man* (London, 1984).

Y. M. Cresswell, *Living with the Wire: Civilian Internment in the Isle of Man during the two World Wars* (Douglas, 1994).

William Cubbon, 'Another Home Rule Crisis', *Truth* (London), 26 December 1917, p. 905.

P. W. Edge, *Manx Public Law* (Douglas, 1997).

Barry Edwards, *The Railways and Tramways of the Isle of Man* (Sparkford, Somerset, 1993).

Sir James Gell, 'Memorandum on Ecclesiastical legislation', *Manx Society Publication*, vol. 31, pp. 21–32.

K. F. W. Gumbley, 'Government Departments and Statutory Boards', 10 *MLB* (1 December 1987–31 May 1988), pp. 61–67.

K. F. W. Gumbley, 'Government Departments and Statutory Boards. An Update', 28 *MLB* (1 January 1997–30 June 1997), pp. 95–96.

Kathleen Jones, *The Making of Social Policy in Britain 1830–1990* (London, 2nd ed. 1994).

Robert Kelly, *The Mail of Mann: The Story of Postal Services in the Isle of Man* (Isle of Man, 1988).

Robert Kelly, *TT Pioneers* (Douglas, 1996).

D. G. Kermode, *The Changing Pattern of Manx Devolution*, Studies in Public Policy No. 52, Centre for the Study of Public Policy (Strathclyde, 1980).

D. G. Kermode, *Devolution at Work: A Case Study of the Isle of Man* (Farnborough, Hampshire, 1979).

D. G. Kermode, 'The Process of Royal Assent to Manx Legislation: A Study of Refusals since 1900', *Proceedings of the Isle of Man Natural History and Antiquarian Society*, VIII, 2, pp. 130–38.

R. H. Kinvig, *The Isle of Man: A Social, Cultural and Political History* (Douglas, 1975).

Angela Kneale, *Against Birching: Judicial Corporal Punishment in the Isle of Man* (London, 1973).

G. N. Kniveton (ed.), *Centenary of the Borough of Douglas 1896–1996* (Douglas, 1996).

G. N. Kniveton (ed.), *A Chronicle of the Twentieth Century: The Manx Experience*, vol. 1: 1901–50 (Douglas, 1999).

G. N. Kniveton (ed.), *A Chronicle of the Twentieth Century: The Manx Experience*, vol. 2: 1951–2000 (Douglas, 2000).

G. N. Kniveton, *The Isle of Man Steam Railway: Official Guide* (Douglas, rev. ed. 1993).

G. N. Kniveton and A. A. Scarffe, *The Manx Electric Railway: Official Guide* (Douglas, rev. ed. 1994).

A. W. Moore, *A History of the Isle of Man* (London, 1900).

Samuel Norris, *Manx Memories and Movements* (Douglas, 3rd ed. 1941).

Samuel Norris, *This Manx Democracy* (Douglas, 1945).

C. G. Pantin, *An Account of the Introduction of the Health Service on the Isle of Man in 1948* (unpublished).

Keith Pearson, *One Hundred Years of the MER* (Hawes, Yorkshire, 1992).

Constance Radcliffe, *Shining by the Sea: A History of Ramsey 1800–1914* (Douglas, 1989).

Vaughan Robinson and Danny McCarroll (eds.), *The Isle of Man: Celebrating a Sense of Place* (Liverpool, 1990).

B. E. Sargeaunt, *The Isle of Man and the Great War* (Douglas, 1920).

B. E. Sargeaunt, *The Military History of the Isle of Man* (Arbroath, 1947).

Tom Sherratt (comp.), *Isle of Man Parliamentary Election Results 1919–1986* (unpublished, Warrington, 1986).

Mark Solly, *Government and Law in the Isle of Man* (Castletown, 1994).

Sue Stuart, *Offshore Finance Handbook: Isle of Man 1996–97* (Narberth, Pembrokeshire, 1996).

A. J. Teare, *Reminiscences of the Manx Labour Party* (Douglas, 1962).

Nicholas Timmins, *The Five Giants: A Biography of the Welfare State* (London, 1996).

George Turnbull, *The Isle of Man Constabulary* (Isle of Man, 1984).

Jeffrey Vaukins, 'The Manx Struggle for Reform' (M.Phil., University of Lancaster, 1984).

Spencer Walpole, *The Land of Home Rule* (London, 1893).

Derek Winterbottom, *Governors of the Isle of Man since 1765* (Douglas, 1999).

# Historical Retail Prices Index from 1900

| Year | Index (1900 = 100) | Factor to Increase to 2000 Prices | Year | Index (1900 = 100) | Factor to Increase to 2000 Prices |
|------|--------------------|-----------------------------------|------|--------------------|-----------------------------------|
| 1900 | 100.0 | 54.031 | 1936 | 168.2 | 32.121 |
| 1901 | 99.2  | 54.470 | 1937 | 174.0 | 31.057 |
| 1902 | 96.9  | 55.771 | 1938 | 179.7 | 30.062 |
| 1903 | 101.0 | 53.493 | 1939 | 176.3 | 30.652 |
| 1904 | 99.1  | 54.525 | 1940 | 206.2 | 26.199 |
| 1905 | 99.5  | 54.304 | 1941 | 227.0 | 23.805 |
| 1906 | 102.2 | 52.861 | 1942 | 230.4 | 23.448 |
| 1907 | 103.7 | 52.092 | 1943 | 229.3 | 23.566 |
| 1908 | 104.9 | 51.493 | 1944 | 230.4 | 23.448 |
| 1909 | 106.4 | 50.763 | 1945 | 232.7 | 23.216 |
| 1910 | 100.0 | 54.031 | 1946 | 233.9 | 23.102 |
| 1911 | 99.0  | 54.580 | 1947 | 235.0 | 22.989 |
| 1912 | 100.5 | 53.761 | 1948 | 248.9 | 21.712 |
| 1913 | 102.7 | 52.602 | 1949 | 254.7 | 21.214 |
| 1914 | 115.4 | 46.824 | 1950 | 265.5 | 20.354 |
| 1915 | 132.5 | 40.780 | 1951 | 278.8 | 19.381 |
| 1916 | 155.5 | 34.738 | 1952 | 311.8 | 17.331 |
| 1917 | 195.9 | 27.586 | 1953 | 326.6 | 16.542 |
| 1918 | 218.9 | 24.683 | 1954 | 330.3 | 16.356 |
| 1919 | 247.7 | 21.812 | 1955 | 341.5 | 15.822 |
| 1920 | 265.0 | 20.390 | 1956 | 363.5 | 14.863 |
| 1921 | 277.7 | 19.459 | 1957 | 373.6 | 14.463 |
| 1922 | 214.3 | 25.213 | 1958 | 389.0 | 13.890 |
| 1923 | 202.8 | 26.646 | 1959 | 395.8 | 13.650 |
| 1924 | 205.1 | 26.347 | 1960 | 393.7 | 13.725 |
| 1925 | 206.2 | 26.199 | 1961 | 404.4 | 13.360 |
| 1926 | 198.2 | 27.266 | 1962 | 421.7 | 12.814 |
| 1927 | 197.0 | 27.425 | 1963 | 435.1 | 12.419 |
| 1928 | 188.9 | 28.596 | 1964 | 441.4 | 12.242 |
| 1929 | 191.3 | 28.251 | 1965 | 461.1 | 11.718 |
| 1930 | 185.5 | 29.128 | 1966 | 480.8 | 11.237 |
| 1931 | 172.8 | 31.265 | 1967 | 497.6 | 10.858 |
| 1932 | 168.2 | 32.121 | 1968 | 514.4 | 10.504 |
| 1933 | 160.1 | 33.739 | 1969 | 546.7 | 9.883 |
| 1934 | 161.3 | 33.498 | 1970 | 574.8 | 9.400 |
| 1935 | 162.5 | 33.260 | 1971 | 625.1 | 8.643 |

| Year | Index (1900 = 100) | Factor to Increase to 2000 Prices | Year | Index (1900 = 100) | Factor to Increase to 2000 Prices |
|------|------|------|------|------|------|
| 1972 | 672.6 | 8.034 | 1987 | 3216.4 | 1.680 |
| 1973 | 727.5 | 7.427 | 1988 | 3367.9 | 1.604 |
| 1974 | 825.6 | 6.544 | 1989 | 3575.1 | 1.511 |
| 1975 | 1000.3 | 5.402 | 1990 | 3867.2 | 1.397 |
| 1976 | 1211.9 | 4.458 | 1991 | 4171.4 | 1.295 |
| 1977 | 1382.8 | 3.907 | 1992 | 4399.2 | 1.228 |
| 1978 | 1520.9 | 3.552 | 1993 | 4509.5 | 1.198 |
| 1979 | 1666.4 | 3.242 | 1994 | 4619.8 | 1.170 |
| 1980 | 2017.8 | 2.678 | 1995 | 4761.6 | 1.135 |
| 1981 | 2254.1 | 2.397 | 1996 | 4909.4 | 1.101 |
| 1982 | 2525.6 | 2.139 | 1997 | 5023.3 | 1.076 |
| 1983 | 2681.9 | 2.015 | 1998 | 5166.3 | 1.046 |
| 1984 | 2811.6 | 1.922 | 1999 | 5264.5 | 1.026 |
| 1985 | 3017.6 | 1.791 | 2000 | 5403.1 | 1.000 |
| 1986 | 3103.7 | 1.741 | | | |

i)  From 1900 to 1914, the index is from E. H. Phelps Brown and Sheila V. Hopkins, 'Seven Centuries of the Prices of Consumables compared with Builders' Wage Rates', *Economica N.S.* (1956).

ii)  For the period 1914 to 1976 then UK Index of Retail Prices has been used.

iii)  The Isle of Man General Index of Retail Prices has been used for the period since 1976.

iv)  From 1914 the index for the end of March has been used.

Martin Caley, Economics Division, Isle of Man Treasury, 11 April 2000

# Appendix 2

# Political Leadership
# 1900–2000

## a) Secretaries of State for the Home Department
## (UK Government)

The UK Home Secretary in his capacity as a Privy Councillor was responsible for Manx affairs throughout the twentieth century; following the UK general election in June 2001, Prime Minister Blair transferred the responsibility for Crown Dependencies, including the Isle of Man, from the Home Office to the Lord Chancellor's Department.

| | | |
|---|---|---|
| Sir M. White Ridley | 1895–1900 | (Conservative, Lord Salisbury) |
| Charles Ritchie | 1900–02 | (Conservative, Lord Salisbury) |
| Robert Ackers Douglas | 1902–05 | (Conservative, Arthur Balfour) |
| Herbert Gladstone | 1905–10 | (Liberal, Sir Henry Campbell Bannerman to 1908 and Herbert Asquith to 1910) |
| Winston Churchill | 1910–11 | (Liberal, Herbert Asquith) |
| Reginald McKenna | 1911–15 | (Liberal, Herbert Asquith) |
| Sir John Simon | 1915–16 | (Coalition, Herbert Asquith) |
| Sir George Cave | 1916–19 | (Coalition, David Lloyd George) |
| Edward Shortt | 1919–22 | (Coalition, David Lloyd George) |
| William Bridgeman | 1922–24 | (Conservative, Andrew Bonar Law) |
| Arthur Henderson | 1924 | (Labour, Ramsay MacDonald) |
| Sir William Joynson Hicks | 1924–29 | (Conservative, Stanley Baldwin) |
| John Robert Clynes | 1929–31 | (Labour, Ramsay MacDonald) |
| Sir Herbert Samuel | 1931–32 | (National, Ramsay MacDonald) |
| Sir John Gilmour | 1932–35 | (National, Ramsay MacDonald) |
| Sir John Simon | 1935–37 | (National, Stanley Baldwin) |
| Sir Samuel Hoare | 1937–39 | (National, Neville Chamberlain) |
| Sir John Anderson | 1939–40 | (National, Neville Chamberlain) |
| Herbert Morrison | 1940–45 | (Coalition, Winston Churchill) |
| Sir Donald Somervell | 1945 | (Coalition, Winston Churchill) |
| Chuter Ede | 1945–51 | (Labour, Clement Attlee) |
| Sir David Maxwell-Fife | 1951–54 | (Conservative, Sir Winston Churchill) |
| Gwilym Lloyd George | 1954–7 | (Conservative, Sir Winston Churchill to 1955 and Sir Anthony Eden to 1957) |
| Richard Austen Butler | 1957–62 | (Conservative, Harold MacMillan) |
| Henry Brooke | 1962–64 | (Conservative, Harold MacMillan to 1963 and Sir Alec Douglas-Home to 1964) |

| | | |
|---|---|---|
| Sir Frank Soskice | 1964–65 | (Labour, Harold Wilson) |
| Roy Jenkins | 1965–67 | (Labour, Harold Wilson) |
| James Callaghan | 1967–70 | (Labour, Harold Wilson) |
| Reginald Maudling | 1970–72 | (Conservative, Edward Heath) |
| Robert Carr | 1972–74 | (Conservative, Edward Heath) |
| Roy Jenkins | 1974–76 | (Labour, Harold Wilson) |
| Merlyn Rees | 1976–79 | (Labour, James Callaghan) |
| William Whitelaw | 1979–83 | (Conservative, Margaret Thatcher) |
| Leon Brittan | 1983–85 | (Conservative, Margaret Thatcher) |
| Douglas Hurd | 1985–89 | (Conservative, Margaret Thatcher) |
| David Waddington | 1989–90 | (Conservative, Margaret Thatcher) |
| Kenneth Baker | 1990–92 | (Conservative, John Major) |
| Kenneth Clarke | 1992–93 | (Conservative, John Major) |
| Michael Howard | 1993–97 | (Conservative, John Major) |
| Jack Straw | 1997–2001 | (Labour, Tony Blair) |
| Lord Irvine (Lord Chancellor) | 2001– | (Labour, Tony Blair) |

## b) Lieutenant-Governors

| | |
|---|---|
| John Henniker-Major, 5th Baron Henniker | 1895–1902 |
| George Somerset, 4th Baron Raglan | 1902–19 |
| Major-General Sir William Fry | 1919–26 |
| Sir Claude Hill | 1926–33 |
| Sir Montagu Butler | 1933–37 |
| Vice Admiral William Leveson-Gower/Earl Granville | 1937–45 |
| Air Vice Marshall Sir Geoffrey Bromet | 1945–52 |
| Sir Ambrose Dundas | 1952–59 |
| Sir Ronald Garvey | 1959–66 |
| Sir Peter Stallard | 1966–73 |
| Sir John Paul | 1974–80 |
| Rear Admiral Sir Nigel Cecil | 1980–85 |
| Major General Sir Laurence New | 1985–90 |
| Air Marshall Sir Laurence Jones | 1990–95 |
| Sir Timothy Daunt | 1995–2000 |
| Air Marshall Ian David MacFadyen | 2000– |

## c) Members of the Executive Council/Council of Ministers

Periods served as a member of the Legislative Council (MLC) are indicated in the third column. The final column applies to the period from 1962 and shows the individuals who served as chair of the Executive Council (EC)/Chief Minister (CM) or as chair of the Finance Board (FB)/Treasury (T).

| | | |
|---|---|---|
| John H. L. Cowin | 1946–50 | MLC |
| Deemster Percy Cowley | 1946–47 | MLC |
| John F. Crellin | 1946–58 | MLC |
| Charles Gill | 1946–51 | MLC |
| George Higgins | 1946–49 and 1958 | |
| Richard Kneen | 1946–51 | MLC 1950–51 |
| Alfred J. Teare | 1946–58 | |

| | | | |
|---|---|---|---|
| Joseph D. Qualtrough | 1947–51 | | |
| Thomas C. Cowin | 1949–55 | | |
| Richard C. Cannell | 1950–58 | | |
| John B. Bolton | 1951–62 and 1967–79 | MLC 1967–79 | FB 1967–76 |
| Henry K. Corlett | 1951–62 | | |
| Jack Nivison | 1951–60 and 1969–72 | MLC 1969–72 | |
| H. Charles Kerruish | 1955–68 | | EC 1962–67 |
| A. Howard Simcocks | 1958–62 and 1970–74 | | |
| Sir Ralph Stevenson | 1958–69 | MLC | |
| George H. Moore | 1958–62 | MLC | |
| James M. Cain | 1960–62 | | |
| Cecil C. McFee | 1962–67 | MLC | |
| James H. Nicholls | 1962–67 | MLC | |
| William E. Quayle | 1962–70 | | |
| Hubert H. Radcliffe | 1962–67 | MLC 1963–67 | |
| Robert C. Stephen | 1962–64 | | FB 1962–64 |
| E. Norman Crowe | 1964–78 | MLC 1970–78 | FB 1964–67 |
| | | | EC 1967–72 |
| R. Edward S. Kerruish | 1967–70 and 1978–85 | MLC 1978–85 | |
| Percy Radcliffe | 1967–85 | MLC 1980–85 | EC 1972–76 |
| | | | FB 1976–81 |
| | | | EC 1981–85 |
| E. Clifford Irving | 1968–81 | | EC 1977–81 |
| R. G. J. Ian Anderson | 1970–82 and 1984–88 | MLC 1984–88 | |
| G. Victor H. Kneale | 1970–74 and 1982–90 | | |
| Colin L. P. Vereker | 1970 | | |
| J. Robert Creer | 1975–77 and 1978–82 | | |
| Roy Macdonald | 1975–78 and 1982–85 | MLC 1982–85 | |
| W. Alexander Moore | 1977–78 | | |
| Noel Q. Cringle | 1978–82, 1982–86 and 1996 | | |
| Edgar Mann | 1980–86 and 1996–99 | MLC 1985–86 and 1996–99 | FB 1981–85 |
| | | | EC 1985–86 |
| Miles Walker | 1982–96 | | CM 1986–96 |
| Matthew Ward | 1982–85 | | |
| Arnold A. Callin | 1985–95 | MLC | |
| Edmond G. Lowey | 1985–96 | MLC | |
| David L. Moore | 1985–86 | | |
| J. Norman Radcliffe | 1985–86 | | |
| Allan R. Bell | 1986–94 and 1996– | | |
| J. Anthony Brown | 1986– | | |
| J. David Q. Cannan | 1986–89 | | |
| Dominic F. K. Delaney | 1986–89 | | |
| Donald G. Maddrell | 1986–88 | | |
| Bernard May | 1988–96 | | |
| Donald G. Gelling | 1988– | | T1989–96 |
| | | | CM 1996– |
| James C. Cain | 1989–91 | | |
| David North | 1989– | | |
| L. Ronald Cretney | 1990–91 | | |
| John Corrin | 1991–95 | | |
| Hazel Hannan | 1991–99 | | |
| Terry R. A. Groves | 1994–96 | | |

| | | |
|---|---|---|
| Richard K. Corkill | 1995– | T 1996– |
| Clare Christian | 1996– | |
| David Cretney | 1996– | |
| Edgar Quine | 1996–99 | |
| Alexander F. Downie | 1999– | |
| Stephen C. Rodan | 1999– | |
| Walter A. Gilbey | 1999– | |

## d) The Presiding Officers of Tynwald

*Presidents of Tynwald*: until 1990 the Lieutenant-Governor presided over meetings of Tynwald. Under the Constitution Amendment Act 1990 the President is elected by Tynwald from among its members.

| | |
|---|---|
| Sir Charles Kerruish | 1990–2000 |
| Noel Q. Cringle | 2000– |

*Presidents of the Legislative Council*: until 1980 the Lieutenant-Governor presided. Between 1980 and 1990 the Council elected its own President. After 1990 the President of Tynwald presided.

| | |
|---|---|
| Jack Nivison | 1980–88 |
| R. G. J. Ian Anderson | 1988–90 |
| Sir Charles Kerruish | 1990–2000 |
| Noel Q. Cringle | 2000– |

*Speakers of the House of Keys*: elected by members of the House.

| | |
|---|---|
| Arthur W. Moore | 1898–1909 |
| Dalrymple Maitland | 1909–19 |
| John Robert Kerruish | 1919 |
| G. Frederick Clucas | 1919–37 (knighted in 1937) |
| Joseph D. Qualtrough | 1937–60 (knighted in 1954) |
| Henry K. Corlett | 1960–62 |
| H. Charles Kerruish | 1962–90 (knighted in 1979) |
| G. Victor H. Kneale | 1990–91 |
| James C. Cain | 1991–96 |
| Noel Q. Cringle | 1996–2000 |
| J. David Q. Cannan | 2000– |

# House of Keys Constituencies and Local Authority Boundary Changes 1866–2000

With the introduction of direct elections to the House of Keys in 1866, provision was made for the four town constituencies to be based on the prevailing local authority boundaries. Thus the distributions of seats for the House of Keys laid down by statute in 1866, 1891, 1956 and 1985 provide only one part of the history of the Island's parliamentary constituencies. The other part, while not affecting the number of seats allocated to the town constituencies, is provided by a series of resolutions and Acts of Tynwald modifying the boundaries of the four towns. In the case of Castletown, Peel and Ramsey throughout the period and Douglas up to 1891, each boundary extension resulted in an equivalent expansion of the respective parliamentary constituency; in the case of Douglas after 1891, resolutions and/or Acts of Tynwald providing for boundary extensions also allocated the extended areas to one of the two constituencies up to 1956 and one of the four after 1956.

This Appendix includes four maps showing the main boundary changes since 1866. It must be stressed that, in contrast to the statutory distributions of 1866, 1891, 1956 and 1985, boundary extensions did not lead directly to any increases in the representation of the town constituencies or to any decrease in the representation of the adjacent sheading constituencies.

## *Castletown*

In 1866 the Castletown constituency was based on the town boundaries detailed in the Towns Act 1852, since when there have been two main boundary extensions:

i)  by resolution of Tynwald on 31 October 1882 and the Castletown Town Act 1883;
ii) by resolution of Tynwald on 20 January 1965 and the Castletown Town Act 1966.

Figure A3.1 illustrates the changes.

Figure A3.1. Castletown Expansion, 1852–2000

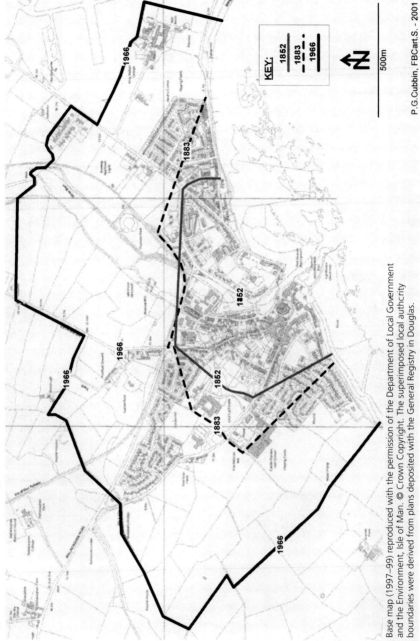

Base map (1997–99) reproduced with the permission of the Department of Local Government and the Environment, Isle of Man. © Crown Copyright. The superimposed local authcrity boundaries were derived from plans deposited with the General Registry in Douglas.

P.G.Cubbin, FBCart.S. - 2001

KEY:

1852
1883
1966

500m

## Figure A3.2. Douglas Expansion, 1852–2000

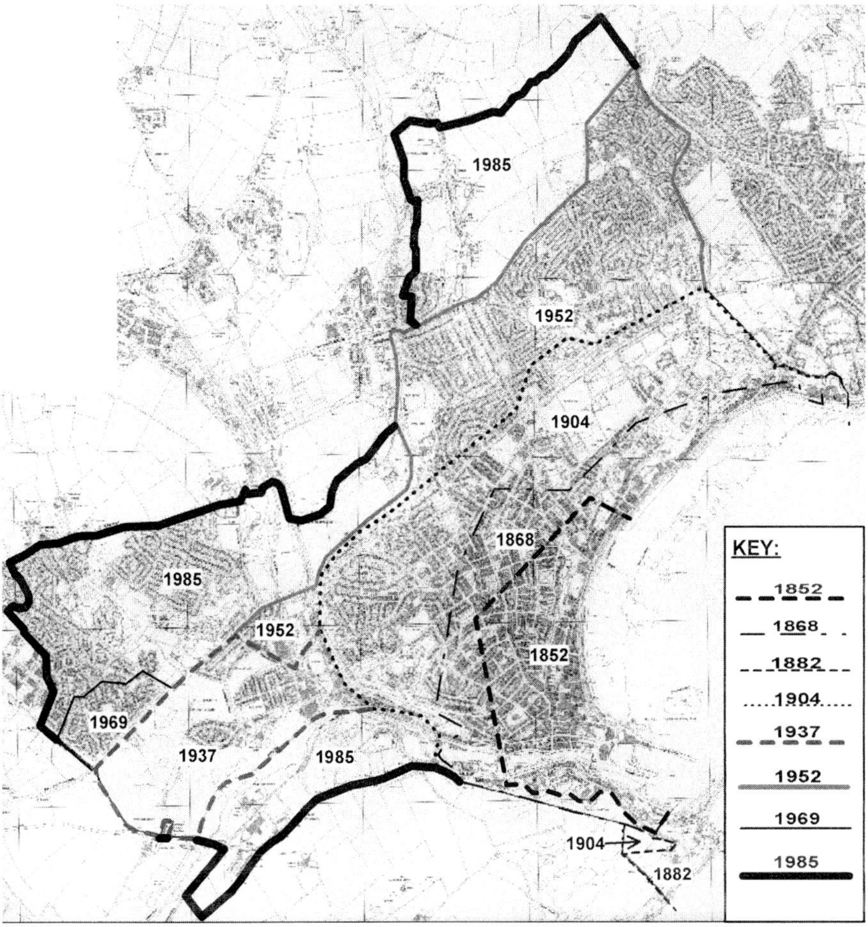

Base map (1997–99) reproduced with the permission of the Department of Local Government and the Environment, Isle of Man. © Crown Copyright. The superimposed local authority boundaries were derived from plans deposited with the General Registry in Douglas.

N

1 km

P.G.Cubbin, FBCart.S. - 2001

# Douglas

In 1866 the single Douglas constituency was based on the town boundaries detailed in the Towns Act 1852 and the Douglas Town Act 1860, since when there have been seven main boundary extensions, two affecting the single three-member constituency, three the two constituencies in existence between 1891 and 1956 and two the four constituencies that have obtained since 1956:

i)    by resolution of Tynwald on 26 March 1868;
ii)   by resolution of Tynwald on 31 October 1882;
iii)  by resolution of Tynwald on 15 July 1903 (implementation deferred to 1 November 1904);
iv)   by resolution of Tynwald on 30 October 1936 and the Douglas (Extension of Boundaries) Act 1937;
v)    by resolution of Tynwald on 12 January 1952 and the Douglas (Extension of Boundaries) Act 1952;
vi)   by resolution of Tynwald on 12 May 1968 and the Douglas (Extension of Boundaries) Act 1969;
vii)  by resolution of Tynwald on 17 October 1984 and the Douglas Extension of Boundaries Act 1985.

Figure A3.2 illustrates the changes.

# Peel

In 1866 the Peel constituency was based on the town boundaries detailed in the Towns Act 1852, since when there have been three main boundary extensions:

i)    by resolution of Tynwald and the Peel Town Act 1883;
ii)   by resolution of Tynwald on 21 February 1956;
iii)  by resolution of Tynwald on 19 October 1971.

Figure A3.3 illustrates the changes.

# Ramsey

In 1866 the Ramsey constituency was based on the town boundaries detailed in the Ramsey Town Act 1865, since when there have been four main extensions:

i)    by resolution of Tynwald on 7 October 1881, approving the transfer of part of the Mooragh and adjacent lands in the parish of Lezayre from the Trustees of Common Lands to the Ramsey Commissioners for the sum of £1,200, and a deed, dated 17 December 1881;
ii)   by resolution of Tynwald on 8 February 1884;
iii)  by resolution of Tynwald on 22 April 1969 and the Ramsey Town Act 1970;
iv)   by resolution of Tynwald on 22 January 1992 and the Ramsey (Boundary Extension) Act 1993.

Figure A3.4 illustrates the changes.

Figure A3.3. Peel Expansion, 1852–2000

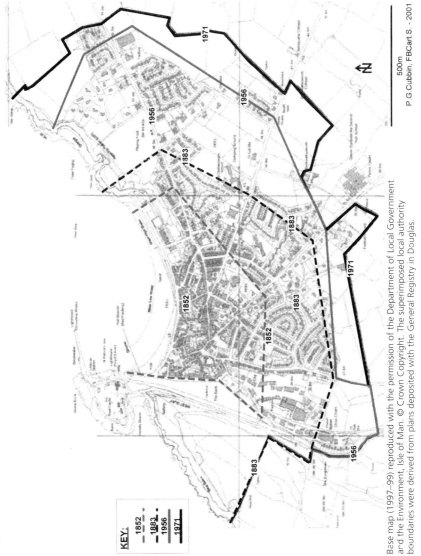

KEY:
- 1852
- 1883
- 1956
- 1971

500m
P.G.Cubbin, FBCart.S. - 2001

Base map (1997–99) reproduced with the permission of the Department of Local Government and the Environment, Isle of Man. © Crown Copyright. The superimposed local authority boundaries were derived from plans deposited with the General Registry in Douglas.

## Figure A3.4. Ramsey Expansion, 1852–2000

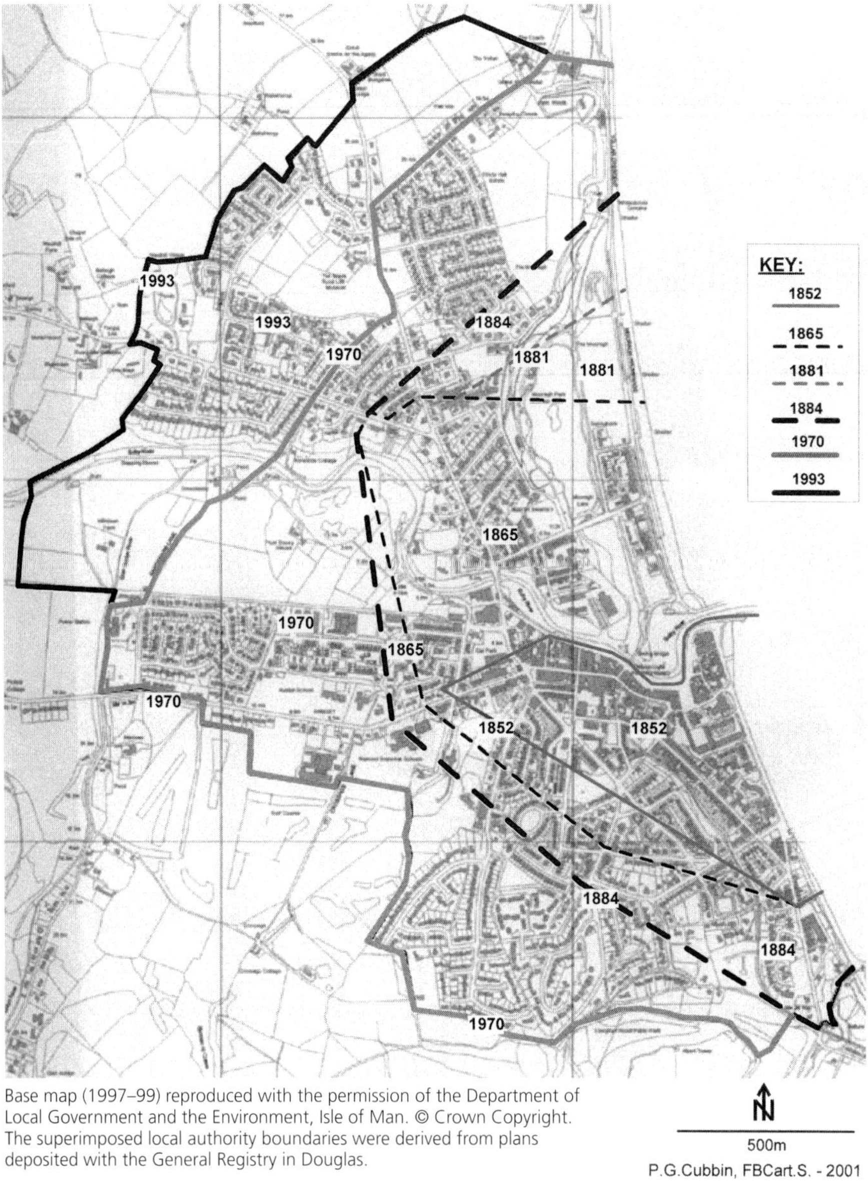

KEY:

| | |
|---|---|
| 1852 | |
| 1865 | |
| 1881 | |
| 1884 | |
| 1970 | |
| 1993 | |

Base map (1997–99) reproduced with the permission of the Department of Local Government and the Environment, Isle of Man. © Crown Copyright. The superimposed local authority boundaries were derived from plans deposited with the General Registry in Douglas.

N

500m

P.G.Cubbin, FBCart.S. - 2001

# Index

Italic page numbers refer to illustrations including maps and photographs.